An Introduction to Work and Organizational Psychology

T0342544

An Introduction to Work and Organizational Psychology

An International Perspective

Third Edition

Edited by

Nik Chmiel, Franco Fraccaroli and Magnus Sverke

WILEY Blackwell

Registered Offices
John Wiley & Sons, Inc., 111 River Street, Hoboken, NJ 07030, USA
John Wiley & Sons Ltd, The Atrium, Southern Gate, Chichester, West Sussex, PO19 8SQ, UK

Editorial Office
The Atrium, Southern Gate, Chichester, West Sussex, PO19 8SQ, UK

For details of our global editorial offices, customer services, and more information about Wiley products visit us at www.wiley.com.

Wiley also publishes its books in a variety of electronic formats and by print-on-demand. Some content that appears in standard print versions of this book may not be available in other formats.

Library of Congress Cataloging-in-Publication Data is available for this title
9781119168027 (paperback)

Cover image: Grant Faint/Gettyimages

Set in 10.5/13 pt ITC Galliard Std by Aptara
Printed and bound by CPI Group (UK) Ltd, Croydon, CR0 4YY

C9781119168027_191223

The Master said, 'If one learns from others but does not think, one will be bewildered. If, on the other hand, one thinks but does not learn from others, one will be in peril.'

Confucius, The Analects, II: 15

Nik

To TA, JA-C, RA-C, you know who you are, may the force be with you.

Franco

To Alba, Cecilia, Nicolò and Pietro.

Magnus

To Ingrid, Emeli, Elina and Ebba, and to all those people who strive to make organizations better places in which to work.

Contents

List of Contributors

Michael Allvin, Associate Professor of Psychology and Sociology, Department of Sociology, Uppsala University, Sweden

Neil Anderson, Professor of Human Resource Management and Director of Research of the HRM-OB research group and the IDEAL (Innovation, Diversity, Employment and Law), Brunel Business School, London, UK

Arnold B. Bakker, Professor of Work and Organizational Psychology and Director of the Center of Excellence for Positive Organizational Psychology, Erasmus University, Rotterdam, the Netherlands. Distinguished Visiting Professor at the University of Johannesburg, South Africa, and Adjunct Professor at Lingnan University, Hong Kong

Talya N. Bauer, Cameron Professor of Management and Management Area Director, School of Business Administration, Portland State University, Oregon, USA. Associate Editor, *Journal of Applied Psychology*

Debby G. J. Beckers, Assistant Professor of Work and Organizational Psychology, member of the research group 'Work, Health and Performance' of the Behavioural Science Institute at the Radboud University, Nijmegen, the Netherlands

Claudia Bernhard-Oettel, Associate Professor and Senior Lecturer, Department of Psychology, Stockholm University, Sweden

Joseph A. Carpini, PhD candidate, Department of Management and Organisation, Business School, the University of Western Australia, Perth, Australia

Nik Chmiel, Professor of Psychology and Head of Department, Department of Psychology and Counselling, University of Chichester, UK. Past president of the European Association of Work and Organizational Psychology (EAWOP)

Catherine E. Connelly, Associate Professor and Canada Research Chair, DeGroote School of Business, McMaster University, Hamilton, Ontario, Canada

Arla Day, Canada Research Chair and Professor of Industrial/Organizational Psychology, Department of Psychology, Saint Mary's University, Halifax, Nova Scotia, Canada. Founding Board Member of the CN Centre for Occupational Health and Safety and Chair of the Nova Scotia Psychologically Healthy Workplace Program

Nele De Cuyper, Associate Professor, Research Group Work, Organizational and Personnel Psychology, Faculty of Psychology and Educational Sciences, KU Leuven, Belgium

Jan de Jonge, Professor of Work, Organizational and Sports Psychology, Department of Industrial Engineering and Innovation Sciences, Human Performance Management Group, Eindhoven University of Technology, the Netherlands. Adjunct Professor, School of Psychology, Asia Pacific Centre for Work Health and Safety, University of South Australia, Adelaide, Australia

Evangelia Demerouti, Professor of Organizational Behavior and Human Decision Processes, Human Performance Management Group, Department of Industrial Engineering and Innovation Sciences, Eindhoven University of Technology, the Netherlands. Distinguished Visiting Professor at the University of Johannesburg, South Africa

Marco Depolo, Professor of Work and Organizational Psychology, Department of Psychology, University of Bologna, Italy. Vice-Rector for Organizational Innovation at the University of Bologna. Past president of SIPLO (Società Italiana di Psicologia del Lavoro e dell'Organizzazione; Italian Society for Work and Organizational Psychology)

James M. Diefendorff, Professor Industrial/Organizational Psychology, Department of Psychology, University of Akron, Ohio, USA

Julie Dinh, Doctoral graduate student researcher, Department of Psychology, Rice University, Texas, USA. National Science Foundation Graduate Research Fellow

Christian Dormann, Professor of Business Education and Management, Department of Law and Economics, Johannes Gutenberg University, Mainz, Germany. Adjunct Professor, School of Psychology, Asia Pacific Centre for Work Health and Safety, University of South Australia, Adelaide, Australia

Constanze Eib, Lecturer in Organisational Behaviour, Norwich Business School, University of East Anglia, Norwich, UK

Allison M. Ellis, Assistant Professor of Management and Human Resources, Orfalea College of Business, California Polytechnic State University, San Luis Obispo, USA

Helena Falkenberg, Post-doctoral researcher, Department of Psychology, Stockholm University, Sweden

Franco Fraccaroli, Professor of Work and Organizational Psychology, Department of Psychology and Cognitive Science, University of Trento, Italy. President of the Alliance of Organizational Psychology and past president of the European Association of Work and Organizational Psychology (EAWOP)

Adrian Furnham, Professor of Psychology, University College London, UK. Adjunct Professor at the Norwegian Business School, Oslo, Norway. Visiting Professor at the University of KwaZulu Natal, South Africa

Stephanie Gilbert, Assistant Professor of Business, Shannon School of Business, Cape Breton University, Sydney, Nova Scotia, Canada

Gudela Grote, Professor of Work and Organizational Psychology, Department of Management, Technology, and Economics, ETH Zürich, Switzerland. Associate Editor of *Safety Science* and President of the European Association of Work and Organizational Psychology

Nic Hammarling, Partner and Head of Diversity, Pearn Kandola, Oxford, UK

Johnny Hellgren, Associate Professor, Department of Psychology, Stockholm University, Sweden. Extraordinary Associate Professor, North-West University, Potchefstroom, South Africa

Daniel P. Hinton, Lecturer in Psychology, Institute of Psychology, University of Wolverhampton, UK

Henry Honkanen, Organizational Psychologist, OD Consultant, Arena Nova, Finland. President of W/O-Psychology Forum in Finland. Former Secretary-General of the European Association of Work and Organizational Psychology (EAWOP), 2003–2011

Göran Kecklund, Professor, Deputy Director and Head of the Sleep and Fatigue Division, Stress Research Institute, Stockholm University, Sweden. International research fellow at Behavioural Science Institute, Radboud University, Nijmegen, the Netherlands

E. Kevin Kelloway, Canada Research Chair in Occupational Health Psychology and Professor of Psychology at Saint Mary's University, Halifax, Nova Scotia, Canada

Christian Korunka, Professor of Work and Organizational Psychology, Department of Applied Psychology, University of Vienna, Austria

Barbara Kożusznik, Professor and Chair of Work and Organizational Psychology, Department of Pedagogy and Psychology, University of Silesia, Katowice, Poland. President-Elect, Division 1, Work and Organizational Psychology, of the International Association of Applied Psychology (IAAP)

Joana Kuntz, Senior Lecturer, Department of Psychology, University of Canterbury, Christchurch, New Zealand

Annika Lantz Friedrich, Professor of Work and Organizational Psychology, Department of Psychology, Stockholm University, Sweden

Gary Latham, Secretary of State Professor of Organizational Effectiveness, Rotman School of Management, University of Toronto, Canada. President of Division 1, Work and Organizational Psychology, of the International Association of Applied Psychology (IAAP)

Pascale M. Le Blanc, Associate Professor of Work and Organizational Psychology, Human Performance Management Group, Department of Industrial Engineering and Innovation Sciences, Eindhoven University of Technology, the Netherlands. Affiliate researcher, Department of Psychology, Stockholm University, Sweden

Constanze Leineweber, Associate Professor and Data Manager of the Swedish Longitudinal Occupational Survey of Health (SLOSH), Division of Epidemiology, Stress Research Institute, Stockholm University, Sweden

Hannes Leroy, Assistant Professor, Department of Organisation and Personnel Management, Rotterdam School of Management, Erasmus University, Rotterdam, the Netherlands

Chang-qin Lu, Associate Professor, Department of Psychology, Peking University, China

Sanna Malinen, Senior Lecturer, Department of Management, Marketing and Entrepreneurship, University of Canterbury, Christchurch, New Zealand

Francisco J. Medina, Professor of Psychology and Dean of the Faculty of Psychology, University of Seville, Spain

Lucas Monzani, Postdoctoral fellow, the Ian O. Ihnatowycz Institute for Leadership, Ivey Business School, Western University, London, Ontario, Canada

Silvia Moscoso, Professor of Psychology and Dean of Faculty of Labour Relations, University of Santiago de Compostela, Spain

Fredrik Movitz, Senior Lecturer, Department of Sociology, Stockholm University, Sweden

Lourdes Munduate, Professor of Organizational Social Psychology, Department of Social Psychology, University of Seville, Spain. Chair of the Spanish Research Agency for Psychology (ANEP)

Megan Murphy, PhD candidate, DeGroote School of Business, McMaster University, Hamilton, Ontario, Canada

Katharina Näswall, Associate Professor, Department of Psychology, University of Canterbury, Christchurch, New Zealand

Karina Nielsen, Professor of Work Psychology and Head of Institute of Work Psychology, University of Sheffield, UK. Research affiliate, Karolinska Institutet, Sweden and CPH-NEW, a Centre of Excellence funded by the National Institute of Occupational Safety and Health, USA

Anne-Sophie Nyssen, Professor of Cognitive Ergonomics and Work Psychology and Head of the Cognitive Ergonomics Laboratory, Department of Psychology, University of Liège, Belgium

Jaco Pienaar, PhD, Senior Lecturer, Department of Psychology, Umeå University, Sweden. Professor, WorkWell Research Unit, North-West University, Potchefstroom, South Africa

Ivan Robertson, Founder Director, Robertson Cooper Ltd., Professor Emeritus, Manchester University, UK

Diana Rus, Organizational Psychologist, Innovation Management Consultant, Creative Peas, the Netherlands

Eduardo Salas, Professor and Allyn R. and Gladys M. Cline Chair, Department of Psychology, Rice University, Texas, USA. Former president of the Society for Industrial and Organizational Psychology (SIOP)

Jesús F. Salgado, Professor of Psychology, University of Santiago de Compostela, Spain. Editor of *Journal of Work and Organizational Psychology*

Guido Sarchielli, Professor Emeritus of Work Psychology, Department of Psychology, University of Bologna, Italy

Matt Smeed, Senior Business Psychologist at Robertson Cooper, now CEO and Business Psychologist, SISU Psychology, UK

Guillaume Soenen, Apicil Chaired Professor of Health and Performance at Work, Associate Professor of Management and Head of the Cognitions-Behaviors-Transformations Research Center, EMLYON Business School, Lyon, France

Christian Stamov-Roßnagel, Professor of Organisational Behaviour, Department of Psychology and Methods, Jacobs University, Bremen, Germany. Scientific Director of Germany's first Age Management Academy (ddn-Akademie)

Magnus Sverke, Professor and Chair of the Division of Work and Organizational Psychology, Department of Psychology, Stockholm University, Sweden. Extraordinary Professor, North-West University, Potchefstroom, South Africa

Philip Tucker, Associate Professor, Department of Psychology, Swansea University, UK. Visiting Researcher at the Stress Research Institute, Stockholm University, Sweden

Daniela Ulber, Professor of Organizational Development and Management, Faculty of Business and Social Sciences, Hamburg University of Applied Sciences, Germany

Anja Van den Broeck, Associate Professor, Research Centre for Work and Organization Studies, Faculty of Economics and Business, KU Leuven, Belgium. Extraordinary Professor, Optentia Research Program, North West University, Potchefstroom, South Africa

Rolf van Dick, Professor of Social Psychology and Director of the Center for Leadership and Behavior in Organizations, Goethe University, Frankfurt, Germany. Visiting Professor at the Work Research Institute (AFI), Oslo, Norway

Matti Vartiainen, Professor of Work and Organizational Psychology, Department of Industrial Engineering and Management, Aalto University, Helsinki, Finland

Mo Wang, R. Perry Frankland Professor of Management and Director of Human Resource Research Center, Department of Management, Warrington College of Business Administration, University of Florida, Gainesville, Florida, USA. Past president of the Society for Occupational Health Psychology (SOHP)

Vicky Ward, Head of Occupational Health and Wellbeing Strategy, Network Rail, UK. A qualified nurse, with over 20 years' experience in health and well-being

Amanda Woods, Doctoral graduate student researcher, Department of Psychology, Rice University, Texas, USA

Stephen A. Woods, Professor of Work and Organizational Psychology and Head of Department, Department of People and Organizations, Surrey Business School, University of Surrey, UK, and a Chartered Occupational Psychologist

Fred R. H. Zijlstra, Professor of Work and Organizational Psychology, Vice-Dean Faculty of Psychology and Neuroscience, Department of Work and Social Psychology, Maastricht University, the Netherlands

Foreword

Current times are exciting, not least for work and organizational psychology. Profound economic changes are taking place because of globalization and technological innovations. Also the workforce is changing as more women, aged workers and workers from ethnic minorities are employed than ever before. In addition, in many countries the level of education is historically high and expectations about work have increased; rather than working only for their pay check, today's employees demand meaningful work.

These changes trickle down to organizations and employees' jobs. Today's workplaces are characterized by continuous change (instead of stability); horizontal networks (instead of vertical hierarchies); self-control and empowerment (instead of external supervision and control); accountability and employability (instead of dependence on the organization); blurred boundaries (instead of fixed schedules and work patterns); team work (instead of individual work); and job crafting (instead of detailed job descriptions). Taken together, this means that mental capital and soft skills have become crucially important for employees and organizations to survive and thrive. For instance, working in teams within horizontal networks requires conflict management skills and empathy, working in a continuously changing environment requires flexibility and adaptability, dealing with uncertainty involves boundary management, and working in jobs that are not clearly defined requires crafting the job yourself.

In other words: a *psychologization* of work is taking place in today's organizations. The usual technical qualifications and competencies need now to be supplemented by psychological skills. For instance, service technicians not only have to fix a broken washing machine (their 'real' job) but they also must leave a satisfied customer (their 'psychological' job).

This *psychologization* of work is, of course, good news. It explains the increasing popularity of work and organizational psychology, for instance in Human Resource Management (HRM) programmes and business schools, as well as in psychology departments of universities. Rather than only focusing on administrative efficiency, HRM is now concerned with increasing employee motivation and performance. Moreover, organizational behaviour is a key element in the curriculum of most business schools.

However, all that glitters is not gold. There are also serious challenges for work and organizational psychology. Because the world of work is rapidly changing, it has to reinvent itself in order not to provide yesterday's solutions for current problems. I see three main areas where change is most urgently needed.

First, many models were developed in the 1950s to the 1970s so that their validity for current workplaces may be questioned. For instance, new stressors have appeared on the scene, which are associated with the use of ICT or the emphasis on customer satisfaction. Also the traditional stress models that associate work with damage, disease, disorder and disability should be supplemented by a more positive approach that views work as enriching, exciting, energizing and engaging.

Second, Spector and Pindek (2016) have recently argued that research should use more exploratory and inductive approaches instead of only testing deductive, theory-driven hypotheses. By investigating burning issues in organizational life, the relevance of work and organizational psychology is increased for professionals in the field. For instance, instead of testing hypotheses about organizational change that have been derived from existing theoretical models, the process of change itself should be described. That way, practitioners receive information about what is actually going on, and researchers may inductively enhance their knowledge of change processes.

Third, although a lot of adequate tools are available, new tools must be developed. Jobs are changing, new leadership concepts are being introduced, and employees need other competencies. Hence these new jobs need to be analyzed, and new assessment tools for leadership and competencies need to be developed. Another important, but relatively neglected area is intervention research. It is important to know which interventions are working so that organizations can spend their resources effectively. By investing in tool development and intervention research work and organizational psychology contributes to evidence based management.

This book is about modern work and organizational psychology that contributes to solving today's problems with today's solutions. It brings together the expertise of a fine selection of top-notch experts, who not only present the current state-of-the-art in their fields, but who, throughout the book, pay much attention to the current challenges of work and organizational psychology.

Wilmar Schaufeli

Reference

Spector, P., & Pindek, S. (2016). The future of research methods in work and occupational health psychology. *Applied Psychology, 65*, 412–431.

Introduction

Nik Chmiel, Franco Fraccaroli and Magnus Sverke

We wanted to produce a book relevant to modern-day work and organizations where psychology rather than management held centre stage, but where the psychology concerned is related to the way managers manage, coworkers behave and organizations function. We wanted the book to be engaging to readers interested in why people behave the way they do at work. So each chapter title is in the form of a question that people at work could ask about their work or workplace because it is important to contemporary organizational life and where the answers matter to how people think, feel and behave when doing their jobs, working with others, grappling with technology, and contributing to the organization they belong to. The answers emerge, as they must do from a science-based field of inquiry, from systematic research into the issues involved and the careful accumulation of evidence that relates working conditions and organizational functioning to people's reactions and behaviour.

Peter Medawar, Nobel Prize-winner and leading light in understanding how the immune system of the body reacts to organ transplants, characterized scientific enquiry as

> a logically articulated structure of justifiable beliefs about nature. It begins as a story about a Possible World – a story which we invent and criticize and modify as we go along, so that it ends by being, as nearly as we can make it, a story about real life. (1969: 59)

In this book our beliefs are formed around questions we might ask about working life and each chapter tries to articulate answers that are justifiable, having been subject to modification and critique through the research process. So what we have are narratives, as close to real life as we can make them with current knowledge, about important issues to people's working lives.

Karl Popper (1991) argued that science itself is a social institution, and therefore knowledge produced by its practice is necessarily influenced by politics, social considerations, economics and the particular interests and experiences of the scientists involved. This book is based, by and large, on a Western perspective, which carries implications for the way in which science and scientists may choose what is important to ask questions about, and what a good answer would look like. Previous editions were sub-titled 'a European perspective' because the authors lived and worked in Europe and were asked to consider the European context in their writing. This edition, however, is sub-titled 'an international perspective'. There are several reasons for this. First, although all the editors and many of the contributors are European (spanning from north to south, east to west) they have an international outlook. Second, other contributors are not from Europe; they live and work, in general, in North America, South Africa and Australasia. We believe widening the social group brings more to the table when a story about real working life requires justification, but also that our desire to bring many contributors to the book means an enriched range of particular interests and experiences are brought to bear on issues important to us all.

In his Foreword Wilmar Schaufeli highlights how much work has changed in the last few years and how much it is continuing to change. He characterizes the change as making mental work and soft skills much more prominent than hitherto, placing people at the heart of organizations and their success, and this observation chimes with that made by Schneider (1987) – that 'the people make the place'. In short, it matters who we are and what we contribute to our organization, both for our own well-being and that of the organization. It is us that are being organized and doing the organization. So it matters what sort of questions we ask of ourselves and our workplaces, and it matters that we understand what type of contribution is made, why and by whom, to our collective endeavour and well-being. The emphasis on people though necessarily entails asking what happens to us when we leave work: What is our work–life balance like? What if we work part time? What if we are unemployed? What if we are moving towards retirement?

We have organized the book into four parts. The first three are: Job-focused; Organization-focused; and People-focused. The chapters in these three parts do just what they should do – focus on jobs, organizations or people, but without ignoring that jobs are offered within organizations and are done by people. Part I highlights that competencies, both technical and with people, have become a focus for organizational recruitment and selection. Thereafter a key message is that when work goals agreed with managers are committed to by employees there is a better outcome for both. Part II points to the ways that organizations gain by paying attention to how well they create healthy workplaces, how people are embraced and come to be a part of them, how well they are led, how fairly they are treated, and how well they are organized into teams. Part III concentrates on how and why people may make their contribution to organizational life as a function of their personalities, attitudes, values, and experiences of their organizations, management and working conditions.

The fourth part is about how organizations may be advised by work and organizational psychologists using the evidence and theorizing produced through the research that is so well discussed in the first three parts of the book. This part is introduced by two practising consultants with an excellent overview of how to advise organizations and the strengths and challenges in our field when doing so. There are also five case studies to demonstrate the kinds of effective contributions work and organizational psychologists can make to the ways organizations and people can function and thrive.

Psychologists trace the dawn of scientific psychology to the laboratory set up by Wilhelm Wundt in Leipzig in 1879, and along the way take in Harvard professor William James' hugely influential book *The Principles of Psychology*, published in 1890. So the fact that Münsterberg, born in Danzig, now modern-day Gdansk, published his book *Psychology and Industrial Efficiency* in an English edition in 1913 means the study of psychology related to the workplace is nearly as old as psychology itself. Throughout the twentieth century the field of work and organizational psychology developed at pace, particularly following World War II, with courses becoming established in universities, and associations being formed devoted to advancing research and practice in this area. The International Association of Applied Psychology (IAAP) was founded already in 1920, making it the oldest international psychology association, and its Division 1 – Work and Organizational Psychology – represents the oldest field of applied psychology.

As editors based in Europe we'd like to make special mention of a person who made important contributions to the further development of work and organizational psychology both as a scientific field and as a profession – Robert Roe – who died recently. Robert was responsible, with others, for establishing the European Association of Work and Organizational Psychology (EAWOP) in 1991 and was its first president. The association has gone from strength to strength providing for a European forum to inform work and organizational psychology that attracts people from around the world to its congresses. Latterly IAAP (Division 1), EAWOP and the American Society for Industrial and Organizational Psychology (SIOP) have founded an Alliance of Organizational Psychology (AOP) to further the impact of work and organizational psychology around the world.

Work and organizational psychology represents the combination of two subdisciplines: work psychology and organizational psychology. We strongly believe that this combination is a fruitful one. Work psychology traditionally embraces areas such as recruitment and selection, career choices, working conditions and safety, as well as stress and health, which involve a focus on individual workers and their well-being. Organizational psychology, on the other hand, typically includes areas such as organizational governance and leadership, employee motivation and performance, and organizational productivity, thus representing a focus on organizations and their prosperity. The combination of these two sub-fields into work *and* organizational psychology thus highlights the importance of studying, and understanding, factors at work that are beneficial to both individual employees and the organizations in which they work. We believe that this *Introduction to Work and Organizational Psychology* contributes to an increased understanding of how jobs, organizations and people are mutually dependent on one another. We also believe that the book's international perspective will make it a valuable tool for work and organizational psychology students in various parts of the world.

References

James, W. (1890). *The principles of psychology.* New York: Holt.

Medawar, P.B. (1969). *Induction and intuition in scientific thought.* London: Methuen.

Münsterberg, H. (1913). *Psychology and industrial efficiency.* Boston: Houghton.

Popper, K. R. (1991). *The poverty of historicism.* New York: Routledge. (first published in 1957)

Schneider, B. (1987). The people make the place. *Personnel Psychology, 40,* 437–453.

PART I

JOB-FOCUSED

What Do People Really Do at Work? Job Analysis and Design

Stephen A. Woods and Daniel P. Hinton

Overview

What do people really do at work? Or to phrase the question differently, what is the content and nature of different jobs in organizations? What *should* people do in their respective jobs in order to deliver organizational strategy? This chapter introduces the means by which these questions are answered: job analysis. In this chapter, job analysis is defined, and its place within a number of wider organizational systems is explored. Following this, the distinction is drawn between two broad types of analysis: *work*-oriented and *worker*-oriented analysis in terms of their focus and the end products that they are used to generate. A number of both work- and worker-oriented methods for the collection of job analysis data are described, after which are considered some specific organizational contexts in which job analysis data is used in the form of training needs analysis and job design. Finally, two modern alternatives to the classical approach to job analysis are described: competency profiling and work analysis. These approaches are explored in terms of the benefits that they can provide to practitioners in overcoming some of the limitations of traditional approaches to job analysis in the modern working world.

1.1 What Is Job Analysis?

What do people really do at work? How do jobs vary such that one person excels in a role, while another struggles? When selecting someone for a job, how do recruiters know what to look for? And, when designing a training programme, how can we make informed decisions about what content should be included and what content is redundant? How can we analyse work design so that we know if it is motivating?

For a role with which you, the reader, are relatively familiar – for example, sales or retail positions – the answers to these questions might seem fairly straightforward.

An Introduction to Work and Organizational Psychology: An International Perspective,
Third Edition. Edited by Nik Chmiel, Franco Fraccaroli and Magnus Sverke.
© 2017 John Wiley & Sons, Ltd. Published 2017 by John Wiley & Sons, Ltd.

However, this becomes much more challenging for jobs with which you are less familiar. If someone were to ask you what makes an effective nuclear power plant operator, or what content might make up a training programme for pathology lab technicians, what would you say? How could a practitioner find out what people really do at work?

The answers to all of these questions may be uncovered through a process called job analysis. Job analysis allows practitioners to gain a thorough understanding of the nature of a job, and the characteristics required for someone to be able to be effective in that job, to a very fine level of detail. Brannick, Levine and Morgeson define job analysis as follows:

> Job analysis is the systematic process of discovery of the nature of a job by *dividing it into smaller units*, where the process results in *one or more written products* with the goal of describing *what is done on the job* or *what capabilities are needed* to effectively perform the job.

> (2007, p. 8; emphasis added)

Bound up in this definition is the idea that job analysis is a robust process whereby a job and the person doing that job are very closely scrutinized. The methods of job analysis all examine work and workers in extremely fine detail, allowing the job analyst the same level of understanding of them as an expert in that field, even if the analyst had, prior to conducting the job analysis, been unfamiliar with the role.

It may appear, at first glance, that job analysis is a rather laborious and unnecessarily complex approach to the understanding of a job. However, it forms the foundation of a diverse range of organizational processes. In recruitment and selection, it provides the criteria by which one can assess a candidate's degree of fit to the job, and their likely level of future job performance. In training and development, it helps to identify gaps between actual performance and the expected level of performance in a job (this gap representing the training needs of an employee or group). In performance management, it allows one to quantify an individual's performance in more objective, behavioural terms. In short, without job analysis, many of the things organizations do would be fundamentally flawed in their approach.

1.2 Types of Job Analysis: Work- and Worker-oriented Analysis

Classically, there are two broad forms of job analysis: *work-oriented analysis* and *worker-oriented analysis* (McCormick, 1976). These forms differ in their focus, and by extension, the types of data which they generate.

Work-oriented analysis seeks to break down a job into its constituent parts through a process of continual narrowing of focus. Within work-oriented analysis, the parts of a job are arranged in a sort of hierarchy. At the top of this hierarchy is the job, which is made up of a number of positions. Positions are composed of duties, which, in turn, are made up of tasks. Tasks can be viewed as collections of activities, which are, themselves, made up of elements, the smallest units of work, which make up the

---

Box 1.1:   Constituent parts of a job

- *Job*: The totality of the work conducted by individuals working in similar *positions* across all organizations (for example, the job of 'receptionist').
- *Position*: A collection of *duties* for which a single individual in a specific organization is responsible (for example, 'the receptionist at Company X').
- *Duty*: A collection of *tasks* that contribute towards a shared goal (for example, customer communication).
- *Task*: A collection of *activities* that contribute towards a related set of specific job requirements (for example, communicating with customers via telephone).
- *Activity*: A collection of *elements* that contribute towards a single job requirement (for example, redirecting customer calls to relevant departments).
- *Element*: The smallest and most basic unit of work, beyond which further meaningful subdivision is impossible (for example, lifting the telephone's receiver).

---

bottom of the hierarchy. The nature of each of these constituent parts is explored further in Box 1.1. By systematically breaking down the job into increasingly smaller parts, work-oriented analysis allows the analyst to understand the nuances of a job role which would otherwise be hidden. The result of work-oriented analysis is a comprehensive picture of every aspect of a job, down to its finest details.

Worker-oriented analysis takes a fundamentally different approach to understanding a job. The aim of worker-oriented analysis is to understand the characteristics that define an effective worker in the role. These characteristics are, collectively, referred to by the abbreviation *KSAOs*, which stands for Knowledge, Skills, Abilities and Other Attributes, the four broad types of characteristics with which worker-oriented analysis is concerned. The distinction between these types of characteristics is explored in Box 1.2. Worker-oriented analysis, therefore, produces a profile of person characteristics that define the ideal person for a job, the person who, at least theoretically, should be a perfect fit to the job.

Box 1.2:   KSAOs

- *Knowledge*: The learning necessary to be able to perform the tasks of a job effectively (e.g. product knowledge; knowledge of processes and procedures).
- *Skills*: Acquired physical, mental, and social capabilities related to specific job tasks, which are acquired through experience and strengthened through practice (e.g. machinery operation; leadership).
- *Abilities*: Innate physical and cognitive capabilities that can be applied flexibly to a number of different job tasks (e.g. verbal reasoning; manual dexterity).
- *Other Attributes*: Any other relevant characteristic of a person that cannot be classified into one of the categories above (e.g. motivation; attitudes; personality traits; values).

1.3 Products of Job Analysis

Work- and worker-oriented analysis can further be separated by their end products. As stated in the operational definition provided above, job analysis results in some form of written product. The end result of work-oriented analysis is the production of a job description. A job description is a statement of the overall purpose of the role and the key tasks and duties for which the job holder will be expected to be responsible.

By contrast, the product of worker-oriented analysis is a person specification. A person specification is a profile of the KSAOs, experience and overt behaviours necessary to perform effectively in the job. Typically, the characteristics in the person specification will be divided into those that are essential for the job (those which the job holder must possess to be effective), and those that are seen as desirable (which are non-essential for effectiveness, but might differentiate job holders in terms of their fit to the role and subsequent level of performance).

Both of these documents are critical to the understanding of the job role. Therefore, work- and worker-oriented analyses should not be viewed as competing processes. Rather, they should be viewed as complementary. Together, they provide a complete picture of the requirements of the job and the attributes which allow the job holder to be effective in it.

1.4 Methods

Job analysts have a very diverse range of methods available to help them understand jobs (see Brannick et al., 2007, for an overview). Different techniques have both strengths and weaknesses, and there is no single technique that can be relied upon to be the 'magic bullet' to be able to effectively analyse all jobs in all contexts. In practice, when conducting job analysis, an analyst is likely to draw upon a number of techniques, as each will provide him or her with a unique perspective on the nuances of the job, providing information that other techniques may well have missed.

1.4.1 Desk research

The easiest and most cost-effective way to find out about the nature of a job is to draw upon work that has already been done. For the vast majority of jobs, it is highly likely that some form of job analysis has been conducted in the past. In all cases, the starting point of job analysis should be an exploration of the data that are already available. Most HR departments hold job descriptions and person specifications for roles in the organization and sometimes retain some of the job analysis data on which they were based. The caveat to doing this is that it is quite possible that much of these data may be old, and, as such, may not be as relevant to the role as they once were. For this reason, this kind of data should be treated as the foundation on which to build a thorough profile of the job and job holder, one that is complemented by current data acquired using other job analysis techniques.

One source of job analysis data that deserves special mention is called *O*NET*. O*NET is an expansive database of job analysis data, curated by the U.S. Department of Labor/Employment and Training Administration (USDOL/ETA). O*NET was created in 2001 as a publicly available database of occupational information that would be continually updated to reflect changes in job roles as technology and society changed. O*NET's content comprises both work-oriented data such as tasks and work context, and worker-oriented data such as required knowledge, skills and abilities. The database contains detailed data on some 974 occupations, the vast majority of which are updated on an annual basis (O*NET, 2016). O*NET is an extremely useful resource, and should be consulted as part of the analysis of any job role. O*NET data have also been used in published research studies (e.g. Judge et al., 1999; Woods & Hampson, 2010), further underlining their robustness and empirical utility.

1.4.2 Work-oriented job analysis methods

Desk research has limitations. For example, it does not fully capture the contextual factors that influence the nature of specific positions within specific organizations. For these reasons, it is always sensible to complement desk research with one or more other job analysis data collection methods.

1.4.2.1 *Observation and shadowing*

One of the most straightforward ways to gather information about the tasks involved in a job is to go into an organization and observe current job holders at work. A job analyst could observe a group of employees, examining behaviour while they carry out specific job tasks. This kind of data collection lends itself particularly well to work that is procedural or repetitive, as specific behaviours in these contexts tend to be demonstrated multiple times a day in a fixed order.

For more complex jobs, the analyst might instead choose to *shadow* a single employee. When shadowing an individual, the analyst will accompany them throughout their working day, recording the behaviours they observe. These methods, however, have some disadvantages: They both represent a relatively narrow 'snapshot' of behaviour, and, as such, are unsuitable for recording behaviours that may be only displayed infrequently or under exceptional circumstances. Additionally, the interpretation of specific behaviours tends to fall to the analyst themselves, so may overlook some of the hidden detail of the observed work tasks. Finally, these methods are unsuitable for tasks in which confidentiality is an issue, as it may be the case that the analyst's presence would expose them to work practices or information to which they should not have access.

1.4.2.2   Diary methods

One approach that can address some of these shortcomings is to ask workers to keep diaries while they perform particular work tasks. Incumbents will typically record their behaviours at work over a relatively short period of time, after which they will pass their diary to the analyst to interpret. Note that diary methods could be quantitative or qualitative, depending on the need of the analysis. Quantitative data could be collected such as daily frequency of certain tasks, whereas qualitative data might capture more open descriptions of the work that people do day-to-day.

1.4.2.3   Task analysis

Observational and diary methods are likely to generate a large amount of data, but that data may not be organized in such a way as to allow for easy interpretation. Task analysis methods are a set of techniques that aim to impose some order upon data of these kinds. The broad aim of task analysis is to create structure to observational data to make it more systematic and quantitative in nature. The analyst observes and records behaviours, their frequency, their duration, the environment in which they occur, the equipment required to perform them, and so on. The analyst then tries to create order from these data to contextualize specific work behaviours as part of wider systems.

One form of task analysis that is widely used in job analysis is *hierarchical task analysis* (HTA). This method aims to understand a work task by breaking it down into a number of subtasks, and then describing how each interacts to contribute towards completion of the task. The task is described in terms of its *goal*, the *operations* needed to be carried out to achieve this goal, and the *plan* that provides the sequence in which these operations need to be conducted.

The HTA technique has the versatility to model tasks to a very fine level of detail. Lane, Stanton and Harrison (2006) used HTA to model the process involved by a medical professional administering a drug to a patient. Though there are only four operations at the top level of the hierarchy ('1. Check chart for medication details', '2. Acquire medication', '3. Administer drug to patient', and '4. Record dosage') that contribute to the goal, they are broken down into an incredibly detailed hierarchy, making for a total of 105 operations in the resultant model of this seemingly simple task.

One further form of task analysis worthy of note is *functional job analysis* (FJA) (Fine, 1955). FJA aims to classify tasks according to similarities in their functional requirements by using a system of coding what a worker does when performing the task. Tasks are broken down into three broad categories by target, the target of a task being data, people, or things. The task is assigned a code based on the action conducted on that target (for example 'analyse data'; 'supervise people'). The end result of FJA is the generation of a task statement that describes the task in terms of the skills needed (*training content*) to perform a specific function (*the task*) to the required standard (*performance standards*). Box 1.3 presents an example of FJA.

Box 1.3: An example of functional job analysis

Fine and Cronshaw (1999) provide an example of the typical form of a task statement generated by FJA, using the task of typing standard form letters and preparing them for mailing. In this example, the task is defined as follows:

> Types/transcribes standard form letter, including information from records provided, following [standard operating procedure] for form letter, but adjusting standard form as required for clarity and smoothness, etc. in order to prepare letter for mailing.
>
> (Fine and Cronshaw (1999, p. 71)

The training content required to do this task is identified as:

- Functional:
  - *How to type: letters.*
  - *How to transcribe material, correcting mechanical errors.*
  - *How to combine two written sets of data into one.*

- Specific:
  - *How to obtain records and find information in them.*
  - *Knowledge of S.O.P. for standard letter format: how/where to include information.*
  - *Knowledge of information required in letter.*
  - *How to use particular typewrite provided.*

(Fine and Cronshaw, 1999, p. 71)

Finally, the performance standards required are:

- Descriptive:
  - *Types with reasonable speed and accuracy.*
  - *Format of letters correct.*
  - *Any changes/adjustments are made correctly.*

- Numerical:
  - *Completes letters in X period of time.*
  - *No uncorrected spelling, mechanical or adjustment errors per letter.*
  - *Fewer than X omissions of information per X no. letters typed.*

(Fine and Cronshaw,1999, p. 71)

1.4.3 Worker-oriented job analysis methods

While these methods will give the job analyst a thorough understanding of the tasks that make up the job in question, what they are unable to do is to provide any insight into the KSAOs that an incumbent requires for the role. By contrast, worker-oriented methods focus on what makes a competent job holder. These methods tend to emphasize the differences in key attributes between good, excellent and poor performers, allowing the job analyst insight into the most relevant person characteristics for the role.

1.4.3.1   Interviews

The most direct way to discover the characteristics that make an effective worker is to speak to some form of *subject matter expert* (SME). SMEs are chosen as they have some insight into the target job which the analyst does not, so they will typically be either job incumbents, or their supervisors or line managers. Interviews are typically conducted one-on-one, though *focus groups* of SMEs can be assembled, allowing the analyst to collect data much more efficiently. However, focus groups can be prone to bias. If one or two group members are substantially more vocal than the others, their opinions may be seen as representing the group as a whole, whereas, in actuality, this may not be the case.

A very useful form of interview for the purposes of job analysis is the *critical incident interview* (Flanagan, 1954). Critical incident interviews are semi-structured interviews in which the interviewee is asked to describe specific incidents in which an employee demonstrated particularly effective or ineffective behaviour. This approach serves two purposes. First, it serves to highlight the specific behaviours that separate good, excellent and poor performers. Second, it provides the analyst with insight into critical aspects of the job that may only occur infrequently, thus would be likely to be overlooked by observational methods.

1.4.3.2   Repertory grids

Repertory grids (Kelly, 1955) are a technique that aims to identify the characteristics that separate good from poor performers. SMEs are presented with sets of three workers drawn from a pool, two of whom have been judged to be alike in terms of their effectiveness and the other as different. The SME then defines a construct of some kind that differentiates between the pair and the single worker. This construct is bipolar, so that the effective worker (or pair) will be characterized by one pole of the construct, and the ineffective worker (or pair) by the other. The SME will then be asked to rate each of the remaining workers in the pool in terms of where they lie on this newly-created continuum. The process then repeats with a new selection of workers and a new construct.

For example, Workers A and B (effective) might be characterized as 'organized' by the SME, whereas Worker C (ineffective) might be characterized as 'disorganized'. Workers D, E, F and G would then be rated according to where on the continuum the SME felt they belonged, assigning each a numerical value. In doing so, the analyst can get a rich understanding of the characteristics that separate effective and ineffective workers, and the relative importance of each aspect compared to others.

1.4.3.3 *Questionnaires*

While interview-based methods tend to provide the analyst with rich descriptions of the characteristics that make for effective job holders, they have a number of drawbacks. First, they tend not to be very quantitative, so can suffer from issues of reliability and validity. Second, they are relatively labour-intensive to run. As an alternative, a number of off-the-shelf questionnaires are available to help the analyst understand the target job quickly and efficiently, all of which are highly quantitative.

The *Fleishman Job Analysis Survey* (F-JAS) (Fleishman & Reilly, 1995) aims to identify the physical, cognitive and social abilities required to perform the tasks of a job. Multiple SMEs complete the survey by rating each of 73 separate abilities in terms of the level required to perform the tasks of a job. The real value of the F-JAS is in its relationship to Fleishman and Reilly's (1992) *Handbook of Human Abilities*. The handbook contains an index of published tests with which to assess each of these abilities, including details on the authors and publishers of the tests. This allows the analyst to interpret the results of the F-JAS in terms of the kinds of assessments that are best suited to measuring each of the abilities most relevant for the job. This allows the results of the job analysis to be easily integrated into other organizational systems such as selection (to identify the suitability of candidates for the job role) and training (to assess trainability and help identify likely training needs).

The *NEO Job Profiler* (Costa, 1996) is a questionnaire designed to identify the personality traits which are desirable for the job. Based on Costa's (1996) NEO PI-R personality trait questionnaire, it examines how desirable in a job incumbent are each of the Big Five Personality Traits (Openness, Conscientiousness, Extroversion, Agreeableness and Neuroticism) and their facets. This results in the generation of an ideal personality profile, against which future candidates' job fit can be assessed at selection, or which can be used in training contexts to identify potential areas of development.

One final questionnaire that deserves mention is the *Position Analysis Questionnaire* (PAQ) (McCormick, Jeanneret, & Mecham, 1972). Unlike the other questionnaires mentioned in this section, the PAQ's focus is work-oriented. It aims to uncover how a job is done through systematic exploration of 189 job elements, classified into seven categories. An SME rates each of these job elements according to six scales, designed to highlight the relative importance of each element. Though the PAQ tends to give very detailed and highly quantitative breakdowns of the tasks involved in a job, it has been suggested that the reliability of its ratings can suffer when analysing the more abstract, less observable elements of a job, such as decision-making and problem-solving (Morgeson & Campion, 1997). For this reason, the PAQ may be better suited to the analysis of highly procedural jobs than it is to those in which task behaviour is less easily observed, such as professional jobs.

Table 1.1 presents a detailed comparison of the job analysis techniques discussed in this chapter.

Table 1.1: Comparing job analysis techniques

Technique	Work/ Worker?	Qualitative/ Quantitative Data?	Good to use when:	Output
Desk research	Both	Neither – accumulation of evidence from pre-existing sources	Jobs are pre-existing, with extensive information available for review.	Portfolio of information concerning focal job
Observation	Work	Qualitative descriptions of behaviour Quantitative frequency data for observations	Procedural or repetitive work	Observed behaviour descriptions plus frequencies
Shadowing	Work	Qualitative – written accounts of work undertaken by a specific individual	Work is complex and varied, requiring a wide cross section of activity to be collected	Structured description of work activities undertaken
Diary Methods	Work	Qualitative: descriptions of work undertaken daily Quantitative: surveys about frequencies of particular activities collected at regular intervals	Work is complex, but privacy of work context prevents shadowing, or when shadowing does not adequately capture full range of tasks	Worker-developed diary return (whether written or survey based)
Hierarchical Task Analysis	Work	Qualitative	The job comprises many procedures that must be carried out precisely and accurately	Hierarchical flow diagram breaking down tasks into smaller subtasks and actions
Functional Job Analysis	Work	Qualitative: key job tasks are content-analysed and classified according to core functional content	Work is generally well defined and predictable in terms of the activities encountered	Set of task statements, that coherently link core tasks together
Interviews with Workers	Worker	Qualitative: exploration of the main person and KSAO requirements of the job	There are multiple stakeholders who may have unique insights (e.g. job holders, managers, customers).	Written outputs of interview sessions
Critical Incidents Interview	Worker	Qualitative: written descriptions of key behaviours differentiating effective versus ineffective performance	Jobs afford high levels of autonomy so that behaviour, decisions, and choices of actions can impact outcomes	Structured descriptions of behaviours influencing effectiveness of performance outcomes

Repertory Grids	Worker	Qualitative: descriptions of performance differentiating characteristics Quantitative: ratings of effectiveness that may be used to establish data structures or relative importance of characteristics	Jobs afford high levels of autonomy, so that individual differences clearly differentiate performance; when raters have a clear oversight of performance of multiple workers doing the focal job	Lists of performance differentiating characteristics and ratings of importance/effectiveness of targets
Questionnaires (e.g. Position Analysis Questionnaire; Fleishman Job Analysis Survey)	Work or Worker	Quantitative	The nature of the job is poorly understood by the analyst, requiring wide assessment of the work tasks or worker characteristics required to perform them; multiple perspectives are to be collected efficiently; jobs are highly multifaceted; comparison with other jobs is necessary, such as in the case of job evaluation	Quantitative data (scores) based on scales and dimensions of the various questionnaires available to the analyst
Combination Job Analysis Methodology	Both	Qualitative: descriptions and statements of key job duties and KSAO requirements Quantitative: ratings of tasks and KSAOs to prioritize content	In-depth analysis is required, and mixed methodology desirable to establish how the outputs of analysis might be used in different Human Resource Management functions	Structured descriptions of key job tasks and duties, and KSAO components required to carry out the tasks and duties

1.4.4 Combination Job Analysis Methodology (CJAM)

A holistic approach to job analysis that considers both work- and worker-oriented approaches is *Combination Job Analysis Methodology* (CJAM) (Pearn & Kandola, 1988). CJAM combines aspects of many different job analysis approaches with the aim of achieving a thorough understanding of both a job's content and the person characteristics that define effective workers in it. SMEs and job analysts form a team, which then uses work-oriented methods to compile a comprehensive list of job tasks. This list is then condensed to form a smaller list of duties of the role, which the team rates according to their importance. A list of the required KSAOs for these duties is then compiled by the team using a variety of worker-oriented methods. This list is then refined, and the resultant KSAOs rated for their relative importance, as for the duties. Though labour-intensive in the extreme, this process results in a job description and a person specification which are likely to be both comprehensive and reliable (Brannick et al., 2007).

1.5 Job Analysis in Training Contexts: Training Needs Analysis

One application of job analysis methods to specific HRM practices is as part of training needs analysis (TNA). TNA is the foundational step in the development of any training programme. It is a systematic process of exploration that identifies where in an organization training is needed, the contextual factors that could influence its success, and the nature of the learning required. Goldstein and Ford (2002) propose a three-stage process for conducting TNA. The first stage is organizational analysis. The aims of this stage are two-fold: (1) this stage provides information about where and when training is required within the organization; and (2) it highlights potential contextual factors that might affect training delivery, such as the culture of the organization, its strategy, and the level of support for the programme from senior management.

The next stage is job/task analysis. This stage aims to define employees' expected level of performance. In doing so, the training needs analyst may draw upon any of the methods described earlier in the chapter. Additionally, it may be useful for the analyst to identify the types of learning necessary for the job. In this case, taxonomies of types of learning (e.g. Gagne, 1984; Merrill, 1983) may be used to match types of learning to training objectives.

Finally, person analysis seeks to assess employees' actual performance. This provides information about who needs to be trained and the content that should be included in the training programme. Any shortfall between the actual and expected performance identified in this stage and the previous one represents a performance gap, which then informs the training needs of the employees. Though the identification of an employee's training needs is traditionally conducted by the analyst, an alternative approach is to ask individuals to self-assess their own training needs. While this is potentially a quicker and more cost-effective alternative to traditional person analysis, data gathered in this way must be treated carefully, as it has been demonstrated that negative attitudes towards the utility of the training can reduce the reliability of self-assessments of an individual's training needs (Ford & Noe, 1987). As well as identifying training needs, person analysis may provide insight into key individual differences between trainees that might affect the delivery of the training.

Box 1.4: How to make 'what people really do at work' really positive, healthy and motivating

Job analysis can serve more than a descriptive function. In a broader sense it helps us to understand whether the work that people do presents a risk or benefit to their motivation and health. The literature on job design and motivation tells us that there are certain characteristics of jobs that make them intrinsically more or less motivating. For example, the Job Characteristics Model (Hackman and Oldham, 1980) included five key characteristics:

- Skill Variety
- Task Identity
- Task Significance
- Autonomy
- Feedback

These and a variety of other social and motivational aspects of jobs were analysed by Humphrey, Nahrgang and Morgeson (2007) in a meta-analysis. They reported that:

- Motivational and social characteristics accounted for 64% of variance in organizational commitment, 87% of variance in job involvement, 35% of variance in subjective job performance, 7% of variance in absence levels and 26% of variance in turnover intentions.

- Motivational, social and work context characteristics accounted for 55% of variance in job satisfaction, 38% of variance in people's experience of work stress and 23% of variance in burnout and exhaustion.

The implications of their work are that by ensuring that certain characteristics and features are present in jobs, they can be designed to be more positive and motivating. These implications are completely consistent with the conclusions of other research into work and well-being (e.g. Warr, 2011), and work stress and health (e.g. Cooper & Marshall, 1976; Cox, 1993). In the case of work stress, job features are modelled as potential psychosocial hazards. So, for example, if role ambiguity (lack of clarity in the job specification), role overload (too much demand in the job specification) or role conflict (aspects of the job specification that clash with one another) are present in a job, the result will tend to be higher levels of stress at work.

The relevance to job analysis is reasonably clear; not only can it identify what people do at work, or what they need to do in a job role, it also serves as a potential diagnostic for whether jobs are likely to be motivating and positive, versus stressful or unhealthy, and demotivating. By intervening (e.g. in ways outlined in Chapter 16 on healthy workplaces), managers and practitioners can ensure that potentially stressful and unhealthy jobs are changed, and better designed to mitigate risks.

On an even broader level, there are potential social and ethical implications of using job analysis in this broader way. Woods and West (2014) highlight the relevance of job design to the "Decent Work Agenda" of the International Labor Organization (ILO). They describe Decent Work as reflecting the aspirations of all people for their working lives, stating it should have:

opportunities for work that is productive and delivers a fair income, security in the workplace and social protection for families, better prospects for personal development and social integration, freedom for people to express their concerns, organize and participate in the decisions that affect their lives and equality of opportunity and treatment for all women and men.

(ILO, 2013)

Continued

The ILO highlight some key aspects of decent work (creating jobs, guaranteeing rights at work, extending social protection, and promoting social dialogue) and provide framework guidelines for assessing it in countries, measuring hard indicators such as labour market participation (e.g. employment and unemployment; numbers of women and children at work), alongside more psychosocial aspects (e.g. number of working hours, and consequent opportunities for balancing work, social and personal life).

The recognition in the Decent Work Agenda is the potential for work to contribute in positive and rewarding ways to people's lives, provided it is organized fairly, ethically, and in the context of sound economic, societal, and governmental structures, with respect for people and their rights at work.

We might see many of the fundamental aspects of decent work as *critical* hygiene factors (this means hygiene in the way that Herzberg, Mausner, and Snyderman (1959) describe hygiene factors, i.e. extrinsic factors including pay and conditions): basic rights and features of work that make it decent.

Morgeson and Dierdorff (2011), in a conference speech, talked about *good* work, and talked about this in the context of job design and the Job Characteristics Model (JCM). Good work is not only *decent*, but is designed to enhance well-being and meaningfulness.

A further implication from the ILO Decent Work Agenda is the need for integrated perspectives on what constitutes decent or good work. From a psychology point of view, there is a need to capture core aspects of job design – the work that people really do – with literature on careers, women at work, diversity and fairness, alongside the real wider context (social, organizational, economic) within which work exists (ILO, 2013).

1.6   Modern Approaches to Understanding Jobs

For some years now, job analysis has been somewhat in decline (Sanchez & Levine, 2012). A key point of criticism that has been levelled at traditional job analysis is that it is static and inflexible: its implicit assumption is that the tasks that comprise a job and the KSAOs necessary to perform it will not change as time passes (Robertson, Bartram, & Callinan, 2002). Clearly this assumption is flawed, given the rapid economic and technological changes that the working world has undergone in the past 30 years. For this reason, many practitioners have sought alternatives to job analysis that are more flexible in their approach, and that can provide outputs that are more 'future proof' than are the outputs of traditional job analysis.

There are two broad approaches that have begun to replace the classical approach to job analysis as the preferred method of understanding jobs in practice. The first is *competency profiling* and the second is *work analysis*.

1.6.1   Competency profiling

One alternative to traditional job analysis that has seen growing popularity in organizations in recent years is competency profiling (sometimes referred to as competency modelling). Competency profiling is similar in its scope to worker-oriented analysis, though, rather than defining effective workers in terms of their KSAOs directly, it defines them in terms of the competencies required to be effective in the job. Competencies are "observable workplace behaviours [that] form the basis of a differentiated measurement [of performance]" (Bartram,

2005, pp. 1185–6). As such, they are patterns of observable, performance-related behaviour that draw upon aspects of KSAOs (Roberts, 2005). This practice of defining performance behaviourally allows competencies to be integrated coherently into a variety of HRM processes such as selection, training and performance management (Soderquist et al., 2010), allowing organizations to assess employees against the same criteria across often disparate processes.

Competencies are arranged into *competency frameworks*, i.e., sets of competencies that seek to cover a wide range of job roles. These frameworks vary widely in their scope. Many organizations have developed their own specific competency frameworks, designed only to describe the performance-related behaviour of their own employees. Other, broader frameworks have been designed to describe behaviour within a family of jobs across organizational settings. One such competency framework is Tett et al.'s (2000) taxonomy of managerial competencies, which describes 53 behaviours related to performance in managers, classifying them according to nine dimensions. At the broadest level, general taxonomies have been developed, such as Bartram's Great Eight (Bartram, 2005; see Box 1.5), which are versatile enough to be used to separate effective and ineffective performers in a wide range of job roles and contexts.

Box 1.5:   Bartram's (2005) Great Eight competencies

- *Leading and Deciding*: Takes control and exercises leadership. Initiates action, gives direction and takes responsibility.

- *Supporting and Co-operating*: Supports others and shows respect and positive regard for them in social situations. Puts people first, working effectively with individuals and teams, clients and staff. Behaves consistently with clear personal values that complement those of the organization.

- *Interacting and Presenting*: Communicates and networks effectively. Successfully persuades and influences others. Relates to others in a confident and relaxed manner.

- *Analysing and Interpreting*: Shows evidence of clear analytical thinking. Gets to the heart of complex problems and issues. Applies own expertise effectively. Quickly learns new technology. Communicates well in writing.

- *Creating and Conceptualizing*: Open to new ideas and experiences. Seeks out learning opportunities. Handles situations and problems with innovation and creativity. Thinks broadly and strategically. Supports and drives organizational change.

- *Organizing and Executing*: Plans ahead and works in a systematic and organized way. Follows directions and procedures. Focuses on customer satisfaction and delivers a quality service or product to the agreed standards.

- *Adapting and Coping*: Adapts and responds well to change. Manages pressure effectively and copes with setbacks.

- *Enterprising and Performing*: Focuses on results and achieving personal work objectives. Works best when work is related closely to results and the impact of personal efforts is obvious. Shows an understanding of business, commerce and finance. Seeks opportunities for self-development and career advancement.

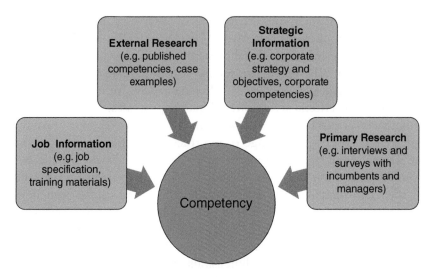

Figure 1.1: Information sources contributing to the design of competency models

Competency profiling is the practice of selecting the relevant competencies for a job. The analyst will select the competencies required for the role based on their own expertise, or will consult SMEs to ensure accuracy. Multiple sources of information (Figure 1.1) are integrated for developing competencies (Campion et al., 2011), for example, including:

- information from existing job analyses, e.g. job descriptions and person specifications;
- external research, e.g. published research papers, case studies;
- strategic information, e.g. corporate strategy, business objectives, corporate values;
- primary research, e.g. data collected using similar techniques to those reviewed earlier for job analysis.

The product of competency modelling is specifications for competencies in terms of what each comprises, and how performance is differentiated at various levels. This represents an advance on conventional job analysis, by specifying not only what people need to do in their role, but how to differentiate when they are doing it more or less effectively. Moreover, because competencies represent combinations of KSAOs, they are more closely aligned to the performance of people at work. This is because almost all job performance behaviour draws on various combinations of knowledge, skills, abilities, personality, attitudes and motivation, and so representing the behaviour in this way in competencies is conceptually sensible. An example competency is shown in Figure 1.2.

PROJECT MANAGEMENT			
The art of creating effective and accurate schedules with a well-defined scope, while being personally accountable for the execution and invested in the success of the project. People who exhibit this competency effectively and continuously manage risks and dependencies by making timely decisions while ensuring the quality of the project.			
Proficiency Level 1	Proficiency Level 2	Proficiency Level 3	Proficiency Level 4
Identifies risks and dependencies and communicates to stakeholders.	Develops systems to monitor risks and dependencies and report change.	Anticipates changing conditions and impact to risks and dependencies and takes preventative action.	Proactively identifies implications of related internal and external business conditions to risks and dependencies.
Appropriately escalates blocking issues when necessary.	Works effectively across disciplines and organizational boundaries to gain timely closure on decisions that impact own project/portfolio/solution.	Effects timely, mutually beneficial outcomes on decisions that impact the whole product, multiple projects or portfolios.	Instills a system and culture that facilitates effective decision-making across organizations, product lines or portfolios.
Understands project objectives, expected quality, metrics and the business case.	Develops methods to track and report metrics, gains agreement on quality and relates it to business value.	Evaluates quality and metrics based on return on investment and ensures alignment to business need.	Evaluates project results against related examples and incorporates best practices and key learning for future improvements.
Champions project to stakeholders and articulates business value.	Asks the right questions to resolve issues and applies creative solutions to meet project objectives.	Proactively inspires others to take action on issues and implications that could prohibit projects success.	Champions business value across multiple organizations and gains alignment and commitment to prioritization to ensure long-term project deliverables.

Figure 1.2: The Competency 'Project Management'
Source: Adapted from Campion et al. (2011).

Campion et al. (2011) note that competency profiling has a number of other tangible benefits over traditional job analysis methods. Senior managers in organizations are likely to pay more attention to competency profiling than they do to traditional job analysis. Competencies tend to be linked directly to organizational goals, meaning they make the alignment of individual performance with these goals easier. They often contain descriptions of how competencies develop with job level, giving them an element of flexibility. Finally, they may be able to accommodate a degree of future change to job requirements, overcoming some of the limitations of the more static traditional job analysis approach. These reasons are most likely why, in practice, competency profiling has overtaken traditional job analysis in recent years as the preferred method of analysing what people really do at work.

1.6.2   Work analysis

Rather than being a truly distinct concept, work analysis is a broadening of the concept of job analysis in response to the criticisms cited above. Work analysis puts greater emphasis upon 'understanding the experience of work' (Sanchez & Levine, 2012, p. 407) than does traditional job analysis. In addition to uncovering both work- and worker-oriented facets of the job itself, work analysis seeks to understand the context in which work is carried out within the role (Morgeson & Dierdorff, 2011). It includes a consideration of wider organizational factors that could affect how a job is done, such as the role's place within a team and organization, and the organization's goals and strategy. In this regard, there are parallels that can be drawn between work analysis and the organizational analysis aspect of TNA described earlier in this chapter. However, where organizational analysis is designed to identify potential barriers to successful delivery of training, work analysis identifies the factors that can influence how work is done. Though in its relative infancy, this approach shows the promise of being able to better understand jobs as the working world itself undergoes changes: Morgeson and Dierdorff (2011) reason that the impacts upon work of factors such as globalization, technological advances, and the changing nature of the global economy could all better be understood through work analysis.

1.7   Job Analysis: A Dynamic Perspective

Clearly, conventional job analysis needs to keep pace with perspectives on management and HRM to remain relevant. In assessing some of the limitations and areas for job analysis to develop, it is helpful to consider some wider aspects of the literature in work and organizational psychology. Techniques that have traditionally been employed to analyse jobs may not adequately capture some of the dynamics of jobs and the realities of how people perform them. A move towards a more developmental, and dynamic view of job analysis would be consistent with trends in other areas of research (e.g., in research on personality and work; Woods, Lievens, De Fruyt, & Wille, 2013). Two elements are particularly relevant to developing a more dynamic view: time, and person–environment fit.

Regarding time, it is critical for the understanding of job roles and the demands they place on incumbents that the influence of time is considered. The performance demands of a job in the first weeks of tenure are different from those that are encountered in year 2 of tenure, for example. Theorizing in this area has distinguished transitional and maintenance periods of job tenure (Zyphur, Chaturvedi, & Arvey, 2008). The transitional period represents the commencement of a new job role and the early months in which the job is learned. The maintenance phase is when the job has generally been learned or mastered. Research findings show that these phases of the job present different demands, such that performance is predicted by different characteristics in each phase (e.g., Lievens, Ones, & Dilchert, 2009; Thoresen, Bradley, Bliese, & Thoresen, 2004). Characteristics that may have been unimportant at the start of the job, become important later on. This is consistent with Trait Activation Theory (Tett & Burnett, 2003) and the idea that the demands of jobs across working life change so as to activate different kinds of KSAOs (Woods et al., 2013).

To account for this, job analysis should more explicitly examine and consider how demands change and evolve. Otherwise, in applying the results of job analysis in, for example, selection and recruitment, there is a real risk that selection decisions may lead to ineffective hiring in the long term.

Regarding person–environment (PE) fit, there is a further potential need for job analysis to extend its scope to encompass a wider perspective on fit. Models of PE fit include examination of fit at different levels of abstraction, for example, person–vocation (PV) fit, person–job (PJ) fit, person–organization (PO) fit, and person–group (PG) fit (Kristof, 1996; Lauver & Kristof-Brown, 2001).

Job analysis has traditionally focused most strongly on PJ fit. Yet, other aspects of PE fit could be equally influential for performance and effectiveness. For example, in a long-term career perspective, PV fit is important. From an organizational strategic point of view, PO fit is key to ensuring that people working in an organization are aligned to its values. PG fit is also critical for ensuring that teams are appropriately diverse, and to manage risks of conflict and cohesion. Moreover, maintaining an emphasis on the dynamic nature of jobs, the notion of fit must also be seen as changeable. That is, people themselves adjust and change in response to their jobs (Woods et al., 2013) and are able to change their jobs to better suit them, through job-crafting, for example (Wrzesniewski & Dutton, 2001).

In short, as job analysis as a technique continues to evolve, psychologists and other practitioners will need to consider not only *what* people really do at work, but also *when, where,* and *why* they do. Recent advances, including work analysis and competency modelling, have already taken steps in these directions.

Summary

Job analysis allows those within organizations to gain insight into what people really do at work. Its methods provide robust information to practitioners about what a job requires, and the key characteristics that predict success within it. As such, it represents a crucial first step in a wide variety of organizational practices. It is the foundation of selection, training, performance appraisal, and work design. However, it may be the case that job analysis in its classical form is no longer truly fit for purpose: The nature of work has changed rapidly in recent history, and it is likely that it will continue to do so in the future as technology advances and the world becomes increasingly globalized. This has led many practitioners to abandon the static and inflexible job analysis in favour of the more dynamic competency profiling. However, new, broader approaches to examining the experience of work in the form of work analysis could allow our understanding of jobs to be better understood in terms of the new contexts in which they may be situated. This has the potential to give many job analysis techniques a new lease of life, to allow them to once again contribute meaningfully to evidence-based practice within modern organizations.

Discussion Points

1 Imagine that you are an occupational psychologist who has been tasked with producing an up-to-date job description and person specification for the position of air traffic controller at a major international airport. What approach would you take to ensure that the end products of your job analysis were accurate reflections of the job and ideal job holder?
2 How can practitioners ensure that, when analysing the demands of jobs, they capture information as widely as possible (including the context, dynamic development of roles, motivational and work-related health aspects of jobs)?

Suggested Further Reading

Bartram, D. (2005). The Great Eight competencies: A criterion-centric approach to validation. *Journal of Applied Psychology*, *90*(6), 1185–1203.

Brannick, M. T., Levine, E. L., & Morgeson, F. P. (2007). *Job and work analysis: Methods, research, and applications for human resource*

management (2nd ed.). Thousand Oaks, CA: Sage.

Campion, M. A., Fink, A. A., Ruggeberg, B. J., Carr, L., Phillips, G. M., & Odman, R. B. (2011). Doing competencies well: Best practices in competency modeling. *Personnel Psychology*, *64*(1), 225–262.

Online Resource

O*NET Available at: http://www.onetonline.org/

References

Bartram, D. (2005). The Great Eight competencies: A criterion-centric approach to validation. *Journal of Applied Psychology, 90*(6), 1185–1203.

Brannick, M. T., Levine, E. L., & Morgeson, F. P. (2007). *Job and work analysis: Methods, research, and applications for human resource management* (2nd ed.). Thousand Oaks, CA: Sage.

Campion, M. A., Fink, A. A., Ruggeberg, B. J., Carr, L., Phillips, G. M., & Odman, R. B. (2011). Doing competencies well: Best practices in competency modeling. *Personnel Psychology, 64*(1), 225–262.

Cooper, C. L., & Marshall, J. (1976). Occupational sources of stress: A review of the literature relating to coronary heart disease and mental ill health. *Journal of Occupational Psychology, 49*(1), 11–28.

Costa, P. T. (1996). Work and personality: Use of the NEO-PI-R in industrial/organisational psychology. *Applied Psychology, 45*(3), 225–241.

Cox, T. (1993). *Stress research and stress management: Putting theory to work.* Sudbury, MA: HSE Books.

Fine, S. A. (1955). Functional job analysis. *Personnel Administration and Industrial Relations, 2,* 1–16.

Fine, S. A., & Cronshaw, S. F. (1999). *Functional job analysis: A foundation for human resources management.* Hove: Psychology Press.

Flanagan, J. C. (1954). The critical incident technique. *Psychological Bulletin, 51*(4), 327–58.

Fleishman, E. A., & Reilly, M. E. (1992). *Handbook of human abilities: Definitions, measurements, and job task requirements.* Palo Alto, CA: Consulting Psychologists Press.

Fleishman, E. A., & Reilly, M. E. (1995). Fleishman Job Analysis Survey (F-JAS). Potomac, MD: Management Research Institute.

Ford, J. K., & Noe, R. A. (1987). Self-assessed training needs: The effects of attitudes toward training, managerial level, and function. *Personnel Psychology, 40*(1), 39–53.

Gagne, R. M. (1984). Learning outcomes and their effects: Useful categories of human performance. *American Psychologist, 39*(4), 377–385.

Goldstein, I. L., & Ford, J. K. (2002). *Training in organizations: Needs assessment, development and evaluation.* Monterey, CA: Brooks Cole.

Hackman, J. R., & Oldham, G. R. (1980). *Work design.* Reading, MA: Addison-Wesley.

Herzberg, F., Mausner, B., & Snyderman, B. (1959). *The motivation to work.* New York: John Wiley & Sons, Inc.

Humphrey, S. E., Nahrgang, J. D., & Morgeson, F.P. (2007). Integrating motivational, social and contextual work design features: A meta-analytic summary and theoretical extension of the work design literature. *Journal of Applied Psychology, 92*(5), 1332–1356.

ILO (2013). *Decent work.* Retrieved from: http://www.ilo.org/global/topics/decent-work/lang—en/index.htm.

Judge, T. A., Higgins, C. A., Thoresen, C. J., & Barrick, M. R. (1999). The Big Five personality traits, general mental ability, and career success across the life span. *Personnel Psychology, 52,* 621–652.

Kelly, G. A. (1955). *The psychology of personal constructs:* vols 1 and 2. New York: W W Norton.

Kristof, A. L. (1996). Person-organization fit: An integrative review of its conceptualizations, measurement, and implications. *Personnel Psychology, 49*(1), 1–49.

Lane, R., Stanton, N. A., & Harrison, D. (2006). Applying hierarchical task analysis to medication administration errors. *Applied Ergonomics, 37*(5), 669–679.

Lauver, K. J., & Kristof-Brown, A. (2001). Distinguishing between employees' perceptions of person–job and person–organization fit. *Journal of Vocational Behavior, 59*(3), 454–470.

Lievens, F., Ones, D. S., & Dilchert, S. (2009). Personality scale validities increase throughout medical school. *Journal of Applied Psychology, 94,* 1514–1535. doi: 10.1037/a0016137.

McCormick, E. J. (1976). Job and task analysis. In M. D. Dunnette (Ed.), *Handbook of industrial and organizational psychology*. Chicago: Rand McNally.

McCormick, E. J., Jeanneret, P. R., & Mecham, R. C. (1972). A study of job characteristics and job dimensions as based on the Position Analysis Questionnaire (PAQ). *Journal of Applied Psychology, 56*(4), 347–368. Merrill, M. D. (1983). Component display theory. *Instructional-Design Theories and Models: An Overview of Their Current Status, 1,* 282–333.

Morgeson, F. P. (2011, May). Who is responsible for good work? Keynote speech at the 15th Conference of the European Association of Work and Organizational Psychology, Maastricht, The Netherlands.

Morgeson, F. P., & Campion, M. A. (1997). Social and cognitive sources of potential inaccuracy in job analysis. *Journal of Applied Psychology, 82*(5), 627–655.

Morgeson, F. P., & Dierdorff, E. C. (2011). Work analysis: From technique to theory. In *APA handbook of industrial and organizational psychology* (vol. 2, pp. 3–41). Washington, DC: APA.

O*NET (2016). *About O*NET.* Available at: http://www.onetcenter.org/aboutOnet.html

Pearn, M. & Kandola, R. (1988). *Job analysis: A manager's guide.* Oxford: IPD.

Roberts, G. (2005). *Recruitment and selection.* London: CIPD.

Robertson, I. T., Bartram, D., & Callinan, M. (2002). Personnel selection and assessment. In P. Warr (Ed.), *Psychology at work,* (pp. 100–152). London: Penguin.

Sanchez, J. I., & Levine, E. L. (2012). The rise and fall of job analysis and the future of work analysis. *Annual Review of Psychology, 63,* 397–425.

Searle, R. H. (2003). *Selection and recruitment: A critical text.* Milton Keynes: Open University Press.

Soderquist, K. E., Papalexandris, A., Ioannou, G., & Prastacos, G. (2010). From task-based to competency-based: A typology and process supporting a critical HRM transition. *Personnel Review, 39*(3), 325–346.

Tett, R. P., & Burnett, D. D. (2003). A personality trait-based interactionist model of job performance. *Journal of Applied Psychology, 88,* 500–517.

Tett, R. P., Guterman, H. A., Bleier, A., & Murphy, P. J. (2000). Development and content validation of a hyperdimensional taxonomy of managerial competence. *Human Performance, 13,* 205–251.

Thoresen, C. J., Bradley, J. C., Bliese, P. D., & Thoresen, J. D. (2004). The Big Five personality traits and individual job performance growth trajectories in maintenance and transitional job stages. *Journal of Applied Psychology, 89,* 835–853.

Warr, P. (2011). *Work, happiness, and unhappiness.* Hove: Psychology Press.

Woods, S. A., & Hampson, S. E. (2010). Predicting adult occupational environments from gender and childhood personality traits. *Journal of Applied Psychology, 95,* 1045–1057.

Woods, S. A., Lievens, F., De Fruyt, F., & Wille, B. (2013). Personality across working life: The longitudinal and reciprocal influences of personality on work. *Journal of Organizational Behavior, 34*(S1), S7–S25.

Woods, S. A., & West, M. A. (2010). *The psychology of work and organizations* (2nd ed.). Boston: Cengage Learning EMEA.

Wrzesniewski, A., & Dutton, J. E. (2001). Crafting a job: Revisioning employees as active crafters of their work. *Academy of Management Review, 26*(2), 179–201.

Zyphur, M. J., Chaturvedi, S., & Arvey, R. D. (2008). Job performance over time is a function of latent trajectories and previous performance. *Journal of Applied Psychology, 93,* 217–224.

How Do I Get a Job, What Are They Looking For? Personnel Selection and Assessment

Silvia Moscoso, Jesús F. Salgado and Neil Anderson

Overview

Personnel selection and assessment (PSA) is one of the most prolific fields of Work and Organizational (W/O) Psychology. PSA is also the most critical process of human resource management (HRM) because it is used by organizations to decide on the person who fits better for a particular position. This fact determines the efficacy of other HRM outcomes (e.g., training success). In this sense, PSA is a decision-making process on the suitability of candidates and, consequently, PSA processes represent the 'barrier to entry' for individuals into any work organization.

This chapter is organized into four main sections. The first section reviews what PSA is and what it aims to predict. This section explores the main theoretical perspectives on PSA and job performance. The second section points out how to choose the most appropriate PSA techniques according to their psychometric properties (e.g., reliability and validity) and according to legal considerations (e.g., adverse impact and indirect discrimination). The third section reviews the most relevant PSA techniques in relation to criterion-oriented validity. The techniques are divided into two main categories: (1) methods of assessment; and (2) procedures for assessing constructs. The fourth section summarizes research on applicant perceptions and reactions carried out since 1990.

As a summary of this chapter, we suggest three conclusions. First, according to the current state-of-the-science, scientific PSA is capable of predicting and explaining over 60% of job performance variance based upon individual differences. Second, future rises in explained variance will probably be based on the development of new assessment technologies and, in particular, on the development of new theoretical approaches for occupational situations. Third, the most valid methods are not necessarily the most widely used in organizations, but paradoxically, also tend to be most popular among applicants.

An Introduction to Work and Organizational Psychology: An International Perspective,
Third Edition. Edited by Nik Chmiel, Franco Fraccaroli and Magnus Sverke.
© 2017 John Wiley & Sons, Ltd. Published 2017 by John Wiley & Sons, Ltd.

2.1   What Is Personnel Selection and Assessment?

Personnel selection and assessment (PSA) is an applied field of both research and practice in Work and Organizational (W/O) Psychology and Human Resource Management (HRM). PSA is used by organizations to determine which of the applicants for a job is the most appropriate for a particular position. In this sense, PSA can be defined as a decision-making process on the suitability of the candidates and, consequently, PSA processes represent the 'barrier to entry' for individuals into any work organization (Anderson, 2005). PSA has a long history of research, mainly in Europe and in North America, but also in other continents (e.g., Asia, Africa and South America). As a scientific discipline, it began around 1900, when the principles and methods of psychology were applied to personnel decisions in Europe and the United States (Salgado, Anderson, & Hülsheger, 2010). The advances in the field were intimately tied to the advances in assessment and measurement procedures and in statistical developments. In our view, PSA is one of the most critical processes in the study of human work behaviour because it determines the efficacy of many other issues of HRM, such as training success, turnover and promotions.

Our PSA concept is based on three important characteristics: (1) it is necessary to use assessment instruments; if this is not done, the process can indeed be considered as one of recruitment, but not of personnel selection, (2) the objective of these instruments is to permit decision-making on the suitability of candidates for a post, and (3) PSA requires a professional who is qualified in the use of such instruments. In order for this process to be carried out in the appropriate manner, it is necessary to know the characteristics of the position (tasks, functions, areas of activity, instruments used in the job, necessary knowledge and training, etc.) and to determine the extent to which the aspirants possess the cognitive abilities, knowledge, aptitude, skills, general abilities, personality dimensions, experience and other characteristics necessary to do the job well. These characteristics (cognitive abilities, knowledge, etc.) have in recent years come to be called competencies, and personnel selection based on their assessment is sometimes called competency-based selection.

2.1.1   Is PSA based on theories?

There are two main theoretical traditions underlying selection processes and candidate assessment methods internationally. The *predictivist perspective* has dominated this area for many years, with thousands of published studies that have adopted this perspective. More recently, attention has turned to the importance of the European approach, perhaps best termed the *constructivist perspective*. Each perspective is not mutually exclusive of course, or wholly attributable to either continent.

2.1.1.1 The predictivist perspective

In essence, the *predictivist* perspective views the job as a given and stable entity for which the most suitable candidate needs to be recruited. *Person–job fit* is therefore of primary importance (e.g., Anderson, 2005). From the predictivist perspective, since the number of applicants usually exceeds the number of job vacancies (and sometimes far exceeds them, depending on labour market conditions), it is the recruiting organization which is seen as making the vital decisions of who to shortlist, and eventually, who to appoint. Selection techniques are therefore referred to as 'predictors' with the more accurate procedures accounting for future job performance more fully than less accurate predictors. The applicant is seen as 'subject' to selection techniques, control of which is vested squarely in the hands of the organization (e.g. Anderson, Born, & Cunningham-Snell, 2010). Recently, however, doubts have been expressed about the on-going viability of this perspective, given the widespread moves toward flexible forms of working and team-based work roles.

2.1.1.2 The constructivist perspective

As job roles become more flexible and as organizations become increasingly aware of the need to compete for the best candidates, selection research from the constructivist perspective has gained momentum. This perspective emphasizes that candidates, as well as organizations, make decisions in selection. Several European authors have described how expectations between the organization and the potential employee build up and how both sides use their meetings during the process to construct a 'viable psychological contract' that underpins their future working relationship. The psychological contract has been defined by Kotter (1973, p. 92) as 'an implicit contract between an individual and his [or her] organization which specifies what each expect to give and receive from each other in their relationship'. The constructivist perspective views selection as a series of social episodes providing an opportunity for both parties to explore whether a future working relationship would be viable. Selection therefore serves as an opportunity for information exchange and the development of mutual expectations and obligations. For example, interactions between the applicant and an organization during selection may affect the applicant's initial expectations and attitudes about the organization. Hence from this perspective, selection not only aims to ensure person–job fit but also *person–organization fit* (i.e., the fit between the applicant's values and the organizational culture), and *person–team fit* (i.e., the fit between the applicant's skills and attitudes and the climate of their immediate working group).

The constructivist perspective is closely related to the Attraction–Selection–Attrition (ASA) paradigm (Schneider, Goldstein, & Smith, 1995). According to the ASA paradigm 'the people make the place'. This means that the attributes of employees (e.g., abilities and personality) are the most relevant factors in job performance. Additionally, candidates are differentially attracted to jobs and organizations select employees whom they view as compatible with the organizational culture and climate and who can be compatible for a number of different jobs. Over time, employees who do not fit in well are more likely to leave. The consequence of this process is that employees who work at the organization become increasingly homogenous.

2.1.2   What does PSA aim to predict?

What is to be predicted? What behaviours and outcomes are relevant for organizations and candidates? For a century, it was believed that the aim of personnel selection was to predict overall job performance (OJP) and that performance was a single entity, whether assessed using a single global dimension or as a composite of multiple dimensions. However, today it is known that some assessment procedures can predict some performance-related behaviours and outcomes (e.g., task performance) very efficiently but are poor predictors of other performance-related behaviours (e.g., contextual performance, counterproductive work behaviours, leadership potential, and so on). Thus, the first step in personnel selection is to determine performance criteria for future employees.

At present, there is consensus among researchers that the job performance domain includes at least three main sub-domains: (1) task performance (TP); (2) contextual (citizenship) performance (CP); and (3) counterproductive work behaviours (CWB). Figure 2.1 represents the performance domain and its dimensions and sub-dimensions.

Task performance is defined as the proficiency with which employees perform core activities that are relevant to the job (Borman, Bryant, & Dorio, 2010). Task performance can be subdivided into individual performance and work-team performance. Contextual performance (also called citizenship performance) relates

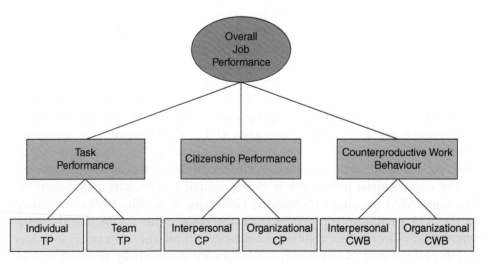

Figure 2.1:   Hierarchical structure of job performance

to the contributions of the employee to the organizational, social and psychological environment to help to accomplish organizational goals (Hoffman & Dilchert, 2012). CWB has been defined as any intentional behaviour of an employee viewed by the organization as contrary to its legitimate interests (Sackett & De Vore, 2001). Two further sub-dimensions of counterproductive performance have been identified, i.e., a sub-dimension related to interpersonal counterproductive behaviour, e.g., abusive supervision, aggression, bullying; and a sub-dimension related to organizational counterproductive behaviour, e.g., theft, voluntary absenteeism, low effort (Hoffman & Dilchert, 2012). Empirical evidence has shown that there is some degree of interrelationship among the three sub-domains (Conway, 1996). There is also meta-analytic evidence that, after controlling for halo error and reliability, a general factor in job performance ratings remains (Viswesvaran, Schmidt, & Ones, 2005), explaining 60% of the total variance.

A note of caution on criterion measurement is required. For some types of job, objective and independent measures of performance are virtually impossible to obtain. This is especially the case for service-related jobs where no physical output is involved (e.g. social workers, police officers, university professors). Often it is problematic to obtain an unbiased rating of performance. A supervisor may, for example, be prone to various errors such as personal-liking bias, or over-estimating performance when they were personally involved in the selection decision (known as *criterion contamination*). Collectively, these difficulties are known as the 'criterion problem'. The crucial point is that 'measures' of performance will almost always be imperfect or biased in some way (e.g., Viswesvaran & Ones, 2001). In connection with this, it is important to note that reliability of supervisory ratings is .52 for a single rater (Salgado, 2015; Salgado, Moscoso, & Anderson, 2016; Viswesvaran, Ones, & Schmidt, 1996), although the interrater reliability can be slightly larger than .60 in the validity studies of personnel selection (Salgado & Moscoso, 1996). The issue of the reliability of job performance measures is important because its effect is to attenuate the true validity of the selection techniques.

2.2 How to Choose Selection Techniques

When choosing between different selection techniques, it is necessary to consider several psychometric characteristics, including *reliability*, *validity*, and *adverse impact*. An important requirement is that a selection technique is reliable. Reliability is the extent to which the selection technique is consistent and free from random variation and other measurement errors. It is axiomatic that reliability is highly desirable and that an organization should be attempting to use selection methods that possess the highest level of reliability practicable. There are several ways to estimate reliability, for instance, internal consistency, parallel forms, and test-retest (see Table 2.1 for a definition). The second, and probably the most important, psychometric characteristic in personnel selection is validity evidence, particularly, evidence of *criterion-related validity*. This can be defined as the degree to which a selection technique can predict a criterion of job performance. Typically, criterion-oriented validity is estimated using a correlation coefficient. Therefore, the higher the correlation is, the greater is the validity. Two additional aspects of validity are construct validity and content validity (see Box 2.1).

Consideration must also be given to the potential *adverse impact* of selection techniques on minority groups protected by law. Adverse impact is a neutral term which reflects potential systematic differences in the assessments of candidates belonging to a protected-by-law group during the hiring processes. The negative consequences of adverse impact not only involve possible legal action, but also the failure to offer employment to candidates who will prove to be the more successful job performers. Across Europe and North America, countries have different legal approaches to dealing with discrimination (see Sackett et al., 2010). The most stringent anti-discrimination legislation exists in the United States and in some countries in the European Union (e.g. the U.K) where long-standing concerns over adverse impact have existed. *Unfair discrimination* may occur either directly or indirectly. *Direct discrimination* involves the conscious decision to

---

Box 2.1:   Types of validity and reliability

1. *Predictive validity*: the extent to which selection scores predict future job performance. Successful applicants are tracked through the selection process and after a period of employment with the organization, a subsequent measure of performance is obtained. The selection and criterion ratings are correlated.

2. *Concurrent validity*: the extent to which selection scores predict current performance. Selection techniques are administered to existing job incumbents and correlated with ratings of job performance taken over the same time period.

3. *Construct validity*: the extent to which selection accurately measures the constructs or dimensions it was designed to assess. The selection method is correlated with another method which is known to accurately reflect the construct.

4. *Content validity*: the extent to which the selection process adequately samples all the important dimensions of the job. This requires a thorough examination of the job description and job specification.

5. *Face validity*: the extent to which the applicant perceives the selection method to be relevant to the job.

6. *Parallel reliability*: the measurement consistency. Each candidate completes two equivalent selection methods and the two scores are correlated.

7. *Test-retest reliability*: the measurement consistency. Candidates complete the same selection method at two time points. The two scores are then correlated.

8. *Split-half reliability*: the measurement consistency. Items from a measure are divided into two halves (e.g. odd-numbered versus even-numbered items) and the scores from each half correlated.

reject certain applicants on the basis of irrelevant criteria, such as race or sex. *Indirect discrimination* is usually unintentional, arising when the selection method turns out to be favourable to one particular group, despite similar treatment for all groups. Anti-discrimination research has tended to define selection fairness, with fairness being measured statistically, as pertaining only to minority groups, purely in terms of the selection outcome and not the process (Hough, Oswald, & Ployhart, 2001).

We have highlighted that a number of vitally important factors or contingencies should influence an organization's choice between different selection methods (Kehoe, Mol, & Anderson, 2016). Figure 2.2 summarizes the main contingencies, but also represents the trade-off which is so often observed between the more valid, reliable and fair methods and their immediate cost, need for expertise, and time-consuming administration. Before we turn our attention to different selection techniques, it is important to note that no procedure is 100% accurate all the time. Choices therefore have to be made between efficacy and administration costs. However, the results from *utility analysis*, which estimate the financial payback of more accurate selection to an organization, demonstrate that substantial financial gains will accrue by using more valid and reliable methods (Hunter & Schmidt, 1982).

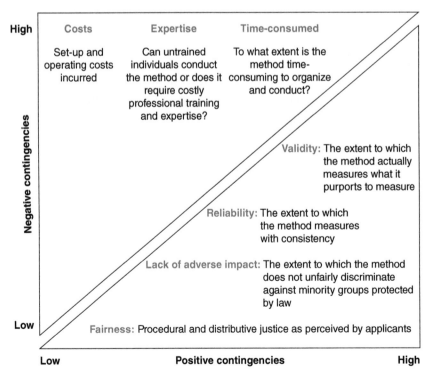

Figure 2.2:   Contingency factors in choosing selection methods

2.3   Selection Techniques and Procedures

Following the suggestion of Hunter and Hunter (1984), we will classify the selection techniques as methods of assessment (this group includes application forms, biodata, interviews, work sample tests, job knowledge and situational judgment tests, assessment centres and reference checks, among others) and procedures for assessing constructs (e.g., general mental ability and specific ability tests, personality inventories and job experience).

2.3.1   Methods of assessment

The meta-analytic evidence of the validity of the methods of assessment is summarized in Table 2.1, which reports the corrected or operational validity of the most common methods of assessment used in personnel selection for predicting overall job performance. Readers should take into account that the corrected or operational validity is typically the correlation between an assessment method (e.g., biodata, interview, etc.) and job performance after correction for job performance reliability and any range restriction in the measure used.

2.3.1.1   *Application forms and curriculum vitae*

Although application forms are very popular in the United Kingdom, there are cultural differences across Europe with standard application documents being more popular in Germany and curriculum vitae being more prevalent in Denmark (Shackleton & Newell, 1997). Both these methods can be used to pre-screen applicants in order to generate a short list to be invited to the next stage. To facilitate effective pre-screening, an application form should ideally be designed to reflect the selection criteria and a systematic screening process adhered to.

Table 2.1: Criterion-related validity of the assessment methods for predicting job performance

Method	Average corrected validity
Biodata	.35[a]
Unstructured interview	.20[b]
Conventional structured interview	.35[c]
Structured behavioural interview	.62[d]
Work sample test	.33[e]
Job knowledge test	.48[f]
Situational judgement test	.26[g]
Assessment centre	.36[h]
Reference check	.26[i]

Note. [a] From Rothstein et al. (1990); [b] from Huffcutt et al. (1996); [c] from Huffcutt et al. (1996); [d] from Salgado & Moscoso (2006); [e] from Roth et al. (2005); [f] from Hunter and Hunter (1984); [g] from McDaniel et al. (2007); [h] from Gaugler et al. (1987); [i] from Hunter and Hunter (1984).

However, research into graduate recruitment suggests that the typical process is far from systematic (Wingrove, Glendinning, & Herriot, 1984) and this can clearly impact negatively on the selection process in the longer term.

2.3.1.2 Biodata

An alternative method for pre-screening is to use biodata, also called biographical information blanks. Biodata are structured forms asking information about a person's past life and work experience. Identification of valid biodata items usually involves establishing significant correlations between biographical data and criterion measures for a group of job incumbents. The significant items are then used as criteria for future selection decisions and the evidence suggests that biodata has a good level of criterion-related validity. A meta-analysis by Rohstein et al. (1990) found an operational validity coefficient (i.e., the observed validity corrected for criterion unreliability and predictor range restriction) of 0.35 for biodata measures against the criteria of job performance. They also found that the correlation of biodata with general mental ability was around .50. Despite its strong validity as an initial stage pre-screening method, biodata is rarely used. This is probably due to the costs involved in setting up a properly designed biodata form along with the poor face validity of biodata as question items may have no obvious connection with the job (e.g., life experience in high school or the military).

2.3.1.3 Interviews

The interview, in all of its guises, remains the most popular method of candidate assessment across Europe and the United States. Applicants also tend to rate the interview highly (e.g., Anderson, Salgado, & Hulsheger, 2010; Kehoe, Mol, & Anderson, 2016). Meta-analyses have found that interviews, especially structured interviews, are considerably more valid and reliable than earlier narrative reviews had suggested (e.g. Conway, Jako, & Goodman, 1995; Salgado & Moscoso, 2006). Indeed, it has become an unfortunate part of human resource management folklore that the interview is fundamentally flawed, but has to remain a component of any selection process simply because it provides the best opportunity for a face-to-face meeting between the organization and the applicant. This received wisdom is widely believed among personnel practitioners, but the unambiguous results of all of the recent meta-analyses indicate that interviews can be almost as valid and reliable as other more costly selection methods. Salgado and Moscoso (2006) summarized the meta-analytic studies on the validity of behavioural structured interviews and found an average operational validity of .62. Huffcutt, Roth, and McDaniel (1996) found that conventional structured interviews showed an operational validity of .35, and that unstructured interviews showed an operational validity of .20. Clearly structured interviews are more valid and reliable than unstructured interviews.

But what exactly is meant by 'structure' in the selection interview? Structured interview designs usually incorporate several of the following elements:

1. in-depth job analyses, commonly using critical incident techniques;
2. standardized questions asked in the same order of all candidates;
3. candidates' replies rated on behaviourally anchored rating scales;
4. interviewer training to ensure that all interviewers understand and adhere to the standardized format;
5. computation of the outcome evaluation via arithmetic combination of ratings on job-relevant dimensions.

Salgado and Moscoso (2002) classified structured interviews into two types, based on the content of the interview questions: (1) conventional interviews; and (2) behavioural interviews. Structured conventional interviews (SCI) are typically composed of questions directed at checking credentials, descriptions of experience and self-evaluative information. Structured behavioural interviews (SBI) include questions concerning job knowledge, job experience and behaviour descriptions. Salgado and Moscoso's (2002) meta-analysis showed that conventional interviews assessed general mental ability, job experience, personality dimensions and social skills, while behavioural interviews mainly assessed job knowledge, job experience and social skills. These findings showed than conventional and behavioural interviews are clearly two different types of interview.

Paradoxically, one of the reasons why the interview remains so popular is that it offers a flexible and unstructured opportunity for recruiters and candidates to exchange information (Dipboye, 1997). The dilemma then is between maximizing predictive validity while simultaneously retaining sufficient flexibility. This has resulted in many organizations developing semi-structured formats which include elements of the highly structured approach but which leave some free time for more open discussion (Dipboye, 1997).

2.3.1.4 *Work sample tests*

Work samples involve identifying tasks representative of the job and using these to develop a representative short test resembling actual components of the job. For example, a typing test may be used as part of the selection process for a secretarial position. Not surprisingly therefore, applicants rate work sample tests very positively, perceiving them as fair, valid and job-related (Anderson et al., 2010). Work sample tests also have highly acceptable predictive validity. Roth, Bobko, and McFarland (2005) carried out the largest meta-analytic study on the validity of work sample tests. These authors reported an average operational validity of .33 for predicting job performance and they also found that work sample test correlated .38 with general mental ability.

Again, perhaps not surprisingly, rating the applicant actually performing key tasks is an accurate means of evaluating their subsequent performance in jobs which require little further training before proficiency can be achieved by the individual.

2.3.1.5 Job knowledge tests and situational judgment tests

Job knowledge tests are techniques for assessing the degree to which the assessees possess the knowledge needed for a specific job. This type of test includes two main assessment methods: (1) job knowledge tests, and (2) situational judgement tests. As with work sample tests, job knowledge tests can be used only for experienced candidates (Schmidt & Hunter, 1998) because this assessment method requires previous practical knowledge of the job requirements.

A meta-analysis by Hunter and Hunter (1984) examined the validity of job knowledge tests for predicting job performance. They found an operational validity of .48 for predicting overall job performance. The meta-analysis of Schmidt, Hunter and Outerbridge (1986) found a corrected correlation of .48 between job knowledge tests and general mental ability.

Situational judgment tests are a type of job knowledge test which present the individual with hypothetical job scenarios and ask the candidates to identify the most appropriate answer for effective job performance. With regard to situational judgement tests, McDaniel, Hartman, Whetzel, and Grubb (2007) found an operational validity of .26. These same researchers found a correlation of .32 between general mental ability and situational judgment tests.

2.3.1.6 Assessment centres

Assessment centres (ACs) involve a combination of selection methods, commonly, in-basket tests, leaderless group discussion, case analysis, role-play and other simulations, but also cognitive ability tests, personality tests and interviews. These are given to a group of candidates over the course of a day, or several days where candidates' behaviours are rated by a number of trained assessors along identified selection dimensions. Organizations may use ACs for selection, promotion and for development purposes. Across Europe, there are wide differences in the use of ACs for selection; they are more common, particularly in large organizations, in the United Kingdom, Belgium, Denmark and Germany, and less common in France, Switzerland, Spain and Italy (Shackleton & Newell, 1997). Overall, applicants tend to favour assessment centres, probably due to their use of work samples and the opportunity that they provide to meet with assessors and to perform job-related exercises alongside other candidates (Anderson et al., 2001; Anderson et al., 2010).

The criterion-related validity of well-designed ACs is relatively strong although higher validities are observed when predicting potential rather than actual performance. In a seminal meta-analysis, Gaugler, Rosenthal, Thornton, and Bentson (1987) found an average operational validity of .36 for predicting job performance when an overall assessment rating (OAR) was used. More recently, Hoffman, Kennedy, Lance, LoPilato, and Monahan (2015) analyzed the validity of the most typical assessment centre exercises, including oral presentations, in-basket tests, case analysis, leaderless group discussions and role-play. They found that the operational validity of these exercises ranged from .18 to .26. Based on these validities and the intercorrelation among the exercises, the best estimate of the corrected validity of the OAR appears to be the coefficient found by Gaugler et al. (1987).

Not every exercise measures every dimension in an AC. Rather, a *targeted matrix* is developed whereby certain exercises are designed to elicit behaviours by candidates relevant to some of the dimensions. Figure 2.3 shows one example of such a targeted matrix with the exercises listed along the top horizontal axis and the dimensions evaluated listed in the first vertical column.

Assessors rate candidates on a five-point scale in this particular matrix, note that the blacked-out boxes indicate that the exercise does not measure that particular dimension. Once all exercises are completed and rated, the assessors then need to meet to agree a final combined rating, the so-called 'Overall Assessment Rating' or OAR. The OAR for the candidate shown in Figure 2.3 is likely to be a '4' and assuming that higher ratings represent stronger within-exercise performance, this candidate is likely therefore to be successful on this occasion.

Not surprisingly, ACs are usually far more expensive than, say, a test of cognitive ability or even a structured interview. From Table 2.1 it is clear that their operational validity is not as high as for these other, less costly techniques.

Dimensions	Interview	Written Analysis Exercise	Exercises Strategic Meeting	Leaderless Group Meeting
Adaptability	4	5		
Analysis		4		
Creativity		4		4
Interpersonal skills	5		4	
Initiative	4		3	
Judgement		4	4	4
Energy				5
Oral Communication				3
Persuasiveness		4	4	5
Planning/organizing		5	4	4
Sensitivity to others	3	4	4	
Tolerance for stress		4	5	
Work standards	5	5	4	5
Written communication		5		

Figure 2.3: Example of a targeted AC matrix

2.3.1.7 Reference checks

This technique is typically used at the end of the selection process. Usually, a reference check consists of collecting information on an individual from a third party, for example, the applicant's previous employer. In the European Union (EU), the use of reference checks is more common in the United Kingdom, Ireland and Belgium than in France, Sweden, the Netherlands and Portugal (Shackleton & Newell, 1997). Reference checks may involve either an open-ended format or a structured format with questions developed from selection criteria. Reference checks may serve at least two purposes: (1) to confirm the accuracy of information provided by the applicant; and (2) to obtain information on the applicant's previous work experience and performance. The reference checks are used in similar ways for high and low complexity jobs and used by large, medium and small companies (Lado, 2012).

With regard to the validity of the reference check, Hunter and Hunter (1984) found an operational validity of .26 for predicting overall job performance. More recently, Lado (2012) found that reference checks correlate .25 with general mental ability and .17 with job experience. Research also suggests that reference checks suffer from leniency errors, with few applicants given negative evaluations (Lado, 2012). Reference checks are therefore rarely used in the decision-making process, but are more likely to be used merely as a final check before any job offer is made.

2.3.2 Procedures for assessing constructs

The evidence from meta-analytic findings for the most common procedures for assessing constructs can be seen in Table 2.2. It includes the corrected validity of cognitive ability tests, personality inventories and job experience.

Table 2.2: Criterion-related validity of the construct-assessing procedures for predicting job performance

Construct	Average corrected validity
General mental ability test	.62[a]
Numerical ability test	.52[a]
Spatial-mechanical ability test	.51[a]
Verbal ability test	.62[a]
Perceptual ability test	.52[a]
Memory test	.56[a]
Conscientiousness [†]	.22[b]
Emotional stability [†]	.11[b]
Job experience	.25[c]

Notes. [†]= validity of the single stimulus (SS) personality inventories.
[a] from Salgado et al. (2003a; 2003b); [b] from Barrick & Mount (1991); [c] from McDaniel, et al. (1986).

2.3.2.1 *General and specific cognitive ability tests*

General mental ability (GMA) can be defined as the capacity of an individual to learn rapidly and accurately in optimal conditions of instruction (Schmidt & Hunter, 1998). Consequently, less time taken and greater accuracy reflect greater GMA. In addition, there are a number of specific cognitive abilities, including verbal, numerical, spatial, memory, perceptual and reasoning, among others (Salgado & Anderson, 2002). Typically, general and specific cognitive abilities are assessed by using psychometric tests. The administration of psychometric tests is governed by fixed procedures and test results are typically interpreted by comparing an individual's score to data collected on previous samples who have taken the same test.

Research on the criterion-related validity of cognitive abilities tests in personnel selection is divided into two main approaches (Schmitt, 2014). The first approach considers that specific cognitive abilities do not add validity beyond the validity of GMA. The second approach maintains that specific cognitive abilities can show incremental validity beyond GMA.

Meta-analyses have demonstrated notably robust predictive validity for cognitive ability tests. For example, Hunter and Hunter (1984), using a database of 515 single studies (n = 38,620) conducted with the US General Aptitude Test Battery (GATB), found an average operational validity of .45 for predicting job performance and of .54 for predicting training proficiency. In the European Union, Salgado, Anderson and their colleagues have carried out several meta-analyses using studies conducted in Belgium, France, Germany, Ireland, the Netherlands, Norway, Spain, Sweden and the United Kingdom (Salgado & Anderson, 2003; Salgado et al., 2003b). The results showed that GMA tests were valid predictors across 12 occupational categories, including drivers, electricians, information clerks, engineers, managers, police, salesmen, typing worker, skilled worked, chemists, mechanics and industrial apprentices. The average operational validity was .62 (n = 9,554) for predicting job performance and .54 (n = 16,065) for predicting training proficiency.

Salgado, Anderson and their colleagues have also examined the validity of several specific cognitive abilities, including verbal, numerical, spatial-mechanical, perceptual and memory (Salgado, Anderson, Moscoso, Bertua, & De Fruyt, 2003a). The results showed that the operational validity of these measures was smaller than the validity of GMA measures. Also examined was the incremental validity of specific abilities beyond GMA validity. They found that incremental validity was practically nil for both job performance and training success.

In summary, the meta-analytic findings across the globe obtained over the last 35 years have demonstrated that: (1) GMA tests or a combination of several specific cognitive ability tests are the most valid predictor of overall job performance for all types of occupations, and .62 is the best estimate of operational validity; (2) the sizes of the estimates of criterion-related operational validity are similar across countries; and (3) specific cognitive tests are also valid predictors of overall performance, but their validity is smaller than the GMA validity.

2.3.2.2 *Personality inventories*

The use of personality measures for selection has become increasingly popular across the world although applicants tend to react somewhat less favourably to these tests than to cognitive ability tests (Anderson et al., 2010). Recent advances in the domain of personality at work were due, in great extension, to the use of the Five Factor Model (FFM) as a construct-oriented approach. The FFM has been supported by compelling research findings although there is an on-going debate over its comprehensiveness (e.g., Judge et al., 2013). The FFM of the structure of personality posits that there are five basic personality dimensions or factors ('the Big Five'), hierarchically organized (Judge et al., 2013):

1. *Emotional stability* (secure, non-anxious, self-confident versus depressed, unstable);
2. *Extroversion* (sociable, assertive versus timid and reserved);
3. *Openness to experience* (creative, curious, versus practical with narrow interests);
4. *Agreeableness* (likeable, co-operative versus antagonistic, rude);
5. *Conscientiousness* (hardworking, dependable, versus lazy, disorganized).

Seminal work on the FFM was conducted by Barrick and Mount (1991), who hypothesized that conscientiousness and emotional stability would be valid predictors of job performance for all occupational groups. Furthermore, they hypothesized that extroversion and agreeableness would be predictive of job performance in occupations with frequent interpersonal interactions (e.g., sales and managerial occupations) and that openness to experience would be a valid predictor for training proficiency. Their results partially supported these hypotheses. Subsequently Salgado (1997) examined the validity of the Big Five in the European Community. The results of Salgado's (1997) study essentially replicated the findings by Barrick and Mount.

Three additional meta-analyses have since added invaluable information. Salgado (2002) showed that conscientiousness and agreeableness were predictors of counterproductive behaviours (i.e. deviant behaviours at work) and that the five dimensions predicted turnover. Salgado (2003) found conscientiousness and emotional stability measures based on the FFM to have higher validity than other measures. More recently, the meta-analyses of Salgado and Tauriz (2014) and Salgado, Anderson, and Tauriz (2015a) examined the validity of the FFM when a forced-choice format is used for the measurement of the personality dimensions. They found that the quasi-ipsative forced-choice response formats increased dramatically the validity of the personality inventories. Table 2.3 reports a comparison of the validity coefficients for the quasi-ipsative and single-stimulus (e.g., Likert scales) formats. As can be seen, for instance, using a quasi-ipsative format, conscientiousness showed an operational validity of .38 *versus* an operational validity of .22 when a single-stimulus format is used. The validity of emotional stability is also greater for the quasi-ipsative formats (.20 *vs.* .11), openness to experience (.22 *vs.* .05) and agreeableness (.16 *vs.* .08).

Table 2.3: Criterion-related validity of the single-stimulus (SS) and quasi-ipsative (QI) personality inventories for predicting job performance (from Salgado et al. (2015a))

Construct	Average corrected validity-SS	Average corrected validity – QI
Conscientiousness	.22	.38
Emotional stability	.11	.20
Extroversion	.12	.12
Agreeableness	.08	.16
Openness to experience	.05	.22

Therefore, the conclusions of the cumulated research on the FFM in the past 25 years can be summarized as follows: (1) the taxonomy of personality traits derived from the FFM has proved to be a very useful framework for organizing various single measures and is now accepted as the paradigm in the field. Widespread use of this taxonomy has allowed personnel selection researchers to adequately respond to the concerns of Guion and Gottier (1965) regarding the lack of a widely accepted personality model; (2) conscientiousness is the best personality predictor of job performance and counterproductive behaviours, and it has shown validity generalization across samples, occupations, and countries. The operational validity of conscientiousness was found to be .39 when a quasi-ipsative forced choice format was used (Salgado, Anderson, & Tauriz, 2015a; Salgado & Tauriz, 2014); (3) emotional stability was the second most relevant personality predictor of job performance and counterproductive work behaviours, (4) conscientiousness, emotional stability and agreeableness are the most valid predictors of overall counterproductive behaviours, interpersonally-oriented counterproductive behaviours and organizationally oriented counterproductive behaviours (Berry et al., 2007); (5) conscientiousness, emotional stability and agreeableness showed incremental validity over GMA for predicting overall job performance (Salgado & De Fruyt, 2005); (6) and the format of the personality inventory is an important moderator of the criterion-related validity of the Big Five dimensions, so that the validity increases dramatically when quasi-ipsative forced-choice formats are used (Salgado & Tauriz, 2014; Salgado et al., 2015a).

In addition to measures of the Big Five, integrity tests (sometimes called honesty tests) are also important techniques for personnel selection. Integrity tests are compound inventories of the Big Five personality dimensions, and meta-analytic research has revealed that the validity of personality-based integrity tests has been estimated at .37 for predicting job performance, and .42 for overall counterproductive behaviours (Ones, Viswesvaran, & Schmidt, 1993). Thus, the joint effect of these three basic personality dimensions explains the high validity of this personality measure.

Typically, personality measures are not used alone in personnel selection processes but alongside other instruments, mainly GMA tests, either at the same stage or at different stages in the overall procedure. Salgado and De Fruyt (2005) demonstrated that three personality dimensions showed incremental validity over GMA: conscientiousness, agreeableness and emotional stability. The first dimensions resulted in strong additions of explained variance beyond GMA, specifically 30.3% and 20.12% for conscientiousness and agreeableness, respectively. Emotional stability also added validity over GMA but the percentage was smaller, 9.07%. With regard to the training proficiency criterion, three personality dimensions showed an important increment in the explained variance over GMA: conscientiousness, openness to experience and extroversion. Agreeableness also showed added validity, but the size of the increment was modest. Conscientiousness, openness and extroversion showed incremental validity by 24.20%, 22.24% and 18.04% respectively, and agreeableness added validity by 7.47% over GMA explained variance.

The results of these two final meta-analyses suggest that a good option for the practitioner, in the majority of cases, is to combine GMA measures with measures of conscientiousness, emotional stability and agreeableness to predict job performance, and to combine GMA tests with measures of conscientiousness, extroversion and openness to predict training proficiency.

2.3.2.3 *Job experience*

In the practice of personnel selection, job experience is usually conceptualized as the number of years of experience on the same or similar job. Therefore, the length of service is used as a proxy for experience on the job.

Schmidt, Hunter, and Outerbridge (1986) found job performance increased linearly as a function of job experience for the first five years, but thereafter the relationship between the two was much reduced. When the amount of job experience was five years or less, the operational validity was .33 for predicting supervisory ratings of job performance.

2.4 Applicant Reactions and Decision Making in Selection

A recurrent theme in this chapter has been the acknowledgement of the increasing importance of the candidates' perspective in selection. Meta-analysis and narrative reviews suggest that candidates prefer methods which appear to be more job-relevant, which are non-intrusive, which do not invade personal privacy, and which in general seem to be fair and objective (Anderson, 2003; Anderson et al., 2010).

In the past few years, a number of frameworks for examining the social issues involved in selection have emerged, providing more detailed insight into the aetiology of the applicants' perspective. Gilliland's (1993) Selection Fairness Model is notable in moving beyond a list of the likely determinants of fairness perceptions, towards developing a framework that is rooted in organizational justice theory (OJT). OJT distinguishes between *procedural justice* and *distributive justice*, referring to the fairness of the selection process and to the fairness of the hiring decision respectively. Consistent with OJT, Gilliland suggests that it is the combined satisfaction or violation of specific rules that produces overall evaluations of procedural and distributive fairness.

Research indicates that candidates' reactions to selection justice can have an impact on three important outcomes (Truxillo et al., 2016). First, perceptions of justice influence applicants' reactions and decisions during hiring, for example, the extent to which the candidate will recommend the organization to others, and their intention to withdraw from the procedure. Second, perceptions of fairness impinge upon candidates' attitudes and behaviours after being hired or rejected, for example, organizational commitment, intention to leave, and work performance in the case of being hired, and the decision of whether to pursue (discrimination) cases if rejected. Third, perceived fairness influences applicants' well-being and self-perceptions, such as self-esteem and self-efficacy.

The second premise that has received considerable attention in applicant reactions research is based on causal attribution theory. This theory pertains to the *attributions* people make as to the causes of all kinds of events, which form the basis for a variety of expectations, intentions, and behaviours. Following this line of thinking, Ployhart and Harold (2004) developed applicant attribution-reaction theory (AART), in which they state that applicants' affective, behavioural and cognitive reactions to selection (e.g., fairness and test perceptions, test performance and motivation) are caused by an attributional process. The focal tenet of the theory is that between objective events (e.g., treatment during the selection procedure, the hiring decision and explanation of the hiring decision) and the formation of reactions, applicants engage in attributional processing of the causes for the particular selection outcome. In a selection situation, for instance, applicants who receive a rejection decision may not react negatively toward the organization if they believe the decision to be based on their own substandard performance during testing. However, if a rejected applicant perceives the rejection as unfair (perceived to be caused by biased tests, unfair procedures, an incompetent committee, etc.), he or she might react more negatively. A third possibility is that the applicant perceives the negative decision as being caused by an external and uncontrollable factor, for example, an extremely low selection ratio (Ployhart & Harold, 2004).

AART also explains the occurrence of a self-serving bias in applicant reactions: Applicants who are hired by an organization generally perceive the procedure and organization as fair, while those who are rejected arrive at the opposite conclusion. Thus, in keeping their self-perceptions intact, rejected applicants lower their perceptions of an organization. To reduce the chances of this bias, organizations may provide applicants with clear information about the selection procedure and decision (Ployhart & Harold, 2004).

A meta-analysis carried out by Anderson et al. (2010) examined applicant perceptions and reactions using studies conducted in 17 countries spread worldwide through Europe, North America, Asia and Africa. With small exceptions, interviews, work sample tests and curriculum vitae were the procedures perceived most favourably. Cognitive tests, personality inventories and reference checks were perceived quite favourably. Finally, personal contacts and graphology were perceived unfavourably. Anderson et al. (2010) also examined the relationship between applicant reactions and the validity of the selection procedures. They found large correlations (over .60) between the validity of the procedures and the perceptions of favourability, scientific evidence, face validity and opportunity to perform.

In sum, rejected applicants' self- and organizational perceptions might be two sides of the same coin: it may be impossible to increase the two types of rejected applicants' perceptions simultaneously. It is axiomatic then, that selected as well as rejected applicants' reactions to selection should remain just as important a concern as validity, reliability, or adverse impact (Truxillo et al., 2016).

Summary

In order to answer the question posed in the chapter title: 'How do I get a job, what are they looking for?', this chapter has given an overview of some of the critical theoretical approaches, research findings and practical ramifications of personnel selection. Our intention throughout has been to provide an introduction to the fast-moving field of research and day-to-day applied practice which today constitutes recruitment and selection. We have explicitly emphasized a 'European' constructivist perspective by arguing that candidates, as well as organizations, reach decisions as a result of their experiences during selection. Finally, we suggest three conclusions. First, according to the current state of the art, scientific personnel selection is capable of predicting and explaining over 60% of job performance variance based on individual differences. Second, future rises in the explained variance will probably be based on the development of new assessment technologies and, specially, on the development of new theoretical approaches for occupational situations. Third, this review presents some interesting and perplexing findings – most notably that the most valid methods, also popular among candidates, are not necessarily the most widely used in organizations (Anderson et al., 2010).

It is our hope that this chapter may stimulate readers to reconsider personnel selection in light of these very practically oriented research findings, many of which have appeared only in recent years, and finally to apply some of the principles of a systems approach to real-life organizational selection procedures.

Discussion Points

1 If you were a personnel manager, which of the two theoretical perspectives on PSA would you find most appropriate and useful?
2 According to the criterion-related validity, which PSA technique would you consider better for predicting job performance? Why?

Acknowledgements

The three authors contributed equally; the order of authorship is arbitrary. This chapter was partially supported by the Ministry of Economy and Competitiveness (Spain) [grant number PSI2014-56615-P] to Jesús F. Salgado and Silvia Moscoso.

Suggested Further Reading

Farr, J. L., & Tippins, N. T. (Eds.). (2016). *Handbook of personnel selection* (2nd ed.). Mahwah, NJ: Erlbaum. The reader will find specific reviews of all the topics covered in the present chapter. This handbook is unique in that it provides an account of the European history of personnel selection. In addition, it includes an important section on legal and ethical issues in employee selection.

Nikolaou, I., & Oostrom, J. K. (Eds.). (2015). *Employee recruitment, selection, and assessment: Contemporary issues for theory and practice.* London: Psychology Press and Routledge Academic. This monograph covers some recent advances on topics such as e-recruitment, the value and impact of video résumés, social networking websites in personnel selection, and selection for innovation.

Ones, D., Anderson, N. R., Viswesvaran, C., & Sinangil, H. K. (2016). *Handbook of industrial, work and organizational psychology* (2nd ed.). London: Sage. An international handbook, volume 1 provides comprehensive, state-of-the-art overviews of personnel assessment and selection, job performance, predictors used for personnel selection, and other important topics such as recruitment, utility analysis, and expatriate selection.

Schmitt, N. (Ed.). (2012). *The Oxford handbook of personnel assessment and selection.* New York: Oxford University Press. Together with Farr and Tippins' handbook, Schmitt's handbook is the most authoritative book on personnel selection. The handbook mainly covers the US approach to personnel selection.

References

Anderson, N. R. (2003). Applicant and recruiter reactions to new technology in selection: A critical review and agenda for future research. *International Journal of Selection and Assessment, 11,* 121–136.

Anderson, N. R. (2005). Relationships between practice and research in personnel selection: Does the left hand know what the right hand is doing? In A. Evers, N. Anderson, & O. Smit-Voskuyl (Eds.), *The Blackwell handbook of selection.* Oxford: Blackwell.

Anderson, N. R., Born, M., & Cunningham-Snell, N. (2001). Recruitment and selection: Applicant perspectives and outcomes. In N. Anderson, D. Ones, H. K. Sinangil, & C. Viswesvaran (Eds.), *Handbook of industrial, work, and organizational psychology*, vol. 1. London: Sage.

Anderson, N. R., Salgado, J. F., & Hulsheger, U. (2010). Applicant reactions in selection: Comprehensive meta-analysis into reaction generalization versus situation specificity. *International Journal of Selection and Assessment, 18,* 291–304.

Barrick, M. R., & Mount, M. K. (1991). The Big Five personality dimensions and job performance: A meta-analysis. *Personnel Psychology, 44,* 1–26.

Berry, C. M., Ones, D. S., & Sackett, P. R. (2007). Interpersonal deviance, organizational deviance, and their common correlates: A review and meta-analysis. *Journal of Applied Psychology, 92,* 410–424.

Borman, W. C., Bryant, R. H., & Dorio, J. (2010). The measurement of task performance as criteria in selection research. In J. L. Farr, & N. Tippins (Eds.), *Handbook of employee selection.* New York: Routledge.

Conway, J. M. (1996). Additional construct validity evidence for the task/contextual performance distinction. *Human Performance, 9,* 309–329.

Conway, J. M., Jako, R. A., & Goodman, D. E. (1995). A meta-analysis of interrater and internal consistency reliability of employment interviews. *Journal of Applied Psychology, 80,* 565–579.

Dipboye, R. L (1997). Structured selection interviews: Why do they work? Why are they underutilized? In N. Anderson, & P. Herriot (Eds.), *International handbook of selection and assessment.* Chichester: John Wiley & Sons, Ltd.

Gaugler, B. B., Rosenthal, D. B., Thornton, G. C., & Bentson, C. (1987). Meta-analysis of assessment centre validity. *Journal of Applied Psychology, 72,* 493–511.

Gilliland, S. W. (1993). The perceived fairness of selection systems: An organizational justice perspective. *Academy of Management Review, 18,* 696–734.

Guion, R. M., & Gottier, R. F. (1965). Validity of personality measures in personnel selection. *Personnel Psychology, 18,* 135–164.

Hoffman, B. J., & Dilchert, S. (2012). A review of citizenship and counterproductive behaviors. In N. Schmitt (Ed.). *Personnel assessment and selection.* New York: Oxford University Press.

Hoffman, B. J., Kennedy, C. L., Lance, C. E., LoPilato, A. C., & Monahan, E. (2015). A review of the content, criterion-related, and construct-related validity of assessment center exercises. *Journal of Applied Psychology, 100,* 1143–1168.

Hough, L. M., Oswald, F. L. & Ployhart, R. E. (2001). Determinants, detection and amelioration of adverse impact in personnel selection procedures: Issues, evidence, and lessons learned. *International Journal of Selection and Assessment, 9,* 152–194.

Huffcutt, A. I., Roth, P. L., & McDaniel, M. (1996). A meta-analytic investigation of cognitive ability in employment interview evaluations: Moderating characteristics and implications for incremental validity. *Journal of Applied Psychology, 81,* 459–473.

Hunter, J. E., & Hunter, R. F. (1984). Validity and utility of alternative predictors of job performance. *Psychological Bulletin, 96,* 72–98.

Hunter, J. E., & Schmidt, F. L. (1982). Fitting people to jobs: The impact of personnel selection on national productivity. In M. D. Dunnette, & E. A. Fleishman (Eds.), *Human performance and productivity: Human capability assessment* (pp. 322–384). vol. 1. Hillsdale, NJ: Erlbaum.

Judge, T. A., Rodell, J. B., Klinger, E. R., Simon, L. S., & Crawford, E. R. (2013). Hierarchical representations of the five-factor model of personality in predicting job performance: Integrating three organizing frameworks with two theoretical perspectives. *Journal of Applied Psychology, 98,* 875–925.

Kehoe, J., Mol, S., & Anderson, N. R. (2016). Managing sustainable selection programs. In J. L. Farr, & N. T. Tippins (Eds.), *Handbook of personnel selection* (2nd ed.). Mahwah, NJ: Erlbaum.

Kotter, J. P. (1973). The psychological contract: Managing the joining-up process. *Californian Management Review, 15,* 91–99.

Lado, M. (2012). Reference checks, general mental ability, and experience: A study of construct validity. *Revista de Psicología del Trabajo y de las Organizaciones, 28,* 119–131.

McDaniel, M. A., Hartman, N. S., Whetzel, D. L., & Grubb, W. (2007). Situational judgment tests, response instructions, and validity: A meta-analysis. *Personnel Psychology, 60,* 201–210.

Ones, D. S., Viswesvaran, C., & Schmidt, F. L. (1993). Comprehensive meta-analysis of integrity tests. *Journal of Applied Psychology, 78,* 679–703.

Ployhart, R. E., & Harold, C. M. (2004). The Applicant Attribution-Reaction Theory (AART): An integrative theory of applicant attributional processing. *International Journal of Selection and Assessment, 12,* 84–98.

Roth, P. L., Bobko, P., & McFarland, L. A. (2005). A meta-analysis of work sample test validity: Updating and integrating some classical literature. *Personnel Psychology, 58,* 1009–1037.

Rothstein, H. R., Schmidt, F. L., Erwin, F. W., Owens, W. A., & Sparks, C. P. (1990). Biographical data in employment selection: Can validities be made generalizable? *Journal of Applied Psychology, 75,* 175–184.

Sackett, P. R., & DeVore, C. J. (2001). Counterproductive behaviors at work. In N. Anderson, D. S. Ones, H. K. Sinangil, & C. Viswesvaran (Eds.), *Handbook of industrial, work and organizational psychology* (vol. 1). London: Sage.

Sackett, P. R., Shen, W., Myors, B., Lievens, F., Schollaert, E., Hoye, G., Cronshaw, S.F., et al. (2010). Perspectives from twenty-two countries on the legal environment for selection. In J. L. Farr, & N. Tippins (Eds.), *Handbook of employee selection* (pp. 651–676). New York: Routledge.

Salgado, J. F. (1997). The Five Factor Model of personality and job performance in the European Community. *Journal of Applied Psychology, 82,* 30–43.

Salgado, J. F. (2002). The Big Five personality dimensions and counterproductive behaviors. *International Journal of Selection and Assessment, 10,* 117–125.

Salgado, J. F. (2003). Predicting job performance using FFM and non-FFM personality measures. *Journal of Occupational and Organizational Psychology, 76,* 323–346.

Salgado, J. F. (2015). Estimating coefficients of equivalence and stability for job performance ratings: The importance of controlling for transient error on criterion measurement. *International Journal of Selection and Assessment, 23,* 37–44.

Salgado, J. F., & Anderson, N. (2002). Cognitive and GMA testing in the European Community: Issues and evidence. *Human Performance, 15,* 75–96.

Salgado, J. F., & Anderson, N. (2003). Validity generalization of GMA tests across countries in the European Community. *European Journal of Work and Organizational Psychology, 12,* 1–18.

Salgado, J. F., Anderson, N., & Hülsheger, U. R. (2010). Psychotechnics and the forgotten history of modern scientific employee selection. In J. L. Farr, & N. Tippins (Eds.). *Handbook of employee selection.* New York: Routledge.

Salgado, J. F., Anderson, N., Moscoso, S., Bertua, C., & De Fruyt, F. (2003a). International validity generalization of GMA and cognitive abilities: A European Community meta-analysis. *Personnel Psychology, 56,* 573–605.

Salgado, J. F., Anderson, N., Moscoso, S., Bertua, C., De Fruyt, F., & Rolland, J. P. (2003b). A meta-analytic study of general mental ability validity for different occupations in the European Community. *Journal of Applied Psychology, 88,* 1068–1081.

Salgado, J. F., Anderson, N., & Tauriz, G. (2015a). The validity of ipsative and quasi-ipsative forced-choice personality inventories for different occupational groups: A comprehensive meta-analysis. *Journal of Occupational and Organizational Psychology, 88,* 797–834.

Salgado, J. F., & De Fruyt, F. (2005). Personality in industrial, work and organizational psychology. In A. Evers, N. Anderson, & O. Smit-Voskuyl (Eds.), *Handbook of selection.* Oxford: Blackwell.

Salgado, J. F., & Moscoso, S. (1996). Meta-analysis of interrater reliability of job performance ratings in validity studies of personnel selection. *Perceptual and Motor Skills, 83,* 1195–1201.

Salgado, J. F., & Moscoso, S. (2002). Comprehensive meta-analysis of the construct validity of the employment interview. *European Journal of Work and Organizational Psychology, 11,* 299–324.

Salgado, J. F., & Moscoso, S. (2006). Utiliser les entretiens comportementaux structures pour la sélection du personnel. In C. Levy-Leboyer, C. Louche, J. P. Rolland, & C. Louche (Eds.),

RH: Les apports de la psychologie du travail. Paris, France: Les Editions d'Organization.

Salgado, J. F., Moscoso, S., & Anderson, N. (2016). Corrections for criterion reliability in validity generalization: The consistency of Hermes, the utility of Midas. *Revista de Psicología del Trabajo y de las Organizaciones, 32,* 17–23.

Salgado, J. F., & Tauriz, G. (2014). The Five-Factor Model, forced-choice personality inventories and performance: A comprehensive meta-analysis of academic and occupational validity studies. *European Journal of Work and Organizational Psychology, 23,* 3–30.

Schmidt, F. L., & Hunter, J. E. (1998). The validity and utility of selection methods in personnel psychology: Practical and theoretical implications of 85 years of research findings. *Psychological Bulletin, 124,* 262–274.

Schmidt, F. L., Hunter, J. E., & Outerbridge, A. N. (1986). Impact of job experience and ability on job knowledge, work sample performance, and supervisory ratings of job performance. *Journal of Applied Psychology, 71,* 432–439.

Schmitt, N. (2014). Personality and cognitive ability as predictors of effective performance at work. *Annual Review of Organizational Psychology and Organizational Behavior, 1,* 45–65.

Schneider, B., Goldstein, H. W., & Smith, D. B. (1995). The ASA framework: An update. *Personnel Psychology, 48,* 747–779.

Shackleton, V. J., & Newell, S. (1997). International selection and assessment. In N. Anderson, & P. Herriot (Eds.), *International handbook of selection and assessment.* Chichester: John Wiley & Sons, Ltd.

Truxillo, D., Bauer, T., McCarthy, J., Anderson, N. R., & Ahmed, S. (2016). Applicant perspectives on employee selection systems. In D. Ones, N. R. Anderson, C. Viswesvaran, & H. K. Sinangil (Eds.), *Handbook of industrial, work and organizational psychology* (2nd ed.). London: Sage.

Viswesvaran, C., & Ones, D. S. (2001). Perspectives on models of job performance. *International Journal of Selection and Assessment, 8,* 216–226.

Viswesvaran, C., Ones, D. S., & Schmidt, F. L. (1996). Comparative analysis of the reliability of job performance ratings. *Journal of Applied Psychology, 81,* 557–574.

Viswesvaran, C., Schmidt, F. L., & Ones, D. S. (2005). Is there a general factor in ratings of job performance? A meta-analytic framework for disentangling substantive and error influences. *Journal of Applied Psychology, 90,* 108–131.

Wingrove, J., Glendinning, R., & Herriot, P. (1984). Graduate pre-selection: A research note. *Journal of Occupational Psychology, 57,* 169–172.

3 How Can I Shape My Job to Suit Me Better? Job Crafting for Sustainable Employees and Organizations

Pascale M. Le Blanc, Evangelia Demerouti and Arnold B. Bakker

Overview

Job redesign is the process through which changes in the jobs, tasks or conditions of individual workers are made with the aim of contributing to their work motivation and performance. Given the unique constellation of working conditions prevalent in each job, traditional top–down job redesign interventions often turn out to be partly ineffective. Currently, organizations recognize that these should be complemented by bottom–up redesign strategies initiated by the job incumbents themselves. This chapter focuses on job crafting as a proactive strategy for employees to 'shape their job to suit them better'. We begin by pointing out the need for sustainable innovation and sustainable employability of the workforce in present-day organizations, and by proposing job crafting as a socially innovative way to achieve both aims. Next, the main theoretical perspectives on job crafting and the measures that have been developed to assess different dimensions of job crafting are discussed. This is followed by an overview of empirical research on the predictors and outcomes of job crafting. In the final section, we explain how organizations can become more sustainable by stimulating the job crafting behaviour of their employees.

3.1 Introduction

Nowadays, business competition is more intense, and the business environment is more uncertain. Organizations are facing dynamic and changing environments that emphasize the importance of flexibility, adaptation, and innovation. Because of this, over the past 20 years, we have seen an increase in business and academic interest in building sustainable organizations that have the capacity to endure and simultaneously satisfy the bottom line of environmental, economic, technological and human performance. Yet, in comparison to the environmental, economic and

An Introduction to Work and Organizational Psychology: An International Perspective,
Third Edition. Edited by Nik Chmiel, Franco Fraccaroli and Magnus Sverke.
© 2017 John Wiley & Sons, Ltd. Published 2017 by John Wiley & Sons, Ltd.

technological dimensions of sustainability, substantially less attention has been focused on the human dimension (Spreitzer, Porath, & Gibson, 2012). This is quite surprising, as a recent Dutch study has demonstrated that only 25% of innovation success can be ascribed to technological innovation and the remaining 75% to social innovation, i.e., to changes in the organization of work and working relations that enhance organizational performance and stimulate employee talent development. Socially innovative companies have a significantly higher percentage of radical (36%) and incremental (29%) innovations, and their market performance is 21% better compared to companies that focus exclusively on technological innovations (Erasmus Concurrentie- en Innovatiemonitor, 2015).

At the same time, in most industrialized countries, the retirement age of employees is high because of the proportional increase in the ageing population. So, the majority of employees will have to work until a later age whereas the influx of young workers in the labour market is declining. Lifetime employment is no longer guaranteed, as the qualifications that are required for jobs are becoming increasingly complex while, simultaneously, the relevance of these qualifications is becoming increasingly less. For all these reasons, the sustainable employability of the workforce nowadays is of vital importance for the economy of these countries as well as for the workers themselves. Sustainable employability implies that, throughout their working lives, workers are able to keep on working continuously while retaining health and well-being (Van der Klink et al., 2016). Highly innovative sectors of industry, such as knowledge-intensive firms that have to cope with frequent technological (and organizational) changes as well as fierce international competition, are particularly in need of a sustainably employable workforce (De Grip, Van Loo & Sanders, 2004).

Technological innovation is still of vital importance to help organizations survive and gain competitive advantage. However, sustainable innovation and sustainable employability can only be realized through complementary changes in the social organization of work that enable employees to utilize and develop their skills, knowledge and abilities more effectively. In this way, organizations can take full advantage of their employees' potential.

The European Agency for Safety and Health at Work coined the term 'workplace innovation', and defined it as 'strategically induced and participatory adopted changes in an organisation's practice of managing, organising and deploying human and non-human resources that lead to simultaneously improved organisational performance and improved quality of working life (2012, p. 8). Thus, it refers to how people are deployed in order to improve performance while at the same time creating 'high quality' jobs. Second, workplace innovation is related to the development and implementation of coherent interventions in the areas of work organisation, control structure and employability of staff. These areas all deal with the design of the organisation, the design of management tasks, and the design of jobs, with the objective of simultaneous improvement of organisational performance and quality of working life.

Complementary to employers' investments in workplace innovation, we suggest that employees themselves could and actually also should take personal responsibility for keeping their professional skills and competencies at an optimal level. This is even more important because of the rapid changes in the nature of jobs over the past decades, including among others the use of new technologies and flexible work methods, and an increase in cognitive tasks and in pressure to provide high quality services in an effective way (e.g., in health care). Moreover, nowadays employees do not merely have to be adaptive (i.e., respond flexibly to job-related and/or organizational changes), but also must be proactive in initiating and co-creating these changes. Job crafting represents employee behaviour that has recently been recognized as something that organizations can stimulate to improve the working conditions for their employees by offering them the opportunity to do so for themselves (Demerouti & Bakker, 2013). It can be seen as a specific form of proactive behaviour in which an employee initiates changes in the level of job demands and job resources to make his or her own job more meaningful, engaging and satisfying. In this way, job crafting uses the potential of the jobholders' own knowledge as they know their job best. Job crafting can be used in addition to top–down approaches to improve jobs, to respond to the complexity of contemporary jobs, and to deal with the needs of the current workforce (Demerouti, 2014).

In this chapter we postulate that organizations and their employees can become more sustainable through job crafting. The chapter starts with a discussion of the main theoretical perspectives on job crafting and the measures that have been developed to assess different dimensions of job crafting. Next, we will zoom in on empirical research regarding its predictors and outcomes. In the final section, we will present some ways to intervene in order to stimulate the job crafting behaviour of employees, and we will link it with sustainable innovation and sustainable employability of the workforce as these represent enduring requirements for contemporary organizations.

3.2   What Is Job Crafting?

Job design describes 'how jobs, tasks, and roles are structured, enacted, and modified, as well as the impact of these structures, enactments and modifications on individual, group, and organizational outcomes' (Grant & Parker, 2009, p. 319). In contrast, job redesign is seen as the process through which something is *changed* in the job, the tasks or the condition of the individual worker (Tims & Bakker, 2010). Traditional job redesign approaches are usually top–down (Oldham & Hackman, 2010), i.e., the structure and content of the work are redesigned by the organization with the ultimate goal of enhancing favourable attitudinal and behavioural work outcomes such as work engagement, well-being and performance. However, most of these approaches have proved to be inadequate to serve the changing nature of current jobs, and therefore the 'one-size-fits-all' approach is no longer sufficient (Aust, Rugulies, Finken, & Jensen, 2010). This has led to the emergence of new, individualized, bottom–up job redesign approaches, such as job crafting that recognize the role of individual employees as proactive agents who form their jobs and change their own job characteristics (Fried et al., 2007; Grant & Parker, 2009). Job crafting has been defined and operationalized based on the perspectives of Wrzesniewski and Dutton (2001) and the Job Demands–Resources (JD–R) model (Bakker & Demerouti, 2007; Demerouti, Bakker, Nachreiner, & Schaufeli, 2001), respectively. Each of these conceptualizations will be explained in more detail in the following section.

3.2.1 Conceptualizations of job crafting

In 2001, Wrzesniewski and Dutton introduced the term 'job crafting' to refer to the process through which employees 'shape' their jobs, and defined it as 'the physical and cognitive changes individuals make in the task or relational boundaries of their work' (Wrzesniewski & Dutton, 2001, p. 179). Changing physical task boundaries refers to altering the form, scope or number of work activities. That is, employees choose to do fewer, more or different tasks than prescribed in their formal job description. In addition, job crafting includes changing cognitive task boundaries, which refers to altering how one sees the job. For example, a cleaner in a hospital may view his or her job either as tidying or as making an important contribution to an agreeable stay for patients. Changing relational boundaries involves changes in the quality and/or the amount of interactions with people at work. For example, employees may avoid colleagues they do not like. By changing any of these elements, individuals themselves change the design of their job and the social environment in which they work.

According to Wrzesniewski and Dutton (2001) job crafting occurs on a daily basis. In order to better capture the 'everyday' changes that employees may pursue, some scholars have proposed conceptualizing job crafting as employee proactive behaviour that is specifically targeted at job characteristics, thereby framing its definition in the Job Demands–Resources model. Tims and Bakker (2010) define job crafting as the changes that employees may make to balance their job demands and job resources with their personal abilities and needs. Rather than restricting job crafting to efforts aimed at altering tasks and relations (cf. Wrzesniewski & Dutton, 2001), they expand the conceptualization of task crafting and relational crafting. Whereas task crafting refers to job demands, i.e., changing one's tasks by increasing challenging demands and/or decreasing demands that hinder, relational crafting refers to job resources, i.e., changing the available social (e.g., support, feedback) and/or structural (e.g., autonomy, variety) resources.

In line with this conceptualization, Petrou et al. (2012) defined job crafting as encompassing: (1) seeking challenges; (2) reducing demands; and (3) seeking resources. Seeking challenges refers to increasing challenging demands, i.e., looking for new challenging tasks at work, keeping busy during one's working day, or asking for more responsibilities once one has finished with assigned tasks. This is done with the primary aim of maintaining motivation and avoiding boredom, and is in line with the proposition of Karasek and Theorell (1990) that workers in active jobs (with high demands and high autonomy) are likely to seek challenging situations that promote mastery and learning. Reducing demands, on the other hand, refers to reducing demands that hinder, for instance, the emotionally, mentally or physically demanding aspects of one's work, in order to reduce one's workload and to make sure that working is not at the cost of one's private life. So, reducing demands can be viewed as a health-protecting coping mechanism when demands are excessively high. Seeking job resources can be viewed as a form of coping with job demands, or completing tasks and achieving goals that foster goal attainment and enhance performance. Examples are seeking feedback or asking for support from one's own direct supervisor or colleagues, and looking for the possibility of learning a new skill in the job. Note that decreasing resources has not been proposed as constituting a form of job crafting, as it does not seem to be a purposeful human behaviour (Hobfoll, 2001). In a diary study by 95 employees from different organizations Petrou et al. (2012) confirmed the validity of conceptualizing job crafting in terms of the three specific behaviours of seeking challenges, reducing demands and seeking resources. Moreover, they found that job crafting indeed occurs on a daily basis, with daily fluctuations in job crafting ranging from 31% (seeking challenges), 34% (seeking resources) to 78% (reducing demands).

Table 3.1 compares the conceptualizations of job crafting of Wrzesniewski and Dutton and the JD–R model with respect to the definition, the purpose and motivation, the target, and the types of job crafting. The main difference between the two conceptualizations is that the JD–R perspective focuses on the behavioural component and excludes the cognitive dimension of job crafting, which results in differences in the targets and types of crafting that are distinguished. In the remainder of this chapter, the JD–R perspective on job crafting is followed because this perspective has stimulated much empirical research over the past decade.

3.2.2   Measurement of job crafting

The first instrument to measure job crafting assesses the three dimensions proposed by Wrzesniewski and Dutton (2001). Unfortunately, there currently is no published information about the psychometric properties of this instrument.

In line with the JD–R conceptualization of job crafting, Tims et al. (2012) developed and validated a scale to measure job crafting behaviour that has four independent job crafting dimensions: (1) increasing social job resources, (2) increasing structural job resources, (3) increasing challenging job demands, and (4) decreasing hindering job demands. The scale shows satisfactory convergent validity (compared to proactive personality, personal initiative and cynicism) and criterion validity (with colleague-ratings of work engagement, employability and performance). Additionally, self-rated job crafting behaviours correlated positively with peer-rated job crafting behaviours. So, job crafting behaviours are also observable by others in the work environment. Finally Petrou et al. (2012)

Table 3.1: Comparison of two perspectives on job crafting

Job-crafting perspectives	Definition	Purpose and motivation	Target	Types
Wresniewski & Dutton (2001)	'the physical and cognitive changes individuals make in the task or relational boundaries of their work' (2001, p. 179)	• To assert control • To create a positive self-image • To connect to others • To increase meaning at work	• Task boundaries • Relational boundaries • Cognitive boundaries	• Task crafting • Relational crafting • Cognitive crafting
Job Demands–Resources Model (Tims et al., 2012)	'the changes that employees may make to balance their job demands and job resources with their personal abilities and needs' (2012, p. 174)	• To improve person–job fit • To enhance work engagement • To avoid health impairment	• Job demands • Job resources	• Seeking challenges • Seeking resources • Reducing demands

Note: Task crafting can be seen as changing job demands. Relational crafting can be seen as changing job resources.

adapted the scale of Tims et al. (2012), operationalizing it with three dimensions: (1) seeking resources, (2) seeking challenges, and (3) reducing demands. Thus, they did not differentiate between structural and social resources. Their findings confirmed the factorial validity and the reliability of the measure at both the general and the daily levels. As mentioned before, they also showed that job crafting behaviours varied significantly from one day to another. In the remainder of this chapter, job crafting will be understood in terms of the three dimensions distinguished by Petrou et al. (2012).

3.3 Predictors and Outcomes of Job Crafting

Before turning to a more detailed discussion of predictors and outcomes of job crafting, we will briefly address the question why individuals are motivated to engage in job crafting. Wrzesniewski and Dutton (2001) state that by fulfilling the three basic human needs for control over their work, to express a more positive sense of self, and to connect with others, job crafting enables workers to experience enhanced meaning in work and attain a positive work identity. In a cross-sectional study among 253 working adults, Slemp and Vella-Brodrick (2013) found that job crafting was related to the satisfaction of the intrinsic needs for autonomy, competence and relatedness at work. According to Petrou et al. (2012) and Tims and Bakker (2010), individuals craft their jobs in order to create conditions in which they can work healthily and with motivation.

3.3.1   Predictors of job crafting

Generally, two approaches can be distinguished regarding research on the predictors of job crafting. In the first approach, situational factors are seen as stimulators of job crafting, whereas, in the second, the focus is on personal attributes as determinants of job crafting.

3.3.1.1   *Situational predictors of job crafting*

Job crafting represents discretionary behaviour on the part of the employee; therefore Wrzesniewski and Dutton (2001) suggested job autonomy was an important stimulating factor of this behaviour. Therefore, individuals who have jobs with more 'degrees of freedom' with respect to how they perform their tasks are more likely to engage in job crafting. Other studies have shown that demanding aspects of the job, for example, task complexity (Githulescu, 2007), are positively related to job crafting too. On a daily level, Petrou et al. (2012) found that on days when work pressure and autonomy were both high, employees showed the highest levels of seeking resources and the lowest level of reducing demands. They argued that jobs with high autonomy and high work pressure (i.e., active jobs) facilitate learning and development and therefore individuals are prone to keep their job stimulating. Consequently, these jobs make employees engage more in seeking resources and less in reducing demands. However, these jobs may already be too demanding for employees to seek (even) more challenges (Wang, Demerouti, & Bakker, 2016).

In addition, job crafting can be triggered by organizational change as a strategy to ensure that their job still fits their preferences after the introduction of change and to make meaning of the changed situation. In a qualitative study during a merger, Kira, Balkin and San (2012) found that relational crafting (e.g., asking for supervisory support) and task crafting (e.g., prioritizing) were used as strategies to deal with the new situation at work. Petrou et al. (2012) found that changes involving new products were negatively associated with daily seeking challenges, while meeting new clients was positively related to daily seeking resources and seeking challenges. Moreover, employees may even be motivated to craft their jobs to proactively prepare for and cope with future job change and uncertainty. For example, they may expand their tasks and relational environments by increasing the scope of job responsibilities, or enhancing the amount of communication with people at work to get more information (Wang, Demerouti, & Bakker, 2016).

3.3.1.2 *Personal predictors of job crafting*

Job crafting has been linked to the individual characteristics of employees too, the first one being proactive personality. Bateman and Crant (1993) defined the prototypic proactive personality as one which is relatively unconstrained by situational forces and which effects environmental change. Individuals with proactive personalities identify opportunities and act on them; they show initiative, take action, and persevere until they bring about meaningful change. Bakker et al. (2012) found that proactive personality (as rated by one's colleagues) was associated with more employee (self-reported) seeking job resources and job challenges. This finding indicates that individuals with a proactive personality are inclined to change their work environment through job crafting.

In addition, daily fluctuations in personal resources, i.e., personal aspects that are generally linked to resilience and refer to individuals' sense of their ability to control and impact upon their environment successfully (Hobfoll, Johnson, Ennis, & Jackson, 2003), may also cause daily fluctuations in job crafting behaviour. For example, on days when employees feel more efficacious about their work, they are more likely to change the characteristics of their job to attain their goals (Tims, Bakker, & Derks, 2014).

Petrou (2013) found that employee regulatory focus, i.e., the way in which individuals regulate their behaviour so that they approach pleasure but avoid pain (Higgins, 1997), might influence the degree to which they craft their jobs. Employees with a promotion focus, who are driven by growth and challenges, were found to show more job crafting behaviour and to be more open to changes, irrespective of how these were presented by the organization. On the other hand, employees with a prevention focus, who are driven by obligations and security, crafted their jobs more when organizational change was communicated in an inadequate way. Thus, insufficient information provided by the organization regarding the change triggered the employees who are focused on security and obligations to craft their jobs in order to be able to fulfil their obligations.

Actually, the study by Petrou (2013) makes clear that, in addition to individual or situational characteristics in isolation, the person x situation interaction also influences job crafting. According to the Person–Environment (P–E) fit approach (Edwards, Caplan, & Harrison, 1998), stress arises from a mismatch between workers' personal characteristics and the characteristics of the job or tasks that are performed at work. An example is a person with a high need for control who has low job control. Tims and Bakker (2010) argue that person–job mismatch particularly triggers job crafting behaviours. Job crafting might result in a better fit between person and job environment and thus reduce stress.

3.3.2 Outcomes of job crafting

The traditional top–down, 'one-size-fits-all' approach that has dominated the job redesign literature for decades has been shown to be partly ineffective in enhancing worker motivation and performance (Grant & Parker, 2009). Complementing the traditional job redesign approaches with new, bottom–up, individualized approaches that employees may use to 'shape their job to suit them better' such as job crafting, may boost their effectiveness. The overall picture of research on the outcomes of job crafting confirms its beneficial effects on both individual and organizational outcomes. Ghitulescu (2007) found a positive link between job crafting and organizational commitment. Tims, Bakker and Derks (2013) found that employees who crafted their structural and social resources reported an increase in job resources, which in turn was positively related to increased job satisfaction two months later. However, crafting job demands (both challenging and hindering ones) was not found to lead to an increase in job satisfaction. In recent years, several studies have demonstrated that employees' job crafting in terms of seeking resources and/or challenges is predictive of higher levels of work engagement, both in general (Bakker et al., 2012) as well as on different days (Petrou et al., 2012). Moreover, in a three-wave longitudinal study, Tims, Bakker and Derks (in press) found dynamic relationships between job crafting intentions, work engagement, and actual job crafting behaviour. Their results showed that job crafting intentions and work engagement were significantly related to actual job crafting behaviour, which in turn was related to higher levels of work engagement. However, in contrast to the other two types of crafting, decreasing hindering job demands was found to be unrelated (Tims et al., 2012) or negatively related to work engagement (Petrou et al., 2012). This might be explained by the fact that reducing demands leads to a less stimulating environment, and thus to lower engagement.

In addition, several studies have demonstrated a positive relationship between job crafting and work performance. Leana et al. (2009) showed that collaborative crafting, i.e., groups of workers discussing and working together to customize how their work is organized and enacted, was positively related to the performance of employees of childcare centres. Bakker et al. (2012) and Tims et al. (in press) found that employees' job crafting was predictive of in-role performance. Petrou, Demerouti and Schaufeli (2015) found that seeking resources predicted task performance one year later. Demerouti, Bakker and Gevers (2015) showed that seeking resources had a positive indirect relationship with supervisor ratings of contextual performance (such as voluntarily helping colleagues with their tasks when they have high work overload), through work engagement and with supervisor ratings of creativity through work engagement and flourishing. Reducing demands, however, was detrimental to both contextual performance and creativity, presumably also because of its negative effect on work engagement. On the daily level, Demerouti et al. (2015) found that seeking resources was positively associated with daily task performance; yet reducing demands was detrimental to task performance.

Taken together, the above studies suggest a favourable impact of seeking resources and seeking challenges and a negative impact of reducing demands on individual and organizational work-related outcomes. However, it is important to realize that the effects of job crafting are also contingent upon situational factors.

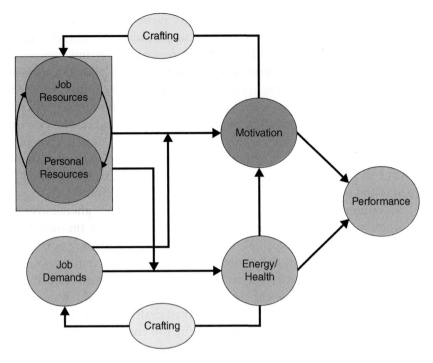

Figure 3.1: Job crafting within the Job Demands–Resources model

For example, in situations of high task interdependence where colleagues have to work closely together to accomplish their tasks, the job crafting behaviour of individual employees is likely to affect their colleagues. This might not always be positive or desirable, e.g., in the case when an employee reduces his/her demands by lowering the number of tasks (s)he performs, which implies that one of his/her colleagues will have to do extra work. Figure 3.1 depicts the role of job crafting within the Job Demands–Resources (JD–R) model.

3.4   Job Crafting Interventions

As mentioned before, the majority of job redesign interventions that are described in the literature use a top–down approach that addresses the same job characteristics for all employees, regardless of the difference in importance each of them attaches to these characteristics. Job crafting, in contrast, can be considered a bottom–up approach that begins specifically from the needs of individual employees. The net result is that each employee might change different job characteristics depending on his/her personal needs, resulting in a better P–E fit and higher level of well-being as well as individual and organizational performance. So both individual workers and their organizations may benefit from interventions aimed at stimulating job crafting.

In the literature, only a few studies on the effectiveness of job crafting interventions are available. All of these interventions scope individual workers. Van den Heuvel, Demerouti and Peeters (2012, 2015) developed a training programme to increase the awareness of employees in different layers of the organization regarding the ways in which they could adjust their job to their own needs so that they experience more pleasure, engagement and meaning in their work. The adjustments refer to the specific job demands and job resources, the two categories of job characteristics that are described in the JD–R Model. That process begins with awareness of the current working situation and the freedom that they have to make those adjustments. In this way, it becomes clear to employees what job demands and job resources they need to adjust or create.

The job-crafting training aims to increase participants' motivation and engagement through two different routes: (1) through promoting the self-directed behaviour of employees; and (2) through the strengthening of personal resources. It consisted of the following elements: (1) a job crafting workshop; (2) a weekly job crafting assignment/logbook; and (3) a reflection meeting. During the workshop, employees got acquainted with the JD–R model and with the concept of job crafting. They learned to draft a Personal Crafting Plan (PCP), which consists of crafting actions, set by the employees themselves, that participants plan to undertake for a period of four weeks. In the second phase, employees kept crafting logbooks, i.e., detailed reports of their crafting activities of each week. During the final refection meeting they discussed the success they had achieved, the problems they had encountered and the solutions they had found. Thus, the training combines learning about what job crafting is and what happens when employees themselves craft their jobs, executing self-specified job-crafting assignments/actions for a period of several weeks and reflecting on the experiences of these job-crafting actions after they have been completed. In this way, individuals are encouraged to integrate job crafting into their daily work by learning to choose and to execute small job-crafting actions. Compared to a control group, it was found that participants in the intervention group showed increased well-being (i.e., more positive and less negative emotions), more job resources (i.e., better contact with the supervisor, more work-related opportunities for development), and higher levels of self-efficacy (Van den Heuvel, Demerouti, & Peeters, 2012).

Gordon et al. (2014) expanded upon their job crafting intervention by making it less demanding for participants and by integrating a new 'thinking-in-action' approach with so-called Situated Experiential Learning Narratives (SELN). The SELN helped participants to create their own job crafting goals more easily, by allowing individuals to learn from their own or others' real-life experiences through sharing stories of how proactive behaviour had changed their thoughts, feelings, or relationships with their jobs. After these reflections, participants were better able to assign their behaviours to specific job crafting strategies. In a study of medical specialists, positive effects of the modified intervention on job crafting behaviors, well-being (i.e., work engagement, health, and reduced levels of exhaustion), and job performance (i.e., adaptive, task, and contextual performance) for the participants in the experimental (vs. control) groups were found.

Based on these two studies, it can be concluded that job crafting behaviour can be stimulated by targeted interventions and that this can have positive effects on employee well-being and performance. However, more research is still needed on how to most effectively stimulate job crafting behaviours leading to favourable outcomes. This research could also be aimed at uncovering the process through which job crafting is related to favourable outcomes: is it because of substantive changes in the work – i.e., job characteristics – itself or does it come from the involvement in the process of making these changes? Or is it a combination of both?

3.5 Building Sustainable Organizations Through Job Crafting

Throughout this chapter, we have attempted to demonstrate that organizations can benefit from job crafting as a means to strengthen the sustainability of their organization as a whole and of their employees in particular. Job crafting can contribute to organizational and employee sustainability in at least three different ways (Demerouti, 2014). First, job crafting can be used as a supplement to more traditional top–down, 'one-size-fits-all' redesign approaches to enhance workers' well being and performance. In this way, job redesign efforts can become more successful as they are better tailored to individual needs, and the improvement of jobs can be a continuing process creating sustainable changes. Second, job crafting represents a means that can be encouraged by organizations to keep their employees enthusiastic for and engaged in their work. For example, managers may motivate their subordinates to craft their jobs and give them the freedom to do so. Thus, organizations can achieve competitive advantage in attracting and retaining employees. Third, job crafting can be a valuable means to adjust jobs according to the needs of specific groups of employees, e.g., older employees, employees with disabilities or health problems, or parents with young children.

A fourth way in which job crafting can add to employee and organizational sustainability, which is particularly relevant in today's transformational work environments, is in successfully dealing with tasks and roles that are 'in flux' (Demerouti & Bakker, 2013). It adds to employee sustainability by enhancing the ability to adapt to the demands that are posed by these environments. Examples of proactive actions that can be useful during organizational change are (1) maximizing the pool of job resources that help employees to deal or cope with change, (2) keeping the work pressure associated with change at an optimal level, and (3) seeking challenges that will transform change to an engaging and efficacious experience (Avey, Wernsing, & Luthans, 2008). These three behaviours are part of job crafting, and thus they form an ideal strategic advantage for employees in the context of change (Petrou et al., 2012).

The results of several studies suggest that job crafting can make individual employees more responsive and adaptive to the context of change and thus facilitate the successful implementation of organizational change and innovations. In a qualitative study during a merger, Kira, Balkin and San (2012) found that, among other activities, relational crafting (e.g., asking for supervisory support) and task crafting (e.g., prioritizing) were used as strategies to deal with the new situation at work. Petrou, Demerouti and Schaufeli (2015) conducted a study during the reorganization of a police department and found that seeking resources was positively associated with work engagement, while reducing demands was negatively associated with work engagement. Moreover, seeking resources and seeking challenges were positively associated with adaptation to change as reported by police officers, whereas reducing demands was negatively related to adaptation. Finally, the health care organization in the above-mentioned study by Gordon et al. (2014) was involved in different forms of change. Results show that by encouraging employees to self-initiate their adaptations to the changes, by providing them with opportunities to self-regulate (gain control) in uncertain, changing environments, and by crafting their changing job, they remained healthier and performed optimally.

Overall, job crafting (i.e., seeking resources and seeking challenges particularly) is the way through which employees become more engaged, responsive and adaptive. In turn, this contributes to the sustainability of employees themselves as well as the organizations they work for.

3.6 Conclusion

In this chapter, we have presented job crafting as a socially innovative approach to proactively involve employees in 'shaping their job to suit them better'. Employees who seek resources and challenges in their job will be better able to fit their job to their preferences so that they can be more motivated and function optimally. Job crafting can also be stimulated through training that helps employees to gain insight into mismatches between their current work situation and their personal needs and preferences, and to tailor their job to better fit these personal needs and preferences. As was shown, job crafting occurs in small steps and is targeted to optimizing the prevailing job demands and resources. Therefore, it can help employees deal with the challenges that they experience in their jobs such as dealing with innovations and organizational change in a sustainable way, i.e., a way that helps them to remain healthy and perform optimally. However, job crafting should not be considered a substitute for, but rather a complement to, the more traditional, top–down approaches for job redesign. Though job crafting is not the answer to all challenges that present-day organizations are facing, it is important to realize that individual employees themselves are the real experts regarding their own jobs and ways to improve these 'to suit them better'.

Summary

The traditional top–down, 'one-size-fits-all' approach that has dominated the job redesign literature for decades has been shown to be partly ineffective in enhancing worker motivation and performance. Complementing the traditional job redesign approaches with new, bottom–up, individualized approaches that employees may use to 'shape their job to suit them better' can boost their effectiveness. In this way, the unique constellation of working conditions prevalent in each job is taken into account. One of these new approaches is job crafting, i.e., the physical and cognitive changes that employees make in their task or relational boundaries by optimizing the level of their job demands and job resources. Recent studies have demonstrated that job crafting can have positive effects on employee motivation and performance. Job crafting can be considered 'everyday' behaviour that many employees display more or less spontaneously already. However, organizations can stimulate this behaviour by explicitly recognizing its existence and by creating conditions that facilitate it. For example, they can offer training to employees to teach them to 'shape their jobs to suit them better' in ways that benefit themselves as well as the larger organization. When organizations successfully promote beneficial job crafting and avoid costly or dysfunctional job crafting, their employees become more responsive and adaptive to change. In turn, this will not only enhance employee sustainable employability but also support sustainable innovation processes of the organizations they work for.

Discussion Points

1 Job crafting is, by definition, self-initiated behaviour that is not part of a given job description. However, organizations could signal to their employees that this type of proactive behaviour is welcomed. In what ways could organizations stimulate or facilitate employees to craft their jobs?
2 Like employees, students are involved in structured, coercive activities (e.g., attending class) that are directed toward a specific goal (e.g., passing exams). Think about the different ways in which students could shape their studies to suit them better by crafting specific demands and/or resources.

Suggested Further Reading

Demerouti, E. (2014). Design your own job through job crafting. *European Psychologist, 19*, 237–247. This article presents an overview of the literature on job crafting and how job crafting can help organizations deal with issues related to specific groups of employees.

Petrou, P., Demerouti, E., Peeters, M. C. W., Schaufeli, W. B., & Hetland, J. (2012). Crafting a job on a daily basis: Contextual correlates and the link to work engagement. *Journal of Organizational Behavior, 33*, 1120–1141. This is the first diary study on job crafting which presents insights and an instrument to capture it on a daily level.

Tims, M., & Bakker, A.B. (2010). Job crafting: Towards a new model of individual job redesign. *SA Journal of Industrial Psychology, 84*, 268–278. This article presents a theoretical overview on job crafting and its relation to existing constructs.

Online Resource

United Nations, available at: http://www.un.org/en/sustainablefuture/jobs.asp#facts This website presents the UN vision on sustainability in relation to work.

References

Aust, B., Rugulies, R., Finken, A., & Jensen, C. (2010). When workplace interventions lead to negative effects: Learning from failures. *Scandinavian Journal of Public Health, 38*(3 suppl.), 106–119.

Avey, J. B., Wernsing, T. S., & Luthans, F. (2008). Can positive employees help positive organizational change? Impact of psychological capital and emotions on relevant attitudes and behaviours. *Journal of Applied Behavioural Science, 44,* 48–70.

Bakker, A. B., & Demerouti, D. (2007). The job demands–resources model: State of the art. *Journal of Managerial Psychology, 22,* 309–328.

Bakker, A. B., Tims, M., & Derks, D.(2012). Proactive personality and job performance: The role of job crafting and work engagement. *Human Relations, 65,* 1359–1378.

Bateman, T. S., & Crant, J. M. (1993). The proactive component of organizational behaviour. *Journal of Organizational Behavior, 14,* 103–118.

De Grip, A., Van Loo, J., & Sanders, J. (2004). The Industry Employability Index: Taking account of supply and demand characteristics. *International Labour Review, 143,* 211–233.

Demerouti, E. (2014). Design your own job through job crafting. *European Psychologist, 19,* 237–247.

Demerouti, E., & Bakker, A. B. (2013). Job crafting. In M. Peeters, J. de Jonge, & T. Taris (Eds.), *An introduction to contemporary work psychology* (pp. 414–433). Chichester: Wiley-Blackwell.

Demerouti, E., Bakker, A. B., & Gevers, J. M. P. (2015). Job crafting and extra-role behavior: The role of work engagement and flourishing. *Journal of Vocational Behavior, 91,* 87–96.

Demerouti, E., Bakker, A. B. & Halbesleben. J. (2015). Productive and counterproductive job crafting: A daily diary study. *Journal of Occupational Health Psychology, 20*(4), 457–469.

Demerouti, E., Bakker, A.B., Nachreiner, F., & Schaufeli, W. B. (2001). The job demands–resources model of burnout. *Journal of Applied Psychology, 86,* 499–512.

Edwards, J. R., Caplan, R. D. & Harrison, R. V. (1998). Person-environment fit theory: Conceptual foundations, empirical evidence, and directions for future research. In C. L. Cooper (Ed.), *Theories of organizational stress* (pp. 28–67). Oxford: Oxford University Press.

Erasmus Concurrentie- en Innovatiemonitor (2015). Rotterdam: INSCOPE – Research for Innovation. Available at: www.erasmusinnovatiemonitor.nl

European Agency for Safety and Health at Work (2012). *Annual Report 2012.* Luxembourg: Office for Official Publications of the European Union.

Fried, Y., Grant, A. M., Levi, A. S., Hadani, M., & Slowik, L. H. (2007). Job design in temporal context: A career dynamics perspective. *Journal of Organizational Behavior, 28,* 911–927.

Ghitulescu, B.E. (2007). *Shaping tasks and relationships at work: Examining the antecedents and consequences of employee job crafting.* Unpublished doctoral dissertation, University of Pittsburgh.

Gordon, H. J., Demerouti, E., Bakker, A. B., Le Blanc, P. M., Bipp, T., & Verhagen, M. A. (2014). Bottom–up job (re)design: Job crafting interventions in health care. Paper presented at the Seventh European Conference on Positive Psychology, July, Amsterdam, The Netherlands.

Grant, A. M., & Parker, S. A. (2009). Redesigning work design theories: The rise of relational and proactive perspectives. *Academy of Management Annals, 3,* 273–331.

Higgins, E. T. (1997). Beyond pleasure and pain. *The American Psychologist, 52,* 1280–1300.

Hobfoll, S. E. (2001). The influence of culture, community, and the nested-self in the stress process: Advancing conservation of resources theory. *Applied Psychology: An International Review, 50,* 337–370.

Hobfoll, S. E., Johnson, R. J., Ennis, N., & Jackson, A. P. (2003). Resource loss, resource gains and emotional outcomes among inner city women. *Journal of Personality and Social Psychology, 84,* 632–643.

Karasek, R. A., & Theorell, T. (1990). *Healthy work.* New York: Basic Books.

Kira, M., Balkin, D. B., & San, E. (2012). Authentic work and organizational change: Longitudinal evidence from a merger. *Journal of Change Management, 12,* 31–51.

Leana, C., Appelbaum, E., & Sevchuck, I. et al. (2009). Work process and quality of care in early childhood education: The role of job crafting. *Academy of Management Journal, 52,* 1169–1192.

Oldham, G. R., & Hackman, J. R. (2010). Not what it was and not what it will be: The future of job design research. *Journal of Organizational Behavior, 31,* 463–479.

Petrou, P. (2013). *Crafting the change: The role of job crafting and regulatory focus in adaptation to organizational change.* Unpublished doctoral dissertation. Utrecht University.

Petrou, P., Demerouti, E., Peeters, M. C. W., Schaufeli, W. B., & Hetland, J. (2012). Crafting a job on a daily basis: Contextual correlates and the link to work engagement. *Journal of Organizational Behavior, 33,* 1120–1141.

Petrou, P., Demerouti, E., & Schaufeli, W. B. (2015). Job crafting in changing organizations: Antecedents and implications for exhaustion and performance. *Journal of Occupational Health Psychology, 20*(4), 470–480.

Slemp, G. R., & Vella-Brodrick, D. A. (2013). The job crafting questionnaire: A new scale to measure the extent to which employees engage in job crafting. *International Journal of Wellbeing, 3,* 126–146.

Spreitzer, G., Porath, C. L., & Gibson, C. (2012). Toward human sustainability: How to enable more thriving at work. *Organizational Dynamics, 41,* 155–162.

Tims, M., & Bakker, A. B. (2010). Job crafting: Towards a new model of individual job redesign. *SA Journal of Industrial Psychology, 84,* 268–278.

Tims, M., Bakker, A. B., & Derks, D. (2012). Development and validation of the job crafting scale. *Journal of Vocational Behavior, 80,* 173–186.

Tims, M., Bakker, A. B., & Derks, D. (2013). The impact of job crafting on job demands, job resources and well-being. *Journal of Occupational Health Psychology, 18,* 230–240.

Tims, M., Bakker, A. B., & Derks, D. (2014). Daily job crafting and the self-efficacy-performance relationship. *Journal of Managerial Psychology, 29,* 490–507.

Tims, M., Bakker, A. B., & Derks, D. (in press). Job crafting and job performance: A longitudinal study. *European Journal of Work and Organizational Psychology.*

Van den Heuvel, M., Demerouti, E., & Peeters, M. (2012). Succesvol job craften door middel van een groepstraining [Successful job crafting through group training]. In J. de Jonge, M. Peeters, S. Sjollema, & H. de Zeeuw (Eds.), *Scherp in werk: 5 routes naar optimale inzetbaarheid* (pp. 27–49). Assen: Koninklijke van Gorcum BV.

Van den Heuvel, M., Demerouti, E., & Peeters, M. (2015). The job crafting intervention: Effects on job resources, self-efficacy, and affective well-being. *Journal of Occupational and Organizational Psychology, 88,* 511–532.

Van der Klink, J. J. L., Bultmann, U., Burdorf, A. et al. (2016). Sustainable employability – definition, conceptualization, and implications: A perspective based on the capability approach. *Scandinavian Journal of Work, Environment & Health, 42*(1), 71–79.

Wang, H., Demerouti, E., & Bakker, A. B. (2016). A review of job crafting research: The role of leader behaviors in cultivating successful job crafters. In S. K. Parker, & U. K. Bindl (Eds.), *Proactivity at work.* London: Routledge.

Wrzesniewski, A., & Dutton, J. E. (2001). Crafting a job: Revisioning employees as active crafters of their work. *Academy of Management Review, 26,* 179–201.

4

What Am I Supposed to Do in My Job? Set Goals and Appraise Your People

Gary P. Latham

Overview

This chapter looks at working with people in teams. The chapter focuses on: (1) the purpose of a performance appraisal, (2) the relevance of goal setting to the performance appraisal, (3) the legal requirements for conducting a performance appraisal, (4) the choice of a measurement scale for appraising job performance, (5) alternatives to the traditional performance appraisal, and (6) the merits of coaching employees on an on-going basis. The chapter concludes with a discussion of (7) self-appraisals.

4.1 Introduction

Once you hire people to be on your team, or once people have been assigned or transferred to your team, you must see to it that the goals they are to pursue are specific and challenging for them. If you fail to do so, you will all but guarantee that you will have a low performing team. This is because goals provide meaning to otherwise meaningless tasks. In the absence of goals, people meander. They have few benchmarks for ascertaining whether their job performance is excellent, average, or inadequate. If the goal is vague rather than specific, some employees will pat themselves on the back undeservedly while others are needlessly self-critical. The attainment of a specific difficult, as opposed to an easy, goal gives people a sense of accomplishment. In doing so, they increase a person's sense of personal effectiveness. When a difficult goal is attained, rather than sitting on their laurels, people generally set an even higher goal to increase their performance (Ilies & Judge, 2005).

Following the goal setting process, you must assess each person's performance on goal pursuit/attainment. Depending on your political viewpoint, one

An Introduction to Work and Organizational Psychology: An International Perspective,
Third Edition. Edited by Nik Chmiel, Franco Fraccaroli and Magnus Sverke.
© 2017 John Wiley & Sons, Ltd. Published 2017 by John Wiley & Sons, Ltd.

advantage/disadvantage of conducting performance appraisals is that the long arm of the law in most western countries (e.g., Canada, the United Kingdom, the United States) specifies what you can and cannot do when conducting a performance appraisal. Most, if not all, employees are aware of their legal rights in this domain, and are quick to file a complaint when they perceive their rights have been violated. Thus, a possible second answer to the question posed in the title of this chapter is do not tarnish your career because of what you did/did not do when you appraised the job performance of your employees in violation of the law.

4.2   Why Conduct Performance Appraisals?

As noted earlier, most western countries, including Australia and Singapore, require documentation of why an individual was promoted, demoted, transferred, laid off, terminated and received or was denied a salary increase or bonus. The law states that these decisions must be based solely on a person's job performance rather than age, sex, race, religion, colour, natural origin, physical disability or sexual preference. In the absence of written documentation, you will find it difficult, and often impossible, to defend in a courtroom the performance appraisals you gave to your employees. The public humiliation your organization endures due to press coverage of a court case alleging that one or more of the above factors influenced your appraisal of one or more of your employees may derail your own career.

A second reason for conducting a performance appraisal is to develop and motivate your employees. Do they have the ability to do what is required of them? Is training required to give them the requisite knowledge and skills to perform their job? Do they receive adequate feedback on the quality and quantity of their performance? Do they have the resources to perform their job? Are they clear as to what is expected of them? These questions suggest the importance of setting specific, challenging goals, and using goal setting theory as a framework for doing so. This theory emphasizes the importance of taking into account an employee's ability in setting goals, providing the employee feedback in relation to goal pursuit, and ensuring the person has the requisite resources to attain the goal. The assumption underlying performance appraisals is that feedback as to how one's performance is viewed by others will lead to an improvement in performance. But this is only half the story. Voluminous studies show that feedback is only information that an employee may heed or ignore. It only leads to an improvement in performance if an employee uses it to set and commit to the attainment of specific, high goals (Locke & Latham, 2002).

4.3   Why Set Goals?

The benefit of relying on theory in the behavioural sciences is that a theory enables you to predict, understand, and influence your employees' behaviour. One such theory is goal setting, a critical variable for creating a high performance team, a variable that is also key to self-management (Latham & Locke, 1991). Goal setting theory (Latham & Locke, 2007) states that a specific, high goal will lead to higher performance than an easier goal or a vague goal, such as urging people to do their best. Moreover, there is a linear relationship between goal difficulty and job performance. However, there are four caveats to these two statements. First, the employee must have the ability to attain the goal that is set. Second, the person must receive feedback on goal progress in order to know what to start, stop, or continue doing to attain the goal. Third, and arguably most important, the person must be committed to attaining the goal. Thus the goal must be seen by an employee as important; the goal must be congruent with the employee's values. Finally, the person must have the resources to attain the goal. Situational constraints must be minimal. Research shows that when supervisors perceive they lack both the resources and the ability to attain the goals that senior management assigns to them, they are likely to abuse their subordinates (Mawritz, Folger, & Latham, 2014).

The reasons why setting specific, high goals are so effective in bringing about high performance is also four-fold: (1) a specific goal leads to the choice to focus on X to the exclusion of Y and Z, (2) commitment to pursuing a specific, high goal leads to an increase in effort, (3) it leads also to persistence until the goal has been attained, and, finally, (4) a specific, high goal gets people to plan ways that it can be attained (Latham & Arshoff, 2015). Over 1000 studies have found evidence supporting one or more aspects of this theory (Mitchell & Daniels, 2003).[1]

There are four types of goals. One is a vague goal (e.g., I am going to do my best to be more productive). This type of goal should never be set because it leads to inferior performance. Its vagueness makes it impossible for an employee to know when the goal has been attained. A second type is a performance goal, sometimes referred to as a cost-related or bottom-line goal. It should be set when the employee has the knowledge and skill to attain it (e.g., increase revenue by X%, reduce costs by Y%, improve typing speed/quality).

Not all measures critical to an individual's or a team's effectiveness are reducible to the bottom line. Moreover, research shows (Greenbaum, Mawritz, & Eissa, 2012; Latham & Wexley, 1994) that a sole focus on the bottom line can lead to counterproductive performance (e.g. falsifying reports). Hence the necessity of setting behavioural goals (e.g. teamplaying, ethics, customer service) instead of, or in addition to performance goals. Behavioural goals specify how bottom-line goals are to be pursued consistent with an organization's values.

When an employee lacks the knowledge and skill to attain a specific, high performance goal, and the desired behaviours are unknown, a specific, high learning goal should be set (Brown & Latham, 2002). The focus of a learning goal is on the discovery or development of a strategy, process or procedure for goal attainment (Seijts & Latham, 2005).

Regardless of whether a specific, high performance, a behavioural or a learning goal is set, proximal or subgoals should also be set when the environment is turbulent or when the goal has a long-term horizon (Latham & Seijts, 1999). This is because in highly dynamic situations, it is important that employees seek and receive feedback, and react quickly to it if the goal is to be attained. Proximal goals facilitate error management because there is an increase in informative feedback for your employees when subgoals are set rather than a distal goal only.

In addition to being informative, setting specific, high proximal goals is motivational relative to only setting a distal goal. The attainment of one proximal goal followed by another and still another increases goal commitment (Latham & Seijts, 1999).

In summary, proximal and distal goals that are specific and challenging provide an unambiguous basis for your employees, as well as you, to appraise their effectiveness. Hence, self-management. They do not need you to tell them how well they are performing their job. They themselves are able to assess their performance relative to their goals (Latham & Locke, 1991).

Interestingly, the relationship between goal attainment and an employee's score on well-being is straightforward. The greater the success in the attainment of challenging goals, the greater the employee experiences job satisfaction. In addition, feelings of competence increase (Latham, 2012; Latham & Brown, 2006).

Research on a broad range of managerial and professional jobs found that feelings of exhaustion did not increase when high goals were set. In fact, a sense of well-being increased only when high rather than easy goals were attained (Wiese & Freund, 2005). Similarly, unionized telecommunication employees had high performance and job satisfaction when their performance appraisal included the setting of specific, high goals (Brown & Latham, 2000).

In the private sector, engineers and scientists with graduate degrees were appraised on the basis of behavioural goals (Latham, Mitchell, & Dossett, 1978). Consistent with goal setting theory, those who were urged to do their best performed no better than those in the control condition despite the fact that they received praise, public recognition or a monetary bonus. Only those who set a specific, high behavioural goal had high performance. This was especially true for those employees who participated in the goal setting process. They set higher goals than the goals that were assigned unilaterally to employees by a supervisor.[2] A study by the US Office of Personnel Management of federal civil service employees showed that specific, high goals have a significant positive relationship with their performance (Selden & Brewer, 2000).

In Italy, law D. Lgsn. 165/01 has changed the mission of the public administration in order to increase agency efficiency and effectiveness. Government employees are now given specific, high goals and are evaluated on their attainment. The result has been an increase in employee commitment to their organization. The employees share knowledge and cooperate with one another for goal attainment (Latham, Borgogni, & Petitta, 2008).

4.4   What Is the Optimum Method for Setting Goals?

Arguably, it is not so important as to *how* goals are set as the fact that specific, challenging goals are set. An assigned goal has been shown in numerous experiments to be as effective in increasing performance as a participatively set goal as long as the logic or rationale for the goal is given (Latham, Erez, & Locke, 1988). However, this is true only when people already have the knowledge and skill to attain the goal.

The advantage of setting goals participatively with an employee is primarily cognitive rather than motivational. When people lack the ability to attain a goal, they ask more questions when they participate in the goal setting process than those who are assigned goals by others (Latham & Saari, 1979). The information gleaned from these questions improves their performance. In addition, doing so can result in an increase in self-efficacy that an effective strategy can be developed for goal attainment (Latham, Winters, & Locke, 1994).

With regard to self-set goals, an experiment conducted in a government agency in Canada found that goal difficulty level, goal acceptance, goal attainment and task performance were as effective as goals that were assigned or set participatively (Latham & Marshall, 1982).

Other studies have shown that self-set goals tend to be lower in difficulty level than goals that are assigned or jointly set with an employee. Nevertheless, there are contexts where only self-set goals are appropriate, such as off-the-job settings. For example, unionized state government employees were taught to self-set goals for job attendance and to monitor their goal process. Three months later, their job attendance was significantly higher than that of individuals in the control condition (Frayne & Latham, 1987).

4.5   What Are the Legal Issues Surrounding a Performance Appraisal?

Countries such as Argentina, Bolivia, Nicaragua and Panama have outlawed job discrimination based on political opinion (Head, Haug, Krabbenhoft, & Ma, 2000). India prohibits job discrimination on the grounds of caste and place of birth or residence in addition to race, sex and religion (Jain, Sloan, & Horowitz, 2003). Australia prohibits employers from taking into account an employee's sex, sexual preference, age, race, religion, mental status, political beliefs, child or elder care responsibilities, pregnancy, physical features or physical impairment when conducting a performance appraisal (Bennington & Wein, 2000). Northern Ireland prohibits making a performance appraisal on the basis of an employee's religion, political opinion, colour, nationality, race and ethnic or national origin (Jain et al., 2003). Similarly, the Race Relations Act in the United Kingdom prohibits making a performance appraisal on the basis of an employee's race, colour, ethnic or national origin as well as citizenship. Canada and the United States have laws similar to those described here. The emphasis is on prohibiting race, sex, age, religion, national origin, sexual preference, or a physical disability from influencing a performance appraisal. In addition, the 1993 US Government Performance and Results Act mandates that every federal agency set goals and be evaluated on goal attainment. In addition, every federal agency must report its progress towards goal attainment annually to Congress.[3]

4.6   What Measurement Scale Should I Use to Appraise an Employee's Performance?

A common way of assessing an employee's performance is to use a trait scale, often consisting of personality dispositions (e.g. conscientious, initiative, assertive). There are three interrelated reasons why this scale should not be used. First, traits are so vague that the probability is low that two or more people (e.g. bosses, peers, subordinates) will agree on the ratings an employee deserves. Second, for this reason the courts dislike them because of the subjectivity inherent in the rating (Latham & Wexley, 1994). Third, it is difficult, if not impossible, to set a specific, difficult goal for exhibiting traits on the job (e.g. show exceedingly high initiative).

At the other end of the continuum is using bottom-line measures to appraise an employee's performance. Bottom-line measures are at the other end of the continuum in that they are seemingly objective rather than subjective (e.g., sold X cars in month Y, reduced costs by Z dollars, increased market share by x%). Specific, challenging goals are easily set for a bottom-line measure. Yet bottom-line measures, as is the case with trait scales, have at least four drawbacks.

One problem with a bottom-line measure is that it is typically affected by factors that have nothing to do with what an employee did on the job (e.g. currency fluctuations that favour exports yet increase the cost of imports). Consequently, employees can be rewarded/penalized undeservedly for factors beyond their control. A second problem is that bottom-line measures are frequently deficient in that they do not include behaviours for which an employee should be held accountable (e.g. ethics, values). In today's legalistic climate, how you perform your job is as important as the results you obtain in any given quarter. A third issue is that a sole focus on the bottom line, as previously noted, encourages a results-at-all-costs mentality (Greenbaum et al., 2012). Finally, bottom-line measures do not lend themselves to coaching employees on what they need to start doing, stop doing or continue doing to be effective. A bottom-line measure is only an indicator of the 'score'.

The solution to the above problems is to use behavioural measures. The behavioural measures are derived from a systematic job analysis that specifies the behaviours that define performance effectiveness, that define an organization's core values, or that define ethical ways to pursue an organization's bottom line. These desired observable behaviours are collected from subject matter experts, namely, an employee's boss, subordinates and customers. The result is a Behavioural Observation Scale (BOS) (Latham & Wexley, 1994) that can be used for self-coaching/appraisals as well as appraisals by one's boss, peers, subordinates and customers. BOS were used in the study involving the performance appraisals of engineers and scientists described earlier (Latham, Mitchell, & Dossett, 1978). An example of a BOS is shown in Figure 4.1.

In a study involving managers and their subordinates at the Israel Airport Company, those who received feedback using BOS reported significantly higher levels of goal clarity and goal commitment relative to those who received feedback using a trait scale (Tziner & Kopelman, 1988). A follow-up study showed that BOS appraisals produced higher levels of satisfaction with the appraisal process than did the trait scales. This is because BOS contain specific behavioural statements that allow employees to understand exactly what they need to do to be viewed as a high performer (Tziner, Kopelman, & Livneh, 1993).

In terms of user reactions, technical managers and programmer analysts in a financial institution in the United States preferred BOS to trait scales for objectivity, providing performance feedback differentiating among performers, setting goals and overall ease of use (Wiersma & Latham, 1986). These results were replicated in two software organizations in the Netherlands (Wiersma, Van de Berg, & Latham, 1995).

An Effective Student					
(1) Attends class					
Almost Never	0	1	2	3	4	Almost Always
(2) Sits in the front half of the classroom					
Almost Never	0	1	2	3	4	Almost Always
(3) Stays up to date on reading assignments					
Almost Never	0	1	2	3	4	Almost Always
(4) Studies reading material daily in a quiet location					
Almost Never	0	1	2	3	4	Almost Always
(5) Attends study groups					
Almost Never	0	1	2	3	4	Almost Always
(6) Is involved in extra-curricular activities					
Almost Never	0	1	2	3	4	Almost Always

Figure 4.1:   Example of a behavioural observational scale

In summary, the use of BOS is conducive to setting specific, high goals (Tziner & Kopelman, 2012). Moreover, bias in ratings is reduced when the appraisal format requires appraisals based on observable behaviour (Varma, De Nisi, & Peters, 1996).

4.7 Are There Alternatives to the Traditional Performance Appraisal?

A seminal study at the General Elective Company (Meyer, Kay & French, 1965) found that as a result of conducting performance appraisals, employee performance frequently decreased, rather than increased and did so in some instances up to 12 weeks following the appraisal. The reasons for this disappointing outcome included not setting specific, high goals, questioning by employees of an appraiser's objectivity, and negative feedback coming as a surprise to an employee.

The importance of goal setting to the appraisal process has already been discussed. With regard to an appraiser's objectivity, most managers are aware of and adhere to their country's laws surrounding performance appraisals (e.g., prohibiting appraisals that are influenced by an employee's age, race, sex or religion). However, appraisers are often unaware of other sources of bias. For example, supervisors often rate smokers lower than non-smokers on professional comportment, working with others and dependability (Gilbert, Hannom, & Lowe, 1998). A series of studies conducted in Canada and Turkey revealed that the appraisal that an appraiser receives from his/her manager influences the ratings that appraiser subsequently gives to direct reports (Latham, Budworth, Yanar, & Whtye, 2008).

There are at least three alternatives to the traditional boss – subordinate performance appraisal: (1) 360° feedback; (2) the feedforward technique; and (3) ongoing coaching including coaching based on feedback from a mystery shopper.

4.7.1 360° feedback

The criticism that my boss does not have a complete picture of what and how I do my job is overcome if multi-source appraisals are conducted. That is, appraisals are made by your employee's subordinates and peers anonymously, in addition to you. In some instances, appraisals may also be done by your employee's customers anonymously as well as by the employees themselves (i.e. self-appraisals). Hence the term 360° feedback. You are getting a complete picture of an individual's performance before you make your assessment. The advantage of this technique for conducting a performance appraisal is that you are receiving input from multiple sources, sources that have different opportunities to observe different aspects of the employee's performance. This allows for an integrated, holistic view of an employee, off-setting the limitations of an appraisal from a single vantage point, namely, yours.

Research shows that 360° feedback accurately distinguishes between high- and low-performing managers (Church, 2000). This same study found that managers who took action to improve their performance based on this feedback saw a decrease in voluntary employee turnover among their direct reports. Action taken on the basis of multi-source feedback correlates positively with bottom-line measures.

4.7.2   Feedforward

An alternative to the traditional performance appraisal is the feedforward interview (FFI). The underlying assumption of the FFI is that employees can, if probed, identify their performance-effective achievements. More importantly, once having done so, employees can develop ways to create conditions for even greater accomplishments. In contrast to the traditional performance appraisal, the FFI focuses on setting goals for future performance rather than on discussing the limitations of an individual's past performance. Employees excel once they recognize their strengths and how to build upon and broaden them in different job-related contexts.

The questions asked in an FFI are as follows: (1) No matter how bad the past year that you have experienced, you had one or more positive experiences. Please tell me about a specific incident where you felt especially good about attaining a goal. (2) What were the circumstances that enabled you to attain it? (3) What exactly did you do? (4) What can you do this coming year to create conditions/circumstances that will enable you to think, feel, and behave on an on-going basis the way you did in the incident you just described?

To test the effectiveness of this technique, employees were randomly assigned to two conditions where half received the traditional performance appraisal and the other half received the FFI. Both groups of employees were evaluated on BOS. Four months later only those who received the FFI had improved their performance (Budworth, Latham, & Manroop, 2015).

Another alternative to the traditional appraisal is coaching an employee, and in some instances doing so based on feedback from a mystery shopper. This technique is discussed in Section 4.8.1 on coaching.

4.8   What Are the Merits of Coaching an Employee on an On-Going Basis?

A primary objective of conducting a performance appraisal is to instill the desire for continuous improvement in your employees. This objective is hampered by the fact that appraisals are done on a discrete basis, namely only quarterly, bi-annually, or annually. In contrast to the traditional performance appraisal, coaching is done on an on-going basis. Consider the performance of an athlete who receives on-coaching versus one who only receives feedback and sets new goals based on feedback that is given quarterly, bi-annually, or annually. Which athlete is likely to perform better?

A study of 400 companies found that cyclical year-round of coaching employees (i.e. feedback, analyzing the results, then setting goals) effectively increases organizational performance (Campbell, Garfinkel, & Moses, 1996). A study of over 1000 managers found that coaching on the basis of 360°/multisource feedback significantly improved their performance as observed by the managers' direct reports and the managers' boss (Smither et al., 2003).

Although on-going feedback to employees on goal progress is indeed beneficial, there also is a downside. The downside is the inability of most managers to find the time to coach each employee continuously. This is problematic because feedback is not only critical for learning, it also influences the decision to exert effort and persist until the goal is attained (Locke & Latham, 2002). Moreover, feedback that is relatively immediate is far more effective for increasing learning and motivation than feedback that is delayed (e.g. provided quarterly, bi-annually, or annually). On-going coaching overcomes the problem of timeliness. The relationship between what an employee is doing and the outcomes that individual can expect are clarified: good performance is praised, ineffective performance is corrected, and the individual knows the behaviours that will lead to high performance (Heslin, VandeWalle, & Latham, 2006).

Employees in this new millennium want relatively immediate feedback (De Stobbeleir & Ashford, 2013). But research suggests that supervisors have little time to observe their subordinates. This is because managerial work has been organized in ways that have greatly expanded a manager's span of control (Ashford & Northcraft, 2003). This makes timely supervisory appraisals an increasingly difficult undertaking.

Another alternative to the traditional performance appraisal and on-going coaching suggests a way to overcome the above issues in the service industry. The service industry is a major driver of economies in the West. This alternative is an adaptation of a technique used in marketing, namely, feedback from a mystery shopper.

4.8.1 Mystery shoppers

The use of mystery shoppers overcomes a problem that confronts most managers – presenting to employees systematic performance feedback in a timely manner. In this instance, the feedback comes from a third party, a customer who is unknown to both the employee and the employee's manager – hence the term, mystery.

Research on schedules of reinforcement call into question the necessity for coaching on a continuous basis (Latham & Dossett, 1978). Once a behaviour is learned, reinforcement (e.g. praise) of that behaviour is no longer required continuously. If praise is given on a fixed interval (e.g. once every hour), the behaviour increases rapidly, but only as the end of the predetermined time period approaches. For example, if students are given an exam at the beginning of each month, most of them do little or no studying during the first three weeks, yet study intensely during the last week, and stop doing so immediately following the exam. But, on a variable interval schedule, a desired behaviour occurs at a high steady rate because it is difficult, if not impossible, for an individual to discern when the behaviour will be appraised. For example, a teacher who gives pop-up quizzes typically has students who are continuously studying the course subject matter because they do not know when they will be quizzed.

Jack Welch (pers. comm.), the former CEO of the General Electric Company, has argued that the words 'leader' and 'coach' should be synonymous. Effective leaders, he said, find the time to 'grow' their subordinates. The critical phrase is 'find the time'.

A coach of a baseball team stands in the dug-out observing the on-going performance of the players on the field; similarly, the hockey coach stands behind the bench watching the players skate. But the typical manager in government or industry is likely to be away from employees, performing other duties (e.g. strategic planning, coordinating implementation of goals with other department heads). To overcome this problem, a restaurant chain hired mystery shoppers to provide relatively immediate feedback for coaching employees on a timely basis (Latham, Ford, & Tzabbar, 2012).

A job analysis was conducted to identify the job behaviours that lead to high customer satisfaction because customer satisfaction increases repeat business. Then each employee sets a goal to be attained for the behavioural measures of customer satisfaction, knowing that goal attainment would increase the restaurant's bottom line. It did.

The advantage of this coaching technique is at least five-fold:

1. A mystery shopper appeared in the restaurant on average, once every 30 days. Because the shopper appeared on a variable interval schedule, the shopper might come into the restaurant two days in a row or not until 45 days after the first visit. But, on average, a shopper visited the store once every 30 days. Because the employees were unaware of the identity of the shoppers, let alone when the person was present, the employees had to maintain a high level of performance if they wanted a good performance appraisal.
2. The feedback given to an employee focused on effective behaviours identified from a job analysis. The job analysis minimized the probability that the relevance of the assessed behaviours would be questioned by the employees, and it increased the probability that the restaurant's bottom line would be affected favourably.
3. The feedback from a mystery shopper is relatively timely. In the present study, it was 18 hours or less before it was posted on the restaurant's computer.
4. The feedback given to an employee comes from a neutral third party, a mystery shopper. This allows a manager to fulfil the role of coach with the minimal likelihood that an employee will view the appraisal as a personal attack. This is because a mystery shopper is, relatively speaking, a neutral party. Nothing is known by the shopper about an employee other than the performance/service that the employee has provided. Thus bias attributed by an employee to the feedback from a manager is minimized, if not eliminated.
5. Only one server is assessed each day. Thus, a manager only had to spend a maximum of 30 minutes daily discussing with an employee the feedback that was provided by the mystery shopper, and setting goals with the employee based on this feedback.

It remains to be explored whether the use of mystery shoppers as a coaching technique can be adapted by managers outside the service industry.

4.9 What About Self-Appraisals?

The key to becoming a high performer is not to wait for formal or informal feedback from others. Instead, actively seek it. 'What am I doing that you would like to see me continue doing?'; 'Is there anything you would like to see me do differently?' Then self-set specific, high goals to attain based on this feedback. Become a self-manager (Latham & Locke, 1991).

In a study involving over 3000 supervisors, 12,000 peers, and nearly 3000 subordinates, there was relative agreement among the sources of appraisal (i.e., you, your boss, peers and subordinates) when a behavioural appraisal scale was used (Facteau & Craig, 2001). People whose self-appraisals are in agreement with the appraisals they receive from others are typically high performers (Fletcher, 1997).

Summary

Performance appraisals are a legal requirement in both the public and private sectors in most countries in the West. Regardless of these legal requirements, employees want feedback as to how they are doing on the job so that they can improve their performance. Performance appraisals are a formal way of providing that feedback. Coaching is an informal way of providing feedback. However, feedback alone will not lead to an increase in performance. To improve performance, specific, high goals must be set.

When giving feedback, a discussion of a person's traits should be avoided. If bottom-line measures are discussed, emphasis must be placed on the behaviours an employee should exhibit to have an impact on the bottom line. A measurement scale that facilitates this discussion is a BOS, derived from a systematic job analysis.

Alternatives to the traditional boss–subordinate appraisal include 360° feedback, the feedforward interview, and on-going coaching. An innovative coaching technique is to coach an employee based on feedback from a mystery shopper that is provided on a variable-interval schedule rather than on an on-going basis.

Even if there were no legal requirements for conducting performance appraisals, there are economic benefits for giving people feedback and setting goals based on this feedback. A utility analysis examined the difference between do-your-best or no goal setting and setting specific, difficult goals (Schmidt, 2013). The analysis was based on four meta-analyses of goal setting experiments that included 19,839 data points. The average increase in employee output per year as a result of a goal setting intervention is $9200. A goal setting intervention over a five-year period, involving only 35 employees, costing $200 per employee yields an organization $1,603,000 due to increases in production. Therefore, the answer to the question in the chapter title, as to what are you supposed to do on your job is clear: set goals and appraise your people.

Discussion Points

1 If you have a defensive employee, or an employee with whom you have had conflicts, how would you go about appraising that person's performance?
2 If your employees work in teams, how would you appraise each individual's performance?

Notes

1 Goals are also effective for improving the performance of teams (Locke & Latham, 2002). Because most laws require appraisals of an employee, this chapter focuses on the individual.
2 Subsequent research shows that when an assigned goal is as high as a participatively set goal, performance is the same. However, on a task that is difficult for an employee to attain, participation in setting the goal can increase the person's self-efficacy that the goal is attainable and lead to the development of a strategy to attain it (Latham, Winters, & Locke, 1994). The relationship between self-efficacy and strategy is reciprocal.
3 The Harvard University Executive Session on Public Sector Performance Management (2001) describes an effective performance management system as one that includes strategic prioritized goals that are challenging yet not overwhelming, and are measurable/fact-based, up-to-date performance data.

Suggested Further Reading

Budworth, M. H., Latham, G. P., & Manroop, L. (2015). Looking forward to performance improvement: A field test of the feedforward interview for performance management. *Human Resource Management, 54,* 45–54. This is the first field experiment that shows the effectiveness of the feedforward interview over the use of supervisory feedback on an employee's past performance.

Latham, G. P., Budworth, M., Yanar, B., & Whyte, G. R. (2008). The influence of a manager's own performance appraisal on the evaluation of others. *International Journal of Selection and Assessment, 16,* 220–228. A disturbing yet fascinating series of three studies, two in Canada and one in Turkey, showing that the appraisal an individual receives influences the appraisals that the individual makes of others.

Latham, G. P., Ford, R. C., & Tzabbar, D. (2012). Enhancing employee and organizational performance through coaching based on mystery shopper feedback: A quasi experimental study. *Human Resource Management, 51,* 213–230. Discusses the use of coaching based on an innovative technique adapted from marketing: the mystery shopper.

Meyer, H. H., Kay, E., & French, J. R. P. (1965). Split roles in performance appraisal. *Harvard Business Review, 43*(1), 123–129. This article is a classic. It is among the first to show what can go wrong when conducting performance appraisals and what to do about it – set goals.

References

Aguinis, H., Joo, H., & Gottfredson, R. K. (2011). Why we hate performance appraisals—And why we should love it. *Business Horizons, 54*(6), 503–507.

Ashford, S. J., & Northcraft, G. (2003). Robbing Peter to pay Paul: Feedback environments and enacted priorities in response to competing task demands. *Human Resource Management Review, 13*, 537–559.

Bennington, L., & Wein, R. (2000). Anti-discrimination legislation in Australia: Fair, effective, efficient or irrelevant? *International Journal of Manpower, 21*, 21–33.

Brown, T. C., & Latham, G. P. (2000). The effects of goal setting and self-instruction training on the performance of unionized employees. *Industrial Relations, 55*, 80–94.

Brown, T. C., & Latham, G. P. (2002). The effects of behavioral outcome goals, learning goals, urging people to do their best on teamwork behavior on a group problem-solving task. *Canadian Journal of Behavioural Science, 34*, 276–285.

Budworth, M. H., Latham, G. P., & Manroop, L. (2015). Looking forward to performance improvement: A field test of the feedforward interview for performance management. *Human Resource Management, 54*, 45–54.

Campbell, J. D., Garfinkel, R. B., & Moses, L. (1996). Strategies for success in measuring performance. *HR Magazine, 41*, 98.

Church, A. H. (2000). Do higher performing managers actually receive better ratings? A validation of multirater assessment methodology. *Consulting Psychology Journal: Practice and Research, 52*, 99–116.

De Stobbeleir, K., & Ashford, S. J. (2013). Feedback seeking behaviour in organizations: Reason theory and implementations. In R. Sutton (ed.) *Handbook of criterion, praise, and advice.* New York: Peter Lang.

Facteau, J. D., & Craig, S. B. (2001). Are performance appraisal ratings from different rating sources comparable? *Journal of Applied Psychology, 86*, 215–27.

Fletcher, C. (1997). Self-awareness—A neglected attribute in selection and assessment? *International Journal of Selection and Assessment, 5*, 183–187.

Frayne, C. A., & Latham, G. P. (1987). The application of social learning theory to employee self management of attendance. *Journal of Applied Psychology, 72*, 387–392.

Gilbert, G. R., Hannan, E. L., & Lowe, K. B. (1998). Is smoking stigma clouding the objectivity of employee performance appraisal? *Public Personnel Management, 27*(3), 285–300.

Greenbaum, R. L., Mawritz, M. B., Eissa, G. (2012). Bottom-line mentality as an antecedent of social undermining and the moderating roles of core self evaluations and conscientiousness. *Journal of Applied Psychology, 97*, 342–359.

Harvard University Executive Session on Public Sector Performance Management. (2001). *Get results through performance management: An open memorandum to government executives.* Cambridge, MA: Harvard University.

Head, T., Haug, R., Krabbenhoft, A., & Ma, C. (2000). Issues and trends in international business law: Implications for OD consultants. *Organization Development Journal, 18*, 62–73.

Heslin, P. A., VandeWalle, D., & Latham, G. P. (2006). Keen to help? Managers' IPTs and their subsequent employee coaching. *Personnel Psychology, 59*, 871–902.

Ilies, R., & Judge, T. A. (2005). Goal regulation across time: The effects of feedback and affect. *Journal of Applied Psychology, 90*, 453–467.

Jain, H. C., Sloan, P. J., & Horowitz, F. M. (2003). *Employment equity and affirmative action: An international comparison.* Armonk, NY: M. E. Sharpe.

Latham, G. P. (2012). *Work motivation: History, theory, research and practice* (2nd ed.). Thousand Oaks, CA: Sage.

Latham, G. P., & Arshoff, A. S. (2015). Planning: A mediator in goal setting theory. In M. Frese & M. D. Mumford (Eds.), *The psychology of planning in organization: Research and applications.* New York: Taylor & Francis.

Latham, G. P., Borgogni, L., & Petitta, L. (2008). Goal setting and performance management in the public sector. *International Public Management Journal, 11,* 385–419.

Latham, G. P., & Brown, T. C. (2006). The effect of learning vs. outcome goals on self-efficacy and satisfaction in a MBA Program. *Applied Psychology: An International Review, 55,* 606–623.

Latham, G. P., Budworth, M., Yanar, B., & Whyte, G. R. (2008). The influence of a manager's own performance appraisal on the evaluation of others. *International Journal of Selection and Assessment, 16,* 220–228.

Latham, G. P., & Dossett, D. L. (1978). Designing incentive plans for unionized employees: A comparison of continuous and variable ratio reinforcement schedules. *Personnel Psychology, 31,* 47–61.

Latham, G. P., Erez, M., & Locke, E. A. (1988). Resolving scientific disputes by the joint design of crucial experiments by the antagonists: Application of the Erez-Latham dispute regarding participation in goal setting. *Journal of Applied Psychology Monograph, 73,* 753–772.

Latham, G. P., Ford, R. C., & Tzabbar, D. (2012). Enhancing employee and organizational performance through coaching based on mystery shopper feedback: A quasi experimental study. *Human Resource Management, 51,* 213–230.

Latham, G. P., & Locke, E. A. (1991). Self regulation through goal setting. *Organizational Behavior and Human Decision Processes, 50,* 212–247.

Latham, G. P., & Locke, E. A. (2007). New developments in and directions for goal setting. *European Psychologist, 12,* 290–300.

Latham, G. P., & Marshall, H. A. (1982). The effects of self-set, participatively set, and assigned goals on the performance of government employees. *Personnel Psychology, 35,* 399–404.

Latham, G. P., Mitchell, T. R., & Dossett, D. L. (1978). The importance of participative goal setting and anticipated rewards on goal difficulty and job performance. *Journal of Applied Psychology, 63,* 163–171.

Latham, G. P., & Saari, L. M. (1979). The importance of supportive relationships in goal setting. *Journal of Applied Psychology, 64,* 151–156.

Latham, G. P., & Seijts, G. H. (1999). The effects of proximal and distal goals on performance on a moderately complex task. *Journal of Organizational Behavior, 20,* 421–429.

Latham, G. P., & Wexley, K. N. (1994). *Increasing productivity through performance appraisal* (2nd ed.). Reading, MA: Addison-Wesley.

Latham, G. P., Winters, D. C., & Locke, E. A. (1994). Cognitive and motivational effects of participation: A mediator study. *Journal of Organizational Behavior, 15,* 49–63.

Linna, A., Elovainio, M., van den Bos, K., Kivimäki, M., Pentti, J., & Vahtera, J. (2012). Can usefulness of performance appraisal interviews change organizational justice perceptions? A 4-year longitudinal study among public sector employees. *International Journal of Human Resource Management, 23*(7), 1360–1375.

Locke, E. A., & Latham, G. P. (2002). Building a practically useful theory of goal setting and task motivation: A 35-year odyssey. *American Psychologist, 57,* 705–717.

Martin, D. C., Barton, K. M. & Kehoe, P. E. (2000). The legal ramifications of performance appraisal: Their growing significance. *Public Personnel Management, 29*(3), 379–405.

Mawritz, M., Folger, R., & Latham, G. P. (2014). Supervisors' exceedingly difficult goals and abusive supervision: The mediating effects of hindrance stress, anger, and anxiety. *Journal of Organizational Behavior, 35,* 358–372.

Meyer, H. H., Kay, E., & French, J. R. P. (1965). Split roles in performance appraisal. *Harvard Business Review, 43*(1), 123–129.

Mitchell, T. R., & Daniels, D. (2003). Motivation. In W. C. Borman, D. R. Ilgen, & R. J. Klimoski (Eds.), *Comprehensive handbook of psychology: Industrial organizational psychology* (vol. 12, pp. 225–254). New York: John Wiley & Sons, Inc.

Schmidt, F. (2013). The economic value of goal setting to employers. In E. A. Locke, & G. P. Latham (Eds.), *New developments in goal setting and task performance*. New York: Routledge.

Seijts, G. H., & Latham, G. P. (2005). Learning versus performance goals: When should each be used? *Academy of Management Executive, 19,* 124–131.

Selden, S. C., & Brewer, G. A. (2000). Work motivation in the senior executive service: Testing the high performance cycle theory. *Journal of Public Administration Research and Theory, 10,* 531–550.

Smither, J. W., London, M., Flautt, R., Vargas, Y., & Kucine, I. (2003). Can working with an executive coach improve multisource feedback ratings over time? A quasi-experimental field study. *Personnel Psychology, 56*(1), 23–44.

Tziner, A., & Kopelman, R. (1988). Effects of rating format on goal setting decisions: A field experiment. *Journal of Applied Psychology, 73,* 323–326.

Tziner, A., & Kopelman, R. E. (2002). Is there a preferred performance rating format? A non-psychometric perspective. *Applied Psychology: An International Review, 51,* 479–503.

Tziner, A., Kopelman, R., & Livneh, N. (1993). Effects on performance appraisal format on perceived goal characteristics, appraisal process satisfaction, and changes in rated job performance: A field experiment. *Journal of Applied Psychology, 127,* 281–291.

Varma, A., DeNisi, A. S., & Peters, L. H. (1996). Interpersonal affect and performance appraisal: A field study. *Personnel Psychology, 49,* 341–361.

Wiersma, U. J., & Latham, G. P. (1986). The practicality of behavioral observation scales, behavioral expectation scales, and trait scales. *Personnel Psychology, 39,* 619–628.

Wiersma, U. J., Van Der Berg, P., & Latham, G. P. (1995). Dutch reactions to behavioral observation, behavioral expectation, and trait scales. *Group and Organization Management, 20,* 297–309.

Wiese, B. S., & Freund, A. M. (2005). Goal progress makes one happy, or does it? *Journal of Occupational and Organizational Psychology, 7*(8), 1–19.

5 Why Is My Job So Stressful? Characteristics, Processes and Models of Stress at Work

Jan de Jonge and Christian Dormann

Overview

Why are jobs stressful? Why does it seem to be a problem for some employees but not for others? Are there differences between bad and good stress? This chapter deals with the issue of job stress in relation to employee health, well-being and performance. We begin with an outline of job stress as a societal problem, illustrating current trends in society, the nature of work, and job stress. We continue with a discussion of the main perspectives on job stress, including bad and good stress, and of the potential role of individual differences in the job stress process. Next, an integrative process model of job stress is presented that will pave the way for a profound discussion of four prominent theoretical models on job stress: (1) the Demand–Control–Support model, (2) the Effort – Reward Imbalance model, (3) the Job Demands–Resources model, and (4) the Demand-Induced Strain Compensation Recovery model. Using the insights gained from these models, this chapter concludes by explaining how a stressful working situation can be transferred into 'healthy work'.

5.1 Why is Job Stress a Societal Problem?

Numerous research studies show that job stress is a major concern in all developing and industrialized countries, affecting not only employees whose health is at stake but also organizations and society as a whole. In economically developing and developed countries, the nature of work has been changing in the past few decades. Current trends are the globalization of economic activities (the '24/7 economy'), increased use of information and communication technology, growing diversity in the workplace (e.g., more women, older, and better educated

An Introduction to Work and Organizational Psychology: An International Perspective, Third Edition. Edited by Nik Chmiel, Franco Fraccaroli and Magnus Sverke.
© 2017 John Wiley & Sons, Ltd. Published 2017 by John Wiley & Sons, Ltd.

people, as well as increased migration), flexible work arrangements, and changed organizational work patterns, such as the new way of working (Peeters, Taris, & de Jonge, 2014). Industrial employment has decreased, while at the same time knowledge work (e.g., consulting) and service work (e.g., nursing) have increased. One of the most striking developments, however, is the changing nature of work itself and increased workloads. Work spaces (e.g., including home offices) and work processes (including flexible work hours) have been redesigned in many ways. New jobs (e.g., web designer and web seller) and new types of companies (e.g., online web stores) have emerged. Nowadays, for many employees, job stress has mainly become a mental and emotional issue rather than being a physical one.

5.1.1 Prevalence and costs of job stress

According to recent figures, the prevalence of job stress is high. For instance, the Sixth European Working Conditions Survey (EWCS) (European Foundation for the Improvement of Living and Working Conditions, 2015) of more than 43,000 employees in 35 different European countries showed that 27% of the employees reported working under tight deadlines (almost) all of the time, and 23% of the employees reported working at very high speed (almost) all of the time. In addition, for two-thirds of the working people, their pace of working is set by direct demands from clients such as customers, patients and passengers rather than supervisors and machines. Moreover, many blue-collar workers remain exposed to high levels of work demands and low levels of job autonomy, job security and employment security.

With regard to job stress and health, 23% of the employees in the Sixth EWCS reported that their health was at risk because of their work (European Foundation for the Improvement of Living and Working Conditions, 2015). Job stress is related to psychological disorders such as burnout and depression (McTernan, Dollard, & LaMontagne, 2013), and also to a number of physical ailments such as cardiovascular diseases (Terrill & Garofalo, 2012), musculoskeletal diseases (Lang, Ochsmann, Kraus, & Lang, 2012), chronic low back pain (Bernal et al., 2015; Lang et al., 2012), and reduced performance and absenteeism from work (McTernan et al., 2013).

Almost needless to say, the expenditures on job stress are huge. Job stress has become as much a business issue as it is a health issue in many countries. For instance, job-related stress costs US companies hundreds of billions of US dollars a year due to burnout, turnover, higher absenteeism and lower productivity (European Agency for Safety and Health at Work, 2014). Even a single job stress outcome such as depression is known to produce direct (through treatment) and indirect (through absence and reduced productivity) costs that add up to billions. One of the lowest estimates for productivity loss caused by depression in the US was $36 billion (Kessler et al., 2009).

The review report by the European Agency for Safety and Health at Work (2014) also provides figures of the costs of job stress for various European countries. According to this report, for example, the costs of depression due to work stress were €617 billion for the 27 member states of the EU in 2013.

The prevalence and costs of job stress have led to stronger labour legislation with regard to psychosocial work conditions. A growing number of countries has introduced legislation to improve employee health, well-being and safety in their work environment. For instance, the EU social partners signed a framework agreement for employers and employees aimed at preventing, identifying, and combating job stress. Nowadays, modern labour legislation emphasizes: (1) a comprehensive approach, integrating health, safety and well-being at work, (2) a broad and positive health concept, which means not only the absence of health problems but also being vital and engaged, (3) active involvement and joint responsibilities of employer and employee, and (4) self-regulation by providing a supportive environment, for instance, by institutionalizing Occupational Health and Safety Services (International Labour Office, 2016).

Thus, job stress is a major concern in both developing and industrialized countries, and it appears that its prevalence is high. This is illustrated by a change in the nature of work, by an increase in job stress-related health and well-being problems, as well as by rising associated costs. Despite the achievements in practice, there is, however, an on-going theoretical debate about the meaning of the term 'job stress' and how job stress emerges.

5.2   What Is Job Stress?

The original meaning of the term 'stress' is derived from the field of engineering. By analogy with physical force on a metal bar, it refers to external pressure that is exerted on a person, which in turn results in tension or stress reactions. These stress reactions are also called 'strain' (Kahn & Byosiere, 1992). Up to a certain level, people are able to deal with this external pressure, can adapt to the situation, and recover when the stress is relieved. A person's adaptability is determined by personal characteristics, for instance, stress tolerance or coping style, and by situational characteristics, for instance, the availability of social support. It is quite normal to experience some stress. Stress releases hormones that speed up the heart rate, make us breathe faster, and give us energy to act. Short-term stress is sometimes experienced as positive activation, however, too much stress is not good for a person as it will deplete a person's resources and energy.

In everyday language as well as in the scientific literature, the term 'stress' is used to refer to the causes as well as the accompanying state of tension, and the consequences of this state. As there is little agreement on how exactly 'stress' should be defined, there is no general and overarching theory of stress. One of the main reasons for this lack of agreement lies in the large number of disciplines with different perspectives that are involved in researching stress, such as biology, sociology, psychology, occupational medicine, ergonomics, industrial engineering, epidemiology, management science, and business administration. Nevertheless, most researchers do agree that three different meanings of the term stress can be distinguished (e.g., Kahn & Byosiere, 1992): (1) stress as a *stimulus* (cause), (2) stress as a *response* (strain), and (3) stress as a *mediational process* between a demand (stimulus) and a stress reaction (response). As our perspective of stress lies within the area of work, we call it 'job stress', which is simply stress related to one's job. We will discuss each of these three perspectives below.

5.2.1   Job stress as a stimulus: Job demands and job resources

Within the domain of job stress, stress-related job characteristics can be categorized under two broad main categories: (1) job demands, and (2) job resources (de Jonge & Dormann, 2003). Job demands refer to those properties of the job that require immediate or sustained cognitive, emotional and/or physical effort. Examples of job demands are workload, time pressure, role conflict, and physical exertion. Job resources are conceptually similar to coping options; they can be broadly conceptualized as work-related assets that can be employed when an employee has to deal with demands at work. Examples of job resources are job autonomy, job variety and workplace social support.

As both job demands and job resources are multi-dimensional constructs, they may basically comprise cognitive, emotional and/or physical components. As far as job demands are concerned, three types can be distinguished (Hockey, 2000): (1) cognitive demands that impinge primarily on the brain processes involved in information processing, (2) emotional demands which refer primarily to the effort needed to deal with organizationally desired emotions during interpersonal transactions, and (3) physical demands that are primarily associated with the musculoskeletal system (i.e., sensomotor and physical aspects of behaviour). Similarly, job resources may have a cognitive-informational component (e.g., colleagues providing information), an emotional component (e.g., colleagues providing sympathy and affection), and a physical component (e.g., instrumental help of colleagues or ergonomic aids).

5.2.2   Job stress as a response: Job-related strain

In psychophysiology and occupational medicine, stress is defined as a combination of psychological and physiological responses of the organism to some kind of threat or danger. This definition of stress is based on Selye's (1956) classical work on the General Adaptation Syndrome (GAS). According to Selye, exposure to a noxious stimulus triggers a complex of non-specific physiological reactions that are intended to protect the individual against harmful consequences. The GAS consists of three stages: (1) the alarm reaction (mobilization by means of physiological and hormonal changes), (2) the resistance stage (optimal adaptation by activating appropriate systems), and (3) exhaustion (depletion of adaptation energy). Although the GAS may be initially adaptive, negative consequences such as fatigue and high blood pressure may occur if the resistance stage persists over longer periods of time.

The GAS is assumed to be non-specific and to be triggered by a huge range of different types of stressful stimuli. Individuals' thoughts and emotions are not proposed to influence the GAS. However, these propositions have proven to be untenable, as a number of studies have demonstrated that different types of physiological and hormonal reactions may occur, depending on the nature and interpretation of the stimulus and the accompanying emotions. For example, in a classic Swedish study among sawmill workers, Frankenhaeuser and Gardell (1976) found that stress, as reflected in the catecholamines' adrenaline and noradrenaline excretion and in self-reports of irritation, was most severe when the job was highly repetitive, when the worker had to maintain the same posture throughout working hours, and when the pace of the work was controlled by machines. The build-up of catecholamine arousal during the working day should be regarded as a warning signal, indicating that the employee is forced to mobilize 'reserve capacity', which in the long run is likely to add to its wear and tear. Indeed, based on interview data they showed that an inability to relax after work was a common complaint among high-stress workers. Moreover, the frequency of psychosomatic symptoms as well as absenteeism was exceptionally high in this group.

So, stress reactions or strains can be expressed in different ways. They can be classified into five different clusters (Le Blanc, de Jonge, & Schaufeli, 2008): (1) affective (e.g., feeling anxious), (2) cognitive (e.g., making wrong decisions), (3) physical (e.g., low back pain), (4) behavioural (e.g., sleeping problems; over-eating), and (5) motivational (e.g., feeling less energetic). In addition, three levels of expression can be distinguished, since stress not only is manifested in the form of individual symptoms (e.g., thoughts and feelings), but is also apparent in the form of interpersonal symptoms (e.g., disliking and struggling), and organizational-level symptoms (costs through reduced productivity, counterproductive work behaviour, and sickness absence).

Stress reactions can also differ in their intensity. In some occasions, the negative effects of stressful stimuli can easily be overcome by recovery. However, in the case of prolonged exposure to stressful stimuli, the individual may not be able to reduce their (physiological) state of stress, and high activation levels are sustained. This can in turn give rise to chronic physical (e.g., coronary heart disease) and/ or psychological stress complaints (e.g., burnout).

5.2.3   Job stress as a mediational process

Whereas both the stimulus approach and the response approach of stress emphasize directly measurable factors (job demands and stress reactions, respectively), the mediational approach focuses on the cognitive, evaluative and motivational processes that intervene between the stressful stimulus (cause) and the stress reaction (response). According to this mediational approach, which is also called a transactional model, stress reactions are the result of the interaction (transaction) between the person and the environment. Potentially stressful stimuli may lead to different types of stress reactions in different individuals, depending on their cognitive evaluations (appraisals) of the situation and the resources they have at their disposal to cope with the stressful situation.

Latack and Havlovic (1992) developed a conceptual framework for coping with job stress. In this framework, a distinction is made between the focus of coping and the method of coping. The focus of coping can be (1) problem-oriented or (2) emotion-oriented. Problem-oriented coping refers to attempts aimed at altering the transaction between person and environment. For instance, it may include behaviour such as seeking help or increasing efforts to counteract the threat. Emotion-oriented coping, on the other hand, is defined as attempts aimed at regulating the emotions of a person (e.g., cognitive strategies such as avoidance and relaxation techniques). With respect to the method of coping, two dimensions are distinguished. First, coping behaviour can be observable (overt) or not observable (covert). Second, each of these two types of coping behaviour can either be aimed at control or at escape (i.e., fight or flight). If the focus and/or method of coping do not match the stressful demand, feelings of stress will be sustained or even intensified. Basically, active ways of coping (e.g., control coping) are to be preferred to passive ones such as escape coping, provided that the situation offers possibilities for active intervention.

In the remaining part of this chapter, job stress is defined as an experienced incongruence between job demands and job or personal resources that is accompanied by cognitive, emotional, physical or behavioural symptoms.

5.3   Bad and Good Job Stress: Two Sides of the Same Coin?

From the outset, the very nature of stress has been debated: is it only 'bad', or does 'good' stress exist as well? Originally, Selye (1956) defined stress as a non-specific biological response to an external demand, meaning that stress in itself is neither bad nor good. He claimed that depending upon the relevant conditions, i.e., 'distress' (from the Latin 'dis' for bad, as in disease) or 'eustress' (from the Greek 'eu' for good, as in euphoria) might occur. Despite this early distinction between good and bad, 'stress' became the scientific and colloquial term for distress, whereas the conceptual development and empirical research on eustress has remained very limited. One promising avenue seems that eustress can be reconceptualized as a positive response to a cognitively appraised demand. For instance, being accountable for a multi-million construction work project might be appraised as a risk for one's reputation because many things can go wrong, or it might be appraised as a huge challenge because it provides an opportunity to progress one's career. The former case would lead to distress, whereas in the latter case eustress might result. Indeed, researchers have found at least two differential physiological response patterns, which are associated with positive and negative appraisals of a given situation. Thus it seems that rather than a non-specific biological response pattern, as originally hypothesized by Selye (1956), two such patterns exist that are associated with negative (distress) and positive (eustress) cognitive appraisals.

At the beginning of the twenty-first century, a new psychological movement has emerged that emphasizes that psychology should cover the entire range of human behaviour instead of being almost exclusively concerned with disease, damage, disability and dysfunction. This movement is called 'Positive Psychology' and looks at the other side of the coin of job stress. It focuses on good stress and its effects on positive health, well-being and optimal functioning (Schaufeli, 2005). This development coincides with major changes in modern organizations that expect their employees to be proactive and show initiative, take responsibility for their own professional development, be committed to high quality performance, and collaborate smoothly with others in teams. Obviously, this cannot be achieved with a workforce that is 'healthy' in the traditional sense of the word; that is, with employees who are merely symptom-free. Instead of just 'doing one's job', employees are nowadays expected 'to go the extra mile' (Lam, Wan, & Roussin, 2016). Thus, well-motivated, dedicated and engaged employees are needed.

5.4 The Role of Individual Characteristics in Job Stress

As employees differ in the probability of encountering job demands, in their appraisal of demands, and in their way of coping with demands, associations between job demands and job strain may not hold for everyone in the same way (Van der Heijden, Van Dam, Xanthopoulou, & De Lange, 2014). The results of individual differences studies seem to indicate that job demands have negative effects on the health of all workers, although these may be more severe for some and less severe for others. Individual characteristics, such as age, gender, level of education, values, and personality, may influence one's coping abilities; they may interact with job demands and either exacerbate or alleviate their effects. In general, we distinguish two main categories of individual characteristics:

1. *dispositional or trait-like characteristics* (such as gender, ethnicity, constitution, coping styles, needs, preferences, resilience, and type A/B behaviour);
2. *acquired or state-like characteristics* (such as education, competences, skills, and social class).

Individual characteristics differ also in their level of objectivity and subjectivity (Van der Heijden et al., 2014). Objective characteristics refer to some demographics such as gender and ethnicity, whereas subjective characteristics refer to those that are experienced or perceived, and manifest themselves through certain behaviours. In this chapter, we will therefore restrict ourselves to the category of individual characteristics that stands out in the literature as being potentially relevant in the job stress process; that is, the dispositional characteristics.

Some job stress studies have shown that the relationship between a certain job demand and a certain stress reaction mainly, or even exclusively, occurs in employees with particular dispositional characteristics. For example, in a study of

Japanese managers, Shimazu, Shimazu and Odahara (2005) found that psychological distress was lowest among managers with high levels of co-worker support combined with high levels of active coping, indicating that job resources worked effectively only for employees who actively cope. According to the Effort–Reward Imbalance (ERI) model (Siegrist, 1996), employees' commitment to work is another important disposition. If people are over-committed to their job, negative consequences for their health occur.

However, it remains unclear at what point in time the individual difference variables influence the job stress process. For instance, do they change the relation between objectively given and subjectively perceived demands, or do they affect the perceptions of job stress as related to affective, cognitive, physical and behavioural outcomes? Moreover, it should also be noted that physical and psychological characteristics, such as physical fitness or a high level of optimism, may not only act as precursors or buffers in the development of stress reactions, but may also change as a result of these effects. For example, if workers are able to deal with job demands, they will be more experienced and self-confident in overcoming similar situations the next time they have to face them (European Foundation for the Improvement of Living and Working Conditions, 2015).

5.5 What Are the Most Important Job Stress Models?

First of all, why is it necessary to look at models on job stress? One could imagine that it is not an easy task for a scientist or practitioner to find characteristics that are both relevant for the numerous different jobs and have predictable effects on stress reactions. The job stress models presented in this chapter are able to reduce the complexity of almost every job into relevant characteristics that are predictive of health and well-being outcomes. This is not only helpful for research purposes, but also for today's practice as theoretical models help practitioners to recognize those job demands that need to be combated to increase employee health and well-being.

In the recent past, many different models focusing on job stress have been highlighted in the literature, and most of them are connected with the process model that is presented in Figure 5.1 (Le Blanc et al., 2008). This process model is based upon insights gained from several theoretical models and empirical studies concerning job stress, on the one hand, and health, well-being, and performance, on the other. For that very reason, it integrates much of what has been outlined before.

According to this integrated process model, different types of job demands can result in different types of stress reactions, such as (adverse) health, (poor) well-being, and (bad) performance. Moreover, the relation between job demands and stress reactions may be moderated by (1) personal resources (e.g., coping styles), and (2) situational resources, such as job autonomy or workplace social support.

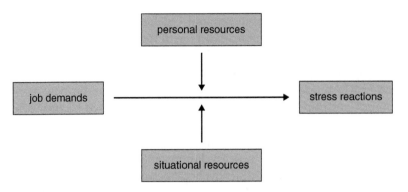

Figure 5.1: A process model of job stress

In this section we discuss four theoretical models that have laid the foundation for contemporary job stress research: (1) the Demand–Control–Support model, (2) the Effort–Reward Imbalance model, (3) the Job Demands–Resources model, and (4) the Demand-Induced Strain Compensation Recovery model. We note that none of these models themselves nor their empirical evidence is contradictory. Rather, they have different foci.

5.5.1   The Demand–Control–Support model

A highly influential model on job stress and health is Karasek and Theorell's Job Demand–Control (DC) model. The model was introduced by Karasek in 1979 and further developed and tested by Karasek and Theorell (1990). The DC model draws upon two research traditions, namely, the occupational stress tradition and the job redesign tradition. The occupational stress tradition focused on demands at work, such as high workload, role conflict, and role ambiguity. The job redesign tradition focused mainly on job characteristics such as job control and skill discretion, as its primary aim was to inform the (re)design of jobs in order to increase motivation, satisfaction, and performance at work.

The DC model postulates that the original and primary sources of stress lie within two basic job characteristics: *job demands* and *job decision latitude.* In the DC model, job demands are primarily associated with expending psychological effort such as time pressure and difficult work. Job decision latitude is a combination of job control and skill use. Job control can be defined broadly as job autonomy. Skill use can be defined broadly as the opportunity to enact one's capabilities. Job control and skill use often occur together in the same jobs. Combining the two dimensions of job demands and job decision latitude reflects four major classes of jobs that are defined by whether the job is high or low on the characteristics of job demands and decision latitude (see Figure 5.2).

The jobs most likely to show extreme job stress reactions (such as exhaustion and cardiovascular diseases) are those that combine high demands and low decision latitude. These jobs are called *high-strain jobs* (quadrant 1) and highlight

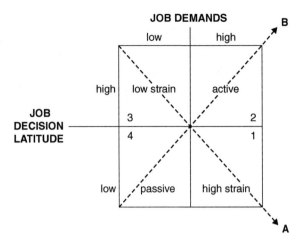

Figure 5.2: The Job Demand–Control model
Source: Adapted from Karasek (1979).

the first important assumption of the model. There is also an opposite situation termed *low-strain jobs*, which are jobs that are low on job demands but high on job decision latitude (quadrant 3). In this situation, lower than average levels of stress reactions can be expected.

The second important assumption of the model is that motivation, learning and personal growth will occur in situations where both job demands and job decision latitude are high: so-called *active jobs* (quadrant 2). This assumption is closely related to what might be called 'good stress' since job demands could be translated into direct action (i.e., effective problem solving) with little strain left to cause job-related stress. The opposite of this situation is formed by *passive jobs*, in which skills and abilities may atrophy (quadrant 4). This situation resembles the 'learned helplessness' phenomenon as described by Seligman (1972).

To summarize, different combinations of job demands and job decision latitude activate two psychological mechanisms, reflected by diagonals A and B in Figure 5.2. The first mechanism influences (adverse) health of the employee (diagonal A), while the other influences work motivation and the learning behaviour of the employee (diagonal B).

Over the years, workplace social support had been added as another factor that is useful in preventing demands from causing strain and in translating demands into growth and motivation. This has been termed the Demand–Control–Support (DCS) model (Johnson & Hall, 1988). Workplace social support is characterized by helpful interactions with supervisors and coworkers. In this extended model, the job strain assumption is split into *isolated* and *collective* conditions, and the processes are consequently redefined. Of particular interest are jobs that are labelled *iso-strain jobs* – these are jobs low on workplace social support and job decision latitude but high on job demands. Iso-strain jobs are jobs considered to be particularly harmful to employee health, including cardiovascular diseases.

In the past, there have been extensive reviews of the empirical evidence on the DCS Model (e.g., de Jonge & Kompier, 1997; Häusser, Mojzisch, Niesel, & Schulz-Hardt, 2010). These reviews show that there is some support for the notion that job decision latitude and workplace social support can offset the adverse health consequences of high levels of job demands. Evidence from a smaller set of studies on the second assumption of the model ('active jobs') indicates job control is linked to motivational and learning outcomes.

Obviously, the strength of the DCS Model lies in its simplicity and practical implications. However, the content, methodology and scope of the model have been commented on in the past. Various authors are of the opinion that a number of theoretical and methodological problems remain to be solved (e.g., Häusser et al., 2010). For instance, one serious problem is that job demands, job decision latitude and workplace social support are concepts that may be too broadly conceptualized and operationalized to be of much theoretical or practical value in deciding how best to optimize work (re-)design for health. A focus on more specific types of demands, control, and support is badly needed. Second, being a situation-centred model, the model focuses on characteristics of the work situation only. As a consequence, many studies have failed to take into account individual differences (such as locus of control and coping styles), considering only the three job factors.

5.5.2   Effort–Reward Imbalance model

Receiving support at work or being allowed to make work-related decisions can be rewarding experiences. Having a job can be rewarding in many more ways. The Effort–Reward Imbalance (ERI) model at work was introduced by Siegrist, Siegrist, and Weber in 1986, and has a more sociological focus than a psychological one. It attempts to combine three issues:

1. sociological factors concerning labour markets, (un-)employment and promotion prospects;
2. psychological factors concerned with individual differences between employees;
3. psychobiological factors concerned with employee ill-health and cardiovascular diseases.

The ERI Model has been very influential in how work and organizational psychologists think of the relation between work, stress and health. As illustrated in Figure 5.3, the work role of an employee is considered a basic tool linking important self-regulatory needs (i.e., self-esteem, self-efficacy and self-integration) with the societal structure of opportunities and rewards. Essentially, the model is based upon the reciprocity principle: employees invest efforts and expect proportionate rewards in return. People who expend high effort at work that is not reciprocated in the form of adequate occupational rewards are at particular risk of job stress. In other words, high effort spent at work in combination with low

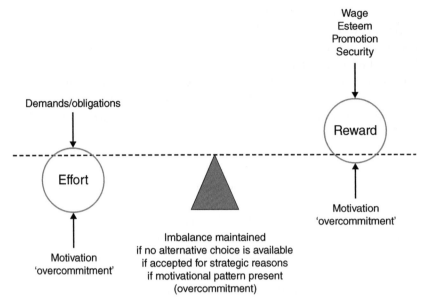

Figure 5.3: The Effort–Reward Imbalance model
Source: Adapted from Siegrist (2012).

reward obtained in turn may cause a state of emotional and physiological distress with an inclination to cardiovascular risks (Van Vegchel, de Jonge, Bosma, & Schaufeli, 2005).

According to the ERI model, occupational rewards are distributed to employees in three different ways: *money* (i.e., adequate salary), *esteem* (e.g., respect and support), and *security/career opportunities* (e.g., promotion prospects, job security, and status consistency). Effort is evaluated as two components: extrinsic effort or *job demands* (such as time pressure, responsibility and physical demands), and intrinsic effort or *overcommitment*. Overcommitment is considered a rather stable personality characteristic, and reflects motivation and ambition with a high need for approval, competitiveness, impatience, and inability to withdraw from work obligations. Highly overcommitted employees underestimate effortful situations and overestimate their own competence, and consequently they tend to invest too much effort. Thus, a mismatch between either high extrinsic effort (i.e., demands and obligations from work) or intrinsic effort (i.e., overcommitment) and low rewards may lead to adverse health effects. In addition, although their excessive efforts often are not met by adequate rewards, overcommitted people tend to maintain their level of involvement and ambition. As this will be exhausting in the long run, overcommitment is also thought to have a direct effect on ill-health (Van Vegchel et al., 2005).

Extensive review studies with the ERI model demonstrate that the combination of high efforts and low occupational rewards represents a short- and long-term risk factor for burnout, depressive symptoms, cardiovascular health diseases, sickness absence, and turnover intention (e.g., Van Vegchel et al., 2005). How-ever, empirical evidence for the effects of overcommitment on adverse health out-comes is mixed and thus less convincing (Van Vegchel et al., 2005).

Although the ERI Model initially looked very promising in the research domain of job stress and health, several concerns have been raised. First, it seems incon-sistent to make a clear distinction between extrinsic and intrinsic efforts, but no clear distinction between extrinsic and intrinsic rewards. Intrinsic rewards, how-ever, seem to be part of the overcommitment construct (i.e., need for approval). Second, one might question the extent to which the overcommitment construct is a stable personality trait and to what extent it is related to the work environment. For instance, will some employees experience more stress because of their charac-ter, or do some job characteristics lead to overcommitment? Moreover, by incor-porating overcommitment, the ERI model suggests that individual characteristics can affect employee health rather than the job characteristics they are exposed to. This might distract from probably more important causes of job stress, and consider the employee as the primary cause of his or her own stress ('blaming the victim'). Finally, a last issue concerns the dynamic nature of the ERI model. It could be that the effort–reward imbalance and adverse health are reciprocally associated. For instance, one might expect that employees who develop signs of ill-health because of a perceived effort–reward imbalance may act to protect their health by restoring the balance by altering the level of effort they put into their work. In a three-wave longitudinal study of Japanese male blue-collar workers, Shimazu and de Jonge (2009) found that the effort–reward imbalance predicted subsequent psychological ill-health, but also that psychological ill-health pre-dicted future effort–reward imbalance. To conclude, the processes underpinning the dynamic relations between effort–reward imbalance and ill-health need fur-ther investigation.

5.5.3   The Job Demands–Resources model

After social support and rewards have been demonstrated to be useful in reduc-ing the negative impacts of demands on strain, it has become clear that offer-ing job control or decision latitude is not the only way to combat the negative effects of job demands. Similarly, it is obvious that Karasek's (1979) focus on job demands in terms of time pressure and difficult work is also too narrow. Addi-tional demands, possibly varying between different occupations, have succes-sively been shown to be important in the development of job strain. Introduced by Demerouti, Bakker, Nachreiner, and Schaufeli (2001), the Job Demands–Resources (JD–R) model has been designed to encapsulate a broad range of job demands and resources unique to various occupations. They used the term resources to summarize various beneficial aspects of the job that are useful in reducing strain. The JD–R model constitutes an overarching framework that can be applied to various occupational settings, irrespective of the particular demands and resources involved.

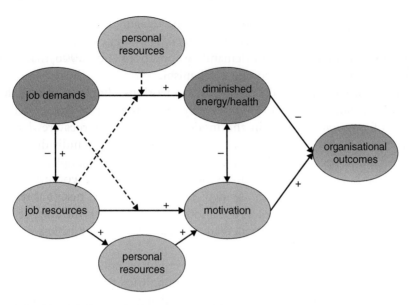

Figure 5.4:   The Job Demands–Resources model

The model generally proposes that two different psychological processes play a role in the development of ill-health and motivation (see Figure 5.4). The first process is called the health impairment process. Chronic job demands (e.g., work overload, emotional demands) exhaust employees' mental and physical resources and may therefore lead to the depletion of energy (i.e., a state of exhaustion) and to ill-health. The long-term effect of this process may be a deterioration of organizational outcomes such as job performance. So, energy depletion and health problems are assumed to (partly) mediate the relation between job demands and organizational outcomes. The second process is motivational in nature: job resources have motivational potential and lead to high work engagement, low cynicism, and consequently to good job performance. Within the JD–R model, job resources may play an intrinsic motivational role because they foster employees' growth, learning and development. So, the presence of job resources leads to engagement, whereas their absence evokes a cynical attitude towards work. In turn, this affective-motivational state fosters positive organizational outcomes, such as organizational commitment and job performance. Thus, motivation and engagement are assumed to (partly) mediate the relation between job resources and organizational outcomes.

Job demands and job resources initiate two different processes, but they could also have joint effects, as reflected by the two dotted lines in Figure 5.4. A first proposition in this respect is that job resources buffer the impact of job demands in predicting employee health and motivation. Or, put differently, the relation between job demands and ill-health will be weaker for employees with a high degree of job resources.

A second proposition is that job resources particularly influence motivation or work engagement when job demands are *high*. This suggests that job resources become most salient under highly demanding conditions and, hence, that employees will use job resources as a coping mechanism.

The JD–R model was initially developed as a work-psychological model, focusing on job demands and job resources only. An extension of the model is the inclusion of *personal resources* in the model. Personal resources are defined as aspects of the self that are linked to resiliency. They refer to an individual's ability to control and impact upon the environment successfully. Examples of personal resources that have been studied within the model are self-efficacy, optimism, and organizational-based self-esteem. As depicted in Figure 5.4, personal resources may have two functions in the JD–R model: (1) to buffer the impact of job demands on ill-health, and (2) to mediate the relation between job resources and motivational outcomes.

The JD–R model has been tested in many countries and cultures (e.g., for an overview, see Demerouti & Bakker, 2011). In line with the general assumptions of the model, most empirical studies provide evidence that irrespective of cultural background and the unique occupation, job demands and resources evoke the two distinct processes as described above. Accordingly, job demands are related to job strain (including lack of energy and development of health problems), and job resources are related to motivation (including engagement and commitment). With regard to the moderating role of personal resources, empirical evidence is mixed. Only a few JD–R studies have confirmed the moderating role in predicting health outcomes. For instance, a longitudinal study by Xanthopoulou, Bakker, Demerouti, and Schaufeli (2009) indicated that job resources predict personal resources and motivational outcomes such as work engagement, and that personal resources and work engagement, in turn, predict job resources.

An overall evaluation shows the JD–R model to be a heuristic, open and flexible job stress model, but with some limitations as well (for an overview, see Schaufeli & Taris, 2014). First, the model's openness and flexibility could also be its Achilles' heel, as this comes at the cost of specificity and the quality of its predictions. It may cause ambiguity, as in some situations a specific characteristic may represent a demand or a resource, or an outcome may be health-related or motivational in nature. For instance, does a high level of work responsibility represent a job demand or a job resource? Is life satisfaction a motivational or a health-related outcome? Perhaps the answer to these questions largely depends on the work context (e.g., a particular constellation of different demands and resources) or the worker's own experience. Second, the model lacks specificity in explaining *why* certain job demands or job resources exert their effects and on which target variable (i.e., adverse health or motivational outcomes) they do so. Also some of the job characteristics are difficult to assign either health or motivational outcomes. This implies that additional explanatory theoretical frameworks are necessary to argue why specific demands interact with specific resources to influence specific outcome variables.

5.5.4   The Demand-Induced Strain Compensation Recovery model

The search for combinations of specific job demands and specific job resources that are particularly suited to predict job strain was one of the triggers of the Demand-Induced Strain Compensation (DISC) model developed by de Jonge and Dormann (2003). The DISC Model unifies principles that are common to earlier job stress models, but it claims to be more comprehensive than other models.

de Jonge and Dormann (2003, 2006) reasoned that stress buffering and motivating effects of job resources largely depend on the so-called 'match' or 'fit' between specific types of job demands and job resources. This idea led to the two main principles of the DISC Model: (1) the multidimensionality principle, and (2) the matching principle. The multidimensionality principle claims that job demands, job resources, and work-related outcomes are multidimensional constructs that contain cognitive, emotional, and physical components (de Jonge & Dormann, 2003). As far as job demands are concerned, three types can be distinguished: (1) cognitive demands that impinge primarily on the human information processing, (2) emotional demands, mainly concerning the effort needed to deal with organizationally desired emotions during interpersonal transactions, and (3) physical demands that are primarily associated with the musculoskeletal system (i.e., sensomotor and physical aspects of behaviour). Similarly, job resources may have a cognitive-informational component (e.g., colleagues or computer systems providing information), an emotional component (e.g., colleagues providing sympathy, affection, and a listening ear) and a physical component (e.g., instrumental help from colleagues or ergonomic aids). Finally, in a similar vein to demands and resources, job-related health, well-being, and performance-based outcomes may also comprise cognitive, emotional and physical dimensions. These outcomes can be either negative or positive. For instance, concentration problems and employee creativity represent cognitively laden outcomes, emotional exhaustion and positive affect represent emotionally laden outcomes, and physical health complaints and physical strength mainly reflect bodily sensations (i.e., physical outcomes).

The second main principle is the *triple-matching principle* (TMP) of concepts (i.e., matching demands, resources, and outcomes). The TMP proposes that the strongest, interactive relations between job demands and job resources are observed if demands *and* resources *and* outcomes are based on qualitatively identical dimensions. For instance, emotional support from colleagues is most likely to moderate (i.e., mitigate) the relation between emotional demands (e.g., irate customers) and emotional outcomes (e.g., emotional exhaustion). So, the TMP suggests not only that job demands and job resources should match, but also that both job demands and job resources should match job-related outcomes.

The two key principles of the DISC model are guided by two further corollaries pertaining to compensation and balance mechanisms (de Jonge, Dormann,

& van den Tooren, 2008). The *compensation* or *stress-buffering* mechanism proposes that the adverse effects of high job demands on worker health and well-being can be counteracted if workers have sufficient job resources to deal with their demanding work tasks. As explained before, job resources from the same conceptual domain as job demands are most likely to counteract these negative effects. The *balance* or *activation-enhancing* mechanism proposes optimal conditions for employee learning, growth, creativity and performance, if there is a balanced mixture of high (but not overwhelming) job demands and high matching job resources. For instance, employees who need to solve complex problems are most likely to be creative if they have sufficient cognitive job resources (e.g., instant access to information or authority to decide the work method themselves) in order to deal with their cognitively demanding job.

The initial DISC model was limited to processes occurring at work, leaving out off-work experiences. However, research has shown that *recovery experiences off the job* interact with job demands and job resources in the prediction of employee health and well-being (e.g., Sonnentag, Binnewies, & Mojza, 2010). Off-job recovery refers to the process where cognitive, emotional and physical systems that were activated on the job unwind and return to their baseline levels (Sonnentag et al., 2010). The recovery process can be regarded as a process opposite to the strain process. Because recovery is so important, it has recently been integrated into the DISC model resulting in the Demand-Induced Strain Compensation Recovery (DISC-R) model as depicted in Figure 5.5 (de Jonge, Demerouti, & Dormann, 2014).

The DISC-R model was introduced by de Jonge and colleagues in 2012. It focuses on the recovery concept of *detachment from work*, which is defined as an "individual's sense of being away from the work situation" (Etzion, Eden, &

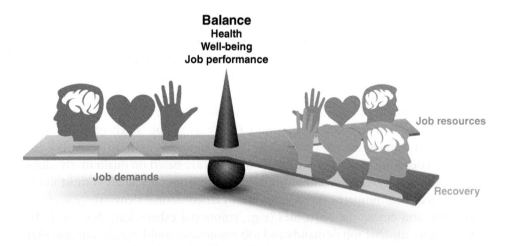

Figure 5.5:   The Demand-Induced Strain Compensation Recovery model

Lapidot, 1998, p. 579), and which is commonly thought of as 'switching off' work. Conversely, not detaching from work implies that the functional psycho-physiological systems remain in a state of prolonged activation. The DISC-R model proposes that detachment from work has an additional, moderating, effect in the relation between job demands, job resources and employee outcomes. More specifically, the DISC-R model proclaims that detachment from work that matches particular demands will be most effective (e.g., emotional detachment to reduce emotional exhaustion that is merely caused by emotional demands). Further, the model proposes that the positive effect of detachment is only valid in the case of high-strain jobs (in Karasek's terms, as discussed before) and health-based outcomes: High detachment from work then buffers the negative effects of job demands on health. In contrast, in active jobs, and with regard to performance-based outcomes, this positive effect of detachment is not expected. Rather, high cognitive detachment from work might interfere with learning and creativity, whereas low cognitive detachment could improve learning and creative behaviour.

The DISC-R model has been tested in different kinds of empirical studies in many countries. Van den Tooren, de Jonge, and Dormann (2011) conducted an extensive review study of 29 high-quality DISC-R studies. The review showed that the TMP was supported largely with regard to the stress-buffering effect of matching job resources (i.e., the compensation mechanism). The review did not lend strong support with respect to the so-called activation-enhancing effect of matching job resources (i.e., the balance mechanism), although more recent DISC-R studies are in favour of this effect (for an overview, see Niks, de Jonge, Gevers, & Houtman, 2013).

Although the JD–R model has been criticized for being overly open and flexible, the DISC model can be criticized for the opposite, namely, its somewhat restrictive focus on the match of only three types of demands and resources. For instance, job demands, such as reorganization and role conflict, and specific job resources, such as developmental possibilities or fairness are difficult to categorize within the DISC-R model and, hence, within the TMP.

5.6   Conclusion: From Job Stress to Healthy Work

A major reason why modern jobs are so stressful is that the nature of work has been changing substantially over the past decades. Job demands are constantly and rapidly changing due to social developments. Nowadays, for many employees, work poses primarily mental and emotional demands rather than physical demands. Job stress is a major concern in both developing and industrialized countries, and it appears that the prevalence and costs of job stress are high. All these changes as well as the high prevalence and costs of job stress have important implications for the theoretical models describing it. All models share some common ground: they share the idea that two key job characteristics (i.e., job demands/efforts and job resources/rewards) can be changed via independent psychological processes to improve employee health as well as to enhance work motivation and work engagement and improve job performance. Furthermore, where the ERI model and JD–R model try to make progress in the direction of the moderating role of personal resources, the DISC-R model tries to extend itself in the direction of the moderating role of off-job recovery (i.e., detachment from work). Both avenues seem to be promising, and offer new opportunities for research and practice.

Nevertheless, all job stress models discussed in this chapter do make it clear that job stress interventions should be targeted primarily at the source of many of the problems; that is, the stressful working situation in terms of too high job demands and lack of job resources/rewards and/or low levels of off-job recovery. Thus, they all are aiming for 'healthy work' and require organizations to provide conditions for healthy workplaces (see also Chapter 16 on the creation of healthy workplaces). For reasons of 'fine tuning', healthy work interventions may be supplemented by interventions targeted at the individual worker (e.g., prevention of becoming overcommitted to the job). This point of view is also supported by modern labour legislation in many countries.

Summary

Why are jobs so stressful? Today's work is still stressful because of substantial societal and job-related changes, for instance, the 24/7 economy, increased use of information and communication technology, growing diversity in the workplace, flexible work arrangements and changed organizational work patterns. Most importantly, the nature of work has changed substantially over the past decades. Nowadays, for modern employees, work poses primarily mental and emotional demands rather than physical demands, which was the case in the past, due to both societal and job-related changes.

Job stress is a major concern and expense for individuals, organizations and societies, and the prevalence and costs of job stress are high. This has important implications for the theoretical models that try to describe and explain job stress. All models are based on the idea that two key job characteristics (i.e., job demands/ efforts and job resources/rewards) can be changed through adopting independent psychological processes to improve employees' health and well-being as well as enhancing work motivation, work engagement and improving employees' job performance.

Moreover, all the job stress models discussed in this chapter indicate that job stress interventions should be targeted primarily at the source of many of the problems, i.e. the stressful working situation. Such work-oriented interventions may be enhanced by measures aimed at the individual worker. This point of view is also supported by modern labour legislation in many countries.

Discussion Points

1 Which job stress model is your personal favourite, and what are its key assumptions? Explain why this model is especially suitable to apply to everyday practice in modern organizations.
2 This chapter has shown that job stress models clearly evolve over time. Explain (1) how the DISC-R model unified principles that are common to other job stress models, (2) how the model elaborates on existing ideas on how to conceptualize and measure job characteristics, and (3) how the model deals with proposed moderating effects of job demands and job resources.

Suggested Further Reading

Griffin, M. A., & Clarke, S. (2011). Stress and well-being at work. In S. Zedeck (Ed.), *APA handbook of industrial and organizational psychology*, Vol. 3. *Maintaining, expanding, and contracting the organization* (pp. 359–397). Washington, DC: American Psychological Association. Reviews major approaches to the stress process, introduces a framework for comparing the major approaches, and summarizes organizational interventions to reduce stress.

Quick, J. C., Wright, T. A., Adkins, J. A., Nelson, D. L., & Quick, J. D. (2013). Organizational consequences of stress. In J. C. Quick, T. A. Wright, J. A. Adkins, D. L. Nelson, & J. D. Quick (Eds.), *Preventive stress management in organizations* (2nd ed.) (pp. 73–86). Washington, DC: American Psychological Association. Addresses the benefits of organizational health and eustress along with the direct and indirect costs of distress, and presents a positive pathway to psychologically healthy organizations.

Schabracq, M. J., Winnubst, J. A. M., & Cooper, C. L. (Eds.) (2003). *The handbook of work and health psychology* (2nd ed.). Chichester: John Wiley & Sons, Ltd. Overview of the theoretical state of the art in Occupational Health Psychology.

Sonnentag, S., Perrewé, P. L., & Ganster, D. C. (Eds.) (2009). *Current perspectives on job-stress recovery*. Bingley, UK: JAI Press. Nice state-of-the art overview in job stress and recovery research.

References

Bernal, D., Campos-Serna, J., Tobias, A., Vargas-Prada, S., Benavides, F. G., & Serra, C. (2015). Work-related psychosocial risk factors and musculoskeletal disorders in hospital nurses and nursing aides: A systematic review and meta-analysis. *International Journal of Nursing Studies, 52*(2), 635–648.

de Jonge, J., Demerouti, E., & Dormann, C. (2014). Current theoretical perspectives in work psychology. In M. C. W. Peeters, J. de Jonge, & A. W. Taris (Eds.), *An introduction to contemporary work psychology* (pp. 89–114). Chichester: Wiley-Blackwell.

de Jonge, J., & Dormann, C. (2003). The DISC model: Demand-Induced Strain Compensation mechanisms in job stress. In M. F. Dollard, H. R. Winefield, & A. H. Winefield (Eds.), *Occupational stress in the services professions* (pp. 43–74). London: Routledge.

de Jonge, J., & Dormann, C. (2006). Stressors, resources, and strain at work: A longitudinal test of the Triple Match Principle. *Journal of Applied Psychology, 91*(6), 1359–1374.

de Jonge, J., Dormann, C., & van den Tooren, M. (2008). The DemandInduced Strain Compensation Model: Renewed theoretical considerations and empirical evidence. In K. Näswall, J. Hellgren, & M. Sverke (Eds.), *The individual in the changing working life* (pp. 67–87). London: Routledge.

de Jonge, J., & Kompier, M. A. J. (1997). A critical examination of the Demand-Control-Support model from a work psychological perspective. *International Journal of Stress Management, 4*, 235–258.

de Jonge, J., Spoor, E., Sonnentag, S., Dormann, C., & van den Tooren, M. (2012). 'Take a break?!': Off-job recovery, job demands and job resources as predictors of health, active learning, and creativity. *European Journal of Work and Organizational Psychology, 21*(3), 321–348.

Demerouti, E., & Bakker, A. B. (2011). The Job Demands–Resources model: Challenges for future research. *SA Journal of Industrial Psychology, 37*, 1–9.

Demerouti, E., Bakker, A. B., Nachreiner, F., & Schaufeli, W. B. (2001). The Job Demands–Resources model of burnout. *Journal of Applied Psychology, 86*, 499–512.

Etzion, D., Eden, D., & Lapidot, Y. (1998). Relief from job stressors and burnout: Reserve service as a respite. *Journal of Applied Psychology, 83*, 577–585.

European Agency for Safety and Health at Work (2014). *Calculating the cost of work-related stress and psychosocial risks: European Risk Observatory Literature Review.* Luxembourg: Publications Office of the European Union.

European Foundation for the Improvement of Living and Working Conditions (2015). *First findings: Sixth European Working Conditions Survey.* Dublin: European Foundation for the Improvement of Living and Working Conditions.

Frankenhaeuser, M., & Gardell, B. (1976). Underload and overload in working life: Outline of a multidisciplinary approach. *Journal of Human Stress, 2*, 35–46.

Häusser, J. A., Mojzisch, A., Niesel, M., & Schulz-Hardt, S. (2010). Ten years on: A review of recent research on the Job-Demand–Control(–Support) model and psychological well-being. *Work & Stress, 24*, 1–35.

Hockey, G. R. J. (2000). Work environments and performance. In N. Chmiel (Ed.), *Introduction to work and organizational psychology: A European perspective* (pp. 206–230). Malden, MA: Blackwell Publishers.

International Labour Office (2016). *Report of the Committee of Experts on the application of conventions and recommendations.* Geneva: ILO.

Johnson, J. V., & Hall, E. M. (1988). Job strain, work place social support, and cardiovascular disease: A cross-sectional study of a random sample of the Swedish working population. *American Journal of Public Health, 78*, 1336–1342.

Kahn, R. L., & Byosiere, P. (1992). Stress in organizations. In M. D. Dunette, & L. M. Hough (Eds.), *Handbook of industrial and organizational psychology* (Vol. 33; pp. 571–650). Palo Alto, CA: Consulting Psychologists Press.

Karasek, R. A. Jr. (1979). Job demands, job decision latitude and mental strain: Implications for job redesign. *Administrative Science Quarterly, 24*, 285–308.

Karasek, R. A., & Theorell, T. (1990). *Healthy work: Stress productivity and the reconstruction of working life.* New York: Basic Books.Kessler, R. C., Aguilar-Gaxiola, S., Alonso, J., et al. (2009). The global burden of mental disorders: An update from the WHO World Mental Health (WMH) surveys. *Epidemiolia e Psichiatria Sociale, 18*(1), 23–33.

Lam, C. F., Wan, W. H., & Roussin, C. J. (2016). Going the extra mile and feeling energized: An enrichment perspective of organizational citizenship behaviors. *Journal of Applied Psychology, 101*(3), 379–391.

Lang, J., Ochsmann, E., Kraus, T., & Lang, J. W. B. (2012). Psychosocial work stressors as antecedents of musculoskeletal problems: A systematic review and meta-analysis of stability-adjusted longitudinal studies. *Social Science & Medicine, 75*(7), 1163–1174.

Latack, J. C., & Havlovic, S. J. (1992). Coping with job stress: A conceptual evaluation framework for coping measures. *Journal of Organizational Behavior, 13,* 479–508.

Le Blanc, P. M., de Jonge, J., & Schaufeli, W. B. (2008). Job stress and occupational health. In N. Chmiel (Ed.), *An introduction to work and organizational psychology: A European perspective* (2nd ed.) (pp. 119–147). Oxford: Blackwell.

McTernan, W. P., Dollard, M. F., & LaMontagne, A. D. (2013). Depression in the workplace: An economic cost analysis of depression-related productivity loss attributable to job strain and bullying. *Work & Stress, 27*(4), 321–338.

Niks, I. M. W., de Jonge, J., Gevers, J. M. P., & Houtman, I. L. D. (2013). Design of the *DIS-Covery* project: Tailored work-oriented interventions to improve employee health, well-being, and performance-related outcomes in health care. *BMC Health Services Research, 13*(66), 1–11.

Peeters, M. C. W., Taris, A. W., & de Jonge, J. (2014). Introduction: People at work. In M. C. W. Peeters, J. de Jonge, & A. W. Taris (Eds.), *An introduction to contemporary work psychology* (pp. 3–30). Chichester: Wiley-Blackwell.

Schaufeli, W. B. (2005). The future of occupational health psychology. *Applied Psychology: An International Review, 53,* 502–517.

Schaufeli, W. B., & Taris, T. W. (2014). A critical review of the Job Demands–Resources Model: Implications for improving work and health. In G. F. Bauer, & O. Hämmig (Eds.), *Bridging occupational, organizational and public health: A transdisciplinary approach* (pp. 43–68). New York: Springer.

Shimazu, A., & de Jonge, J. (2009). Reciprocal relations between effort-reward imbalance at work and adverse health: A three-wave panel survey. *Social Science and Medicine, 68*(1), 60–68.

Shimazu, A., Shimazu, M., & Odahara, T. (2005). Divergent effects of active coping on psychological distress in the context of the Job Demands Control Support Model: The roles of job control and social support. *International Journal of Behavioral Medicine, 12,* 192–198.

Seligman, M. E. P. (1972). Learned helplessness. *Annual Review of Medicine, 23,* 407–412.

Siegrist, J. (1996). Adverse health effects of high-effort/low-reward conditions. *Journal of Occupational Health Psychology, 1,* 27–41.

Siegrist, J. (2012). *Effort-reward imbalance at work: Theory, measurement and evidence.* Düsseldorf: University of Düsseldorf.

Siegrist, J., Siegrist, K., & Weber, I. (1986). Sociological concepts in the etiology of chronic disease: The case of ischemic heart disease. *Social Science and Medicine, 22,* 247–253.

Selye, H. (1956). *The stress of life.* New York: McGraw-Hill.

Sonnentag, S., Binnewies, C., & Mojza, E. J. (2010). Staying well and engaged when demands are high: The role of psychological detachment. *Journal of Applied Psychology, 95,* 965–976.

Terrill, A. L., & Garofalo, J. P. (2012). Cardiovascular disease and the workplace. In R. J. Gatchel, & I. Z. Schultz (Eds.), *Handbook of occupational health and wellness* (pp. 87–103). New York: Springer.

Tooren, M. van den, de Jonge, J., & Dormann, C. (2011). The Demand-Induced Strain Compensation Model: Background, key principles, theoretical underpinnings, and extended empirical evidence. In A. Caetano, S. A. Silva, & M. J. Chambel (Eds.), *New challenges for a healthy workplace in human services* (pp. 13–59). Mering: Rainer Hampp Verlag.

van der Heijden, B., van Dam, K., Xanthopoulou, D., & de Lange, A. (2014). Individual characteristics and work-related outcomes. In M. C. W. Peeters, J. de Jonge, & A. W. Taris (Eds.), *An introduction to contemporary work psychology* (pp. 243–266). Chichester: Wiley-Blackwell.

van Vegchel, N., de Jonge, J., Bosma, H., & Schaufeli, W. B. (2005). Reviewing the Effort-Reward Imbalance Model: Drawing up the balance of 45 empirical studies. *Social Science and Medicine, 60*(5), 1117–1131.

Xanthopoulou, D., Bakker, A. B., Demerouti, E., & Schaufeli, W. B. (2009). Reciprocal relationships between job resources, personal resources, and work engagement. *Journal of Vocational Behavior, 74,* 235–244.

6 Digital Technologies at Work Are Great, Aren't They? The Development of Information and Communication Technologies (ICT) and Their Relevance in the World of Work

Christian Korunka and Matti Vartiainen

Overview

The digitalization of working life and Information and Communication Technologies (ICT) are essential components of working environments nowadays and are important working tools. ICT affect knowledge-intensive work as well as manual and industrial work and critically influence various aspects of the work environment due to their impact on organizational structures, division of work, relationships between people and productivity, and beneficial outcomes. Many of these influences are positive. For instance, work processes are improved and there is better access to knowledge. On the other hand, ICT may be responsible for producing negative impacts, such as decreases in the quality of working life or increased ICT-related demands for self-control and learning, for instance. To achieve the expected beneficial outcomes, job design and management of the implementation process of ICT are important.

The chapter begins with a short description of the history of ICT and its rapid development at work. Next, an overview of the use of ICT for individual and group work in different locations is given. New forms of work based on the internet and applications of ICT in the industry are described. In the following section, an overview of the positive and sometimes negative consequences of ICT at work at different levels – the individual, the job, the organization, and outside of work – is given. This is followed by the presentation of the sociomaterial approach as an example of an approach to job design in this field. Finally, successful management of ICT-related change processes is described as a support measure that may be used to develop positive effects and prevent negative effects of ICT use.

An Introduction to Work and Organizational Psychology: An International Perspective,
Third Edition. Edited by Nik Chmiel, Franco Fraccaroli and Magnus Sverke.
© 2017 John Wiley & Sons, Ltd. Published 2017 by John Wiley & Sons, Ltd.

6.1 Digital Technologies Are Essential Components of Work Systems

6.1.1 The development of technologies

The role of technology in working life has greatly increased since the 'computerization' of work, which began in the 1970s. However, its influence has pervaded throughout as technological innovations seem to play a crucial role in the development of economies and whole societies. The process of long-term growth of the economy, including crucial changes in the production and organization of work has been theorized to occur as 'Kondratieff waves' (Kondratieff, 1979) or 'great surges' (Perez, 2014). The 'long wave theory' (e.g., Perez, 2014) argues that there are repeating phases over 50–60 years that are associated with technological innovations (Figure 6.1). According to this theory, the present 'computerization' is just one phase in the developmental chain. Kondratieff (1979) and several other scholars found that British industrial growth accelerated around 1780, primarily in the cotton and iron industries. Driven by water power, this rapid growth constituted the first great surge or the Industrial Revolution, which lasted approximately from 1780 until 1840. The second surge revolved around the steam engine and railways, while the third revolution is known as the age of steel, electricity and heavy engineering. The fourth surge took place in the age of oil, the automobile and mass production. Finally, the fifth surge, called the 'Age of Information and Communications', occurred in the 1970s with chips, hardware and new materials, followed by software and telecommunications equipment, e-services such as email, the internet, and new forms of electronic communication.

GREAT SURGE		INSTALLATION PERIOD	TURNING POINT	DEPLOYMENT PERIOD
		'Gilded Age' Bubbles	Recessions	'Golden Ages'
1st	1771 The Industrial Revolution Britain	Canal mania	1793–97	Great British leap
2nd	1829 Age of Steam and Railways Britain	Railway mania	1848–50	The Victorian Boom
3rd	1875 Age of Steel and heavy Engineering Britain/USA Germany	London funded global market infrastructure build-up (Argentina, Australia, USA)	1890–95	Belle Époque (Europe) 'Progressive Era' (USA)
4th	1908 Age of Oil, Autos and Mass Production/USA	The roaring twenties Autos, housing, radio, aviation, electricity	Europe 1929–33 USA 1929–43	Post-war Golden age
5th	1971 The ICT Revolution USA	Emerging markets dotcom and internet mania financial casino	2007 –???	Sustainable global knowledge-society 'golden age'?

Figure 6.1: Great surges of technological, economic, and institutional development and their turning points

Source: Perez (2014), Figure 1, p. 13. Reproduced with permission of Routledge.

6.1.2   The social acceleration of work

A well-known pattern in the development of new technologies at work is the perception of an accelerated pace of changes, which leads to new demands for employees. In his sociological framework, Rosa (2005) describes a general process of social acceleration as one of the main characteristics of late capitalism. Social acceleration consists of three interrelated facets:

* Technological acceleration – results from the rapid deployment of technologies. An increasing amount and pace of information both in daily life and in the world of work require employees to respond more intensively at increasing speeds. The constant introduction of new technologies permanently forces employees to learn new competences.
* Acceleration of social change – describes the increasing speed at which formerly valid structures in organizations are changing. At work, employees have to expand their knowledge and skills in order to adapt to rising rates of change in organizational processes.
* Acceleration of the pace of life – is the increase in the number of actions and experiences per time unit. Breaks and interruptions are increased, downtime between work activities is reduced, and different actions are performed at the same time (multitasking).

The development of technologies at work is not only a singular aspect of social acceleration, it is also an important driver for the other two elements of acceleration.

The development of the internet and social media over the past few decades is a good example of accelerated technology development. Predecessors of the internet already existed in the 1960s when researchers were able to connect several computers for the first time, establishing the so-called ARPANET. It took another 25 years until the first web browser (1989) was developed at the CERN research centre in Geneva. The 'World Wide Web' (WWW) was founded in 1991, and in 1993 it was opened to non-technical users. Figure 6.2 shows the development of internet use since 1993.

In the early 1990s, internet use was confined to the United States and Western Europe. Increases in internet use in developed countries have only been observable since 2000. At that time, nearly 50% of all computer users were inhabitants of the United States and about 25–35% were inhabitants of European countries, but only 1–5% in developed countries were connected to the internet. In 2015, 88% of North Americans, 74% of Europeans, 40% of Asians, and 29% of African inhabitants were connected to the internet (Internet World Stats, 2015).

Computer use at work is also increasing. The Fifth European Working Conditions Survey (EWCS) shows the development of the use of computers at work in five selected countries in the European Union (Figure 6.3).

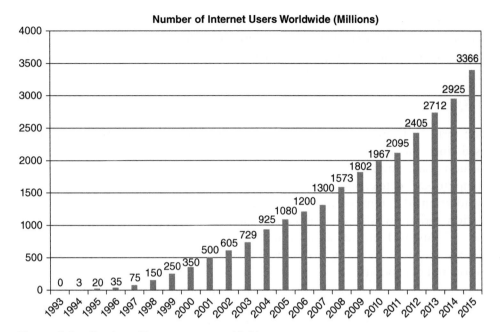

Figure 6.2: Number of internet users worldwide

Source: Internet World Stats, 2015, NUA. Adapted from Korunka & Hoonakker (2014), Figure 2.2, p. 12.

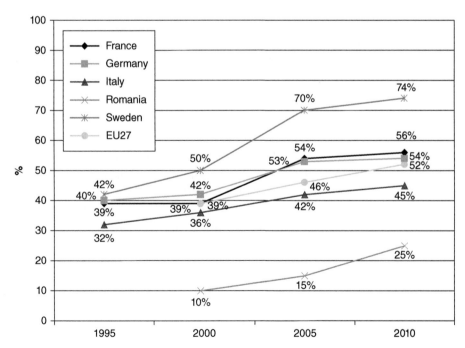

Figure 6.3: Percentages of workers working with computers at least 25% of the time in selected European countries

Source: Korunka & Hoonakker (2014), Figure 2.5, p. 15. Reproduced with permission of Springer Science+Business Media Dordrecht.

The data show that in more than 50% of the workplaces in Europe, ICT are used regularly, although remarkable differences still exist, for example, between Northern and Eastern European countries.

6.1.3   Digital technologies are used for individual and collaborative work

The term 'Information and Communications Technologies' (ICT) has been used since the 1980s as an extended synonym for information technologies, including and emphasizing the aspect of communication technologies such as computer-aided telecommunications, smartphones and email communication. In addition to communication, ICT are used to process and store data, information and knowledge in a digital form as combinations of the digits 0 and 1 (bits). Thus, ICT include all uses of digital technology that exist to help individuals, businesses and organizations access and use information for communication and collaboration.

In addition to individual work on data and information, ICT are used to enhance knowledge sharing, co-ordination and co-work, and co-creation in group work, and when building communities. Collaboration technologies or 'groupware' could be grouped into those allowing synchronous, online communication and to those allowing asynchronous, offline communication (Table 6.1).

Today collaboration environments typically integrate and fuse diverse tools, creating an internet ecosystem of different technologies, resources and services. For example, smartphones not only integrate the functionalities of a mobile phone, such as a personal digital assistant, a calendar, browser, email, audio conferencing, chat, and document reading; they also allow access to potentially millions of applications and data resources.

6.1.4   Digital work on the internet

Today, the internet exploits cloud technologies and Big Data and its analytics, and enables fully digital work. Cloud computing involves the storage of data in networked data centres and its processing and distribution as applications and services for individuals and organizations (Mosco, 2014). 'Big Data' refers to the vast amounts of information that is gained, for example, from data transfers on the internet and end-users' smart devices and their behaviour. Services provided through cloud platforms are often constructed based on the analysis of Big Data. Three types of actors participate in organizing work in cloud computing platforms: (1) cloud companies providing the platform and possibly services, (2) organizations using the platform and building their own services there, and (3) finally, often global workers. Digital workers access cloud data by using networked client devices such as desktop computers, laptops, tablets and smartphones, and any Ethernet-enabled 'Internet of Things' device, such as gadgets in a smart home, or a machine on an industry shop floor.

Table 6.1: Examples of information and collaboration tools and services

ICT	Different location		Same location
	Tools for asynchronous, offline communication	Tools for synchronous, online communication	Tools for face-to-face communication
Information sharing systems	• email • bulletin board • multimedia mail (text, voice, image) • websites • cloud and software services • offline browsing • data and file storage • wiki	• call (voice and video) • microblogging • live streaming • online bulletin board • online browsing	• face-to-face • presentation systems
Co-ordination and co-work systems	• group-calendar • event manager • shared planning • shared workflow management systems • subgroup spaces	• chatting • teleconference • videoconference • virtual world meeting • notification systems, e.g., active batch	• command and control centre support systems
Co-creation systems	• document co-authoring, e.g., Google Drive	• shared CAD, whiteboard, word processor, spreadsheet • brainstorming systems	• group decision support systems (meeting support systems, e.g., agenda, voting)
Community systems	• social media, e.g., LinkedIn and Facebook • weblog • social news websites	• social networking, e.g., yammer • media spaces	

Source: Adapted from: Andriessen, 2003, Table 1.1, p. 12. Reproduced with permission of Springer.

Clouds are increasingly serving as crowdsourced workplaces. One such workplace, Amazon Mechanical Turk, acts as an employment agency. An employer posts digital tasks for the site's users to complete. A worker enters the site using their owned or borrowed device, selects a task, completes it, is credited with the proceeds, and selects the next task. Each completed task earns the worker a remuneration. A whole 'digital working class' has emerged worldwide, working for international employers (Scholz, 2013). Digital delocalized labour is characterized as being of two types: work as partly relocalized elsewhere and delocalized work that is dispersed. Relocalization is exemplified by offshored work and dispersed work by crowdsourced work and microwork. Virtual or digital work means, for example, working as a freelancer on the internet doing microtasks from a remote place using digitalized working environments. A major difference versus conventional jobs is the fact that this kind of work is entrepreneurial, and often without any kind of social protection.

6.1.5   The role of ICT in industry

ICT have also permeated traditional industries that produce goods and products for everyday life and the various means of production. The application of digital technologies started from the design of new products. For example, enabled by the rapid development of technical capabilities of computers, Computer-aided design (CAD) started in the 1970s to aid in the creation, modification, analysis or optimization of a design (Narayan et al., 2008). CAD is used in electronic design, mechanical design, in architecture, and in many other fields. Computer-aided manufacturing (CAM) is the use of computer software to control machine tools and machinery in the manufacturing of designed workpieces. Early applications of CAM were implemented in the automobile industry in the 1960s. Since then, CAD and CAM technologies have altered working conditions in production to a high degree.

The 'Internet of Things' ('Industrie 4.0' in Germany) is the latest development of the use of ICT and digitalization in industries. The 'Internet of Things' embraces the vision and execution of 'smart factories', where comprehensive applications of ICT allow the merging of production processes and logistic processes, including all the resources needed. 'Intelligent' production and logistic systems exchange their information and make artificial intelligence-based decisions. Products are highly customized in highly flexible mass production conditions. As expected, there have been serious effects on employment and on the qualification levels of the employees. For example, 3D printing allows the local manufacturing of products, thereby reducing transporting and storing of parts and thus a shortening of the logistic chains. 'Internet of Things' workplaces will be highly flexible with regard to work contents, work times and work places.

Industrial digitalization has led to renewed organizational structures through the replacement of old jobs with new ones, and demands for increased employee competence. Such changes have led to some beneficial but also controversial outcomes. For example, CAM systems have eliminated heavy and dangerous work by replacing manual work with control work, but such systems have also reduced the number of employees working in production. However, the competency levels of the remaining workers have become higher, although new stressors affecting workers have been identified – their constant monitoring of CAM systems has led to job boredom (Edwards, 1989). Studies on the quality of working life of CAD workers have shown mainly positive effects. CAD workers are often well-educated and show a positive attitude towards CAD work (e.g., Korunka et al., 1995). On the other hand, because of the rigid body postures associated with this type of work, musculoskeletal complaints may be observable in workers involved with high degrees of CAD work.

6.2 Consequences of ICT at Work for the Individuals, the Jobs, and the Organizations

The consequences of ICT in the world of work are wide-ranging. However, they are not limited to work itself; they are also found in other life domains. Developments in ICT are one important example of how ICT has permeated both work and non-work domains. ICT has many benefits and positive effects, but of course there are also many new challenges and even negative outcomes. Table 6.2 shows examples of such challenges and related outcomes at the individual, job, organization, work–family and societal levels.

Table 6.2: Examples of challenges and possible positive and negative consequences related to ICT

Level	Challenges	Potential positive outcomes	Potential negative outcomes
Individual	• Need for ICT-related competences • Adequate recovery from work • Finding a personal work-age balance	• Availability and easy access to a wide range of information • Increased independence because of better information	• Technostrain • Technoaddiction • Alienation
Job	• Work intensification • Work interruptions • Lack of training • Frustration because of technical problems	• More and better feedback • Many new opportunities to learn	• Burnout
Organization	• Over-controlling • Need for development of trust • Permanent adaptation needs	• Better service quality • Increased productivity • Cost reductions	• ICT dependency • Complex interdependencies between subsystems of organizations
Work–Family	• Adequate telework design	• Enhanced productivity • More 'quality time'	• Reduced privacy
Society and certain groups	• Need for new forms of learning • Development of opportunities for people with disabilities	• Bridging distances • Inclusion of all minority groups	• ICT dependency

Source: Korunka & Hoonakker 2014, Table 13.1, p. 208. Reproduced with permission of Springer Science+Business Media Dordrecht.

6.2.1   Consequences for individuals at work

There are many positive consequences for individuals who use ICT. ICT allow everyone to access a wide range of information and knowledge. Better informed people are more autonomous and are less dependent on others. New communication and collaboration technologies have the potential for a better social embeddedness, and they bridge distances in location and time. At the same time, individuals are required to find their personal 'balance' (Carayon & Smith, 2014) on many levels. Self-control is needed to effectively deal with information overload and the permanent access to communication tools. 'Technostrain' and even 'technoaddiction' could be negative ICT-related individual outcomes.

In addition, 'technostress' at work is a negative psychological state associated with the use (and the abuse) of new information and communication technologies, as well as the threat of technology use in the future (Salanova et al., 2013). The experience of technostress is related to negative psychological experiences such as feelings of anxiety, fatigue, burnout, inefficacy beliefs and addiction to technology.

Technoaddiction is defined as a specific technostress experience due to an uncontrollable compulsion to use technology 'anywhere and any time' and 'to use them for long periods of time in an excessive way' (Salanova et al., 2013). 'Technoaddiction' is comparable to the concept of 'workaholism'. Both these addictive behaviours might be observable at the same time since there is a connection between working excessively and the use of technology. They may be even more observable with new information and communication technologies, which enable the worker to work anywhere at any time (Andriessen & Vartiainen, 2006).

To avoid such negative consequences of ICT use, one needs to recognize the specific demands related to technologies, their context of use, and the certain resources needed to buffer these demands. Examples of technology-related demands are task overload, multitasking, the increasing pace of technology, social demands (e.g., triggered by virtual work settings), job insecurity (triggered by lacking technology-related competences), and increased work–family conflicts (triggered by the opportunity to use technologies anywhere and any time). Important organizational resources to deal with the demands triggered by technologies include participation and organizational support in the implementation phase of new technologies (Korunka et al., 1995), and the offer of high-quality training opportunities to deal with certain demands of new technologies (e.g., software changes).

6.2.2   New ICT-related job demands

There are many obvious advantages to using ICT at work. Most jobs are no longer conceivable without the use of ICT. ICT contribute to cost reductions and the generation of economic advantages in organizations. Work with ICT has resulted in a decline in workload in many work areas. Even work intensity, which was found to be generally increasing, seems to decrease at least for certain groups of ICT workers (Kubicek, Korunka, Paskvan, Prem, & Gerdenitsch, 2014). Improvements in production technologies have resulted in a strong decrease in workloads in many production jobs. Nearly all aspects of productivity and quality have increased (Carayon & Smith, 2014). In addition, ICT offer many opportunities for high-quality task feedback. New technologies always have an inherent potential for learning opportunities. On the other hand, there are new job demands related both to social acceleration processes and the increased use of ICT (Paskvan, Kubicek, & Korunka, 2015).

- Intensified autonomy demands refer to the increasing need for employees to plan and structure their working days autonomously. Such demands are triggered by reduced levels of hierarchy, which come about by fostering team and project work as well as managerial practices such as Management by Objectives (Drucker, 1954). ICT create and increase the opportunity to work any time in any place. For instance, emails may be checked not only in the workplace, but also at any time from nearly every location in the world by a smartphone user. Thus, ICT have the potential to increase intensified autonomy demands even further. 'Autonomy' (i.e., job control) is described in the classic models of work stress (e.g., in the Job Demand-Control model; Karasek, 1979) as a job resource. Job design should aim to increase job control. Intensified autonomy demands describe the fact that autonomy may become a demand, at least at high levels of autonomy (likely induced by ICT, which makes working possible at any time in any place).

- Intensified learning demands refer to the increasing learning needs in modern workplaces. Knowledge of technological devices, work practices, and guidelines needs to be updated at shorter time intervals (Obschonka et al., 2012) because rapid technological innovations render technological equipment outdated more quickly. Intensified learning demands comprise knowledge-related demands and skill-related demands (Paskvan et al., 2015). Similar to job control, knowledge and skills are generally important job resources. The intensified need for learning, necessitated by the demands of rapidly developing ICT, may transform this resource into a demand too. Again, job design in the context of ICT should focus on the right amount of new knowledge and skill development.

Because of the technological advances in communication technologies, there is an increased expectation for employees to respond to all queries quickly. Email communication is a good example. In many workplaces, there are no defined rules about how and when to respond to emails from supervisors and colleagues. This leads to an additional pressure on the employees. Email communication is also an example of why work interruptions triggered by ICT have increased. In many circumstances, email communication has contributed to the fragmentation of work.

6.2.3   Life outside work and societal effects

ICT has established the opportunity for many workers to work at home and at other places outside the main workplace (telework). Telework at home allows better integration of job-related and family-related tasks. Commuting times are reduced completely. On the other hand, studies confirm increases in work–family conflicts and generally higher levels of stress for many teleworkers. An intense use of ICT outside the work environment may result in reduced privacy and diminished relaxation from work.

Some observers point to the risk of a 'digital divide' in society. Certain groups in society may have better access to ICT and thus better life chances (Weber & Zink, 2014). To bridge such a digital divide, similar access to ICT and ICT-related education is necessary for all groups in society. In the case of a diverse workforce, recognizing the needs of all groups of workers is a cornerstone before putting the many positive potentials of ICT into practice.

6.3   Design of ICT-Related Work: The Sociomaterial Approach

Work practices in physical, digital and social environments are designed and developed, on the one hand, by using the widely accepted models of work and organizational psychology and by using more specific models related to ICT adaption, diffusion and use, on the other. The central question focuses on the relationship of the psychological, social and material characteristics of the working life and developing human practices based on this knowledge. As an important example of the design of ICT-related work, the sociomaterial approach is introduced here.

The sociomaterial approach provides a broad framework to understand and further develop digital technologies in physical and social work environments that can benefit human work. It adds new features to the traditional socio-technical systems approach (e.g., Trist & Bamforth, 1951) by enlarging 'technology' to 'materiality' (Carlile et al., 2013). 'Material' refers to all objects, artifacts and technologies that mediate human activities. The central idea of sociomaterialism is that materiality is integral to organizing, positing that the social and the material are constitutively entangled in everyday life, and hence, neither human nor technical elements of a system enjoy a privileged status. Every organizational practice is always bound by materiality, especially in the digital age. The social and the material are considered to be inextricably related – there is no social that is not also material, and no material that is not also social. Therefore, when discussing the consequences of ICT use, technology is not directly influencing human perceptions and experiences, but they are produced in everyday activities. These activities include uncertainties and risks and produce both intended and unintended outcomes.

6.3.1 Work analysis as the basis for job design

When studying and designing digital computerized work from the socio-technical and sociomaterial perspectives, it is crucial to focus on the task to be done, the context of the work to be done, by what processes it will be done, and the identification of its human and performance outcomes (Vartiainen, 2014). Task contents of knowledge work vary from the creation of new ideas, plans and solutions to the application of rules and the execution of well-internalized routine tasks. Although knowledge-intensive work is understood as high-level cognitive work, knowledge workers also perform mundane routine tasks, such as storing and retrieving information, and managing calendars, telephone calls and emails, which can occupy a substantial amount of their time. In knowledge work, the requirements of the activity environment are defined as the context. In addition to the task characteristics, the context refers to those types of knowledge work processes and levels of mental action regulation that are needed to perform and produce outcomes. The meaning of context has evolved during the last decade because knowledge workers typically use multiple work locations along with smart devices and remote connections to communicate and collaborate. Thus, work analysis approaches need to take the context into consideration.

6.4 Managing ICT-Related Change Processes

The rapid development of ICT leads to strong demands on organizations and companies. New developments in hardware and software often trigger organizational change. In many cases, new ICT will bring about the restructuring of organizational processes. Thus, careful management of such change processes is needed. The following section describes characteristics and elements of such change processes.

6.4.1 Implementation and adaption of ICT

The implementation of an ICT system refers to: 'all activities related to deployment and adoption of a new technology, namely requirements specification, acquisition and/or design and development, installation, training and internalization of routines for effective utilization' (Munkvold, 2003, p. 3). The adoption refers to individual acceptance and willingness to use the system. The implementation of an ICT system entails two adoption processes at the same time, namely, the adoption of technology and the adoption of new ways of working.

An organizational ICT system implementation process is usually conceptualized as a series of stages. Davis (1989) presented the Technology Acceptance Model (TAM) to predict and explain ICT usage behaviour; that is, what causes potential adopters to accept or reject the use of information technology. Theoretically, TAM is based on the Theory of Reasoned Action (e.g., Fishbein & Ajzen,

1975). In TAM, two theoretical constructs, perceived usefulness and perceived ease of use, are the fundamental determinants of system use and predict attitudes towards the use of the system – that is, the user's willingness to use the system. Perceived usefulness refers to 'the degree to which a person believes that using a particular system would enhance his or her job performance' and perceived ease of use refers to 'the degree to which a person believes that using a particular system would be free of effort' (Davis, 1989, p. 32).

The Unified Theory of Acceptance and Use of Technology (UTAUT) (Venkatesh et al., 2003) further develops the TAM model. In addition, the purpose of UTAUT is to explain a user's intentions to use ICT and the subsequent user behaviour. The model considers four constructs as direct determinants of user acceptance and usage behaviour, namely, performance expectancy, effort expectancy, social influence, and facilitating conditions. Accordingly to the model, the link between these four constructs and user acceptance/behaviour is moderated by four key variables: gender, age, experience, and voluntariness of use. For instance, the link between performance expectancy and user behaviour may become stronger when users are more experienced. The authors state that UTAUT provides a tool for managers to assess the likelihood that technology introductions will be successful and to understand the drivers of acceptance in order to design interventions such as training or marketing. UTAUT focuses on users who may be less willing to adopt and use new systems.

6.4.2   Implementation of change

Kwon and Zmud (1987) developed a six-stage model of an ICT system implementation process (Table 6.3). The stages are based on Lewin's (1952) change model from unfreezing to change and to refreezing. Lewin referred to the 'unfreezing'

Table 6.3: The model of an ICT system implementation process (based on Kwon and Zmud, 1987)

Stages	Activities
1. Initiation	Scanning organization needs and ICT solutions.
2. Organizational adoption	Negotiations to get organizational backing for novel ICT implementation.
3. Organizational adaption	Developing, installing, and maintaining the ICT system.
	Developing new organizational procedures. Training users both in the new procedures and in the use of ICT.
4. User adoption and acceptance	Including the members of the organization to use the technology.
5. Established use	Use the ICT system is encouraged among employees as a normal activity.
6. Infusion	The intended benefits of the technology are obtained through effective use of the technology.

Source: Korpelainen, Vartiainen, & Kira, 2010, Table 1, p. 54. Reproduced with permission of *Journal of Organizational and End-User Computing.*

of existing norms, 'changing' and 'refreezing' them. The six-stage model covers an implementation process from the scanning of organizational needs to a full and effective use of the technology in daily practices. However, an actual implementation process is rarely linear, but often iterative, and the different stages partly overlap (Munkvold, 2003). The model helps an understanding of the different stages, the activities connected to each stage, and the prominence of each stage in an ICT implementation process. However, alternative models for organizational change and especially for ICT implementation have been presented, for example, from the sociomaterial perspective. These models challenge the neat step-wise progression of a planned change and pay more attention to the unpredictable and emergent nature of social change and its incremental progress (see e.g., Orlikowski & Scott, 2008).

6.4.3 Adoption: Psychological needs, information, and participation in change processes

The implementation of ICT and their subsequent use often fail because employees do not fully accept the new ICT and/or are not motivated to use them. Self-determination theory (SDT; e.g., Deci & Ryan, 2000) helps to explain lack of motivation in ICT use (Mitchell et al., 2012). SDT proposes that different types of motivation, varying in their degree of self-determination, define human behaviour. An important aspect of SDT theory is the expansion of extrinsic motivation by assuming different regulation and introjection processes. 'Identified regulation' is an autonomous, internalized type of extrinsic motivation where a person is involved in an activity because the activity is personally meaningful (see also Chapter 19 on motivation). In ICT use, people may like to use ICT because it has proven to be useful and it helps to get work done (Mitchell et al., 2012). Both intrinsic motivation and identified regulation are autonomous forms of motivation supporting positive behaviour outcomes.

Another important proposition of ICT is that the three basic psychological needs of competence, autonomy, and relatedness are positively related to both autonomous forms of motivation (Deci & Ryan, 2000). By promoting experiences of competence through optimal challenges and feedback, by removing pressure and increasing control at work, and by offering a positive interpersonal environment through open communication and teamwork, employees will be more likely to adopt autonomous motivation styles (Mitchell et al., 2012).

Positive outcomes for all forms of employee participation in change processes have been confirmed since the 1970s (see the seminal meta-analysis of Cotton et al., 1988). There are many empirically based guidelines and recommendations of how to implement new ICT. Some of the most important recommendations are:

- Planned introductions of new ICT (hardware changes, software changes, etc.) need to be communicated to the end users in advance. The advantages of the new systems need to be communicated in a realistic way.

- Users should have the opportunity to participate to some degree in the implementation processes. User participation has many facets. Users may be assigned some responsibilities regarding system selection and the implementation process, or they may be offered some other choices in the implementation process. Their involvement may be direct or indirect, e.g., they may serve as consultants by contributing input about system design while actual implementation is handled by experts.
- The amount of change and the timing of change processes need to be carefully planned. Criteria used for positive evaluation by the users of new systems should include questions about the meaningfulness of the change process, expected improvements, and the usefulness and ease of use of the new system.
- Comprehensive support should be offered during an implementation phase. High-quality training measures need to be offered. There should be enough time for users to adapt to new systems. There should also be a contact person available for support when problems occur.

Figure 6.4 shows a comprehensive multi-level framework that identifies the antecedents and consequences of individual, work group, and organizational readiness for change as developed (Rafferty, Jimmieson, & Armenakis, 2013). Rafferty and colleagues highlight the affective and cognitive nature of change processes. They propose that an individual's readiness for organizational change is influenced by: (1) the individual's beliefs (a) that change is needed, (b) that he or she

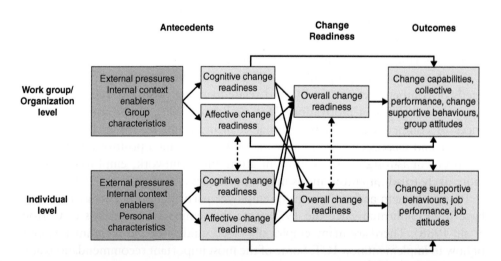

Figure 6.4: Multi-level framework of the antecedents and consequences of readiness for change

Source: Rafferty, Jimmieson & Armenakis (2013), Figure 1, p. 113. Reproduced with permission of SAGE Publishing.

has the capacity to successfully undertake change, and (c) that change will have positive outcomes for his or her job/role; and, (2) the individual's current and future-oriented positive affective emotional responses to a specific change event. A work group's change readiness and an organization's change readiness are influenced by: (1) shared cognitive beliefs among work group or organizational members (a) that change is needed, (b) that the work group or organization has the capability to successfully undertake change, (c) that change will have positive outcomes for the work group or organization; and, (2) the occurrence of current and future-oriented positive group or organizational emotional responses to an organizational change.

Summary

Currently, new technologies such as environmental technologies, biotechnology, nanotechnology and healthcare technologies are being invented and put into use. Their effect is leveraged by digitalization and the exponential rise of computational power that create circumstances for new products and services – and the 'sixth smart wave' (Wilenius & Kurki, 2012).

In the future, additional and renewed ICT and digital applications will be designed and used in organizations. More powerful microprocessors, Big Data and its analysis, 4G and 5G infrastructures, mobile internet, and cloud services will lead to the availability of various applications and services for both employees and employers to use in flexible collaboration environments. Organizations in industry will use process automation tools as an alternative to using people, new software, and other technologies such as 3D printing, robotics, and fully integrated systems. Increasing digitalization will have an impact on existing and future job contents and organizational structures. Frey and Osborne (2013, p. 38) forecast that '47 percent of total US employment is in the high risk category, meaning that associated occupations are potentially automatable over some unspecified number of years, perhaps a decade or two'.

However, these calculations are only rough estimations, which do not necessarily take into account changes in people's needs, minds and consuming habits. They ignore powerful societal forces such as prevailing regulation and established organizational structure that may hinder technological advances. In any event, it seems clear that new tasks and jobs are emerging. They may be fully digital, but they are still jobs, occupations and professions needed to produce goods, products and services globally and locally. Digital work is just a form of work that adds surplus value to products and services for the benefit of people. Labour input is exchanged for monetary compensation – digital workers earn their living to satisfy their daily needs as was the case with 'old' jobs. New forms of organizing, emerging jobs, and renewed task contents have their beneficial outcomes. Institutional and psychological contracts are still needed to balance the needs of people with implementation and use of technologies in the context of work.

Discussion Points

1 What do you think are the most important consequences of further increases in ICT use in the near future in the world of work?
2 What are the most important demands made on individuals at work as the result of increased ICT use?

Suggested Further Reading

Korunka, C., & Hoonakker, P. (Eds.) (2014). *The impact of ICT on quality of working life.* Heidelberg: Springer. This book gives a good overview on the wide range of possible impacts of ICT on quality of working life.

Orlikowski, W. J., & Scott, S. V. (2008). Sociomateriality: Challenging the separation of technology, work and organization. *Academy of Management Annals, 2*(1), 433–474. This chapter is a good introduction to the sociomateriality approach.

Vartiainen, M., & Hyrkkänen, U. (2010). Changing requirements and mental workload factors in mobile multi-locational work. *New Technology, Work and Employment, 25*(2), 117–135. This article gives an overview on the needs and workload aspects of multi-locational work.

Journals

- *Behaviour & Information Technology*
- *Computers in Human Behavior*
- *Computer Supported Cooperative Work (CSCW)*
- *The Journal of Collaborative Computing and Work Practices*
- *Organization Science*

References

Andriessen, J. H. E. (2003). *Working with groupware: Understanding and evaluating collaboration technology.* London: Springer.

Andriessen, J. H. E., & Vartiainen, M. (Eds.). (2006). *Mobile virtual work: A new paradigm?* Heidelberg: Springer.

Carayon, P., & Smith, M. J. (2014). The balance concept revisited: Finding balance to reduce stress in a frantic world of IT. In C. Korunka, & P. Hoonakker (Eds.), *The impact of ICT on quality of working life* (pp. 105–121). Heidelberg: Springer.

Carlile, P. R., Nicolini, D., Langley, A., & Tsoukas, H. (2013). *How matter matters: Objects, artifacts, and materiality in organization studies.* Oxford: Oxford University Press.

Cotton, J. L., Vollrath, D. A., Froggatt, K. L., Lengnick-Hall, M. L., & Jennings, K. R. (1988). Employee participation: Diverse forms and different outcomes. *Academy of Management Review, 13*(1), 8–22. doi:10.5465/AMR.1988.4306768

Davis, F. D. (1989). Perceived usefulness, perceived ease of use, and user acceptance of information technology. *MIS Quarterly, 13*(3), 319–340. doi:10.2307/249008

Deci, E. L., & Ryan, R. M. (2000). The "what" and "why" of goal pursuits: Human needs and the self-determination of behavior. *Psychological Inquiry, 11,* 227–268.

Drucker, P. F. (1954). *The practice of management.* New York: Harper & Row.

Edwards, J. R. (1989). Computer-aided manufacturing and worker well-being: A review of research. *Behaviour & Information Technology, 8*(3), 157–174.

Eurofound (2012). *Fifth European Working Conditions Survey.* Luxembourg: Publications Office of the European Union.

Fishbein, M,. & Ajzen, I. (1975). *Belief, attitude, intention and behaviour: An introduction to theory and research.* London: Longman.

Frey, C. B., & Osborne, M. A. (2013). The future of employment: How susceptible are jobs to computerisation? *OMS Working Papers,* September 18. Available at: http://v.gd/iViQ0L

Hoonakker, P., & Korunka, C. (2014). Information and communication technology and quality of working life: Backgrounds, facts, and figures. In C. Korunka, & P. Hoonakker (Eds.), *The impact of ICT on quality of working life* (pp. 8–26). Dordecht: Springer.

Internet World Stats. (2015, November 30). *World's internet usage and population statistics.* Available at: http://www.internetworldstats.com/stats.htm

Karasek, R. A. (1979). Job demands, job decision latitude, and mental strain: Implications for job redesign. *Administrative Science Quarterly, 24*(2), 285–308. doi:10.2307/2392498

Kondratieff, N. D. (1979). The long waves in economic life. *Review (Fernand Braudel Center), 2*(4), 519–562. Available at: http://www.jstor.org/stable/40240816

Korunka, C., & Hoonakker, P. (2014). The future of ICT and quality of working life: Challenges, benefits, and risks. In C. Korunka, & P. Hoonakker (Eds.), *The impact of ICT on quality of working life* (pp. 205–219). Heidelberg: Springer.

Korunka, C., Weiss, A., Karetta, B., & Huemer, K. H. (1995). The effect of new technologies on job satisfaction and psychosomatic complaints. *Applied Psychology: An International Review, 44*(2), 123–142.

Korpelainen, E., Vartiainen, M., & Kira, M. (2010). Self-determined adoption of an ICT system in a work organization. *Journal of Organizational and End User Computing, 22*(4), 51–69. doi:10.4018/joeuc.2010100103

Kubicek, B., Korunka, C., Paškvan, M., Prem, R., & Gerdenitsch, C. (2014). Changing working conditions at the onset of the twenty-first century: Facts from international datasets. In C. Korunka, & P. Hoonakker (Eds.), *The impact of ICT on quality of working life* (pp. 25–41). Heidelberg: Springer.

Kubicek, B., Paškvan, M., & Korunka, C. (2015). Development and validation of an instrument for assessing job demands arising from accelerated change: The intensification of job demands scale (IDS). *European Journal of Work and Organizational Psychology, 24*(6), 898–913. doi:10.1080/1359432x.2014.979160

Kwon, T. H., & Zmud, R. W. (1987). Unifying the fragmented models of information systems implementation. In R. J. Bolan, & R. A Hirschheim (Eds.), *Critical issues in information systems research* (pp. 227–251). New York: John Wiley & Sons, Inc.

Lewin, K. (1952). Group decision and social change. In G. E. Newcombe, & E. L. Hartley, (Eds.), *Readings in social psychology* (pp. 459–473). New York: Henry Holt.

Mitchell, J. I., Gagné, M., Beaudry, A., & Dyer, L. (2012). The role of perceived organizational support, distributive justice and motivation in reactions to new information technology. *Computers in Human Behavior, 28*(2), 729–738. doi:10.1016/j.chb.2011.11.021

Mosco, V. (2014). *To the cloud: Big data in a turbulent world.* Boulder, CO: Paradigm Publishers.

Munkvold, B. E. (2003). *Implementing collaboration technologies in industry: Case examples and lessons.* London: Springer.

Narayan, K. L., Rao, K. M., & Sarcar, M. M. M. (2008). *Computer aided design and manufacturing.* New Delhi: PHI.

Obschonka, M., Silbereisen, R. K., & Wasilewski, J. (2012). Constellations of new demands concerning careers and jobs: Results from a two-country study on social and economic change. *Journal of Vocational Behavior,* 80, 211–223. doi:10.1016/j.jvb.2011.08.002

Orlikowski, W. J., & Scott, S. V. (2008). Sociomateriality: Challenging the separation of technology, work and organization. *Academy of Management Annals,* 2(1), 433–474.

Paškvan, M., Kubicek, B., & Korunka, C. (2015). Development and validation of an instrument for assessing job demands arising from accelerated change: The intensification of job demands scale (IDS). *European Journal of Work and Organizational Psychology,* 24, 898–913.

Perez, C. (2014). Financial bubbles, crises and the role of government in unleashing golden ages. In A. Pyka, & H-P. Burghof (Eds.), *Innovation and finance* (pp. 11–25). London: Routledge.

Rafferty, A. E., Jimmieson, N. L., & Armenakis, A. A. (2013). Change readiness: A multilevel review. *Journal of Management,* 39(1), 110–135.

Rosa, H. (2005). *Beschleunigung. Die Veränderung der Zeitstrukturen in der Moderne.* Frankfurt am Main: Suhrkamp.

Ryan, R. M., & Deci, E. L. (2000). Self-determination theory and the facilitation of intrinsic motivation, social development, and well-being. *American Psychologist,* 55, 68–78.

Salanova, M., Llorens, S., & Cifre, E. (2013). The dark face of technologies: About the concept and measurement of technostress experience. *International Journal of Psychology,* 48, 422–433.

Scholz, T. (Ed.). (2013). *Digital labor: The Internet as playground and factory.* New York: Routledge.

Trist, E., & Bamforth, K. (1951). Some social and psychological consequences of the long-wall method of coal getting. *Human Relations,* 4(1), 3–38.

Vartiainen, M. (2014). Hindrances and enablers of fluent actions in knowledge work. In: P. Sachse & E. Ulich (Eds.), *Psychologie menschlichen Handelns: Wissen und Denken – Wollen und Tun* (pp. 95–111). Langerich: Pabst Science Publishers.

Vartiainen, M., & Hyrkkänen, U. (2010). Changing requirements and mental workload factors in mobile multi-locational work. *New Technology, Work and Employment,* 25(2), 117–135.

Venkatesh, V., Morris, M. G., Davis, G. B., & Davis, F. D. (2003). User acceptance of information technology: Toward a unified view. *MIS Quarterly,* 27(3), 425–478.

Weber, H., & Zink, K. J. (2014). Boon and bane of ICT acceleration for vulnerable populations. In C. Korunka, & P. Hoonakker (Eds.), *The impact of ICT on quality of working life* (pp. 177–190). Heidelberg: Springer.

Wilenius, M., & Kurki, S. (2012). *Surfing the sixth wave. Exploring the next 40 years of global change.* Finland Futures Research Centre, FFRC eBook 10. Turku: University of Turku.

7

Whose Side Is Technology on, Really? On the Interdependence of Work and Technology

Michael Allvin and Fredrik Movitz

Overview

This chapter is divided into three parts. In the first part the close relationship between work and technology is outlined. By describing how the modern conception of work was established through the spreading of industrialization, it is argued that work, in fact, originated as a residue of technology. This implies a broader understanding of technology than what one might normally think of. Technology is not just about machines and gadgets, but also about the general systems they are a part of. These technological systems can be divided into: (1) general systems for *production*, and (2) various local systems for coordinating and enabling *work* within the production. The second part of the chapter discusses how the general technologies that are sustaining globalization are changing the possibilities for production today. The third part describes how, following these changes, a second order of local technologies for promoting and governing work are being developed, and how these technologies change the conditions for contemporary work.

7.1 Introduction

Work, or more specifically 'paid work', is probably the most thoroughly and unconditionally regulated situation most people will ever find themselves in. Regular working hours and a regular working place are a general standard from which all deviations must be formally negotiated and approved. Also, standard operating procedures, whether prescribed or acquired by practice, and a fixed area of responsibility both delimit and define the work as such. Within this general framework there are a variety of different regulations, standards and technical requirements that are more or less specific to individual jobs.

An Introduction to Work and Organizational Psychology: An International Perspective,
Third Edition. Edited by Nik Chmiel, Franco Fraccaroli and Magnus Sverke.
© 2017 John Wiley & Sons, Ltd. Published 2017 by John Wiley & Sons, Ltd.

Furthermore, these limitations not only define the work, they also differentiate it from that which is not work. Everything workers do outside of their stipulated working hours and workplace is, per definition, not work. If they deviate from a prescribed operating procedure, or make decisions beyond their formal jurisdiction, they are technically not doing their job. The fact that transgressions of the rules in most cases are not acted against, does not mean that the rules are not enforced. If an accident, or some other serious occurrence, could be attributed to the fact that the people involved were 'not doing their job', in other words, not following the rules laid down for their work, the repercussions would definitely be noticeable.

Even if we generally do not think about work as a bundle of rules and regulations, especially since they tend to disappear from our view as we learn to abide by them, it is not difficult to see why this must be so. Unless we are all alone in our work and in our field, work is necessarily part of a larger organized production process, whether of products or of services. Work, then, is merely the human aspect of such an organization. As humans we share this organization with a variety of artefacts, from machines and systems to charts and directives. The artefacts interact with each other as more or less functional systems, and together they constitute the backbone of the organization. These systems of artefacts are generally referred to as 'technologies' (Hughes, 2012).

7.2   Work as a Consequence of Technological Developments

Just because 'work' is a common word in our vocabulary, most people seem to think of it as a natural, even intrinsic part of human life. Technically speaking, that is not the case. In fact, before the spread of industrialization during the nineteenth century, work, as we now know it, did not even exist. Work was not generally conceived of as a distinctive area of life. Most people lived in a household type of economy that did not distinguish between their lives and the way they made their living. Nature and tradition generally set their schedules. The conditions were certainly crude, insensitive and exhausting, but they were not hectic and not very efficient. The social element was often just as important as the functional.

All this changed with industrialization and the emergence of the 'factories'. At the heart of the factories were the large industrial machines that could do 'the work of hundred men' (Ricardo, 1817). Since the machines were both crucial and expensive pieces of hardware, they had to be operated almost continuously in order to pay for themselves. This demanded regular and precise working hours of the workforce maintaining the machines. Also, the power supply dictated the arranging of the machines within the factory, which in turn determined the necessary locations of the workers. The factory floor thereby formed a social grid governing the physical position of the workers vis-à-vis each other, a grid that had to be continuously manned and supervised for the factory to operate properly. There had to be, as Foucault (1977) put it, a space for everybody, and a body for every space.

The necessities of the machines thus formed a rudimentary 'work organization', that is an organization of the workforce. The work organization was communicated through a set of rules that were written down and nailed to the wall for all to see. These rules, simply referred to as 'factory rules', typically stressed conformity to the conditions of time, space and self-discipline required by the machines (Pollard, 1965). At the same time, they also articulated the first responsibility of management: making sure that the workforce remained in their place and performed consistently over a fixed period of time (Zuboff, 1988). The organization, then, in so far as it involves humans, is a set of rules for work implied by the technical infrastructure. As such, it is also the principal instrument of management. Management both writes the rules and oversees the observance of them. It is important here to note this innate mutuality between 'organization' and 'management', since they are usually talked about as two different things following their development into different areas of expertise.

Compared to work done by hand, the machines did not alter anything in terms of its compositional content. They did, however, blow the traditional structure of work out of proportion by first reducing it to a mere fraction of its content, and then repeating that fraction a 'hundred' times. Producing cloth, for instance, involved several interdependent stages, including carding, spinning and weaving, not to mention the various social and aesthetic elements. When James Hargreaves introduced his 'Spinning Jenny' in 1764, it only addressed the single functional element of spinning, and only with wool. But, on the other hand, it made it possible for one person to work up to 120 spindles at the time, instead of just one (Espinasse, 1874, pp. 294ff).

Through this the machines shifted the focus of the working procedure, from that which had been socially meaningful to that which was functionally meaningful. The human contribution was subsequently reduced to the relatively simple task of feeding, servicing and maintaining the machines, as well as forwarding the results. In other words, the 'production process' was a coordinated effort between machines and humans, the machines carried out the 'production' and the humans constituted the 'process'.

Hence, the industrial machines did not just determine the conditions for work, they even defined the work as such. When production is industrialized, the work becomes subordinated to the mechanized production. This was emphasized by another important artefact, the employment contract. Unlike previous agreements for labour, the modern employment contract is both more open and more limited. It is open in the sense that the employees are not hired for a specific task. They are hired to labour, that is, to follow the rules of work, whatever they may be. In other words, the employees dispense their labour at the employer's discretion. The employment is, at the same time, more limited in the sense that it does not involve the employed individuals. It only applies to their labour. The distinction between the hired labour and the person doing the labour is an important one, not just for understanding organizations but from a legal point of view as well. While the employers literally 'own' the *labour* they hire, as Marx (1847) liked to point out, they of course cannot own the actual *person* behind it. This is an important difference between a market economy and a slave economy (Stanley, 1998). This means that, unlike the preindustrial master–servant agreement, the employer has no legal responsibility for the person being employed. On the other hand, the employer has no legal right to make decisions on behalf of the person in matters outside of work either. The modern employment contract is a 'limited responsibility' for both parties.

Out of these 'technical' requirements arose the modern conception of work, not as a specific practice with an expressed objective but as a 'job', a 'multi-purpose' function clearly delimited in time, space and commitment. As a consequence, new techniques for measuring, managing and bringing attention to these arrangements were progressively employed. Regional infrastructure was developed, local time zones were integrated, timetables and clocks came into regular use, as did punch clocks, time cards and factory whistles. Housing was provided within close proximity of the factories. The factories themselves were fenced in, allowing only workers through the factory gates. The layout of the factory separated workers, activities and functions, making them easier to observe and supervise. Management and administration, for instance, were typically located above and overviewing the factory floor. As the factories spread and society became more reliant on industry, the clear divisions in time and space ultimately dictated by the machines no longer just coordinated the workers directly involved, but those indirectly, even peripherally, involved who were gradually forced to adapt as well. By the beginning of the twentieth century pretty much the whole of modern society was revolving around the factories and their rhythm, making the work-leisure distinction and regular working hours one of its main features.

As the technical development proceeded during the twentieth century, the rules for work became ever more finely tuned. The complexity of the production process increased, along with the technical and production specific *competences* required for the work. As a consequence, the workforce became more specialized, and its coordination more sophisticated. The technical requirements of the production process itself provided most of the micro-management, leaving little control in the hands of the individual worker. When the pressure from the production process increased, the workers had little room for manoeuvring. This made it difficult for them to counteract the demands, causing the specific form of fatigue or 'stress' associated with low control and high demands (Karasek & Theorell, 1990). On the other hand, the limited responsibility and the subsequent lack of commitment at work, along with the clear division between work and leisure, made it relatively easy to disconnect oneself from the pressure of work once it was over (Wilensky, 1960). This recurrent dissociation from work was further facilitated by the absorbing world of consumption made possible in the post-war period by the expanding production itself.

7.3 What *Is* Technology and What Does It *Do*?

In this short and sketchy flashback on the origin of 'work', it becomes clearer how technology, in the broadest sense, operates. When rationalization and mechanization are introduced, they not only enable a novel and more effective production process, they also determine the technical and economic infrastructure necessary for that process. In order to maintain, support, manage, administer and supervise the production, a second order of technologies is introduced. These technologies follow, utilize and develop the already existing infrastructure and are consequently treated as resources facilitating the work in and around the production. The more they actually do facilitate the work, the more we use and become dependent on them, the more they entrench the established infrastructure. In other words, the resources that improve and make work easier are also the main agents governing the conditions for work.

From this we can also begin to understand what technology actually 'is made of'. The first and most obvious feature is that it *enhances* human performance. It does what humans do, only more so. It also enables human performance by first copying human action, and then substituting it when the human constitution is inadequate. When, for instance, humans are too big, too small or too fragile. Or when humans are not strong, fast, persistent, or accurate enough. Technology is thus inherently related to human action, as replication and extension.

At the same time technology also *objectifies* performance, by establishing a material routine for it. Inherent in human action is a continuous learning experience, allowing it to change and adapt according to circumstances. This is a source of both creativity and errors. Introducing technology to replace human performance will consequently delimit the room for both errors and creativity. Technology, thus, stabilizes performance, thereby allowing it to transcend the human performance in time, space and achievement.

When a technology is eventually put in place, it will establish, through its very existence, a rationale for doing things. Its material quality allows it to bridge the successions of individual human beings, thereby linking their individual actions into one continuous performance. It does this by forcing the individual actors to adjust their actions to its own rationale for doing things. In this way, technology becomes a formidable force of *regulation*, making deviations impractical, as well as irrational.

The fact that technology regulates action, also means that the action will be consistent and uniform. Technology will, in other words, standardize the action. This is important because that makes technology-based actions *predictable* and therefore something to depend on. It allows other people to relate their own actions to it beyond the immediate 'here and now'. This makes it possible for them to plan and invest in future actions. Once they do this, others will be able to do the same, thereby creating a growing network of interdependent actions, effectively 'normalizing' each other.

Once technology is functionally analysed in such a way, it becomes obvious that the artefacts usually talked about and thought of as technology – such as machines, appliances, tools and mechanical devices – are only the surface and instruments of the systems, architecture, infrastructure and organizations actually sustaining society. To this end, laws, decrees and contracts, materialized in writing and backed up by the authority of a legislator, as well as institutionalized forms of knowledge in the form of scientific disciplines, generally accepted theories, methods and authorities, must also be thought of as technologies regulating performance and allowing them to transcend the limitations of the individual.

'Work', then, is only the historically specific arrangement of such an interdependent and multiple layered network of 'technologies' regulating our (economic) interactions and performances. Even if a lot of these technologies are reinforcing each other, giving the impression of an overly static society, the fact that they are interdependent also means that the resulting network is highly dynamic. Even small changes can reinforce each other and cause chain reactions spreading throughout the network. Also, most of these technologies are not as tightly coupled as they might appear when everything is working 'normally'. One only has to read the 'crash reports' from the latest financial crisis to realise how volatile the system actually is.

7.4   New Forms of Work as a Consequence of New Technological Developments

Although much changed during the twentieth century, the general business model for industry remained essentially the same. This was an economy of scale focusing on mass markets and built to capitalize on the machines. The Italian Marxist, Gramsci (1971) famously dubbed it Fordism, after the Ford Motor Company's influential business model. It was adopted by many other industries, such as retail, tourism and health care, regardless of their reliance on actual machines. The Fordist model had matured and been perfected through a continuous process of rationalization following an economic logic wholly committed to lowering the threshold to where the heavy investments started producing surplus. This typically meant increasing the output in every stage of the manufacturing process that involved heavy investments. If the production as a whole was to generate a maximum surplus, the stages in the production that cost the most also had to be used the most.

Until the 1970s, the economic logic of business was, consequently, heavily biased towards the supply side of the economy. This meant that business in general, and industry in particular, relied firmly on 'passive consumption'. In other words, it was generally presumed that consumers bought, or could be made to buy, everything that was put before them. It was only a matter of price. From the 1970s on, however, the markets in the western hemisphere started to shift towards 'active consumption'. People became more selective in their consumption patterns, regardless of price (Cohen, 2004). Consumption started to replace work as an identity marker, as we entered what consequently came to be called the consumer society (Bauman, 1998). The fact that people started to consume in accordance with their professed or desired life style was not just another trend or fashion, however, but also a sign of noticeably saturated markets.

The increasingly saturated markets forced companies to grow by diversifying their business *across* markets. This was facilitated by several important developments. The first being the rapidly expanding efficiency and global reach of the transportation system, in the air, on land and by sea, embodied for example by the development of a worldwide container system (Hoovestal, 2013). This, in turn, was facilitated by an expanding global trade, following the increasingly pervasive trade agreements negotiated through GATT, and later WTO. These were all technological achievements in their own rights, bridging not only geographical distances but social, political and cultural differences as well. They are technologies in the sense that they shape, standardize, ensure and regulate the terms of agreements by 'materializing' them in laws, contracts, records, taxonomies and infrastructure, thereby facilitating collaboration on a larger scale (Rodrik, 2012).

Perhaps even more important was the deregulation of the financial system in the 1980s, allowing banks to more freely lend out money and companies to move the money more freely across borders. Financial services literally exploded as banks and other financial advisors supplied companies with new instruments for 'financial engineering', that is, finding the most profitable ways to finance business. These instruments made it possible to increase the scope and scale of finance, and should perhaps more appropriately be understood as triggering an industrialization process in financial speculation. Since money was cheap and freely available following the deregulation, most of these instruments involved the use of credits (Krippner, 2012). The extensive use of credits had, in turn, a profound impact on the Fordist business model and the way it organized the production.

This became painfully clear to the American and European manufacturers during the 1980s as they were dethroned by their Japanese counterparts. Japanese manufacturers had developed the Fordist business model beyond its focus on the mechanized production process. To the Japanese, the production as such was merely one element in a larger and more comprehensive 'business process'. When looking at and valuating the *entire* business process, the fixed costs (the heavy investments in machines and buildings) are dwarfed by the total investments made in the products themselves. Since the investments are financed by credits, the products continue to accumulate costs, in the form of interest payments, unrealized value, etc., even after they have been put together. Holding finished products in stock, for instance, is especially expensive since their costs continue to accumulate, even though their value does not. Rather than continuing to produce as much as possible, it becomes imperative to cash in on the finished products as quickly as possible so as to realize the value they have accumulated on their way through the production process. From an economic standpoint then, minimizing total throughput time becomes more important than maximizing the output. The manufacturer that became a symbol of this business model was the Toyota Motor Corporation. As a consequence, Fordism was replaced by *Toyotism* (Dohse, Jürgens, & Nialsch, 1985).

It is, however, the information technology process – from the development of numerically controlled lathes and cutting machines in the 1960s, the synthesis of the satellite-based global positioning system (GPS) and the construction of the microprocessor in the 1970s, to the specification and implementation of the transmission control protocol for internet (TCP/IP) in the 1980s (all of which were started as US government defence initiatives) – that has become synonymous with our current dependence on modern technology (Castells, 2003).

Even if 'containerization', free trade agreements and global financing helped flatten the world for global collaboration and competition, it was the precision and reliability of the information technology that finally paved it (Friedman, 2005). It made the transactions between companies efficient and reliable enough to reduce the risks involved, thereby making the 'transaction costs' predictable and even calculable. Information technology made it possible, not only to use subcontractors on a global scale, but also to synchronize their deliveries with a tightly coordinated production process without sacrificing momentum, speed and quality. It also made it possible to globally orchestrate several different companies around a single business process, thereby reducing the risks and costs for everybody involved. Finally, information technology made it possible for companies themselves to take part in financial transactions on a global scale, both in order to finance their business and to make some money 'on the side' while doing it.

All of these technologies interacted to facilitate, and later necessitate, the *decoupling* of the economic enterprise of business from its roots in the physical production process. As an economic enterprise, the sole purpose of business is to maximize shareholder value. This can be done in various ways, but it invariably means making strategic decisions with shareholder interests in mind. As a production process, on the other hand, the purpose of business is to organize the production and manage the workforce in such a way that the output exceeds the input (Fligstein, 1990). Traditionally these two sides of business went hand in hand. If the output exceeded the input, the shareholders made a corresponding profit. But the development of the economic side of business facilitated by new technologies, from financial instruments to real-time communication technology, has substantially increased the conceivable ways to make profit. And, unlike the production side of business, these ways are not restricted to a physical place with a local workforce, nor a comparatively convoluted and lengthy production process.

This does not mean that production has become obsolete as a creator of value. It does mean, however, that it has been subjected to new and increasing demands for economic achievement. To meet these demands nearly all organizations adopt various forms of process-oriented layouts for their production in accordance with the Toyotist paradigm. As a consequence, the traditional boundaries separating functionally organized departments and areas of responsibilities become obstacles and bottlenecks restraining the business process, and demanding reorganization.

The changing infrastructure for production puts new demands on work. Participating in various joint ventures, for instance, involves coordination beyond one's own organization. The traditional time–space framework for performance does not necessarily serve to coordinate instruments *between* different organizations, and definitely not on a global scale. Instead deadlines and projects become more important as conditions for work. Furthermore, having collaborative partners accessible on the same basis as colleagues within a regular workplace, may not always be possible. Interacting over the internet and travelling are therefore becoming a more common requirement of work. As a consequence, the time–space framework that generated the traditional distinction between work and leisure is gradually broken down as a condition for many jobs. This means that the concern for the practical structuring of both work and everyday life is increasingly being left to the individual person, resulting in recurrent negotiations between colleagues, spouses, family, friends and others. It also means that the technical restraints for how much one can work are being taken apart. Instead, it is up to the individuals themselves to schedule their involvement in all areas of life, as well as to pace themselves and allocate enough time for personal recuperation so as not to 'burn out' (Allvin et al., 2011).

As we can see, new developments in general technology alter the conditions for production which, in turn, alters the conditions for work. Out of these conditions, a second order of new and more targeted technologies for facilitating and governing work emerges.

7.5 New Technologies as a Consequence of the New Forms of Work

When an established infrastructure is challenged by a new technological infrastructure, it tries to cope with the challenge by making minor adjustments. This results in various transitional 'hybrid' techniques. When, for instance, regular working hours no longer form a common requirement for white-collar workers, the traditional punch clock is upgraded to register time quotas, on a weekly, monthly, or even yearly basis. This means that workers can come and go as they please, within certain limits, as long as a set time quota is filled. Hence, flexitime. It is, in a sense, a compromise to please both the old and the new infrastructures. The clock can, for instance, be integrated with the company payroll and security system to monitor the whereabouts of the employee (Ellis, Gage, & Signor, 2007). The problem is of course that it does not facilitate the work. As a consequence, it just makes the obsolescence of an old technology even more apparent, while not doing anything to satisfy the new one. It is still possible to 'underperform' and fill the time quota. Regular office hours are, for many jobs, rapidly becoming a non-issue.

Another such hybrid technique is telework. The personal computers, cell phones, and the new communication technology of the 1990s made it possible to do the work from home instead of commuting to work every day, contributing to and wasting time in the traffic 'rush hours'. But, like regular office hours, a fixed office space was still considered an intrinsic feature of work, necessary to coordinate and supervise the workforce. Telework appeared as a compromise.

Through a formal agreement with the employer, allowing the employee to work 'out of the office' one or two days a week, the necessary office equipment and sometimes even office space closer to home, are supplied and furnished by the employer. Of course, being available on phone or email during regular office hours is still a requirement. Just like flexitime, telework does not really satisfy either system. The employee is just as enclosed in time and space as before, albeit in two different locations. When trying to meet a deadline, it does not really matter if the job is done at home or at the office, it still needs to be finished on time. Insisting on a fixed framework in time and space runs the risk of being more frustrating than supportive.

What is interesting, though, is to see just how entrenched the previous system has become. Telework, for instance, is discussed in terms of its legal ramifications. How far does the employer's responsibility for the employee reach? If one trips in the shower while working from home, should that constitute an occupational accident, making the employer responsible? If so, how far are we prepared to let our employer furnish and supervise our home in order to ensure a safe working environment? The questions are more argumentative than practical, but they point towards the deeply institutionalized relation between, on the one hand, the employee representatives, who are afraid of losing their influence over the conditions for work, but not wanting to antagonize their members who appreciate telework, and, on the other hand, the employers who want to reduce their responsibility for their employees, while still keeping control of their labour (Allvin, 2001).

Both flexitime and telework are descendants of the twentieth century and reflect the dazed reactions to what Manuel Castells (2009) talked about as an emerging 'network society', where new technologies have changed the way we use and understand space, from a historically specified place to the 'flow' of our *recurring social exchange and interactions*, which, in turn, has changed the way we relate to and experience time, from a relentless progression to a *perpetual present*, a 'timeless time'. The fact that flexitime and telework are still used, and referred to as viable forms for work, has probably more to do with our prevailing institutions, administrative and negotiating systems, than the practical requirements of work itself.

Organizations are slowly adapting to the new technological conditions, however. New techniques for facilitating and monitoring work in a new time–space framework, sometimes called flexible work, are gradually being put into place. These techniques can schematically be identified on three different but interdependent levels within the organization.

First, and most apparently, we encounter these techniques as mundane 'resources' for communication and administration. Most people today have access to computers both at home and at work. Furthermore, these computers are becoming increasingly more powerful as well as more portable. The paradoxical consequence of this is that the actual device is functionally becoming correspondingly less and less significant. It is gradually being reduced to a mere vehicle for the communicative and administrative functions enabled by the software inside.

Aesthetically, however, it is the other way around. The design is becoming more and more significant, which indicates that the user experience is becoming more personalized. This has a functional value in itself, since it tells us that the device and the user are being integrated with each other. This is important because it means, first: that we will always carry it with us, second; that we will become more and more comfortable and trusting in our relation to it and, third; that we, as a consequence, will become more proficient, but also more accommodating, users of its applications (Cieslak & Van Winkle, 2004).

The new technology, of course, excels in applications facilitating administration, coordination, and 'productivity', from 'to do' lists and merged calendars to collaborative writing features and project administration programmes. These applications have an expressed focus on localized, even individual, self-administration and coordination, explicitly bypassing common office hours and office space as formally acknowledged constraints for coordinating work. More subtle, perhaps, are the proliferation and specialization of media for communication. The increasing specialization tend to differentiate the communication into functional and social forms. Texting, email services, word-processing and presentation programmes, for instance, have facilitated, improved, but also standardized the functional communication. Additional features are continuously added to improve functionality. There are even functions compensating for dysfunctional side effects following the increasing demand for our attention, such as the possibility to automatically sort incoming mail, self-learning junk mail filters, grammatical and spelling functions, suggested templates, etc. There are also functions for subscribing and filtering news and information retrieval into what is deemed to be functionally or socially relevant. Social communication is, on the other hand, of course serviced by the more or less targeted 'social' forums on the internet (Crowe & Middleton, 2012).

The interesting thing here is that the technology supports and encourages us to distinguish, categorize and objectify that which is essentially a subjective and decided distinction between what is 'functionally' and 'socially' relevant. It allows us to focus on and become more attentive to relevant information, regardless of when or from where we receive it. As a consequence, this distinction is rapidly becoming more significant than the traditional distinction between work and leisure. Unlike the traditional work–leisure distinction, the functional-social distinction is not limited to that which is provided and not provided through the 'office', nor does it have to be. It is as counterproductive and frustrating to be prevented from updating Facebook during office hours, as it is to be prevented from reading job emails after (Hochschild, 1997; Nippert-Eng, 1996).

Second, techniques for supervising flexible work can, of course, also be observed from a managerial aspect. In fact, the obsolescence of regular office hours and office space as principal techniques for monitoring flexible work was proclaimed already in the 1980s when cell phones and personal computers first appeared. Local management, however, was understandably sceptical since there were no feasible and acknowledged alternatives readily available at the time. Ironically, the most obvious alternative for supervising flexible work, was Peter Drucker's (1954) half a century-old technique for monitoring the local managers themselves. Since they have to tackle problems that are not readily foreseeable, managers ultimately have to act on their own initiative and rely on their own capability. Managers, therefore, cannot be micro-managed. Instead, they must have a clear objective for what to attain, and then be provided with the appropriate resources to attain that objective. The rest is up to them. Managing by objectives, consequently, not only shifts the *focus* of work, from the procedure to the result, it also shifts the *responsibility* for work, from the organization predetermining the procedure to the individuals' capability to attain the result on their own. For Drucker, this was a question of using the competence inherent within the organization, and of trust in those who embodied that competence (Drucker, 1954).

Although management may be enthusiastic advocates for using the competence of their workforce, they do not seem to be equally enthusiastic about trusting their capability. The modern managerial toolbox involves a host of techniques for piloting performance and assessing the results. These include the systematic use of 'best practices', benchmarking, manualized (or 'evidence-based') practices, as well as performance appraisals and various forms of audits (Merchant & Stede, 2011).

Third, new techniques can finally be identified on an overall level, where they are used to create a new *framework* for performance. Unlike the traditional time–space framework, the immediate function of these techniques is not so much supervising the individuals directly, but to integrate them within a shared social context. Such a context is intended to enclose the individuals within a functional and symbolic universe, rendering *meaning* to their functions, roles and work. The ultimate purpose of such a fabricated culture is, of course, to promote identification with the organization, its values and self-prescribed objectives, making the individual think, feel and act 'organizational' without having to be told to do so. Such cultures are, of course, generally not as powerful as they might appear and perhaps are intended to be, but they can be quite successful in creating a general awareness of what is expected of the workers (Kotter, 2008; Kunda, 1992).

Of course, there is nothing new in trying to create an awareness of what is expected of a worker. Traditionally, however, this was accomplished through explicit rules, like the early factory rules. What is new are the subtle, implicit, almost subconscious way in which they are conveyed. Also, the rules are not directed at individual actions, but at the attitudes and values behind the actions. Nor are they preventive in their ambition, but promotive and encouraging, even inspiring. They are, what political scientists call 'soft rules' (Mörth, 2004).

We recognize these rules in various symbolic *rituals* of an organization, such as 'rites of passages' when newly employed, promoted, or retired are celebrated; for acknowledging achievements, as when closing a business deal, finishing a project, or launching a new product; for consolidation social bonds, through recurrent social events like 'five o'clock beer', the company Christmas event, company-sponsored activities, such as health promotion and sports contests; etc. (Alvesson & Willmott, 2002; Holmqvist, 2009).

We also recognize these soft rules in various forms of 'storytelling" and 'corporate narratives', distinguished by their typical 'from rags to riches' theme, inviting the individual worker to take part in a grand and inspiring success story. Finally, we also recognize the rules in the specific usage of language for distinguishing and differentiating within or between organizations, such as, for instance, 'management speak', a language that is functional on the surface, but socially excluding or including underneath (Brighton, 2002; Greatbatch & Clark, 2005; Hinton, 2002).

From the techniques governing the new forms of work we can, therefore, deduce that just filling a slot in the functional grid of the organization is no longer good enough. Instead there are other requirements implied by the techniques. The technological system presupposes, first, that the worker is a self-relying and self-guiding operator, able to find, recognize, and put together the means necessary to accomplish the task. Second, it is no longer enough to be proficient in the performance of work, the important thing is to achieve results. Third, the managerial focus on assessments and evaluations suggests that the demand for continuous rationalization previously restricted to the overall production, has penetrated all the way down to the individual worker. Being good enough is clearly no longer good enough. Fourth, even though it is important to be self-relying and operate independently, you also have to be a 'team player' and act within the shared cultural framework of the organization. This may seem contradictory, but in fact it is quite the opposite. It is because workers have to operate independently, and thus cannot be closely supervised, that it becomes important to know that they are acting within the restraints of an accepted framework.

Describing the techniques for governing work in this way may not reflect the working conditions of most jobs today. The majority of work may well be performed within a relatively traditional framework. However, the new framework is steadily making itself more manifest, meaning that many, if not most, jobs are presently run by both frameworks, although in various degrees. Generally speaking, a traditional framework is more commonly used for 'blue-collar' jobs, while 'white-collar' jobs have more elements of a newer framework. Independent and highly skilled jobs are also more likely to be governed by a new framework (Allvin et al., 2013).

To conclude, work is still as regulated today as it was a hundred years ago, if not more so, only in a different way. Instead of (just) being regulated through a fixed time–space framework, it is (also) being regulated through a general commitment culture. And, depending on the job, instead of being regulated by fixed operating procedures with limited responsibilities, it is being regulated by goals, deadlines and recurrent audits. The more independently we have to operate at work, the more pervasive and personally penetrative technology has to become in order to ensure our acceptable performance. When looking at the technological development during the last hundred years from this perspective, it does indeed become difficult to tell whether it is we who use the technology, or the technology that is using us.

Summary

The aim of this chapter has been to demonstrate the relationship between work and technology. The relationship is most clearly seen when looking at the development of work itself. Industrialization started with the machines, and labour was hired to do what they could not. The work was consequently organized for and around the machines. Various technologies were introduced as resources to facilitate and promote the work. As the technologies developed, the organization and conditions for work changed accordingly. This means that organizations should be understood as technological infrastructures of production, involving both humans and artefacts. In this sense, technology is the vehicle through which we, as humans, perform and interact within the organization. When we use technologies to achieve something, which is what we do when we work, we also confirm the functionality of that technology, thereby reproducing the organization it is a part of. To work is to be regulated by technology.

Discussion Points

1   The technologies that facilitate your job the most are also the technologies that condition your performance the most. Think about the techniques that you use regularly, and discuss in what ways they condition what you do.
2   The various techniques used for governing new forms of work presupposes a self-reliant, goal-oriented, flexible worker with social skills. Why are these qualities so important in today's work?

Suggested Further Reading

Allvin, M., Aronsson, G., Hagström, T., Johansson, G., & Lundberg, U. (2011). *Work without boundaries: Psychological perspectives on the new working life*. Chichester: Wiley. For an overview of the 'new' conditions for work.

Grint, K., & Woolgar, S. (1997). *The machine at work: Technology, work and organization*. Cambridge, UK: Polity. For a classic discussion of technology, work and organization.

Matthewman, S. (2011). *Technology and social theory*. Basingstoke: Palgrave Macmillan. A general and comprehensive book on technology.

MacKenzie, D., & Wajcman, J. (Eds.). (1999). *The social shaping of technology* (2nd ed.). Buckingham: McGraw-Hill. For many good and classical examples of the relationship between humans and technology.

References

Allvin, M. (2001). Distansarbete: Ett instrument för frihet eller kontroll? *Arbetsliv i Omvandling/ Work Life in Transition, 10.*

Allvin, M., Aronsson, G., Hagström, T., Johansson, G., & Lundberg, U. (2011). *Work without boundaries: Psychological perspectives on the new working life*. Chichester: Wiley.

Allvin, M., Mellner, C., Movitz, F., & Aronsson, G. (2013). The diffusion of flexibility: Estimating the incidence of low-regulated working conditions. *Nordic Journal of Working Life Studies, 3*(3), 99–116.

Alvesson, M., & Willmott, H. (2002). Identity regulation as organizational control: Producing the appropriate individual. *Journal of Management Studies, 39*(5), 619–644.

Bauman, Z. (1998). *Work, consumerism, and the new poor*. Buckingham: Open University Press.

Brighton, A. (2002). Introduction – management speak: a master discourse? *Critical Quarterly, 44*(3), 1–3.

Castells, M. (2003). *The Internet galaxy: Reflections on the Internet, business, and society*. New York: Oxford University Press.

Castells, M. (2009). *The rise of the network society: vol. I, The information age: Economy, society, and culture* (2nd ed.). Oxford: Blackwell.

Cieslak, D. M., & Van Winkle, M. (2004). Carry your office in the palm of your hand. *Journal of Accountancy, 198*(2), 52.

Cohen, L. (2004). A consumers' republic: The politics of mass consumption in postwar America. *Journal of Consumer Research, 31*(1), 236–239.

Crowe, R., & Middleton, C. (2012). Women, smartphones and the workplace. *Feminist Media Studies, 12*(4), 560–569.

Dohse, K., Jürgens, U., & Nialsch, T. (1985). From 'Fordism' to 'Toyotism'? The social organization of the labor process in the Japanese automobile industry. *Politics & Society, 14*(2), 115–146.

Drucker, P. (1954). *The practice of management*. New York: Harper & Row.

Ellis, R., Gage, G. R., & Signor, T. (2007). A multi-tasked human resources and payroll accounting system. In *United States patent application publication*. Google Patents.

Espinasse, F. (1874). *Lancashire worthies*. London: Simpkin, Marshall, & Co.

Fligstein, N. (1990). *The transformation of corporate control*. Cambridge, MA: Harvard University Press.

Foucault, M. (1977). *Discipline and punish: The birth of the prison*. New York: Pantheon.

Friedman, T. L. (2005). *The world is flat: A brief history of the twenty-first century*. New York: Farrar, Straus and Giroux.

Gramsci, A. (1971). Americanism and Fordism. In *Selections from the prison notebooks* (pp. 362–403). New York: International Publishers Co.

Greatbatch, D., & Clark, T. (2005). *Management speak*. London: Routledge.

Hinton, D. A. (2002). Triangulating the circle: the three laws of Management Speak. *Critical Quarterly, 44*(3), 55–62.

Hochschild, A. R. (1997). *The time bind: When work becomes home and home becomes work*. New York: Henry Holt & Co.

Holmqvist, M. (2009). Corporate social responsibility as corporate social control: The case of work-site health promotion. *Scandinavian Journal of Management, 25*(1), 68–72.

Hoovestal, L. E. (2013). *Globalization contained*. Basingstoke: Palgrave Macmillan.

Hughes, T. P. (2012). The evolution of large technological systems. In W. E. Bijker, T. P. Hughes, & T. Pinch (Eds.), *The social construction of technological systems: New directions in the sociology and history of technology* (Anniversary Edition). Cambridge, MA: MIT Press.

Karasek, R., & Theorell, T. (1990). *Healthy work: Stress, productivity, and the reconstruction of working life*. New York: Basic Books.

Kotter, J. P. (2008). *Corporate culture and performance*. New York: Simon & Schuster.

Krippner, G. R. (2012). *Capitalizing on crisis: The political origins of the rise of finance*. Cambridge, MA: Harvard University Press.

Kunda, G. (1992). *Engineering culture: Control and commitment in a high-tech corporation*. Philadelphia, PA: Temple University Press.

Marx, K. (1847). Wage labour and capital. Marx/Engels Internet Archive. Available at: www.marxists.org.

Merchant, K., & Stede, W. V. der. (2011). *Management control systems: Performance measurement, evaluation and incentives* (3rd ed.). Harlow: Prentice Hall.

Mörth, U. (2004). *Soft law in governance and regulation: Aan interdisciplinary analysis.* Cheltenham, UK ; Edward Elgar Publishers.

Nippert-Eng, C. E. (1996). *Home and work: Negotiating boundaries through everyday life.* Chicago: University of Chicago Press.

Pollard, S. (1965). *The genesis of modern management: A study of the industrial revolution in Great Britain.* Cambridge, MA: Harvard University Press.

Ricardo, D. (1817). *On the principles of political economy and taxation.* London: John Murray.

Rodrik, D. (2012). *The globalization paradox: Democracy and the future of the world economy.* New York: W. W. Norton & Company.

Stanley, A. D. (1998). *From bondage to contract: Wage labor, marriage, and the market in the age of slave emancipation.* Cambridge: Cambridge University Press.

Wilensky, H. (1960). Work, careers, and social integration. *International Social Science Journal, 12*(3), 543–560.

Zuboff, S. (1988). *In the age of the smart machine.* Oxford: Heinemann.

Why Did I Choose That Career Path? Approaches to Vocational Choices and People's Readiness to Self-Manage their Own Career Paths

8

Guido Sarchielli

Overview

A choice of training and/or occupation is made after a long process initially. This is an example of a developmental task that has to be met to address entry into adult life with a reasonable chance of success. Currently, changes to the working context make these decisions even more complicated and anxiety-inducing than in earlier times. In fact, it is increasingly uncommon for anyone now to find a 'job for life'. Thus choice becomes a recurring process, not dealing with a single job but rather a career path, difficult to plan in advance. This chapter examines the main theoretical approaches to vocational choices, which emphasize different aspects of choice: as a match between person and job; as a developmental process; as an outcome of social learning; as career construction and as decision-making process. This chapter illustrates how such aspects of the career process may depend on various prerequisites for a career choice that is experienced as at least satisfactory to the individual. The crucial roles of preparation and readiness for career choices are underscored and the personal factors that need to be developed to make the choice easier are addressed. From such a perspective, the final process of decision-making should face fewer concerns about failure.

8.1 Introduction

Career choices, whether made as a university student or as a worker, are usually conceived of as an important *developmental task* in the transition to adulthood (Savickas, 2002) and for a better adjustment to employment during working life. Successful achievement of this task is expected to develop personal independence,

An Introduction to Work and Organizational Psychology: An International Perspective,
Third Edition. Edited by Nik Chmiel, Franco Fraccaroli and Magnus Sverke.
© 2017 John Wiley & Sons, Ltd. Published 2017 by John Wiley & Sons, Ltd.

lead to success in later personal and social tasks as well as to the imminent beginning of an autonomous life-career.

The complexity of these choices is growing as an indirect result of changes in the world of work. These external factors have important effects not only on the degree of openness of the labour market (e.g., strong imbalances between demand and labour supply are reflected in an extraordinary high unemployment rate; CEDEFOP, 2012) but also on the ways people face their professional futures and on the need to make a reasonable vocational choice (Brown et al., 2010). Examples of these latter effects are: increased competition for a job; being better prepared to focus on new professional pathways; the need for skills to cope with recurrent transitions and role changes; an awareness of a harder match between expectations and work reality and of the reduced possibility of designing a long-term career; being prepared to adjust to a variable quality of work; and the need to be well equipped (Akkermans et al., 2013) to manage uncertain employment relationships and ever-changing work demands (e.g., need for new technical and soft skills).

Until recently, finding the 'right job' was the main objective of choices related to a professional future. At present, this goal has become more risky and challenging because the assumption that an individual will choose the right 'job for life' is no longer valid, or at least not generally true. Consequently, if we ask someone, 'Why did you choose the job you're doing?', he/she will find it difficult to reply in a simple, immediate way. A common general response is almost impossible. The choice and entry into employment are not made in the same way among different social groups, even within the same society, because of differences in available resources (e.g., social and psychological capital, family support, educational qualifications or previous work experience) and socio-economic, cultural and ethnic origins. Thus, traditional work histories that linearly sequence education (before) and then apprenticeship and work apply to a dwindling number of people.

It is now much more likely that individuals will move from an employee role with a predictable organizational career path (often anticipated during the school period) to an 'entrepreneur for themselves role'. This is a challenging new condition in which individuals have to face all the risks of unsuitable decisions concerning their occupational future and balance the necessary resources and efforts to manage them. In addition, people have to re-decide many times about their job. Whereas established ideal research models of the career process took a single early choice as point of departure, these models have gradually been replaced by models that emphasize a series of choices or often forced transitions that individuals make over a life span, depending more on contextual contingencies than on personal desires and projects. This is why employability rather than getting an initial job is now considered a key to success in the world of work (Watts, 2006). Employability is a set of desirable personal characteristics, self-perceptions and learning achievements relevant to the world of work that enhances the probability of being able to move self-sufficiently within the labour market. This capacity to master the skills, knowledge and attitudes to engage and re-engage with the labour market seems to be a more important challenge for individuals in self-managing their career development than their initial choice of a specific job.

The questions addressed by vocational psychology (Fuad, 2007) about choosing and building a satisfying working future (How do people make career decisions? What factors influence career choices? Which barriers make the choice process difficult?) have to be re-focused by considering people's readiness to design and implement a career path. This long process will be summarized in this chapter, taking into account different theoretical perspectives that focus on traditional factors considered for a vocational career. Consequently, 'readiness to choose a career' and the 'decision-making process' will be examined to find a reasonable answer to the question raised in the title of this chapter.

8.2 Main Conceptual Approaches to Career Choice

Some of the main approaches to vocational choice will be briefly examined, advancing the judgement that none of them is alone sufficient to explain the complexity of the contemporary career choice process (Patton & McMahon, 2006). These theories are not in competition since each explores particular aspects of the phenomenon, aiming to find an answer to different questions, but all are interested in supporting professional help in career choice. Table 8.1 shows the main questions these conceptual approaches try to answer. The short answer given by each approach summarizes the prevailing meaning attributed to the vocational choice that will be set out in the following paragraphs.

Table 8.1: Overview of the main conceptual approaches to vocational choice

Basic questions	Main answers Vocational choice as...	Reference
Which contents (interests or personality characteristics) are important for better adaptability to work?	a matching process (*trait-factor theories*)	Holland & Gottfredson (1992)
Which processes characterize the construction of a career over a life span?	a developmental process (*developmental theories*)	Super (1980; 1996)
What are the effects of learning on the choice and development of a career?	a learning process (*social learning theories*)	Krumboltz (1994); Lent, Brown, & Hackett (2002)
How does someone construct a significant career path in a given context?	a career construction process (*career construction theory*)	Savickas (2002)
What is the nature of decision-making processes, and what are the barriers to be overcome?	a decision-making process (*decision-making approaches*)	Amir, Gati, & Kleiman (2008) Hirschi & Läge (2007)

There is one common element to the various approaches: the importance given to self-knowledge in implementing a satisfactory career path. In the most recent theories (Hirschi & Dauwalder, 2015), careers are no longer conceived in linear terms or with the same developmental opportunities for everyone. In fact, the traditional linear career patterns that had a clear upward direction (a sort of 'career ladder') and denoted cumulative development through time have in many cases been replaced by sequences of discontinuous (and sometimes inconsistent) job experiences with both gains and losses of skills and positions and sudden changes in career goals. This reveals a final picture of a segmented personal work history that involves an increasing percentage of workers greatly diversifying their chances for satisfactory careers. Essentially, current careers are flexible, multi-directional (with many options from which to choose to achieve success; Baruch, 2004) and highly dependent on the dynamics of change and instability in work contexts. Furthermore, individuals' active roles affect the construction of a career path in close relationship to the contexts with which they interact.

8.2.1   Vocational choice as a matching process

A theoretical perspective that regards vocational choice as a process of matching between personal and job features has been developed by Holland (Holland & Gottfredson, 1992). This is one of a category of approaches (trait-factor theories) developed in the early twentieth century, which suggests that people look for jobs that allow for the best fit with their individual abilities, interests and personal attributes. When people are adequately self-aware and informed about the world of work, they can make vocational choices that are true (rational) and congruent with their way of being and thinking and with their expectations. This perspective focuses on the vocational personality. It represents a dispositional personality model, described by Holland, that proposes six basic personality types (called RIASEC) corresponding to six emblematic professional contexts that allow people to carry out their interests and to express their skills, attitudes and values. The six RIASEC types are:

1. *Realistic*: preference for working with hands, objects, machines, tools, animals and for environments that allow one to be active, practical, adventurous.
2. *Investigative*: preference for analytical approaches, observational activities, systematic and creative investigation of different kinds of natural phenomena.
3. *Artistic*: preference for unsystematized activities focused on manipulation of physical, verbal, or human materials, and for literary, musical and artistic activities.
4. *Social*: preference for activities that help people such as training, informing, educating and caring and for environments characterized by cooperation, social support and empathy.

5. *Enterprising*: preference for activities attaining organizational or business goals and for influencing and leading people.
6. *Conventional*: preference for data processing, working with written records and numbers in a systematic way, and for planning, organizing and providing order and efficiency.

These vocational personality types are identified empirically and are graphically represented as the points of a hexagon (Figure 8.1) (Holland, 1992).

Although all contribute to the full profile, three types are sufficient to describe a personality that can be used as the basis for making career choices (especially, but not exclusively, the three types placed at adjacent points). Holland's inventories for identifying personality types have been shown to be psychometrically sound, and are still the basis for professional career guidance and counselling. This model has, however, been criticized (Nauta, 2010) for its static vision of people and jobs. In fact, such person–environment matching appears less and less probable given the current volatility of the labour market and the growing pressure on individuals to prepare for numerous career changes. Moreover, the model is not particularly sensitive to differences of a cross-cultural nature, to gender, to social background or to the numerous situational factors affecting the construction of concrete careers.

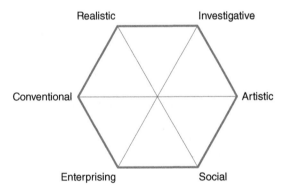

Figure 8.1: Simplified representation of Holland's hexagon of vocational personality types

8.2.2 Vocational choice as a developmental process

An approach that tries to give additional meaning to vocational choices is the life-span, life-space approach to career development (Super, 1980; Super, Savickas, & Super, 1996). This developmental process theory proposes that each job requires a certain pattern of abilities, knowledge and personal characteristics and that, at the same time, such attributes correspond to important aspects of the individual's self-concept. Even this theoretical approach assumes the importance of person–environment fit but argues that such a correspondence cannot be taken for granted after the first comparison between personal desires and employment information. It can become an optimal outcome only of a lifelong process in which people continually strive to match their ever-changing career goals and self-concept to the reality of the world of work. In fact, the self-concept is not a static entity (as are Holland's personality traits), but is enriched over time and works as a useful cognitive tool to give continuity to the subjective experience of different roles and social contexts in the course of a person's life stages: growth (birth to age 14), exploration (ages 15–24), establishment (ages 25–44), maintenance (ages 45–64) and decline (over 65). The exploration stage has crucial relevance to career choice. It involves mastering three developmental tasks: (1) crystallization (cognitive processes of defining one's own vocational goals), (2) task specification (specifying goals and planning vocational direction), and (3) implementation (engagement in training activities aimed at the successive entrance into a chosen occupation).

Successfully facing the environmental requirements of each stage of a career depends on the individual's career maturity defined as individual readiness to face the problems of a career at each stage in a realistic and age-appropriate manner. This includes the person's physical, social and psychological resources (e.g., resilience, career motivation, emotional stability) as well as how much has been learned in successfully passing the previous stages of the career. Over the course of a career, the individual constructs a professional self (an overall evaluation of one's worth, value and interests as a worker) through interaction between personal resources, the role played in the work context and the evaluations of superiors and colleagues. Work and career satisfaction will depend on the congruence between professional self and the characteristics of the job. Empirical evaluation of the model has given encouraging but not unequivocal results. The five age-related stages are by now outdated due to the rapid changes of current work that continually require transitions within a stage and between stages. Thus, it is very hard to generalize age-related patterns and think that people will experience these stages in the same way. On the contrary, a cyclical life-span perspective (neither normative nor strictly age-linked) focused on the transitions and unpredictable changes that people face during their working life seems more realistic. Such stages are, moreover, not very sensitive to the numerous gender, ethnic, cultural and socio-economic differences in life cycles, which also have a notable differentiating effect on their duration.

Box 8.1 summarizes two criticisms of both theoretical perspectives centred on person–environment congruence.

Box 8.1:   Two criticisms of person–environment congruence models

- *Occupational opportunity structure* – Roberts (1995; 2009), since the late 1960s, has criticized approaches to vocational choices based on the congruence between the self and the job. He points out that most people experience a mismatch between the self and the concrete job. This depends on lack of work opportunities, variability of the labour market and notable individual differences in social capital due, in particular, to the social class of origin, types of social support, level of education and gender. Roberts (1995) also criticizes the concepts of project, 'free choice of employment' and strategies of self-realization because they prevalently refer to people from a middle-high social class who have genuine decisional possibilities regarding a future career. For the great majority of people carrying out jobs of middle or middle-low qualification, it seems more realistic to conceive of vocational choice as an adjustment to the occupational opportunity structure in a specific historical and social moment.

- *Resources availability* – Blustein (2011) has recently re-examined the influence of sociocultural and economic context on work and career choice. He underscores how every work-related decision is not the result of individual agency or of intentions elaborated in a social vacuum, but is rather shaped by the context, i.e., by the different availability of personal and social resources, the opportunities for self-determination and the quality of relationships with the people who can contribute to the construction of the working experience. Thus, an individual's career is not necessarily linked to the original projections for a professional future consistent with their own desires and preferences. It is much more likely that it is dependent on progressive adaptation to situations over which people have little or no control.

8.2.3 Vocational choice as a learning process

The theoretical perspective that emphasizes learning highlights a third meaning of vocational choices that enriches the picture. Social learning theory of career decision-making (Krumboltz, 1994) and social cognitive career theory (Lent, Brown, & Hackett, 2002) are examples of theories that emphasize the role of learning in explaining how individuals develop their interests and become ready for decision-making. These approaches are influenced by the notion of self-efficacy elaborated by Bandura (1986).

According to Krumboltz (1994), with learning, an individual acquires self-observation generalizations (e.g., self-efficacy, interests, work values) and task-approach skills (i.e., the ability to face a range of contexts and manage affective elements). Through such knowledge and skills, it is possible to plan a series of steps: commitment to information researching, defining career objectives, clarifying the value attributed to such objectives and finding alternatives to evaluate and choose. It is worth noting that beliefs and skills influence successive experience; they can change as a result of new learning and affect work aspirations and action strategies. Therefore, if dysfunctional or incorrect beliefs develop, regarding the workplace, self-attributes or real capabilities, it is foreseeable that there may be negative consequences on choices and a reduction in the probability of staying employable (Froehlich et al., 2014).

Considering the current variability of the job market, it is also necessary to be ready to manage situations in which there is limited personal control and little possibility of planning. With happenstance learning theory, Krumboltz (2009) supplements the previous version of social learning theory of career decision-making, illustrating how unpredictable social factors, chance events and contingent environmental factors can act as obstacles to choices, even when such choices have been planned in a clear, rational manner. Such factors can, however, be faced with a positive attitude if people have been prepared for unforeseen events and changes and certain qualities have been reinforced, such as curiosity to explore contingent events such as learning opportunities; persistence to deal with obstacles; flexibility to address varying circumstances; and optimism to maximize benefits also from unplanned events. Social cognitive career theory (Lent, Hackett, & Brown, 1996) enriches the role of learning processes through two elements:

1. *outcome expectations*: i.e., beliefs about the results of a performance. If workers understand that they are competent at an activity and gain pleasure from the results, it is probable that they will develop an interest in that type of activity and explore the vocational choice possibilities in that direction.
2. *goals*: i.e., criteria that guide decisions and outcomes in the long term. These have an important motivational function when they are clear and well-specified and stimulate personal involvement. The selection of goals forms the translation of vocational interests into concrete objectives and consequently into action plans. Such a process is influenced by the perception of valid social support by significant others and by the level of social and economic opportunities (and restraints).

8.2.4   Vocational choice as career construction

The following perspective views career choices and development as a complex and ever-evolving socially constructed process that reflects a person's subjective interpretation and meaning attributed to situations, events, and social interaction. Savickas' theory of career construction (2002) is an example of a modern constructivist approach to careers (Hirschi & Dauwalder, 2015; Vondracek et al., 2010). It considers people's expectations, worries and actions about their professional futures without isolating them from their socio-economic, cultural and historical context. This engenders a greater acceptance of rapid changes in the working environment and overcomes the idea that career development is linear, follows a pre-ordered sequence of stages, and has a normative value for everyone.

The person–environment relationship is not conceived in terms of congruence (how people fit into work) but rather as an active mutual interaction (Savickas, 2002), as an active process that individuals can control through the attribution of meaning to their own real experiences, the memories of past experiences and their future hopes. In this way, a subjective path is constructed, linked to all life roles (not only work roles) and based on three main factors: vocational personality, career adaptability and life themes.

Savickas (2002) redefines vocational personality by concentrating on the fact that interests, values and personal characteristics (e.g., those diagnosed by Holland's RIASEC inventory) are descriptions of a totality of temporary qualities that are only significant in relationship to the socio-cultural context that determines them. Therefore, rather than considering personal traits as objective characteristics or genuine predictors of the match between individual and job, it is better to look at how people can use this information about themselves to guide their personal histories in a desired direction and adapt to the sequence of changes brought by the context in which they live (while remaining faithful to themselves and recognizable to others).

Interest in the self and its development over time is represented in the notion of career adaptability, which replaces the career maturity used by Super (1980). Career adaptability indicates the individual's capacity and resources to face vocational developmental tasks imposed by society, professional transitions, and the requirements to adapt to changes in work and non-work roles. It represents both a capacity for resilience (resisting changes and career disruptions) and an active strategy of self-control that allow the individual to link self-concept to work roles, thus constructing a satisfying professional career. To do so, the individual should develop four components of adaptability: (1) concern (interest in one's own future as a worker), (2) control (agency and personal responsibility for one's own future), (3) curiosity (exploration of possible selves and future scenarios), and (4) confidence (belief in being able to achieve one's own aspirations).

The last of these factors concerns the narrative of events experienced in a given context (place, time and roles carried out). Recounting a career history brings out life themes defined as typical thematic patterns (events, actions carried out, typical relationships) that make up the common thread of the personal histories narrated, and reveal the meanings at the core of the choices made. Life themes reflect the individual's needs, dominant worries and self-concept attributes. In other words, the content of the individual's work history is also selected regarding current objectives perceived as important, and can reveal why the individual intends to build a particular professional development. They can therefore be extrapolated to become the basis for future career choices. Basically, awareness of one's own life themes helps in understanding why one should aim at a particular job. This achieves full satisfaction when it leads to the enactment of the individual's own self and the development of one's life themes in a given area of employment.

8.3 Readiness to Choose a Career

The important phase of preparation for choosing a career is explored through the construct of career readiness. This indicates to what extent a person is capable of exploring his/her work situation and aspirations with the goal of mastering knowledge of the world of work and of specific professional development that fits his/her expectations. To be career-ready means mastering knowledge (academic, technical and workplace knowledge) and self-concept, being committed to life-long learning and being responsive to exploring and planning new career paths.

Various aspects of career readiness have been considered. For instance, Stringer, Kerpelman and Skorikov (2011) consider three dimensions in the personal commitment to career construction that can be linked to Savickas' (2002) notion of career adaptability. These are indicators of being career-ready: (1) career decision-making (knowing how to make decisions), (2) career planning (using active strategies to outline career goals), and (3) career confidence (belief in the possibility of achieving the expected goals). Their longitudinal study (Stringer et al., 2011) on students in the passage into work or university demonstrates that such dimensions are directly related and can be used to determine how to create a career identity. Career confidence grows in a linear fashion in the course of the transition from high school to work. Young adults commit to the activity of exploration, progressively gain confidence about the possible choices and learn how to make their hopes consistent with actual working reality. Although positively linked to confidence, career planning, according to this perspective, remains relatively more stable, probably because people are not sure of their career paths and delay planning while waiting to acquire new experiences in other contexts. Career indecision, by contrast, tends to decrease rapidly at the beginning of the transition and more slowly successively.

In a longitudinal study on high school students, Hirschi, Niles, and Akos (2011) demonstrate how engagement in career choices (defined as self- and environmental exploration and active career planning) is linked to social support (particularly from teachers, parents and friends) in clarifying goals and self-efficacy. Individuals with high self-efficacy are more optimistic about their careers and more open to adjusting their plans, since they are more confident of their ability to succeed. Goal clarity (defined as level of specification and goal decidedness) is also linked to more effective career exploration and planning. Creed et al.'s (2011) longitudinal study of Australian students demonstrated the link between goal orientation and career. Students who define their goals more clearly tend to be more focused on labour market information and more flexible in defining their future plans. Taber and Blankemeyer (2015) concentrate on the future dimensions of self-concept outlining the construct of the future work self (what a person hopes to become in the future). Their research with university students demonstrates that future work self-salience predicts proactive career behaviour (defined as career planning, skills developments and networking) and is linked to the resources of career adaptability. Thus, people should be made aware of this future perspective and encouraged to foster it during the transition phases from school to work or of return to work after periods of unemployment.

Career readiness also has notable practical relevance since it represents an important element to implement in career development support initiatives, making them more effective (Sampson et al., 2013). Box 8.2 identifies some key personal and social barriers to benefit from career readiness preparation programmes. Such obstacles should be treated with career interventions (Sampson et al., 2013) aimed at reducing the risk that people do not take direct responsibility for their choices; develop negative perceptions about their abilities and interests; are poorly motivated to face the effort of the process of choosing; use an incomplete set of information about the reality of work and about themselves too early; and 'endlessly' prolong the search for information (e.g., on the internet) without having rational criteria to evaluate the various options.

Box 8.2:   Obstacles in the use of support interventions for career readiness

The main factors of low readiness in the subject of career preparation interventions are summarized in the following list (based on Sampson et al., 2013, p. 100):

1. inadequate personal characteristics (e.g., a tendency to suffer from acute and/or chronic negative thoughts and feelings, reduced linguistic aptitude and proficiency and limited IT skills);

2. acute or chronic external barriers (e.g., excessive family pressure or conditions of limited availability of social and economic resources);

3. limited knowledge of self, options, and decision-making procedures;

4. limited familiarity with IT resources for careers;

5. unrealistic expectations of being able to make the 'perfect choice' immediately;

6. inappropriate expectations about career services;

7. unsuccessful experiences in previous career interventions.

For example, Hirschi and Läge (2008) studied the effects of a support service on career choices during sessions dedicated to developing (1) career decision-making knowledge (self-knowledge and occupational knowledge), (2) decision-making skills (generic information processing skills), and (3) executive processing (meta-cognitions in terms of self-talk, self-awareness, and control). The outcomes of the course were measured with a scale of career decidedness (level of commitment to choices), career planning, career exploration and vocational identity (personal interests, strengths and values). The results demonstrate that even three months after the intervention, career readiness was enhanced on all four dimensions used to measure it.

On the whole, studies into career readiness remark on the need for vocational research to render the notion of human agency operational. They stress the subjective resources and competencies that draw people into forecasting their future and using self-reflection to conceive and attain objectives not only in the phase of starting a career, but also in the organizational life course.

This perspective aligns with studies on self-management of careers (Akkermans et al., 2013). Attitudes of openness to the future and of optimism and skills for initial career planning are substantially the same as those (e.g., reflective, communicative, social and behavioural competencies) that serve in successfully facing subsequent career phases and are considered as important as those required to perform a specific job.

This attention given to the development of skills could represent a point of convergence (Arnold, 2011) between the approaches of vocational psychology and those of work, organization and personnel psychology, which are more directly focussed on: (1) the organizational career, seen as the expression of the worker's social exchange processes with his/her specific context; and (2) career management skills or competencies. A classic example is Nicholson's approach (1984), which concentrates on a cycle of recurrent phases to self-manage a career, not linked to age but to competence in facing career-related tasks (preparation, encounter, adjustment and stabilization) for adjusting to new circumstances or trying to adapt the job to one's needs (career role innovation).

The notion of career competencies (King, 2004) refers to a skill set for self-managing working and learning experiences to achieve a desired career. They include proactivity; self-reflection; motivation reflection (e.g., investment in skills training) and work exploration capacities; career directedness (planning and taking actions); networking (influence capacity); and boundary management (balancing the demands of work and non-work domains). Without such competencies, it is difficult to develop an efficacious plan both at the beginning and in the course of a career. Consequently, individuals often become discouraged with their career progress, disillusioned with their job situations and worried about personal obsolescence.

8.4 Empowering Career Readiness: Two Promising Perspectives

The development of readiness in creating satisfying career paths over time can be faced from two different perspectives. The first comes indirectly from social cognitive career theory. Lent (2013) proposes integrating career planning activities into the framework of life preparedness. This is defined as a healthy state of vigilance and responsiveness in knowing how to respond to uncertainty and unforeseen events and as the ability to find opportunities, activate proactive strategies to manage setbacks and advocate for one's own career-life future. People should also be prepared to face obstacles and changes, bearing them in mind at least because of events that might happen. The process of career planning, too often limited to the search for a rational match between the individual and the environment, is thus enriched, and career adaptability becomes more effective. Lent (2013) emphasizes that career readiness has been explored, identifying a set of attitudes and attributes of the self that help the planning of an attractive career. This is undoubtedly important when there are notable individual differences in the possession of such attributes. Nevertheless, it is equally important to develop coping skills and strategies, or rather a set of capabilities (cognitive, behavioural, social, and emotional), to be used in overcoming difficulties. Developing life preparedness (also defined as resilience-building) means developing: (1) the ability to handle barriers and unforeseen events that might hinder the decisions to be taken; and (2) the ability to identify valid social support to implement projects.

The second perspective refers to life designing (Nota & Rossier, 2015), a programme of research and vocational interventions focused on the life trajectories that an individual progressively constructs. Concrete interactions in different contexts also contribute to the construction of the self, accomplished with modalities of dialogue and self-reflection in the course of life (Guichard, 2009). Such modalities are shaped by having the knowledge and skills with which to outline and manage one's own career history and face the developmental tasks, vocational traumas and frequent occupational transitions that characterize present-day situations. It focuses on developing capabilities to reflect on oneself and one's resources and to foresee current and future changes. Hirschi and Dauwalder (2015) insist on the necessity from early on of promoting proactive career behaviour, strengthening people's readiness and resources to construct and manage their working lives. Consequently, career preparation interventions should aim to develop:

1. human capital resources (e.g., education and work-relevant knowledge and skills);
2. social resources (e.g., networking and social support);
3. psychological resources (e.g., attitudes, motivation and affective resources in relationship to work roles);
4. career identity resources (e.g., self-awareness as a future worker; knowledge of one's interests, goals and values: 'at the core of career identity is the question: who am I and how is my work meaningful to me?' (Hirschi & Dauwalder, 2015, p. 35)).

Closely related to the concept of career identity resources, career anchors (Schein, 1990) represent another way to consider personal resources for career construction and management. They are defined as a set of self-perceived talents, values, motives, needs and attitudes established during the first stages of a working career as a learning outcome of past experience. They are significant because they not only influence the initial occupational choice – or the move from one job to another – but also serve to guide, stabilize and integrate a person's career path, providing continuity of individual identity over time. As a result, career anchors can contribute to people's responsiveness to self-managing their career paths.

8.5 The Career Decision-Making Process

Since career paths are becoming less predictable and require greater flexibility, people now find it more difficult to plan their future and make informed decisions. Three broad categories of factors that increase the complexity of the career decision-making process are:

1. *contextual*: macro-social factors that reduce access to decision-making processes such as social origins, quality of anticipatory socialization, gender role, ethnicity; unequal social support availability from family, peer groups, guidance and other information sources;
2. *personal*: perception of being unable to make ideal choices immediately, but having to reach compromises; anxiety about the risk of making mistakes in an important life phase;

3. *task-related*: the high number of alternatives to choose from, at least for those who have had the chance to pursue prestigious university studies; having to weigh up at the same time subjective elements (wishes and preferences, self-attributes, acquired skills, etc.) and objective ones referring to both the self (e.g., type, quality and period of education/training, school results and qualifications, pre-work experiences, etc.) and external context (e.g., labour market opportunities); and obsolescence of information about work contexts that change rapidly after the initial decisions.

Amir, Gati and Kleiman (2008) have developed a taxonomy of three major difficulties or barriers to career choice that can be used to assess their different natures before and during the actual decision-making process. Table 8.2, based on Gati, Krausz and Osipow (1996) and Amir, Gati and Kleiman (2008, p. 284), presents these difficulty clusters, each including different categories of difficulty and their sources.

Being aware of a decision-making difficulty does not necessarily mean a loss of self-efficacy or confidence to overcome contingent obstacles. For some individuals the difficulty actually creates a stimulating challenge, for others, it represents an incentive to correct their limits, for yet others it means a push towards better choice preparation by developing their career readiness (e.g., by searching for

Table 8.2: Taxonomy of career decision-making difficulties

Prior to the process	During the process	
Lack of readiness	Lack of information	Inconsistent information
• Lack of motivation (low volition and engagement in decisions) • Indecisiveness (general and systematic difficulty in making decisions in various life contexts) • Dysfunctional beliefs (distorted perception of careers, irrational expectations and dysfunctional thoughts about the decision-making process)	• About the career decision-making process (lack of knowledge about the steps in the career decision-making process) • About the self (low self-efficacy perceptions and lack of information about career preferences, abilities and skills) • About the labour market and occupations (lack of knowledge about career alternatives and their characteristics) • On how to obtain information (difficulties in searching for information and getting help from others about career decision-making)	• Unreliable information (contradictory information about themselves and possible occupations) • Internal conflicts (difficulty in reaching compromises on incompatible factors that individuals consider important) • External conflicts (disagreements between personal preferences or opinions and those of significant others)

more accurate information), and, finally, yet other people might find a more logical justification for a reasonable compromise between different career objectives.

It is therefore possible to reach a satisfactory decision by accurately distinguishing a correct decisive direction ('a good decision modality') from the result of the decision process itself. The latter may, however, prove unsatisfactory due to other factors beyond the individual's control, such as excessive time pressure, reduced opportunities in the economic context or lack of social support. But how can this complex obstacle course be explored?

Almost all conceptual models divide the decision-making process into different phases, even though they identify different numbers of phases with different denominations. For example, Peterson et al. (2002) have conceived of career decision-making as a problem-solving task based on information processing skills focused on different domains and in different phases of the process. They have developed a cognitive information processing model for the systematic exploration of multiple options visualized as a pyramid.

At the base of the pyramid are self- and occupational knowledge, that is, people's awareness of their professional interests, values and skills, and knowledge of the main job characteristics and requirements needed to work. In the middle are skills for managing the five typical phases of the decision-making process (CASVE): *Communication* (being aware I need to make a choice); *Analysis* (understanding myself and my options); *Synthesis* (producing and narrowing my list of options); *Valuing* (prioritizing programmes of study or job alternatives); and *Executing* (implementing my choice). At the top of the pyramid is the executive processing domain, which has the meta-cognitive function of monitoring the decision-making process (e.g., a person can ask, 'How is the process working? What adjustments should I make?').

Hirschi and Läge have integrated the phases proposed by various decision-making models, outlining a sequential model composed of six phases:

> (1) becoming concerned about career decision-making (awareness), (2) generating possible career alternatives based on one's own interests, skills, and values through self- and environmental exploration, (3) reducing the career alternatives to a manageable number for more in-depth exploration, (4) deciding among a few alternatives, (5) confirming one's choice and building a commitment to it, and (6) being firmly decided and committed to a choice. (2007, p. 165)

Tests of this model have proved very promising (at least among Swiss students), although we should be careful about generalizing such phases, considering the notable inter-individual differences in managing each of the proposed steps.

The final career choice will depend on how much a person manages to evaluate such options in terms of advantages and disadvantages, while also being prepared to consider reasonable forms of compensation. It is, however, necessary to remember that vocational choice is a special case of decision-making under uncertainty (urgency, incomplete knowledge of employment options or personal capabilities). These issues can be addressed in a systematic and rational way, not subject to emotion influences, but people often tend to use mental shortcuts and simplification (based on gut feeling, rules of thumb and availability heuristics), by which they avoid accurately calculating the cost-benefit ratio of each decision option, as Kahneman (2003) explained by distinguishing between rational and intuitive modes of processing information and making decisions.

However, it is not necessarily true that the use of such heuristics always results in a wrong decision. Sometimes, career decisions have to be limited to being merely satisfactory since they are affected by a high number of factors not always under the person's control. The important thing is not to become stuck at the point of these acceptable choices, but to continue weighing one's own decisions to see how they are working, and engaging in periodic check-ups useful to provide for corrective adjustments or substantial changes to the career path initially undertaken.

Usually, the decision-making situation activates emotions and states of internal conflict in the face of alternatives. In general, there is a distinction between indecision (temporary, caused by one of the difficulties described in Table 8.2, but that can be quite easily resolved) and indecisiveness. The latter is a more severe condition, longer-lasting, that reoccurs in numerous decision-making occasions. Gati et al. (2012) recognize three major clusters of emotional and personality-related difficulties:

- pessimistic views (negative perceptions of work and career, low career decision-making self-efficacy, external locus of control);
- anxiety (pre-decision-making anxiety, uncertainty about the future, fear of personal involvement in decisions, worrying about the results);
- self-concept and identity (low self-esteem, uncrystallized identity, inadequate relationships with significant others).

In their longitudinal research on a heterogeneous sample of students and workers, Gati et al. (2012) demonstrate that pessimistic views can diminish over time. Therefore, early support interventions should be carried out to reduce such mistaken beliefs; extended counselling interventions might mitigate situations of decision-making strain (indecisiveness) and help self-concept adjustments.

In summary, it is not easy to proceed immediately toward the 'right' career decision. One must be aware of different contextual, task-related and personal factors that increase the complexity of choice and be able to recognize different types of obstacles regarding lack of readiness and poor or inconsistent information. It is therefore important to try early to overcome the cognitive aspects and phases of information processing for career decision-making in addition to emotional and personality-related difficulties. Furthermore, the belief that 'there is one career for me and I will choose it on the first shot' is misleading. Actually, career decisions can be seen as a long-term process of adaptation that involves arranging and rearranging information into a course of action and adjustment and changes that make it possible to build a satisfying career path.

8.6 Conclusion

The question that is the title of this chapter (Why did I choose that career path?) leads to various answers because of the increasing heterogeneity of career paths managed by current workers and future candidates to enter into the workforce. It is quite probable that the person asked will not give a short reply, but rather a narration of his/her original journey through the labour market, and more or less distant from the initial career development plan designed during their school/university preparation period.

Moreover, making a career choice takes on different meanings. It can be viewed, in some cases, as a rational and objective matching process between self-knowledge and occupational knowledge. But such a matching opportunity, entirely achieved in a single moment of life, becomes more and more rare. Conversely, career choices and career path building can be better represented as a long developmental process driven by self-concept/career anchors that is shaped progressively through the interaction between people and their environment. In this process, self-efficacy beliefs and skills learned to handle repeated transitions play an important function. In fact, such learning allows people to maintain an active role as creators of their actual and future lives within the constraints of personal and environmental factors, and prepares them better to accommodate unexpected events.

All in all, career paths are more easily interpreted as an original individual construction which expresses how people are trying to adapt working into their life projects. Career development thus requires strong career commitment and adaptability to cope with changes of self and situation over time. Therefore, a reasonable and comprehensive response to our initial question can be: 'I've created my career path focussing less on the choice of my initial job in favour of a wider vision of the significant goals I wanted to achieve in my life. So I've tried as much as possible to prepare the necessary resources to self-manage my career, not only the work aspects. I boosted two kinds of resources: (1) attitudes such as curiosity by exploring new social possibilities; confidence in achieving goals; concerns such as a positive attitude to the future, commitment to different activities and projects and not only on a particular job; and (2) career adaptive competencies to achieve self-efficacy, career and environmental explorations; define significant, achievable goals; and accomplish critical self-reflection for a better understanding of the longer-term consequences of ongoing experiences and decisions.'

What must be emphasized is the value of choice preparation (career readiness) as the acquisition of attitudes and skills useful not only in the initial phase of work-entry, but also for self-managing one's professional development over time.

Summary

This chapter has presented some characteristics of the vocational decision-making process, starting from the assumption that it nowadays has different features from those of the past. In fact, in a growing number of cases, vocational choice is no longer directed toward a single desired job but rather towards a career, constructed progressively as a sequence of work experiences over time. Various theoretical approaches have been presented, chosen not with the aim of giving a complete picture, but of emphasizing the different connotations of vocational choice made relevant by the concrete interaction between the individual and the current social context, and of which the individual should be made aware.

Vocational choice – in the most favourable cases – can be understood as a rational process of matching personal interests to the reality of work. It can, however, also be seen as a developmental process allowing the achievement of professional maturity and as a learning process leading to suitable attitudes and skills to negotiate entry into work. Above all, vocational choice is becoming more and more a personal path of career construction requiring different resources and skills to reach the desired goals. In particular, what is clear is the importance of the capacities for personal involvement and adaptability which guarantee career readiness in planning one's own future and taking meaningful decisions. These should be developed in the phases of choice preparation to allow the individual not only to face the decision-making process successfully, but also to self-manage subsequent stages in career development.

Discussion Points

1 Thinking again about the various theoretical approaches to the problem of vocational choices, do you find them to be true alternatives? Or do you think that each of them makes a useful contribution to understanding an individual career construction process? Justify the reasoning behind your point of view.
2 Given the complexity and instability of labour market demands, career choice has changed from a single event to a recurrent process leading to an individual path which is not easily standardizable. What does it mean today to be well-prepared to set up and manage a career?

Suggested Further Reading

Akkermans, J., Brenninkmeijer, V., Schaufeli, W. B., & Blonk, R. W. B. (2015). It's all about CareerSKILLS: Effectiveness of a career development intervention for young employees. *Human Resource Management, 54*(4), 533–551. This study analyses a career development intervention based on six career competencies (reflection on motivation, reflection on qualities, networking, self-profiling, work exploration, and career control) which aims to stimulate career self-management. It investigates the effectiveness of the CareerSKILLS program and the results allow the reader to reflect on the important practical implications of this method for improving career competencies.

Brown, D. and Associates (Eds.). (2002). *Career choice and development* (4th ed.). San Francisco: Jossey-Bass. This classic handbook presents a selection of the main modern and postmodern career development theories. Explanations of how people develop certain skills and personality characteristics and how these developments influence career decision-making in different contexts are extensively discussed. Thus the reader can easily recognize and compare the strengths and weaknesses of each theoretical approach.

Jaensch, V. K., Hirschi, A., & Freund, P. A. (2015) Persistent career indecision over time: Links with personality, barriers, self-efficacy, and life satisfaction. *Journal of Vocational Behavior, 91,* 122–133. This longitudinal study explores the persistence of career indecision, focusing on its stable component (indecisiveness) and its relationships with core self-evaluation and career-related variables (e.g., occupational self-efficacy, perceived career barriers). The results are important not only for distinguishing between state and stable indecision, but also to better finalize professional intervention, taking into account the different responsiveness of undecided (temporary indecision) and indecisive (stable indecision) individuals.

Nota, L., & Rossier, J. (Eds.). (2015). *Handbook of life design: From practice to theory and from theory to practice.* Göttingen: Hogrefe Publishing. This book aims to explain the theory and the main concepts of life design from a new perspective of career development and change, suitable for facing the current social and cultural transformation of work and career. It shows the results of research and interventions across different age-groups and social contexts, devoted to activating personal resources to construct meaningful life-careers.

References

Akkermans, J., Schaufeli, W. B., Brenninkmeijer, V., & Blonk, R. W. B. (2013). The role of career competencies in the Job Demands–Resources model. *Journal of Vocational Behavior, 83,* 356–366.

Amir, T., Gati, I., & Kleiman, T. (2008). Understanding and interpreting career decision-making difficulties. *Journal of Career Assessment, 16,* 281–309.

Arnold, J. (2011). Career concepts in the 21st century. *The Psychologist, 24,* 106–109.

Bandura, A. (1986). *Social foundations of thought and action: A social cognitive theory,* Englewood Cliffs, NJ: Prentice Hall.

Baruch, Y. (2004). Transforming careers: from linear to multidirectional career paths. Organizational and individual perspectives. *Career Development International, 9*(1), 58–73.

Blustein, D. L. (2011). A relational theory of working. *Journal of Vocational Behavior, 79,* 1–17.

Brown, A., Bimrose, J., Barnes, S. A., Kirpal, S., Grønning, T., & Dæhlen, M. (2010). *Changing patterns of working, learning and career development across Europe: Final report (EACEA/2007/07).* Brussels: Education, Audiovisual & Culture Executive Agency.

CEDEFOP (European Centre for the Development of Vocational Training) (2012). *Future skills supply and demand in Europe.* Luxembourg: Publications Office of the European Union.

Creed, P., Tilbury, C., Buys, N., & Crawford, M. (2011). The school to work transition for young people in state care: Perspectives from young people, careers and professionals. *Child and Family Social Work, 16*(3), 345–352.

Froehlich, D. E., Beausaert, S. A. J., Segers, M. S. R., & Gerken, M. (2014). Learning to stay employable. *Career Development International, 19*(5), 508–525.

Fuad, N. A. (2007). Work and vocational psychology: Theory, research, and applications. *Annual Review of Psychology, 58,* 543–564.

Gati, I., Asulin-Peretz, L., & Fisher, A. (2012). Emotional and personality-related career decision-making difficulties: A 3-year follow-up. *The Counseling Psychologist, 40*(1), 6–27.

Gati, I., Krausz, M., & Osipow, S. H. (1996). A taxonomy of difficulties in career decision making. *Journal of Counseling Psychology, 43,* 510–526.

Guichard, J. (2009). Self-constructing. *Journal of Vocational Behavior, 75,* 251–258.

Hirschi, A., & Dauwalder, J-P. (2015). Dynamics in career development: Personal and organizational perspectives. In L. Nota, & J. Rossier (Eds.), *Handbook of life design: From practice to theory and from theory to practice* (pp. 27–39). Göttingen: Hogrefe Publishing.

Hirschi, A., & Läge, D. (2007). The relation of secondary student's career choice readiness to a six-phase model of career decision-making. *Journal of Career Development, 34*(2), 164–191.

Hirschi, A., & Läge, D. (2008). Increasing the career choice readiness of young adolescents: An evaluation study. *International Journal for Educational and Vocational Guidance, 8,* 95–110.

Hirschi, A., Niles, S. G., & Akos, P. (2011). Engagement in adolescent career preparation: Social support, personality and the development of choice decidedness and congruence. *Journal of Adolescence, 34,* 173–182.

Holland, J. H. (1992). *Making vocational choices* (2nd ed.). Odessa, FL: Psychological Assessment Resources, Inc.

Holland, J. L., & Gottfredson, G. D. (1992). Studies of the exagonal model: An evaluation. *Journal of Vocational Behavior, 40,* 158–170.

Kahneman, D. (2003). A perspective on judgment and choice: Mapping bounded rationality. *American Psychologist, 58,* 697–720.

King, Z. (2004). Career self-management: Its nature, causes and consequences. *Journal of Vocational Behavior, 65,* 112–133.

Krumboltz, J. D. (1994). Improving career development theory from a social learning perspective. In M. L. Savickas, & R. W. Lent (Eds.), *Convergence in career development theories* (pp. 9–31). Palo Alto, CA: CPP Press.

Krumboltz, J. D. (2009). The happenstance learning theory. *Journal of Career Assessment, 17*(2), 135–154.

Lent, R. W. (2013). Career-life preparedness: Revisiting career planning and adjustment in the new workplace. *The Career Development Quarterly, 61,* 1–14.

Lent, R. W., Brown, S. D., & Hackett, G. (2002). Social cognitive career theory. In D. Brown & Associates (Eds.), *Career choice and development* (4th ed.) (pp. 255–311). San Francisco: Jossey-Bass.

Lent, R. W., Hackett, G., & Brown, S. D. (1996). A social cognitive framework for studying career choice and transition to work. *Journal of Vocational Education Research, 21,* 3–31.

Nauta, M. M. (2010). The development, evolution, and status of Holland's theory of vocational personalities: Reflections and future directions for counseling psychology. *Journal of Counseling Psychology, 57*(1),11–22.

Nicholson, N. (1984). A theory of work role transitions. *Administrative Science Quarterly, 29*(2), 172–191.

Nota, L., & Rossier, J. (Eds.). (2015). *Handbook of life design: From practice to theory and from theory to practice.* Göttingen: Hogrefe Publishing.

Patton, W., & McMahon, M. (2006). *Career development and system theory: Connecting theory and practice.* Rotterdam: Sense Publishers.

Peterson, G. W., Sampson, J. P. Jr., Lenz, J. G., & Reardon, R. C. (2002). Becoming career problem solvers and decision makers: A cognitive information processing approach. In D. Brown & Associates (Eds.), *Career choice and development* (4th ed.) (pp. 312–369). San Francisco: Jossey-Bass.

Roberts, K. (1995). *Youth employment in modern Britain.* Oxford: Oxford University Press.

Roberts, K. (2009). Opportunity structures then and now. *Journal of Education and Work, 22*(5), 355–368.

Sampson, J.P. Jr., McClain, M-C., Musch, E., & Reardon, R. C. (2013). Variables affecting readiness to benefit from career interventions. *The Career Development Quarterly, 61,* 98–109.

Savickas, M. L. (2002). Career construction: A developmental theory of vocational behavior. In D. Brown & Associates (Eds.), *Career choice and development* (4th ed.) (pp. 149–205). San Francisco: Jossey-Bass.

Schein, E. H. (1990). *Career anchors: Discovering your real values.* San Francisco: Jossey-Bass Pfeiffer.

Stringer, K., Kerpelman, J., & Skorikov, V. (2011). Career preparation: A longitudinal, process-oriented examination. *Journal of Vocational Behavior, 79,* 158–169.

Super, D. E. (1980). A life-span, life-space approach to career development. *Journal of Vocational Behavior, 16,* 282–298.

Super, D. E., Savickas, M. L., & Super, C. M. (1996). The life-span, life-space approach to careers. In D. Brown, L. Brooks, & Associates (Eds.), *Career choice & development* (3rd ed.) (pp. 121–178). San Francisco: Jossey-Bass.

Taber, B. J., & Blankemeyer, M. (2015). Future work self and career adaptability in the prediction of proactive career behaviors. *Journal of Vocational Psychology, 86,* 20–27.

Vondracek, F. W., Gomez Fereira, J. A., & Ribeiro Dos Santos, E. J. (2010). Vocational behavior and development in times of social change: New perspectives for theory and practice. *International Journal for Educational and Vocational Guidance, 10,* 125–138.

Watts, A. G. (2006). *Career development learning and employability.* Heslington, UK: Higher Education Academy.

PART II

ORGANIZATION-FOCUSED

How Do We Get New Entrants 'On Board'? Organizational Socialization, Psychological Contracts, and Realistic Job Previews

Allison M. Ellis and Talya N. Bauer

9

Overview

Organizational socialization is a critical time when new employees 'learn the ropes' at their new organization and go from being organizational 'outsiders' to organizational 'insiders' over the course of their first year on a new job. Individual differences exist and research finds that more proactive individuals are more successful. In addition, organizations that are able to help new employees navigate this time successfully are more likely to benefit from a workforce that is more satisfied, more committed, and less likely to leave the organization. The Five C's model (which focuses on compliance, clarity, connection, confidence, and culture) (Bauer, 2011) characterizes different levels of socialization and onboarding programmes from those most basic to those that are more sophisticated. This chapter will also review the organizational socialization process in detail; including a look at what organizations and new employees can do to facilitate successful adjustment, and what short- and long-term outcomes can be expected as a result of these efforts. Finally, we review current and emerging challenges for organizational socialization, including onboarding virtual teams, mitigating stress for new employees, and considering the potentially darker sides of socialization. Further readings, a case study, and a best practice checklist are also included.

9.1 Introduction

A key function of organizations is getting new employees onboard and up to speed as quickly and efficiently as possible so they can begin contributing to the organization. This process is often called onboarding, or organizational socialization, and refers to the process by which 'an individual acquires the social knowledge and skills necessary to assume an organizational role' (Van Maanen & Schein, 1977, p. 3). Importantly, the process of organizational socialization goes beyond learning about

An Introduction to Work and Organizational Psychology: An International Perspective,
Third Edition. Edited by Nik Chmiel, Franco Fraccaroli and Magnus Sverke.
© 2017 John Wiley & Sons, Ltd. Published 2017 by John Wiley & Sons, Ltd.

the technical aspects of one's new job or role (i.e., formal job or position within the organization), towards developing an understanding of the culture of the organization, the unwritten norms for how one is to behave and interact with others, and finding one's place in the social fabric of the new organization (Chao et al., 1994). Simply put, organizational socialization is about transforming from an organizational 'outsider' to an organizational 'insider' (Louis, 1980), and this transition occurs not only for young adults entering their first job, but any time there is a significant change in the context within which one is doing work; for instance, when one is promoted or changes roles, or when one transitions to bridge employment at the end of their career. During this time new employees learn about their new role, coworkers, and the organization. It is also a time when new employees form their first impressions of their new organization and decide whether or not they will be a good fit, whether the job is what they thought it would be, and whether or not they will stay in the long term with the organization. As such, the time between an employees' first day on the job through becoming a true 'organizational insider' is critical and typically lasts one year in duration (Bauer & Erdogan, 2011).

In fact, research suggests that half of all new hourly employees will leave their organization in their first year; and half of outside senior hires will fail to effectively onboard during this same time period (Bauer, 2011). This is costly for organizations and individual employees alike, as both invest significant time and energy into coming together. Research also shows that those with more positive organizational socialization experiences are more likely to be satisfied with their job, more committed to their organization, and are less likely to leave the organization (Bauer et al., 2007; Saks & Ashforth, 1997).

One of the dominant theoretical themes in organizational socialization and onboarding research is a focus on uncertainty reduction. Being new is a stressful time as noted by Berger and Calabrese decades ago (1975). New employees are facing a new work environment, including new colleagues, a new manager and new work tasks. They may wonder, 'Will I fit in with others?', 'Will I be able to learn my new job?', and 'Will my boss like me and help me?' Thus, a central goal of any organizational socialization process is providing helpful and useful resources to newcomers that reduce ambiguity and facilitate greater understanding of their roles and their new organizations.

The organizational socialization process is not a one-off event, but a process of learning and adjusting that can take up to one year after an employee starts in a new role, as depicted in Figure 9.1. However, research shows that events and experiences that occur within an employee's first 30–90 days are especially important. For example, having a new employees' desk and equipment ready on the first day, or being welcomed by one's supervisor send signals to the new employee that they are valued and their arrival is important. Beyond that, a number of other factors play a role in the effective onboarding, or socialization, of new employees.

The following sections will cover the features of a successful onboarding programme, what organizations and newcomers themselves might do to facilitate the socialization process, and the outcomes that can be expected from the socialization process. It makes sense to think of the onboarding process as a special period

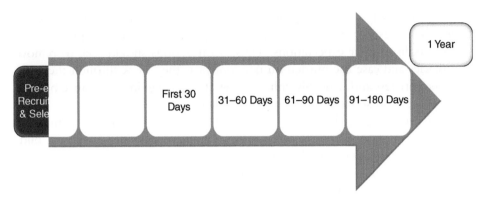

Figure 9.1: The socialization process unfolds over a newcomer's first year

Note. Darker grey boxes indicate the more intense socialization time periods such that pre-entry and the first 30 days tend to be more intense transitions than the period between 180 days to 1 year post-entry.

Source: Ellis, Bauer & Erdogan (2015).

of training. As such, factors such as what new employees need, what they know, and how they feel will also influence their learning during the socialization/onboarding process. Finally, we discuss current and emerging issues facing organizations and researchers related to organizational socialization.

9.2 What Are the Features of a Successful Onboarding Programme?

9.2.1 The five C's model of onboarding

There are five factors which relate to onboarding, which were originally described by Bauer (2011). These include compliance, clarity, connection, confidence, and culture, the five C's.

1. *Compliance* refers to the on-the-job requirements such as tax forms, legal paperwork, and employee identification (e.g., employment paperwork, government-issued identification) which must be in place as part of the onboarding process for legal and logistical reasons, which vary across industries and countries. Organizations must engage in these activities but there is variance in how strategically they engage in them. For example, is paperwork available prior to the first day so it can be completed and turned in rather than spending time at the initial orientation going over it? Do new employees spend 2 minutes or 2 hours waiting to get their badges and work stations assigned to them? The way these things are approached send signals to the new employee about how much their organization values them and how committed they are to ensuring the new employee is successful. The more strategically organizations can focus attention early on in a newcomer's tenure, the better, as compliance must be

done but it only serves as a problem if not implemented well. In other words, newcomers expect smooth sailing, so if they experience an easy process, this only confirms their expectations. Thus, organizations should seek to remove obstacles and ease the burden on newcomers as they work through the compliance process and generally enhance how they engage in compliance but this is not the most strategic aspect of onboarding.

2. *Clarification* refers to how much information and understanding a new employee has. Organizations can influence this by providing information, assigning buddies or mentors to new employees, or having materials available so that newcomers can gather information. Similarly, newcomers can influence this by proactive behaviours such as how much information they seek and the questions they ask. For example, Morrison (1993) collected data from 240 new staff accountants and found that those who sought out more information by asking questions of their colleagues and supervisors reported greater mastery and understanding of their new role, a greater understanding of the organizational culture, and felt more socially integrated with others in their workplace. Whether acquiring information through formal socialization programmes or informally through reaching out to others, the more ability to clarify what is expected and garner a greater understanding of how things work in a new organization, the better adjusted newcomers will be and the higher their on-the-job performance.

3. *Connection* refers to how well integrated and accepted the new employee feels within their new organization. Early on, this is based on how welcomed they feel. And as time goes on, relationship building influences this as well (Ashford & Black, 1996). Organizations can affect this feeling of connection by sending signals that they value diversity and individual identity (Ashforth, 2012), assigning buddies or mentors, and creating affinity groups. For example, at Google, thousands of special interest groups (SIGs) exist. They range from formal interest groups such as Google Women Engineers and Greyglers for older employees to more informal groups bound together by a love of bowling, flea markets, or Dooglers who bring their dogs to work at Google. These groups range in size and scope and allow employees to find their own 'micro' groups in a very large organization. In addition, new employees can influence how connected they feel by how engaged they are with joining such groups or how social they are at work. One study of new healthcare employees showed that newcomers who developed a high quality relationship with their leader and had coworkers on whom they could rely for support and advice, reported better socialization, less role stress, and were less burned out compared to those who did not have the same social resources (Thomas & Lankau, 2009).

4. *Confidence* refers to how much the new employee feels they can succeed at the tasks associated with their new role. Confidence ensures that when setbacks occur or things do not go exactly as planned, newcomers will be able to bounce back and keep moving forward. The higher the degree the organization can help the newcomer understand what it is expected and enhance their role clarity and support them as they attempt to learn new things, the more confident new employees

should be. In addition, new employees come with their own unique levels of core self-esteem and self-efficacy and approaches to new and challenging assignments, which also influence how they feel in terms of confidence level. Bauer and colleagues (2007) conducted a meta-analysis of 70 socialization studies and found that newcomer self-efficacy was positively related to job performance, newcomers' intentions to remain with their organization, and was negatively related to actual turnover. Generally, the more confident the newcomers are, the more effective and positive they are in their new jobs over time.

5. *Culture* refers to the organizational culture of the organization they are joining. Much like individuals, organizations vary. A great deal of the onboarding process is communicating to new employees the organization's mission, values, and helping them understand the way things are done in the organization. This influences their outcomes and also helps them understand if they are a good fit for the organizations which is related to onboarding success. As organizations evolve, so do their cultures, so it is imperative that the stories, rituals and artifacts are updated over time as well.

9.3 The Socialization Process

9.3.1 What do organizations do to onboard new employees?

Organizations with the most successful socialization programmes are those that take into consideration new employees' experiences from the moment a vacancy is posted until they are fully integrated with the organization at the end of one year. Figure 9.2 highlights some specific strategies that organizations may use to ensure the socialization process is successful.

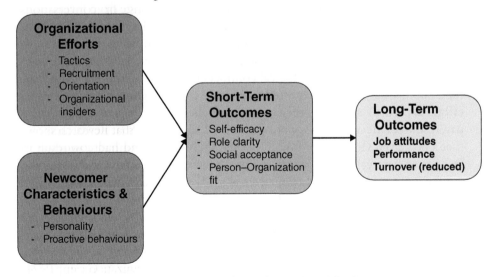

Figure 9.2: Antecedents and outcomes of organizational socialization.
Source: Ellis, Bauer & Erdogan (2015a).

- *Recruitment*: Even before an employee joins an organization, they are forming impressions of the organization: what the organization values, whether they would be a good fit with the organization, and what it would be like to work there. Therefore, the recruitment phase during which the organization and potential new employee interact and assess one another is an important time that will shape a new employee's expectations and perceptions about the organization. While historically researchers and those in practice have thought of recruitment and onboarding separately, more and more these are being seen as aspects of the same process as the recruitment process is the organizational reality and expectation setting frame for newcomers before they enter their organizations.

- *Realistic job previews*: Realistic job previews are one specific recruitment technique that has received research attention. Realistic job previews (RJPs) provide both favourable and unfavourable information about the role, thereby adjusting a candidate's expectations of the role in line with reality (Rynes, 1991). For instance, a realistic job preview might include providing job candidates a realistic idea of what the job entails, such as the benefits of the role and what resources are going to be available, as well as the challenges or difficulties that can be expected in a given role, so they are better able to self-select into organizations to which they feel they would be successful. Research shows that when candidates are provided with RJPs, they are less likely to drop out of the recruitment process, and, once at work, they have lower turnover and higher performance (Phillips, 1998).

- *Expectations and psychological contracts*: As we previously noted, by the time a newcomer starts on their first day of work, they will have already interacted with the organization a number of times; for instance, through interviews, compensation (i.e., wage, salary, benefits) negotiations, or conversations related to the logistics of starting at the organization. Each interaction gives the newcomer small but important pieces of information that serve as the basis for the development of the psychological contract between the newcomer and the organization. Psychological contracts represent the beliefs individuals hold about what they are expected to provide to the organization (e.g., time, effort, expertise) and what they expect that they will receive in return (e.g., pay, resources, development opportunities) (Rousseau, 1989). Research shows that a perceived violation or breach of this psychological contract can result in feelings of betrayal and anger on the part of newcomers and can damage the employment relationship (Lapointe et al., 2013). On the other hand, when employees feel that their experiences and the things they receive from the organization (e.g., training, high quality relationship with their supervisor) are in line with their expectations, they are more likely to engage in the socialization process more fully and experience better outcomes such as greater role clarity and understanding of the organization's values (Bauer & Green, 1994; Delobbe, Cooper-Thomas, & De Hoe, 2015). If RJPs are in place and accurately reflect organizational realities, met expectations should be higher.

- *Orientations.* One of the most common ways that organizations attempt to help new employees understand their new organizations is the new employee orientation given early on in their tenure with the firm. New employee orientations typically refer to formal, organization-led training programmes in which new employees are given information about their new job and work environment, as well as the larger organization (Klein & Weaver, 2000). Orientations are often held the first day or first week for new employees. Research finds that new employees find orientations helpful (Louis, Posner, & Powell, 1983) but they also report that so much information at once can be challenging to digest. Thus, some organizations hold an initial orientation programme early on and have either follow-up conversations to clarify key information or another orientation session later on once the new employee has had a chance to acclimatize to their new organization. Orientation trainings should seek to focus on helping new employees understand the five C's of onboarding and they tend to vary in terms of how much they focus on each of them.
- *Organizational socialization tactics.* Organizations vary a great deal in the degree to which they have formal or more informal onboarding tactics (Saks et al., 1997; 2007). All of these things, called organizational socialization tactics, influence how adjusted new employees feel as they join their organizations. For example, does the organization hire individuals one at a time or in a large group? Do they have formal training procedures or do new employees learn on-the-job? Are mentors formally assigned to newcomers? How empowered are new employees? Research shows that socialization programmes that are more structured and formalized are related to better adjustment outcomes for newcomers (Saks et al., 2007).
- *Organizational insiders.* While much of our chapter has focused on the importance of the new employee, they are not the only ones affected by onboarding. Research shows that organizational insiders both influence and are influenced by newcomers (Allen et al., 1999; Allen, Eby, Chao, & Bauer, in press; Kammeyer-Mueller et al., 2013). Managers and peers are important in terms of influencing the five C's of onboarding. For example, they influence how much new information is given to newcomers. They influence how welcomed they feel. And they influence the organizational culture. Thus, one primary way that organizations influence the onboarding process is through organizational insiders. When thinking about onboarding programmes, this is an important factor to keep in mind. Figure 9.3 presents the manager's perspective on the onboarding process.

9.3.2 What do new employees do to 'learn the ropes'?

If you've ever started at a new job, you might recall that you yourself looked for opportunities to learn about your new organization or role, or perhaps you found a colleague or two that you could go to for questions and advice. Indeed, research supports the idea that the organizational socialization process is a dual process in

---

Onboarding New Employees

Best Practices Checklist for Fostering Connection

☐ *Make the first day special for new employees.* Meet with them, make sure someone takes them to lunch, and that the atmosphere is welcoming. This simple connection matters for success over the long run.

☐ *Recognize that the manager plays a special role.* Make a special effort to connect with the new employee on their first day of the job even if it is just to say hello and welcome.

☐ *Check in with new employees to make sure they have what they need on their first day* as well as a week later when new questions may have arisen.

☐ *Remember new employees are anxious to make a good impression. Tell them how happy you are to have them join your team.* Doing this early on has a much bigger positive impact than waiting until later.

☐ New employees need to learn specific rules and procedures. *The most effective way to do this is to get them comfortable with the other best practices below so they are receptive and able to focus on learning.*

☐ *Be consistent with onboarding practices for new employees.* Some issues about your organization may be 'old news' to you, but it's all new to them. Have a written onboarding plan in place and enact it every time.

☐ *Make sure your values and culture are projected in how you treat and greet new employees.* Stories tell who you are.

☐ *Establish time-based milestones to check in with new employees to see how things are going.* For example, 30-, 60-, 90-, and 180-day milestones are good markers to consider.

Figure 9.3: Best practices during onboarding

Source: Talya N. Bauer, re:Work blog post which originally appeared on March 4, 2016 on https://rework. withgoogle.com/blog/connections-onboarding-and-the-need-to-belong/.

which both the organization and the new employee have an important role to play. Scholars have referred to this as the *interactionist perspective* and it suggests that while the organization may provide certain opportunities to help new employees adjust to their new role, it is up to the newcomers to take advantage of those opportunities, or in some cases create new opportunities for learning (Reichers, 1987). Certain individual features can make this easier for the newcomers:

- *Personality*: Not surprisingly, there are some individuals who are more likely to seek out opportunities to learn about their new organization or take advantage of chances to get to know their colleagues. For example, those high on *proactive personality*, which refers to the tendency to take action to bring about change in one's environment, are more likely to be successful in the socialization process (Seibert, Kraimer, & Crant, 2001). These individuals are not afraid to seek out information from others, they are willing to take steps to develop their own skills and relationships, and they are more motivated to learn. Those who are higher on *extraversion* and *openness to experience* also tend to experience better adjustment to their new roles. Extraversion refers to the tendency to be social, gregarious and assertive, while openness to experience is characterized by curiousness, intelligence and willingness for adventure (Wanberg & Kammeyer-Mueller, 2000). Research supports that those high on *self-efficacy*, which refers to those who believe they are capable of being successful in their new role, also tend to have better adjustment outcomes, such as higher job satisfaction and organizational commitment, in part because they are more willing to seek out information and feedback from others (Gruman, Saks, & Zweig, 2006).

- *Proactive behaviours*: New employees' willingness to take initiative to learn about their role, their colleagues, and the larger organization is an important ingredient in successful socialization. Researchers have found that there are some specific behaviours that new employees can engage in that help them get up to speed more quickly. First, new employees can *seek out information* and *feedback* from their fellow colleagues or their supervisor (Ashford & Black, 1996). New employees who actively seek out information can better understand how their role is related to other roles in the organization, or what the expectations are for how employees interact in the organization (Bauer et al., 2007). Those who seek feedback can achieve more clarity with regard to their role and understand whether they need to make adjustments in their work. In both cases, one added benefit is that through asking for information and feedback, new employees are interacting with others in the organization to a greater extent and this provides opportunities to get to know others and begin to develop meaningful relationships with them. Indeed, other forms of newcomer proactive behaviour are focused specifically on *building relationships, networking,* and *socializing* with other insiders in the organization and have been found to predict higher job satisfaction among newcomers (Cooper-Thomas et al., 2014; Wanberg & Kammeyer-Mueller, 2000).

9.3.3 Outcomes of adjustment

The final components of the socialization process are the adjustment outcomes. By examining certain outcomes we can understand how successful the socialization process has been.

- *Short-term outcomes*: Short-term outcomes can occur early on in the socialization process and can be thought of as indicators of successful adjustment. Research conducted by Bauer and colleagues (2007) reviewed 70 studies on organizational socialization and found support for three key short-term outcomes. The first is *role clarity* which refers to knowing what is expected of you in your role; the second is self-*efficacy* or being confident in yourself that you can perform your job successfully; and, the third is *social acceptance* or feeling like you belong and have friends at your organization. Other research has also identified *perceived fit*, or believing that your values and goals are a match to those of the organization, and *knowledge of organizational culture,* meaning an understanding of the organization's norms and way of doing things, as additional short-term outcomes of the socialization process (Cooper-Thomas, Van Vianen, & Anderson, 2004; Chao et al., 1994, respectively). These outcomes map onto the five C's of onboarding discussed earlier.

- *Long-term outcomes*: Long-term outcomes of the socialization process include better job attitudes and more effective newcomer behaviours. For instance, effective socialization programmes are related to increased *job satisfaction, organizational commitment, organizational identification* and reduced *intentions to leave the organization* (Ashforth & Saks, 1996; Bauer et al., 2007; Saks et al., 2007). At the same time, employees who are well adjusted to their new roles and organizations are more likely to show higher levels of job performance both in the form of completing assigned work tasks as well as helping fellow coworkers and colleagues (Bauer et al., 2007). Finally, research supports that those who report more positive socialization experiences are less likely to turnover or exit the organization (Griffin & Clarke, 2011).

9.4   Current Issues in Organizational Socialization

Although we have learned a great deal about the factors that make for a successful onboarding programme, the workforce and work environments continue to change, which introduces new challenges and requires new thinking about how to best manage this critical time for new employees. The following reviews three current issues in organizational socialization: (1) virtual onboarding, (2) mitigating stress for newcomers, and (3) the potential dark sides of socialization.

9.4.1   Virtual onboarding

Increasingly, organizations are adopting virtual working arrangements that are made possible by better technology. While these arrangements can provide greater access to talent across the globe, and important flexibility to workers managing multiple home and work demands, one challenge that virtual arrangements present is the ability to effectively onboard new employees. Specifically, how do technology-mediated communication channels like email, videoconferencing, and instant messaging change the way orientations can be delivered or how willing new employees are to reach out to colleagues for information? How can organizations ensure that both new employees and current organizational insiders are aware of each other and have opportunities to help each other? Wesson and Gogus (2005) found that online orientation was related to lower connection-type outcomes while it was not related to the more information-based content offered in the orientation. Thus, we know that orientations conducted online can help with clarity and perhaps confidence but are not as effective for connection in terms of these early indications. However, as technology becomes more enhanced, perhaps this will evolve as well.

9.4.2   Mitigating stress for newcomers

Entering a new organization is characterized by a high degree of uncertainty which can be experienced as stressful for new employees (Berger & Calabrese, 1975; Ellis et al., 2015b). In addition to feeling uncertain about one's role and what is to be expected, newcomers face many other challenges, such as having to learn new tasks, systems and processes; having to make new friends and learn new social norms (Nelson, 1987). Newcomers may be met with open arms by organizational insiders, or they may be viewed with scepticism or as a threat. One recent study found that conflict between newcomers and organizational insiders was common (Nifadker & Bauer, 2016). They found that this conflict caused newcomers to feel anxious around their coworkers and made them less likely to seek out information from them. Factors like these make navigating this time period fraught with potential for stress and burnout. How can organizations support new employees and ensure they have the resources they need to rise to the occasion? How can an understanding of demands and resources in the environment help organizations to better design onboarding programmes? Box 9.1 shows how L'Oréal, a global beauty company, integrates newcomers into its organization.

Box 9.1:   Case study: L'Oréal Paris' Fit programme helps ensure onboarding success

As we have noted in this chapter, the formality and comprehensiveness of onboarding programmes vary widely across organizations, and those considered 'best in class' for onboarding have more formal onboarding programmes. For example, L'Oréal Paris has a highly structured approach to their onboarding process starting with a first-day welcome. Global beauty company L'Oréal says, 'Our aim is to develop successful, committed and mutually beneficial relationships with each of our employees.' The company supports onboarding with a two-year, six-part integration programme called 'L'Oréal Fit'. The programme includes:

- Training and roundtable discussions.
- Meetings with key insiders.
- On-the-job learning supported by line management.
- Individual mentoring and HR support.
- Field and product experiences such as site visits and shadowing programmes.

By taking a structured approach to new employee onboarding, they have taken positive steps towards preventing employees from feeling lonely in their first weeks, they help to get them connected to organizational insiders early on, and they send out the signal that the company cares about and values all its employees.

Source: Bauer (2011).

9.4.3   The dark side of socialization

Effective socialization is generally considered a positive goal for newcomers and organizations, however, there may be times when socialization can backfire. For instance, a toxic organizational culture that impedes individual creativity or where employees are hostile towards one another may create situations where socialization is unwanted. Rather, organizations may hope that by bringing in new employees, they will change the organizational culture. You might also imagine an organization in which certain unethical or counterproductive behaviours are the norm. New employees who want to 'get along' and feel accepted by their colleagues might feel pressure to conform to these sorts of behaviours against the will of the organization (Liu et al., 2015). A study conducted by Kammeyer-Mueller, Simon, and Rich (2012) showed that among new attorneys, when the organizational socialization system encouraged newcomers to adopt the norms and ethical standards of the organization over their own belief system, they felt more ethical conflict, and reported being more emotionally exhausted. Really socialization can fail by either two of the extremes of over-conformity or nonconformity, as Schein (1988) notes. How can organizations guard against potential negative outcomes of socialization? Research shows that when newcomers feel valued and able to bring their authentic selves to work, their socialization is more effective. When there is alignment between newcomers' true identity and the person they are at work, they can focus their resources and effort on learning about their role and their new work environment, rather than dealing with the stress that could occur when newcomers feel they cannot be who they really are (Cable, Gino, & Staats, 2013; Kammeyer-Mueller, Simon, & Rich, 2012).

Summary

The period of time when a newcomer first joins an organization is a critical time. This is the time when newcomers go from being organization 'outsiders' to organizational 'insiders' and is commonly referred to as organizational socialization, or onboarding. This chapter explains how organizations should operate to get new entrants on board. Designing effective onboarding programmes requires consideration of the five C's of effective onboarding (compliance, clarity, confidence, connection, and culture). Our detailed review of the socialization process showed that organizations can focus on recruitment, new employee orientations, structured organizational tactics, and organizational insiders to improve the chances that new employees will be successful. At the same time, new employees can be proactive through seeking out information and feedback and making efforts to build relationships with their colleagues and supervisor. Research shows that successful adjustment to a new organization is seen in short-term outcomes such as a sense of self-efficacy or mastery of work tasks, clarity with regard to one's role, a feeling of being accepted by one's peers and knowledge about the organizational culture. Together these factors have been associated with a number of long-term outcomes, including better performance, more positive job attitudes, and reduced likelihood of turnover. Finally, this chapter considered important special topics and current challenges related to organizational socialization including virtual onboarding, reducing stress for new employees, and the potential dark side of socialization.

Discussion Points

1 As an organization, how could you know whether employees were being successfully onboarded?
2 In your next job or role, what could you do to help facilitate your own adjustment?

Suggested Further Reading

Bauer, T. N. (2011). Onboarding new employees: Maximizing success. *SHRM Foundation's Effective Practice Guidelines Series*. Alexandria, VA: SHRM. Retrieved from https://www.shrm.org/about/foundation/products/Documents/Onboarding%20EPG-%20FINAL.pdf. This is a White Paper which reviews key research on organizational socialization and translates it for practitioner use. It includes several case studies.

Bauer, T. N., Bodner, T., Erdogan, B., Truxillo, D., & Tucker, J. S. (2007). Newcomer adjustment during organizational socialization: A meta-analytic review of antecedents, outcomes, and methods. *Journal of Applied Psychology, 92,* 707–721. This is a meta-analysis of organizational socialization research and includes a test of a summary model of the findings of 70 studies on the topic.

re:Work @ Google: https://rework.withgoogle.com/The Google rework website includes information to help inform research and practice. They did a specific focus on onboarding which can be found at this url.

Wanberg, C. (2012). *The Oxford handbook of organizational socialization*. Oxford: Oxford University Press. This book includes chapters on key aspects of onboarding and is a good comprehensive review of the literature.

References

Allen, T., Eby, L., Chao, G., & Bauer, T. N. (in press). Taking stock of two relational aspects of organizational life: Tracing the history and shaping the future of socialization and mentoring research. *Journal of Applied Psychology*.

Allen, T. D., McManus, S. E., & Russell, J. E. A. (1999). Newcomer socialization and stress: Formal peer relationships as a source of support. *Journal of Vocational Behavior, 54,* 453–470.

Ashford, S. J., & Black, J. S. (1996). Proactivity during organizational entry: The role of desire for control. *Journal of Applied Psychology, 81,* 199–214.

Ashforth, B. E. (2012). The role of time in socialization dynamics. In C. Wanberg (Ed.), *The Oxford handbook of organizational socialization*. Oxford: Oxford University Press, pp. 161–186.

Ashforth, B. E., & Saks, A. M. (1996). Socialization tactics: Longitudinal effects on newcomer adjustment. *Academy of Management Journal, 39,* 149–178.

Bauer, T. N. (2011). Onboarding new employees: Maximizing success. *SHRM Foundation's Effective Practice Guideline Series*. Retrieved January 14, 2016 from http://www.shrm.org/about/foundation/products/Pages/OnboardingEPG.aspx

Bauer, T. N., Bodner, T., Erdogan, B., Truxillo, D. M., & Tucker, J. S. (2007). Newcomer adjustment during organizational socialization: A meta-analytic review of antecedents, outcomes, and methods. *Journal of Applied Psychology, 92,* 707–721.

Bauer, T. N., & Erdogan, B. (2011). Organizational socialization: The effective onboarding of new employees. In S. Zedeck (Ed.). *APA handbook of industrial and organizational psychology* (vol. 3) (pp. 51–64). Washington, DC: American Psychological Association.

Bauer, T. N., & Green, S. G. (1994). The effect of newcomer involvement in work-related activities: A longitudinal study of socialization. *Journal of Applied Psychology, 79,* 211–223.

Berger, C. R., & Calabrese, R. J. (1975). Some explorations in initial interaction and beyond: Toward a developmental theory of interpersonal communication. *Human Communication Research, 1,* 99–112.

Cable, D. M., Gino, F., & Staats, B. R. (2013). Breaking them in or eliciting their best? Reframing socialization around newcomers' authentic self-expression. *Administrative Science Quarterly, 58,* 1–36.

Chao, G. T., O'Leary-Kelly, A. M., Wolf, S., Klein, H. J., & Gardner, P. D. (1994). Organizational socialization: Its content and consequences. *Journal of Applied Psychology, 79,* 730–743.

Cooper-Thomas, H. D., Paterson, N. L., Stadler, M. J., & Saks, A. M. (2014). The relative importance of proactive behaviors and outcomes for predicting newcomer learning, well-being, and work engagement. *Journal of Vocational Behavior, 84,* 318–331.

Cooper-Thomas, H. D., Van Vianen, A., & Anderson, N. (2004). Changes in person–organization fit: The impact of socialization tactics on perceived and actual P–O fit. *European Journal of Work and Organizational Psychology, 13,* 52–78.

Delobbe, N., Cooper-Thomas, H. D., & De Hoe, R. (2015). A new look at the psychological contract during organizational socialization: The role of newcomers' obligations at entry. *Journal of Organizational Behavior.* Online access only. doi: 10.1002/job.2078

Ellis, A. M., Bauer, T. N., & Erdogan, B. (2015). New employee organizational socialization: Adjusting to new organizations, insiders, and roles. In J. E. Grusec, & P. D. Hastings (Eds.), *Handbook of socialization: theory and research.* New York: Guilford Press.

Ellis, A. M., Bauer, T. N., Mansfield, L. R., Erdogan, B., Truxillo, D. M., & Simon, L. S. (2015). Navigating uncharted waters: Newcomer socialization through the lens of stress theory. *Journal of Management, 41,* 203–235.

Griffin, M. A., & Clarke, S. (2011). Stress and well-being at work. In S. Zedeck (Ed.), *APA handbook of industrial and organizational psychology* (vol. 3) (pp. 359–397). Washington, DC: American Psychological Association.

Gruman, J. A., Saks, A. M., & Zweig, D. I. (2006). Organizational socialization tactics and newcomer proactive behaviors: An integrative study. *Journal of Vocational Behavior, 69,* 90–104.

Kammeyer-Mueller, J. D., Simon, L. S., & Rich, B. L. (2012). The psychic cost of doing wrong: Ethical conflict, divestiture socialization, and emotional exhaustion. *Journal of Management, 38,* 784–808.

Kammeyer-Mueller, J. D., Wanberg, C., Rubenstein, A., & Song, Z. (2013). Support, undermining, and newcomer socialization: Fitting in during the first 90 days. *Academy of Management Journal, 56,* 1104–1124.

Klein, H. J. & Weaver, N. A. (2000). The effectiveness of an organizational-level orientation training program in the socialization of new hires. *Personnel Psychology, 53,* 47–66.

Lapointe, É., Vandenberghe, C., & Boudrias, J. S. (2013). Psychological contract breach, affective commitment to organization and supervisor, and newcomer adjustment: A three-wave moderated mediation model. *Journal of Vocational Behavior, 83,* 528–538.

Liu, S., Wang, M., Bamberger, P., Shi, J., & Bacharach, S. B. (2015). The dark side of socialization: A longitudinal investigation of newcomer alcohol use. *Academy of Management Journal, 58,* 334–355.

Louis, M. R. (1980). Surprise and sense making: What newcomers experience in entering unfamiliar organizational settings. *Administrative Science Quarterly, 25,* 226–251.

Louis, M. R., Posner, B. Z., & Powell, G. N. (1983). The availability and helpfulness of socialization practices. *Personnel Psychology, 36,* 857–866. Morrison, E. W. (1993). Longitudinal study of the effects of information seeking on newcomer socialization. *Journal of Applied Psychology, 78,* 173–183.

Nelson, D. L. (1987). Organizational socialization: A stress perspective. *Journal of Occupational Behavior, 8,* 311–324.

Nifadker, S. S., & Bauer, T. N. (2016). Breach of belongingness: Newcomer relationship conflict, information, and task-related outcomes during organizational socialization. *Journal of Applied Psychology, 101,* 1–13.

Phillips, J. M. (1998). Effects of realistic job previews on multiple organizational outcomes: A meta-analysis. *Academy of Management Journal, 41,* 673–690.

Reichers, A. E. (1987). An interactionist perspective on newcomer socialization rates. *Academy of Management Review, 12,* 278–287.

Rousseau, D. M. (1989). Psychological and implied contracts in organizations. *Employee Responsibilities and Rights Journal, 2,* 121–139.

Rynes, S. L. (1991). Recruitment, job choice, and post-hire consequences. In M. D. Dunnett, & L. M. Hugh (Eds.), *Handbook of industrial and organizational psychology* (pp. 399–444). Palo Alto, CA: Consulting Psychology Press.

Saks, A. M., & Ashforth, B. E. (1997). A longitudinal investigation of the relationships between job information sources, applicant perceptions of fit, and work outcomes. *Personnel Psychology, 50,* 395–426.

Saks, A. M., Uggerslev, K. L., & Fassina, N. E. (2007). Socialization tactics and newcomer adjustment: A meta-analytic review and test of a model. *Journal of Vocational Behavior, 70,* 413–446.

Schein, E. H. (1988). Organizational socialization and the profession of management. *MIT Sloan Management Review*. Retrieved January 13, 2016 from http://sloanreview.mit.edu/article/organizational-socialization-and-the-profession-of-management/

Seibert, S. E., Kraimer, M. L., & Crant, J. M. (2001). A longitudinal model linking proactive personality and career success. *Personnel Psychology, 54,* 845–874.

Thomas, C. H., & Lankau, M. J. (2009). Preventing burnout: The effects of LMX and mentoring on socialization, role stress, and burnout. *Human Resource Management, 48,* 417–432.

Van Maanen J., & Schein E. H. (1979). Toward a theory of organizational socialization. In Staw B. M. (Ed.), *Research in organizational behavior, 1* (pp. 209–264). Greenwich, CT: JAI Press.

Wanberg, C. R., & Kammeyer-Mueller, J. D. (2000). Predictors and outcomes of proactivity in the socialization process. *Journal of Applied Psychology, 85,* 373–385.

Wesson, M. J., & Gogus, C. I. (2005). Shaking hands with a computer: an examination of two methods of organizational newcomer orientation. *Journal of Applied Psychology, 90,* 1018.

10 How Does Power Affect Those Who Have It and Those Who Don't? Power Inside Organizations

Lourdes Munduate and Francisco J. Medina

Overview

This chapter begins with the assumption that power is a critical resource for organizational actors. A person with power commands prominence, respect and influence in the eyes of others. Possessing power means that a person is able to influence others more easily and perform his/her job more effectively, facilitating the achievement of personal and organizational objectives. Power relationships affect how managers and employees work together to make decisions and manage. Therefore, it is essential to understand how some individuals acquire power when others do not: What are the origins of power in organizational settings? The possession of power transforms individuals psychologically, shapes their behaviour, and produces an enduring effect on individual status and influence with teammates. This long shadow cast by power on the mental state of either powerful or powerless actors is the second question addressed by this chapter: How does power influence those who possess it and those who don't? Third, the metamorphic effects of power can lead to both positive and negative consequences such as creative thinking or cooperative behaviour versus selfish, corrupt, and risky behaviour. When does the experience of power lead to positive cognitive and behavioural outcomes?

10.1 What Is Power and Why Is It Important?

Power is a basic force of human interaction. Who has power, who is affected by power and how power is exercised provide the foundation for understanding human relations (Lammers & Galinsky, 2009). Power is defined as the ability to influence others through the control over resources or the capacity to punish them (Anderson et al., 2015; Emerson, 1962). This concept is rooted in theories of dependency and interdependency (Thibaut & Kelly, 1959). The idea is that

An Introduction to Work and Organizational Psychology: An International Perspective,
Third Edition. Edited by Nik Chmiel, Franco Fraccaroli and Magnus Sverke.
© 2017 John Wiley & Sons, Ltd. Published 2017 by John Wiley & Sons, Ltd.

high power individuals have more control over valued resources and can often act at will without serious consequences. Low power individuals, on the other hand, have to be more careful because they are more dependent on other people for their interests to be met. Because low power individuals are more dependent on the resources of higher power individuals, the powerful are more easily able to satisfy their own needs and desires (Lammers & Galinsky, 2009).

One important characteristic of power is that it is *contextual or relational*. Power emerges from a specific set of social relations and can be understood only in relation to others, whereas a low-power party depends on a high-power party to obtain rewards and avoid punishments (Emerson, 1962). The power does not reside in the person but rather in the relationship. In general, power is derived from the situation in which the person operates and in the event of the situation changing, the person's power also changes. For example, an individual's prominence and potential power in the textile company taskforce described below can be understood only with reference to his or her relationships with the group. This inherently relational nature of power differentiates it from dominance, or the tendency for individuals to behave in assertive, forceful and self-assured ways across a variety of groups (Anderson & Berdahl, 2002). In that sense although different, dominance is often a predictor of an individual's power in specific contexts (Anderson, John, & Keltner, 2012).

A second characteristic reflects that *power is potential* and, as a result, a person can have power without necessarily deploying it. The availability of resources does not mean that they have to be used (Munduate & Medina, 2004).

Social influence can be seen as a primary consequence of power. Power often involves putting pressure on others to engage in behaviours that will help the powerful accomplish their own objectives (Lammers, Stoker, Rinks & Galinsky, 2016). Thus, power has been defined as the *capacity to* influence others in psychologically meaningful ways. In fact, some have even defined power as actual influence, such that power occurs only when a person directly causes or alters the behaviour of another person. French and Raven (1959) likened power to potential energy and influence to kinetic energy, both metaphorically and literally, so that one can think of control over resources as a potential source of influence in the same way energy can be stored and later released.

French and Raven (1959) defined *influence* as a force one person exerts on someone else to induce a change in behaviours, attitudes and values. Influence is 'power in action' just as power is 'potential influence'. Power may be present even when no direct behavioural effects are observed. Thus, in principle, individuals do not need to use their power to be considered powerful.

Power has also been differentiated from leadership, status or authority, which are social roles that can endow individuals with power (Anderson & Berdahl, 2002). Empirical research shows that these constructs are correlated, in the sense that individuals with power are more respected and admired, and those who are respected tend to be given control over valued resources. Leaders tend to have more power than followers because groups give them control over important decisions, information and group processes. However, powerful individuals do not always serve as leaders (Anderson et al., 2015). It is possible that people who do not have high status inside their organization have an important capacity to influence others due to their experience, relations or even by personality variables such as dominance (Anderson et al., 2012).

The personal *sense of power* is the perception of one's ability to influence another person or other people (Anderson et al., 2012). When individuals have control over resources and punishment, they often realize that they have an increased capacity to influence others. Powerful individuals are less likely to pay attention to, and think about, the less powerful than vice versa (Keltner, Gruenfeld, & Anderson, 2003). Powerful parties tend to have higher aspirations, to demand more and to concede less (De Dreu, 1995). Power also increases action orientation and goal-directed behaviour (Galinsky, Gruenfeld, & Magee, 2003).

The CEO of a textile company has set a first meeting of a cross-departmental task-force created to develop a tailored employee wellness programme, aimed at encouraging healthier lifestyle behaviours. The taskforce has been created with the members of some of the offices and with a lot of functional diversity, as well as diversity in their academic background, age and gender. Colleagues from international offices are participating via Skype or videoconference. The CEO has started asking all of them to help start a new programme, and he expects that innovative ideas to start the project will arise during the meeting. The members of the taskforce see this programme as an opportunity for their career development. They are eager to make a good impression in this first meeting and to get a position to manage the programme and achieve its successful implementation in all the international offices.

Who will be the star of the group? Will it depend on their previous position in the organization? Will it depend on his/her knowledge of the subject? Will it depend on his/her personal characteristics? Will the reinforcement of their position be sustained in the future? How will they carry out the programme in each geographic area? How will they involve all employees from different offices in the process?

These questions touch on why power is important to employees, and how they may try to acquire power in organizations, how power is maintained and what the personal and organizational consequences of having power are. As Anderson and Brion (2014) state, possessing power has some advantages such as stronger job security and better financial rewards, being able to influence others more easily, and perform one's job more effectively (see Magee & Galinsky, 2008). By contrast, lacking power means less autonomy and control in one's job, being susceptible to unfair treatment, and experiencing lower job satisfaction and low morale (Keltner, Gruenfeld & Anderson, 2003; Lammers, et al., 2016).

Given the importance of power for individuals' well-being, social scientists have spent decades studying how individuals achieve power within organizational groups – that is, how they gain respect, prominence and influence in the eyes of others (Galinsky & Kilduff, 2013). Two complementary theoretical approaches have addressed these questions: *the bases of power* and the *consequences of having power*. The bases of power approach examines the sources of power and the specific resources used to influence others. From this perspective, power is conceived as a structural variable and as a property of social relationships. The second approach argues that power can also become a psychological property of powerful individuals. Power is not simply the control over resources. Differences in control over valued resources lead to differences in dependence, and these differences transform individuals psychologically (Keltner et al., 2003). This way of understanding power, derived from social cognition, has emerged as an indispensable level of analysis for the understanding of how and why being in a powerful or powerless position affects individuals. This approach provides insight on how power influences those who possess it and those who do not.

10.2   The Bases of Power

Research on the bases of power examines the specific resources used by the power holder to influence the beliefs, attitudes and behaviour of others (Kipnis, 1976; Yukl & Falbe, 1991). To analyze the influence of power bases we look first to responses to influence attempts, and then the link between power bases and these responses.

10.2.1   Influence processes

In studies looking at people's responses to power holder influence attempts, there is a clear difference between yielding to direct or indirect social pressure from an individual and being genuinely persuaded (Emans et al., 2003). For example, the power holder's influence may be strong enough to wield control over the target's behaviour, ensuring public agreement, regardless of whether they are privately convinced. On other occasions the influence process may change the targets' private attitude or opinion and make them committed to the power holder's request. Therefore social psychologists made a distinction between three different types of influence process (Kelman, 1958).

- *Compliance* refers to a surface change in behaviour and expressed attitudes, often as a consequence of coercion or the target's desire to obtain a reward. As compliance does not reflect internal change, it usually only persists while behaviour is under surveillance.
- In contrast to compliance, *internalization* means subjective acceptance that produces true internal change that persists in the absence of surveillance. The norm becomes an internalized standard for behaviour. There is genuine support for the powerful's proposals because they appear to be intrinsically desirable and are suited to the targets values and beliefs.
- *Identification* is based on the power holder's attractiveness to the targets, who imitate his or her behaviour and attitudes in order to gain approval. The maintenance of a close relationship with the powerful involves the target's need for acceptance and esteem.

The outcomes of these different forms of social influence in terms of compliance, internalization and identification may occur at the same time. For example, a person who works in an NGO with exploited children in the Third World may accept a proposal from his/her superior to design a new programme because this person will obtain tangible rewards for carrying it out (compliance), besides believing in the necessity and effectiveness of said programme (internalization), and at the same time, this person is proud of working with his/her superior on this project and this will increase the level of satisfaction in the relationship (identification).

10.2.2 Bases and sources of power

To understand the different ways that power can be exercised, it is best to look at the various bases and sources of power. French et al., (1959) considered five *bases of power* with a sixth one that was added later: reward, coercion, legitimacy, reference, expertise, and information. A powerful individual possesses these resources and can use them to change the beliefs, attitudes, or behaviours of the targets. Some types of power correspond closely to some of Kelman's influence processes (1974). There is evidence that the nature of the resource that a power holder controls may affect how others respond to that power (Cialdini & Goldstein, 2004; Munduate & Dorado, 1998; Overbeck, 2010) (see Figure 10.1).

- *Reward* and *coercive power* rely on others believing the powerful can provide them with the desired rewards or can punish them, respectively. Using either of these bases will induce only a superficial change in the targets. In other words, none of the targets' privately held beliefs, attitudes or values are changed. Only compliance is obtained, the continuation of which depends on successful surveillance of the targets.

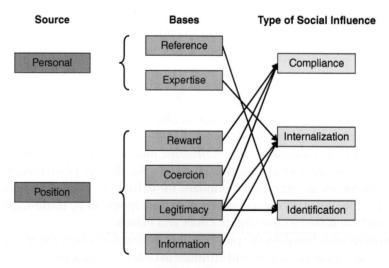

Figure 10.1: Relationships between sources and bases of power and outcomes of influence attempts

- A person possesses *legitimate power* when others believe that he or she has a legitimate right to exert influence over them, and they are obliged to accept this influence. It cuts across all the three types of influence processes and as a result may share elements of each of them.
- *Referent power* refers to targets' identification with the powerful. It leads to private acceptance by targets by enabling them to maintain a satisfactory relationship with the powerful person and see themselves as similar to the powerful in certain important areas.
- *Expert power* depends on targets' perception of having expertise or knowledge, in a specific domain. If a target perceives a powerful person as an expert, this will result in private acceptance on the part of the target.
- Finally, *informational power* leads to internalized and lasting changes in the targets' beliefs, attitudes, or values. Compared to other social power bases, the changed behaviour resulting from information is maintained without continued social dependence on the actor, and is instead based on the perceived importance and validity of the information. Only informational power leads to cognitive change in targets because it immediately becomes independent of the actor.

Another related dimension of power refers to *sources of power*. When dealing with the bases of power, the focus was on the resources available to a person to influence the other party or the environment. In terms of sources of power, the focus points towards the way a person comes to control these resources. Two different sources of power have been identified (Yukl & Falbe,1991). *Position power* arises from the status held in a group or organization, while *personal power* arises from personal attributes and the kind of relationship established with the other party. In the former source of power, potential control is derived from legitimate authority, the control over resources and punishment, and the opportunity to access certain information that is important for the members of the group or organization. People with high personal power use their previous relationships, prestige, knowledge of the task, and expectations to generate a situation of mutual help with others.

So far, we have identified two sources of power, six bases of power and three influence processes. Figure 10.1 presents the relationships between these aspects of power.

10.3   The Consequences of Having Power

The psychological consequences of power emerge not just from the amount of resources one possesses but on how power is conceptualized, acquired and wielded (Lammers & Galinsky, 2009). Power is not simply the control over resources or composed solely of one's social position within organizational groups. Power is also a psychological state – a perception of one's capacity to influence others (Anderson et al., 2012; Galinsky et al., 2003). For example, the 'powerless parents' research (Bugental & Lewis, 1999) states that parents have control over resources that are important to their children, such as food, safety, comfort, and nurturance. However, many parents feel themselves as lacking power over their young children and attribute the child's behaviour to factors outside their control, such as the child's disposition or personality. Further, this mental state of powerlessness can lead parents to use ineffective and coercive influence tactics which do reduce their actual influence (Anderson et al., 2012). The focus on the consequences of power is based on the assumption that the effects of power are dependent on how the power holder conceptualizes his or her power and on the interdependence relationship between the powerful and the powerless (Lammers & Galinsky, 2009).

Scholars who examine the psychological effects of power argue that power has a transformative impact on an individual's psychological state, leading the powerful to roam in a very different space from the powerless (Keltner, Gruenfeld & Anderson, 2003; Kipnis, 1972). As in the case of 'powerless parents', individuals' beliefs about their power can shape their actual influence over others, above and beyond the effects of their social network position, so that those who perceive themselves as powerful behave in more effective ways that increase their actual power (Anderson et al., 2012).

The psychological associations between power and behavioural tendencies have been built based on research on *behavioural priming* (Tost, 2015). Behavioural priming studies focus on how cognitive representations of concepts can be made psychologically salient and can consequently affect behaviours, often outside conscious awareness. The idea is that over time people's experiences produce a set of learned associations between and among concepts, and these associations are stored in memory. Consistent with this approach, Smith and Galinsky (2010) state that power is a mental concept linked in memory to a host of cognitive, affective and behavioural tendencies, so that when the concept of power is activated, other concepts are activated as well. It has been found that even only the experience of power makes individuals perceive personal control (Fast, Gruenfeld, Sivanathan, & Galinsky, 2009). Therefore, power can be activated experimentally, making the participants feel powerful through making them imagine a situation in which they had power over others (e.g. Galinsky et al., 2003) or when carrying out the role of a general manager with several subordinates (e.g. Guinote, 2008).

The pattern of results in the existing literature suggests that the cognitive constellation of power is broadly composed of concepts related to agency (for reviews, see Anderson & Brion, 2014; Tost, 2015). Agency is defined as the experience of the self as an independent entity with a focus on self-expression and self-expansion, and, as such, a proactive orientation to behaviour (Tost, 2015). Concepts such as confidence, being decisive, active, persistent, and independent, belong to the cognitive constellation of power. Therefore, the psychological experience of power has been shown to be associated with behavioural tendencies close to agency, such as action-orientation, risk seeking, and a focus on goal pursuit (Anderson & Galinsky, 2006; Guinote, 2008; Kelter et al., 2003).

Compared with individuals who lack power, possessing power leads individuals to experience more positive and less negative affect, to pursue a more assertive approach to the world, taking action to make it a better place, to be less averse to potential losses, and to enjoy higher self-esteem, physical health and longevity (see Anderson et al., 2012, for a review). From this perspective, power has group-serving functions and power roles involve social responsibility (Van Vugt et al., 2008). The powerful should not just influence others but attend and care to their needs. But power can also lead to negative consequences (see also Chapter 27 in this volume). Fuelling the dark side of power are findings that support the idea that power often promotes corruption, selfishness, and aggression, decreases empathy and attention towards others, and increases prejudice. Power has also been identified as a springboard to sexual harassment (see Lammers & Galinsky, 2009, for a review). Lammers and Galinsky (2009) argue that how power is conceptualized by the powerful and by the powerless will have different downstream effects on behaviour and cognition. In this way, Galinsky and colleagues (2003) found that, contrary to conventional beliefs about corruption, power does not always have the goal of one's own interest. Having power increments the tendency to act, independently of it having prosocial or antisocial consequences.

Keltner et al. (2003) provided one of the first theoretical formulations of power's affective, cognitive and behavioural effects. They argued that power activates the behavioural *approach system*, in that power leads to approach behaviours that pursue rewards, whereas a lack of power activates the behavioural *inhibition system*, leading to behavioural inhibition and avoidance of threats.

The activating behaviour of power comes from two characteristics of the dynamics of power. First, elevated power is associated with the increase in access to higher benefits from having more resources. Second, powerful people find fewer obstacles to achieve benefits, or put differently, they have more freedom to carry out actions which lead to benefits. In the same way, the lack of power facilitates the inhibition system due to the fact that individuals with less power have less access to benefits and they receive more material and psychological threats when they pursue these benefits. While powerful people have more opportunities in their environment, less powerful people find more potential damage threatening them. In summary, there is an asymmetry between benefits and threats perceived by those individuals who maintain relationships of power. Thus, in a certain environment, powerful people will receive more opportunities than the less powerful, who will receive more threats than the powerful. These perceptive asymmetries in an equal environment would facilitate a response of approach in the more powerful and a response of inhibition in the less powerful.

The differences in the activation of both systems involve the activation of affective states, cognitions and different behaviours (Anderson et al., 2012). For example, the hierarchical position of an individual inside a group will determine the level of situational pressures which he/she will be subject to. People with low power obey explicit demands of people with high power and are also easily influenced. In contrast, people with high power can behave more freely and manifest a higher diversity in interpersonal relations. Thus, the activation of the approach system manifests in the power holder's propensity to experience more positive

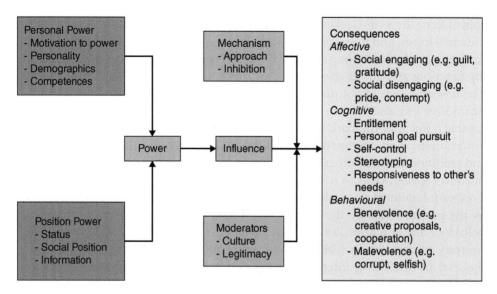

Figure 10.2: Psychological effects of power

affect, take action more readily, and focus on rewards and opportunities in the environment (Anderson & Brion, 2014). For complementary reasons, when people have low power, they are subject to more social and material threats. Thus, the activation of the inhibition system has been equated to an alarm system that triggers avoidance and response inhibition (Anderson & Brion, 2012).

Following this approach/inhibition theory, different studies suggest that the psychological effects of power can be expected to vary across individuals and across cultures (Figure 10.2). Between the moderators of the effects of power (for a review, see Tost, 2015), personal experiences related with the legitimacy of power or socialization processes have been the most studied (Anderson et al., 2014; Chen, Lee-Chai, & Bargh, 2001; Zhong, Magee, Maddux, & Galinsky, 2006).

10.4   What Moderates the Psychological Effects of Power?

10.4.1   Legitimacy

Following the approach/inhibition theory (Keltner et al., 2003), a series of studies explored how power and legitimacy affect the basic tendencies associated with power. Lammers and Galinsky (2009) state that the power-approach link is tempered by the perceived legitimacy of power. Although legitimate power puts a focus on gains (approach) and legitimate powerlessness on preventing losses (inhibition), under conditions of illegitimacy, this effect could be diminished. Consistent with this notion, power and legitimacy were manipulated in several studies –for example, asking participants to recall a time when they had power or were in a state of low power and whether that power was legitimate or illegitimate

(Lammers et al., 2008). Although legitimate power led to more approach tendencies than legitimate powerlessness, the opposite effect occurred under conditions of illegitimacy: illegitimate powerlessness led to more behavioural approach than illegitimate power.

Similar results were found for the propensity to negotiate (Magee et al., 2007) or the preferences for risk (Anderson & Galinsky, 2006; Chen et al., 2001). Across different studies, legitimate power consistently led to more approach but when power was conceived or expressed under the shadow of illegitimacy, the powerful no longer showed more approach than the powerless (Lammers & Galinsky, 2009).

In the case of the effects of power on tendencies to cooperate, it is relevant to note that the literature is full of contradictory findings, with some studies showing that the powerless are more inclined to cooperate than the powerful (Tjosvold & Wu, 2009) and other studies demonstrating the opposing pattern of the powerful being more inclined to cooperate (van Knippenberg, van Knippenberg, & Wilke, 2001). As Lammers and Galinsky (2009) argue, these effects may depend on the degree to which the various power manipulations were seen as legitimate. In fact, their study suggests that when power was seen as legitimate, the powerful cooperate less than the powerless, but when power was seen as illegitimate, the powerful cooperated more than the powerless.

These findings have important implications not only for when power leads to approach and cooperation but also to understand to what extent the consequences of power are dependent on how power holders conceptualize their power (Lammers & Galinsky, 2009). We now focus on how power is conceived not in terms of legitimacy but in terms of cultural differences.

10.4.2   Culture

With the benefit of a cross-cultural perspective, scholars have analyzed how culture affects the conceptualizations of power and the behavioural consequences of power. They focus in particular on how culture moderates the previously demonstrated positive relationship between power and attention to rewards and assertive actions (Magee & Smith, 2013; Zhong et al., 2006).

Western cultures tend to be characterized by independence, as people tend to be socialized to think of themselves as separate, unconnected entities and are encouraged to forge their own way independent of the expectations of others. In contrast to the self-focused traditions of the West, East Asian cultures lead individuals to consider others explicitly, stressing the notion that productive societies should have a relationship and group-centred focus (Markus & Kitayama, 1991; Zhong et al., 2006). On average, Westerners tend to perceive themselves as relatively independent, whereas East Asians tend to perceive themselves as relatively interdependent.

Based on this different conceptualization of the self, Zhong et al. (2006) argue that (1) power is conceptually and experientially connected to the dominant values of one's culture, and (2) culture therefore produces different cognitive and behavioural outcomes of power. As a result, they proposed that power is conceptualized around influence and entitlement in the West, and Westerners behave assertively to satisfy themselves. In contrast, East Asians conceptualize power around responsibility and tend to consider how their behaviour affects others. Consistent with this notion, Park and colleagues (2013) found that expansive postures symbolizing self-expression, independence and entitlement were associated with power for individuals of Western culture but not for individuals of East Asian culture.

Research has demonstrated that individuals from different cultural backgrounds have different associations between the concepts of power and the concepts of reward, responsibility and restraint (Galinsky et al., 2003; Zhong et al., 2006). For example, power was conceptually linked to influence in the West but to responsibility in the East: power increased assertive actions and claims of self-interest among Westerners but the experience of power by East Asians reduced self-interest claims and hence increased the potential preservation of a commonly shared resource (Zhong et al., 2006). It has been also shown that, for Westerners, power was negatively correlated with cooperation, but for East Asians a sense of power was positively related to cooperation (Galinsky et al., 2003).

These results suggest that culture moderates the psychological effects of power with relevant practical implications. First, relatively independent versus interdependent self-construals moderate individuals' social behaviour with respect to power. Second, the current findings suggesting a strong association between power and agentic traits and behaviours may be specific to Western cultures, or to individuals who personally hold values that associate power with entitlement. And, third, consequently, individual-level variables may determine whether power engenders positive or negative outcomes.

Box 10.1:   How to gain power

We started this chapter with the first meeting of the CEO of a company with a taskforce created to develop an employee wellness programme. We wondered who would be the star of the meeting and why. We also wondered whether their position would be sustained in the future. Finally, we asked how they would carry out the programme in each geographic area and if they would involve all employees from different offices and geographic areas in the process. After analysing the dynamics of power in organizational settings and how they affect people who have power, we can now start exploring these questions.

To begin with the question of who would be the star of the meeting, we argue that personality characteristics will predict individual power attainment. Based on the personal need of power, individuals who desire power are more proactive in their attempts to acquire it. Thus, the taskforce members who are looking for power will try to increase their visibility in the first meeting to help highlight any valued competence or skill they might possess and to build alliances strategically. Personal stable traits such as narcissism, dominance and self-monitoring, for example, contribute to power attainment.

The ability to socially influence others may emerge from a variety of sources, such as argumentative skill, interpersonal liking and reciprocity. However, as Tost (2015) points out, the ability to enforce desires even when others in the company have not been persuaded to comply is dependent on resource control. That is, control over anything of value that others in this taskforce could depend on, such as information, technology, professional security, decision-making opportunities, or access to important people in the company for the development of the wellness programme. The social network position in the group therefore counts because one's network centrality influences one's ability to obtain information, and consequently to obtain power. For example, Burt (2000) found that bridging structural holes (connecting two otherwise disconnected individuals) provides control over the flow of information. It can also apply to personal characteristics. An outstanding taskforce member can also be construed as controlling valued resources if he or she possesses personal skills, knowledge or expertise that others need.

Therefore, a taskforce member who wants to have influence on the ways the CEO and other members feel, think or behave, will gain respect in the eyes of others because he or she has control over one or more of these resources. Both his/her personal attributes and his/her position in the social network will work in his/her favour. In this sense, as Galinsky and Kilduff state (2013, p. 1), demographics matter:

> People of the historically dominant race and gender and a respected age (white men over 40 in the western corporate world) are typically afforded higher status than everyone else ... Appearance also plays a role (the tall and the good-looking are favoured over those less genetically blessed) as does personality (confident extroverts win out).

In addition to demographics and morphologic characteristics, more legitimate measures will command others' respect, such as expertise, competence and reciprocity.

We have seen that cultures differ in how power is understood and interpreted. Accordingly, the first meeting of the taskforce with the CEO will be moderated by the culture of taskforce members. Following the rationale of Sassemberg, Ellemers and Scheepers (2012) that power can be understood as opportunity versus responsibility in different cultures, we can expect advantages for some members in the current taskforce. The power construed as opportunity to advance in personal career development will be perceived as more attractive than power construed as responsibility for others, among promotion-oriented Western members.

We argue that the first actions of the person who stands out in the group will cast a long shadow. We have seen that power transforms those who possess it because it instils an elevated sense of power that changes their frame of mind. The psychological experience of power can encourage self-expression in power holders, as well as a transformation of their thoughts, emotions and actions. As Galinsky and Kilduff (2013) point out, the phenomenon is similar to what chaos theorists call the 'butterfly effect': the idea that a small change in conditions in the natural world, even the mere flap of a butterfly's wing, can have profound consequences, such as setting off a hurricane weeks later and thousands of miles away.

In any case, we know that personal and cultural differences can affect the psychological effects of power, and this is an important aspect to consider in a company with international scope, and with employees from different cultures. Thus, experiences related to the legitimacy of trying to implement a programme which changes the lifestyle of workplace behaviours can moderate the effects of power holders. Legitimate power consistently leads to more approach behaviours but when power is conceived under the shadow of illegitimacy, as could be the case in instituting a workplace wellness programme, the powerful no longer show more approach behaviours than the powerless.

Continued

The nature of the resource that the taskforce member controls may affect how other members in the organization respond to that power. In the long term, the ways that they have been used (e.g., reward and coercion versus information and social approval) to influence the adoption of healthy workplace behaviours will also affect the type of response to influence attempts. For example, the key to having a successful corporate wellness programme is how it is promoted and perceived by employees. To build a supportive, positive climate of fun and camaraderie would help people adopt or maintain a healthy way of living. An example would be an employee's engagement with a month-long 'Challenge to Not Drive to Work'. Employees' responses will differ from mere compliance (with or without being inclined to do so by him/her self), to internalization and identification, which generate genuine persuasion and true internal change that persist in the absence of pressure or reward. For example, employees who participate in the Challenge and enjoy the experience to walk, ride a bike, take public transportation, or car-share to work, may then appreciate the additional benefits to the environment that the Challenge promoted, generating a true internal change to their lifestyle behaviour.

Summary

In this chapter we have discussed how individuals gain respect, prominence and influence in the eyes of others. To this end, we have focused on two approaches to the study of power: the bases of power and the consequences of having power. The first approach examines the specific resources used by individuals to change the beliefs, attitudes, or behaviours of others; provides a taxonomy of the different bases of power; and identifies the responses of the targets of influence to different bases of power. From this perspective power is conceived of as a structural variable and as a property of social relationships.

The second approach to the study of power argues that power can also become a psychological property of the individuals. The experience of holding power in a particular situation generates a constellation of characteristics and propensities that manifest themselves in affect, cognition and behaviour. The behavioural approach theory of power provides a foundation for understanding how the experience of power can change the power holders in specific ways. Power holders' actions are a product of increased activation of the behavioural approach system (which regulates behaviour associated with rewards); however, those who lack power experience increased activation of the behavioural inhibition system (which equates to an alarm system).

Some individual-level variables such as the experiences of legitimacy and culture moderate the effects of power on cognition and behaviour, explaining that the psychological consequences of power depend on how power is conceptualized, acquired and wielded.

Discussion Points

1 What can managers and employees do to ensure power is not abused but is used wisely?
2 Why does culture produce different behavioural and cognitive outcomes of power? Do you agree with the notion summarized in this Spiderman quote: 'With great power comes great responsibility'?

Suggested Further Reading

Anderson, C., & Brion, S. (2014). Perspectives on power in organizations. *Annual Review Organizational Psychology and Organizational Behavior, 1,* 67–97. This article addresses power as a process that unfolds over time. It explores how individuals gain, as well as lose power.

Galinsky, A. D., & Kilduff, G. J. (2013). Be seen as a Leader. *Harvard Business Review*, December. Available at ;https://hbr.org/2013/12/be-seen-as-a-leader. A practical overview on how the temporary mind-set that individuals bring to an initial group project can have a lasting effect on their status and influence with the group members.

Guinote, A., & Vescio, T. K. (2010). *The social psychology of power*. New York, NY: Guildford Press. The book undertakes an extensive review of theorizing on power in social science.

Tjosvold, D., & Wisse, B. (2009). *Power and interdependence in organizations*. Cambridge: Cambridge University Press. This book provides a good introductory text focused on the positive and negative features of power, especially in the context of both individuals and organizations.

References

Anderson, C., & Berdahl, J. L. (2002). The experience of power: Examining the effects of power on approach and inhibition tendencies. *Journal of Personality and Social Psychology, 83,* 1362–1377.

Anderson, C., & Brion, S. (2014). Perspectives on power in organizations. *Annual Review of Organizational Psychology and Organizational Behavior, 1,* 67–97 doi: 10.1146/annurev-orgpsych-031413-091259

Anderson, C., & Galinsky, A. (2006). Power, optimism, and risk-taking. *European Journal of Social Psychology, 36,* 511–536.

Anderson, C., Angus, J., Hildreth, D., & Howland, L. (2015). Is the desire for status a fundamental human motive? A review of the empirical literature. *Psychological Bulletin, 141,* 574–601.

Anderson, C., John, O. P., & Keltner, D. (2012). The personal sense of power. *Journal of Personality, 80,* 313–344.

Bugental, D.B., & Lewis, J.C. (1999). The paradoxical misure of power by those who see themselves as powerless: How does it happen? *Journal of Social Issues, 55,* 51–64.

Burt, B. M. (2000). The network structure of social capital. *Research in Organizational Behavior, 22,* 345–423.

Chen, S., Lee-Chai, A. Y., & Bargh, J. A. (2001). Relationship orientation as moderator of the effects of social power. *Journal of Personality and Social Psychology, 80,* 183–187.

Cialdini, R. B., & Goldstein, N. J. (2004). Social influence: Compliance and conformity. *Annual Review of Psychology, 55,* 591–621.

De Dreu, C. K. W. (1995). Coercive power and concession making in bilateral negotiation. *Journal of Conflict Resolution, 39,* 646–670.

Emans, B., Munduate, L., Klever, E., & Van de Vliert, E. (2003). Constructive consequences of leaders' forcing influence styles. *Applied Psychology: An International Review, 52,* 3–17.

Emerson, R. M. (1962). Power dependence relations. *American Sociological Review, 27,* 31–41.

Fast, N. J., Gruenfeld, D. H., Sivanathan, N., & Galinsky, A. D. (2009). Illusory control: A generative force behind power's far-reaching effects. *Psychological Science, 20,* 502–508.

French, J. R. P., & Raven, B. (1959). The bases of social power. In D. Cartwright (Ed.), *Studies in social power* (pp. 118–149). Ann Arbor, MI.: Institute of Social Research.

Galinsky, A. D., Gruenfeld, D. H., & Magee, J. C. (2003). From power to action. *Journal of Personality and Social Psychology, 85,* 453–466.

Galinsky, A. D. & Kilduff, G. J. (2013). Be seen as a leader. *Harvard Business Review*. Available at: https://hbr.org/2013/12/be-seen-as-a-leader'

Guinote, A. (2008). Power and affordances: When the situation has more power over powerful than powerless individuals. *Journal of Personality and Social Psychology, 95,* 237–252.

Kelman, H. C. (1958). Compliance, identification, and internalization: Three processes of attitude change. *Journal of Conflict Resolution, 2,* 51–60.

Kelman, H. C. (1974). Further thoughts on the processes of compliance, identification, and internalization. In J. T. Tedeschi (Ed.), *Perspectives on social power.* Chicago, IL: Aldine.

Keltner, D., Gruenfeld, D. H., & Anderson, C. (2003). Power, approach, and inhibition. *Psychological Review, 110,* 265–284.

Kipnis, D. (1972). Does power corrupt? *Journal of Personality and Social Psychology, 24,* 33–41.

Kipnis, D. (1976). *The powerholders.* Chicago: University of Chicago Press.

Kipnis, D., Schmidt, S. M., & Wilkinson, I. (1980). Intraorganizational influence tactics: Explorations in getting one's way. *Journal of Applied Psychology, 65,* 440–452.

Lammers, J., & Galinsky, A. D. (2009). The conceptualization of power and the nature of interdependency: The role of legitimacy and culture. In D. Tjosvold, & B. Wisse (Eds.), *Power and interdependence in organizations* (pp. 67–82). Cambridge: Cambridge University Press.

Lammers, J., Galinsky, A. D., Gordijn, E. H., & Otten, S. (2008). Illegitimacy moderates the effects of power on approach. *Psychological Science, 19,* 558–564.

Lammers, J., Stoker, J. I., Rink, F., & Galinsky, A. D. (2016). To have control over or to be free from others? The desire for power reflects a need for autonomy. *Personality and Social Psychology Bulletin, 42,* 498–512.

Magee, J. C., & Galinsky, A. D. (2008). Social hierarchy: The self-reinforcing nature of power and status. *Academy of Management Annuals, 2,* 351–398.

Magee, J. C., Galinsky, A. D., & Gruenfeld, D. H. (2007). Power, propensity to negotiate, and moving first in competitive interactions. *Personality and Social Psychology Bulletin, 33,* 200–212.

Magee J.C. & Smith, P.K. (2013). The social distance theory of Power. *Personality and Social Psychology Review, 17,* 158–186.

Markus, H. R., & Kitayama, S. (1991). Culture and the self: Implications for cognition, emotion, and motivation. *Psychological Review, 98,* 224–253.

Munduate, L., & Dorado, M. A. (1998). Supervisor power bases, cooperative behavior and organizational commitment, *European Journal of Work and Organizational Psychologist, 7,* 16–26.

Munduate, L., & Medina, F. J. (2004). Power, authority and leadership. In C. Spielberger (Ed.), *Encyclopedia of applied psychology* (pp. 91–99). San Diego, CA: Academic Press.

Overbeck, J. R. (2010). Concepts and historical perspectives on power. In A. Guinote, & T. K. Vescio (Eds.), *The social psychology of power* (pp. 19–27). New York, NY: Guildford Press.

Park, L. E., Streamer, L., Huang, L., & Galinsky, A. D. (2013). Stand tall, but don't put your feet up: Universal and culturally-specific effects of expansive postures on power. *Journal of Experimental Social Psychology, 49,* 965–971.

Sassenmerg, K., Ellemers, N., & Scheepers, D. (2012). The attraction of social power. The influence of construing power as opportunity versus responsibility. *Journal of Experimental Social Psychology, 48,* 550–555. doi: 10.1016/j.jesp.2011.11.008

Smith, P. K., & Galinsky, A. D. (2010). The nonconscious nature of power: Cues and consequences. *Social and Personality Psychology Compass, 4,* 918–938. doi:10.1111/j.1751-9004.2010.00300.x 4,918–38

Thibaut, J. W., & Kelley, H. H. (1959). *The social psychology of groups.* New York: John Wiley & Sons, Inc.

Tjosvold, D., & Wu, P., (2009). Power in cooperation and competition: Understanding the positive and negative faces of power. In D. Tjosvold, & D. Wisse (Eds.), *Power and interdependence in organizations* (pp. 83–100). Cambridge: Cambridge University Press.

Tost, L. P. (2015). When, why, and how do power-holders "feel the power"? Examining the links between structural and psychological power and reviving the connection between power and responsibility. *Research in Organizational Behavior, 35,* 29–45.

Van Knippenberg, B., Van Knippenberg, D., & Wilke, H. A. (2001). Power use in cooperative and competitive settings. *Basic and Applied Psychology, 23,* 291–300.

Van Vugt, M., Hogan, R., & Kaiser, R. B. (2008) Leadership, followership, and evolution: Some lessons from the past. *American Psychologist,* 63, 182–196. Available at: http://dx.doi.org/10.1037/0003-066X.63.3.182

Yukl, C., & Falbe, C. M. (1991). The importance of different power sources in downward and lateral relations. *Journal of Applied Psychology, 76,* 416–423.

Zhong, C-B., Magee, J. C., Maddux, W. W., & Galinsky, A. D. (2006). Power, culture, and action: Considerations in the expression and enactment of power in East Asian and Western societies. In E. A. Mannix, M. Neale, & Y. R. Chen (Eds.), *Research on managing groups and teams* (pp. 53–73). Greenwich, CT: Elsevier.

11 Does It Matter Who Leads Us?: The Study of Organizational Leadership

E. Kevin Kelloway and Stephanie Gilbert

Overview

Leaders are often saddled with the enormous responsibility of ensuring the success of organizations. The influence any single leader can exert on organizational-level performance continues to be debated, but other important individual-level outcomes of leadership have been more confidently supported. A very large body of academic literature across the fields of both organizational psychology and management has explored how leaders influence followers and what makes them effective. Organizational leadership research focuses on individual-level attitudinal, health, and performance outcomes, primarily for employees.

This chapter introduces the various approaches to the study of leadership and how they have evolved over time. We will review how each approach uniquely describes effective leadership, discuss some of the key outcomes of each leadership approach, and cover the strengths and weaknesses of each approach. The chapter begins with a discussion of the earliest trait-based leadership theories dating back to the early 1900s, followed by behavioural, contingency and modern leadership theories, as well as negative forms of leadership. Taken together, the findings suggest that leadership matters significantly, and we conclude that it is not *who* leads us but rather *how* those in leadership positions behave, adapt to different situations, and create positive relationships with followers that matters.

11.1 Does Leadership Matter?

Perhaps no question in organizational studies has attracted as much attention as the simple question of whether leadership matters (Barling, Christie, & Hoption, 2011). Certainly organizations and individuals act as if leadership matters. Sports teams on a losing streak change their coaching or managerial staff (e.g., Roma's firing of soccer

An Introduction to Work and Organizational Psychology: An International Perspective,
Third Edition. Edited by Nik Chmiel, Franco Fraccaroli and Magnus Sverke.
© 2017 John Wiley & Sons, Ltd. Published 2017 by John Wiley & Sons, Ltd.

coach Rudi Garcia after his team lost 9 of 10 matches). Businesses respond to adverse economic conditions by changing their Chief Executive Officers (e.g., Target firing Greg Steinhafel after a $1 billion failed expansion into Canada). In short, we behave as if leadership is one of the most important factors in organizational success, and is associated with numerous organizational outcomes (Barling, 2014).

It is not entirely clear that this faith in leadership is justified. One problem with studying leadership effectiveness is that we tend to judge whether a leader is effective or not based on the success of the organization he or she leads. Our evaluation of an individual's 'leadership' is confounded with the success of the organization. We often fail to recognize that the success or failure of organizations is most likely due to a multitude of factors. Consistent with the idea that we romanticize and exaggerate the importance of leadership, one longitudinal study found that the charisma of CEOs was not predictive of organizational financial performance. However, when firms were successful, their leaders were judged to be more charismatic (Agle, Nagarajan, Sonnenfeld, & Srinivasan, 2008). In a sense, leadership – or at least the attribution of effective leadership – may be the outcome, rather than the cause, of successful organizational performance.

Although researchers continue to debate the effect of leadership on organizational performance, there is less debate about the effect of leadership on more micro-level outcomes such as employee attitudes, behaviours and performance. Leadership has been associated with attitudes such as commitment to the organization (Barling, Weber, & Kelloway, 1996), satisfaction with and trust in the leader (Judge & Piccolo, 2004), and employee intent to leave the organization (Bycio et al., 1995). Leadership has also been associated with employee creativity and motivation (Dvir et al., 2002). Leadership also predicts performance outcomes (Barling et al., 1996).

Leaders also have an effect on employee well-being. For example, negative interactions with leaders have been linked to higher blood pressure among employees (Wong & Kelloway, 2016). Leadership also predicts employee safety (e.g., Mullen & Kelloway, 2009). In their review, Kelloway and Barling (2010) concluded: 'In short, virtually every outcome variable in the field of occupational health psychology is empirically related to organizational leadership' (p. 260). Taken together, these data clearly suggest that leadership matters, and we now turn our attention to identifying which aspects of leadership are important in predicting individual and organizational outcomes.

11.2   What Makes a Good Leader?

To begin, we should spend a few minutes thinking about what we mean when we refer to 'leadership' or 'leaders' in organizations. There are, perhaps, as many definitions of leadership as there are researchers interested in the topic (Kelloway & Barling, 2010). However, when individuals study leadership, they tend to focus on one of two basic definitions. First, researchers have been concerned with leadership emergence or role occupancy (Barling et al., 2011). The question here is how and whether an individual takes on a formal leadership role in the organization.

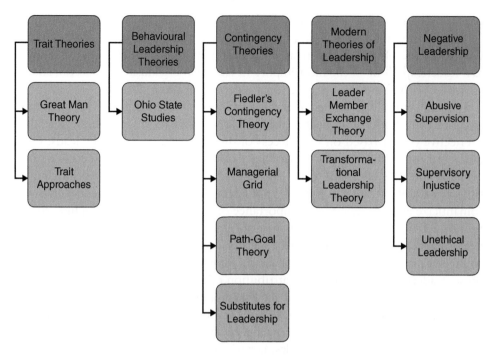

Figure 11.1:   Overview of leadership theories covered in this chapter

Another definition has focused on the question of leadership style, that is, the focus has been on how leaders behave (e.g., towards their subordinates) and how effective these behaviours are. In this sense, everyone is, or can be, a leader in that they can influence other people. In their review, Kelloway and Barling (2010) put these definitions together to suggest that, in general, when we talk about organizational leadership, we are talking about the behaviour and effectiveness of individuals who hold formal leadership roles in the organizations. Thus, most extant research has focused on the behaviour of supervisors and managers in organizations.

This is the approach we adopt in this chapter – focusing on how formal leaders behave. Historically, the focus of leadership research has shifted from leaders' own traits, to the importance of the situation, to modern theories of leadership that focus on leaders' behaviours and their relationships with followers. We discuss each, in turn, below, to explain how we have arrived at the modern theories that are the focus of today's leadership research. Figure 11.1 provides an overview of theories to be discussed in this chapter.

11.3   Trait Theories

We will first discuss trait theories of leadership, comprised of Great Man theory and the examination of stable leader characteristics that relate to leadership and leader effectiveness. Historically, this is where leadership research begins.

11.3.1   Great Man theories

The very earliest approach to understanding leadership was based on the notion that the history of the world was shaped by 'great men'[1] [*sic*] (Carlyle, 1907). By studying the lives and characteristics of leaders, such as Napoleon or Alexander the Great, it was believed that we would be able to learn about the characteristics that led to effective leadership. To some extent, this approach has died out as a research technique, although biographies of successful leaders (e.g., Jack Welch, the former CEO of General Electric Co.) and the study of leaders' actions (e.g., the 'I have a dream' speech of Martin Luther King) are still popular ways of learning about leaders and leadership.

11.3.2   Other trait theories

The Great Man approach to leadership resulted in a focus on identifying the characteristics or traits associated with these leaders. Traits are relatively stable and enduring characteristics of an individual. Both physical characteristics (e.g., height) and psychological characteristics (e.g., personality) are considered traits. One of the earliest approaches to studying leadership was the attempt to identify traits that differentiated 'leaders from non-leaders'.

The trait approach to understanding leadership dominated the early part of the twentieth century but was largely dismissed when major reviews of this literature concluded that there was little or no evidence supporting an association between traits and leadership. More recently, researchers have pointed to flaws in these early reviews (e.g., Zaccaro, 2012) and provided evidence that there may well be consistent associations between traits and leadership.

For example, leadership is positively associated with intelligence (Judge, Colbert, & Ilies, 2004) and height (Judge & Cable, 2004). The traits comprising the "Big 5" model of personality (i.e., agreeableness, conscientiousness, openness to experience, extraversion, and neuroticism; (see also Chapter 17 in this volume) are also associated with leadership – particularly extraversion and a lack of neuroticism (Judge et al., 2002). The consistency of these findings suggests that some individual characteristics are associated with leadership and that organizations may improve their leader selection processes by selecting individuals based on these traits.

Another approach has considered other characteristics of individuals such as gender. Although the fact that the 'Great Man' approach to leadership excluded women, this is now recognized as an error. However, it remains true that men are more likely than women to be in leadership roles and the difference becomes remarkably pronounced when one considers more senior leadership roles such as CEO or board members. There are a number of factors that might contribute to this disparity. One is that women may hit the 'glass ceiling' – a set of barriers in organizations that might prevent their advancement into more senior management positions. Ryan and Haslam (2007) also identified the 'glass cliff' that exists for women in organizations – women may be more likely to be selected for leadership positions on 'high risk' projects that are more likely to fail. When the project does fail, the failure is blamed on the woman in charge. Both of these factors reflect an underlying stereotype of women as ineffective leaders (Ryan & Haslam, 2007). Women may also be less motivated to pursue advancement into senior leadership positions either because they continue to bear a disproportionate amount of family responsibilities or because they are aware of the stereotypes about women as leaders.

A wealth of empirical data now speaks to the differences between men and women in terms of leadership. In contrast to any stereotype about women being less effective in leadership roles, the data actually suggest that women leaders tend to be less autocratic, more participative, and engage in more effective leadership behaviours than do men (Eagly, Johannesen-Schmidt, & van Engen, 2003).

In terms of our guiding question, the trait approach to leadership suggested that it does matter who leads – leaders with certain traits (e.g., high intelligence, extraverted personality) are more likely to be effective than individuals without those traits. However, the findings with regard to gender suggest a reason for these links between individual characteristics and leadership. Women are not more effective just because they are women – they are more effective in leadership roles because they tend to engage in more positive leadership behaviours. This suggests that it may be more productive to change the question from 'does it matter who leads us?' to 'does it matter how our leaders treat us?' This latter question has been the focus of considerable research since about the middle of the twentieth century.

11.4 Behavioural Theories

Although we now have a clearer idea of the role of traits in predicting leadership, early findings were often counter-intuitive. Thus, although leadership might be associated with height, it is easy to think of examples where individuals who were not very tall emerged as leaders (e.g., Napoleon). Moreover, although some leaders were good students, others had a more mixed record during their schooling (e.g., Winston Churchill). The lack of clarity regarding the role of traits led researchers to turn from traits to examining behaviours. That is, rather than asking, '*who* is an effective leader?' researchers began asking, '*what* do effective leaders do?'

Perhaps the most influential answer to this question emerged from a series of studies known as the Ohio State Studies (e.g., Kerr, Schriesheim, Murphy, & Stogdill, 1974). These researchers identified two aspects of leaders' behaviour that seemed to be important. 'Consideration' was the label given to behaviours that were focused on people rather than on tasks. For example, working to build trust and showing concern for the welfare of others would be examples of consideration behaviours (Kerr et al., 1974). In contrast, 'initiating structure' comprised behaviours that were focused on the task – establishing clear guidelines

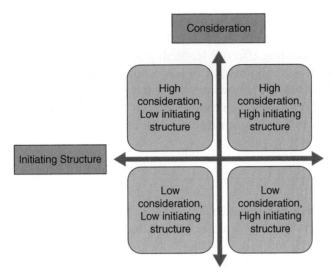

Figure 11.2: Four combinations of Ohio State Studies' behavioural leadership dimensions

and procedures for how the work was to be done. Setting clear goals, scheduling and defining standards of performance are examples of initiating structure (e.g., Kerr et al., 1974). Figure 11.2 depicts the four combinations of consideration and initiating structure, according to this theory.

Although the Ohio State Studies generated a great deal of research, the results were not always consistent and this led to increasing questions about the validity of this approach to understanding leadership. However, just as with the trait approach to leadership, a recent reappraisal of the research evidence provides convincing evidence for the validity of the basic propositions relating to initiating structure and consideration. In their meta-analysis of behavioural leadership research, Judge et al. (2004) show that the previous inconsistencies in findings were a result of methodological problems with the research. When these problems are accounted for, there is good evidence that consideration is moderately to strongly correlated with morale and employee attitudes. Initiating structure is associated with task and group performance. To some extent, the propositions of the behavioural theory of leadership seem to be quite well supported by the empirical data.

One problem with this behavioural approach and how it defines effective leadership remains. Initially, it was thought that the most effective leadership style would involve high levels of both initiating structure and consideration – that is, effective leaders would be equally highly concerned with both task and people. Empirically though, the correlation between these two types of behaviours is quite small (i.e., r = .17; Judge et al., 2004), suggesting that this is not the case. Indeed, in some studies, the relationship is negative; suggesting, for example, that leaders high on initiating structure may have demonstrated little or no consideration for employees, and vice versa.

The importance of these early studies of leadership may not lie in the particular findings obtained. Rather, the behavioural study of the leadership introduced a new way of understanding effective leadership by focusing on what leaders actually do. In turn, this paradigm shift in leadership research opened up the possibility that leaders could be trained or taught the behaviours that comprise effective leadership. This focus on behaviour has been continued and underpins much of the current research on organizational leadership.

11.5 Contingency Theories

The behavioural approach to leadership was based on the notion that there was a single set of behaviours that would be effective under all conditions. Partially as a result of the perception that the Ohio State Studies had inconsistent findings, researchers introduced a new notion of contingent leadership. The idea underpinning contingency models was that leaders would need to demonstrate different behaviours in different circumstances – that is, the most appropriate leadership style to be displayed depends on the situation.

For example, when people are in danger (e.g., stuck in a building fire), it might be more appropriate to be solely focused on getting people to safety rather than being concerned about their feelings. In terms of behavioural theories, emergencies may require high initiating structure and low consideration. However, when it is important for a group to reach consensus on an issue, it may be more important for leaders to demonstrate high consideration (i.e., ensuring that individuals have a chance to express their views and that all group members are heard) with less emphasis on initiating structure.

11.5.1   Fiedler's contingency theory

Fred Fiedler (1967) is frequently identified as the first true contingency theorist of leadership. Like the behavioural theorists, Fiedler viewed leaders as being primarily motivated around task (i.e., initiating structure) or people (i.e., consideration). However, Fiedler extended his analysis to consider three situational aspects thought to be particularly important in determining the appropriate style of leadership. Fiedler thought that: (1) the quality of leader–follower relationships (see section on leader member exchange theory below), (2) the existence of formal authority or power in the relationship, and (3) the clarity of performance goals all contributed to what he termed the favourableness of the situation. He predicted that task-motivated leaders would be most effective when favourableness was either very high or very low. In contrast, relationship-motivated leaders were predicted to be more successful in more moderate situations.

Thus, in an emergency, a leader may not know the people he/she is working with, there is little or no established structure, and nobody knows what is happening. Fiedler would suggest that in this very unfavourable situation, a task-motivated leader would be effective. Task-motivated leaders were also thought to be effective in more favourable situations where there are strong and positive relationships between the employees and the leaders, the goals are clear and there is a clearly established power structure (e.g., a military unit on a training exercise). However, when conditions are more mixed – for example, when a leader is new to the situation or does not have any formal power – then a relationship-motivated manager might be more effective.

There is fairly good evidence for the basic notion that different leader behaviours are more effective under different circumstances (e.g. Peters, Hartke, & Pohlmann, 1985). Perhaps the more problematic aspect of Fiedler's theory was his view that one had to change the leader to suit the situation, since he believed that leaders' orientation was stable and trait-like. This was a difficult proposition for organizations as it implied that one had to switch managers whenever the situation changed and this would obviously create some practical problems within the company.

11.5.2   The Leadership Grid

Blake and Mouton (1964) developed their managerial leadership grid, recently renamed the Leadership Grid® (Blake & McCanse, 1991), based on the idea that some situations require different leadership styles. Their grid places concern for results (achieving tasks) and concern for people (meeting the needs of followers) along two dimensions, and along these two axes the authors identify five key leadership styles:

1. *Country club management*: leader pays special attention to attending to the needs of followers and building relationships, placing little emphasis on achieving results.
2. *Impoverished management*: leader shows concern neither for people nor for results, putting in a minimum of leadership effort.
3. *Middle-of-the-road management*: a leadership approach that balances people- and results-focused behaviours.
4. *Team management*: high people-orientation combined with high results-orientation leads to high levels of follower commitment to work and high efficiency.
5. *Authority-compliance management*: leader focuses primarily on efficiency and achieving results, demonstrating low concern for people.

The two dimensions are very similar to the behavioural leadership dimensions of the Ohio State Studies discussed above. According to this model, leaders must choose a style that best fits the needs of both people and results, and a team-oriented style of management is most effective for high productivity. See Figure 11.3 for a depiction of the Leadership Grid, which shows each of the five styles of leadership along the two axes of concern for results and concern for people.

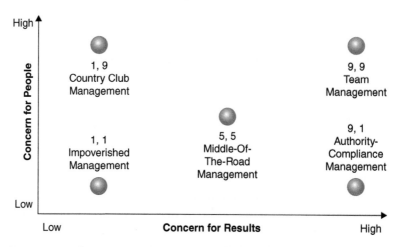

Figure 11.3: Five leadership styles according to the Leadership Grid®
Source: Blake & McCanse (1991).

11.5.3   Path–goal theory

Proposed by House (1971), path – goal theory also emerged based on the notion that leaders had to adapt their behaviour to different circumstances. House (1971) thought that the leader's role was: (1) to align the goals of the organization and the followers, and (2) to help followers achieve those goals. Leaders could help followers by focusing on either the path (i.e., the means to achieving goals) or the goal (i.e., the value that followers placed on the goal or the sense that followers could accomplish the goal).

Four leadership styles (ranging from very relationship-oriented to very task-oriented) were proposed as leader behaviour that could be used to motivate followers. These included:

1. *participative leadership* – engaging followers in decision-making and inviting feedback;
2. *supportive leadership* – demonstrating concern for the needs of followers;
3. *directive leadership* – providing task structure, clear goals and contingent feedback; and
4. *achievement-oriented leadership* – setting high standards for performance and challenging followers to achieve these standards.

Path–goal theory suggests that the effectiveness of these four leadership styles varies according to the situation (i.e., work environment characteristics, such as amount of task structure, and follower characteristics, such as ability). There is some support for propositions of the theory (Wofford & Liska, 1993). However, as Barling et al. (2011) noted, the complexity of the theory where leaders must evaluate follower characteristics and work environment characteristics and then modify their leadership style accordingly makes it difficult to test and to implement in organizations.

11.5.4   Substitutes for leadership theory

Kerr and Jermier (1978) proposed an additional contingency theory of leadership based on the idea that situational characteristics may either replace (they termed these 'substitutes') or nullify (such characteristics are called 'neutralizers') the effects of leadership. For example, professionals such as physicians are typically highly interested in the work they do and are highly skilled with a great deal of training. Such individuals may not need a leader to motivate them in order to be satisfied and effective in their job. Although this theory makes intuitive sense (Barling et al., 2011), there is not a lot of evidence supporting substitutes for leadership theory (Dionne, Yammarino, Atwater, & James, 2002).

11.6   Modern Theories of Leadership

Although most of the theories discussed above have some supporting evidence, they have largely been supplanted by what might be called the modern theories of leadership. Two theories in particular – leader member exchange (LMX) and transformational leadership theory – dominate the modern research on organizational leadership. Barling et al. (2011) reported that LMX and transformational leadership were the foci of 63% of all leadership research conducted between 1980 and 2007, with the latter theory dominating the research.

11.6.1   Leader member exchange (LMX) theory

Rather than focusing on the characteristics or behaviours of the leader, LMX focuses on the quality of the relationship between the leader and the follower (Gerstner & Day, 1997). LMX theory is premised on the idea that leaders and followers influence each other and that it is the quality of the relationship between the two that is most important. When leaders and followers like and support each other, when they are loyal to and trust one another, positive outcomes result, such as employee commitment, satisfaction and performance (see Gerstner & Day, 1997).

Two problems emerge with this perspective on leadership. From a practical perspective, the theory offers little guidance to leaders as to what they should do to improve the quality of their relationships with followers (Barling et al., 2011). That is, the theory suggests that the relationship is important but does not really articulate how to improve the relationship. Second, leaders and followers may disagree on the quality of the relationship (Gerstner & Day, 1997). Leaders may, therefore, be unaware that this important relationship is not a strong one from the employees' perspective and be unmotivated to improve the relationship.

11.6.2   Transformational leadership theory

In their meta-analysis and review, Judge and Bono (2002) pointed out that more research had been conducted on transformational leadership theory than on all

Figure 11.4: Full-range transformational leadership theory (Bass, 1985) depicting leadership styles ranging from active-constructive to passive-avoidant leadership

other theories of leadership combined (see also Barling et al., 2011). Transformational leadership theory (Bass, 1985) begins by making a distinction between 'transactional' and 'transformational' leadership behaviours. Transactional leadership behaviours are based on a transaction or an exchange between the leader and the follower. The leader engages in certain behaviours (e.g., praising or criticizing) in response to the follower's behaviour. Transformational leadership behaviours are those that go beyond the level of transactions by focusing more on the 'big picture' processes and outcomes to result in higher levels of performance. All leadership styles described in full-range transformational leadership theory may be described as lying along a continuum from active-constructive to passive-avoidant leadership (e.g., Bycio et al., 1995). Active-constructive leaders are involved, effective, and positive, whereas passive-avoidant leaders exert the minimum level of effort, avoiding leadership responsibilities altogether (see Figure 11.4).

11.6.3   Transactional leadership

Both negative and positive forms of transaction are considered. First, *laissez-faire* leadership is really the absence of leadership, where no transactions are made. It occurs when the leader has no response to the behaviour of followers. Such leaders avoid or deny responsibility and refuse to take any action in the workplace. Different types of management are:

- *Management by exception* occurs when transactions are primarily negative. In this style, leaders only respond to employee mistakes and failures to meet standards. In *active management by exception*, leaders actively look for employee mistakes. They micro-manage, closely supervise, and constantly check up on employees to ensure that tasks are properly performed. When mistakes occur, the leader criticizes and punishes the follower – which may lead to employees experiencing this form of leadership as abusive.
- *Passive management by exception* combines elements of both styles discussed above. For the most part, such leaders act as *laissez-faire* leaders – essentially ignoring followers. However, when mistakes or failures to meet standards are brought to their attention, then leaders respond with criticism and punishment. In contrast to the more active form, passive management by exception does not involve actively looking for failure but incorporates the same negative response to failure.
- *Contingent reward* behaviours are based on positive, rather than negative, transactions. Leaders engaging in this style set clear goals for employees and provide immediate and contingent feedback based on behaviour. In this case, contingent means that the behaviour of the leader is based on the behaviour of the follower. If mistakes are made, then the leader gives negative feedback and correction. However, when all goes well, leaders offer praise and support to employees.

Judge and Piccolo's (2004) meta-analytic review found that the more leaders engaged in *laissez-faire* and management by exception behaviours, the more employees expressed dissatisfaction with leaders and their jobs and the less effective they rated leaders. In their study of workplace safety, Kelloway, Mullen, and Francis (2006) found an additional destructive effect. Their data showed that when leaders were passive and ignored safety, the safety of the workplace was impugned. Kelloway et al. (2006) suggested that by being passive and ignoring safety issues, leaders sent the message that safety does not matter, and this influenced how followers thought and behaved with regard to workplace safety.

Transactions are not exclusively negative and when leaders engaged in more positive contingent reward behaviours, employees reported greater satisfaction and motivation. Importantly, contingent reward behaviours are also associated with increased individual and organizational performance (Judge & Piccolo, 2004). Thus, although contingent reward is classified as 'transactional' leadership behaviour, employees see it as a very positive form of leadership that is closely associated with transformational leadership (Bycio et al., 1995).

11.6.4   Transformational leadership

Transformational leadership is based on four forms of behaviour (Bass & Riggio, 2006). *Idealized influence* occurs when leaders are concerned with what is best for followers and the organization (i.e., doing the 'right' thing rather than taking the easiest course of action). Leaders who act in this way create a sense of shared mission and build trust and respect among their followers because they can be counted on to go beyond self-interest to do what is right. *Inspirational motivation* is evidenced by leaders who set high but achievable standards and who encourage followers to achieve more than they thought. Telling stories and using symbols are integral to inspirational motivation, which is aimed at increasing employees' sense of motivation and self-efficacy. *Intellectual stimulation* involves challenging existing beliefs and encouraging employees to think for themselves to generate solutions to long-standing problems. Adopting a questioning stance, encouraging creativity and facilitating independent thought are all characteristics of leaders who demonstrate intellectual stimulation. Finally, leaders demonstrate *individualized consideration* when they recognize individual strengths and weaknesses and pay attention to followers as individuals. Coaching, mentoring, and supporting individuals are all characteristic of individualized consideration.

Given the amount of research that has focused on transformational leadership, it is not surprising that there is a great deal of evidence supporting the effectiveness of transformational leadership behaviours. Leaders who are rated by their followers as being transformational (i.e., displaying the behaviours described above) are seen as more productive, elicit better performance from their followers at the individual, team and organizational levels, and have followers who are more satisfied with their jobs and their leaders (Judge & Piccolo, 2004).

Importantly, there is evidence that transformational leadership can be taught to managers (see, e.g., Barling et al., 1996; Mullen & Kelloway, 2009). Moreover, when leaders learn and demonstrate the behaviours associated with transformational leadership, employees demonstrate improved attitudes and performance (Barling et al., 1996; Mullen & Kelloway, 2009), translating into improved organizational performance. Overall, transformational leadership is consistently related to individual, team and organizational performance.

11.7   Comparison of Leadership Approaches

Most of the above theories share in common an emphasis on both task or production concerns and relationship concerns to explain various leadership styles and behaviours. Table 11.1 shows how each theory addresses each of these two dimensions and specifies which dimensions of each approach relate most to either 'task/production concerns' or 'relationship concerns'. All approaches address each dimension, except leader-member exchange theory, which does not explicitly

Table 11.1: Leadership theories addressing task/production and relationship concerns

				Leadership theories		
	Behavioural leadership	*Managerial grid*	*Path–goal theory*	*Fiedler's contingency theory*	*Leader member exchange*	*Transformational leadership*
Task/production	√(Initiating structure)	√(Concern for results)	√(Directive and achievement-oriented)	√(Task motivated leadership)		√(Intellectual stimulation and inspirational motivation)
Relationship	√(Consideration)	√(Concern for people)	√(Participative and supportive)	√(Relationship motivated leadership)	√(Relationship quality)	√(Individualized consideration and idealized influence)

Note: √ theory addresses this concern.

address task/production concerns. However, enhanced employee performance may be an indirect outcome of high-quality leader-member relationships (see Gerstner & Day, 1997).

11.8 Negative Leadership

Most leadership theory has focused on identifying the characteristics of effective leadership in organizations. However, researchers have also focused on negative or destructive aspects of leaders' behaviour (see, e.g., Kelloway et al., 2005) including abusive supervision, supervisory injustice, and unethical leadership.

11.8.1   Abusive supervision

When individuals in a formal leadership role engage in aggressive or punishing behaviour towards their employees, they are demonstrating abusive supervision (Tepper, 2007). Abusive supervision includes yelling at or ridiculing subordinates, name-calling, or threatening employees with punishment or job loss.

It is probably not surprising to find that such behaviour on the part of leaders is associated with increased employee stress. Employees of abusive supervisors report lower levels of job and life satisfaction, lower levels of affective commitment, increased work–family conflict, and psychological distress (Tepper, 2000), as well as psychosomatic symptoms, anxiety and depression. Employees exposed to this behaviour might engage in retaliatory behaviour (Townsend, Phillips, & Elkins, 2000; see case study on humiliation, Chapter 27 in this volume).

Wong and Kelloway (2016) examined how interactions with supervisors affected employees in long-term care facilities. Their data showed that when individuals had negative interactions with supervisors, their blood pressure went up. Moreover, the rise in blood pressure persisted into the after-work evening period. These data suggest that negative interactions with supervisors have consequences for physical, as well as psychological, well-being.

11.8.2   Supervisory injustice

Somewhat related to abusive supervision, a great deal of research has focused on the consequences of being treated unfairly by supervisors (see Chapter 15 in this volume). Based on their meta-analysis, Colquitt et al. (2001) reported that experiencing injustice was associated with job dissatisfaction and reduced organizational commitment. Kivimäki and colleagues (Kivimäki et al., 2005) have shown that both procedural (organizational) and relational (supervisory) injustice are predictors of minor psychiatric morbidity as well as sickness absence.

Supervisory injustice is also linked to a variety of physical health outcomes such as heavy drinking, impaired cardiac regulation, and use of sick time. Cardiovascular disease is linked to the experience of injustice: In their prospective cohort study, Elovainio, Leino-Arjas, Vahtera and Kivimäki (2006) found that employees reporting more favourable experiences of justice at work had a 45% lower risk of cardiac death than respondents reporting lower levels of justice.

11.8.3   Unethical leadership

In the wake of recent corporate scandals, a great deal of interest has been paid to the topic of unethical leadership in organizations. Brown et al. (2005) define ethical leadership as 'the demonstration of normatively appropriate conduct through personal actions and interpersonal relationships, and the promotion of such conduct to followers through two-way communication, reinforcement, and decision-making' (p. 120). Unethical leaders would be those who do not adhere to this standard.

Unfortunately, being unethical does not mean that these leaders are ineffective. Pseudo-transformational leaders place their own self-interest above the good of the group. Although they have a powerful ability to motivate and inspire others, they do not care about the welfare of followers and, therefore, may induce others to similarly act upon their own best interests rather than focus on attaining group goals (Barling et al., 2011).

Perhaps in a return to an earlier focus on the traits of leaders, there has been increased interest in the notion that leaders might possess more of the 'dark personality' traits (see Chapter 17 in this volume). For example, in their popular book, *Snakes in Suits*, Babiak and Hare (2006) suggest that some leaders may demonstrate psychopathic tendencies. Such leaders are thought to be incapable of empathy or loyalty to others and are solely focused on achieving their own goals at the expense of others. Babiak and Hare note that such characteristics might actually assist individuals to rise through the ranks of organizational leadership. That is, to the extent that psychopathy includes manipulating others, it may help individuals get promoted to increasingly senior leadership positions.

Similarly, in their meta-analytic review, Griljava, Harms, Newman, Gaddis, and Fraley (2015) found that narcissists are more likely to emerge as leaders in their organizations, although narcissism had no effect on leadership style. Individuals high in narcissism have a grandiose sense of self-importance, a tendency to feel entitled, and are often arrogant and exploitative. Narcissists are self-absorbed, crave attention, and tend to self-promote. It is possible that leaders become more narcissistic as a result of their corporate success (rather than narcissism predicting emergence as a leader).

Whatever the direction of the relationship, these findings are troubling in that they suggest individuals with 'dark personality' traits such as narcissism and psychopathy can emerge as leaders in organizations. Such personality characteristics are often associated with manipulation and exploitation of others and may lead to unethical behaviour by organizational leaders.

11.9　Conclusion

This chapter has reviewed the historical development of leadership theory, from trait, to behavioural, to contingency, to modern leadership theories, as well as negative forms of leadership. This development is important to understand as a foundation for where the leadership literature stands today. For example, after reviewing the key leadership theories, it is apparent that, in most of these theories, effective leadership often takes into consideration the need to achieve results and the need to build positive relationships with followers. Modern leadership theories, which have built upon decades of prior research, suggest that leaders' behaviour and the relationships they create with followers are critical to achieving positive outcomes.

Summary

In this chapter, we have described the evolution of leadership theory, introducing each individual theory in the process. First, we discussed the early Great Man and trait-based theories of leadership, which suggested that certain characteristics of the leader do matter. Behavioural-based theories furthered our understanding of leadership by addressing whether it matters how leaders treat followers. Evidence from this approach suggested that leaders could learn to exhibit more effective leadership behaviour. Contingency theories addressed the complex and varied environments in which leaders work, and this research discovered that it matters how leaders can adapt to situations and individuals. Modern leadership theories focus more on the relationships that are created between the leader and each individual follower, and this literature has suggested that leaders who create positive relationships with followers are more effective. Negative styles of leadership such as abusive, unethical, and pseudo-transformational leadership as well as acts of supervisory injustice were also discussed. Although these negative forms of leadership may sometimes still have good performance outcomes, they tend to be related to other poor employee outcomes. The important contributions that each of the above theories have made to the leadership literature inform how and why leadership is so critical to organizational success.

Taken together, over 100 years of research into organizational leadership suggest that it might not matter who leads – but it does matter how they lead. That is, the characteristics of individual leaders seem less important than how they treat, and interact with, their followers. The behaviour of the leaders, and the resultant relationships with employees, are critical to both individual and organizational success.

Discussion Points

1 Describe a manager you have had in the past who took a transactional approach and a manager you have had who was transformational. What effect did each leader have on your attitudes and performance?
2 Compare and contrast Fiedler's contingency theory and House's path-goal theory. What are the similarities and differences? Which do you think would be more easily applied in organizations?

Note

1 Historically, a strong gender bias excluded the consideration of 'great women' although a great deal of research now speaks to the leadership effectiveness of both men and women in organizations.

Suggested Further Reading

Barling, J., Christie, A., & Hoption, C. (2011). Leadership. In S. Zedeck (Ed.), *Handbook of industrial and organizational psychology* (vol. 1). Washington, DC: APA Books. For a review of negative forms of leadership, including abusive leadership.

Kelloway, E. K., Sivanathan, N., Francis, L., & Barling, J. (2005). Poor leadership. In J. Barling, & E. K. Kelloway (Eds.), *Handbook of work stress* (pp. 89–112). Thousand Oaks, CA: Sage. For a further review of leadership theories as well as key leadership issues such as gender and leadership.

Journals

The following journals regularly publish high-quality leadership articles:

- *Journal of Applied Psychology*
- *Journal of Occupational and Organizational Psychology*
- *Journal of Organizational Behaviour*
- *Leadership Quarterly*
- *Leadership and Organizational Development Journal*

References

Agle, B. R., Nagarajan, N. J., Sonnenfeld, J. A., & Srinivasan, D. (2006). Does CEO charisma matter? An empirical analysis of the relationships among organizational performance, environmental uncertainty, and top management team perceptions of CEO charisma. *Academy of Management Journal, 49,* 161–174.

Babiak, P., & Hare, R. (2006) *Snakes in suits: When psychopaths go to work.* New York: Harper Books.

Barling, J. (2014). *The science of leadership: Lessons from research to organizational leaders.* New York: Oxford University Press.

Barling, J., Christie, A., & Hoption, A. (2011). Leadership. In S. Zedeck et al. (Ed.), *Handbook of industrial and organizational psychology.* Washington, DC: American Psychological Association.

Barling, A. J., Weber, T., & Kelloway, E. K. (1996). Effects of transformational leadership training on attitudinal and financial outcomes: A field experiment. *Journal of Applied Psychology, 81,* 827–832.

Bass, B. M. (1985). *Leadership and performance beyond expectations.* New York: Free Press.

Bass, B. M., & Riggio, R. E. (2006). *Transformational leadership* (2nd ed.). Mahwah, NJ: Erlbaum.

Blake, R. R., & McCanse, A. A. (1991). *Leadership dilemmas: grid solutions.* Houston, TX: Gulf Publishing.

Blake, R. R., & Mouton, J. (1964). *The managerial grid: Key orientations for achieving production through people.* Houston, TX: Gulf Publishing.

Bono, J. E., & Judge, T. A. (2004). Personality and transformational and transactional leadership: A meta-analysis. *Journal of Applied Psychology, 89,* 901–910.

Brown, M. E., Treviño, L. K., & Harrison, D. A. (2005). Ethical leadership: A social learning perspective for construct development and testing. *Organizational Behavior and Human Decision Processes, 92:* 117–134.

Bycio, P., Hackett, R. D., & Allen, J. S. (1995). Further assessments of Bass's (1985) conceptualization of transactional and transformational leadership. *Journal of Applied Psychology, 80,* 468–478.

Carlyle, T. (1907). *Heroes and hero worship.* Boston, MA: Houghton Mifflin.

Colquitt, J. A., Conlon, D. E., Wesson, M. J., Porter, C. O. L. H., & Ng, K. Y. (2001). Justice at the millennium: A meta-analytic review of 25 years of organizational justice research. *Journal of Applied Psychology, 86,* 425–445.

Dionne, S. D., Yammarino, F. J., Atwater, L. E., & James, L. R. (2002). Neutralizing substitutes for leadership theory: Leadership effects and common-source bias. *Journal of Applied Psychology, 87,* 454–464.

Dvir, T., Eden, D., Avolio, B. J., Shamir, B. (2002). Impact of transformational leadership on follower development and performance: A field experiment. *Academy of Management Journal, 45,* 735–744.

Eagly, A. H., Johannesen-Schmidt, M. C., & van Engen, M. L. (2003). Transformational, transactional, and laissez-faire leadership styles: A meta-analysis comparing women and men. *Psychological Bulletin, 129,* 569–591.

Elovainio, M., Leino-Arjas, P., Vahtera, J., & Kivimäki, M. (2006). Justice at work and cardiovascular mortality: A prospective cohort study. *Journal of Psychosomatic Research, 61,* 271–274.

Fiedler, F. E. (1967). *A theory of leadership effectiveness.* New York: McGraw-Hill.

Gerstner, C. R., & Day, D. V. (1997). Meta-analytic review of leader-member exchange theory:

Correlates and construct issues. *Journal of Applied Psychology, 82,* 827–844.

Grijalva, E., Harms, P. D., Newman, D. A., Gaddis, B. H. and Fraley, R. C. (2015), Narcissism and leadership: A meta-analytic review of linear and nonlinear relationships. *Personnel Psychology, 68:* 1–47.

House, R. J. (1971). A path goal theory of leader effectiveness. *Administrative Science Quarterly, 16,* 321–339.

Judge, T. A., & Bono, J. E. (2000). Five-factor model of personality and transformational leadership. *Journal of Applied Psychology, 85,* 751–765.

Judge, T. A., Bono, J. E., Ilies, R., & Gerhardt, M. W. (2002). Personality and leadership: A qualitative and quantitative review. *Journal of Applied Psychology, 87,* 765–780.

Judge, T. A., & Cable, D. M. (2004). The effect of physical height on workplace success and income: Preliminary test of a theoretical model. *Journal of Applied Psychology, 89,* 428–441.

Judge, T. A., Colbert, A. E., & Ilies, R. (2004). Intelligence and leadership: A quantitative review and test of theoretical propositions. *Journal of Applied Psychology, 89,* 542–552.

Judge, T. A., & Piccolo, R. F. (2004). Transformational and transactional leadership: A metaanalytic test of their relative validity. *Journal of Applied Psychology, 89,* 755–768.

Judge, T. A., Piccolo, R. F., & Ilies, R. (2004). The forgotten ones? the validity of consideration and initiating structure in leadership research. *Journal of Applied Psychology, 89,* 36–51.

Kelloway, E. K., & Barling, J. (2010). Leadership development as an intervention in occupational health psychology. *Work & Stress, 24,* 260–279.

Kelloway, E. K., Mullen, J., & Francis, L. (2006). Divergent effects of transformational and passive leadership on employee safety. *Journal of Occupational Health Psychology, 11,* 76–86.

Kelloway, E. K., Sivanathan, N., Francis, L., & Barling, J. (2005). Poor leadership. In J. Barling,

& E. K. Kelloway (Eds.), *Handbook of work stress* (pp. 89–112). Thousand Oaks, CA: Sage.

Kerr, S., & Jermier, J. M. (1978). Substitutes for leadership: Their meaning and measurement. *Organizational Behavior and Human Performance, 22,* 375–403.

Kerr, S., Schriesheim, C.A., Murphy, C. J., & Stogdill, R. M. (1974). Toward a contingency theory of leadership based upon the consideration and initiating structure literature. *Organizational Behavior and Human Performance, 12,* 62–82.

Kivimäki, M., Ferrie, J. E., Brunner, E., Head, J., Shipley, M. J., Vahtera, K., & Marmot, M. (2005). Justice at work and reduced risk of coronary heart disease among employees: The Whitehall II Study, *Archives of Internal Medicine, 165,* 2245–2251.

Mullen, J. E., & Kelloway, E. K. (2009). Safety leadership: A longitudinal study of the effects of transformational leadership on safety outcomes. *Journal of Occupational and Organizational Psychology.82,* 253–272.

Peters, L. H., Hartke, D. D., & Pohlmann, J. T. (1985). Fiedler's contingency theory of leadership: An application of the meta-analysis procedures of Schmidt and Hunter. *Psychological Bulletin, 97,* 274–285.

Ryan, M. K., & Haslam, S. A. (2007). The glass cliff: Exploring the dynamics surrounding the appointment of women to precarious leadership positions. *Academy of Management Review, 32*(2), 549–572.

Tepper, B. J. (2000). Consequences of abusive supervision. *Academy of Management Journal, 43,* 178–190.

Tepper, B. J. (2007). Abusive supervision in work organizations: Review synthesis, and research agenda. *Journal of Management, 33,* 261–289.

Townsend, J., Phillips, J. S., & Elkins, T. J. (2000). Employee retaliation: The neglected consequence of poor leader-member exchange relationships. *Journal of Occupational Health, Psychology, 5,* 457–463.

Wofford, J. C., & Liska, L. Z. (1993). Path-goal theories of leadership: A meta-analysis. *Journal of Management, 19,* 857–876.

Wong, J. H. K. & Kelloway, E. K. (2016). What happens at work stays at work? Workplace supervisory social interactions and blood pressure outcomes. *Journal of Occupational Health Psychology, 21,* 133–141.

Zaccaro, S. J. (2012). Individual differences and leadership: Contributions to a third tipping point. *The Leadership Quarterly, 23*(4), 718–728.

12 Why Are We in a Team? Effects of Teamwork and How to Enhance Team Effectiveness

Annika Lantz Friedrich and Daniela Ulber

Overview

Many organizations have structured their work around teams, and most people have an experience of teamwork when they have felt the joy of accomplishing things together, learning from others, and getting good and rewarding results. There are many reasons why people work in teams, including managerial beliefs that teamwork can be beneficial to organizational effectiveness. We start this chapter by describing positive outcomes of teamwork for the individual, the team and the organization. In a second step, we define teams and distinguish them from other groupings. Teams are not always effective. How can the effects of teamwork be explained and thus be enhanced? In the following sections, we first outline a model of effective teamwork and then go deeper into aspects and processes that research has shown to be important for team effectiveness. We finish with an overview of the main findings and discuss how contextual and situational aspects can influence team processes, and how factors on individual, team and organizational levels interact.

12.1 Why Teams?

Throughout history people have been living and working in groups and families. Doing things together, whether it is hunting, harvesting, playing games, bringing up children or doing research, has been shown to be more rewarding and effective than doing things individually. Lieberman, a prominent psychologist and neuroscientist, states that evolution has designed our modern brains to be wired for 'reaching out to and interacting with others' (Lieberman, 2013, p. 9). Individuals are social animals: they have social needs for affiliation and know how *to make use* of social interaction. There are many ways of organizing work, and

An Introduction to Work and Organizational Psychology: An International Perspective, Third Edition. Edited by Nik Chmiel, Franco Fraccaroli and Magnus Sverke.
© 2017 John Wiley & Sons, Ltd. Published 2017 by John Wiley & Sons, Ltd.

although it all depends on social interaction, social needs can be met in different ways. Why should organizations invest in teams as the work unit? The main reason for organizing work in teams is probably the idea of synergy: 'The whole is more than the sum of its parts.' When teamwork in the workplace functions well, it may result in *outcomes for individual, team, and organizational levels*. Researchers have investigated what enables specific team processes that result in worthwhile outcomes for organizations. Work and organizational psychologists help teams to accomplish these outcomes with a minimum of expenditure of time and effort (see Chapter 25 in this volume). We start by describing the outcomes of teamwork, as these are what organizations strive for.

12.2 Outcomes of Teamwork

In descriptions of production systems and organizational strategies, statements like 'teamwork is a pillar for innovation' are common. Organizations invest in teamwork, believing it can be an effective way of organizing work and attaining their goals. Organizations benefit from outcomes at the individual and the team level. Organizational learning, change and development can be a bottom–up process, and so we first begin with describing outcomes for the individual.

Most people like to work with others, and meeting this social need through teamwork is important for an employee's commitment and well-being. Maslow (1943) identified our basic love and esteem needs as a motivational force, and in work psychology the principle of 'social and societal embeddedness' is seen as an important criterion for a humane work situation. Ulich and Weber (1996), among many others, report high intrinsic motivation, personal development, enhancement of skills and qualification as well as a reduction of workload and stress as positive effects of teamwork. Mutual support in teams promotes health and satisfaction and reduces burnout rates (see e.g., van Dick & Haslam, 2012).

At the team level, well-functioning teamwork will over time give the team a sense of efficacy and a belief in the team's viability. Viability is the 'team's capacity for the sustainability and growth required for success in future performance episodes' (Bell & Marentette, 2011, p. 279). It is a team-level outcome that is important to the team taking on future challenges. Moreover, team learning and knowledge management are supported because team members share their expertise and are involved in a mutual learning process (West, 2012).

Organizations profit from the outcomes of the individual and team level. Work results are obtained faster and more effectively, since teams can structure their sub-tasks more flexibly. Quality management is increased, and innovations and changes are eased, because team members can bring different perspectives. An organization based on teams works with less structural complexity and a flatter hierarchy. Decision-making can be decentralized to lower levels. A team structure is a good answer to the requirements of organizational complexity, since teams can be connected and involved when needed (West, 2012).

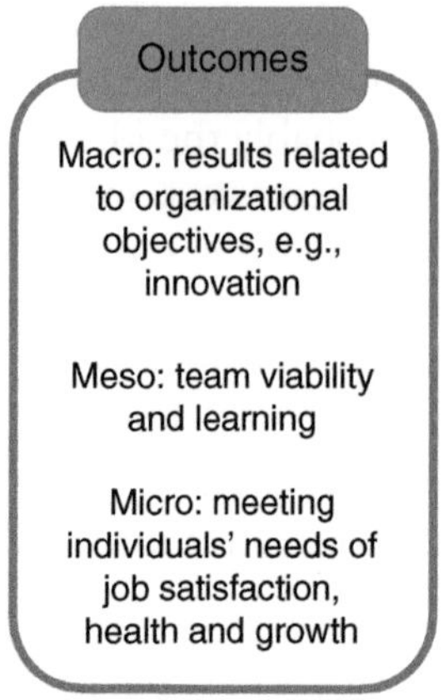

Figure 12.1: Outcomes of teamwork

Some of the reasons for teamwork are due to contextual and societal change: In the past few decades, environments have become much more turbulent and dynamic, because of increasing global competition and demands for individualized specialized products and services. This means that organizations are faced with the necessity to be flexible and with a pressure to innovate. Figure 12.1 summarizes the expected results of teamwork.

Teamwork has been introduced in many organizations to ensure good working conditions for employees, team-based learning and effective and flexible production. Although there is substantial evidence that teamwork is an effective means of working, positive effects of teamwork cannot be generalized to all organizational contexts. A meta-analysis of 61 studies (Richter, Dawson, & West, 2011) showed that teamwork in general has significant, but only small or moderate, effects on organizational performance, personal attitudes (such as job satisfaction and organizational commitment) and well-being. The conclusion is that it takes a lot to create the right conditions for teams if they are to be effective, and the outcomes depend on, among other things, how dependent team members are on each other.

12.3   What Is a Team?

Many different kinds of groupings exist. Are persons working in the same unit or in the same room a team? Not necessarily. It depends on how closely they work together, and that is why it is important to distinguish work teams as a specific unit of analysis in relation to other groupings.

Kozlowski and Bell (2013) give a basic definition of work groups:

> Groups are composed of two or more individuals, share one or more common goals, exist to perform organizationally relevant tasks, exhibit task interdependencies, interact socially, maintain and manage boundaries, and are embedded in an organizational context that sets boundaries, constrains the team, and influences exchanges with other units in the broader entity. (p. 415)

Groups differ in how closely team-members are connected, and in some cases they hardly need to communicate while working. West and Lyubovnikova (2012) identified four characteristics that distinguish teams from other groupings or 'pseudo-teams' – groups called teams but in which members mainly carry out their work individually. Teams are characterized by:

- *Reflexivity*: Teams discuss, reflect upon, and evaluate their on-going work and cooperation. They review their performance systematically, while pseudo-teams' communication is restricted, to, for example, the sharing of information for coordination of individual tasks. Teams *reflect* on habitual routines, such as how to coordinate work, and how these habitual routines might impede effectiveness and satisfaction – creating an opportunity to develop a shared understanding of the tasks and how to perform.

- *Task interdependence*: Tasks vary in how closely team members need to work together to complete the task. Task interdependence is the degree to which members of the team are mutually dependent on the others. High task interdependence means that the main task requires that the team members work in close collaboration to complete sub-tasks that are coordinated and aligned with overall goals. Task interdependence puts demands on collective regulation processes, and a shared understanding about what to do and how. A low level of task interdependence exists in a pooled form – team members make different contributions to the outcome, but do not interact with each other. Team members can also be connected sequentially, so that the chronological sequence of team members' actions is fixed, for example, in an assembly line where one member collects parts that the next one assembles into a machine, and then a third member tests the quality of the machine. In teams with reciprocal task interdependence, single team members interact with another team member one-to-one, and back and forth. It can be questioned whether teams with pooled or sequential team interdependence are real teams. Task interdependence put demands on both 'task work', how to carry out the work, and 'teamwork', how to interact.

- *Shared objectives*: In pseudo-teams there is no shared understanding of what the goal is, and what the team should strive for. A team has a common goal that *regulates* what different team members do and how.

- *Boundedness*: In a team, members identify with their specific team. Pseudo-teams are permeable to a degree that creates uncertainty about who the team players are. If team members do not have a sense of belonging to the team, they will be less motivated to contribute to the team and invest less in creating relationships with the others.

With the advent of the internet, the nature of teams has been changing rapidly in the past few years. Teams can be virtual, i.e. team members do not meet physically, but they still meet personally over the internet. A virtual team with members situated in distant locations and using communication technology to interact is a relatively new phenomenon but is quite common in many international companies and in research collaborations. Often employees work in ad hoc teams for a limited time, for example, forming a team to solve a complex technical production problem, or working in several teams simultaneously.

12.4   What Is an Effective Team?

Team effectiveness is the result of dynamic team processes, which depend on a broader system context that drives team task demands (Kozlowski & Bell, 2013). A team is inter-linked to other teams and functions, and exists in a workflow that will put external demands on the team. A team is effective when it accomplishes results and performs in line with external expectations, and within given prerequisites. The key here is that that these external expectations are not always so obvious, or easy for the team to interpret. An organization has an overall goal, key values, and a culture that sets the rules for how things should be done. Task demands are always determined by the surrounding organizational system, but they may sometimes be contradictory or vague, and different stakeholders, e.g. customers and labour unions, may have different priorities. Kozlowski and Ilgen (2006) describe the essence of team effectiveness pragmatically: 'When team-processes are aligned with environmentally driven task demands, the team is effective: when they are not, the team is not' (p. 78). Now let us turn to factors that make effective teamwork possible.

12.5   What Characterizes Effective Teamwork?

More than 50 years ago, McGrath (1964) proposed an Input–Process–Outcome (IPO) framework for studying team phenomena. The model describes how team effectiveness can be achieved. Inputs (I) describe antecedents that enable and constrain team processes. Processes (P) are interactions between team members. Outputs (O) are the outcomes of teamwork. This static model (i.e. it does not take into account how teams develop over time) has been interpreted causally (i.e. inputs impact processes and processes impact outcomes) and although contemporary perspectives on team effectiveness often use the basic IPO framework, and we do too, *we stress the dynamic process* that underlies it. Important inputs are individual team members' characteristics (e.g. skills, generic team competencies, and personality), team-level antecedents (e.g. task, job design, and interdependencies) and contextual factors (e.g. organizational structure and organizational support). The task is obviously the most important input. Processes are interactions between team members, such as coordination of work, but also leadership processes such as coaching and supporting the team.

The original IPO model has been developed subsequently to take into account the fact that teams develop over time, feedback loops exists, and processes and outcomes will over time influence the prerequisites for team processes. For example, a team reflects on work routines and learns to organize their work in a better way (processes), it becomes more productive (output), and needs less performance management and a different kind of managerial support (inputs). Mathieu et al. (2008) summarized previous extensive research on how inputs, processes and outputs are related in an organization in a model that is presented in Figure 12.2. Major research reviews have shown that team processes not only influence, but also drive outcomes of teamwork, and there is solid and growing evidence that team processes mediate the relation between input factors and outcomes. This is why processes are described as mediators (M) in Figure 12.2. Further, Figure 12.2 shows that individuals (the micro-level) are embedded in a team context (the meso-level), the team is embedded in an organizational context (the macro-level), and contexts on different levels influence each other. The model serves our purposes in addressing how inputs, processes and outcomes are inter-related in a multi-level context, and in describing what it takes for a team to be effective. We will use the model in Figure 12.2 to guide us from inputs, to processes and to the outcomes that were described at the beginning of this chapter.

Figure 12.2 shows that individual members comprise the team as a collective entity that also serves as a context that influence individual team members.

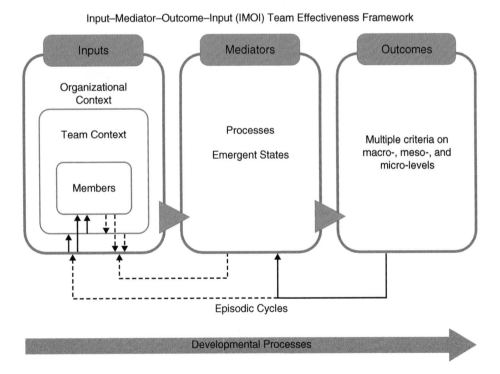

Figure 12.2: A model of team effectiveness

Source: Adapted from Mathieu et al. (2008). Reproduced with permission of SAGE Publications.

Linkages across micro-, meso- and macro-levels (team members, team context and organizational context) are key resources or demands that necessitate aligned team processes in order for the team to be effective. The arrows represent the feedback loops that over time will bring changes in both contexts and processes. Contemporary perspectives on team effectiveness regard teams as part of a multilevel system, put emphasis on the dynamic nature of teamwork, and view team processes as emergent phenomena that develop over time. Over time, teams develop e.g. a relatively stable way of work division and coordination.

The model is generally accepted by team researchers, and it is often used as a framework for empirical research. Substantial research has shown the complexity of interactions between factors on different levels and how context-specific prerequisites interact with team processes over time. The model takes into account how teams develop over time through feedback loops. The model is different from, and does not follow, the popular models of team process development through stages, so often used in consultancy. Tuckman and Jensen (1977), for instance, postulate, that after a phase of forming, there is a storming phase, where team members are resistant to norms, and controversies appear. After this, teams develop cohesiveness and a group identity (norming), and the following performing stage stands for effective group working. The final stage is adjourning: the dissolution of the team. Different stage models of group development are remarkably similar to Tuckman and Jensen's original work that was based on how therapy groups interact over time. There is little empirical evidence for stage models, and in contrast to the model above, the context, work task specifics, and their implications for the team are neglected (Kozlowski & Bell, 2013). We now turn to important inputs that affect outcomes through team processes.

12.6 Inputs

In line with the model in Figure 12.2, we distinguish between inputs at the individual, team, and organizational level. The main point is that these are contextually determined, and interlinked. Individuals differ in many respects (micro-level), team characteristics differ (meso-level), and organizational goals and structures differ between different organizations (macro-level). All these inputs affect team processes.

12.6.1 Inputs at the individual level

Team members differ from each other in experiences, personality, skills, and in many more ways, and hence contribute with different things; each member gives an individual input to the team. Team researchers have identified some characteristics that affect team processes more than others.

There is ample evidence that an employee's motivation may affect their performance. In a team context, motivation is also a question of being motivated to work closely with others. Bell (2007) regards *preference for teamwork*, the degree to which individuals have strong preferences for teamwork rather than autonomous work, as a value of great importance for teamwork. It is difficult to form a dynamic team if team members are not engaged in working together to accomplish the team task.

What are important individual team members' characteristics for team processes? Research has found that *team working skills*, such as a cooperative and supportive orientation, active listening and communication, as well as self-regulation skills (e.g., understanding how one reacts to and deals with criticism), promote an amicable climate in the team. To have team members who are kind and generous certainly is an asset when working together. *Personality and general cognitive ability* predict individual performance, and team performance, too. For example, when inter-dependence between team members is high, conscientiousness is important for team effectiveness. One needs to be able to rely on the others' order and self-discipline. Several studies have been conducted in this field. For instance, Bradley et al. (2013) researched conflicts and found that openness and emotional stability affect positively how teams resolve task conflicts. In sum: there is support that individual characteristics such as conscientiousness, extraversion, preference for teamwork, KSAOs (knowledge, skills, abilities and other characteristics), and team working skills predict team performance.

12.6.2 Inputs at the team level

Another important type of input concerns the team level, including team composition, team size, and, importantly, characteristics of the work task:

- *Team composition* looks at the characteristics of individual team members and how these characteristics are balanced. Personality factors such as team minimum agreeableness, team mean conscientiousness, openness to experience, collectivism, and preference for teamwork are strong predictors of good team performance (Bell, 2007). The more complex and innovative a team task is, the more heterogeneity is needed (West et al., 2004). There is broad agreement that heterogeneity of task-related attributes has a positive impact on team effectiveness, because it brings a broader knowledge base. But not only complementary professional expertise is important for team success. Belbin (2010) advocates heterogeneity of team roles: 'Teams are a question of balance. What is needed is not well-balanced individuals but individuals who balance well with one another' (p .73). A team needs specialists and innovators, as well as people who coordinate and implement processes, and those who focus on quality of social relations.
- *Diversity* refers to all the characteristics in which team members can differ (such as age, gender, social and cultural background, physical ability, etc). It is assumed that it takes time for heterogeneous teams to become an effective and cohesive group, because they need to establish common

norms. This may be challenging a common language has to be found, there must be an acceptance of different rationalities and perspectives and resulting conflicts have to be managed constructively. After this period, 'surface diversity' (for example gender, age, nationality) should no longer be a problem. But 'deep diversity' in attitudes, vision and goals can persist as a negative factor.

- *Team composition* matters, but also the size of a team sets a frame for team processes. There are different opinions on how many persons should be in a team. It is often said that the ideal size for a team is 6–8 members, because the larger the team, the more difficult it is to collectively regulate team processes. The team should include as many as it takes to carry out the job.
- *Team size* affects communication and interactions between team members, and the probability of social loafing is increased the more members in a team, the more probable it is, that they will reduce their effort. Team research has a long history. In Box 12.1, one of the first experiments on social loafing is described and explained.

The characteristics of the task affect team interactions. It is well known that work *task complexity* is crucial for team effectiveness (West et al., 2004). A challenging complex task is likely to be interesting to discuss and drives dynamic team learning, while routine tasks that put little demand on cognition can be accomplished without collective problem-solving, collective regulation or communication. Work psychologists use the term completeness to describe team tasks. A work task is complete when it includes goal-setting, planning and execution, as well as an evaluation of the outcome, and feedback. Complete team tasks imply team decisions – and for decision-making, teams need autonomy. With a complete job, the team has to discuss many aspects of work and take decisions on how to perform. Team *autonomy* refers to the amount of control and the margin of discretion a team has. Greater autonomy and degrees of freedom increase

---

Box 12.1:   Experiment on social loafing

In 1913, Maximilien Ringelmann, a French agricultural engineer, researched how much force people use at rope pulling. People pulling together as a team exerted less effort than individuals. The more people pulling, the less force they applied individually (the social loafing effect). Team members reduce their effort, they work and strive less in groups than alone. How can this be interpreted? There are two complementary explanations:

- *free riding*: individual team members think that the others will work enough to attain team goals without their individual effort;
- *sucker effect*: team workers notice that others do less, which causes a reduction in their own efforts, so that justice is served and effort is perceived to be fairly distributed between team members.

Box 12.2:   Tasks for teamwork

Tasks that are suitable for teamwork are:

- *complex* – so that they put demand on team cognition and team learning;
- *autonomous* – so that teams can find out how they best perform;
- *interdependently carried out* – so the tasks demand teamwork;
- *complete* – so that the team is responsible for a chain of inter-related tasks that are varied, make use of different KSAOs and provide task identity.

---

scope for using intellectual skills and influence collective regulation processes. If the task is standardized, such that there is only one way of doing it, there is no autonomy and no reason for the team to discuss what to do or how to do it. Autonomy in decision-making makes discussions about the task meaningful since such discussions can lead to a change in how to carry out the task or what should be aimed for. Task complexity and autonomy are inter-related, and are the criteria used for deciding whether teamwork is meaningful at all. Box 12.2 summarizes tasks that make teamwork worthwhile.

There are even more inputs on the meso-level that affect team interactions (see Wildman et al., 2012): What are the ways and structure of communication and information flow? How are team members distributed locally and can they interact face to face? How is work divided among team members and how far are these roles fixed or interchangeable?

12.6.3   Inputs at the organizational level

Teams do not operate in isolation; they are embedded in an organizational context that should support their processes. Such support may take various forms (Hackman, 1990):

- an adequate reward system, oriented toward team outputs, and an appropriate, needs-based qualification system;
- an information system for task-relevant news;
- material resources, for instance, space, equipment, finances, etc.

HR practices influence team effectiveness (Richter, Dawson, & West, 2011), for example, by giving teams feedback, and developing a transparent reward system (West, 2012). West et al. (2004) argue in favour of establishing an *organizational climate* of learning, development and innovation to ensure innovative teams.

It is the management's responsibility to supply organizational support in line with team demands, and human resource management is a useful tool.

Figure 12.3: Inputs that affect team processes and outcomes of teamwork

Managers need to believe in teamwork, support teams accordingly and invest in creating a climate of trust, shared responsibility, psychological empowerment and cooperation. Leadership is a core component of teamwork. What is specific for team leadership? It is a bit confusing as leadership is both an input and a process intertwined with team processes. *Leadership structure* is important for how closely team processes and leadership processes interact. Teams can have an external manager, or a designated team leader who belongs to the team and is responsible for all leadership functions. Types of shared leadership involve the team members. There can be temporary leadership, where leadership tasks and decisions are delegated to a team member for a certain period of time, a rotating model, in that different team members take on leadership responsibility consecutively, and distributed leadership, where leading different tasks is done by different team members. In a rotating, or a distributed model, leadership and team processes are practically the same thing. Leadership as an input factor means creating adequate conditions for the performance of team work, such as making sure that the task is explicit, searching for and structuring relevant information, ensuring that the necessary resources are available, and that team boundaries are clear (Burke et al., 2006). Figure 12.3 provides a summary of team inputs that affect outcomes through team processes.

12.7   Processes as Mediators between Inputs and Outcomes

Inputs are an important prerequisite for teamwork, but teams in the same setting can work very differently. Team and leadership processes play a crucial role as mediators for team effectiveness. On-going processes are dynamic and difficult to capture empirically. Kozlowski and Bell (2013) characterize emergent processes as dynamic, interactive, and multilevel, process-oriented and temporal in nature. But teams as well as leaders develop routinized patterns of interaction. Over time, processes become *emergent states* through: habitual ways of thinking, somewhat stable affective states and typical patterns of behaviours. The team can save energy by relying on usual ways of doing things, and habitual ways of interacting that also guide future processes. Over time these emergent states/phenomena change, as team members and leaders encounter new situations, integrate new information, and so think, feel and behave differently. We distinguish between leadership processes and team processes although they are interlinked.

12.7.1 Leadership processes

A team leader is a social problem solver (Zaccaro, Rittman, & Marks, 2001). Process tasks of team leadership are (West, 2012):

- building and maintaining the team as a functioning unit, in other words making sure that the right team members are in the team and that team processes are functioning well;
- coaching and supporting, in the form of direct interaction, interventions (when needed), establishing communication and exchange in the team, and creating and supporting learning processes.

Hackman and Wageman (2005) describe three ways of team coaching that in practice are most often integrated. Motivational coaching focuses the effort of team members, consultative coaching aims to influence the performance strategy of a team, and educational coaching addresses the knowledge and skills of team members. An important aspect of coaching is to help the team reflect on on-going processes. What processes impede performance? Simple methods, such as team debriefs, have been shown to enhance team effectiveness by up to 20–25% (Tannenbaum & Cerasoli, 2012). A team debrief reflects on specific team processes, such as helping behaviours and information sharing. These can be carried out at the end of a project, or throughout the process. It is a way to stop working and start reflecting on both task-work and teamwork.

It cannot be stressed enough: a key task for team leaders is to encourage reflexivity so that processes that impede effectiveness can be changed. But what is the impact of leadership behaviour in general on team effectiveness? A meta-analysis by Burke et al. (2006) shows mostly moderate positive effects of different leadership behaviours, such as structuring work, on team productivity and efficiency, with a remarkable relationship between empowerment by the leader and team learning.

12.7.2   Team processes

Processes fluctuate and are difficult to capture, but at a certain time we can describe emergent states to characterize dynamic processes. These states influence performance; think of the difference between a state of mutual trust versus conflict and tension. An important issue for research is to identify crucial emergent states for team effectiveness. The term 'process' applies to something that goes on or takes place, and is a series of progressive and interdependent actions by which an end is attained. There are a lot of things going on in human interactions, and to bring some order and make research possible, team researchers distinguish between three kinds of team processes: cognitive, affective-motivational, and behavioural processes.

12.7.2.1   *Cognitive processes*

Effective teamwork requires a shared understanding of what to do, why and how. DeChurch and Mesmer-Magnus (2010) define *team cognition* as 'an emergent state that refers to the manner in which knowledge important to team functioning is mentally organized, represented, and distributed within the team and allows team members to anticipate and execute actions' (p. 33). Some argue that the term *team knowledge* is a more suitable term, as cognition can include a wide range of cognitive phenomena at the team level. Knowledge facilitates performance. An effective team has, through discussions and reflexivity, identified key stakeholders, available resources, external expectations, and understood how the team is interlinked to others and why. This knowledge will guide team members in carrying out everyday work.

Learning and knowledge go together. Team learning as a social process of constructing knowledge is conceptualized as the building of a shared understanding of the problem or the task at a certain moment. Teams learn and develop by sharing inputs from outside the team, team activity, team reflexivity, and managing constructive conflict about task-work and teamwork. Team learning brings about an integrated shared understanding of what do to and why, that later will guide performance. Over time, this shared understanding may be altered and changed through reflexivity and feedback from stakeholders outside the team. Team learning is a collective thought process combined with reflexivity. Reflexivity allows teams to understand their own belief-systems that impede performance and learning behaviours. There is enough empirical evidence to show that team learning as a process of building shared meaning is crucial for team effectiveness (Van den Haar, Segers, & Jehn, 2013). For example, a meta-analysis of the impact of information sharing on performance, showed that information sharing, especially the sharing of unique information that is not available to all in the team, is positively related to all performance outcomes (Mesmer-Magnus & DeChurch, 2009).

The team's *awareness* of its knowledge base, the collection of knowledge of each team members' knowledge, and a shared collective understanding of who knows what, enable team members to communicate effectively and coordinate work in the team. This awareness of who knows what is often referred to as *transactive memory*. It helps team members to know whom to turn to, and integrates team members' behaviour in alignment with overall goals. Lewis, Lange and Gillis (2005) were the first to show that transactive memory is related to knowledge transfer. Transactive memory is important for both carrying out a given task, and for learning transfer, so that the team can go beyond and take on other, and perhaps more challenging tasks.

Then, what kind of knowledge is important for team performance and effectiveness? Team members have a mental model of their individual tasks and their environment, and when team members share similar team mental models (TMM), they can communicate more easily, and perform more effectively. TMMs are shared knowledge structures that enable the team to form accurate explanations and expectations of work, to communicate and coordinate actions, and adapt their behaviour to task demands and other team members. TMMs guide performance and enable teams to anticipate what needs to be done, and prepare for that. Four types of TMMs impact on team effectiveness according to Kozlowski and Ilgen (2006):

1. knowledge about the task, expected results, performance requirements, standards, task-related problems (task mental model);
2. knowledge about equipment, tools, and resources, (equipment mental model);
3. knowledge about each other; team composition and resources, team members' preferences, values, habits and KSAOs (team member mental model);
4. knowledge of effective ways of interacting in teams (team interaction model).

Team mental models are shared understandings of what to do. *Team climate* refers to the team's shared understanding of *what should be aimed for*. This is more general in nature, and the team climate depends on the team's shared understanding of external expectations and demands. Pirola-Merlo et al. (2002) defined it as 'the set of norms, attitudes, and expectations that individuals perceive to operate in a specific context' (p. 564). Many organizations describe principles for its production. This can, for example, be an imperative to continuously improve working methods, to economize, or always to bear in mind to treat others with respect and dignity when carrying out the main task. Such task demands need to be identified and interpreted by the team. An effective team understands and completes not only its specific in-role or main task, but also performs extra-role tasks as continuous improvements in accordance with expectations from stakeholders outside the team. Research has consistently shown the importance of team climate for organizational outputs, and also for individual learning and well-being. Some teams have a team climate of resisting change; others have a climate of proactivity and are on the lookout for opportunities to do things better, i.e., the teams have a team climate for innovation. Team climate for innovation influences the team's involvement in change and developmental work. Team safety climate is related to the team following regulations and safety routines to avoid accidents. Further, as TMMs describe what to do, they are related to team climate. To conclude: team knowledge gives the team a task focus, and *all cognitive processes influence how performance is regulated*.

12.7.2.2 *Affective–motivational processes*

Social interactions are full of emotions. It is obvious to most people who have worked in a team that affective processes influence performance. Feelings of mutual trust and an amicable climate make everything easier. Affective processes influence cognitive processes, such as team learning. Amy Edmondson (1999) introduced the concept of *psychological safety* that describes how safe it is to take risks in challenging the status quo, and of questioning habitual routines and the usual way of thinking. This certainly is an important input to team reflexivity. Raising critical viewpoints is possible when the affective climate is safe for inter-personal risk-taking. Team members feel free to speak up without risking being ridiculed or personally criticized.

Psychological safety is related to *team trust*. With experiences over time a climate might develop where team members rely on each other, and have confidence in each other. To trust is to be willing to be vulnerable to another's actions as you feel confident that the other will perform a particular action important to you, without you being able to control what happens. Psychological safety and team trust are important for team reflexivity and team learning, as people tend to act in ways that inhibit learning when they face a potential threat or embarrassment (Edmondson, 1999). Team trust has been shown to help teams handle conflicts, as task conflicts can be tolerated and dealt with without turning into destructive inter-personal conflicts.

The team members' commitment to the team is described as *cohesion*, 'the resultant of all the forces acting on the members to remain in the group' (Festinger, 1950, p. 254). A vast amount of research (see, for a meta-analysis, Beal et al., 2003) has shown that three dimensions of cohesion – interpersonal, pride, and task – are all, and fairly equally, related to performance (effect sizes around .25). Individuals may want to be in a team for different reasons, and taking pride in the team is one of these important motives. Team cohesion is of greater importance to teams that work in a complex workflow that demands close cooperation and interdependence, than to teams with a simple task structure.

Another important affective – motivational characteristic is *collective efficacy*: a shared belief in the team's collective capability of organizing and executing actions to attain a certain level of performance in relation to a goal. Different experiences of carrying out challenging tasks and performing well will over time give the team a sense of collective efficacy. It is not the mean value of different team members' appraisal of their self-efficacy, but a concept describing the team members' appraisal of the team's collective efficacy in a specific task. Team efficacy grows with the team taking on challenging tasks, and hence it is closely related to whether the task is complex and puts demands on learning.

Conflicts can be primarily cognitive, but typically evoke tensions and involve emotions. Without conflict management, conflicts can escalate and cause severe problems for team members and the organization. A meta-analysis (Dreu & Weingart, 2003) demonstrated the negative effects of conflicts on team performance and team member satisfaction. On the other hand, conflicts can also be useful, if they influence the quality of decisions, team learning, creativity and innovation positively (Robbins & Judge, 2015).

Psychological safety, team trust, cohesion and collective efficacy are affective and motivational states that we hope will emerge over time. They affect learning and the team's performance. Conflicts occur, and if handled well, might be useful and contribute positively to better ways of handling both task and teamwork. It is easy to cooperate in an amicable climate, and team members are more motivated to reflect on their performance in an amicable climate.

12.7.2.3 *Behavioural processes*

Now, back to what teams *do* in order to accomplish their task in line with expectations. What teams strive to do in order to achieve a goal, resolve task demands, and coordinate activities, is their performance. Performance is not an outcome. How the team does things, how they perform, will bring different results. Salas, Cooke and Rosen (2008) describe the team's ability to adapt its performance processes in response to changes in the external demands from the surrounding system as a first core characteristic of teamwork. Other core characteristics of teamwork are: mutual performance monitoring to ensure that the performance is on track; team members support each other; and they maintain a team orientation to ensure effective teamwork also under pressure or when in difficulty. This is what effective teams do. Team members coordinate, cooperate and communicate.

Communication regulates activities, and is based on team knowledge that guides regulation processes. Communication is most typically regarded as the means to coordinate individual activities, and it supports both task work and teamwork. The *coordination* of individual team members' activities is central so that different persons' activities are combined and aligned, not only in terms of sub-tasks in relation to the team's task and shared goal, but also in terms of timing. Coordination is: (1) the combination of disparate team member actions and efforts; and (2) temporal and action synchronization when combining team member actions and efforts. Wagner (1995) defined cooperation as: 'the wilful contribution of personal efforts to the completion of interdependent jobs' (p. 152), and when giving this definition a second thought, it is a demanding concept. It implies that team members by themselves initiate what needs to be done, and then do it. This is the opposite of social loafing.

We have now identified what teams should strive for in order to become effective, and have highlighted the importance of discussions about task-relevant subjects, reflexivity on routinized patterns of interaction, and the team's learning process. Effective teams continuously evaluate habitual routines to identify what impedes their performance. Help the team to start thinking is very good advice to team leaders and team coaches. Cognitive processes guide performance and affective processes may smooth both team learning and carrying out tasks. Figure 12.4 summarizes these findings.

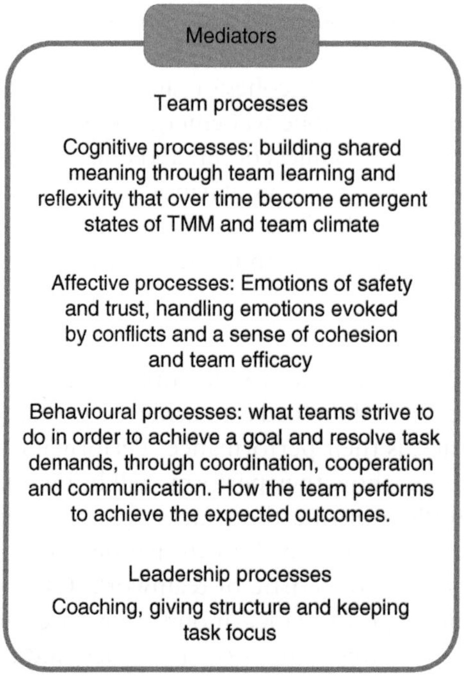

Figure 12.4:   Team processes and leadership processes that impact outcomes

12.8 Conclusion

Team effectiveness depends on contextual resources and demands (inputs) and team processes. Inputs are contextually determined and hence vary from one organization to another. Individuals differ in KSAOs, personality, general cognitive ability, etc., while team characteristics and task design depend on organizational structure and goals. When inputs on different levels are aligned, they positively impact outcomes through processes. Leadership processes and team processes are interdependent, and the team's performance is enhanced by team knowledge, on-going reflection and keeping a task focus also under pressure. An amicable climate, feelings of mutual trust and belief in the team's efficacy make team learning possible and will motivate the team to take on future challenging tasks. We have extended Figure 12.2 by incorporating the previous boxes and summarize in Figure 12.5 how team effectiveness can be understood.

We said earlier that individual members comprise the team as a collective entity that also serves as a context that influences individual team members. Linkages across multiple levels (team members, team context, and organizational context) are key resources or demands that necessitate aligned team processes in order for the team to be effective. This is not easy to grasp. As an example: individual resources, such as openness and general cognitive ability, a team resource, such as complex tasks and close interdependence, and an organizational resource,

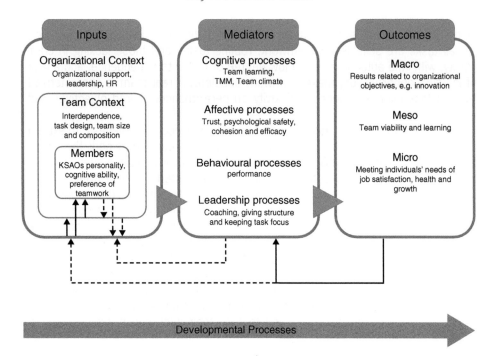

Figure 12.5: A summary and a model for enhancing team effectiveness
Source: Adapted from Mathieu et al. (2008). Reproduced with permission of SAGE Publications.

such as competence development measures, are resources that are interlinked, and positively impact team processes. Complex tasks, that can be idiosyncratically interpreted and redefined, impact on team learning. This is because they put a demand on the mental regulation process whereby the team, through communication, will share different understandings of the task, have controversies and co-construct the meaning of both the expected results and the task that might go beyond the stipulated task. Expert coaching by a team leader and affections of team trust and psychological safety will stimulate reflexivity on habitual work routines in relation to external expectations and form a team climate of readiness for change and innovation. This in turn will impact team performance and result in the team's taking part in change and developmental activities that result in innovation (a new process, service or product).

Summary

There is substantial evidence that teamwork can be an effective means of working and that it is an important aspect of a humane work situation. Teamwork may help in fulfilling individuals' needs for growth and health, and be a source of motivation and satisfaction. Team learning and team viability make teams take on future challenges that together with individuals' motivation and gained competence will influence outcomes

Continued

at the organizational level (such as productivity, efficiency, innovation). However, not all tasks are suitable for teamwork; routine tasks, and those lacking in complexity, with little autonomy, with a low degree of task interdependence, and a lack of learning opportunities, make teamwork obsolete. A real team is characterized by high task interdependence, reflexivity on performance, shared objectives and boundedness.

A main task for team research is to find ways to enhance effectiveness. To explain team effectiveness on different levels, a model has been introduced: the Input–Mediator–Outcome–Input (IMOI) model, in which team processes are seen as mediators between inputs and outcomes. Individual characteristics and KSAOs, team composition, team characteristics, task design as well as organizational support are some of the Input variables. Leadership processes, for instance, team coaching to facilitate team reflexivity, as well as cognitive, emotional and behavioural team processes play a crucial role as mediators. Important team processes are cognitive (as building team knowledge and team mental models through team learning), emotional (for instance, psychological safety, team trust, collective efficacy) and behavioural (coordination, cooperation and communication). All these contextual aspects are inter-related and impact team processes. Therefore, it takes a multi-level approach to describe team effectiveness – and to take their interactions into account to enhance team effectiveness.

Discussion Points

1 Find different examples of linkages between inputs, processes and outcomes, and put your own questions (use Figure 12.5 to guide you). One such interesting question could be: Why is it, that autonomy highly impacts team reflexivity?
2 If you were a new manager in an organization, what information about the individual team members and the team task would you need if you were to make decisions on team leadership structure and team composition? What would you analyse?

Suggested Further Reading

Hackman, J. R. (1990). *Groups that work (and those that don't)*. San Francisco: Jossey-Bass. An influential and still valid book about team effectiveness (and its tripwires), also giving detailed descriptions of several types of work groups.

Kozlowski, S. W. J., & Bell, B. S. (2013). Work groups and teams in organizations: Review update. In N. Schmitt & S. Highhouse (Eds.), *Handbook of psychology*: Vol. 12. Industrial and organizational psychology (2nd ed.) (pp. 412–469). Hoboken, NJ: Wiley. This chapter in the *Handbook of Psychology* describes profoundly and in detail the actual state of the art of team research, including many meta-studies and theoretical models.

West, M. A. (2012). *Effective teamwork: practical lessons from organizational research*. Chichester: John Wiley & Sons, Ltd. Michael A. West, is one of the most profiled team researchers, his book is praxis-orientated and evidence-based, bringing together relevant and comprehensive knowledge about factors impacting team effectiveness with diverse examples, tools and exercise material.

Wildman, J. L., Thayer, A. L., Rosen, M. A., Salas, E., Mathieu, J. E., & Rayne, S. R. (2012). Task types and team-level attributes: Synthesis of team classification literature. *Human Resource Development Review, 11*, 97–129. For an overview of the team classification literature and resulting team typologies on task and core team characteristics.

References

Beal, D. J., Cohen, R. R., Burke, M. J., & McLendon, C. L. (2003). Cohesion and performance in groups: A meta-analytic clarification of construct relations. *Journal of Applied Psychology, 88*, 989–1004.

Belbin, M. R. (2010). *Team roles at work.* London: Routledge.

Bell, S. T. (2007). Deep-level composition variables as predictors of team performance: A meta–analysis. *Journal of Applied Psychology, 92*, 595–615.

Bell, S. T., & Marentette, B. J. (2011). Team viability for long-term and ongoing organizational teams. *Organizational Psychology Review, 1*, 275–292.

Bradley, B. H., Klotz, A. C., Postlethwaite, B. E., & Brown, K. G. (2013). Ready to rumble: How team personality composition and task conflict interact to improve performance. *Journal of Applied Psychology, 98*, 385–392.

Burke, C. S., Stagl, K. C., Klein, C., Goodwin, G. F., Salas, E., & Halpin, S. (2006). What type of leadership behaviors are functional in teams? A meta-analysis. *Leadership Quarterly, 17*, 288–307.

DeChurch, L. A., & Mesmer-Magnus, J. R. (2010). The cognitive underpinnings of effective teamwork: A meta-analysis. *Journal of Applied Psychology, 95*, 32–53.

De Dreu, C. K. W., & Weingart, L. R. (2003). Task versus relationship conflict and team effectiveness: A meta-analysis. *Journal of Applied Psychology, 88*, 741–749.

Edmondson, A. (1999). Psychological safety and learning behavior in work teams. *Administrative Science Quarterly, 44*, 350–383.

Festinger, L. (1950). Informal social communication. *Psychological Review, 57*, 271–282.

Hackman, J. R. (1990). *Groups that work (and those that don't).* San Francisco: Jossey-Bass.

Hackman, J. R., & Wageman, R. (2005). A theory of team coaching. *Academy of Management Review, 30*, 269–287.

Ilgen, D. R., Hollenbeck, J. R., Johnson, M., & Jundt, D. (2005). Teams in organizations: From input-process-output models to IMOI models. *Annual Review of Psychology, 56*, 517–543.

Kozlowski, S. W. J., & Bell, B. S. (2013). Work groups and teams in organizations: Review update. In N. Schmitt, & S. Highhouse (Eds.), *Handbook of psychology*, vol. 12. *Industrial and organizational psychology* (2nd ed.) (pp. 412–469). Hoboken, NJ: Wiley.

Kozlowski, S. W. J., & Ilgen, D. R. (2006). Enhancing the effectiveness of work groups and teams. *Psychological Science in the Public Interest, 3*, 77–124.

Lewis, K., Lange, D., & Gillis, L. (2005). Transactive memory systems, learning and learning transfer. *Organization Science, 16*, 581–598.

Lieberman, M. D. (2013). *Social: Why our brains are wired to connect.* New York: Crown.

Maslow, A. H. (1943). A theory of human motivation. *Psychological Review, 50*, 370–396.

Mathieu, J., Maynard, M. T., Rapp, T. L., & Gilson, L. (2008). Team effectiveness 1997–2007: A review of recent advancements and a glimpse into the future. *Journal of Management, 34*, 410–476.

McGrath. J. E. (1964). *Social psychology: A brief introduction.* New York: Holt, Rinehart & Winston.

Mesmer-Magnus, J. R., & DeChurch, L. A. (2009). Information sharing and team performance: A meta-analysis. *Journal of Applied Psychology, 2,* 535–546.

Pirola-Merlo, A., Hartel, C., Mann, L., & Hirst, G. (2002). How leaders influence the impact of affective events on team climate and performance in R&D teams. *The Leadership Quarterly, 13,* 561–581.

Richter, A. W., Dawson, J. F., & West, M. A. (2011). The effectiveness of teams in organizations: A meta-analysis. *The International Journal of Human Resource Management, 22*(13), 2749–2769.

Ringelmann, M. (1913). Recherches sur les moteurs animés: Travail de l'homme. *Annales de l'Institut National Agronomique, 12,* 1–40.

Robbins, S., & Judge, T. (2015). *Organizational behavior.* Harlow: Pearson Education Limited.

Salas, E., Cooke, N. J., & Rosen, M. A, (2008). On teams, teamwork and team performance: Discoveries and developments. *Human Factors, 3,* 550–547. doi 1015180001872008X288457

Tannenbaum, S. I., & Cerasoli, C. P. (2012). Do team and individual debriefs enhance performance? Meta-analysis. *Human Factors: The Journal of the Human Factors and Ergonomics Society.* doi: 10.1177/0018720812448394

Tuckman, B. W. & Jensen, M. A. (1977). Stages in small group development revisited. *Group and Organisation Studies, 2,* 419–427.

Ulich, E. & Weber, W. G. (1996). Dimensions, criteria and evaluation of work group autonomy. In M. A. West (Ed.), *Handbook of work group psychology* (pp. 247–282). Chichester: John Wiley & Sons, Ltd.

Van der Haar, S., Segers, M., & Jehn, K. A. (2013). Towards a contextualized model of team learning processes and outcomes. *Educational Research Review, 10,* 1–12.

Van Dick, R. & Haslam, S.A. (2012). Stress and well-being in the workplace: Support for key propositions from the social identity approach. In J. Jetten, C. Haslam, & S. A. Haslam (Eds.), *The social cure: Identity, health, and well-being* (pp. 175–194). New York: Psychology Press.

Wagner, J. A. (1995). Studies of individualism-collectivism: Effects on cooperation in groups. *Academy of Management Journal, 1,* 152–173.

West, M. A. (2012). *Effective teamwork: Practical lessons from organizational research.* Chichester: John Wiley & Sons Ltd.

West, M. A., Hirst, G., Richter, A. & Shipton, H. (2004). 12 steps to heaven: successfully managing change through developing innovative teams. *European Journal of Work and Organizational Psychology, 13*(2), 269–299.

West, M. A., & Lyubovnikova, J. R. (2012). Real teams or pseudo teams? The changing landscape needs a better map. *Industrial and Organizational Psychology, 5*(1), 25–28.

Wildman, J. L., Thayer, A. L., Rosen, M. A., Salas, E., Mathieu, J. E., & Rayne, S. R. (2012). Task types and team-level attributes: Synthesis of team classification literature. *Human Resource Development Review, 11,* 97–129.

Zaccaro, S. J., Rittman, A. L., & Marks, M. A. (2001). Team leadership. *Leadership Quarterly, 12,* 451–483.

How Do We React When Our Organization Changes? Perspectives on Employees' Appraisal of Change, Consequences and Mitigating Factors

13

Magnus Sverke, Helena Falkenberg, Johnny Hellgren, Chang-qin Lu and Jaco Pienaar

Overview

Everyone experiences organizational change at some point during his or her work career. How individuals meet with and react to the changes they face in their careers as well as in life in general depends on many factors and circumstances. A factor that has been shown to be important for how employees react to an organizational change is how the change is perceived and appraised – whether as a threat or as an opportunity. If a change is seen as something stressful, individuals tend to take on a defensive stance and use various defence mechanisms in order to handle the situation. If a change, however, is interpreted positively, with the hopes that certain wishes and expectations will be met, the individual may instead welcome the change and even work towards it. As most people naturally seem to prefer predictability, security and stability when it comes to their employment and work situation, organizational changes tend to be experienced as stressful, at least to some degree. This chapter presents the most common models for organizational change and describes different types of organizational changes, along with several of the most important aspects for understanding and explaining individuals' perceptions and reactions concerning organizational changes.

An Introduction to Work and Organizational Psychology: An International Perspective,
Third Edition. Edited by Nik Chmiel, Franco Fraccaroli and Magnus Sverke.
© 2017 John Wiley & Sons, Ltd. Published 2017 by John Wiley & Sons, Ltd.

13.1 Introduction

There are many types of organizational changes, which affect organizations and their employees in various ways. What is central to the concept of organizational change, however, is that it implies a transition from one state to another; such a transition may concern an organization as a whole or only certain parts or aspects of the organization. Organizational changes are typically considered in terms of pre-change (present state) and post-change (desired state). The basic premise is that organizations are in a more or less permanent or stable state between changes, and that the differences that arise between the pre- and post-change states are a result of the change itself. Organizational changes are planned and carried out because there is a need for change (the current situation is not satisfactory) and the purpose of the change is often to make the organization better in some way (e.g., improved finances, quality, new innovations, new operational conditions). There are a number of aspects that influence and shape the change and improvement needs of an organization. Changes in business cycles, increased competition (globalization), new and more efficient technologies, new markets, new products, altered consumer demands, and the actions of stakeholders and politicians are some of the most common driving forces behind organizational changes.

In order for an organizational change to be considered successful, it has to have, completely or to a large extent, fulfilled and established the state that was desired before the change process started. Research has found that at least two-thirds of all completed organizational changes in one way or another are unsuccessful and that this is mainly due to organizations underestimating the key role of employees in the change process (Choi, 2011). Obviously, it is easier for management to implement an organizational change if employees are supportive of the change and actively participate in the change process rather than resisting it. The reactions and behaviour of employees are thus of central importance in order for an organizational change to succeed in reaching the goals of the change set up by the organization.

In order for an organizational change to be successful, the employees need to have a positive attitude towards the change and its goals, and actively contribute to reaching them (Herscovitch & Meyer, 2002). This presents, however, a fundamental problem in that, for employees, all or nearly all organizational changes carry with them some degree of uncertainty, threat, or loss of control over the situation. These reactions relate to various aspects of work that the individual values, or even take the form of a threat to one's future employment in the organization. How strongly an individual reacts to different types of organizational change depends on many different factors. An important factor is how distant the change seems to be to the concerned individuals, along with how much they perceive the change will affect them. If the change is perceived to be close and to have the potential to significantly affect one's work situation (a proximal change), employees tend to react more strongly than if the change is perceived as distant with little chance of affecting their work situation (a distal change). Research has found that those who react negatively to organizational changes report poorer attitudes towards both the job and the organization (Oreg, 2006). When it comes to behavioural reactions, employees tend to use various kinds of defence mechanisms, including apathy and withdrawal or active resistance. Such attitudes and reactions, in turn, can have a negative impact on individuals' health and well-being as well as on their work performance.

How individuals assimilate and react to an organizational change therefore not only has consequences for the individual employee but is also important for whether an organization is able to meet the objectives of the change. This chapter outlines different perspectives on organizational change and describes some of the most common types of organizational changes. How employees evaluate and react to change efforts is also examined along with the potential consequences of organizational change, paying particular attention to the role of job insecurity. Finally, the chapter addresses individual and organizational factors that may affect the consequences of organizational change for employees.

13.2   The Various Focuses of Organizational Changes

What is it that can actually change in an organization? The answer to this question depends in large part on what one considers an organization to be. One way to describe an organization is to view it as comprised of five central components. The first component is the *people* in the organization. Changes that relate to people include changes in the number of employees, as when an organization expands and hires new employees or shrinks and reduces personnel. The competence of individuals in an organization can also change, for example, by further educating the current staff and by recruiting new employees with competencies not already present in the organization, or through lay-offs and retirements which could lead to certain competencies disappearing from the organization. The second component is the *activities* that are carried out in an organization, that is, what the employees do in an organization. Activities change when new technologies are introduced, when new products begin to be produced, when new services are offered to customers or when new work practices are introduced. The third component that can change is the *goals* of the organization. Existing goals can be adjusted and new goals can arise. A privatization, for example, often leads to organizational goals becoming more profit-oriented. The fourth component is the *structure* of the organization. The structure changes when an organization's leadership and management change. It may, for example, take the form of increased or decreased centralization. The fifth component is the *culture* of an organization. The culture of an organization is difficult to change. One reason for this is that organizational culture permeates all of the above-mentioned components of an organization. Even if several of an organization's components change, the culture can carry on in the components that did not change.

Considering these five components, a further question is how *many* and how *much* of them need to change in order for an organizational change to have occurred. There are several perspectives on this question. The two most predomi-nant perspectives in the literature are presented below, one viewing an organiza-tional change as a radical change and the other viewing it as a gradual process, as well as an introduction to conceptual models to understand what organizational changes are and how they can be implemented.

13.2.1   Radical or evolutionary change

One way of looking at the concept of organizational change is to view it as refer-ring to large-scale changes that occur relatively seldom. In contrast, another per-spective is to view organizational change as something that occurs continually and on a smaller scale. There are various labels for the kinds of changes associated with these different views (see, e.g., French, Bell, & Zawacki, 2005; Kanter, Stein, & Jick, 1992). Large-scale changes, for example, have been termed revolutionary, discontinuous, radical, transformational, and as second-order change. What all of these terms have in common is that they attempt to describe comprehensive changes that affect an entire organization or large parts of it. These kinds of changes are often carefully planned and strategically initiated by top management and are intended to take place during a limited period. There is also a variety of corresponding contrasting names, including evolutionary, continuous, conver-gent, transactional, and first-order change. All of these terms attempt to rep-resent ongoing changes that are continually occurring in an organization. They may include adjustments or improvements that are initiated and carried out by employees without a directive from management. Such changes affect different parts of the organization on different occasions.

The distinction between large-scale (radical) changes and small-scale (evolu-tionary) changes is not an absolute dichotomy, but these changes can rather be seen as endpoints of a continuum. This distinction also reflects different theoreti-cal perspectives on what an organization is, what an organizational change rep-resents, and how change processes occur and can be managed. It is also important to keep in mind that organizational changes can be understood as an organiza-tional phenomenon, in that it affects the organization of work and the structuring of the organization as a whole (for instance, the outsourcing of central services, such as HR), and also as an individual-level phenomenon that affects individuals' employment situation (such as a change in their job descriptions following an outsourcing or their job positions becoming threatened). Typically, it is the more large-scale, radical or revolutionary changes that are described in the literature on organizational change, and they are also the main focus of this chapter.

13.2.2   Sequential change models

Many types of change models have been developed to facilitate our understanding of how organizational changes are planned and implemented. While most of them presuppose that organizational changes are large-scale and revolutionary and also

Figure 13.1: A sequential model of organizational change
Source: Adapted from Lewin (1951).

initiated by management for a limited period, they are still useful for providing an overall understanding of the change processes in general. Since these models are built on a series of steps or phases that are gone through in order for a change to be realized, they are called sequential change models. A classic sequential change model is Kurt Lewin's (1951) three-step model (see Figure 13.1). According to Lewin, in order to successfully carry out an organizational change, any resistance to the change must be dealt with by working with the group norms. If there is a group-level acceptance of a change, the individual members of the group will end up adapting to the norm and thereby more easily accept the change. In order to create this acceptance on the group level, Lewin maintains, the first step is to get everyone to understand and accept the purpose of, and the need for, the change. This involves getting those who will be affected by the change to realize that the current situation is not working or will not work in the future. The current structure must therefore be dissolved in what Lewin calls the *unfreezing* phase. Then the *moving* (or change) phase occurs, when the actual change is implemented by the organization. This is followed by the *refreezing* phase, as the new system settles and stabilizes within the organization. Lewin maintained that people often revert to how things used to be done unless acting according to the new system is reinforced through repetition. This final step in the change process is therefore critical.

This relatively simple three-step model – unfreeze, change, and refreeze – essentially laid the groundwork for all subsequent sequential step-based models of change. The three steps are often broken down into smaller steps or phases that the organization is to follow in order to succeed with the change. Sequential change models are based on at least three central assumptions: (1) an organizational change can have a starting point; (2) it is possible to direct and control the direction and nature of the change; and; (3) an organizational change can come to an end and it is possible to make the change permanent. Sequential change models have received a good amount of criticism for their relatively static nature and presumption that all organizations can go through such predetermined steps in an order postulated by the models. The criticism asserts, to the contrary, that organizational changes are dynamic in nature and difficult to plan and control. This perspective presumes that the changes are continuous and evolutionary without a clear beginning or end; models based on this perspective depict organizational change as a circle, with new change sequences emerging as previous sequences end.

13.3   Different Types of Organizational Changes

What is considered to be an organizational change and how large or small the change is perceived to be depend to a large extent on the individual: one person's large and radical change may be another person's insignificant change. This section presents several of the most common types of relatively large-scale organizational changes which often span throughout entire organizations or at least large parts of them.

13.3.1   Organizational development

While many organizational changes are perceived as frightening or threatening by employees, not all changes evoke negative or defensive behaviour. One such example is referred to as organizational development. Organizational development programmes vary in their degree of comprehensiveness and duration and may affect only certain employees or units or the whole organization. The goal of such programmes is typically to equip individuals or the organization with competencies that can provide further advancement and be used for handling future organizational challenges. They are thus proactive and future-oriented by nature. Organizational development programmes can be described as a system of planned measures by management to alter an organization's structure and/or operations with the purpose of stimulating increased functionality in the organization (French, Bell, & Zawacki, 2005). These kinds of programmes are usually implemented when organizations are doing well and expanding, as they aim to increase the organization's market shares, find new outlets for its products, or enlarge its staff by hiring new employees.

13.3.2   Downsizing

Another type of organizational change, which could be regarded as the opposite of organizational development, is downsizing. Although downsizing in an organization can take different shapes and pertain to different aspects of an organization, it nearly always involves letting staff go and has thus essentially come to be synonymous with personnel reductions. Downsizing has been defined as a deliberate and planned reduction of an organization with the purpose of increasing profitability (Cameron, Freeman, & Mishra, 1991). There are different methods of reducing personnel but the most common is through lay-offs. The specific lay-off process, however, can differ considerably in different countries depending on the laws, collective agreements between employers and unions, employment contracts, and common practice. Other tactics for reducing personnel include offering a voluntary retirement package to those employees who have reached a certain age (e.g., in which they receive a percentage of their pay until their regular pension activates) and the more gradual approach of not hiring new employees when old ones leave.

However, the most common type of downsizing is that which involves a hasty and rather panicked reduction in the number of employees in an organization. It entails individuals losing their jobs and becoming unemployed, with all the consequences that unemployment carries with it (see McKee-Ryan, Song, Wanberg, & Kinicki, 2005, for a review of the consequences of unemployment). Downsizing also entails that some individuals remain working in the downsized organization, as opposed to a closure where everyone becomes unemployed, and those remaining have been termed 'survivors' in the literature.

It is then the survivors who are expected to 'save' the organization from the troubles that led to the downsizing and re-establish its vitality and competitiveness going forward. It has been found, however, that downsizing is not a cure-all for organizations in distress, as research shows that organizations that have carried out a downsizing are likely to continue with further downsizing and that many downsized organizations may end up shutting down completely. One reason why downsizing is such a difficult strategy to succeed with concerns the reactions of the survivors, which include poorer attitudes towards their work and the organization, lower performance, increased absence, and sickness absence (Cascio, 1998). Another hurdle is to keep staff turnover to a minimum, as it is likely that more employable survivors, with competencies that the organization would like to retain, often choose to leave the organization (Pfeffer, 1998). For these reasons, it can prove difficult for organizations to pull themselves out of the financial straits that first led to their downsizing and avoid falling into a negative spiral of further downsizings.

13.3.3 Mergers and acquisitions

Another common type of organizational change is the merger, where two or more organizations are joined together to form a larger organization (Burke & Nelson, 1998). This can occur through two or more rather similar organizations combining under relatively equal terms and building a new organization (mergers, sometimes called amalgamations). The power balance between the organizations in this case may be uneven with one organization dominating the new constellation. Organizations can also combine through acquisition, which is when a larger organization purchases or incorporates one or more smaller organizations which dissolve into the larger organization (sometimes called absorptions). Acquisitions are often a matter of one organization buying out another and forcing it to give up its current name and organizational structure as it is completely absorbed into the dominant, acquiring organization. Both mergers and acquisitions may be subject to downsizing in the form of personnel reductions; in cases where the motivation for the combining is to some degree financial, savings from rationalizations are likely to be sought, for instance, by eliminating redundant human resources or security services. In these situations research has found that employees from the absorbed organization tend to react with feelings of uncertainty, antipathy and antagonism as well as stress symptoms, especially in cases of hostile takeover, when one organization is forced to dissolve into the other (Burke & Nelson, 1998).

13.3.4   Privatization

There are also other kinds of ownership and operational changes that constitute types of organizational change. One example is when public operations and
organizations become privatized, but this can certainly apply also to other types
of ownership changes besides privatization. The main argument for this kind of
deregulation and privatization of public operations is based on the premise that
the operations will be more cost effective and the quality of the organization's
products or services will improve when the organization has to compete on the
open market. The effects of privatization have been studied in work and organizational psychology by mainly focusing on the areas of work environment, leadership, and attitudes towards the organization. A study from Great Britain found
that both job satisfaction and general well-being among the staff deteriorated
after the organization underwent privatization (Nelson, Cooper, & Jackson,
1995). Other studies, however, have found that physicians at a privatized hospital
tended to report more positively on their work environment and had more positive work-related attitudes than physicians working at a publicly administrated
hospital (Hellgren, Sverke, Falkenberg, & Baraldi, 2005). As these findings suggest, research cannot yet provide a clear picture of what the effects of privatization are on individual employees, and there are relatively few published studies
on the effects of privatization. Some researchers have even argued that changes in
ownership type are a distal (i.e., distant) type of change and therefore do not have
a strong effect on the immediate working conditions of individual employees
(Burke & Cooper, 2000).

13.4   How Do Employees Appraise Organizational Change?

What employees think about an organizational change can greatly impact its success. Many attempts have been made to explain how employees perceive and
react to organizational changes, and two aspects have emerged as central to their
appraisals. The first of these concerns the nature and content of the change. This
aspect involves not only the type of organizational change (e.g., downsizing,
merger) and whether it is likely to affect the individual's immediate work situation
(proximal change) or not (distal change), but also how the individual evaluates
the usefulness and legitimacy of the change effort. Employees' overall evaluation
of the change to a large extent depends on whether it is interpreted as necessary,
legitimate, and adequate (see Barnett & Carroll, 1995, for a comprehensive literature review). However, even if individuals understand why the organization
needs to undergo change and accept the content of the change, their appraisal
of how the change is being implemented is also vital – especially in regard to
whether they are comfortable with it and feel they are being treated fairly by the
organization. This represents the second key aspect that determines individual

reactions to change. The implementation of the change – the process – is at least as important and sometimes even more important for individual reactions than the change itself.

Stress theory is often used to shed light on how employees evaluate and react to circumstances in their environment, such as organizational changes. One theory that is of particular relevance is Lazarus and Folkman's (1984) transactional stress theory, according to which the appraisal of any event is essential in determining individual reactions. An understanding of the mechanisms that may explain how aspects of organizational change translate into employee reactions is not only of interest from a research perspective but also highly valuable for management. Transactional stress theory posits that individuals' interpretations and appraisals of how a situation may affect them are essential in shaping their reactions. Although Lazarus and Folkman's model is suitable for describing appraisals of any situation, Figure 13.2 illustrates the logic of this model in the context of organizational change.

The basic premise of Lazarus and Folkman's (1984) model is that individuals interpret the situation or event they encounter, and this interpretation determines how they will react. In this evaluation, or appraisal process, individuals try to make sense of what the situation – in our case, an organizational change – may mean to them. According to the model, the first phase of this evaluative process

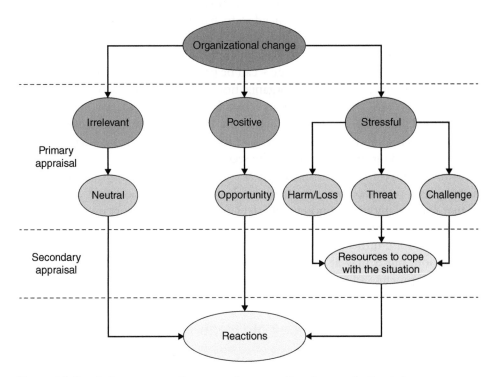

Figure 13.2: A stress perspective on employee reactions to organizational change
Source: Adapted from Lazarus and Folkman (1984).

(primary appraisal) is when individuals seek to determine whether the organizational change is at all relevant to them. If it is found to be relevant, they then
judge whether it is a positive or potentially stressful occurrence. An organizational
change that is deemed irrelevant is, in other words, a change that the individual
does not expect to be affected by. The employee can continue to work as usual
and the situation is not expected to result in any gains or losses. Individuals who
judge an organizational change as positive or benign appraise it as an opportunity
that may lead to positive consequences, such as increased meaningfulness at work
and greater job satisfaction. The primary appraisal can also result in an evaluation of the organizational change as potentially stressful, that is, as a situation
that involves actual harm or loss, carries with it a threat of such harm or loss, or
represents a challenge. These appraisals of expected or threatened harm or loss
normally concern negative impact to one's job, certain work tasks, colleagues,
security and/or stability in connection with the organizational change. A primary
appraisal of the situation as a challenge often relates to facing work demands that
are seen as difficult, yet possible to meet, at least to some extent, through hard
work, perseverance and adjustment to the situation.

For organizational changes that are judged as stressful, according to the model,
this primary appraisal is followed by a second phase, secondary appraisal, where an
evaluation is made of how the situation could be managed. Regardless of whether
the stressful situation is deemed to involve a loss, threat, or challenge, individuals
need to assess what resources are needed to handle the situation and evaluate
whether they can use any of their available strategies for coping with the perceived
stress associated with the situation. While these different types of stressful primary
appraisals – loss, threat, and challenge – can be presumed to lead to different consequences in connection with an organizational change, the consequences that
occur depend on the resources that are identified in the secondary appraisal. The
two appraisal phases are not singular events but can, rather, be understood as constituting a cyclical and dynamic process, as individuals re-appraise their primary
appraisal depending on the results of the secondary appraisal.

In this context it should also be mentioned that the categories of threat and
challenge are not necessarily mutually exclusive. An organizational change or,
for that matter, any type of potentially stressful situation can contain elements of
both threat and challenge. For example, a change can be perceived as involving
demands that are difficult to meet and which pose a threat to one's role in the
organization, but it may at the same time also present opportunities for competency development and taking on greater responsibilities.

13.5 Consequences of Organizational Change

As described above, there are many types of organizational changes and these
changes impact both organizations and employees to various degrees. Both
the type and the extent of a change are factors that influence the effects that the

Focus of consequence:	Type of consequence: Time aspect	
Who is concerned?	Short-term	Long-term
Employee	Psychological reactions Spillover effects from work to home	Mental and physical health Work–life balance
Organization	Work-related attitudes	Work-related behaviour

Figure 13.3: Consequences of organizational changes
Source: Adapted from Sverke et al. (2002).

change brings with it. In addition, an individual's appraisal of the change process plays a key role in determining how she or he will react, as an organizational change is likely to have different consequences depending on if it is appraised as irrelevant, positive, or potentially stressful. The consequences of organizational change may be grouped in several ways. One way is to draw distinctions among the consequences according to whether they concern work-related attitudes (such as job satisfaction, organizational commitment and work engagement), health (mental and physical health) or behaviour (e.g., job performance and turnover). The consequences may also be evaluated from different perspectives, such as the employee's or the organization's perspective. Another aspect to the consequences of organizational change is time, as certain consequences tend to arise more immediately while others take more time to develop. Figure 13.3 presents an attempt to systematize these various approaches, based on a figure developed by Sverke, Hellgren, and Näswall (2002). Figure 13.3 combines the aspect of time with whether the consequences primarily concern the employee or the organization.

13.5.1 Consequences for the employee

It is not unusual for the anticipation and implementation phases of a change process to be characterized by turmoil and rumours. In these situations the impact that the change will have on employees is often largely unknown, which makes it difficult for individuals to assess their situation (cf. primary appraisal) as well as the resources that may be needed to effectively cope with it (cf. secondary appraisal). As noted in various stress theories (e.g., Lazarus & Folkman, 1984), uncertainty over whether something stressful will occur may in fact be more demanding for the individual than actually experiencing such a stressful event. When something stressful has occurred, or when it is known that it will occur, the individual can start evaluating what resources can be used to start coping with the situation.

Being uncertain about what will happen, in contrast, makes it problematic to cope, as it is difficult to know what strategies would be needed to handle the situation.

Given that the early phases of an organizational change are characterized by uncertainty, the short-term consequences of organizational changes often involve feelings such as irritation, dejection and indifference. Employees can thus take a defensive stance and use various defence mechanisms in order to handle the situation. Other short-term consequences can include anticipating that the content of the job may change and even become less meaningful, along with worrying about how the change will affect one's employment and future financial situation. More long-term consequences mainly regard various aspects of health and well-being. A considerable amount of research has found that organizational changes are related to an increase in mental health problems (Bamberger et al., 2012). While it seems that such negative effects on health and well-being tend to diminish over time, they can in some cases still be present several years after a change.

Box 13.1:   Case study: Downsizing

This case study concerns a large-scale downsizing that was conducted within a large organization in the grocery and retail business. The economic viability of the organization had been gradually deteriorating over a longer period until the situation finally became acute. The organization decided at this point to drastically rationalize their operations and reorganize the entire company. Their slogan for success became 'back to what once made us great' and so they sold off all of their subsidiaries that were in business sectors outside of their core area of operations. The reorganization not only had widespread effects on all of the operations below the parent organization but also impacted the parent organization itself, including the main offices. The change included rationalizations that led to the elimination of a large number of administrative positions from the main offices. This especially affected the administrative staff in the financial and logistics departments as well as the entire payroll department along with other, smaller divisions within the main offices.

Specifically, the change meant that 1,570 office employees were reduced to 880 over the course of two years. Initially, all of these office employees were given notice about their employment dismissal and then told that they could apply and compete for one of the 880 positions that would remain after the change. Consequently, 690 employees were to lose their employment in the organization, of whom 200 were offered a retirement package in which they continued to receive 75% of their pay until they reached 65, when their regular pension would come into effect. This offer was made to everyone who was 60 or older – and the only options it contained were acceptance of the retirement package or unemployment. One year later another round of notices was given, resulting in 70 of the 880 employees re-hired after the first round losing their jobs.

Approximately two years after receiving the first round of dismissal notices, the original pool of 1,570 employees can be divided into four groups:

1. those who still worked in the organization (approx. 810);
2. those who retired after accepting the offer (approx. 200);
3. those who acquired employment elsewhere (approx. 330);
4. those who became unemployed (approx. 230).

When it comes to the consequences of the change among these four groups, it is the retirees (group 2) who appear to have fared best. They reported the fewest health problems and had the most positive attitudes towards the organization and their previous work. The group who acquired employment elsewhere, typically after having been unemployed (group 3), also reported having positive attitudes as well as a decrease in stress symptoms and health problems compared to when they were initially unemployed. Those worst impacted were those who remained (the survivors; group 1) and those who were still unemployed after two years (group 4). Both of these groups reported high levels of stress-related symptoms and ill-health as well as dissatisfaction and disappointment towards the organization and, in the case of the survivors, also a dissatisfaction with their current work situation.

These results (that are in line with other similar studies) demonstrate the importance of looking after those who remain in the organization after a downsizing, as there is a risk that their reactions may be similar to those of long-term unemployed individuals.

Sources: Hellgren & Sverke (2003); Isaksson, Hellgren, & Pettersson (2000); Isaksson, Pettersson, & Hellgren (1998).

The nature and strength of the consequences of organizational changes can vary among employees. The consequences also depend, at least to a certain extent, on the type of organizational change that is being carried out. Changes that involve extensive staff reductions have stronger negative consequences for employees than other types of changes. Brockner and colleagues, who investigated this in several studies, coined the terms 'survivor guilt' and 'survivor syndrome' (e.g., Brockner, Grover, Reed, DeWitt, & O'Malley, 1987) to describe how the remaining staff reacted after extensive reductions. These reactions can take the form of feelings of guilt towards those colleagues who lost their jobs as well as negative attitudes towards the organization and the management. A recently published review article concluded that most types of organizational change and restructuring tend to have negative consequences for employees' well-being, regardless of whether the changes include staff reductions or not (de Jong, Wiezer, de Weerd, Nielsen, Mattila-Holappa, & Mockałło, 2016). Especially negative consequences seem to occur when employees undergo repeated changes (Westerlund, Ferrie, Hagberg, Jeding, Oxenstierna, & Theorell, 2004) or when employees experience prolonged uncertainty over whether their organization will undergo a change or not (Falkenberg, Fransson, Westerlund, & Head, 2013).

As we have seen, there are a number of factors that determine the consequences of organizational change for the employees. Large-scale, radical changes tend to impact employees more than small-scale, evolutionary changes. Changes that involve layoffs (e.g., downsizing, but also other types of changes that result in staff reductions) affect not only those let go but also the remaining staff (i.e., the survivors). The consequences also depend on whether the effects of the change are more proximal or distal. Finally, appraisal of the change – as something irrelevant, positive, or stressful – not only guides how individuals cope with the situation but also determines what consequences the change will produce.

	Passive	**Active**
Constructive	Loyalty	Voice
Destructive	Neglect	Exit

Figure 13.4:   Categorization of employee responses to organizational change
Source: Adapted from Hirschman (1979) and Mishra and Spreitzer (1998).

A useful conceptual framework for examining individuals' behavioural reactions to organizational change is provided by Mishra and Spreitzer (1998). Their framework originates from Hirschman's (1970) description of behavioural reactions to decline in organizations and nations. According to this framework, employees' responses to organizational changes can be separated into two sets of dimensions: passive versus active responses and destructive versus constructive responses (see Figure 13.4). These two sets of dimensions can then combine into four types of responses: exit, voice, loyalty, and neglect. When these are applied to the consequences of organizational change, the combination of active and destructive responses is chiefly associated with employees leaving the organization (exit). Exiting from an organization is an active individual response that, while at times representing a constructive solution to a problematic situation, can be considered destructive in the sense that it interrupts a stable relationship with the organization. The exit option typically requires that there are alternative employment opportunities and that the individual is employable. Another alternative, which combines active and constructive responses, is for employees to signal what they think about the organizational change and express their opinions about what should happen in order to improve the situation for themselves and potentially also for the organization (voice). This alternative is often exercised by those who have a strong position in the organization, allowing their voice to be heard and listened to. Employees at lower levels, in contrast, could signal and express to their coworkers what they think about the changes in a way which could shape opinion and in turn potentially influence the change, or make use of more collective forms of voice through their trade union. Still another alternative, that is described as passive and constructive, is to show loyalty to the organization and hope that it pays off when the turbulence in the organization is over. For those with a weak position in the organization and in the labour market, the only alternative may be to withdraw and try to avoid dealing with the situation (neglect). This passive and destructive response results in impaired work performance and increased risk of ill-health.

Although most of the research on the effects of organizational change on employees has focused on consequences such as emotional reactions, well-being and job changes, there has also been an increasing amount of research on how life outside of work can be affected. For example, studies have shown that individuals who have gone through organizational changes for a prolonged period may react with spillover effects from work to home, such as sleeping problems and increased alcohol consumption. In the long term, such spillover effects can result in conflicts between work and the rest of life. In the longer run, these spillover effects may also affect the well-being of other members of the family and even have an impact on the children's views on working and their career aspirations.

13.5.2 Consequences for the organization

Many of the consequences of organizational change that affect employees also have an effect on the organization itself. For instance, a number of studies have found organizational changes to be related to a lower degree of job satisfaction, decreased commitment to the organization, and an increased desire to leave the organization, which in turn will also be detrimental to the organization. Furthermore, studies have shown that organizational changes can lead to a lower degree of trust in the organization and decreased confidence in its management (for an overview, see e.g., Bamberger et al., 2012; Brockner et al., 1987; Burke & Nelson, 1998). These effects may arise shortly after a change process is announced, in connection with an onset of considerable uncertainty about the future. In the longer term, poorer attitudes tend to manifest themselves in behaviour, such as decreased or poorer job performance and increased absenteeism (e.g., sickness absence). Organizational changes can also lead to greater employee turnover. Those with the highest employability, that is, who have competencies that are attractive to the labour market, are most likely to leave since they can more easily find comparable employment in another organization (cf. Pfeffer, 1998). For those with less attractive competencies and fewer options in the labour market, it may be necessary to stay even if they would like to leave the organization, which is sometimes referred to as being 'locked-in' in their current organization. Finally, there is also research indicating that dysfunctional or counterproductive behaviour can arise in the form of employees working against the organization in various ways. For example, individuals may start neglecting their work, mishandling equipment, or even stealing from the organization. Organizational changes can thus result in impaired productivity and increased costs for the organization.

13.6 The Role of Job Insecurity

As mentioned above, all types of change carry with them an element of uncertainty over the future and what might happen after the change. A common type of uncertainty associated with organizational change relates to the future of one's employment in the organization, known as job insecurity. More specifically, for many employees organizational change is perceived as a threat to their current position in the organization. It should be emphasized that job insecurity can also be experienced in situations that do not contain a specific threat or involve an upcoming change; employees still may find themselves experiencing constant insecurity over what the future may bring and how the organization is going to handle and react to outside changes, market slumps or other external pressures. Given how common the phenomenon is, considerable research attention has been devoted to investigating job insecurity perceptions, both as a singular phenomenon and in connection with different types of organizational changes (Sverke & Hellgren, 2002).

One of the earliest theoretical conceptualizations of job insecurity was put forward by Greenhalgh and Rosenblatt (1984), whose theoretical model includes the potential causes, effects and organizational consequences of job insecurity perceptions. Job insecurity, in their work, is defined as 'a perceived powerlessness to maintain desired continuity in a threatened job situation (1984, p. 438). Later research has defined job insecurity as 'the subjectively experienced anticipation of a fundamental and involuntary event' that concerns one's future employment (Sverke, Hellgren, & Näswall 2002, p. 243). These definitions are based on two main premises. First, the insecurity is understood to be subjective in the sense that different individuals in the same situation can experience different degrees of it, depending, for example, on individual characteristics such as age, gender, education, personality, and employability. The second premise is that insecurity perceptions are involuntary in the sense that they reflect an involuntary change from a secure state to an insecure state – or that the individual would rather have a more secure employment situation than she or he currently has (see also De Witte, 1999). The concept of job insecurity has been expanded to relate not only to threats to employment in general (quantitative insecurity) but also to threats to qualities of the job that are meaningful and valuable for individuals, such as opportunities for career progression or skill enhancement (qualitative insecurity) (Greenhalgh & Rosenblatt, 1984; Hellgren, Sverke, & Isaksson, 1999). Both of these dimensions of job insecurity have been found to result in negative consequences.

A number of researchers have classified job insecurity as a classic work stressor (e.g., Barling & Kelloway, 1996), involving uncertainty about the future, often experienced for a prolonged time, that evokes stress reactions in individuals. This is in line with stress theories postulating that individuals who live under threat of a negative event occurring will eventually experience consequences from this uncertainty that are just as, if not more, negative than those which the actual event would carry with it (cf. Lazarus & Folkman, 1984). The uncertainty that employees with job insecurity have over their future job situation and whether they will lose their job can be difficult to deal with as it also involves a loss of control over the situation. Indeed, lack of control or feelings of powerlessness over one's employment situation and how it should be handled are considered key aspects of the job insecurity concept by many researchers (Ashford et al., 1989; De Witte, 1999; Sverke & Hellgren, 2002). This unpredictability and lack of control appear to be closely connected to feelings of stress and tension about the situation.

When it comes to the consequences of job insecurity, two meta-analyses (Cheng & Chan, 2008; Sverke et al., 2002) have revealed that perceptions of job insecurity have negative consequences for both the individual and the organization. For example, both meta-analyses found negative associations between job insecurity and a number of job- and organization-related attitudes, including job satisfaction, job involvement, organizational commitment and trust in the organization. They also conclude that perceived job insecurity has consequences for individuals' health and well-being in the form of negative associations with both mental health and physical health. In addition, both meta-analyses found negative effects on behavioural aspects such as performance and the intention to remain in the organization.

In more recent years, there has also been a focus on how perceived job insecurity can spread within an organization through individuals interacting with one another, which can create a climate of insecurity that may affect certain groups or units or the entire organization. Such a job insecurity climate has also been linked to negative work- and health-related outcomes (Låstad, Näswall, Berntson, Seddigh, & Sverke, 2016; Sora, Caballer, Peiró, & De Witte, 2009). All in all, research has found that perceived job insecurity often arises in connection with organizational changes and is associated with a number of negative consequences. For organizations implementing change, the challenge is to try to minimize employee perceptions of insecurity and, in particular, perceived threats to future employment and valued aspects of the job.

13.7 Factors that Affect the Appraisal and Consequences of Change

As we have discussed above, stress theory can assist in shedding light on how a situation, such as an organizational change, can be appraised and experienced in different ways by different individuals. Just as these experiences can differ among individuals, so can the consequences they face. In comparison to the research that has focused on the consequences of organizational change, less is known about the factors that may affect these consequences. A model that complements Lazarus and Folkman's (1984) transactional stress theory is the model described by Katz and Kahn (1978). Basically, this model emphasizes that the appraisal of a situation – in our case, an organizational change – depends on two major sets of factors, individual and organizational factors, which also affect the consequences resulting from the individual's experience of the situation (see Figure 13.5).

13.7.1   Importance of individual factors

Individual factors, such as personality traits, coping strategies, and demographic characteristics, are not only important for the appraisal of a given situation but may also affect how an employee's experience of that situation translates into

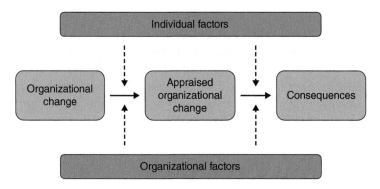

Figure 13.5: The importance of individual and organizational factors for the appraisal and consequences of organizational change
Source: Adapted from Katz and Kahn (1978).

consequences. In terms of dispositions, there is research to suggest that personality characteristics, such as low emotional stability and low openness to experience, may evoke resistance to change, which, in turn, is of importance for work-related attitudes and behaviour (e.g., Oreg, 2006). In addition, proactive traits such as resilience, hardiness, and persistence may facilitate individuals' ability to deal with the stress associated with organizational change. A strong belief in one's own capacities, such as in the form of strong self-esteem or self-efficacy, may also give employees more confidence for mastering stress in connection with organizational change and turmoil. Also, other individual dispositions, such as the tendency to hold a negative view on life in general (negative affectivity) and the tendency to attribute causes to things that happen either internally or externally (locus of control), tend to alter the consequences that arise from organizational change. It is possible that the importance of personality characteristics, however, varies depending on the effects in question, as a study on organizational change has found that personality characteristics are only of limited importance in affecting work- and health-related outcomes of job insecurity (Näswall, Sverke, & Hellgren, 2005).

Research has also found that other individual factors, such as individuals' coping strategies, play an important role in organizational change. Coping, as noted by Lazarus and Folkman (1984), is an important factor in determining the consequences of any stressful situation. Typically, a distinction is made between emotion-focused and problem-focused coping strategies, where emotional coping may involve anything from mentally avoiding a stressful situation to grieving over what has been lost or what is perceived to be under the threat of loss. Problem-oriented coping may involve, for example, attempting to influence the process of change by protesting against circumstances that are deemed unsatisfactory or it may mean actually exiting from the organization (cf. Mishra & Spreitzer, 1998). While early research on coping typically viewed problem-oriented coping as a more effective strategy, more recent research acknowledges that emotional coping may be a necessary first step in getting individuals used to the situation and preparing them for more problem-focused strategies (for an overview of coping research, see Pienaar, 2008). Also, coping resources, such as perceived employability, may be central in determining the consequences of organizational change. Employability essentially reflects the individual's perceived possibilities of obtaining new employment. High employability may not only make it easier for individuals to signal their discontent with an organizational change and make them more prone to leave the organization, but it can also affect their level of commitment to the change process. For instance, employability has been found to be an important coping resource during organizational restructuring by mitigating the negative effects of job insecurity on the staff's commitment to change (Kalyal, Berntson, Baraldi, Näswall, & Sverke, 2010).

Another factor influencing how employees are impacted by an organizational change is social position. The increased uncertainty that is associated with organizational changes (Bordia, Hunt, Paulsen, Tourish, & DiFonzo, 2004) may be felt unevenly among the various hierarchic positions in an organization. Employees in higher positions often have access to more information about the change as well as greater opportunity to influence and control the change process. These are factors that decrease uncertainty and lead to a belief that the situation can be handled, which lessens the stress experienced in connection with the change (cf. Lazarus & Folkman, 1984). In contrast, employees at lower positions often have less control and less opportunity to influence a change. Uncertainty, for these individuals, may be perceived as more difficult to handle and the change can feel more stressful. Another aspect that can differ with social position is the nature of the demands that are associated with an organizational change. Since employees at higher positions often have greater responsibility for carrying out changes, an organizational change can entail an increase to their already heavy workload. Furthermore, employees at higher positions have more social status and power to lose than those in lower positions. However, most empirical studies suggest that it is the employees in lower positions who report the most negative consequences of organizational changes (de Jong et al., 2016). In addition, there are studies showing that employees in middle positions experience more negative consequences than employees at both lower and higher levels. It has been suggested that this is due to those in the middle positions having greater demands placed on them to contribute to carrying out the change than those in lower positions as well as not having the same access to change-effecting resources as employees in higher positions (Falkenberg, Näswall, Sverke, & Sjöberg, 2009). Other studies have shown that self-reported health becomes worse for all employees in connection with a comprehensive organizational change, regardless of social position or gender (Falkenberg et al., 2013).

Concerning gender, there are different conceptions about how facing organizational changes differs between women and men. The dissolution and re-organization of the power structure that may accompany a major organizational change have been viewed as creating an opportunity for women to advance in the organization. However, with women often being overrepresented in lower positions and on temporary contracts, and organizational change presumed to be particularly detrimental to employees in these positions, organizational changes are therefore likely to affect more women than men. Organizational changes also often carry with them increases in workload as well as greater demands for flexibility and work presence, and as long as women continue to carry most of the responsibility for unpaid domestic work, these demands will be more difficult to handle for women than for men (Karambayya, 1998).

13.7.2   Importance of organizational factors

While research has shown that certain individual factors may mitigate or buffer the consequences of organizational change, applying these results in practice may be problematic as individual factors tend to be relatively stable over time. Since they are difficult to alter or improve in order to increase individuals' ability to deal with the challenges associated with organizational change, focusing on individual characteristics could be construed as 'blaming the victims'. There is a risk that the negative consequences of organizational change may be attributed to individuals having the 'wrong' gender, education, hardiness or openness to change. Partly because of this, a great deal of research has focused on what organizations can change within their own operations to mitigate the negative consequences of organizational change.

There is a considerable amount of research showing that certain organizational factors may affect the consequences of organizational change. Such organizational factors include fair treatment from the organization, social support from supervisors and colleagues, open communication structures in the organization, and HR strategies that provide opportunities for employee participation in decision-making. One central aspect in this context concerns organizational justice, which refers to the degree to which employees perceive that they are being fairly treated by the organization. Justice perceptions are typically conceived of in terms of distributional aspects (such as who is let go and who is kept during a downsizing), but can also include perceptions of the procedures followed in an organizational change (e.g., the process for determining redundancies) as well as interactional aspects concerning information-sharing and interpersonal treatment, i.e., interactional justice (see also Chapter 15 in this volume). If employees feel they are being fairly treated by the organization, it results in them having a better understanding of the necessity of the change, which can also improve their understanding of the goals of the change process and reduce the likelihood of resistance to change. For example, in the context of job insecurity, which typically arises in many organizational change processes, it has been shown that organizational justice moderates the negative effects of job insecurity such that high levels of justice result in less negative effects of job insecurity on job performance (Wang, Lu, & Siu, 2015).

There is also research to suggest that support from the organization, supervisors or colleagues may also be influential in determining the strength of association between how an organizational change is perceived and the outcomes it may result in. Social support has, for some time, been acknowledged as an important factor in helping individuals deal with stressful situations at work (e.g., Karasek & Theorell, 1990). Indeed, social support provides employees with the resources that are needed to effectively cope with a stressful situation in that it can involve receiving instrumental advice as well as emotional understanding. Yet another important organizational factor that has been found to affect the consequences of organizational change concerns the opportunities for participation in the change process. Such participation may not only provide an increased understanding of the change process and result in an acceptance of the necessity of the restructuring, but can also provide management with alternative perspectives – and thus result in a more effective change process (cf. Heller, Pusić, Strauss, & Wilpert, 1998).

An interesting combination of the various organizational factors that may be effective in addressing the potential negative consequences of organizational change is provided by what is sometimes called a proactive stance to change by management. As noted above, very often organizations make use of organizational change as a reaction to circumstances in the environment, such as decreasing market shares, a declining financial situation, or intensified competition (e.g., Cascio, 1998; Pfeffer, 1998). In contrast to this reactive stance (sometimes called a tactical or short-term stance) to implementing organizational change is the proactive stance (sometimes called a strategic or long-term stance), which involves, for example, the organization actively seeking employee participation in the change process and doing its best to implement fair procedures during the change process (Parker, Chmiel, & Wall, 1997). Such a proactive or strategic stance towards organizational change, which considers long-term organizational goals and visions, has been shown to lessen the negative consequences of downsizing and to be associated with more favourable health- and work-related outcomes (Parker et al., 1997; Sverke, Hellgren, Näswall, Göransson, & Öhrming, 2008). All in all, these results suggest that while organizational changes often tend to be negatively received by the staff, there are also a number of factors that may mitigate their negative consequences.

Summary

Organizational changes tend to take place at a rapidly increasing pace in contemporary working life. There are many reasons why such changes and restructurings take place, often involving a tighter financial situation and increased demands for organizational competitiveness. Organizational changes can represent gradual adjustments to environmental demands or take the form of dramatic alterations to established work practices. There are many types of organizational change, including organizational development, downsizing, mergers

Continued

and acquisitions and privatization. Common to all of these is that they are likely to affect the employees, at least to the extent they feel personally affected by the change. Although some employees may appraise an organizational change as irrelevant while others embrace it, most are likely to experience the change process as stressful – and such stressful experiences are likely to have consequences. Organizational changes can have a number of consequences for individuals' health, well-being, experiences of job insecurity and views on working. The consequences of organizational change affect not only the employees, but may also be detrimental to the organization. There are also a number of factors that influence how strong the consequences of organizational change will be. These include individual factors such as personality, coping strategies, social status, and demographic characteristics as well as organizational factors such as organizational justice, opportunities for participation, and social support. On a general level it seems that a proactive, or strategic, stance to organizational change may reduce resistance to change and lead to less negative consequences.

Discussion Points

1　Why might people be resistant to organizational change? What are the theoretical explanations for such reactions?
2　What strategies can organizations use to try to prevent or minimize the potential negative consequences of organizational change among the employees? How can the organization communicate the reasons and expected benefits of the change throughout the organization?

Suggested Further Reading

Burke, W. W. (2014). *Organizational change: Theory and practice*. Thousand Oaks, CA: Sage. This book gives a comprehensive description of theories, models, and research on organizational change, and combines a theoretical perspective with practical cases.

Datta, D. K., Guthrie, J. P., Basuil, D., & Pandey, A. (2010). Causes and effects of employee downsizing: A review and synthesis. *Journal of Management, 36*, 281–348. This article outlines, discusses, and critically examines the theoretical approaches and empirical results that are the basis of our knowledge of downsizing and its consequences.

van de Ven, A. H. & Poole, M. S. (1995). Explaining development and change in organizations. *Academy of Management Review, 20*, 510–540. This article is an attempt to synthesize various views on why systems change. It describes four motors of change (life cycle, teleology, dialectics and evolution) and argues that all theories of organizational change can be placed in one or more of these four motors.

Weick, K. E., & Quinn, R. E. (1999). Organizational change and development. *Annual Review of Psychology, 50*, 361–386. This classic article distinguishes between episodic and continuous change, two important and contrasting theoretical perspectives on organizational change.

References

Ashford, S. J., Lee, C., & Bobko, P. (1989). Content, cause, and consequences of job insecurity: A theory-based measure and substantive test. *Academy of Management Journal*, *32*(4), 803–829.

Bamberger, S. G., Vinding, A. L., Larsen, A., Nielsen, P., Fonager, K., Nielsen, R. N., Ryom, P., & Omland, Ø. (2012). Impact of organisational change on mental health: A systematic review. *Journal of Occupational & Environmental Medicine, 69*(8), 592–598.

Barling, J., & Kelloway, E. K. (1996). Job insecurity and health: The moderating role of workplace control. *Stress Medicine, 12*(4), 253–259.

Barnett, W. P., & Caroll, G. R. (1995). Modeling internal organizational change. *Annual Review of Psychology, 21*, 217–236.

Bordia, P., Hunt, E., Paulsen, N., Tourish, D., & DiFonzo, N. (2004). Uncertainty during organizational change: Is it all about control? *European Journal of Work and Organizational Psychology, 13*(3), 245–365.

Brockner, J., Grover, S., Reed, T., DeWitt, R., & O'Malley, M. (1987). Survivors' reactions to layoffs: We get by with a little help for our friends. *Administrative Science Quarterly, 32*(4), 526–541.

Burke, R. J., & Cooper, C. L. (2000). The new organizational reality: Transition and renewal. In R. J. Burke, & C. L. Cooper (Eds.), *The organization in crisis: Downsizing, restructuring, and privatization* (pp. 4–18). Oxford: Blackwell Publishers.

Burke R. J., & Nelson, D. (1998). Mergers and acquisitions, downsizing, and privatization: A North American perspective. In M. K. Gowing, J. D. Kraft, & J. C. Quick (Eds.), *The new organizational reality: Downsizing, restructuring, and revitalization* (pp. 21–54). Washington, DC: APA.

Cameron, K. S., Freeman, S. J., & Mishra, A. K. (1991). Best practices in white-collar downsizing: Managing contradictions. *Academy of Management Perspectives, 5*(3), 57–73.

Cascio, W. F. (1998). Learning from outcomes: Financial experiences of 311 firms that have downsized. In M. K. Gowing, J. D. Kraft, & J. Campbell Quick (Eds.), *The new organizational reality: Downsizing, restructuring, and revitalization* (pp. 55–70). Washington, DC: APA.

Cheng, G. H.-L., & Chan, D. K.-S. (2008). Who suffers more from job insecurity? A meta-analytic review. *Applied Psychology: An International Review, 57*(2), 272–303.

Choi, M. (2011). Employees' attitudes toward organizational change: A literature review. *Human Resource Management, 50*(4), 479–500.

de Jong, T., Wiezer, N., de Weerd, M., Nielsen, C., Mattila-Holappa, P., & Mockałło, Z. (2016). The impact of restructuring on employee wellbeing: A systematic review of longitudinal studies. *Work & Stress, 30*(1), 91–114.

De Witte, H. (1999). Job insecurity and psychological well-being: Review of the literature and exploration of some unresolved issues. *European Journal of Work and Organizational Psychology, 8*(2), 155–177.

Falkenberg, H., Fransson, E., Westerlund, H., & Head, J. (2013) Short- and long-term effects of major organizational changes on minor psychiatric disorder and self-rated health: results from the Whitehall II Study. *Occupational & Environmental Medicine, 70*(10), 688–696.

Falkenberg, H., Näswall, K., Sverke, M., & Sjöberg, A. (2009). How are employees at different levels affected by privatization? A longitudinal study of two Swedish hospitals. *Journal of Occupational and Organizational Psychology, 82*(1), 45–65.

French, W. L., Bell, C., & Zawacki, R. A. (2005). *Organization development and transformation: Managing effective change.* Maidenhead: McGraw-Hill.

Greenhalgh, L. & Rosenblatt, Z. (1984). Job insecurity: Toward conceptual clarity. *Academy of Management Review, 9*(3), 438–448.

Heller, F., Pusić, E., Strauss, G., & Wilpert, B. (1998). *Organizational participation: Myth and reality*. Oxford: Oxford University Press.

Hellgren, J., & Sverke, M. (2003). Does job insecurity lead to impaired well-being or vice versa? Estimation of cross-lagged effects using latent variable modeling. *Journal of Organizational Behavior, 24*, 215–236.

Hellgren, J., Sverke, M., Falkenberg, H., & Baraldi, S. (2005). Physicians' work climate at three hospitals under different types of ownership. In C. Korunka, & P. Hoffmann (Eds.), *Change and quality in human service work* (pp. 47–65). Munich: Rainer Hampp.

Hellgren, J., Sverke, M., & Isaksson, K. (1999). A two-dimensional approach to job insecurity: Consequences for employee attitudes and well-being. *European Journal of Work and Organizational Psychology, 8*(2), 179–195.

Herscovitch, L., & Meyer, J. P. (2002). Commitment to organizational change: Extension of a three-component model. *Journal of Applied Psychology, 87*(3), 474–487.

Hirschman, A. O. (1970). *Exit, voice and loyalty: Responses to declines in firms, organizations and states*. Cambridge, MA: Harvard University Press.

Isaksson, K., Hellgren, J., & Pettersson, P. (2000). Repeated downsizing: Attitudes and well-being for surviving personnel in a Swedish retail company. In K. Isaksson, C. Hogstedt, C. Eriksson, & T. Theorell (Eds.), *Health effects of the new labour market* (pp. 85–101). New York: Plenum.

Isaksson, K., Pettersson, P., & Hellgren, J. (1998). Utvecklingscentrum: En verksamhet för uppsagda tjänstemän i KF [Development centre: Activities for redundant staff in KF]. *Arbetsmarknad & Arbetsliv, 4*(1), 33–43.

Kalyal, H., Berntson, E., Baraldi, S., Näswall, K., & Sverke, M. (2010). The moderating role of employability on the relationship between job insecurity and commitment to change. *Economic and Industrial Democracy, 31*(3), 327–344.

Kanter, R. M., Stein, B. A., & Jick, T. D. (1992). *The challenge of organizational change: How companies experience it and leaders guide it*. New York: Free Press.

Karambayya, R. (1998). Caught in the crossfire: Women and corporate restructuring. *Canadian Journal of Administrative Science, 15*(4), 333–338.

Karasek, R. A., & Theorell, T. (1990). *Healthy work*. New York: Basic Books.

Katz, D., & Kahn, R. L. (1978). *The social psychology of organizations* (2nd ed.). New York: Wiley.

Låstad, L., Näswall, K., Berntson, J., Seddigh, A., & Sverke, M. (2016). The roles of shared perceptions of job insecurity and job insecurity climate for work- and health-related outcomes: A multilevel approach. *Economic and Industrial Democracy*. Advance online publication: doi: 10.1177/0143831X16637129

Lazarus, R. S., & Folkman, S. (1984). *Stress, appraisal, and coping*. New York: Springer Publishing Company.

Lewin, K. (1951). *Field theory in social science: Selected theoretical papers*. New York: Harper & Brothers Publishers.

McKee-Ryan, F., Song, Z., Wanberg, C. R., & Kinicki, A. J. (2005). Psychological and physical well-being during unemployment: A meta-analytic study. *Journal of Applied Psychology, 90*(1), 53–76.

Mishra, A. K. & Spreitzer, G. M. (1998). Explaining how survivors respond to downsizing: The roles of trust, empowerment, justice, and work redesign. *Academy of Management Review, 23*(3), 567–588.

Näswall, K., Sverke, M. & Hellgren, J. (2005). The moderating role of personality characteristics on the relation between job insecurity and strain. *Work & Stress, 19*(1), 37–49.

Nelson, A., Cooper, C. L., & Jackson, P. R. (1995). Uncertainty amidst change: The impact of privatization on employee job satisfaction and well-being. *Journal of Occupational & Organizational Psychology, 68*(1), 57–71.

Oreg, S. (2006). Personality, context, and resistance to organizational change. *European Journal of Work and Organizational Psychology, 15*(1), 73–101.

Parker, S. K., Chmiel, N., & Wall, T. D. (1997). Work characteristics and employee well-being within a context of strategic downsizing. *Journal of Occupational Health Psychology, 2*(4), 289–303.

Pfeffer, J. (1998). *The human equation: Building profits by putting people first.* Boston, MA: Harvard University Press.

Pienaar, J. (2008). Skeleton key or siren song: Is coping the answer to balancing work and well-being? In K. Näswall, J. Hellgren, & M. Sverke (Eds.), *The individual in the changing working life* (pp. 235–257). Cambridge: Cambridge University Press.

Sora, B., Caballer, A., Peiró, J. M., & De Witte, H. (2009). Job insecurity climate's influence on employees' job attitudes: Evidence from two European countries. *European Journal of Work and Organizational Psychology, 18*(2), 125–147.

Sverke, M., & Hellgren, J. (2002). The nature of job insecurity: Understanding employment uncertainty on the brink of a new millennium. *Applied Psychology: An International Review, 51*(1), 23–42.

Sverke, M., Hellgren J., & Näswall, K. (2002). No security: A meta-analysis and review of job insecurity and its consequences. *Journal of Occupational Health Psychology, 7*(3), 242–264.

Sverke, M., Hellgren, J., Näswall, K., Göransson, S., & Öhrming, J. (2008). Employee participation in organizational change: Investigating the effects of proactive vs. reactive implementation of downsizing in Swedish hospitals. *German Journal of Human Resource Research, 22*(2), 111–129.

Wang, H.-J., Lu, C.-Q., & Siu, O.-L. (2015). Job insecurity and job performance: The moderating role of organizational justice and the mediating role of work engagement. *Journal of Applied Psychology, 100*(4), 1249–1258.

Westerlund, H., Ferrie, J., Hagberg, J., Jeding, K., Oxenstierna, G., & Theorell, T. (2004). Workplace expansion, long-term sickness absence, and hospital admission. *Lancet, 636,* 1193–1197.

14

How Do We Feel and Behave When We're Not Permanent Full-Time Employees? The Case of the Diverse Forms of Non-Standard Work

Claudia Bernhard-Oettel, Nele De Cuyper, Megan Murphy and Catherine E. Connelly

Overview

This chapter discusses how it feels to work in non-standard employment that deviates from the traditional full-time permanent arrangement. Non-standard employment is frequently used by organizations today and often tailored to organizational needs. Therefore, a diversity of arrangements has developed, which means that employment and working conditions and their consequences for the individual and the organization may vary a lot. The chapter first provides a typology of most commonly used non-standard contracts and discusses their comparability across national employment protection legislation and labour markets. It further illustrates that workers may view alternative employment differently, depending on organizational or labour market structures that create working conditions for specific contracts, and individual perspectives that are shaped by different needs and perceptions of the employment. These structural issues and individual perceptions may well explain the variety of consequences, positive as well as negative, which are discussed in this chapter in terms of work attitudes, organizational behaviour, individual health and well-being and career development.

14.1   Introduction

Not having a full-time and/or permanent employment contract means that the employee does not have what is typically seen as a 'standard' employment relationship. The standard employment relationship is: (1) full-time, with an average working week of about 40 hours, (2) open-ended, with no fixed end date, and

An Introduction to Work and Organizational Psychology: An International Perspective,
Third Edition. Edited by Nik Chmiel, Franco Fraccaroli and Magnus Sverke.
© 2017 John Wiley & Sons, Ltd. Published 2017 by John Wiley & Sons, Ltd.

(3) organized such that work is carried out at the employing organization. In most industrialized countries, permanent full-time employment is still the norm, even though the numbers of part-time and temporary arrangements have been increasing steadily over the past three decades. The average rate of part-time employment across all OECD countries (based on the OECD definition of working 30 hours/week or less) was 17% in 2014 (OECD, 2015). There are considerable country and demographic differences with percentages varying from below 5% to over 30% across countries, and with more women than men in part-time jobs (OECD, 2015). On average, 11% of all employees were on temporary contracts in OECD countries in 2014 (estimates from national labour force surveys; OECD, 2015). However, again, there are considerable differences between countries, but in all countries, the share of temporary work is higher for young workers (15–24 years) (OECD, 2015).

This increase over the past decades has mainly been driven by organizational needs for flexibility. Many organizations compete globally and face fluctuating demands, both quantitative and qualitative. Quantitative demands may relate to business cycles of expansion and recession. Qualitative demands may concern the need to innovate, for example, in terms of introducing and implementing new products. Organizations thus need flexibility in terms of how many staff (quantity) and which competences (quality) to employ. Non-standard employment arrangements may help organizations to achieve this with respect to both *quantitative (numerical) flexibility* and *qualitative (functional) flexibility* (Kalleberg, 2001). The observation that the increase in non-standard employment is mainly driven by employers' needs has raised concerns about the potential implications for employees: non-standard employment may serve the organization's needs, but what about the workers? How do they feel? However, before these topics can be discussed, we first want to provide the reader with a more profound understanding of the most typically used forms of non-standard employment.

14.2   Different Forms of Non-Standard Employment

14.2.1   A typology of different forms of non-standard employment

There is general agreement that 'standard employment' is full-time, open-ended, and with the employing organization being identical with the organization in which work is carried out (De Cuyper et al., 2008). This implies that non-standard employment deviates from the standard on one or more of three dimensions: (1) number of working hours, (2) length of contract, and (3) responsibility of the employer. Table 14.1 illustrates how different types of contracts compare to the standard of permanent full-time work. Importantly, differences can exist in one or several of these dimensions.

Regarding (1), number of working hours: full-time employment means working about eight hours for five days per week. The number of hours can vary somewhat between countries: from 35–40 hours per week in Western European countries to 40 hours in Eastern Europe, Asia and South America. Part-time work, then, is

Table 14.1: Typology of different non-standard employment forms

Employer responsibilities	Contract length	Number of working hours		
		Full-time	*Part-time*	*Minimal hours*
Organization = employer	Permanent	'Standard'	Permanent part-timer	Mini jobs
	Temporary	Seasonal employees, project workers, substitutes		On call, zero hours contract
Organization = client	Temporary[1]	Temporary agency workers, subcontractors		

Note: [1] Temporary agency workers and subcontractors may be employed by their own employer on a permanent contract, but work temporarily for the client organization.

any work arrangement less than this threshold. As a result, *part-time workers* can work any number of working hours from 1 up to between 30 and 34 hours per week. An example of a part-time arrangement on minimal hours is the minimum job arrangement (*mini job;* see Table 14.1) in Germany, in which workers can earn up to 450 euros/month, and thus work an average of 13 hours/week if paid minimum wages (Federal Ministry of Labour and Social Affairs, Germany, 2014).

Regarding (2), length of contract: open-ended employment means working in a permanent contract as opposed to being 'non-permanent' or 'temporary'. Under a temporary contract, both parties in the employment relationship – the employee and the employer – are aware that the contract will end at a specific date (e.g., after six months) or when a specific condition is fulfilled (e.g., upon the return of a permanent employee). Temporary contracts can stretch from a few hours or days to several months or years. Short-term temporary contracts are often used to cover for the absence of regular staff or to provide extra resources when workload is high (e.g., retail workers during holiday periods). An example of this arrangement is the *on-call contract* sometimes called '*zero hour*' contracts (see Table 14.1). These workers have no fixed or minimum working hours, but are called in when needed (Office of National Statistics, 2015). This form of contract is rather typical in the retail, catering industry, cleaning, health-care, and educational sectors. Another form of temporary work concerns *seasonal employment*, typically used in tourism or agriculture. This contract is restricted for the duration of a season but may reoccur year after year. Longer-term contracts are often used for *project workers* who are employed for the predefined duration of a project or until a certain task is done. For example, PhD students are working on a temporary basis on their PhD project. Another typical arrangement is that of '*substitutes*' who fill in for a permanent worker on long-term sick leave or parental leave.

Regarding (3), responsibility of the employer: there are two parties in the standard employment relationship: the employer and the employee. Employees are hired directly by the employer to perform work at the employer's organization. In contrast, some non-standard employment relationships may be tripartite: the employee performs work at the client organization but is contractually bound to

> ### Box 14.1:   Emerging types of non-standard employment forms
>
> 1. The 'sharing economy' worker (e.g., the Uber driver, the Amazon Mechanical Turker) who finds work through an intermediary, but neither the intermediary nor the client are employers. The contracts are typically short-term, and workers may vary in the extent to which they depend upon a single intermediary. Thus far, the popular discussion about this form of work arrangement has focused on the performance of these workers and the legality and appropriate regulation of these workers.
> 2. The 'astronaut' or long-distance commuting worker. These work arrangements involve an employee spending a short period of intensive work at a client site or other work location, frequently in shared accommodation provided by the employer. These arrangements are becoming typical in resource extraction industries (e.g., forestry, mining, fisheries, oil and gas), but the occupations involved are support functions (e.g., cooks, mechanics, nurses, administrators) as well as more stereotypical roles.

another organization. The client organization is the *de facto employer* and responsible for the day-to-day management of the employee, including safety training, for example. The hiring organization is the *de jure* employer and carries responsibility over hiring and pay. For example, *temporary agency workers* are contracted by an agency and then sent to client organizations to work there. Another example are *subcontracted or outsourced workers* who are hired by an organization for their specific expertise (e.g., IT, payroll) and then sent to client organizations.

Apart from this classification of the most common types of non-standard employment forms presented here, it can be noted that new contractual arrangements keep emerging to provide flexibility and services that are sought by organizations, but also by customers or employees. Box 14.1 presents two of these emergent forms that have become more influential in many different labour markets, but have – thus far – received fairly little research attention: (1) 'Sharing economy' worker, and (2) the 'astronaut' or long-distance commuting worker.

14.2.2   How comparable are typologies of employment forms across national legislations?

Even though the typology of non-standard employment arrangements may appear fairly straightforward, it should be tempered with the understanding that the legal definitions of these types of work vary considerably between countries. In particular, there are systematic differences in the protections and benefits offered to workers with different non-standard arrangements.

In the European Union, anti-discrimination laws prohibit employers from treating part-time or temporary workers differently from full-time employees because their work is part-time or temporary (Institute of Business Ethics, 2015). This means that these workers should receive the same treatment as permanent and full-time employees when it comes to pay rates, leave (e.g. sickness or parental leave), pension, benefits and holidays. However, since many of these benefits are tenure- and seniority-based or conditional upon a minimal contribution period in most organizations, permanent workers typically enjoy more privileges. There are also considerable differences within the EU. For example, Sweden, compared to most other EU countries, has a very generous system for parental leave that allows mothers or fathers to work part-time until their child is 8 years old. In Canada and the United States, part-time employees may be paid a lower wage and they may receive fewer (or none) of the employment benefits given to permanent workers, but also here differences exist between these two countries. For example, temporary agency workers must be provided with details such as the name of the client organization, the length of the contract, the wage, and the nature of the job duties in Canada. The temporary agency cannot discourage the client from hiring the temporary worker on a permanent basis at the conclusion of the contract. These protections are not available to temporary agency workers in the United States. Moreover, in some countries (e.g., Sweden), temporary agency workers can be permanently employed by their temporary agency, but hired temporarily to clients, whereas in most countries, temporary agencies only offer temporary contracts to their workers.

Conclusions about how workers with non-standard contracts feel may not be easily translated from one context to another. It may be especially difficult to make comparisons between regions with very different legal environments; these variations can mask potential differences. The fact that research on non-standard employment has received more attention in some regions (e.g., Europe and North America) than in others (e.g., Africa, South America) also influences our understanding of international differences (Connelly & Murphy, in press).

14.3   The Nature of Non-Standard Employment Forms: The Organizational and Individual Perspectives

In order to better understand how workers in non-standard employment may feel, researchers have mainly taken either an organizational or an individual perspective (De Cuyper et al., 2008). The organizational perspective highlights what function different employment contracts have for organizations, since this has implications for how workers in these contracts are being treated. The individual perspective holds that such objective functions or organizational structures are perceived and interpreted by each individual and therefore, individuals may arrive at different appraisals of what their employment conditions mean, and hence, may react differently to them. Thus, how it feels to work in a less than full-time or non-permanent employment contract is believed to be a function of both organizational and structural factors, as we will explain in the section outlining the organizational perspective, and of perceptual and individual factors, that are discussed in the individual perspective section.

14.3.1   The organizational perspective

Aronsson, Gustafsson, and Dallner (2002) proposed the centre–periphery model, which highlights potential structural and organizational differences between permanent full-time and various forms of *temporary* employment, and is rooted in earlier conceptualizations, such as the flexible firm (Atkinson, 1984) and the dual labour market theory (Doeringer & Piore, 1971). The core–periphery model divides the organization into a core segment and several layers of periphery to illustrate the fact that various employment forms serve different functions to the organization. Accordingly, workers in different employment contracts are treated differently. Permanent full-time work with the employing organization is seen as the standard, and all other forms of employment are considered to be outside of the core of the organization and in one of the more or less peripheral layers. In this chapter, we extend Aronsson's centre–periphery model to include both temporary *and* part-time arrangements (see Figure 14.1), and discuss the implications of this model for how these workers may feel.

Full-time permanent (i.e., core) employees are thought to be the most skilled and experienced employees in a company; they usually have longest tenure and experience. This provides employers with functional flexibility, meaning that full-time permanent employees can each perform many different tasks. In order to attract and retain these workers with the most valuable skills, and to guarantee high quality work, full-time permanent employees usually receive the most training and benefits, as well as the highest job security and the most desirable career opportunities (Atkinson, 1984).

Part-time permanent employees are the first peripheral layer around the core because part-time employees – even though they often are provided with a permanent contract, at least in Europe – are not present in the organization to the same extent as full-time employees. Also, part-time workers are more likely to be employed during nights, evenings and weekends. Not being at the workplace to

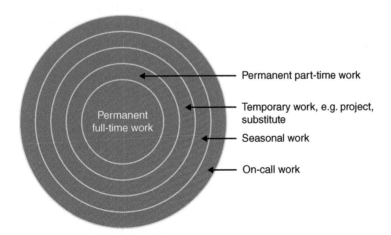

Figure 14.1:   The core–periphery perspective

the same extent as full-time workers may reduce their inclusion in the organization, access to information, and opportunities for participation, and all together, this may result in less desirable working conditions (Thorsteinson, 2003).

A second segment of peripheral employees includes temporary workers, such as substitutes or project workers. These employees may work full- or part-time, but because the duration of their employment contract is limited, these workers do not receive the same training. They also have less job security and, depending on the legal jurisdiction, they may also miss out on benefits that are based on seniority (Kalleberg, 2001).

The next circle of the periphery includes seasonal temporary employees. These workers have less contact with permanent employees because the majority of the workers in the organization are employed temporarily. They may not have job security, unless (as sometimes is the case), they are rehired the same season the year after. This, however, implies long spells of absence from the organization, and thus results in a more peripheral position.

Finally, the outer circle in the model is comprised of on-call workers who have no guarantee of a minimum of working hours per month. These workers are only hired when there are urgent short-term needs for their services in the organization (i.e., when many employees have called in sick). On-call workers thus have to be available on short-term notice, and can never plan when and how much to work, which adds to their job insecurity and makes their amount of income rather unpredictable (De Cuyper et al., 2008).

It has been argued that the degree of periphery may, at least to some extent, explain how part-time or temporary workers perceive their situation (Aronsson et al., 2002). With increasing job insecurity and income unpredictability and limited access to training, those in more peripheral positions may feel less attached to their organization, less committed and less knowledgeable about organizational routines and standard procedures. This may lead to higher strain or sub-standard safety behaviour (Aronsson et al., 2002). Furthermore, the degree of periphery may also affect the type of work and services that can be provided. For example, the shorter the duration of an employment is, the more it is important that a temporary worker quickly adjusts to the new environment and performs what is expected. This means that more interdependent or complex tasks that require a long-term engagement cannot be given to temporary employees. Inevitably, this has consequences for job demands, and opportunities to learn and develop through work.

In this core–periphery perspective, we have deliberately omitted the case of temporary agency workers, because they are not employed directly by the organization. These employees can be portrayed as peripheral to the company, but, depending on the tasks they are hired for, their status in the periphery may vary. This also illustrates one of the main problems with the core–periphery perspective: there are many possible exceptions. For example, one may argue that a part-time worker with minimal hours is more peripheral to the organization than a temporary worker who works full-time for a year or more. The core–periphery model only partly explains how workers in peripheral positions may feel. Individuals may differ considerably in how they perceive their situation, which is further discussed in the following section highlighting the individual perspective.

14.3.2   The individual perspective

Individual attitudes and behaviour are shaped by individual appraisals of a situation rather than by objective reality (Scott & Marshall, 2009). Using psychological contract theory, the implication is that employees in non-standard contracts may not feel either 'good' or 'bad' only as a function of their peripheral position to the organization. Instead, how they feel may be conditional upon their individual interpretation of the situation, or their perception of choice in pursuing that type of position. Outcomes related to employees attitudes and behaviour may furthermore also be shaped by objectively given and subjectively perceived work conditions – as outlined in stress–strain frameworks. Furthermore, the degree of choice or volition has been found to be a decisive predictor of part-time and temporary workers' attitudes and well-being. Therefore, next we will discuss psychological contract theory, stress frameworks and the role of volition in more depth, in order to shed more light on the question concerning how workers in non-standard contracts may feel.

14.3.3   Psychological contract theory

The psychological contract concerns an exchange between two parties (e.g., employee and employer), and includes perceptions of reciprocal promises and obligations that have been given to each other (Guest et al., 2010). In contrast to legal contracts, psychological contract terms are implicit and unwritten, and exist only in the mind of the beholder. Although the psychological contract is not legally binding, it is a strong driver of employee attitudes and behaviour. Generally, psychological contracts are defined as 'individual beliefs regarding terms of an exchange between individuals and their organization' (Rousseau, 1995, p. 9).

The psychological contract has particular resonance in the context of alternative employment. Not surprisingly, the actual employment contract shapes the content of the psychological contract (Rousseau & Schalk, 2000). Time in the organization appears to be a critical aspect, both in terms of number of working hours and length of contract; a shorter time span induces a narrower psychological contract, in the sense of fewer (perceived) mutual obligations and entitlements. Also, a shorter time span may induce a predominantly transactional and less relational deal. A transactional deal means there are more short-term, economic and specific exchanges (e.g. pay for performance) and few if any dynamic and socio-emotional exchanges (e.g. job security for loyalty) that build a long-term relationship and trust and characterize a relational deal. In line with this, temporary, as compared to permanent, employees tend to have fewer and mainly transactional expectations about what they should get from the organization and what they should give in return (Guest et al., 2010).

These findings can be understood from the perspective of the different parties to the employment deal. From the perspective of the organization, non-core workers are only partially included in the organization (see the core–periphery model), implying that non-standard workers are less entitled to scarce organizational resources, such as training or promotion opportunities. From the employee perspective, part-time workers may have other priorities and responsibilities outside work, and temporary workers may see their assignment as a stepping stone to jobs elsewhere. The implication is that they may invest less personal resources in the current employment relationship.

Consequences for employee attitudes and behaviour of non-standard workers with such a psychological contract are twofold. On the negative side, the narrower and more transactional psychological contract that is typical for non-standard workers may provide few incentives for attitudinal or behavioural engagement; rather, to the contrary. On the positive side, the narrower and more transactional psychological contract of non-standard workers is less susceptible to breach because there are fewer mutual obligations and they are less ambiguous. Psychological contract breach occurs when employees feel that the organization has failed to fulfil key promises, for example, when employees miss out on a promotion that they feel entitled to. Breach brings about strong negative emotions (e.g., anger, betrayal), stress and withdrawal, both in terms of attitudes (e.g., reduced organizational commitment, increased turnover intention) and behaviour (e.g., less willing to work hard or to go the extra mile).

In conclusion, it is clear that the psychological contract may affect how non-standard workers (compared with standard workers) feel and behave. It is, however, difficult to predict *a priori* whether the psychological contract of non-standard workers will produce 'worse' or 'better' outcomes, because of two related yet conflicting mechanisms: (1) the psychological contract content, and (2) the psychological contract breach.

14.3.4   Stress frameworks

Stress frameworks such as Karasek's Job Demand–Control model (Karasek & Theorell, 1990) or the Job Demands–Resources model (Bakker & Demerouti, 2007) are built on the idea that strain results from perceived imbalance between demands and resources at work (see also Chapter 5 in this volume). It is often assumed that non-standard work comes with fewer resources (see psychological contract theory), which has been demonstrated in results from the European Surveys on Working Conditions (e.g., Benach, Gimeno, & Benavides, 2002). For example, non-standard workers may experience few opportunities for autonomy, limited influence on workplace decisions, and little control over the design, implementation and nature of work tasks. Non-standard workers, moreover, may be less likely to receive or seek social support because they are considered 'outsiders' and this outsider view is shared by supervisors, permanent coworkers and the union. However, the picture for demands is less straightforward: non-standard work has been associated with job insecurity and role ambiguity, but also with lower workload (Parker, Griffin, Sprigg, & Wall, 2002). To complicate the picture even further, the large heterogeneity in non-standard employment forms likely brings about large differences in job demands and resources. In conclusion, it is difficult to portray non-standard work as good or bad in terms of job quality and as stressful or not: what is needed is a balanced view that accounts for both job resources and demands and for the large pool of non-standard work forms.

14.3.5 Volition and motives to work in non-standard employment forms

A major hypothesis in research on non-standard workers is that they appraise their situation more positively when non-standard work matches their individual desires and needs, and they appraise it more negatively when they feel forced into this type of work. This phenomenon has been studied under the heading of volition (i.e., the workers' preferences for non-standard work arrangements).

Part-time employment is often portrayed as largely voluntary; many workers choose part-time assignments to achieve greater balance between work and non-work activities and obligations (e.g., care for dependent children or other relatives). However, many workers, in particular, women, would prefer to work more hours but are forced into part-time employment because of poor economic conditions and the associated inability to find full-time employment (OECD, 2015). Temporary employment is often framed as involuntary because it brings about few tangible benefits for the workers and is mostly driven by the employer's need for more flexibility. Voluntary temporary employment is often framed in the context of boundaryless careers in which (mostly highly skilled) workers proactively pursue work across organizational boundaries. This picture seems quite inaccurate: the numbers of involuntary temporary workers far outweigh the number of voluntary temporary workers (Eurostat, 2014).

Volition is a continuum, but it has mostly been studied as a dichotomy between 'involuntary' versus 'voluntary' non-standard workers. However, this dichotomy may be too simple, because reasons behind non-standard work vary widely and the distinction between voluntary and involuntary is sometimes blurred (Bernhard-Oettel, Isaksson, & Bellaagh, 2008). For example, part-time work may be chosen despite a worker's own preferences for full-time work when family commitments are too burdensome. As another example, some temporary workers may prefer permanent employment but nevertheless see benefits associated with temporary employment, such as opportunities for skill development or experience in different jobs or industries, or in opportunities for permanent employment. Such motives targeted towards a specific outcome have sometimes also been termed stepping-stone motives (de Jong, de Cuyper, De Witte, Silla, & Bernhard-Oettel, 2009). For example, non-standard work may serve as a 'foot in the door' technique that leads to higher quality or permanent employment.

The idea behind research on workers' motivations is that both voluntary and involuntary reasons may simultaneously lead workers to accept non-standard employment. Voluntary motives are aspects that pull workers into non-standard work and that enable the pursuit of personal goals, and include the need to combine work with non-work commitments, financial incentives, or skill development. Involuntary motives are aspects that push workers towards non-standard work, often to avoid an even more negative state; the most notable examples are lack of viable alternatives, economic recession or avoiding unemployment.

In sum, not only the perceptions of the psychological contracts or work conditions, but also volition and motives are important to consider if one aims to understand how it feels to work in a non-standard employment contract. For example, a more peripheral position in the organization may have less negative consequences for those who have accepted this arrangement since it matches their needs, or if they feel their demands to be manageable and their psychological contract to be unambiguous. In contrast, a position closer to the core may prove more stressful if job demands are felt to be high, and control fairly low, or if the only reason to accept this position was that there was no better employment opportunity.

One issue that has been left out in this discussion of the organizational vs. individual perspective relates to stigmatization and social comparison processes. However, as illustrated in Box 14.2, an individual's position in the core–periphery of an organization, as well as the distribution of core vs. periphery positions in that organization, may create norms that influence individual as well as shared perceptions of what it feels like to work in a certain contract, and that may in turn also have an impact on workers' reactions.

Box 14.2:   A social comparison and workplace perspective

There has been limited discussion on the effect that different ratios of standard vs. non-standard employment forms at a workplace may have. However, working together with other temporary vs. permanent workers may evoke social comparison processes that are likely to have consequences for how satisfied different workers may become with their own psychological contract terms, how justice and fairness are perceived and how that generally affects organizational behaviour, work attitudes or well-being. For example, it has been found that temporary workers have an outgroup–favouritism, that is, instead of favouring their own in-group (the temporary workers), they favour the out-group (permanent workers) and rather 'switch than fight' (van Hippel, 2006). This illustrates that core standard employment still is viewed as a norm, whereas a more peripheral non-standard contract may be stigmatized (Boyce, Ryan, Imus, & Morgeson, 2007). However, also core workers are affected by having many coworkers in more peripheral positions, since an extensive use of temporary workers at a workplace leads to higher job insecurity climate among permanent workers (De Cuyper, Sora, De Witte, Caballer, & Peiró, 2009). In sum, how workers in core and periphery positions in an organization perceive and compare each other's position has implications for how they feel on an individual level, as well as in a work-group.

14.4 Consequences of Non-Standard Employment

As described above, it is often assumed that part-time and temporary workers will have more negative job attitudes, fewer positive organizational behaviours, and reduced well-being; however, empirical evidence shows that this is not always the case. Instead, how these workers feel often depends on a mixture of the organizational and individual factors that are at play. In the following, we discuss consequences with respect to work attitudes, workplace behaviour, health and well-being, as well as career development in more detail.

14.4.1 Work attitudes of non-standard workers

There are three prominent work attitudes which are often examined in the context of non-standard work arrangements, namely, (1) job satisfaction, (2) organizational commitment, and (3) turnover intentions. For workers in non-standard employment – and temporary workers in particular – the evidence regarding job satisfaction is inconclusive. For temporary workers with more passive tasks and lower working life quality, more negative work attitudes than for permanent workers have been reported (Wagenaar et al., 2012). However, other studies have found opposite effects or no differences at all in job satisfaction, perhaps because temporary workers may fill highly qualified jobs or differ in their motives to work in a non-standard contract (De Cuyper et al., 2008). Job satisfaction is known to be related to organizational commitment (see also Chapter 22 in this volume), and although non-standard employees display similar levels of organizational commitment, developing and maintaining that commitment may require different actions by the organization, such as scheduling procedures and development opportunities (Epstein, Seron, Oglensky, & Saute, 2014). Also, preferences for temporary employment and expectations of being offered a new contract seem to increase both job satisfaction and organizational commitment among those with a temporary contract (Clinton, Bernhard-Oettel, Rigotti, & de Jong, 2011). Whereas permanently employed full- or part-timers have to make an active decision in leaving their organizations, temporary employees are by definition forced to think about leaving the organization. They may be thinking about finding a new employer, especially one that offers them a permanent contract, more often. This may mean that engaging in job search when the end of the contract approaches has negative effects both for the workers' well-being but also for their organizational performance (Clinton et al., 2011).

One way to foster more job satisfaction and commitment for part-time but also temporary workers may be to monitor employees' psychological contract, in order to balance expectations, for example, in terms of contract renewal or scheduling of working hours (Conway & Briner, 2002). An understanding of the importance of finding a good match between the job role and employee expectations can also provide significant benefits for both the firm and the employee. Even for organizations employing part-time and temporary workers, negative work attitudes can be quite costly. Increased turnover and unhappy employees can lead to a toxic work environment and increased costs related to recruitment, selection and training of new employees. It is therefore important for managers of part-time and temporary employees to understand the situational but also individual factors which may affect the work attitudes of their employees. This suggestion is supported by research by Wittmer and Martin (2011), who found that part-time employees are not one homogeneous group, but rather several different types of workers with different needs and attitudes related to their role (e.g., primaries, college students and moonlighters). The study found that factors such as psychological involvement and other life demands (the individual's roles outside of work) of the employees were stronger predictors of work attitudes, than being a part-time versus full-time employee. Similar conclusions have been reached in the comparisons of permanent to temporary employees when it comes to work attitudes (De Cuyper et al., 2008).

14.4.2   How do non-standard employees act at work?

Other desirable outcomes of the employment relationship, such as organizational citizenship behaviour, workplace safety and performance are also important when considering non-standard work arrangements. Especially for organizations with a high proportion of part-time or temporary workers, the contributions made by these employees are crucial for the performance of the firm (Künn-Nelen, De Grip, & Fouarge, 2013). Encouraging part-time and temporary workers and providing a supportive work environment are therefore both important factors in fostering in-role and extra-role behaviours that increase performance. Empirical findings show that temporary workers who feel that they are receiving fewer benefits than their permanent counterparts (or less than expected), are less likely to engage in positive civic behaviour in their organization (Chambel & Castanheira, 2006). However, those in temporary work who believe they can get renewed or prolonged employment, tend to report higher levels of job performance than workers without such expectations (Clinton et al., 2011). Here again, the complexity of contractual arrangements, together with individual perceptions, provide the answer to how workers in non-standard work act at work.

Another critical outcome for both organizations and individuals relates to safety at work, that is, safety knowledge and safety behaviour (Probst & Brubaker, 2001; see also Chapter 21 in this volume). Scheduling safety training can be challenging when employing non-standard workers, as can engaging and motivating them to participate in safety initiatives. This, however, is highly important for non-standard workers, because many of them are younger and less experienced or educated, and therefore more likely to be injured. Generally, workers feeling job insecure have been found to be less likely to report minor injuries or near misses because they are afraid that they will be fired (Probst & Brubaker, 2001) or, if they are temporary employees, they may not have their contracts renewed (Aronsson, 1999). Complicating the research on workplace safety of these workers is the fact that the hiring of non-standard workers may be associated with higher injury rates for both these workers and permanent employees, because their hiring is often associated with production line speed-ups arising because of increased demands for a particular product.

14.4.3   Non-standard workers' well-being and health

Particularly in Europe, many studies have analysed stress, uncertainty, well-being and health, but also here findings have been mixed. For part-time workers, where job security may be less of a concern, well-being can have a positive effect by reducing turnover intentions (Mauno, De Cuyper, Tolvanen, Kinnunen, & Mäkikangas, 2014). Research on temporary workers has found them to report higher levels of psychological distress and non-optimal self-rated health than permanent employees, which may indicate that organizations should move away from temporary contracts (Waenerlund, Virtanen, & Hammarström, 2011). A recent longitudinal study of temporary workers in Italy has also found significant negative health effects when the temporary employment is prolonged (Pirani & Salvini, 2015), or, as shown in a European sample, when workers repeatedly work in temporary contracts (Clinton et al., 2011). These findings support the position that employees are more significantly affected when their job role does not align with their expectations over a longer period of time.

Interestingly, a recent study of temporary workers in Britain has found that permanent workers with reduced mental health may choose to switch to a temporary position, which means that previous studies of the effects of temporary work may overemphasize the effect of work status on mental health (Dawson, Veliziotis, Pacheco, & Webber, 2015). Organizations which emphasize employees' well-being may see improvements with initiatives related to mental health, disease prevention and employee absenteeism. All workers benefit from accessible services, but organizations should emphasize opportunities for non-standard workers, who may be less likely to engage in services they feel are oriented towards full-time employees. Supervisor support and positive communications can increase the likelihood that part-time and temporary workers will utilize these services. Organizations may also choose to offer additional services targeted at employees in non-standard contracts where different needs are identified.

14.4.4   Career development

What appears largely missing in non-standard work research is a focus upon careers throughout the lifespan. This is the more so surprising for two reasons. First, non-standard work is often framed as a transition period that eventually lands workers in standard jobs. Examples are temporary employment as a stepping stone to permanent employment, part-time employment as a way to reintegrate after a period of inactivity or unemployment, or as a way to balance paid work with other demands. This framing seems to suggest that non-standard workers, perhaps more than standard workers, make job transitions, and that many of these job transitions concern upward mobility. Evidence for this hypothesis is again mixed, and figures vary dramatically across studies and countries: the best conclusion to date is that non-standard work arrangements are a stepping stone to standard employment for some workers but a dead end for others, with a significant share of workers cycling between non-standard employment and unemployment (De Cuyper, Notelaers, & De Witte, 2009). Job transitions between non-standard and standard work, and the success factors driving such transitions and associated career outcomes should be probed in greater detail. This probing could help to answer the question whether non-standard employment may help workers to build portfolios that are valued on the labour market and that may lead to a successful career or instead whether non-standard work is a negative signal for employers.

Second, non-standard work appears more prevalent at life events that are often experienced as shocks, both positive and negative. Examples are young graduates who accept a temporary job as an orientation on the labour market, parents who decide to work part-time in order to meet family demands, or workers who take up part-time leave to take care for a seriously ill family member. Shocks are seen as career markers, yet they are not often considered in the realm of non-standard work research.

Summary

This chapter started with the general question: 'How do we feel and behave when we are not permanent, full-time employees?'. The answer is complicated. Non-standard workers are a heterogeneous group. Non-standard employment is an umbrella term consisting of arrangements that differ in working hours and permanency, and can involve a tripartite employment relationship including the worker, the employer and the organization for which work is carried out. Non-standard employment arrangements are nested within organizations, each with specific motives for using non-standard employment work and corresponding human resource practices. Organizations are again embedded within specific labour markets, and these come with specific employment protection regulations, all affecting how non-standard workers feel and behave.

Despite the complicated nature of non-standard employment, we believe this chapter provides some useful insights for practice. We have discussed potential risks associated with non-standard work arrangements in terms of job design and psychological contract expectations, and highlighted the role of individual preferences. These factors seem to interact and this in turn may explain the inconsistent findings regarding effects on work attitudes, behaviour, well-being and health. As the prevalence and the variety in the nature of these arrangements continue to increase, organizations will need to be more aware of the expectations that employees in non-standard as well as standard employment forms may have, or face elevating costs related to sickness, turnover, absenteeism and counterproductive workplace behaviours.

Discussion Points

1 Imagine you are an HR manager: Would you hire temporary workers with the prospect of becoming a permanent worker, even if you knew that not all temporary workers could become permanent workers? What are advantages and disadvantages?
2 Imagine you are an HR manager: How could you try to find an optimal ratio of temporary to permanent workers at a workplace?

Suggested Further Reading

Guest, D., Isaksson, K., & De Witte, H. (2010). *Employment contracts, psychological contracts, and employee well-being.* Oxford: Oxford University Press. Findings from a large European study on non-standard work, its psychological contracts and consequences.

Koene, B., Garsten, C., & Galais, N. (2014). *Management and organization of temporary agency work.* London: Routledge. Read about the special case of temporary agency work.

Online resources

International Labour Organization (ILO): http://www.ilo.org/global/research/global-reports/weso/2015-changing-nature-of-jobs/lang–en/index.htm The world employment social outlook, the changing nature of jobs, and statistics for many different countries.

OECD: www.oecd.org: Statistics and employment outlooks, reports on temporary, part-time or temporary agency work in OECD countries.

References

Aronsson, G. (1999). Contingent work and health and safety. *Work, Employment & Society, 13*(3), 439–459.

Aronsson, G., Gustafsson, K., & Dallner, M. (2002). Work environment and health in different types of temporary jobs. *European Journal of Work and Organizational Psychology, 11*(2), 151–175.

Atkinson, J. (1984). Manpower strategies for flexible organisations. *Personnel Management, 16*(8), 28–31.

Bakker, A. B., & Demerouti, E. (2007). The Job Demands–Resources model: state of the art. *Journal of Managerial Psychology, 22*(3), 309–328.

Benach, J., Gimeno, D., & Benavides, F. G. (2002). *Types of employment and health in the European Union.* Luxembourg: European Foundation for the Improvement of Living and Work Conditions.

Bernhard-Oettel, C., Isaksson, K., & Bellaagh, K. (2008). Patterns of contract motives and work involvement in temporary work: Relations to work-related and general well-being. *Economic and Industrial Democracy, 29*(4), 565–591.

Boyce, A. S., Ryan, A. M., Imus, A. L., & Morgeson, F. P. (2007). 'Temporary worker, permanent loser?' A model of the stigmatization of temporary workers. *Journal of Management, 33*(1), 5–29.

Chambel, M. J., & Castanheira, F. (2006). Different temporary work status, different behaviors in organization. *Journal of Business and Psychology, 20*(3), 351–367.

Clinton, M., Bernhard-Oettel, C., Rigotti, T., & de Jong, J. (2011). Expanding the temporal context of research on non-permanent work: Previous experience, duration of and time remaining on contracts and employment continuity expectations. *Career Development International, 16*(2), 114–139.

Connelly, C. E., & Murphy, M. (in press). Alternative work arrangements. In D. Ones (Ed.). *The SAGE handbook of industrial, work & organizational psychology* (vol. III) (2nd ed.).

Conway, N., & Briner, R. B. (2002). Full-time versus part-time employees: Understanding the links between work status, the psychological contract, and attitudes. *Journal of Vocational Behavior, 61*(2), 279–301.

Dawson, C., Veliziotis, M., Pacheco, G., & Webber, D. J. (2015). Is temporary employment a cause or consequence of poor mental health? A panel data analysis. *Social Science and Medicine, 134,* 50–58.

De Cuyper, N., de Jong, J., De Witte, H., Isaksson, K., Rigotti, T., & Schalk, R. (2008). Literature review of theory and research on the psychological impact of temporary employment: Towards a conceptual model. *International Journal of Management Reviews, 10*(1), 25–51.

De Cuyper, N., Notelaers, G., & De Witte, H. (2009). Transitioning between temporary and permanent employment: A two-wave study on the entrapment, the stepping stone and the selection hypothesis. *Journal of Occupational and Organizational Psychology, 82*(1), 67–88.

De Cuyper, N., Sora, B., De Witte, H., Caballer, A., & Peiró, J. M. (2009). Organizations' use of temporary employment and a climate of job insecurity among Belgian and Spanish permanent workers. *Economic & Industrial Democracy, 30*(4), 564–591.

de Jong, J., De Cuyper, N., De Witte, H., Silla, I., & Bernhard-Oettel, C. (2009) Motives for accepting temporary employment: A typology of temporary workers. *International Journal of Manpower, 30*(3), 237–252.

Doeringer, P. B., & Piore, M. J. (1971). *Internal labour markets and manpower analysis.* Lexington, MA: Heath Lexington Books.

Epstein, C. F., Seron, C., Oglensky, B., & Saute, R. (2014). *The part-time paradox: Time norms, professional life, family and gender.* New York: Routledge.

Eurostat (2014). Temporary employees as percentage of the total number of employees, involuntary temporary employees. Retrieved February 2, 2016 from http://ec.europa.eu/eurostat/

Federal Ministry of Labour and Social Affairs, Germany (2014). 450 Euro mini jobs/marginal employment. Retrieved November 30, 2015 from http://www.bmas.de/EN/Our-Topics/Social-Security/450-euro-mini-jobs-marginal-employment.html

Guest, D., Isaksson, K., & De Witte, H. (2010). *Employment contracts, psychological contracts, and employee well-being.* Oxford: Oxford University Press.

Institute of Business Ethics (2015). Fairness in the workplace: Staffing and employment contracts. *Business Ethics Briefing, 47.* Retrieved 19 March 2016 from: https://www.ibe.org.uk/userassets/briefings/b47_staffing_and_employment_contracts.pdf

Kalleberg, A. L. (2001). Organizing flexibility: The flexible firm in a new century. *British Journal of Industrial Relations, 39*(4), 479–504.

Karasek, R., & Theorell, T. (1990). *Healthy work. Stress, productivity, and the reconstruction of working life.* New York: Basic Books.

Künn-Nelen, A., de Grip, A., & Fouarge, D. (2013). Is part-time employment beneficial for firm productivity? *Industrial & Labor Relations Review, 66*(5), 1172–1191.

Mauno, S., De Cuyper, N., Tolvanen, A., Kinnunen, U., & Mäkikangas, A. (2014). Occupational well-being as a mediator between job insecurity and turnover intention: Findings at the individual and work department levels. *European Journal of Work and Organizational Psychology, 23*(3), 381–393.

OECD (2015). *Labor Force Statistics: Data on temporary employment and part-time employment.*

Retrieved January 27, 2016 from http://stats. oecd.org/index.aspx?DatasetCode=TEMP_I

Office of National Statistics (2015). *Analysis of employment contracts that do not guarantee a minimum number of hours*. Retrieved November 30, 2015 from http://www.ons.gov.uk/ ons/dcp171776_396885.pdf

Parker, S. K., Griffin, M. A., Sprigg, C. A., & Wall, T. A. (2002). Effect of temporary contracts on perceived work characteristics and job strain: A longitudinal study. *Personnel Psychology, 55*(3), 689–717.

Pirani, E., & Salvini, S. (2015). Is temporary employment damaging to health? A longitudinal study on Italian workers. *Social Science & Medicine, 124,* 121–131.

Probst, T. M., & Brubaker, T. L. (2001). The effects of job insecurity on employee safety outcomes: Cross-sectional and longitudinal explorations. *Journal of Occupational Health Psychology, 6*(2), 139–159.

Rousseau, D. M. (1995). *Psychological contracts in organizations. Understanding written and unwritten agreements.* Thousand Oaks, CA: SAGE Publications.

Rousseau, D. M., & Schalk, R. (2000). *Psychological contracts in employment. Cross-cultural perspectives.* Thousand Oaks, CA: SAGE Publications.

Scott, J., & Marshall, G. (2009). *A dictionary of sociology* (3rd ed.). Oxford: Oxford University Press.

Thorsteinson, T. J. (2003). Job attitudes of part-time vs. full-time workers: A meta-analytic review. *Journal of Occupational & Organizational Psychology, 76*(2), 151–177.

von Hippel, C. D. (2006). When people would rather switch than fight: Out-group favoritism among temporary employees. *Group Processes & Intergroup Relations, 9*(4), 533–546.

Waenerlund, A.-K., Virtanen, P., & Hammarström, A. (2011). Is temporary employment related to health status? Analysis of the Northern Swedish Cohort. *Scandinavian Journal of Public Health, 39*(5), 533–539.

Wagenaar, A. F., Kompier, M. A., Houtman, I. L., van den Bossche, S., Smulders, P., & Taris, T. W. (2012). Can labour contract differences in health and work-related attitudes be explained by quality of working life and job insecurity? *International Archives of Occupational and Environmental Health, 85*(7), 763–773.

Wittmer, J. L., & Martin, J. E. (2011). Work and personal role involvement of part-time employees: Implications for attitudes and turnover intentions. *Journal of Organizational Behavior, 32*(5), 767–787.

15

Why Should Organizations Treat Their Employees Fairly? Definition, Relevance, and Consequences of Justice at Work

Constanze Eib and Guillaume Soenen

Overview

At its most general level, organizational justice is an area of psychological inquiry that focuses on perceptions of fairness in the workplace. (Byrne & Cropanzano, 2001, p. 4)

This chapter explains why organizations should treat employees fairly and what happens when they do not. In the context of work and organizational psychology, organizational justice typically refers to the perceived fairness of an authority's decision-making. Authority figures such as supervisors or managers, who are perceived as behaving fairly, are trusted, which, in turn, can affect performance positively. Conversely, employees who feel treated unfairly are more likely to exhibit behaviour that harms the organization or its members. In this chapter, we explore why justice is important for individuals in general and, in the work context, under what circumstances someone is likely to feel fairly, or unfairly, treated, what the characteristics of a fair decision are and the rules managers have to follow in order to be perceived as fair. Then, we review whether all people are equally affected by the presence or absence of justice. Finally, we consider how fair organizations can be built.

15.1 Introduction

In developed countries, since the first industrial revolution, the relationship between an employer and an employee has been an economic one. Employees put their skills and effort at the service of an employer who in return pays compensation. Yet, this relationship is also a social relationship. Employees may require not just money in exchange for their involvement but they may want intangible things, such as recognition, belonging, development opportunities, and fulfilling

An Introduction to Work and Organizational Psychology: An International Perspective,
Third Edition. Edited by Nik Chmiel, Franco Fraccaroli and Magnus Sverke.
© 2017 John Wiley & Sons, Ltd. Published 2017 by John Wiley & Sons, Ltd.

relationships. Employers are looking for strong engagement above and beyond the formal obligations set out in the employment contract.

Organizational justice is one important dimension of the psycho-social dimension of work. It refers to perceptions that someone, or something, is fair, for instance, managers and colleagues, or recruitment procedures or performance appraisals. Fairness has been described as the glue that holds employer and employee together (Cropanzano, Bowen, & Gilliland, 2007). Employees who feel fairly treated by their employer are more committed to the organization, trust the managers, perform better, and have lower turnover, as we will describe later in the chapter. Perceptions of injustice, on the other hand, have negative consequences for employees and employers alike, such as employees being on sickness absence due to health problems, or employees who are less willing to help and who are inclined to use company resources for private means. Justice and injustice perceptions are subjective ('do I feel fairly treated?'), and this sets the study of organizational justice in psychology apart from how justice is considered in disciplines like philosophy which is concerned with normative prescriptions ('what is just?').

15.2   What is Justice in the Work Context?

Justice became a topic of interest in organizational psychology and management science in the early 1980s, after it already had enjoyed a long tradition in criminology and social psychology. The term 'organizational justice' was coined to designate the study of justice perceptions in the workplace. Historically, the field of organizational justice has focused on the perceptions of employees with regard to their employer or organization in general, their supervisor or specific work-related events. However, there are other strands of research that are relevant to grasp the richness of organizational justice scholarship. The literature may be structured along two dimensions: the unit of analysis, and the nature of the variable of interest. Regarding the *unit of analysis*, social scientists have distinguished between the recipient, the observer and the actor. The recipient, usually the employee, is the person who is faced with the actions of a decision-maker, for instance, an employee is confronted with a decision made by his/her manager. Observers are those individuals like colleagues, customers, or clients, who happen to witness the interaction between the decision-maker and the recipient. Research has shown that customers and clients, for instance, are influenced by how employees of an organization are treated by their managers. Finally, research on the actor perspective, a more recent development, involves looking at the motives of decision-makers to treat others fairly, and, for example, whether their behaviour towards subordinates is influenced by how fairly they feel treated by top managers. Also, there is evidence that managers sometimes behave unfairly without intention. The second dimension is the *nature of the variable*. When organizational justice is studied to understand how it may relate to work attitudes and behaviour, such as job satisfaction or performance, it is studied as an independent variable.

Unit of analysis:	Nature of the variable Organizational justice as: Predictor	Outcome
Recipient	- 1 - How do employees react when they feel treated unfairly?	- 2 - What are the characteristics of a fair process?
Observer	- 3 - How do customers react upon hearing a company mistreats its employees or suppliers?	- 4 - Who is more likely to notice and react to injustice done to others?
Actor	- 5 - Does fair treatment of senior managers trickle down to how line managers treat their team members?	- 6- What are the motives for managers to behave fairly?

Figure 15.1: A simple typology of organizational justice scholarship – with sample research questions across different streams of justice research

When researchers try to understand if and why perceptions of justice vary across people and contexts, then it is studied as a dependent variable. Combining these two dimensions results in a 3 by 2 matrix, presented in Figure 15.1. Each cell represents a distinct thread of justice research, and is illustrated with a sample research question.

Cells 1 and cell 2 correspond to the perspective of the recipient of justice, or the victim of injustice; most of the time, this refers to employees' perceptions. This is a perspective which is studied widely. Studies of how perceptions of fairness affect employees' attitudes and behaviour fall in cell 1, while studies of the characteristics of the personality or the environment that affects whether a situation is perceived as fair or not, belong to cell 2. Cells 3 and 4 refer to the perspective of the observer. Research concerned with questions such as how team members or customers react to witnessing unfairness, in terms of trust or consumer behaviour, falls in cell 3. Research in cell 4 is focused on personality and situational characteristics that affect whether observers notice or react to unfairness. Cells 5 and 6 refer to the actor perspective of organizational justice which is a comparatively less researched area. Cell 5 is about research on the consequences of fair and unfair behaviour at a higher level of the organization, on the fairness of behaviour at lower levels. Studies that aim to understand the various motives for adhering to justice rules, also called justice enactment, fall in cell 6.

15.2.1 Dimensions of justice

From largely mono-dimensional, the conceptualization of organizational justice gradually became multi-dimensional. From the 1950s to the 1970s, justice was mainly studied from an outcome, or distributive, perspective. Distributive justice refers to the fairness of decision outcomes such as pay, promotions, or desirable assignments. A decision, or 'distribution', is considered fair when it conforms to a chosen norm of allocation. Outcomes can be allocated according to merit. This is the case when better performers get better pay; this is referred to as the 'equity norm'. Outcomes may also be allocated on the basis of needs, whereby those with greater needs receive greater benefits ('need norm'). The 'equality norm' calls for the same outcomes to be allocated to all. Within organizations, notably those of Anglo-Saxon origin, the equity rule is dominant, as it is believed to be the one most conducive to individual performance (Adams, 1965).

The second important dimension of justice is procedural justice, which refers to the fairness of the process that leads to decision outcomes. This dimension was first investigated in courtroom settings in which the fairness of the sentence was distinguished from the fairness of the process leading to the sentence (Thibaut & Walker, 1975). Individuals tend to be more satisfied with decision outcomes and tend to perceive outcomes as more fair when they had a say during the process (this is referred to as 'voice', for instance, the opportunity for employees to contribute information during the appraisal process). These findings led to a stream of research on the 'fair process effect', which refers to the fact that individuals react more positively to a decision or outcome when they perceive the decision was arrived at by a fair procedure.

A third dimension, interactional justice, was introduced in the late 1980s (Bies & Moag, 1986) on the premise that fairness perceptions are influenced by not only outcome allocations or processes but also by the treatment individuals receive from organizational representatives. The notion of interactional justice was later split into interpersonal and informational justice. Interpersonal justice refers to the fairness of the interpersonal treatment and informational justice refers to the fairness of explanations and information provided regarding decision-making. The debate about the number of justice dimensions (two, three, or four) is still on-going although less actively than a decade ago (see Colquitt, 2001). Nowadays, different scholars use different numbers of dimensions but most scholars adopt a four-dimensional understanding of the organizational justice phenomenon.

Aside from the different dimensions of justice, some researchers focus instead on overall justice (Ambrose & Schminke, 2009). It is suggested that overall justice better captures individuals' justice experiences as it has been argued that individuals make a holistic judgement when they form impressions of justice. It is further suggested that individuals approach justice as a 'Gestalt' and that overall justice perceptions drive individuals' behaviour. Therefore, a focus on the different justice dimensions may not represent how individuals form and use justice evaluations. Although discussions are still on-going, overall justice is now seen as a useful and relevant construct in parallel to the traditional four justice dimensions.

A further recent development is the attention given to further distinguishing between justice and injustice than has traditionally been the case. Justice can be seen as something that is expected, whereas injustice is something that is noticed. Similarly, justice can be described as the cognitive ('cold') aspect of rule adherence whereas injustice is a more affective-laden concept ('hot'). Some scholars argue that injustice is easier to perceive, and, because of the negative connotation, also has stronger effects on outcomes. In a recent study, it was found that justice and injustice can be measured separately and have independent effects on a variety of different outcomes. However, the correlation was −.80 (on a scale from −1 to +1) which is very high. At this point, further research is needed to establish whether justice and injustice are the two polar extremes of one continuum or distinct phenomena (see Colquitt, Long, Rodell, & Halvorsen-Ganepola, 2014).

15.2.2   Why justice matters to people

The literature distinguishes between three accounts of why justice matters to individuals: (1) instrumental reasons, (2) relational reasons, and (3) deontic reasons. In broad terms, it is argued that individuals care about justice because justice can fulfil fundamental psychological needs, such as the need for control, belonging, positive self-regard and meaningfulness (Cropanzano, Byrne, Bobocel, & Rupp, 2001). Conversely, injustice threatens the fulfilment of those same needs.

There are several accounts of why justice matters to individuals. According to the instrumental model (Cropanzano et al., 2001), individuals are concerned about justice because it ensures the predictability and favourability of their outcomes. Justice is therefore a control mechanism to receive favourable outcomes in the future. According to relational models, individuals care about justice because it provides them with information about their status, self-worth, and hence contributes to their social identity. Fairness communicates to individuals that they have a good relationship with the organization and are recognized as full members of the group. These perceptions elicit pride in group membership, and can fulfil psychological needs of belonging and positive self-regard. According to deontic models, individuals care about justice out of a respect for human worth and dignity, such that every employee deserves to be treated fairly or that some people may not want to work for an organization with a bad reputation. Justice is hereby stated as a virtue in itself and can fulfil the need for meaningfulness.

These three different views do not exclude each other; in fact, they can be present to differing degrees at the same time. Individuals have different psychological needs that can be fulfilled by fairness considerations. All three perspectives have in common that fairness is important and relevant to individuals in general, and at work.

15.3 How Individuals Form Justice Perceptions

In the previous section, we have defined organizational justice and explained why it matters to individuals at work. We now turn our attention to the processes by which justice perceptions are formed, and transformed. When individuals experience an event, for instance, a managerial decision, they assess its fairness by assessing the extent to which the justice rules are followed or not. Equity theory provides an important answer as to how individuals experience fairness. Fairness heuristic theory complements equity theory and is useful particularly to explain how justice perceptions evolve. Both are explained next.

15.3.1 Justice rules and equity theory

When an event occurs, such as a performance appraisal review, it is suggested that an employee assesses the fairness of the event by considering the fairness of the outcome, the process, and whether the interpersonal treatment was fair. Figure 15.2 presents the rules for the four justice dimensions, and also a brief description of each rule (Cropanzano et al., 2007). For instance, if judging the process of specific event like a recruitment, applicants might use the rule of process control and ask themselves whether they had sufficient opportunities to talk about their past work experiences. Applicants might also look for any signs of bias or prejudice against themselves or other applicants. After considering the relevant justice rules, individuals form their perception of the fairness of the recruitment process and that of the hiring organization.

Among the many justice rules listed in Figure 15.2, the most well-known is the one stemming from equity theory (Adams, 1965). The basic tenet of equity theory is that employees try to maintain a balance between what they bring to their job and what they get in return from their organization compared to the inputs and outputs of comparable others. In this sense, equity theory deals with the perceived fairness of the allocation of resources (distributive justice). The critical part for perceptions of fairness is that the ratio between inputs and outputs should be equal to that of relevant others. Even if colleagues receive more outputs, this can be seen as fair as long as the colleagues also have bigger inputs. Ratios are considered unfair if the ratio of the comparable other is more favourable (more output for less input) or if it is less favourable (more input for less output). If the ratio is unfair, individuals experience distress and are motivated to re-establish fairness. Individuals can attempt to change their input or their output. For instance, it has been shown that factory workers who are over-rewarded, for instance, react by increasing the quality of their work (Adams, 1963). It is argued that over-reward elicits guilt which motivates the individual to balance out the inequity. Employees may also change the reference group they compare their ratio to. Individuals can compare their ratio not only to others within or outside of the organization but also to themselves at a previous employer. In order to remedy inequity, employees can potentially also

	Rule	Description
Distributive Justice: *Fairness of outcomes*	Equity	Rewarding employees based on their contributions
	Equality	Providing each employee roughly the same compensation
	Need	Providing a benefit based on one's personal requirements
Procedural Justice: *Fairness of the allocation proces*	Consistency	All employees are treated the same
	Lack of Bias	No person or group is singled out for discrimination or ill-treatment
	Accuracy	Decisions are based on accurate information
	Representation of all Concerned	Appropriate stakeholders have input into a decision
	Correction	There is an appeals process or other mechanism for fixing mistakes
	Ethics	Norms of professional conduct are not violated
Interpersonal Justice: *Fairness of interactions*	Respect	Treating an employee with courtesy and politeness
	Propriety	Not making improper remarks to an employee
Informational Justice: *Fairness of the communication*	Truthfulness	Employees are provided with honest information
	Justification	Providing thorough explanations to employees

Figure 15.2: Justice rules

Source: Adapted from Cropanzano et al. (2007).

modify their perceptions of the inputs and outputs, or the relative importance of them. Inputs include time, energy, dedication, knowledge, skills, and abilities. Outputs include pay, benefits, work conditions, job security, attention, enjoyment, reputation.

Equity theory has received widespread attention from other disciplines than psychology, particularly as a theory to explain motivation. Employees are more satisfied and motivated if they think they are being fairly compensated for their work. If an employee notices that another person is getting more recognition or is being promoted for the same quantity and quality of work, the employee is likely going to be dissatisfied. However, it is often perceived as acceptable if a more senior colleague receives a promotion as experience or education is seen as a higher input.

Despite its popularity, equity theory has been criticized for its neglect of other justice dimensions, and the lack of specificity of the consequences described. Equity theory also does not take into account that even though the equity between colleagues is sustained, the entire compensation system in the organization can be perceived as unfair. For instance, if everyone gets a similar low pay, equity is sustained but motivation will still be low. Another criticism alludes to the fact that perceptions of input and outputs are subjective. Some people may think of a specific aspect as input whereas others perceive it as an output, for example, responsibility. Also, employees ascribe personal values to specific inputs and outputs, making subjective comparisons difficult to deal with from the manager's point of view. Furthermore, the choice of the comparison other is not explained in much detail. And, finally, the impact of individual differences is neglected in equity theory.

15.3.2 Justice heuristics and fairness heuristics theory

Broadly defined, heuristics are cognitive shortcuts. Individuals use cognitive shortcuts to minimize the use of their cognitive resources, of which there is only a finite quantity. Equity theory posits that justice perceptions are the result of a complex cognitive process involving multiple comparative assessments of input–output ratios. Fairness heuristics theory (Lind, 2001) posits that individuals form overall justice judgements about an organization or a supervisor very quickly (as soon as they enter an organization and even before that during the hiring process). These overall justice judgements are then used to assess the fairness of subsequent events and experiences so that assessing multiple justice dimensions is not necessary. Once formed, overall justice perceptions are stable and are used as cognitive heuristics. Sometimes, however, individuals can re-evaluate their overall justice judgements. This happens either because an event (e.g., a harsh costs reduction programme) presents a serious deviation from the expected fairness level, or because there are signs that the relationship the individual has had with the organization is changing (e.g., an employee used to enjoy a lot of personal autonomy in her work now founds herself constrained by a new set of top–down driven rules and regulations).

Research on cognitive processes, in general, and on justice reasoning in particular, can benefit from a recent integration of social science methods with neuroscientific methods (Becker, Cropanzano, & Sanfey, 2011). Evidence suggests that there is a neural basis for fairness that is different from self-interest and economic gain. For instance, studies using brain imaging techniques have shown that receiving a fair offer activates brain areas dealing with processing rewards, whereas receiving unfair treatment triggers an increased activation of negative affective systems. In another study, study participants could accept or reject an unfair allocation which would provide economic gain; for those who accepted the offer there was no increase in the activity of the brain areas related to satisfaction. In another study, it was found that distributive and procedural injustice activated different brain regions (Dulebohn, Conlon, Sarinopoulos, Davison, & McNamara, 2009). This line of research, while preliminary, looks promising.

15.4   Consequences of Justice Perceptions

After we have explained what justice perceptions are, why they matter and how they are formed and evolve, we turn to their consequences for recipients, observers and actors. Below we briefly present research showing that organizational justice perceptions of employees are related to work attitudes, work behaviour, health and well-being of employees. Moreover, organizational justice appears relevant to the wider society as it influences the climate in work groups, affects supervisors' and subordinates behaviour, as well as the attitudes and behaviour of customers and observers.

15.4.1   Consequences for employees' work attitudes and behaviour

There is a large amount of evidence showing that justice perceptions are related to a wide array of work-related outcomes. In an effort to summarize the literature, Conlon and colleagues divided the studied outcomes into three categories: the good, the bad and the ugly (Conlon, Meyer, & Nowakowski, 2005). Meta-analyses (see e.g., Colquitt et al., 2013; Rupp, Shao, Jones, & Liao, 2014) have revealed that perceptions of justice are related to many desirable, 'good' outcomes, like trust, perceived organizational support, job satisfaction, organizational commitment, and performance. Employees who feel fairly treated have positive expectations regarding the other party (trust), see the organization as supportive (perceived organizational support), enjoy their work and their workplace (job satisfaction), and are more dedicated to their workplace (organizational commitment). The most often studied outcome has been organizational citizenship behaviour, which includes helping colleagues voluntarily, the willingness to go through difficult times with the organization, and behaviour that improves the working environment.

In terms of 'bad' outcomes, employees who feel unfairly treated have stronger intentions to search for new jobs. They are also more likely to hold back information, suggestions, or new ideas. The so-called 'ugly' outcomes refer to behaviour that companies want to avoid under all circumstances because they go directly against the companies' interest. There is strong evidence that injustice perceptions at work may result in more counterproductive behaviour and workplace deviance, which may include small norm violations like leaving early, coming in late, or taking long lunch breaks. But it may also include interpersonal counterproductive behaviour, such as stealing, harassment, gossiping about a colleague, aggression, or even violence. Behaviour directed at the organization can include theft, or sabotage.

15.4.2   Consequences for employee health

In addition to work-related outcomes, justice perceptions also have consequences for employee health and well-being. Not only are individuals and the society as a whole interested in healthy workers, also organizations have (next to a moral obligation) economic reasons to be interested in their employees' health (see also Chapter 16 in this volume). Healthy employees are much more productive than unhealthy employees. It can be very costly to organizations when employees are absent or on sick leave, when they are dissatisfied, or wish to leave the organization.

One study from Finland has calculated the relationship between fairness perceptions at work and the risk of mortality due to cardiovascular diseases. In this study, it was found that those with high perceptions of supervisory treatment had a 45% lower risk of dying of cardiovascular diseases than those with low levels of fair treatment (Elovainio, Leino-Arjas, Vahtera, & Kivimäki, 2006). This result was found even after demographical information, health, and working conditions were accounted for.

Organizational injustice perceptions can be considered a possible organizational stressor. A meta-analysis showed that perceptions of injustice are associated with health-related outcomes such as:

* burnout: a state of emotional exhaustion and decreased working ability;
* mental health: including symptoms like depression, anxiety, psychological distress;
* physical health problems such as health complaints and diseases, unhealthy behaviours like smoking, sedentary lifestyle or consuming alcohol;
* other outcomes: perceived stress, negative emotional states like anger and hostility, and absences from work (Robbins, Ford, & Tetrick, 2012).

The strongest effects across different justice dimensions were found with burnout, mental health, stress, and negative emotional states.

With regards to studies on health, there is the view that unhealthy employees perceive the behaviour of managers differently or that these employees are treated differently. Therefore, studies that investigate the relationship between organizational justice and health outcomes over time are important. So far, there is strong evidence to suggest that justice perceptions are associated with health outcomes over time. But there is also some evidence that health status is also associated with justice perceptions over time, such that unhealthy individuals perceive their workplace as less fair. This needs to be investigated more in the future. However, in general, researchers have found evidence that justice perceptions are related to employee health. Comparing the effects of justice on work and health-related outcomes shows that associations with work outcomes tend to be stronger than associations with health-related outcomes. In sum, there is strong evidence to suggest that justice and injustice are important aspects to consider for individuals and organizations.

15.4.3   Consequences for other individuals of interest

It has been proposed that companies that are viewed as being fair towards their employees generate higher firm performance than when they are viewed as unfair (Bosse, Phillips, & Harrison, 2009). There is evidence that colleagues react to witnessing unfairness committed by peers or managers. Witnessing unfairness in the workplace has negative effects on cooperation and helping, on levels of performance and creativity. One mechanism that is being discussed is negative emotions: witnessing an unfair act triggers negative emotional states like anger which undermines productive thinking patterns (see Skarlicki, O'Reilly, & Kulik, 2015).

Besides colleagues as observers, unfairness is also relevant for supervisors, for subordinates and for customers. For instance, supervisors' own fairness perceptions can 'trickle down' to their subordinates because supervisors follow the norm of reciprocating how they are treated themselves. If supervisors perceive themselves to be unfairly treated, their feelings of anger and frustration are likely to be expressed not towards the source of the unfairness, the manager, but to their own subordinates (Wo, Ambrose, & Schminke, 2015). Also, the treatment of others impacts how a work group sees the fairness overall, that is a fairness climate is formed which affects levels of teamwork and cooperation in the workplace. Fairness also has an impact on customers. When customers observe unfairness between two employees, customers are more likely to make negative generalizations of the employees working for the company, the organization itself, and the organizations' products. For instance, it has been shown that the loyalty of hotel guests is reduced by unfair acts of the hotel management towards staff (see Skarlicki et al., 2015).

15.4.4   Overview of the consequences of organizational justice

This overview of outcomes shows that organizational justice perceptions have relevant consequences for individuals, colleagues, supervisors and subordinates, customers, and maybe even the wider society. Figure 15.3 presents an overview of the outcomes discussed.

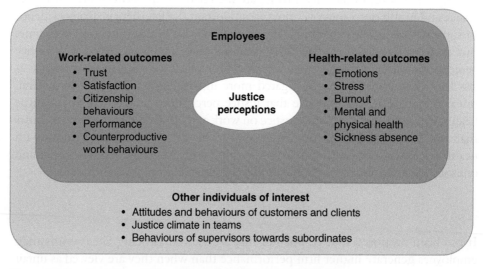

Figure 15.3:   Overview of the consequences of justice perceptions

15.5　The Relevance of Individual and Situational Characteristics

In this part, we consider whether justice has similar effects across personality types and across situations. In other words, we now explore the 'boundary conditions' of the theories we have reviewed so far. We first focus on individual characteristics before reviewing some important situational characteristics.

15.5.1　Individual characteristics

Among important individual characteristics, personality has often a central role. There is one individual trait that is highly relevant to reactions to justice and injustice perceptions. Indeed, people differ in how strongly they react when witnessing unfairness. While some may barely notice an unfair event, others are outraged. Research has established the existence of stable individual differences in sensitivity to justice issues, i.e., justice sensitivity (Schmitt, 1996). An individual with high justice sensitivity is someone who (1) frequently notices unfair situations, (2) tends to react with anger in such cases, (3) experiences intrusive thoughts about the issue, and (4) typically intends to punish those who committed the injustice (Schmitt, Neumann, & Montada, 1995). Individuals with high justice sensitivity are more likely to perceive injustices because, as a result of this personality trait, their attention is guided towards injustice cues in their environment. Furthermore, they are likely to interpret ambiguous situations – from a fairness standpoint – as less fair than those who have low justice sensitivity. Individuals with high justice sensitivity are also more likely to take action to restore justice as a result. One reason for this is that individuals with high justice sensitivity are able to rely on more accurate memories about past unfair situations as greater memory performance leads to greater confidence in one's judgements. Feeling more confident about their assessment of an unfair situation, individuals with high justice sensitivity are thus more likely to take action to right the injustices. To summarize, justice sensitivity increases attention, interpretive processes and memory for justice-related information. These effects are domain-specific, i.e. justice sensitivity does not reflect a superior cognitive functioning. This personality trait exerts an influence whether individuals observe injustice or benefit from it. It is typically associated with concerns for fairness and high moral standards. It also extends to situations where individuals are themselves a victim of injustice; in such circumstances, however, justice sensitivity simultaneously reflects genuine moral concerns and self-protective motives.

In addition to personality traits, there are also within-individual differences in justice dynamics. Recent research has shown that justice trajectories, i.e., levels and trends of individual fairness perceptions over time, influence employees' attitudes and intentions above and beyond the absolute levels of fairness perceptions (Hausknecht, Sturman, & Roberson, 2011). For instance, let us consider two employees, who, after their annual review, both feel treated slightly unfairly by their supervisor. While employee A, last year, had been fairly treated, employee B had not. As a result of having different justice trajectories, employee A is likely to react more negatively than employee B, even though they currently have the same level of justice perceptions.

15.5.2 Situational characteristics

Aside from individual characteristics, there are a number of situational characteristics that determine, if, and how, people react to justice, including status, uncertainty, culture, and organizational structure. People perceive fairness and react according to their status in the situation, that is, whether they are a victim, or an observer (Mikula, 1993). An individual can be the victim of unfair treatment. In this case, the feeling of injustice is linked to the physical, psychological or moral wrong he/she has endured. A person may also be an observer of an injustice done to someone else. Alternatively, an individual can benefit from an unfair and at the same time positive event, such as an undue advantage. Even though feelings of injustice may arise among victims, observers, or even beneficiaries, it may not cause the same reactions. For instance, people attend to injustice more frequently when they themselves are directly affected than when the unfair situations affect someone else.

Justice matters particularly in situations requiring individuals to cooperate while outcomes, or the trustworthiness of authority figures, are uncertain. In such situations, which are quite common at work in particular in times of organizational changes, individuals have to assess the risks of exploitation, that is whether their cooperation will be rewarded or if the organization will exploit their goodwill without reciprocating. According to uncertainty management theory (see Lind & van den Bos, 2002, for a review), people rely heavily on justice perceptions in uncertain situations, and use fairness as a surrogate for trust, as a cognitive heuristic. These effects have been shown in several experiments. For instance, the impact of receiving the opportunity to express oneself during a decision process (this is known as 'voice') on satisfaction with an authority figure is stronger when the trustworthiness of that authority is uncertain. Likewise, in experimental settings, the effect of procedural justice on emotions has been found to be stronger when people were reminded of their own death or when they had to remember situations in which they feel uncertain about themselves than for people who were not confronted with uncertainty.

In situations involving groups, violations of procedural justice may have greater consequences than otherwise, especially if the membership of that group is important to the identity of the individual. Individuals perceive a direct link between how fairly their group treats them and their standing with respect to that group. When an individual identifies strongly with a group, hence deriving part of his or her social identify from it (cf. social identity theory), unfair treatment received from the group is perceived as an identity threat, which increases the intensity of the affective reactions to injustice.

Justice is socially constructed, and therefore it is influenced by cultural norms (see the meta-analysis of Shao, Rupp, Skarlicki, & Jones, 2013). For instance, organizational justice effects are stronger in cultures emphasizing individual achievements (this cultural dimension is referred to as individualism; see Hofstede, 2001). Another salient dimension of culture, according to Hofstede, is power distance, which refers to the degree to which the less powerful members of a society accept and expect that power is distributed unequally. In countries where power distance is low, justice effects are stronger. In addition, cultural norms also influence justice standards. For instance, in countries where corruption is widespread, the threshold above which a behaviour is regarded as unfair might be higher than in countries with less corruption. A given action might thus be perceived fair in one setting while failing to meet the fairness standards of another culture. The effects of norms are not limited to cultural norms; industry, occupation or organizational norms have a similar influence.

Moreover, organizational structure influences justice in complex ways. There is some research that tends to indicate that in organizations with a strong hierarchy, procedural justice plays a greater role in predicting fairness-related outcomes. Conversely, in organizations characterized by open and more flexible communication lines, interactional justice plays a more central role.

15.6 Building Fair Workplaces

After reviewing the importance of justice at the workplace, we now turn our attention away from descriptive analyses of organizational justice, and focus on normative approaches and tackle the difficult yet important issue of building fair workplaces. There are a number of actions that have been suggested to create fair workplaces, although, by comparison to theory-oriented research, pragmatic guidelines have received less attention. For instance, it has been proposed that justice and fairness should be incorporated in key HR practices like recruitment, rewards systems, conflict management, performance appraisals, and layoffs (Cropanzano et al., 2007).

Consider the case of recruitment, for instance. The appropriateness of the questions and criteria used during the recruitment process are critical because they affect procedural justice perceptions, which will contribute to the new recruit's overall justice perceptions (see also Chapter 2 in this volume). Even if the candidate does not get the job, recruitment should be handled fairly. Indeed, through word of mouth, and online forums, unfair hiring processes may harm the organization's reputation as an employer. To establish fairness, it is particularly important that candidates are given adequate opportunity to perform during the selection process. Recruitment processes ought to give job candidates the chances to make a case for themselves, and allow sufficient time in interviews. Overly personal questions and some screening procedures may be perceived as inappropriate and an invasion of privacy. Unfortunately, many of the selection tests that have the best predictive validity for performance, including cognitive ability and personality tests, are also often perceived as unfair. Questions on these tests are often not related to the job, and applicants do not feel they have an opportunity to display their true potential. On the other hand, other forms of selection processes such as unstructured interviews, while perceived to be fair by most job applicants, have been shown to have low validity. Remedies to this paradox include using work sample tests and performance-based simulations, which have both reasonable predictive validity and are perceived as fair, or conducting interviews with both structured behavioural questions, in order to maximize predictive validity, and unstructured questions to give applicants room to display their potential (for more details, refer to Cropanzano et al., 2007).

In addition, management may consider training managers to make them more aware of justice issues, and better at putting justice principles into practice. The effectiveness of training has been demonstrated in field studies. For example, Greenberg (2006) studied nurses, comparing a group who had experienced a pay cut with a group who had not. Half of the supervisors of the nurses whose pay was cut and half of the supervisors of the nurses whose pay was unchanged received training in providing interactional justice. Following the pay cut, and during the following six months, nurses reported their sleep quality. Results showed that the degree of insomnia among lower-paid nurses was significantly higher than that for those whose pay was unchanged. However, lower-paid nurses whose supervisors received training in interactional justice reported significantly less insomnia symptoms than those whose supervisors who did not go through such training.

Even when management is aware and willing to create a fair workplace, it is probably next to impossible to avoid perceptions of injustice completely. Thus, part of building a fair workplace involves managing justice-related conflicts, so that they do not escalate. This is especially important with justice-sensitive persons, who tend to interpret ambiguous situations as potential cases of injustice. In such cases, it is recommended to avoid ambiguity by increasing the transparency of decisions (Schmitt & Dörfel, 1999), by providing explanations for decisions (Shaw, Wild, & Colquitt, 2003), and by setting up conflict resolution programmes (Montada, 2007). Given research on justice trajectories' influence, managers may find it useful to consider employees' unique histories of perceived treatment.

While managerial practices should be the focus when attempting to build a fair workplace, cultural issues should not be neglected. Indeed, it is perfectly possible for people to recognize that a process has been handled fairly, yet feel that the overall system and the values upon which it is based are unfair. This could be the case, for instance, in a multinational firm with operations in some countries where equity is the dominant distributive justice norms, and operations in countries where the dominant justice rule is need or equality. People from the latter group of countries may perceive that the HR practices set up by the corporation are fair from a procedural standpoint, as the rules are the same for every subsidiary. However, they might still reject the basis on which outcomes are allocated.

Clearly there is no easy way out of such dilemmas. However, when organizations choose to enforce uniform justice rules across multinational operations, other justice dimensions like informational justice or giving voice become even more important. For instance, this means that giving voice to those individuals who feel their justice rules are violated is particularly important under those circumstances.

Summary

This chapter has reviewed research on organizational justice, which typically refers to individuals' perceptions that someone, or something, is fair or unfair. Organizations should treat their employees fairly because justice provides them with a sense of control, belonging, positive self-regard and meaningfulness – and also, because it is the right thing to do. Originally focused on issues of distributive fairness, the concept of organizational justice has developed into a multi-dimensional construct. Often it is now characterized as having four components: distributive, procedural, interpersonal and informational. Also, we have shown that while the majority of research has focused on the justice recipients, typically employees, there are two alternative strands of research, one focusing on third-party observers and the other on justice actors, including supervisors and managers. Another distinction was introduced to round up the overview of justice scholarship, namely, the nature of the variable. Organizational justice may be studied as a dependent variable, as something to be explained. However, in most research studies justice has been explored as a potential antecedent of a wide range of outcomes. Such outcomes fall into two broad categories: work-related outcomes and health-related outcomes. Beyond employees, organizational justice also matters for a number of other individuals, including clients and customers, and thus may be associated with firms' performance and other group-level outcomes. Following our review of the consequences of justice, we have highlighted a number of boundary conditions, including individual characteristics, such as personality, and context variables, such as uncertainty and culture, that modify the impact of justice. The last section was devoted to more practical guidelines on how to build fair workplaces. It was suggested to embed fairness considerations in the design and implementation of HR practices, and to use justice sensitivity training for managers. Finally, attention was drawn to the intercultural issues of such interventions.

Discussion Points

1 One of the implications of the subjectivity of justice perceptions is that managers cannot make every employee feel fairly treated. Do you think organizational justice is a useful concept for managerial practice? Why?

2 Every culture has a different understanding of justice and fairness. How do you think this affects multicultural teams or multinational corporations?

Suggested Further Reading

Cropanzano, R., & Ambrose, M. L. 2015. *The Oxford handbook of justice in the workplace.* New York: Oxford University Press. The second and newest handbook, a comprehensive overview of the justice literature from the most well-known justice scholars around the world.

Cropanzano, R., Bowen, D. E., & Gilliland, S. W. (2007). The management of organizational justice. *The Academy of Management Perspectives, 21*(4): 34–48. This review of the justice literature from distinguished scholars includes practical guidelines for building fair management activities in areas such as hiring, performance appraisal, reward systems, conflict management and downsizing.

Fortin, M. (2008). Perspectives on organizational justice: Concept clarification, social context integration, time and links with morality. *International Journal of Management Reviews, 10*(2): 93–126. Another comprehensive review which includes discussions about conceptual clarity, context and time, and outlines areas for future research.

Online resource

Online Harvard University course on justice: http://www.justiceharvard.org/. This free online course explains the views of the best-known philosophers in interactive lectures and blog entries in relation to the big questions of our time such as immigration, affirmative action, and same-sex marriage.

References

Adams, J. S. (1963). Wage inequities, productivity and work quality. *Industrial Relations, 3*(1), 9–16.

Adams, J. S. (1965). Inequity in social exchange. In L. Berkowitz (Ed.), *Advances in experimental social psychology*, vol. 2 (pp. 267–289). New York: Academic Press.

Ambrose, M. L., & Schminke, M. (2009). The role of overall justice judgments in organizational justice research: A test of mediation. *Journal of Applied Psychology, 94*(2), 491–500.

Becker, W. J., Cropanzano, R., & Sanfey, A. G. (2011). Organizational neuroscience: Taking organizational theory inside the neural black box. *Journal of Management, 37*(4), 933–961.

Bies, R. J., & Moag, J. F. (1986). Interactional justice: Communication criteria of fairness. In R. J. Lewicki, B. H. Sheppard, & M. H. Bazerman (Eds.), *Research on negotiations in organizations*, vol. 1. Greenwich, CT: JAI Press.

Bosse, D. A., Phillips, R. A., & Harrison, J. S. (2009). Stakeholders, reciprocity, and firm performance. *Strategic Management Journal, 30*(4), 447–456.

Byrne, Z. S., & Cropanzano, R. (2001). The history of organizational justice: The founders speak. In R. Cropanzano (Ed.), *Justice in the workplace: From theory to practice*, vol. 2 (pp. 3–26). Mahwah, NJ: Lawrence Erlbaum Associates.

Colquitt, J. A. (2001). On the dimensionality of organizational justice: A construct validation of a measure. *Journal of Applied Psychology, 86*(3), 386–400.

Colquitt, J. A., Long, D. M., Rodell, J. B., & Halvorsen-Ganepola, M. D. K. (2014). Adding the "in" to justice: A qualitative and quantitative investigation of the differential effects of justice rule adherence and violation. *Journal of Applied Psychology, 100*(2), 278–294.

Colquitt, J. A., et al. (2013). Justice at the millennium, a decade later: A meta-analytic test of social exchange and affect-based perspectives. *Journal of Applied Psychology, 98*(2), 199–236.

Conlon, D. E., Meyer, C. J., & Nowakowski, J. M. (2005). How does organizational justice affect performance, withdrawal, and counterproductive behavior? In J. A. Colquitt, & J. Greenberg (Eds.), *Handbook of organizational justice*. Mahwah, NJ: Lawrence Erlbaum Associates.

Cropanzano, R., Bowen, D. E., & Gilliland, S. W. (2007). The management of organizational justice. *The Academy of Management Perspectives, 21*(4), 34–48.

Cropanzano, R., Byrne, Z. S., Bobocel, D. R., & Rupp, D. E. (2001). Moral virtues, fairness heuristics, social entities, and other denizens of organizational justice. *Journal of Vocational Behavior, 58*(2), 164–209.

Dulebohn, J. H., Conlon, D. E., Sarinopoulos, I., Davison, R. B., & McNamara, G. (2009). The biological bases of unfairness: Neuroimaging evidence for the distinctiveness of procedural and distributive justice. *Organizational Behavior and Human Decision Processes, 110*(2), 140–151.

Elovainio, M., Leino-Arjas, P., Vahtera, J., & Kivimäki, M. (2006). Justice at work and cardiovascular mortality: a prospective cohort study. *Journal of Psychosomatic Research, 61*(2), 271–274.

Greenberg, J. (2006). Losing sleep over organizational injustice: Attenuating insomniac reactions to underpayment inequity with supervisory training in interactional justice. *Journal of Applied Psychology, 91*(1), 58–69.

Hausknecht, J. P., Sturman, M. C., & Roberson, Q. M. (2011). Justice as a dynamic construct: Effects of individual trajectories on distal work outcomes. *Journal of Applied Psychology, 96*(4), 872–880.

Hofstede, G. (2001). *Culture's consequences: Comparing values, behaviors, institutions and organizations across nations* (2nd ed.). Thousand Oaks, CA: Sage.

Lind, E. A. (2001). Fairness heuristic theory: Justice judgments as pivotal cognitions in organizational relations. In J. Greenberg, & R. Cropanzano (Eds.), *Advances in organizational justice* (pp. 56–88). Stanford, CA: Stanford University Press.

Lind, E. A., & van den Bos, K. (2002). When fairness works: Toward a general theory of uncertainty management. In B. M. Staw, & R. M. Kramer (Eds.), *Research in organizational behavior*, vol. 24 (pp. 181–223). Boston: Elsevier.

Mikula, G. (1993). On the experience of injustice. *European Review of Social Psychology, 4*(1), 223–8.

Montada, L. (2007). Justice conflicts and the justice of conflict resolution. In K. Y. Törnblom, & R. Vermunt (Eds.), *Distributive and procedural justice: Research and applications* (pp. 255–268). Aldershot: Ashgate.

Robbins, J. M., Ford, M. T., & Tetrick, L. E. (2012). Perceived unfairness and employee health: A meta-analytic integration. *Journal of Applied Psychology, 97*(2), 235–272.

Rupp, D. E., Shao, R., Jones, K. S., & Liao, H. (2014). The utility of a multifoci approach to the study of organizational justice: A meta-analytic investigation into the consideration of normative rules, moral accountability, bandwidth-fidelity, and social exchange. *Organizational Behavior and Human Decision Processes, 123*(2), 159–185.

Schmitt, M. (1996). Individual differences in sensitivity to befallen injustice (SBI). *Personality and Individual Differences, 21*(1), 3–20.

Schmitt, M., & Dörfel, M. (1999). Procedural injustice at work, justice sensitivity, job satisfaction and psychosomatic well-being. *European Journal of Social Psychology, 29*(4), 443–453.

Schmitt, M., Neumann, R., & Montada, L. (1995). Dispositional sensitivity to befallen injustice. *Social Justice Research, 8*, 385–407.

Shao, R., Rupp, D. E., Skarlicki, D. P., & Jones, K. S. (2013). Employee justice across cultures: A meta-analytic review. *Journal of Management, 39*(1), 263–301.

Shaw, J. C., Wild, E., & Colquitt, J. A. (2003). To justify or excuse?: A meta-analytic review of the effects of explanations. *Journal of Applied Psychology, 88*(3), 444–458.

Skarlicki, D. P., O'Reilly, J., & Kulik, C. T. (2015). The third-party perspective of (in)justice. In R. Cropanzano, & M. L. Ambrose (Eds.), *The Oxford handbook of justice in the workplace* (pp. 235–255). New York: Oxford University Press.

Thibaut, J., & Walker, L. (1975). *Procedural justice: A psychological analysis.* Hillsdale, NJ: Erlbaum.

Wo, D. X. H., Ambrose, M. L., & Schminke, M. (2015). What drives trickle-down effects? A test of multiple mediation processes. *Academy of Management Journal, 58*(6), 1848–1868.

What Does Our Organization Do to Help Our Well-Being? Creating Healthy Workplaces and Workers

16

Arla Day and Karina Nielsen

Overview

Although workplaces can be a significant source of stress and ill-health for many workers, they also can be a source of well-being and provide support and meaning to people's lives. Helping to improve and maintain employees' well-being is essential, not only because it is important to have healthy people at work (and in society in general), but also because a healthy workforce is associated with good organizational performance. However, creating and maintaining well-being are not always easy. Therefore, in this chapter, we discuss how organizations can make explicit attempts to foster employee well-being by developing respectful cultures, providing competent and supportive leadership, and implementing specific healthy workplace initiatives (e.g., to encourage a good life balance, create safe and healthy work practices, increase employee involvement, etc.). To provide a framework to examine how organizations can increase well-being, we use the term 'psychologically healthy workplaces'. We discuss not only how to decrease negative workplace factors (e.g., work overload; bad or 'toxic' leaders), but also how to increase the positive factors (e.g., work-life balance, employee growth and development). We provide examples of how organizations can create healthy workplaces through initiatives that target: (1) the way work is organized, designed and managed (i.e., changing the organization itself), (2) the social relationships (i.e., the work groups), (3) the leaders or line managers who are responsible for worker well-being, and (4) the development of individual resources. We discuss the importance of having a multi-focus on supporting organizational change with group, leader and individual initiatives.

An Introduction to Work and Organizational Psychology: An International Perspective,
Third Edition. Edited by Nik Chmiel, Franco Fraccaroli and Magnus Sverke.
© 2017 John Wiley & Sons, Ltd. Published 2017 by John Wiley & Sons, Ltd.

16.1   Introduction: Improving Workers' Well-Being

Given the importance of having healthy workers, and given that a healthy work-force is associated with good organizational performance, fostering worker well-being should be an integral goal for all organizations. However, many organizations often do not consider the well-being of their employees, or even worse, they may inadvertently worsen employees' health. Therefore, the umbrella term of 'psychologically healthy workplaces' is used in this chapter to help us discuss the ways in which organizations can foster individual well-being by focusing on the organization, the workgroup, leaders and individual employees. In order to understand what constitutes psychologically healthy workplaces, it is important to understand first what is meant by individual well-being and health.

16.2   What Is Meant by Well-Being and Health?

Health and well-being can be considered in very broad terms. Overall, well-being is defined as 'comprising the various life/non-work satisfactions enjoyed by individuals (i.e., satisfaction and/or dissatisfaction with social life, family life, recreation, spirituality, and so forth), work/job-related satisfactions (i.e., satisfaction and/or dissatisfaction with pay, promotion opportunities, the job itself, co-workers, and so forth), and general health' (Danna & Griffin, 1999, p. 359). General health may be viewed as a component of well-being. For example, according to Danna and Griffin (1999), health is 'a sub-component of well-being and comprises the combination of such mental/psychological indicators as affect, frustration, and anxiety and such physical/physiological indicators as blood pressure, heart condition, and general physical health' (p. 359).

Similarly, the World Health Organization defined health as 'a state of complete physical, mental, and social well-being and not merely the absence of disease or infirmity' (WHO, 2015).

Although these two definitions use health and well-being interchangeably, they both highlight two issues that are important to understanding (and improving) worker health/well-being:

1. Health should be viewed as holistic. That is, we must take a complete view of health, including not only physical health, but also psychological (mental) and social health.
2. Health involves not only a lack of negative factors, but also the presence of positive factors. That is, health is not merely the absence of disease. A healthy person also tends to be engaged, have high self-efficacy, feel respected, and involved in their work and life.

Therefore, healthy employees can be defined as those who have low levels of physical symptoms, stress, burnout, and negative mental health symptoms and who possess positive indicators of physical health, satisfaction, engagement, energy, professional efficacy, integrity and respect towards others, their environment, and

> ## Box 16.1: Healthy workers and workplaces
>
> How do the terms health, well-being, and healthy workplaces interrelate? The general term of individual well-being encompasses health, and healthy workplaces encompass what is known about individual health and well-being, but ascribe these ideas to the workplace.
>
> - *Well-being* is made up of 'the various life/non-work satisfactions enjoyed by individuals (i.e., satisfaction and/or dissatisfaction with social life, family life, recreation, spirituality, and so forth), work/job-related satisfactions (i.e., satisfaction and/or dissatisfaction with pay, promotion opportunities, the job itself, co-workers, and so forth), and general health' (Danna & Griffin, 1999, p. 359).
> - *Health* is defined as a state of complete physical, mental, and social well-being. It is not merely the *absence* of disease or infirmity, but it also should include the *presence* of positive factors (WHO, 2015).
> - *Healthy workplaces* are workplaces in which workers are treated with respect, and organizational members engage in activities that foster the psychological and physical health of all of its workers. These workplaces are dedicated to promoting and supporting the physical and psychological health and well-being of their employees while simultaneously incorporating solid business practices to remain as an efficient and productive business entity and having a positive impact on their clients and community (Day & Randell, 2014).

themselves. Healthy employees are employees who feel good at work, have positive work attitudes, and feel passionate about their contributions to their work, and generally enjoy the people with whom they interact with at work on a daily basis (see Box 16.1 for definitions).

Understanding the concept of health and well-being is our first step to understanding how our organization may impact on our health. As Jan de Jonge and Christian Dormann noted in Chapter 5 in this volume, job stress can arise from many aspects of the work environment, and can have a negative impact on worker health. A lot of research has demonstrated how work can create stress and ill-health, so that there is a good understanding of what makes employees stressed at work (see, e.g., Kivimäki, Virtanen, Elovainio, Kouvonen, Väänänen, & Vahtera, 2006; Sonnentag & Frese, 2003).

However, the workplace can have many positive impacts on workers and it can be a great platform to promote and improve the mental and physical health and well-being of workers (Day & Helson, 2016). For example, one of the key positive things people may like about their work is that it provides them with a salary, and this money enables them to afford a house or apartment, to buy food and necessities, and engage in fun activities, such as sports, hobbies, eating out and travel. Work also can provide people with less tangible things that positively affect their health. Gaining new skills, or simply doing a job well, may help them develop a high sense of self-esteem and mastery. Many people form strong friendships with their coworkers. This sense of community and social support is important for their health and well-being. Work can provide a sense of positive routine and structure for them, and it has the potential to be a positive environment to help behaviour change and maintenance (Day & Helson, 2016; see Box 16.2 to help you think about what your work provides for you). Therefore, although work can decrease employee health, it also has

---

**Box 16.2:   It's all about you … what does
your work provide for you?**

Think about different jobs that you have had … hopefully, they all paid you and gave you benefits. Now ask yourself …

• What else did those jobs provide to you?
  ☐ *Social interaction?*
  ☐ *Job training?*
  ☐ *Development opportunities?*
  ☐ *Other? Please explain:* _____

• How did you feel about the job?

Typically, people like jobs that are more meaningful and engaging, and that provide more 'benefits'.

---

the opportunity to act as a viable resource for employees to help prevent, protect and recover from mental and physical ill-health (Kelloway & Day, 2005).

When examining how organizations can improve worker well-being, it is clear that they need to focus on reducing the negative factors that create stress and ill-health as well as focus on increasing the positive factors that promote satisfaction, self-esteem, health and well-being. Organizations may accomplish these tasks by developing psychologically healthy workplaces.

16.3   Psychologically Healthy Workplaces

The term 'psychologically healthy workplace' (PHW) is becoming a popular umbrella term to refer to a workplace that aims to foster employee health by reducing negative stressors and demands and promoting organizational resources to enhance well-being (Kelloway & Day, 2005). That is, similar to the conceptualization of individual health, a healthy workplace is defined both in terms of the absence of negative factors and the presence of positive factors.

Psychologically healthy workplaces are workplaces that integrate practices, policies and initiatives that promote and enhance positive employee health and well-being, as well as initiatives that focus on preventing and minimizing worker stress and other negative components that may jeopardize employee health (Day & Randell, 2014). By integrating the works of prominent occupational health researchers (e.g., Cooper & Cartwright, 1994; Cooper & Patterson, 2008; Grawitch, Gottschalk, & Munz, 2006; Kelloway & Day, 2005), Day and Randell (2014) developed a working definition of psychologically healthy workplaces as workplaces:

> that are dedicated to promoting and supporting the physical and psychological health and well-being of their employees while simultaneously incorporating solid business practices to remain as an efficient and productive business entity and having a positive impact on their clients and community … (p. 10)

This definition also introduces the idea that a healthy workplace is also a productive workplace. It is essential to have a workplace that is financially stable and productive; if a workplace is not financially viable, it would soon fail and have to fire its employees (which would not improve employee health). It also is important to note that there is no 'one-size-fits-all' approach to fostering healthy workplaces. That is, each organization will have their own problems and their own solutions to create a healthy workplace. Part of the process of becoming a healthy workplace (and promoting worker well-being) is to understand the unique challenges and resources of each workplace.

16.4 What Does a Psychologically Healthy Workplace Look Like?

The concept of a healthy workplace is not new. In fact, not only has there been a lot of research identifying the aspects of work that can create job stress (e.g., Kelloway & Day, 2005) and ill-health (e.g., Demerouti, Bakker, Nachreiner, & Schaufeli, 2001), but there also has been research identifying how organizations can improve worker health and well-being through improving the physical health and safety of workplaces, promoting individual health, and addressing a multitude of psychosocial aspects of the job (e.g., Cooper & Cartwright, 1994), such as increasing resources (e.g., positive leadership, fairness and autonomy) and reducing job demands (e.g., conflict, work overload; see Box 16.3).

Box 16.3:   Creating change in the organization

How can organizations create healthy workplaces? To answer this question, it is important to look at terms used to describe specific organizational change and practices:

- *Work psychosocial factors* refer to workplace conditions (e.g., design of work, interpersonal relationships, fairness, leadership, and conflict, and the interactions among these conditions that can affect employee health and well-being (Burton, 2004, ILO, 1986).

- *Job demands* are aspects of the job that require a sustained physical, emotional or cognitive effort (Demerouti, Bakker, de Jonge, Janssen, & Schaufeli, 2001).

- *Job resources* are 'those objects, personal characteristics, conditions, or energies that are valued by the individual or that serve as a means for attainment of these objects, personal characteristics, conditions' (Hobfoll, 1989, p. 516).

- *Organizational interventions* can be defined as planned, behavioural, theory-based actions that aim to improve the health and well-being of workers (Nielsen, 2013). These planned actions are integral to organizational change and creating healthy workplaces.

- *Organizational initiatives* are more broadly defined than interventions, so that they can involve not only these behavioural interventions, as well as both formal and informal work practices, organizational communications (e.g., mission statements, newsletters), and programmes.

Given the notion that work may create ill-health (e.g., Kelloway & Day, 2005), an organizational focus on health often has been on how to get rid of the negative aspects of work. Some of the work has focused on improving the dangerous physical working conditions and reducing risks. For example, many organizations have established health and safety committees, implemented mandatory safety training and/or equipment, and taken additional safety precautions.

As is evident, it is insufficient to simply get rid of negative working conditions. An environment must be created that promotes positive employee health and functioning. This philosophy involves initiatives on workplace health promotion, in which organizations provide resources to individuals to choose and maintain healthy lifestyles, such as educating about healthy behaviours (e.g., healthy eating seminars and mindfulness education sessions; Cartwright & Cooper, 2005; Cox, 1997; Day & Helson, 2016). The organization can be an ideal platform to promote healthy lifestyles (Cox, 1997) because of the huge influence that the work and the social environment can have on individual behaviours. Finally, research has demonstrated how psychosocial factors, such as interpersonal or social workplace conditions (e.g., design of work, interpersonal relationships), culture, and leadership, may influence employee health and well-being (Burton, 2004). Therefore, organizations can look to increasing positive psychosocial factors (e.g., supervisor support) and minimizing negative factors (e.g., toxic leaders, group incivility). For example, organizations may promote employee health and functioning by designing jobs that foster employees' professional and personal development through collaborative decision-making (Nielsen, Randall, & Christensen, 2010).

16.5   Promoting Worker Well-being: Building a Model of Psychologically Healthy Workplaces

Researchers around the world have integrated these different perspectives and organizational health initiatives to help us understand the different components of a psychologically healthy workplace. Although there are various models that list different components, there are a great number of similarities between the models, and their general focus is the same. For example, all healthy workplace models define healthy organizations as ones that systematically work towards fostering employee health and well-being, through organizational processes, while still maintaining effective organizational outcomes (Day & Randell, 2014; Grawitch, Gottschalk, & Munz, 2006; Kelloway & Day, 2005; Salanova, Llorens, Cifre, & Martinez, 2012). Figure 16.1 illustrates an integrated model of components of a psychologically healthy workplace.

16.5.1   Healthy workplace components

Healthy workplaces are characterized as those that provide organizational resources and practices to provide meaningful work and to support their

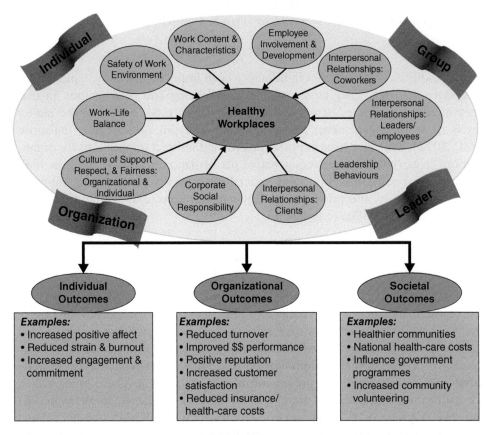

Figure 16.1: A reflective framework of the various healthy workplace models. Illustrative healthy workplace model based on previous healthy workplace models (Day & Randell, 2014; Grawitch et al., 2006; Kelloway & Day, 2005; Salanova et al., 2012)

employees to do their work efficiently (e.g., task autonomy, clarity, feedback, colleague and leader support, skills training; Kelloway & Day, 2005; Salanova et al., 2012). In addition to providing resources and encouraging engaging work, ensuring the physical and psychological health and safety in the workplace is a key component of a healthy workplace. Supporting a positive work–life balance, providing opportunities for growth and development, and recognizing employees' efforts are all initiatives that acknowledge the importance of the individual to the organization. Fostering positive interpersonal relationships at work (relationships among coworkers, clients, subordinates, and leaders) and providing opportunities for meaningful employee involvement and voice in the work process are both integral to a healthy workplace (e.g., Day & Randell, 2014; Grawitch et al., 2006; Kelloway & Day, 2005; see Figure 16.1). Moreover, the extent to which the organization involves its employees in corporate social responsibility, seeing itself as being part of a larger community, and developing this sense of community among its employees also may be viewed as a component of healthy workplaces (Day & Randell, 2014).

16.5.2   Healthy workplace outcomes

These resources and practices can influence both important employee and organizational outcomes. They target employee well-being and performance, in that they increase employees' sense of ability to achieve tasks, and promote higher levels of work engagement, job satisfaction, and job performance (Salanova et al., 2012). They also have important direct and indirect implications for organizations (e.g., reduced turnover, increased performance, positive reputation, high levels of customer satisfaction) and societal outcomes (e.g., providing supports in the community, and providing healthy work options; Day & Randell, 2014; Kelloway & Day, 2005; see Figure 16.1).

16.6   How Do Organizations Support and Create Healthy Workers and Workplaces?

There are many types of interventions or initiatives that organizations can implement to promote worker well-being. Initiatives are broadly defined as any planned interventions, as well as formal and informal work practices, organizational processes, or organizational communication (e.g., mission statement). These initiatives may be organizational policies or mission statements. They could involve formal health programmes or training interventions specifically implemented to improve employee well-being and effectiveness (e.g., leadership training). They also may include informal practices and behaviours, such as informal walking groups at lunch or supportive, open-door practices.

These initiatives and interventions can integrate the components identified in the healthy workplace models at various levels of the organization by targeting the following areas:

1. the entire organization (organization-level interventions);
2. the work groups and units (group-level interventions);
3. the organizational leaders (leader-level interventions);
4. the individual worker (worker interventions).

Although the distinction among the levels is difficult to define at times, this framework helps to disentangle the focus of the initiative to ensure that all areas of the organization are being targeted. That is, in order to have a healthy organization, there should be a balance of initiatives that are looking at the overall organization, groups, leaders and individual employee. An over-reliance on only one of these areas (e.g., focusing solely on the individual) can create an imbalance and a perception that the problem always is at the individual level (without trying to fix the problem at a higher level). Example initiatives that target the components of a healthy workplace using this four-level framework are found in Table 16.1.

Table 16.1: Examples of intervention research and organizational best practices

Level of intervention	Research and organizational examples		Healthy workplace component
Organization	Research example	Work programmes such as PIOP are participatory intervention programmes aimed at empowering employees and managers. By analysing how demands and resources relate to employee well-being and health, employees and managers jointly agree to change the way work is organized, designed, and managed, and they work together to systematically implement these changes and evaluate whether they have the intended effects.	Employee Involvement and Development
	Organizational best practice	Acknowledging the high pressure in the financial sector, the Danish Lån & Spar bank has developed the 'DO IT NOW' project. The aim is to improve efficiency by giving employees the tools to change the way work is designed and organized so that they can complete work in a more structured way and reduce wasted time.	Employee Involvement and Development
Group	Research example	Research intervention programmes, such as CREW, involve a team focus, with coworkers working together to improve workplace conduct and to develop effective interpersonal skills with the goal of reducing incivility and improving employee outcomes.	Interpersonal relationships: Coworkers
	Organizational best practice	Schuberg Philis in the Netherlands is an IT outsourcing company. Work is designed in small tightly knit and independent teams aimed at giving employees the opportunity to ask for help and be open about their personal strengths and weaknesses. The 'scrum method' is used to assess and divide work into manageable blocks. Teams also hold 'stand-up' meetings every day to discuss progress, and to prevent individual members from becoming overloaded or isolated.	Interpersonal relationships: Coworkers

Continued

Level of intervention	Research and organizational examples		Healthy workplace component
Leader	Research example	Programmes like the Mental Health Awareness Training (MHAT) provide leaders with the resources and knowledge necessary to recognize, address and support their employees at work when confronted with mental health issues and promote an open and destigmatized environment. Although designed to help leaders, this programme also may have indirect effects on the subordinates in the workplace.	Leadership behaviours and Interpersonal relationships between leaders and employees
	Organizational best practice	Employee feedback from Siemens organizations all over the world resulted in the development of 'Life in Balance' (LiB). Key components of this initiative are stress management training for managers and the two-day health seminars that are run targeting managerial staff. Both initiatives promote employee health and well-being and highlight how managers can support both prevention and rehabilitation.	Leadership behaviours and Interpersonal relationships between leaders and employees
Individual	Research example	Research intervention programmes like ABLE help employees deal with their work and non-work demands, set goals, improve health, and manage these demands and stressors. By focusing on the individual, sessions are tailored to each worker's needs, and helps them improve psychological well-being and satisfaction.	Work–Life Balance; Health
	Organizational best practice	Toronto Police Service is serious about helping their staff balance the demands of their job and their family life. They offer maternity and parental leave, multi-site childcare programme, emergency childcare programme, paid dependent sick leave, job sharing opportunities, and on-site exercise facilities to make the juggling of work and non-work a bit easier.	Work–Life Balance; Health

16.7 Organizational-Level Initiatives

Organization-level interventions provide resources to change the organization, in terms of addressing the psychosocial factors of work, such as increasing resources to workers and/or decreasing demands. Organizational-level interventions can be defined as planned, behavioural, theory-based actions that aim to improve the health and well-being of participants by changing the way work is organized, designed and managed (Nielsen, 2013). Generally it is recommended to use participatory approaches (EU-OSHA, 2010) to achieve these changes. In this context, a participatory approach means that employees and managers jointly define the process and the methods used in the intervention; they jointly plan which actions to make to the way work is organized, designed and managed, and they collaborate to implement and evaluate the effects of these actions. Participation involves employees and managers at all levels working in cooperation to decide which changes to make through a stepwise approach (Nielsen, Randall, Holten, & Rial-Gonzalez, 2010).

This participatory process may empower employees and managers through a range of mechanisms. First, it creates a culture where employees and managers in collaboration reflect on their own well-being. Second, a respectful culture may be created where the participatory process creates an awareness and insight of managers into employees' work situation and vice versa, employees develop an awareness and understanding of wider organizational issues and constraints. Third, the participatory process may also create self-direction and self-management because employees and managers become aware of the importance of jointly discussing work-related problems. Finally, a supportive culture is created when employees and managers collaborate to implement changes of mutual benefit to employees and the organization (Nielsen, 2013; Nielsen, Stage, Abildgaard, & Brauer, 2013). The extent to which employees are engaged in the participatory process can be linked to actual changes in working procedures being reported and to improved social support and employee well-being (Nielsen & Randall, 2012).

16.7.1 Organizational-level intervention research example: PIOP

Participatory Intervention from an Organizational Perspective (PIOP) is a programme designed to make changes in the way work is organized, designed and managed (Nielsen et al., 2013; Nielsen, Abildgaard, & Daniels, 2014). The programme aims to identify demands and resources particular to the organization in question, allowing employees and managers to systematically develop and implement changes to the way that work is organized, designed and managed, with the aim of creating a psychologically healthy workplace.

As with other participatory intervention methods, employees and managers go through a stepwise, systematic process (Nielsen et al., 2010b). In the first stage, barriers and facilitators to change are identified and analysed, and a steering group (consisting of employee, HR, Occupational Health and manager representatives) is established. In the second stage, a systematic analysis of job demands and resources is conducted. Employees and managers are interviewed about the most important demands and resources in the particular workplace. A key strength of the PIOP method is that it focuses not only on the psychosocial risks but also on the strengths and resources of the organization and the work teams and this dual approach may help ensure engagement (Nielsen et al., 2014). On the basis of these interviews, a tailored questionnaire is developed that taps into the local language and the specific working conditions of the employees and managers. Results are fed back to employees and managers and employees, and managers jointly prioritize which demands and resources they wish to change.

In the third stage, work teams jointly develop detailed and concrete action plans. It is recommended to have no more than three to five action plans. Each action plan should include detailed information about who does what, when, why, and how the action plan can be evaluated (i.e., when do employees and managers know they have achieved what they wanted to achieve?) In the fourth stage, action plans are implemented. Systematic follow-up of action plans is incorporated into existing meeting structures. In the fifth, and final, phase, work teams and the steering group evaluate: (1) whether any changes in the way work is organized, designed and managed have taken place, (2), whether these changes are associated with reduced demands and better resources, and employee well-being, and (3) the intervention process. For example, what was the level of experienced participation? Has there been any learning in how to manage job demands and resources? The evaluation provides valuable information on whether existing action plans need to be amended, new action plans need to be developed that better target the prioritized issues and at a higher level, or whether changes in strategies and policies to manage employee well-being need to be made (Nielsen et al., 2013; Nielsen et al., 2014). The PIOP programme has been evaluated using a 12-month follow-up and has been found successful in reducing job insecurity in groups where action plans focused on job insecurity and on improving team functioning and employee well-being when employees are ready for change (Nielsen, Daniels, von Thiele Schwarz, Hasson, Hasson, & Ogbonnaya, 2014).

16.8 Group-Level Initiatives

Group-level initiatives are those that target teams and units and whose goals are to improve group-level processes and the quality of workplace interactions and relationships. Initiatives may be aimed at groups of employees who work together to encourage a workplace culture of people who treat each other and their physical environment with respect and dignity. A culture of respect may be reflected in the organization's mission statement to promote supportive and respectful interpersonal interactions. Training may help leaders and employees develop greater interpersonal skills, and increase respect towards others and levels of civility.

16.8.1   Group-level Initiatives Research Example: CREW

The Civility, Respect, Engagement in the Workplace (CREW) training programme is a group-based programme initially developed for Veterans Health Administration hospitals in the United States (Osatuke, Moore, Ward, Dyrenforth, & Belton, 2009). This intervention is a tailored and flexible intervention, in which each workplace gets to decide how they define 'incivility' and what they need to focus on in order to improve civility in their own work environment. Coworkers worked together to develop standards of behaviours and effective interpersonal skills in the workplace in order to reduce incivility and improve employee outcomes. It was successful in the Veterans Health Administration, in that civility significantly increased at the worksites implementing the CREW programme (Osatuke et al., 2009).

Further work was done with CREW in health care organizations in Canada (Leiter, Laschinger, Day, & Oore, 2011; Leiter, Day, Oore, & Laschinger, 2012). Compared to workers who did not participate in CREW, workers engaged in this programme reported that their coworkers behaved more civilly after the intervention, and they to a higher extent respected and trusted their supervisors. They also reported a decrease in the amount of incivility from their supervisors and felt less cynical at work. Finally, workers who participated in the CREW training were absent less often from work (Leiter et al., 2011). Moreover, in studying these workers a year after the intervention, work attitudes gains were maintained. However, the reduction in absenteeism that was initially found was not maintained over the year, such that they returned to pre-intervention levels. This initiative suggests that group-based interventions for incivility may improve collegiality, which in turn should help foster a healthier workplace. These findings suggest that group-level interventions have the potential for fostering a more positive social environment in the workplace.

16.9   Leader-Level Interventions

It is widely acknowledged that leaders' behaviour towards employees can influence the well-being of these employees (Skakon, Nielsen, Borg, & Guzman, 2010). Leader-focused interventions are those in which training and resources are provided to leaders to help foster worker (and leader) health and well-being, either directly (e.g., by providing leaders with information about improving their own health and the health of subordinates) or indirectly (e.g., by training leaders to become better leaders more generally, which can lead to positive effects on workers' health). Unlike interventions at other levels (i.e., the organizational, group and individual level), interventions targeting the leader are aimed not only at enhancing the resources and the well-being of the leader, but also the resources and well-being of the leader's subordinates (Kelloway & Barling, 2010). Leadership interventions may focus more specifically on increasing awareness among leaders about health and well-being, and more broadly on developing their ability to manage employees.

16.9.1   Leader-level intervention research example #1: MHAT

Mental Health Awareness Training (MHAT) is a programme designed to improve leaders' mental health literacy in an organizational context (Dimoff & Kelloway, 2013a; 2013b; http://ohpsychology.ca/organizational-solutions#_ftn1). This programme aims to improve leaders' awareness of mental health issues of their employees (i.e., equip leaders to work towards their employees' health and well-being directly). It offers leaders the resources and knowledge necessary to address mental health concerns among individuals. Leaders who took part in the MHAT demonstrated greater knowledge of mental health concerns, decreased stigmatization of workers suffering from mental illness, greater self-efficacy for dealing with individuals with concerns, and improved intentions for promoting mental health at work (Dimoff & Kelloway, 2013a). Each 3-hour training session is tailored to the host organization to ensure leaders receive training on the organizational resources and policies that help them better deal with and promote mental health in an organizational setting. This programme helps leaders foster a psychologically heathy workplace and improves their own well-being by providing them with the appropriate knowledge, resources, and attitudes in order to feel confident to deal with problems in the workplace (Dimoff & Kelloway, 2013a; http://ohpsychology.ca/organizational-solutions#_ftn1).

16.9.2   Leader-level interventions research example #2: Managing teams

Teamwork has become an increasingly popular way of organizing work (Mathieu, Maynard, Rapp, & Gilson, 2008), but this type of job design puts demands on leaders to involve employees and facilitate employee decision-making, growth and development, in other words, function as transformational leaders (Nielsen et al., 2010a). Training leaders to manage teams effectively may indirectly ensure employee health and well-being because developing leaders' general leadership competences will create better leader behaviours (which are associated with employee well-being). Managing Teams is a leadership-training programme that focuses on equipping leaders with the necessary resources to implement and manage teams. Over a period of six months, leaders engage in six full days of training. Leaders are trained in recognizing what is a team and how to implement and manage teams. As part of the training they are provided with tools they can use to develop the team structure and their own leadership style. They also develop action plans on how to implement teamwork and improve their own leadership style. Between each session, leaders are given homework and network groups are established, encouraging leaders on the programme to support each other in working with teams (Nielsen et al., 2010a). Evaluating the programme among managers in eldercare centres, Nielsen et al. (2010a) found that 12 months after the training programme had been completed, employees reported being more involved in and satisfied with their jobs.

16.10 Individual-Level Interventions

Another way that organizations can improve worker well-being is by providing resources directly to the individual to support them and to foster their well-being. These types of interventions help workers improve and maintain their well-being by engaging in recovery activities, having positive coping styles and strategies, and developing their individual resilience.

That is, these programmes are not intended to change the organization or the leaders or the work environment. The aim of these types of programmes is to help the individual deal with the demands of the workplace and demands outside of work as well. In essence, any programme that is designed to help the employee can be considered an individual initiative. These types of initiatives may be aimed directly at employee health (e.g., healthy eating programmes), or they may help the individual have sufficient personal resources (e.g., providing training to do their work more effectively) to deal with work and non-work demands. They may even be job-related training, that helps employees be better able to do their job, which may not only increase productivity, but also may increase well-being.

16.10.1 Individual-level intervention research example: ABLE

Another individual program is the ABLE (Achieving Balance in Life & Employment) Program, which is a phone-based coaching programme that is tailored to the individual needs of each worker (Day, Francis, Stevens, Hurrell, & McGrath, 2015). ABLE is based on the premise of using personal coaching to help workers address demands, and to attain their work and life goals. ABLE is a 10–12-week programme in which workers are paired up with a coach, who helps each of them identify their personal work and non-work challenges, set goals to improve individual well-being and functioning at work and in life overall, identify work and non-work demands that may hinder success, and identify work and non-work resources to increase success. Participants like the format for several reasons: It allows more flexibility than other methods (such as workshops) as workers can schedule the meetings and work at their convenience. It is more time-sensitive because workers do not have to travel to receive coaching. Participants like the personalized, tailored content of the programme, and the ability to seek extra information and guidance in specific areas. The coaches help workers go through the programme manual, web-based supplementary materials, and activities on a weekly basis to assist in achieving set work and life goals by creating effective action plans. ABLE has been shown to be effective in improving individual well-being. That is, compared to a control group, ABLE participants showed improved engagement (vigour and dedication), and increased job satisfaction. Moreover, compared to the control group, ABLE participants reported decreased negative mood, cynicism and emotional exhaustion, as well as greater positive mood and improved life satisfaction (Day et al., 2015).

16.11   Conclusion

Given the increased attention given to both the physical and psychological aspects of health and wellness, and given the importance of increasing positive aspects of health, rather than just minimizing the negative aspects, the critical question is, what can organizations do to help employees' well-being? Despite the number of competing models of healthy workplaces, they all share similar characteristics. In addition to the focus on both physical and psychological health and well-being as noted above, most models explicitly highlight the importance of including both individual and organizational outcomes. They look at similar initiatives involving well-studied constructs (e.g., autonomy, involvement, work-life balance), and there is either an implicit or explicit assumption about the importance of culture and respect.

To aid in the understanding of the material, the interventions are classified into four levels: the organizational, the group, the leader, and the individual level, and their impacts are examined in terms of individual, organizational, and societal impacts. These levels are not mutually exclusive: That is, this classification does not mean that organizations should focus only on one of the levels. For example, it may be necessary to strengthen leaders' project management skills before initiating an organizational-level intervention. As seen in the Managing Teams project, training leaders was an important prerequisite for the teamwork implementation, as well as for the organizational and group-level intervention. Interestingly, the key driver for all of these specific initiatives under the different components is having a genuine respect for all members of the workplace.

Summary

The aim of this chapter was to address the question of what organizations do to improve employees' well-being. In answering this question, it was first necessary to examine what was meant by healthy workers and workplaces. Healthy workplaces integrate concerns for employee health and well-being with the considerations for performance and quality. That is, healthy, sustainable organizations need to consider both worker well-being and organizational performance to build resilience in a global competitive environment. There are many initiatives that organizations can undertake to promote a psychologically healthy workplace. Organizations can initiate interventions that target individuals (e.g., health awareness training), target the work group (e.g., group climate training), target leaders (e.g., leadership development programmes), as well as target the organization itself (e.g., changes to HR practices and the way work is organized, designed and managed). However, it is important to note that healthy workplaces are built by multi-level interventions. A synergistic effect can be observed when interventions targeting different levels are implemented. Therefore, either alone or in combination, these initiatives may create a psychologically healthy workplace that not only improves worker well-being, but also that may provide benefits for the organization and the wider society. Interestingly, the actual practices and interventions used may be less important than the overall organizational culture of respect and the motivation for these initiatives. Having mutual respect among organizational members may be the key to having a healthy workplace and helping worker well-being.

Discussion Points

1 You are the CEO of a medium-sized business with approximately 250 employees and employee records indicate that absenteeism is steadily on the rise. You also notice that health care costs for your employees are increasing as well. What programmes, policies, initiatives, or organizational changes would you implement to foster a more psychologically healthy workplace and alleviate these threats to organizational performance?

2 You are the HR responsible in a large, multinational finance company. In the annual attitude survey, employees report dissatisfaction with their departmental managers. To get a better understanding of these issues, you conduct a series of focus groups with employees. During these interviews it becomes clear that employees feel that their managers do not listen to their suggestions and problems and use their power to implement unpopular decisions. What initiatives would you propose to the organization to address this situation with the managers?

Suggested Further Reading

Bauer, G., & Jenny, G. (2013). *Concepts of salutogenic organizations and change: The logics behind organizational health intervention research*. Dordrecht: Springer. You can find inspiration on how to develop organizational interventions in the Bauer and Jenny book, which provides examples of how organizational interventions can be developed that focus on promoting employee health and well-being and that ensure employees thrive in their jobs.

Biron, C., Burke, R., & Cooper, C. L. (Eds.). (2014). *Creating healthy workplaces: Stress reduction, improved well-being, and organizational effectiveness*. Farnham, UK: Gower. Various interventions at the individual, group, leader/manager, and organizational levels are discussed in the Biron et al. book, emphasizing the importance of health and well-being not only in terms of the absence of ill health, but also in terms of promoting a psychologically healthy workplace.

Day, A., Kelloway, E. K., & Hurrell Jr, J. J. (Eds.). (2014). *Workplace well-being: how to build psychologically healthy workplaces*. Chichester: John Wiley & Sons Ltd. The Day et al. book is an essential compendium to understanding and implementing the principles of a psychologically healthy workplace. Each chapter addresses a separate component of psychologically healthy workplaces as well as the contextual aspects to consider in developing healthy workplaces, focusing on both research and practice.

Online resources

There are several websites that provide information about creating healthy workplaces, best practices in workplace health, and worker health. You can check them out at:

- https://www.apaexcellence.org/resources/creatingahealthyworkplace/
- http://www.smu.ca/centres-and-institutes/cncohs.html
- http://www.who.int/occupational_health/5_keys_EN_web.pdf?ua=1
- http://www.mentalhealthcommission.ca/English/issues/workplace/national-standard
- https://osha.europa.eu/en

References

Burton, J. (2004). *Creating healthy workplaces.* Retrieved February 2, 2016, from http://www.iapa.ca/pdf/2004

Burton, J. (2010). WHO Healthy workplace framework and model: Background and supporting literature and practice. Retrieved February 2, 2016, from http://www.who.int/occupational_health/healthy_workplaces_background_original.pdf

Cartwright, S. & Cooper, C. (2005). Individually targeted interventions. In J. Barling, E. K. Kelloway, & M. R. Frone (Eds.), *Handbook of work stress* (pp.607–622). Thousand Oaks, CA: Sage Publications, Inc.

Cooper, C. L., & Cartwright, S. (1994). Healthy mind; healthy organization—A proactive approach to occupational stress. *Human Relations, 47*(4), 455–471.

Cooper, J., & Patterson, D. (2008). Should business invest in the health of its workers?. *International Journal of Workplace Health Management, 1*(1), 65–71.

Cox, T. (1997). Workplace health promotion. *Work & Stress, 11*(1), 1–5.

Danna, K., & Griffin, R. W. (1999). Health and well-being in the workplace: A review and synthesis of the literature. *Journal of Management, 25*(3), 357–384.

Day, A., Francis, L., Stevens, S., Hurrell, Jr., J. J., & McGrath, P. (2015). Improving employee health and work-life balance: Developing and validating a coaching-based ABLE Program. In C. Biron, R. Burke, & C. L. Cooper (Eds). *Creating healthy workplaces: stress reduction, improved well-being, and organizational effectiveness.* (pp. 68–90).Farnham: Gower.

Day, A., Hartling, N., & Mackie, B. (2015). The psychologically healthy workplace: fostering employee well-being & healthy businesses. In P. Perrewe, & J. Meurs (Eds.), *Stress and quality of working life* (pp. 199–217). Charlotte, NC: Information Age Publishing.

Day, A. L., & Helson, T. (2016). Workplace health promotion. In S. Clarke, T. M. Probst, F. W. Guldenmund, & J. Passmore (Eds.), *The Wiley Blackwell handbook of the psychology of occupational safety and workplace health* (pp. 377–413). Chichester: John Wiley & Sons, Inc.

Day, A., & Randell, D. (2014). Building a foundation for psychologically healthy workplaces and well-being. In A. Day, E. K. Kelloway, & J. J. Hurrell Jr. (Eds.), *Workplace wellbeing: How to build psychologically healthy workplaces* (pp. 3–26). Chichester: John Wiley & Sons, Ltd.

Day, A., Kelloway, E. K., & Hurrell Jr, J. J. (Eds.). (2014). *Workplace well-being: How to build psychologically healthy workplaces.* Chichester: John Wiley & Sons, Ltd.

Demerouti, E., Bakker, A. B., Nachreiner, F., & Schaufeli, W. B. (2001). The job demands–resources model of burnout. *Journal of Applied Psychology, 86*(3), 499–512.

Demerouti, E., Bakker, A. B., de Jonge, J., Janssen, P. P., & Schaufeli, W. B. (2001). Burnout and engagement at work as a function of demands and control. *Scandinavian Journal of Work, Environment & Health, 27,* 279–286.

Dimoff, J., & Kelloway, E.K. (2013a). Mental health awareness training. Paper presented at the bi-annual conference, Work Stress and Health, Los Angeles, CA.

Dimoff, J., & Kelloway, E.K. (2013b). Mental health awareness training (MHAT): The evaluation of an intervention for leaders. Paper presented at The European Congress of Psychology, Stockholm, Sweden.

EU-OSHA (2010). European Agency for Safety and Health at Work. *European Survey of Enterprises on New and Emerging Risks,* 2010. Retrieved from http://www.esener.eu.

Grawitch, M. J., Gottschalk, M., & Munz, D. C. (2006). The path to a healthy workplace: A critical review linking healthy workplace practices, employee well-being, and organizational improvements. *Consulting Psychology Journal: Practice and Research, 58*(3), 129–147.

Hobfoll, S. E. (1989). Conservation of resources: A new attempt at conceptualizing stress. *American Psychologist, 44,* 513–524.

ILO (International Labour Organization) (1986). *Psychosocial factors at work: Recognition and control.* Report of the Joint ILO/ WHO Committee on Occupational Health, Occupational Safety and Health Series No. 56, Geneva: ILO, 18–24 September 1984. Available at: http://www.who.int/occupational_health/publications/ILO_WHO_1984_report_of_the_joint_committee.pdf.

Kelloway, E. K., & Barling, J. (2010). Leadership development as an intervention in occupational health psychology. *Work & Stress, 24*(3), 260–279.

Kelloway, E. K., & Day, A. L. (2005). Building healthy workplaces: What we know so far. *Canadian Journal of Behavioural Science, 37*(4), 223–235.

Kivimäki, M., Virtanen, M., Elovainio, M., Kouvonen, A., Väänänen, A., & Vahtera, J. (2006). Work stress in the etiology of coronary heart disease. A meta-analysis. *Scandinavian Journal of Work, Environment & Health, 32*(6), 431–442.

Leiter, M. P., Day, A., Oore, D. G., & Laschinger, H. K. S. (2012). Getting better and staying better: Assessing civility, incivility. distress, and job attitudes one year after a civility intervention. *Journal of Occupational Health Psychology, 17*(4), 425–434.

Leiter, M. P., Laschinger, H. K. S., Day, A., & Oore, D. G. (2011). The impact of civility interventions on employee social behavior, distress, and attitudes. *Journal of Applied Psychology, 96*(6), 1258–1274.

Mathieu, J. E., Maynard, M. T., Rapp, T., & Gilson, L. (2008). Team effectiveness 1997–2007: A review of recent advancements and a glimpse into the future. *Journal of Management, 34*, 410–476.

Nielsen, K. (2013). Review article: How can we make organizational interventions work? Employees and line managers as actively crafting interventions. *Human Relations, 66*(8), 1029–1050.

Nielsen, K., & Abildgaard, J. S. (2013). Organizational interventions: A research-based framework for the evaluation of both process and effects. *Work & Stress, 27*(3), 278–297.

Nielsen, K., Abildgaard, J. S., & Daniels, K. (2014) Putting context into organizational intervention design: Using tailored questionnaires to measure initiatives for worker well-being. *Human Relations, 67*(2), 1537–1560.

Nielsen, K., Daniels, K., von Thiele Schwarz, U., Hasson, H., Hasson, D. & Ogbonnaya, C. (2014). Are you ready? The role of organizational readiness for change when implementing interventions to improve employee well-being. Adelaide: ICOH-WOPS (International Commission of Occupational Health – Work and psychosocial factors).

Nielsen, K., & Randall, R. (2012). The importance of employee participation and perceptions of changes in procedures in a team-working intervention. *Work & Stress, 26*(2), 91–111.

Nielsen, K., Randall, R. & Christensen, K. B. (2010). A longitudinal field study of the effects of team manager training. *Human Relations, 63*, 1719–1741.

Nielsen, K., Randall, R., Holten, A.-L., & Rial-Gonzalez, E. (2010). Conducting organizational-level occupational health interventions: What works? *Work & Stress, 24*(3), 234–259.

Nielsen, K., Stage, M., Abildgaard, J. S., & Brauer, C. V. (2013). Participatory intervention from and organizational perspective: Employees as active agents in creating a healthy work environment. In G. Bauer, & G. Jenny. (Eds.), *Concepts of salutogenic organizations and change: The logics behind organizational health intervention research* (pp. 327–350). Dordrecht: Springer Publications.

Osatuke, K., Moore, S. C., Ward, C., Dyrenforth, S. R., & Belton, L. (2009). Civility, Respect, Engagement in the Workforce (CREW) Nationwide organization development intervention at Veterans Health administration. *The Journal of Applied Behavioral Science, 45*(3), 384–410.

Salanova, M., Llorens, S., Cifre, E., & Martínez, I. (2012). We need a hero! Toward a validation of the Healthy and Resilient Organization

(HERO) model. *Group & Organization Management, 37,* 785–822.

Skakon, J., Nielsen, K., Borg, V., & Guzman, J. (2010). The impact of leaders on employee stress and well-being: A systematic review of 29 years of empirical research. *Work & Stress, 24,* 107–139.

Sonnentag, S., & Frese, M. (2003). *Stress in organizations.* Hoboken, NJ: John Wiley & Sons.

WHO (World Health Organization) (2015) Who definition of health. Retrieved February 02, 2015 from http://www.who.int/about/definition/en/print.html

PART III

PEOPLE-FOCUSED

Does It Matter Who We Are? Personality at Work

Adrian Furnham

17

Overview

This chapter examines the research on the relationship between personality traits and all aspects of work-related behaviour. Personality, along with other characteristics such as ability and motivation, are important correlates of all sorts of behaviour in the workplace. Most psychologists now support the Big Five personality system. The chapter describes each trait (Neuroticism, Extraversion, Openness, Agreeableness and Conscientiousness) and how it relates to all sorts of work outcomes from accidents to satisfaction. Overall, the traits do not change much over time once adulthood is achieved.

The chapter looks at the research findings on the relationship between personality and organizational level, promotion level and salary, all of which are related. The results suggest that personality plays an important part in all these outcomes and that three traits are constantly found to be implicated. The higher people score on trait Conscientiousness and Extraversion, and the lower they score on trait Neuroticism, the better they do at work. It is possible thus to describe, in personality terms, the profile of high flyers.

Finally the chapter looks at the more recent interest in management derailment. This is based on the 'dark side' traits and the paradoxical finding that some sub-clinical personality disorders actually correlate with management success.

17.1 Introduction

Every manager knows that, in the workplace, some people are more engaged, happy and productive than others. Some go absent a lot and others very rarely. Some work happily in teams, others not. The most productive workers achieve roughly two and a half times that of the least productive.

Most managers are, quite rightly, concerned with recruiting and selecting people who will have job commitment, involvement and satisfaction. They look for people

An Introduction to Work and Organizational Psychology: An International Perspective,
Third Edition. Edited by Nik Chmiel, Franco Fraccaroli and Magnus Sverke.
© 2017 John Wiley & Sons, Ltd. Published 2017 by John Wiley & Sons, Ltd.

who will be both happy and productive; those who will enjoy job satisfaction and be highly effective. The question is, what do they look for and how do they measure it?

People differ on a number of different factors relevant in the workplace:

- *Ability*: This refers to the extent to which a person can *efficiently* carry out multiple processes in coordination to achieve a specified goal based on their skills and gifts. Skills extend from relatively simple dexterous, hand-eye coordination tasks to complex intellectual decision processes, and are thus related to intelligence – but are distinguished from it. Sometimes abilities are called competencies. Different jobs call for different abilities.
- *Demographic factors*: This refers to background factors such as sex, age, class, or education. Demographic factors usually relate to biographical factors in the life of a particular person, e.g., birth order, occupation of parents, type of school attended, and are distinguishable from psychographic factors, which refer to beliefs and values. It is illegal to base selection decisions on the basis of some of these factors, such as ethnicity or religion, and the illegality of these factors differs from country to country.
- *Intelligence*: This refers to the individual's capacity for abstract and critical thinking. Many controversies surround this concept, for instance, whether it is uni- or multi-dimensional, to what extent it is inherited or learnt, and how it should be measured. Despite all the concerns of investigators, few doubt the effect of general intelligence on performance at work. The more complex and sophisticated the job, the more a person needs high intelligence to perform it well.
- *Motivation*: Like intelligence, this is a multidimensional abstract concept that refers to the drive to cause some actions. It is notoriously difficult to measure, partly because people cannot or will not talk about the things that motivate them. Hence, one talks of the strength of particular motivations, such as the need for achievement. The higher the generalized need for achievement, the stronger the motivation for success at work. Motivation is often measured by values such as how much people want recognition or power or the opportunity to be altruistic at work.
- *Personality*: This refers to all those fundamental traits or characteristics of the person (or of people generally) that endure over time and that account for consistent patterns of responses to everyday situations. Personality traits supposedly account for the what, why and how of human functioning. Definitions of personality are as varied as writers of textbooks. It is argued people are unique, but can be described and categorized parsimoniously along various fundamental dimensions or into specific categories. Personality dimensions are behavioural dispositions in the sense that they correlate with determination and drive, to affect social behaviour. Personality dimensions are relatively stable over time and manifest consistently and coherently over varying social situations. The personality of a person can, and must, be decomposed into its specific and fundamental parts, elements and building blocks, but also combined into an organized whole system in order to understand its functions.

17.2 The Taxonomy of Personality

Psychologists have argued with each other for around 100 years over the basic dimensions of personality. Some argued there were three, others five and some even 16. For many years the *Gigantic Three* of Hans Eysenck dominated the research but this was replaced by the now widely accepted *Big Five* of Paul Costa and Donald McCrae. There remains a lot of overlap between them.

The Eysenckian model still has three – and only three – super-factors: (1) Psychoticism, (2) Extraversion, and (3) Neuroticism (known as P-E-N). Eysenck was quite convinced that these three conceptual and descriptive categories are necessary and sufficient for a thorough understanding of individual differences in personality. On the other hand, the Big Five model, which is now very widely established, has been employed in most studies looking at personality at work. The Big Five dimensions are set out in Table 17.1.

Table 17.1: The Big Five traits

High	Average	Low
1. Neuroticism Sensitive, emotional and prone to experience feelings that are upsetting.	Generally calm and able to deal with stress, but sometimes experience feelings of guilt, anger or sadness.	Secure, hardy and generally relaxed, even under stressful conditions.
2. Extraversion Extraverted, outgoing, active and high-spirited. Prefer to be around people most of the time.	Moderate in activity and enthusiasm. Enjoy the company of others but also value privacy.	Introverted, reserved and serious. Prefer to be alone or with a few close friends.
3. Openness-to-experience Open to new experiences. Have broad interests and are very imaginative.	Practical but willing to consider new ways of doing things. Seek a balance between the old and the new.	Down-to-earth, practical, traditional and pretty much set in your ways.
4. Agreeableness Compassionate, good-natured and eager to cooperate and avoid conflict.	Generally warm, trusting and agreeable, but can sometimes be stubborn and competitive.	Hard-headed, sceptical, proud and competitive. Tend to express anger directly.
5. Conscientiousness Conscientious and well organized. Have high standards and always strive to achieve goals.	Dependable and moderately well organized. Generally have clear goals but are able to set work aside.	Easy-going, not very well organized, and sometimes careless. Prefer not to make plans.

Source: Adapted from Costa and McCrae (1987).

Table 17.2: Possible relationships between personality traits and work outcomes

Trait	Positive				Negative			
	Creativity	Engagement	Productivity	Promotion	Absenteeism	Accidents	Derailment	Turnover
Neuroticism	+	−−	−−	−	+++	+	+	+
Extraversion	+	+		++	+	+++	+	+
Openness-to-Experience	+++						+	+
Agreeableness		+			−	−	−	−
Conscientiousness		+++	+++	+++	−−	−	−	−

There have been as many speculations as studies that have investigated the relationship between the Big Five dimensions and different work outcome which could be classified as positive or negative. Table 17.2 presents some of these hypotheses. This is not a meta-analysis though hopefully in time that might be done. Three points about Table 17.2 are noteworthy. First, the strongest and most consistent personality correlate of work-related behaviour is Conscientiousness. The second most consistent predictor is Neuroticism (low Adjustment). Third, Extraversion seems to be related to both positive and negative work outcomes.

17.2.1   Extraversion

Extraversion is perhaps the best known as it is at the very 'heart' of many theories of personality and is well understood by lay-people. Introversion-extraversion is a dimension from very high to very low. So most of us are *ambiverts*: in the middle and not strongly the one or the other. Extraverts are seen as more likeable, interesting and popular; introverts are more honest, stable and reliable. Extraverts are attracted to 'people jobs' such as sales and the service industry and do well.

Extraverts are less distracted than introverts. Their world is ever more busy, noisy and distracting. The open-plan office, the mobile phone, the relentless meetings all favour extraverts who like stimulation, whereas introverts are only distracted by people, noise, or stimulants of any kind. They are less comfortable, less efficient, and less helpful in the noisy world of work.

Introverts take longer to retrieve information; longer to marshal their ideas and thoughts and longer to respond to the demands of the world around them.

From a motivational point of view, we know extraverts respond better to carrots and care less about sticks, while introverts are less motivated by rewards and more sensitive to and inhibited by threats of punishments. Perhaps, therefore, extraverts are easier to manage. They are certainly easier to read.

People like extraverts because they tend to be more socially confident and comfortable. Children move towards, away from or against people. The stimulus-seeking extravert learns early on that people can be lots of fun. So most learn social and emotional intelligence earlier.

However, there have always been serious known *disadvantages* of being a (strong) extravert:

- *Accidents*: Extraverts are risk takers. They drive fast and choose risky recreational activities. They trade off accuracy for speed. They are prone to all sorts of gaffes, preferring to think before they speak.
- *Crime*: Extraverts are social and impulsive. They are excitement-seekers interested in novel experiences, which often leads them to be poorer learners than introverts at many tasks, including the acquisition of general social rules. They are difficult to train, naughty and rebellious. They are more likely than introverts to become delinquents or criminals, though it does depend on the nature of the criminal activity.
- *Learning:* Extraverts do well at primary school but less well at university. The idea of sitting in a quiet room for hours learning complicated abstract ideas just does not suit the extravert.
- *Sex:* Extraverts tend to be less prudish and nervous than their introverted cousins and more excited and satisfied with sex. But extraverts are more likely to have premarital sex and more likely to experiment.

Most people are able to accurately rate themselves and others on Introversion and Extraversion.

17.2.2 Neuroticism

Neuroticism is also called 'negative affectivity' or 'poor emotional adjustment'. Researchers believe it is based on activation thresholds in the sympathetic nervous system or visceral brain. This is the part of the brain that is responsible for the fight-or-flight response in the face of danger.

Neurotic persons have a low activation threshold: when confronted with even mild stressors or anxiety-inducing situations, they quickly and easily experience negative emotions and moods and quickly, and sometimes seriously, become upset. These manifestations can range from physiological changes in heart rate, blood pressure, cold hands, sweating, and muscular tension, to feelings of apprehension and nervousness, to the full effects of fear and anxiety.

In contrast to Neurotics (or emotionally unstable and labile persons), their emotionally stable peers have a much higher activation threshold, and thus will experience negative affect only when confronted by major stressors. Such individuals tend to be calm even in situations that could be described as anxiety-inducing or pressure-laden. They are stable not moody; robust not vulnerable; hardy not overly sensitive.

The World Health Organization's International Classification of Diseases (ICD-10) (WHO, 1992) uses Neuroticism as a central organizing principle, considering the stress-related, somatoform and dissociative disorders. Neuroticism is a correlate and predictor of many different mental and physical disorders.

Neuroticism is most clearly described in three disorders: Generalized Anxiety, Panic and Phobic disorders. Specific phobias detailed to overlap with Neuroticism include agoraphobia, social phobia, obsessive compulsive disorder and post-traumatic stress disorder.

Many higher-order theories of personality – like the Eysenckian Giant Three, the Big Five, the six-factor HEXACO model or the seven-factor Hogan Personality Inventory – describe and measure Neuroticism at the Domain, but also at the Facet level, though there remains very little agreement in the description of these facets. For instance, the *Eysenck Personality Profiler* (EPP) has seven N facets labelled: Inferiority, Unhappiness, Anxiety, Dependence, Hypochondria, Guilt and Obsessiveness; the HEXACO model four facets labelled: Fearfulness, Anxiety, Dependence and Sentimentality; and the Multidimensional Personality Questionnaire (MPQ) has three facets labelled Stress Reaction, Alienation and Aggression.

Even the name of the domain changes: for the EPP it is *Neuroticism,* for the HEXACO it is *Emotionality* and for the MPQ it is *Negative Emotional Temperament.* This indicates subtle but important differences in the conceptualization of Neuroticism.

People who score high on Neuroticism are prone to anxiety, depression and psychosomatic illness and hence higher levels of stress at work. However, they are very vigilant and able to pick up the emotional tones around them better than stable individuals.

17.2.3   Psychoticism

Psychoticism is the most under-developed and debated of Eysenck's three super-factors. This dimension is also called tough-mindedness. People who score high on this dimension tend to manifest a higher probability of engaging in aggression and demonstrating the kind of cold, tough-mindedness that characterizes psychopathy and persons more likely to engage in crime.

Psychoticism also has a biological basis. There are few positive correlates of this dimension in the workplace except creativity. It has been argued that people who score highly on this factor have a thinking style (latent inhibition) that is associated with creativity. However, there is evidence that high P scorers are cold, aggressive, unreliable and difficult to manage.

It was the psychometric and definitional problems associated with this dimension that led to the development of the Big Five. Essentially Psychoticism was split into three Dimensions, all of them expressed positively. They are Agreeableness, Conscientiousness and Openness-to-Experience.

17.2.4   Agreeableness

The trait Agreeableness is associated with being altruistic, appreciative, compliant, trusting and tender-minded. People high in Agreeableness have been shown to be generous, kind, sympathetic and warm. Agreeableness facets include Easy to Live With, Sensitive, Caring, Likes People and No Hostility. Others have suggested facets labelled forgiveness, gentleness, flexibility, patience and altruism vs. antagonism.

To some extent, Agreeableness has been the 'Cinderella' trait of the Big Five, as it seems less related to many education, health and work outcomes. Also doubt has been expressed as to whether it is a trait (as opposed to a social desirability or social-relational concept). Further, it is often seen to be a disadvantage to be high in Agreeableness. Those low, rather than high in, Agreeableness, have been associated with success as a business leader.

Studies on Agreeableness in children have demonstrated that it predicts academic performance and social competence. Agreeableness is often highly valued in the workplace. People like to work with others who are helpful, kind and empathic. They tend to be liked and valued. However, the workplace is often a competitive and 'win-lose' philosophy environment where those who are more disagreeable, egocentric and tough-minded do best.

17.2.5   Openness-to-Experience

Of all the Big Five personality traits, Openness-to-Experience is often shown as the strongest correlate of ability, particularly creativity and intelligence. In the Big Five personality system, trait Openness is associated with having a vivid imagination and an active fantasy life; a deep appreciation for art and beauty; a receptivity to one's own and other's emotions; a willingness to try new experiences; intellectual curiosity and a readiness to examine political, social and religious values. People high in Openness have been shown to be unconventional, questioning and emotionally literate. Other personality theories and systems have described Openness as Intellect or Culture and had different ideas about the facets of the super-factor or domain. These include Aesthetic Appreciation, Inquisitiveness, Creativity and Unconventionality. While there is confusion and disagreement about facets of Openness, there seems agreement that it is a stable trait that reflects intellectual curiosity, imaginativeness and inquisitiveness.

Those interested in personality correlates of educational, health and occupational outcomes have tended to show that, of the Big Five traits, Neuroticism and Conscientiousness account for most of the variance, with Openness being related to very specific issues such as aesthetic preferences or leisure pursuits. In most individual difference studies, therefore, personality traits are the predictor variables and some salient beliefs or behaviours are the criterion variable. One relevant theory is Cattell's (1971) investment theory which suggests personality and fluid intelligence contribute to the development of crystallized intelligence. An alternative research question is, what are the early determinants, including intelligence, of Openness in adulthood? Few studies have investigated this question because of the difficulty of obtaining longitudinal data, though there are some recent exceptions (Furnham & Cheng, 2015).

There is an extensive literature on Openness. Many studies are concerned with the extent to which Openness is related to cognitive ability. Studies have used different measures of both Openness and intelligence and have all tended to show a significant positive correlation (Chamorro-Premuzic, Moutafi, & Furnham, 2005; DeYoung, Quilty, Peterson, & Gray, 2014). One study (Ziegler, Danay, Heene, Asendorpf, & Bühner, 2012) was developmental and measured parent-rated Openness in 172 adolescents at 17 years, and both Openness and Fluid and Crystallized intelligence at 23 years. The correlation between the two measures of Openness was .49 and those between Openness and Intelligence between .23 and .49. In another study, Schretlen and colleagues tested 335 healthy adults and found that Openness was more strongly correlated with verbal/crystallized intelligence ($r = .44$) than with executive functioning ($r = .16$) and fluency ($r = .26$).

Gow, Whiteman, Pattie and Deary (2005) found that intelligence measured in childhood and late adulthood was significantly correlated with Intellect (Openness) but that when the association in old age was controlled for childhood intelligence, it fell to almost zero. Their conclusion was that the relationship between intelligence and Openness in adulthood is through the lifelong stable trait of intelligence. However, showing that childhood variables predict adult variables does not unambiguously show environmental effects (regardless of what the childhood variables are) because there could be genetic forces that influence both predictor and criterion variables (i.e., the third-variable problem).

17.2.6   Conscientiousness

Trait Conscientiousness is associated with being efficient, organized, reliable and responsible. People high in Conscientiousness have been shown to be achievement-oriented, competent, dependable and productive. It is not surprising therefore that parents, teachers and employers value the trait and attempt to shape and encourage it in their children, students and employees. Students who were more Conscientious earned university grades higher than their intelligence scores would predict.

There are consistent findings from correlational studies that show a very small, but significant positive, association between Conscientiousness and educational achievement and occupational prestige. There is also some evidence to suggest sex differences in Conscientiousness which has been used to explain why females outperform males in school grades despite the evidence of very small differences in intelligence between the genders (Furnham, 2008).

The taxonomists of Conscientiousness argue that there are eight distinguishable but related parts:

1. *Industriousness:* This is about working hard, always putting in an effort and frequently exceeding expectations. In industries, people push themselves (and others) very hard to succeed.
2. *Perfectionism:* This is aiming for high quality, no mistakes, no reject work. It is about being detail-orientated and striving always to be the best.
3. *Tidiness:* This is strong preference for order, regularity, and the 'everything-in-its-place philosophy'. Conscientious people have a strong aversion to disorder and mess. They like things correctly filed and tasks completed.
4. *Procrastination Refrainment:* The really Conscientious are not types easily distracted or have difficulty getting started. They don't put off all unpleasant tasks, starting only the easy ones. They go to work at once: they prioritize and spend their time and effort wisely.
5. *Control Preference:* This should not be confused with control freakery. It's about being planful, thoughtful and decisive. It is also about understanding the role of authority. The opposite is rushed, rash, impulsive behaviour.
6. *Caution:* Because of the above, the Conscientious person is careful to avoid mistakes, get their facts right and think ahead. They think before they speak; they choose their words carefully.
7. *Task Planning:* The Conscientious person is planful. They carefully devise a plan, a schedule, a considered path. They stick to it and require others to do likewise. They like to work out an efficient routine and stick to them.
8. *Perseverance:* The Conscientious deal well with frustrations and setbacks. They don't give up easily, they don't wait or avoid responsibility, they don't lose interest. They are calm under pressure.

17.3 Change Over Time

There is considerable debate about the stability of personality over time. The debate about the equivocal nature of both findings and conclusions regarding continuity vs. change revolves around a number of issues: the reliability and validity of personality tests used (to account in part for measurement error); the moderator variables considered (i.e., sex, education and ethnicity); the age at which people are measured (i.e., adolescents, adults, old age); the time span that shows most change and stability; how change is measured (such as mean level change, rank order, ipsative change); the stability of the environments of people and what, if anything, leads to change.

There inevitably remain many disagreements, however, all agree that there is evidence of *both* stability *and* change. Personality seems most stable between the ages of 30 and 60 years, particularly using established Big Five measures to assess it and there are modest increases in emotional ability and agreeableness over this period with Extraversion and Neuroticism showing least change (both with a slight decline) and Conscientiousness showing most change (an increase).

17.4 Personality and Work Success: Organizational Level, Promotion History And Salary

Those interested in personality correlates of educational, health and occupational outcomes have tended to show that, of the Big Five traits, Neuroticism and Conscientiousness account for most of the variance, with Openness being related to very specific issues, such as aesthetic preferences or leisure pursuits. Again and again studies have shown that being high on Conscientiousness and low on Neuroticism are the two best predictors of success at work.

The question is how to measure success at work. This can be measured either objectively or subjectively.

1. *Subjective*: Most people have a sense of how successful they have been in the workplace, though both their criteria and their evaluations may differ significantly. There are two ways in which the concept of subjective may be used. The first is in terms of a personal overall or specific rating of success at work. The second is that the reporting is subjective, such as reporting one's salary, promotion speed, etc. The issue here is the reliability and accuracy of these reports which could be distorted for a number of reasons, like poor memory, social desirability, etc.
2. *Objective*: There are a whole range of criteria that may be considered to be markers of occupational success. This includes salary, rank, job title, speed of promotion, etc. There are essentially three problems associated with these variables. The *first* is that it is difficult to compare across jobs, organizations or sectors. Second, there are great differences between regions, countries and time periods. Therefore, the salary of a highly successful person from a developing country may be a third of that of somebody with identical criteria (even working in the same organization) in a developed country. Third, in times of growth (which may be specific to a sector, or region or product), people are likely to be paid more than in times of stagnation.

The question is, what sort of questions have been asked? Consider three:

1. *Are people at different levels of an organization different in their personality profile?* A number of studies using different tests have compared people at different levels from supervisor level, through management and senior management to chief executive. While there are a number of these studies there is a major issue that is not easily solved. The question is whether the person's

personality profile in some way was responsible for their level. Thus, because Conscientious people are more reliable, responsible and productive, and less Neurotic people less stress-prone, these traits lead to greater productivity, which is rewarded by promotion or appointment to senior levels. On the other hand, it is possible that personality may change as a person moves up levels in organizations, learning to become better organized and less stressed. While the studies in the area inevitably give equivocal results, it seems that more senior people tend to be more Extraverted and Conscientious and less Agreeable and Neurotic.

2. *Is there evidence that personality profile is related to both the speed and number of promotions at work?* It is possible to do either a retrospective or a prospective study to determine how long it takes people to get promoted to middle or senior management within any organization as well as between organizations in the same sector. Of course, many factors are related to promotion but these can be taken into account.

3. *Is personality linked to salary?* Many factors dictate a person's salary. These include the type of job they do (bankers tend to get paid more than bar-staff; doctors more than dock-workers) as well as their seniority and age. However, it is possible to take many confounding factors into account and demonstrate that indeed personality is related to personal wealth as a function of salary.

The central question for the researcher is to describe and explain the mechanism or process whereby personality traits are related to various related aspects of work success. For most researchers, the idea is that personality is related to various specific behaviours that directly impact on work productivity:

a) *Personality and life style*: this includes diet and personal habits, including exercise. Thus traits influence mental and physical health which impacts on such things as efficiency and absenteeism, which impacts on productivity at work.

b) *Personality and risk taking*: this includes such things outside work like driving and hobbies but also risk taking in the workplace.

c) *Personality and stress*: this includes the extent to which people cause and experience personal stress, which can have many consequences.

d) *Personality and social support*: this includes a person's ability to establish personal bonds, support networks and succeed in teams.

17.5 High Flyers Personality

There have been many attempts over the years to develop models and measures of 'high flyers' or talented people who succeed in organizations. The idea is to identify those abilities, motives and traits that are, in most organizations, clearly linked to occupational success.

MacRae and Furnham (2014) have developed the High Potential Traits Inventory (HPTI) (formerly the High Flying Personality Inventory), a measure of personality traits directly relevant to workplace behaviours, thoughts and perceptions of the self and others at work. The HPTI can be used to investigate which personality traits in the workplace might predict career success and thus predict high potential (MacRae & Furnham, 2014). Six scientifically validated personality traits are involved: Conscientiousness – planning, organization, strong work ethic, achievement drive; Openness/Curiosity – openness to new information, adopting new approaches; Approach to Risk – willingness to confront difficult situations, thrive during adversity, solve difficult problems, have difficult conversations; Stress Reactivity – resilient to the impact of stressors, not overly worried about others' judgement; Tolerance of Ambiguity – approach to ambiguous situations and information, make use of mixed information, cope (and thrive) with ambivalence; and Competitiveness – need to achieve, drive to exceed one's own or another's performance, desire for control.

17.6   The Dark Side of Personality at Work

Over the past 15 to 20 years there has been a great interest in the relationship between what have been called the dark side traits and work failure rather than the bright side traits and work success.

Psychologists are interested in personality traits; psychiatrists in personality disorders. Psychologists interested in personality have made great strides in describing, taxonomizing and explaining the mechanisms and processes in normal personality functioning.

Both argue that the personality factors relate to how people think, feel and act. It is where a person's behaviour 'deviates, markedly' from the expectations of the individual's culture where the disorder is manifested. The psychiatric manual is very clear that 'odd behaviour' is not simply an expression of habits, customs, religious or political values professed or shown by a people of particular cultural origin.

Psychiatrists and psychologists share some simple assumptions with respect to personality. Both argue for the *stability* of personality. The DSM criteria talk of 'enduring pattern', 'inflexible and pervasive', 'stable and of long duration' (APA, 2001; 2014). The pattern of behaviour is not a function of drug usage or some other medical condition. The personality pattern furthermore is not a manifestation or consequence of another mental disorder.

The manuals are at lengths to point out that some of the personality disorders look like other disorders: anxiety, mood, psychotic, substance-related, etc., but have unique features. The essence of the argument is

> Personality Disorders must be distinguished from personality traits that do not reach the threshold for a Personality Disorder. Personality traits are diagnosed as a Personality Disorder only when they are inflexible, maladaptive, and persisting and cause significant functional impairment or subjective distress. (APA, 2000, p. 633)

One of the most important ways to differentiate personal style from personality disorder is flexibility. There are lots of difficult people at work but relatively few whose rigid, maladaptive behaviours mean they continually have disruptive, troubled lives. It is their inflexible, repetitive, poor stress-coping responses that are marks of disorder.

Personality disorders influence the *sense of self* – the way people think and feel about themselves and how other people see them. The disorders often powerfully influence interpersonal relations at work. The anti-social, obsessive-compulsive, passive-aggressive and dependent types are particularly problematic in the workplace. People with personality disorders have difficulty expressing and understanding emotions. It is the intensity with which they express them and their variability that make them odd. More importantly, they often have serious problems with self-control.

The most progress in this area occurred when the Hogans developed the Hogan Development Survey (HDS) (Hogan & Hogan, 1997). Their idea was to use the categories of the Personality Disorders but to conceive of 'dark side' tendencies rather than disorders. The test that is now widely used contains 168 true/false items that assess dysfunctional interpersonal themes. These dysfunctional dispositions reflect one's distorted beliefs about others that emerge when people encounter stress or stop considering how their actions affect others. Over time, these dispositions may become associated with a person's reputation and can impede job performance and career success. The HDS is not a medical or clinical assessment. It does not measure personality disorders, which are manifestations of mental disorder. Instead, the HDS assesses self-defeating expressions of normal personality. The DSM 5 makes this same distinction between behavioural traits and disorders – self-defeating behaviours, such as those predicted by the HDS, come and go, depending on the context. In contrast, personality disorders are enduring and pervasive across contexts. Table 17.3 compares the DSM IV criteria and the HDS.

The research in this area has revealed three consistent findings. The first is that paradoxically some of the dark side traits are implicated in (temporary and specific) management success. Thus, the 'naughtiness' of the anti-social mischievous type, the boldness and self-confidence of the arrogant narcissist; the colourful emotionality of the histrionic and the quirky imaginativeness of the schizotypal type may in fact help them climb up the organization. The second issue refers to the curvilinearity or optimality of these traits. That is, that at high levels these traits are nearly always 'dangerous' and associated with derailment and failure but at moderate levels they may even be beneficial. Third, some of these dark side traits are nearly always associated with lack of success at work. Thus Cautious/Avoidant and Reserved/Schizoid people rarely do very well at work except in highly technical jobs where they work on their own. Their low social skills and inability to charm and persuade others mean that they very rarely occupy positions of power and influence.

Table 17.3: The DSM IV and the HDS

DSM labels	PROFILE Theme	PROFILE Scale	HDS Theme	HDS Scale	Theme
Borderline	Inappropriate anger; unstable and intense relationships alternating between idealization and devaluation	Unstable Relationships	Flighty; inconsistent; forms intense albeit sudden enthusiasms and disenchantments for people or projects	Excitable	Moody and hard to please; intense, but short-lived enthusiasm for people, projects or things
Paranoid	Distrustful and suspicious of others; motives are interpreted as malevolent	Argumentative	Suspicious of others; sensitive to criticism; expects to be mistreated	Sceptical	Cynical, distrustful, and doubting others' true intentions
Avoidant	Social inhibition; feelings of inadequacy and hypersensitivity to criticism or rejection	Fear of Failure	Dread of being criticized or rejected; tends to be excessively cautious; unable to make decisions	Cautious	Reluctant to take risks for fear of being rejected or negatively evaluated
Schizoid	Emotional coldness and detachment from social relationships; indifferent to praise and criticism	Interpersonal Iinsensitivity	Aloof; cold; imperceptive; ignores social feedback	Reserved	Aloof, detached, and uncommunicative; lacking interest in or awareness of the feelings of others
Passive-Aggressive	Passive resistance to adequate social and occupational performance; irritated when asked to do something he/she does not want to	Passive-Aggressive	Sociable, but resists others through procrastination and stubbornness	Leisurely	Independent; ignoring people's requests and becoming irritated or argumentative if they persist
Narcissistic	Arrogant and haughty behaviour or attitudes; grandiose sense of self-importance and entitlement	Arrogance	Self-absorbed; typically loyal only to himself/ herself and his/her own best interests	Bold	Unusually self-confident; feelings of grandiosity and entitlement; overvaluation of one's capabilities

Antisocial	Disregard for the truth; impulsivity and failure to plan ahead; failure to conform with social norms	Untrustworthiness	Impulsive; dishonest; selfish; motivated by pleasure; ignoring the rights of others	Mischievous	Enjoying risk taking and testing limits; needing excitement; manipulative, deceitful, cunning and exploitative
Histrionic	Excessive emotionality and attention seeking; self-dramatizing, theatrical, and exaggerated emotional expression	Attention-seeking	Motivated by a need for attention and a desire to be in the spotlight	Colourful	Expressive, animated, and dramatic; wanting to be noticed and needing to be the centre of attention
Schizotypal	Odd beliefs or magical thinking; behaviour or speech that is odd, eccentric, or peculiar	No Common Sense	Unusual or eccentric attitudes; exhibits poor judgement relative to education and intelligence	Imaginative	Acting and thinking in creative and sometimes odd or unusual ways
Obsessive-Compulsive	Preoccupations with orderliness, rules, perfectionism, and control; over conscientious and inflexible	Perfectionism	Methodical; meticulous; attends so closely to details that he/she may have trouble with priorities	Diligent	Meticulous, precise, and perfectionistic; inflexible about rules and procedures; critical of others' performance
Dependent	Difficulty making everyday decisions without excessive advice and reassurance; difficulty expressing disagreement out of fear of loss of support or approval	Dependency	Demand for constant reassurance, support, and encouragement from others	Dutiful	Eager to please and reliant on others for support and guidance; reluctant to take independent action or go against popular opinion

17.7   Conclusion

To answer the question: Does it matter who you are at work? The answer is 'Profoundly yes, and a great deal'. In the workplace personality traits are *pro-active, re-active and evocative*. We know from vocational psychology that personality plays a large part in job selection. On the basis of our trait preferences we are attracted to different jobs in different organizations (Furnham & Palaiou, 2016). Further, personality traits play a big part in how we react to situations at work. Thus the identical situation may be thought of as fun for some people, challenging for others, and stressful for many. Third, personality traits have an evocative function: that is, they determine how people react to us. Thus extraverts are more sociable at work and neurotics more stressed and coworkers may be attracted to the outgoing and optimistic extravert while shunning the anxious and depressed neurotic.

However there are three important caveats that need to be considered. The first is that personality traits are but one factor determining behaviour at work. Other important factors such as ability and motivation are equally and sometimes more important in determining work outcomes than traits. Second, while nearly all researchers in this area have looked at the relative power of different traits, these tend to interact, which is more difficult to describe and explain. It is the total personality profile that needs to be taken into account to properly understand how personality factors work. Third, workplaces are dynamic and complex places and there are many different facets to a work outcome. Thus some personality traits might more strongly related to some work behaviours rather than others.

Further, it should never be forgotten that most people work in teams and are neither dependent nor independent at work but interdependent. Thus work outcomes are a function of group interaction and dynamics which is a part function of the personality of all the members.

Summary

There are lots of ways to describe who we are. We could do so in terms of our gender or ethnicity; our height and weight; our education and self-perceived ability. Most of us, however, describe ourselves and others in terms of our personality. 'He is an Extravert'; 'She is Neurotic'; 'I am very Conscientious'. A personality trait is a stable disposition, largely biologically based that influences our preferences both inside and outside the workplace. After years of disagreement psychologists have mostly accepted the Big Five model of personality. These dimensions are now well understood.

Work psychologists have spent a great deal of time trying to understand how these traits affect behaviour in the workplace. This is relevant to both the selection and management of people. The central question has been which traits are related to which work outcomes and how the process works. It has always been difficult to measure 'work success' and this has been done objectively and subjectively. The results suggest that three traits seem most important in predicting nearly all work outcomes: Conscientiousness (as it is related to hard work, being organized and reliable), Neuroticism (as it is related to anxiety, ill-health and worry) and Extraversion (as it is related to being optimistic, sociable and active).

There are some recent studies on the personality of 'high flyers' but perhaps the most innovative work in this area is on managerial derailment and how personality disorders, rather than traits, are indicative of behaviours that lead to business failure.

Discussion Points

1 What recommendations would you give to those who planned to use personality tests in selecting people at work?
2 What characteristics would you look for in a person who had recently applied for promotion?

Suggested Further Reading

Chamorro-Premuzic, T., & Furnham, A. (2010). *The psychology of personnel selection.* Cambridge: Cambridge University Press.

Furnham, A.(2015). *Backstabbers and bullies.* London: Bloomsbury.

Howard, P., & Howard, J. (2010). *The owner's manual for personality at work* (2nd ed.). Atlanta, GA: Bard Press.

Macrae, I., & Furnham, A. (2014). *High potential.* London: Bloomsbury.

References

American Psychiatric Association. (2000). *Diagnostic and statistical manual of mental disorders.* (4th ed. rev.). Washington, DC: APA.

American Psychiatric Association. (2014). *Diagnostic and statistical manual of mental disorders.* (5th ed.). Washington, DC: APA.

Cattell, R. (1971). *The scientific analysis of personality.* Hardmondsworth: Penguin.

Chamorro-Premuzic, T., Moutafi, J., & Furnham, A. (2005). The relationship between personality traits, subjectively-assessed and fluid intelligence. *Personality and Individual Differences, 38*(7), 1517–1528.

Costa, P., & McCrae, R. (1987). *Your NEO summary.* Odessa, FL: Psychological Assessment Resources.

DeYoung, C. G., Quilty, L. C., Peterson, J. B., & Gray, J. R. (2014). Openness to experience, intellect, and cognitive ability. *Journal of Personality Assessment, 96*(1), 46–52.

Eysenck, H. (1970). *The structure of human personality.* London: Methuen.

Gow, A. J., Whiteman, M. C., Pattie, A., & Deary, I. J. (2005). Goldberg's 'IPIP' Big-Five factor markers: Internal consistency and concurrent validation in Scotland. *Personality and Individual Differences, 39*(2), 317–329.

Furnham, A. (2008). *Personality and intelligence at work.* London: Routledge.

Furnham, A., & Cheng, H. (2015). Early indicators of adult trait Agreeableness. *Personality and Individual Differences, 73,* 67–71.

Furnham, A., & Palaiou, K. (2016). The dark side of the CEO. Unpublished paper.

Hogan, R., & Hogan, J. (1997). *Hogan development survey manual.* Tulsa: OK. Hogan Assessment Centers.

Macrae, I., & Furnham, A. (2014). *High potential.* London: Bloomsbury.

Schretlen, D. J., van der Hulst, E., Pearlson, G. D., & Gordon, B. (2010). A neuropsychological study of personality: trait openness in relation to intelligence, fluency, and executive functioning. *Journal of Clinical Experimental Neuropsychology, 32,* 1068–1073.

WHO (World Health Organization). (1992). *The ICD-10 classification of mental and behavioural disorders: Clinical descriptions and diagnostic guidelines.* Geneva: World Health Organization.

Ziegler, M., Danay, E., Heene, M., Asendorpf, J., & Bühner, M. (2012). Openness, fluid intelligence, and crystallized intelligence: Toward an integrative model. *Journal of Research in Personality, 46*(2), 173–183.

How Do I Learn What to Do? How the Science of Training Supports Learning

Amanda Woods, Julie Dinh and Eduardo Salas

18

Overview

Organizations bring together individuals of varying abilities and experiences, in the hopes of creating an effective and cohesive workforce. In order to create a common ground of understanding, it is critical to appreciate how individuals learn and how to best optimize this through training. This chapter is intended to give a broad overview of the organizational learning and training landscape. It will begin with foundational information, defining and providing theoretical facets of learning and training. We will then discuss the psychological antecedents of training – that is, processes that drive and influence learning – before moving into more practice-oriented aspects. The chapter will cover training content and delivery methods, particularly as they impact learning processes. In addition to understanding how training can be designed and implemented, it is also critical to understand its consequences and usefulness after the fact. We will conclude the chapter with a discussion on how individuals transfer what they have learned to the post-training world, as well as ways that organizations can assess the overall effectiveness of programmes. When implemented well, training establishes long-term learning, benefiting both the organization in terms of effectiveness and the individual through increased competency.

18.1   How Do I Learn What to Do?

Pitaya Inc. is a quickly growing (fictional) software company, determined to make the leap from mid-sized company to tech giant. Recently, they implemented a number of personnel changes in an effort to better utilize their workforce. Alexandra, an engineer, transferred from research & development to administration and management. Marcus, a young professional from a rival company, was hired to lead the customer success division. Gita, an older employee

An Introduction to Work and Organizational Psychology: An International Perspective,
Third Edition. Edited by Nik Chmiel, Franco Fraccaroli and Magnus Sverke.
© 2017 John Wiley & Sons, Ltd. Published 2017 by John Wiley & Sons, Ltd.

in the operations department, was promoted, moving from supporting small initiatives to managing large-scale projects. How can Pitaya teach each of these employees the *knowledge, skills, abilities,* and *other characteristics* (KSAOs) they need in their new roles? In order to identify how people learn best, we can refer to the vast body of knowledge on training, coaching and mentoring.

Training, coaching and mentoring have grown in popularity and practice as the workforce has grown and become more diverse and fluid. As such, organizations have poured substantial sums of money into training. According to a recent industry report by the American Society for Training and Development, organizations in the United States alone have spent upwards of $135 billion annually on employee training and development – an average of $1,208 per employee in 2013 (Miller, Ho, Frankel, Jones, & Bello, 2014). These dollars are spent across diverse industries, from industry (such as corporate project teams) to the military (e.g., special forces) and even to the stars (in space flight teams). Furthermore, this increasing public awareness has sparked a demand for more rigorous science on training in interdisciplinary fields, such as psychology, human resource management and human factors.

The booming industry of training has been driven forward by several trends, including globalization and advances in science and technology. In order to remain competitive in a global economy, organizations must ensure that their workforce continually learns and develops (Salas, Tannenbaum, Kraiger, & Smith-Jentsch, 2012). Furthermore, novel technology has made the world much smaller and training much stronger. Recent decades have seen the promulgation of learning systems such as distance learning, virtual reality training, computer-based training, intelligent tutoring systems, and Web-based trainings (Goldstein & Ford, 2001). The processes made possible by these novel platforms have pushed learning to new boundaries. Indeed, the growth of science and industry has revolutionized learning within organizations, resulting in robust academic and applied research.

18.2   Definitions and Theory

In order to fully comprehend the nuances and impact of learning and training, it is important to first establish definitions and clarify their relationship to one another. While the two concepts are related, they are not the same. Training, when successful, will produce learning – but, if ineffective, can fail to yield such outcomes. Furthermore, learning occurs in numerous contexts outside of the training (Salas et al., 2012). That said, learning and training, when studied side by side, can help boost understanding that is more than the sum of its parts.

18.2.1   Learning and training

Learning is the acquisition of new knowledge and skills as a result of practice, study, or experience. It involves relatively permanent changes, which can be measured through types of outcomes: cognitive outcomes, including enhanced knowledge and better mental models; behavioural outcomes, such as acquiring new skills or the honing of new ones; and affective outcomes, which could mean improved motivation and self-efficacy (Kraiger, Ford, & Salas, 1993; Salas et al., 2012). Learning is the desired result when designing and implementing a training program. Training is one of the many ways through which learning can be achieved. Training provides for the systematic acquisition of skills, rules, concepts or attitudes that result in improved performance in another environment (Goldstein & Ford, 2001). Such performance can be measured at the individual, team or organizational level.

In much the same way, training can also be driven by individual, social and situational factors. People bring their unique abilities and previous experiences to the table, which may influence the overall effectiveness of training programmes. For example, individual characteristics such as motivation and personality can determine how receptive trainees are to any particular programme. However, it is important to note that training never occurs in a vacuum, as it requires organizational initiative and trainer expertise. As such, social factors can have a great impact on the outcomes of training. Supportive work climates and formal and informal feedback can encourage trainees to retain learning long after training sessions have finished. Finally, contextual characteristics can shape training effectiveness enormously. To illustrate, organizations can vary in how many opportunities it offers its employees to use their KSAOs developed through training; this will, in turn, influence how much trainees retain their learning. This last point deserves special attention in that it touches upon the topic of training transfer.

As mentioned above, the objective of training should be to impart learning to its participants. However, learning is not helpful if it is only temporary or nongeneralizable. Training transfer is the extent to which learning during training is subsequently applied on the job or affects later job performance. In a practical sense, transfer is critical because, without it, an organization is not likely to receive any tangible benefits from its training investments (Salas et al., 2012). In this way, training does not simply involve the development and deployment of a programme, but the evaluation of its effectiveness well beyond the last training session.

Thus, effective training is not a one-time event, but a system. It is an iterative process, involving elements preceding the training as well as important factors after its delivery (Salas et al., 2012). The success of training revolves around learning outcomes, with the additional, critical goal of training transfer. Table 18.1 illustrates the stages of the training process discussed in the following sections of the chapter, beginning with needs analysis, followed by design considerations, which feed into training delivery, and finishes with training evaluation. It is important to note, however, that training alone is not a panacea. While training has been shown to be generally very effective, it must also be designed and implemented appropriately in light of the specific context

Table 18.1: Phases of the training process and guiding principles

Training phase	Guiding principle
Analyze training needs	Conduct due diligence
	Define performance requirements
	Define cognitive and affective states
	Define KSAO attributes
	Delineate learning objectives
Develop training content	Forge instructional experiences
Implement training	Set the stage for learning
	Deliver blended solution
	Support transfer and maintenance
Evaluate training	Execute evaluation plan
	Gauge trainee learning
	Gauge team learning
	Gauge organizational impact
	Disseminate training results

Source: Adapted from Salas and Stagl (2009).

(Salas et al., 2012). It would be unwise to simply implement training for 'training's sake' – rather, to truly maximize return on investment, organizations should understand their needs and constraints before hoping to maximize learning.

18.3   Analyzing Training Needs

When designing training, it is key to first understand the needs and resources of an organization. After all, what good is a training programme if it doesn't address the appropriate or target topic? Worse yet – what if the training is not necessary in the first place? Organizations should be optimizing their labour force when they implement training, not wasting resources on irrelevant development. To this end, experts in the field commonly recommend conducting a preliminary evaluation before any undertaking any training in earnest.

A *training needs assessment* (TNA) is an on-going process of gathering data to determine what training needs exist, which then helps design programmes to best help the organization accomplish its objectives (Brown, 2002). In order to make accurate and comprehensive conclusions, a successful TNA will carefully examine organizational goals, personnel, production, resources, and other factors. Box 18.1 describes the functions of an effective TNA, while Table 18.1 demonstrates the detailed considerations involved in a training needs analysis (Brown, 2002). This process of identifying training needs can also be organized into three different levels of analysis: organizational, task, and individual.

Box 18.1:   Functions of training needs assessments

1. Help identify specific problem areas in the organization.
2. Help obtain management support.
3. Develop data for evaluation.
4. Determine the costs and benefits of training.

Source: Brown (2002).

Organizational analysis focuses on where training is needed within the organization and under what conditions the training will be conducted (Brown, 2002). The examination of human resources data, such as hiring statistics and performance reviews, can help paint this 'big picture' of training needs. Importantly, this level of analysis also requires forecasting and anticipating how organizational aspects may change in the future (for example, how necessary skills, the labour pool, or laws and regulations might evolve over time). Other examples of these steps can be found under the 'conduct due diligence' guiding principle of the "analyze training needs" step in Table 18.1. Furthermore, developing organizational expectations can help set solid goals and create opportunities for learners to apply their new KSAOs in real-life environments. By understanding the short- and long-term goals of an organization, a needs assessment can address and set up conditions for optimal learning (Goldstein & Ford, 2001).

Job analysis (also known as task analysis) involves looking at specific roles, identifying job requirements and comparing employee KSAOs to determine training needs (Brown, 2002). By examining job descriptions and performance, we can determine gaps that would indicate a need for training. In addition to clarifying the responsibilities of an employee, a task analysis would also reveal aspects of the job such as working conditions, frequency of duties, and necessary resources. In Table 18.1, these characteristics are targeted by guiding principles 'define performance',' 'define cognitive and affective statements', and 'define KSAO attributes' within 'analyze training needs'. This step not only identifies the components and context of a job, but can also help obtain holistic, structural understanding – for example, which KSAOs are most critical to the job and at which point in the employee's tenure they should be learned. Without a thorough task analysis, it would not be possible for an organization to fully understand the concrete objectives of learning.

Individual analysis, the most microscopic of these analyses, occurs at the person level. It targets individual employees and how they perform in their jobs. Trainers often use information (criteria) from performance reviews or self-report measures to determine programme needs and help employees meet organizational standards. For example, examining progress reports from a classroom of students can help assess which necessary KSAOs have been learned, thereby reducing training time spent on redundant material. Once the training needs analysis understands the fine-grained needs of individuals within organizations, it can then properly 'delineate learning objectives' as listed in Table 18.1. The individual analysis is the most personal level of the needs analysis, as it directly addresses what and how unique individuals and groups learn.

Taken together, the stages of the training needs analysis helps us understand how to create an effective learning environment. It allows organizations to make the best use of their resources and ensures that trainees are guided towards meaningful and useful learning outcomes.

18.4 The Learning Climate

Moving on from the training needs analysis to the environment in which the training will occur, factors that comprise this environment should be considered. Needs identified through previous analyses cannot be addressed if workplace factors are not conducive to learning. Many variables make up the learning climate, also referred to in this chapter as the pre-training environment. Factors that combine to influence the pre-training environment are categorized broadly as either *individual characteristics* or *organizational characteristics*.

18.4.1   Individual characteristics

General mental ability, hereby referred to as individual cognitive ability, is a salient factor affecting the training processes; however, there are individual characteristics that stem from, or are influenced by, cognitive ability that affect training processes as well. As stated previously, individual cognitive ability, or g i.e. general intelligence) is a strong predictor of performance outcomes in many settings, and it is no different in the current context. Cognitive ability predicts how well a trainee can attain knowledge, and also positively affects trainee self-efficacy- another individual difference that can influence training performance (Salas & Cannon-Bowers, 2001). Self-efficacy, as it relates to training, is an individual characteristic that refers to how capable an individual feels they are at executing necessary actions to achieve training objectives. Self-efficacy enhances learning and performance, both in the form of trainee initial self-efficacy and self-efficacy gained during training (Stevens & Gist 1997). For example, it has been well established that if an individual has high self-efficacy, they are more likely to continue attending and remain actively engaged in the training programme. Participating in learning and adapting to challenges or setbacks in training is critical to the learning process, hence the implications for self-efficacy should be emphasized.

The propensity for an individual to approach a situation with a disposition towards setting goals that promote learning, in comparison to goals that focus solely on the appearance of competence (e.g. 'looking good'), can also influence learning. This goal-setting propensity is labelled *goal orientation*, separated into learning, also referred to as mastery, and performance goal orientation (Dweck, 1986). Individuals with a learning orientation strive to actively enhance their own learning (Fisher & Ford, 1998), and as such, are prime candidates for training. Surprisingly, learning-oriented trainees are often seen as exhibiting poor performance during training, but excel in areas of knowledge acquisition and retention as they are more open to making and learning from their mistakes (compared to performance-oriented individuals who attach a stigma to errors and negative evaluations).

As cognitive ability has been found to affect self-efficacy, motivation can also be influenced by individual characteristics, such as general intelligence level and self-efficacy (Colquitt et al., 2000), and organizational environmental factors (Salas & Cannon-Bowers, 2001). Training motivation can be thought of as individually expressed interest, intention, and exertion of effort towards actively participating in the training programme, and achieving learning-related training goals outlined by the programme. An individual's motivation to learn predicts the degree to which learning will occur as a result of the training programme (Baldwin Magjuka & Loher, 1991). Motivation can also influence how participants perceive the training. If an individual lacks motivation, they could perceive the training as useless or a waste of time; furthermore, behaviour resulting from this attitude can negatively influence other trainees. Conversely, highly motivated trainees can set a precedent in training, raising the bar regarding overall performance, while promoting overall positivity.

18.4.2 Organizational characteristics

The individual characteristics that can influence training tell only half of the story. The bigger picture of training contains both individual and organizational factors. Organizational characteristics are comprised of workplace factors and factors influenced by people (Lim & Morris, 2006). These influential aspects of training involve organizational support, autonomy level afforded to trainees, attendance requirements, and framing. The level of an organization's commitment and support of the training effort can also impact training effectiveness (Darden, Hampton, & Howell, 1989). Without organizational backing, training may never get off the ground or transfer may not occur, leading to an extreme waste of time and resources. Organizations should also allow individuals to set their own goals in an attempt to enhance the likelihood that knowledge gained during training will transfer to the work setting (Baumgartel, Sullivan, & Dunn, 1978). As we will discuss later in the chapter, the transfer of this knowledge is critical to achieving training-related goals and objectives. Whether a programme is either voluntary or mandatory is also an important factor to consider, with Baldwin and Magjuka (1997) contending that organizational characteristics such as this can influence motivation to learn. Though it has been widely demonstrated that trainees learn more when they choose to participate in training voluntarily, the issue of lack of participation ties the hands of organizations with regard to adopting this voluntary approach.

18.5   Design and Delivery Methods Impacting Learning

The needs analysis and organizational climate provide boundaries and constraints within which the training and subsequent learning will occur, and as such, instructional strategies must be adapted accordingly. Instructional strategies refer to how information targeting learning outcomes is designed and how it should be delivered. It is during the design and delivery phase of training that training competencies (i.e. knowledge, skill and attitudes) and organizational goals are systematically identified. Essentially, this phase of training development could be thought of as the 'blueprint' of the training programme. This blueprint must be theoretically grounded, drawing upon past research and theory that have been found to affect the training process with respect to the environmental constraints and organizational objectives. Fortunately, the science of training has developed a robust literary foundation concerning design and delivery of programmes aimed at the promotion of learning outcomes (Kraiger, 2003). Calling upon this literature, key themes and practices have emerged that span across many training domains.

18.5.1   Theoretical drivers

We must first consider the theories that tie into training techniques in the context of learning and knowledge acquisition. Various theories pertaining to the overall learning process have been previously discussed; however, theories that focus specifically on the learning environment and delivery methods warrant further discussion. Though a comprehensive examination of all theories informing the design and delivery process are beyond the scope of this chapter, central theories derived from the cognitive psychology, industrial and organizational psychology, and educational domains are discussed with the caveat that theoretical and empirical developments are not limited to these areas.

The realm of cognitive science promotes the organizational adoption of a 'learner-centered' perspective (Cooke & Fiore, 2010). This perspective dictates that training design and delivery should focus on how the trainees form knowledge structures, and what tools can enhance the development of these structures (Cooke & Fiore, 2010). Cooke and Fiore point out that, though a learner-based perspective is beneficial to understanding the process of knowledge acquisition, environmental factors should also be taken into consideration. In the same vein, Mayer (1989) highlights the development of knowledge structures ('mental models'), or the manner in which people organize and conceptualize knowledge, as a way of enhancing how a trainee interprets, processes, and recalls the information being delivered. Conceptual model usage has been found to influence how an individual processes information and subsequently performs on a given task (Bayman & Mayer, 1984).

Moving from cognition to behaviour, one of the most common behavioural theories pertaining to learning is Bandura's (1977) social learning theory, commonly considered when selecting instructional strategies. First, social learning theory contends that an individual exhibits certain behaviour based on: what they expect as a consequence of certain behaviour, how they can adapt their behaviour to achieve a desired outcome, and level of belief in their ability to exhibit this behaviour, these are referred to as 'expectancies'. Second, 'incentives' refer to the individual's perceptions or values attributed to the desired outcomes. This, again, supports the idea that learning strategies should place heavy importance on individual-level factors as they pertain to the learning process, since they have been found to significantly impact training programme effectiveness.

18.5.2 Active learning

Born out of these theories, specifically in regard to the learner-centred approach, the idea has emerged that trainees should play an active part in their own learning (Bell & Kozlowski, 2008). This notion of "active learning" has received a lot of attention and ties into the forging of instructional experiences in Table 18.1: promoting the development of instructional strategies that keep the individual engaged in the training (Salas & Stagl, 2009). Active learning differentiates itself from other learner-centred approaches by integrating formal training design elements into the learning process in an effort to influence and shape affective, behavioural, and cognitive processes relevant to knowledge and skill acquisition. This learning approach manifests itself in a variety of training techniques, including error management training, behavioural modelling training and self-regulatory training.

A good example of active learning can be seen in Keith and Frese's (2008) investigation into error-management training. The researchers adopted a meta-analytic approach to looking at the effectiveness of error management training and found that trainees who participated in error management training yielded better training outcomes compared to trainees who were encouraged to avoid making errors (Keith & Frese, 2008). This finding supports Noe and Colquitt's (2002) assertion that effective training programmes should encourage learners to make errors, and learn from them without fear of negative evaluation.

Another example of active learning comes in the form of behaviour modelling training (BMT), which is derived from Bandura's (1977) social learning theory discussed above. Taylor, Russ-Eft, and Chan (2005) describe BMT as the incorporation of all prescribed training characteristics, which include:

> (a) describing to trainees a set of well-defined behaviors (skills) to be learned, (b) providing a model or models displaying the effective use of those behaviors, (c) providing opportunities for trainees to practice using those behaviors, (d) providing feedback and social reinforcement to trainees following practice, and (e) taking steps to maximize the transfer of those behaviors to the job. (p. 692)

BMT is a classic example of all three types of delivery methods (e.g. information, demonstration, and practice) being used in the training programme. In a recent meta-analysis, Taylor and colleagues (2005) examined how BMT affects training outcomes, finding that the significant positive effect of BMT on learning-related outcomes was greater than the effect of BMT on job behaviour and work-related productivity. Their conclusion highlights the utility of BMT in the context of enhancing learning outcomes.

Finally, we will briefly touch on self-regulation as an important facet of training programmes in the context of learning. According to Salas et al., 'self-regulation refers to learner cognitions that help them sustain focused attention on learning through self-monitoring of performance, comparison of progress to an end goal, and adjustment of learning effort and strategy as appropriate' (2012, p. 87). Salas and colleagues (2012) assert that, due to the benefits of self-regulation as a tool for promoting learning outcomes coupled with the relative ease of implementation, trainers should attempt to integrate this process into the programme design. The promotion of self-regulatory processes during training has been found to enhance learners' procedural (e.g. how to perform certain tasks) and declarative knowledge (e.g. facts or information), effects that persisted over time after the training had concluded (Sitzmann, Bell, Kraiger, & Kanar, 2009). This process helps the individual focus on what they should be learning, reflect on their current progress and set goals that align with learning objectives.

18.5.3   Delivery methods

Because theoretical drivers and resulting active learning approaches address the design of training (i.e. content and learner-centred factors), we will examine how this content should be delivered. The delivery aspect of training can be seen under the *Implement Training* phase outlined by Salas and Stagl (2009) in Table 18.1, which highlights the methods of delivery, and supports the use of multiple methods as well as the importance of transfer, all of which will be discussed. There are three umbrella categories under which most delivery methods fall: information, demonstration and practice, followed by feedback (Kraiger & Culbertson, 2013; Noe & Colquitt, 2002). It is important to note that these methods are most commonly used in combination with one another, not as standalone strategies, and can even be thought of as more of a cyclical process (see Figure 18.1). These categories can also be thought of as stages, with informational components preceding the demonstration of training competencies that should in turn be supplemented with opportunities for the learner to practise newly learned KSAOs. During the informational stage, trainers should clearly convey the goals of the training programme as well as its utility in an effort to increase the learner's motivation upon entering the programme (Kraiger & Culbertson, 2013; Noe & Colquitt, 2002). It is also during this stage that programme content is delineated. The demonstration stage requires that trainers actively portray the competencies that need to be learned. It has been found that learning aids are particularly helpful if administered during this stage of training (Salas & Stagl, 2009). Finally, learners should be provided with opportunities to practise in a psychologically safe setting that encourages the exploration of these KSAOs in such a way that they can make and

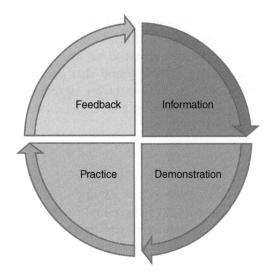

Figure 18.1:   The training delivery cycle

learn from their mistakes (Keith & Frese, 2008; Kraiger & Culbertson, 2013). So far the theories and delivery methods that comprise effective training programmes have been outlined; next, we elucidate how these factors are synthesized to form actual training characteristics and approaches to learning.

18.5.4   Feedback

So far the first three stages of this cycle discuss the stage at which individuals receive *information*, then watch as it is *demonstrated* to them, and subsequently *practise*; now the role of feedback in this processes will be delineated. Feedback should be considered a key element in any training programme, as it enables individuals to learn from their mistakes and make plans for the future (Salas & Cannon-Bowers, 2001). Feedback comes into play after individuals have been given the opportunity to practise learned KSAOs. This information on their performance helps further the trainees' understanding of how well they have performed. Taking a finer lens to design and delivery considerations, there are many factors that should be taken into account regarding feedback. One must look at the constraints of the learning environment, when feedback should be delivered, and its content. When feedback is accurate, developmental, specific, and delivered at the appropriate time in the appropriate quantity, then feedback can significantly bolster the learning process.

   After Action Reviews (AARs) are a prime example of a widely used feedback delivery tool that has been employed across many military and organizational settings. AARs allow learners to reflect upon their performance, and the outcome that occurred as a result of that performance, and have been shown to enhance performance (Villado & Arthur, 2013). This finding is further supported by recent meta-analytic efforts revealing that debriefs, which can also be referred to as AARs, were found to increase effectiveness in the context of teams by 25% (Tannenbaum & Cerasoli, 2013). From the behavioural modelling approach, Smith-Jentsch, Salas, and Baker (1996) found that performance feedback and practice enhanced behavioural outcomes that were targeted during training. This leads into another component pertaining to instructional strategies that merits further attention, practice.

18.5.5   Technology

We have already touched on various types of training such as self-regulatory training, error management training, and behavioural modelling training; however, there are other large bodies of literature surrounding the specific use of technology in training. The use of technology as a tool in the learning environment is rapidly increasing, and research has followed this movement closely. With the growing use and availability of technology, trainers and educators have attempted to capitalize on this movement by integrating technological elements into existing training programmes, as well as creating entirely new programmes delivered on web-based platforms that can be accessed through computers, tablets and smart phone devices. The primary aim of technological integration is to reduce long-term costs associated with staffing, facilitating, and conducting training (Kraiger & Culbertson, 2013). Another benefit to technology-enhanced delivery methods is the ability for many systems to generate immediate, objective feedback, which is a critical component to feedback effectiveness (Bedwell & Salas, 2010). Computer-based training methods have demonstrated the ability to successfully educate individuals, regardless of the level of prior computer experience. This is promising in that it addresses the concern of usability, or 'ease of use', as it applies to the general population containing varying levels of technological expertise. Though research has yet to arrive at a definitive conclusion in regard to which method is better, instructor-led or technology-delivered instruction, the benefits to incorporating the use of technology should not be ignored because at the very least they add another tool to the belt of trainers. Beyond this, future research may demonstrate circumstances under which technology outperforms traditional instructor-led courses. Though this avenue has not yet proven to be a fruitful endeavour (Sitzmann, Kraiger, Stewart, & Wisher, 2006), many technological tools are still in their nascent stages of development.

18.5.6   Simulation-based training

Simulation-Based Training (SBT) refers to the creation of a simulated environment, mimicking the real-world setting in which the trained KSA will need to be used, to teach targeted competencies (Baldwin, 1992; Salas, Wilson, Burke, & Priest, 2006). During these training exercises, the learner is able to practise using the information learned, and receive immediate feedback on his or her performance

(Oser, Cannon-Bowers, Salas, & Dwyer, 1999; Salas et al., 2006). These simulations do not necessarily have to be highly technologically based, simulations can adhere to varying levels of fidelity. They can range from simple role play and paper-based scenarios to high fidelity technologically enhanced training environments, such as surgical simulators used in the medical field to simulate (e.g., different scenarios in the operating room). The main aspect of fidelity that has been shown to influence training effectiveness is *psychological fidelity*, or better put, how relevant the material in the simulation is to the setting in which the learner will need to apply the information. This highlights the importance of training content, as it fits into the larger picture of programme design. Here we also see again the impact of feedback and practice on the learning process.

18.5.7   Team training

Team training has come to the forefront in the past three decades as a viable option to address many training needs in organizational, scholastic and military settings. Teams are defined as a group consisting of two or more members who are united under a common goal, and who must interact with one another through the completion of interdependent tasks in order to achieve a certain set of objectives (Salas & Cannon-Bowers, 2000; see also Chapter 12 in this volume). The use of teams can be seen in classroom settings with a larger emphasis being placed on group work, they can also be seen with increasing frequency in organizations facing the need to adapt and manage complex problems that require collaborative solutions. When looking at training design and delivery, factoring in team-level dynamics only adds another layer of complexity to the mix. Now not only do individual characteristics such as personality traits, cognitive ability and past experience need to be factored in, but trainers must consider the processes and emergent states resulting from team-level attitudes, behaviours and cognitions (Salas & Cannon-Bowers, 2000). A popular example of a team training strategy is Team Coordination Training, also known as Crew Resource Management (CRM), and Team Coordination and Adaptation Training (TACT), which is the most widely utilized form of team training (Salas & Cannon-Bowers, 2000).

18.6   Transfer

The primary goal of training is to ensure knowledge/skills being learned are transferred beyond the training environment because in the end, the purpose behind learning is to develop information that is deemed important to the learner's subsequent development and competence. Hence, the inclusion of transfer and maintenance (e.g. maintaining learned content over time) as a final consideration under the implementation phase (see Table 18.1). The importance of learner development and retention of KSAOs is why an abundance of transfer literature focuses on learning outcomes (Blume, Ford, Baldwin, & Huang,

2010; Colquitt, LePine, & Noe, 2000). Learning transfer can be heavily influenced by the learning climate. The aforementioned learning climate affects the learning process because after training has taken place, events that occur subsequently determine how successfully trained competencies transfer back into the post-training environment. The definition of transfer is dependent upon context, in the training sense, transfer refers to the ability for the learner to apply their trained attitudes, skills, or knowledge to their job setting (Baldwin & Ford, 1988; Wexley & Baldwin, 1986). Training transfer can be thought of as an extension of learning transfer, in that it not only takes into account learning that occurs during training, but also factors in subsequent performance outcomes. Since the science of training has informed best practices applicable across many domains, including the learning environment (Salas et al., 2012), we will now expound upon transfer from the training perspective.

Baldwin and Ford's (1988) model of training transfer is one of the most commonly used models in the training literature. This model analyzes the impact that trainee characteristics, training design and delivery, and organizational environment has on facilitating learning, and the generalization and maintenance of trained competencies over time after training (Baldwin & Ford, 1988). The main factors that impact training transfer are organizational support, transfer climate and situational constraints (Kraiger, 2003). Organizational support refers to how the organization facilitates and rewards behavioural, attitudinal or cognitive changes that result from training. The extent to which trainees think they are able to apply trained skills to the work environment, and receive support from their peers and supervisors are all aspects that pertain to the transfer climate. Situational constraints do not encompass an individual's perceptions, and are slightly more granular than organizational context. Situational constraints relate to objective peer and supervisor support as well as opportunities to practise. Within the context of this model, specific factors pertaining to the learning environment and training content that should be considered when looking at training transfer have been identified, that shape transfer effectiveness. Baldwin and Ford (1988) explain how the probability of successful transfer is a function of fidelity, such that when the training environment is closely translatable to the work or real-world environment, then transfer is more likely to occur. Learning outcomes have also been known to impact this element of training. Specifically, the relationship between training transfer and characteristics of the learner was stronger in situations where the goals of training centred on the retention and transfer of learning concepts (Blume, Ford, Baldwin, & Huang, 2010).

18.7 Evaluation

In order to determine the overall effectiveness of the training programme, training must be systematically evaluated (Kraiger, Ford, & Salas, 1993). This leads to an important question, followed by a series of questions put forward by

Goldstein and Ford (2001); the overall question being how do we know if a training programme is effective? The first question that addresses this is if the trainees' subsequent performance is a result of the training programme. Essentially, can improvements in performance or behaviour be tied directly back to what was taught during training, or could this improvement be the result of some external factor? Another question pertains to how generalizable the training programme is, so it begs the question, if another person were put through the same training programme, would it be just as effective? These are just a few examples, but when put together, these questions provide a clear answer to how effective the training programme was overall.

As stated before, there is a need to be systematic about the evaluation process. This need for a methodological approach paved the way for Kirkpatrick's (1959) four-level model of training evaluation, which remains the most popular training evaluation model to this day, and is the backbone for the final training phase, the *Evaluation of Training* phase, and corresponding guiding principles (see Table 18.1). This four-level model includes, in order: (1) Reactions, (2) Learning, (3) Behaviour, and (4) Results of the training programme (see Figure 18.2). Reactions capture trainee perceptions of the training programme (Kirkpatrick & Kirkpatrick, 2005). Learning is assessed through measuring how much knowledge enhancement has taken place during training (Kirkpatrick & Kirkpatrick, 2005). This is commonly captured through administering knowledge tests that assess trainees' retention of the course material. We have already discussed behaviour at length, known by its other name, transfer. The third level of Kirkpatrick's model closely aligns with one of the questions put forward by Goldstein and Ford (2001), and determines how much behaviour that occurs in the post-training environment is attributable to the training programme. Results refer to broader organizational objectives such as reductions in turnover, higher levels of retention, or increased productivity (Kirkpatrick & Kirkpatrick, 2005). Sometimes it can be challenging to assess the fourth level because it is so broad, attributing the results of a training programme to overall sales, for example, can be confounded by external factors such as the current state of the economy.

Evaluating training programme effectiveness allows trainers and organizations to take a step back and look at strengths and weaknesses of the programme objectively. From this, it can be determined if a training programme should continue to be used, if revisions are needed, or if it is no longer useful. Due to the costly nature of training, in the form of development and implementation, evaluation is extremely important from an economic standpoint.

Figure 18.2:   The four levels of training evaluation
Source: Kirkpatrick (1959).

18.8   Conclusion

While we have spoken about training at the individual, team and organizational levels, it is important to recognize its contributions to larger societal issues. By examining and applying training and development strategies, we can help improve worker and public safety; for example, more effective programmes can produce higher-performing first responders, clinicians, and vehicle drivers and airplane pilots. Indeed, academia and industry have invested in training exactly because of its potential to improve functioning, both horizontally and vertically. Today, the training literature continues to grow exponentially, both through empirical science and theoretically-based modelling. Recalling the example provided at the beginning of this chapter, we can conclude that organizations may consult a robust body of work to help facilitate learning through appropriate, innovative and effective training.

Summary

An effective organization will understand that they must support the continual learning of their workforce, as proper training can yield more effectiveness and cohesion overall. In order to maximize these outcomes, organizations should first analyze and understand their needs and target them through design. However, training as a whole is only as strong as its constituent parts. Elements of design and delivery must be derived from theory and tailored to suit both individual differences and organizational objectives. Moreover, training should yield opportunities to practise the trained competencies and receive specific, immediate feedback on performance. The role of the learner as an active agent in their own learning process has remained a common thread connecting all aspects of training development; however, the onus ultimately falls on the trainer, coach or mentor to ensure that they are setting up the trainee for success (that is, through selecting training tools and delivery methods that promote optimal learning outcomes). Furthermore, the use of computer-based instructional strategies has shown promise, and arrives at an opportune time when technology is rapidly advancing learning and training environments. As the use of teams increases, many training programmes will also need to adopt a multilevel approach to enhancing KSAO acquisition. Fortunately, organizational science has made great strides towards identifying best practices for training design and delivery, supported by theory and tested empirically. In both the laboratory and the field, researchers and practitioners are recognizing and responding to the pivotal role that learning can play in organizations.

Discussion Points

1 What are the consequences of not conducting a thorough training needs analysis?
2 How can society benefit from the investment of organizations in learning and training?

Acknowledgements

This work was supported in part by contract NNX16AB08G with the National Aeronautics and Space Administration (NASA) to Rice University, Texas. The views expressed in this work are those of the authors and do not necessarily reflect the organizations with which they are affiliated or their sponsoring institutions or agencies.

Suggested Further Reading

Aguinis, H., & Kraiger, K. (2009). Benefits of training and development for individuals and teams, organizations, and society. *Annual Review of Psychology, 52,* 451–474. This journal article provides a comprehensive overview of the current state of training in organizations, summarizing research between 2000 and 2009.

Goldstein, I. L., & Ford, J. K. (2001). *Training in organizations* (4th ed.). Belmont, CA: Wadsworth. This handbook is a valuable resource containing all aspects pertaining to training, intended to reach a wide audience with a vested interest in expanding their knowledge of the training process in the workplace.

Kraiger, K., & Culbertson, S. S. (2013). Understanding and facilitating learning: Advancements in training and development. In *Handbook of psychology*, vol. 12 (pp. 244–261).

Wiley Online Library. This chapter describes various other learning theories that were beyond the scope of the current chapter as well as further expounds on theories presently discussed. The chapter also aids in drawing the connection between training and learning in the workplace.

Salas, E., & Stagl, K. C. (2009). Design training systematically and follow the science of training. In E. A. Locke (Ed.), *Handbook of principles of organizational behavior: indispensable knowledge for evidence-based management,* (2nd ed.) (pp. 59–84). Chichester: John Wiley & Sons, Ltd. To further understand the science behind training in the context of organizations, we recommend this source as it provides an expanded view of training phases, by supplementing the included principles with corresponding guidelines.

References

Aguinis, H., & Kraiger, K. (2009). Benefits of training and development for individuals and teams, organizations, and society. *Annual Review of Psychology, 60,* 451–474.

Baldwin, M. W. (1992). Relational schemas and the processing of social information. *Psychological Bulletin, 112*(3), 461.

Baldwin, T. T., & Ford, J. K. (1988). Transfer of training: A review and directions for future research. *Personnel Psychology, 41*(1), 63–105.

Baldwin, T. T., & Magjuka, R. J. (1997). Training as an organizational episode: Pretraining influences on trainee motivation. In K. Ford and Associates (Eds.), *Improving training effectiveness in work organizations* (pp. 99–127). LEA.

Baldwin, T. T., Magjuka, R. J., & Loher, B. T. (1991). The perils of participation: Effects of choice of training on trainee motivation and learning. *Personnel Psychology, 44*(1), 51–65.

Bandura, A. 1977. *Social learning theory.* Englewood Cliffs, NJ: Prentice-Hall.

Baumgartel, H., Sullivan, G. J., & Dunn, L. E. (1978). How organizational climate and personality affect the pay-off from advanced management training sessions. *Kansas Business Review, 5,* 1–10.

Bayman, P., & Mayer, R. E. (1984). Instructional manipulation of users' mental models for electronic calculators. *International Journal of Man-Machine Studies, 20*(2), 189–199.

Bedwell, W. L., & Salas, E. (2010). Computer-based training: capitalizing on lessons learned. *International Journal of Training and Development, 14*(3), 239–249.

Bell, B. S., & Kozlowski, S. W. J. (2008). Active learning: Effects of core training design elements on self-regulatory processes, learning, and adaptability. *Journal of Applied Psychology, 93*, 296–316.

Blume, B. D., Ford, J. K., Baldwin, T. T., & Huang, J. L. (2010). Transfer of training: A meta-analytic review. *Journal of Management, 36*(4), 1065–1105.

Brown, J. (2002). Training needs assessment: A must for developing an effective training program. *Public Personnel Management, 31*(4), 569–578.

Chen, G., Gully, S. M., Whiteman, J. A., & Kilcullen, R. N. (2000). Examination of relationships among trait-like individual differences, state-like individual differences, and learning performance. *Journal of Applied Psychology, 85*(6), 835.

Colquitt, J. A., LePine, J. A., & Noe, R. A. (2000). Toward an integrative theory of training motivation: A meta-analytic path analysis of 20 years of research. *Journal of Applied Psychology, 85*(5), 678.

Cooke, N. J., & Fiore, S. M. (2010). Cognitive science-based principles for the design and delivery of training. In S. W. J Kozlowski and E. Salas (Eds.), *Learning, training, and development in organizations* (pp. 169–201). New York: Routledge.

Darden. W. R., Hampton. R., & Howell, R. D. (1989). Career versus organizational commitment: Antecedents and consequences of retail salespeople's commitment. *Journal of Retailing, 65*, 80–105.

Dweck, C. S. (1986). Motivational processes affecting learning. *American Psychologist, 41*(10), 1040.

Fisher, S. L., & Ford, J. K. (1998). Differential effects of learner effort and goal orientation on two learning outcomes. *Personnel Psychology, 51*(2), 397–420.

Ford, J. K., Quiñones, M. A., Sego, D. J., & Sorra, J. S. (1992). Factors affecting the opportunity to perform trained tasks on the job. *Personnel Psychology, 45*(3), 511–527.

Goldstein, I. L., & Ford, J. K. (2001).The criterion choices: Introduction to the evaluation process. In *Training in organizations* (4th ed.). Belmont, CA: Wadsworth.

Hunter, J. E. (1986). Cognitive ability, cognitive aptitudes, job knowledge, and job performance. *Journal of Vocational Behavior, 29*(3), 340–362.

Keith, N., & Frese, M. (2008). Effectiveness of error management training: A meta-analysis. *Journal of Applied Psychology, 93*, 59–69.

Kirkpatrick, D. L. (1959). Techniques for evaluating training programs. *Journal of the American Society of Training Directors, 13*, 3–9, 21–26; *14,* 13–18, 28–32

Kirkpatrick, D. L., & Kirkpatrick, J. (2005). *Transferring learning to behavior: Using the four levels to improve performance.* Oakland, CA: Berrett-Koehler Publishers.

Klein, H. J., Noe, R. A., & Wang, C. (2006). Motivation to learn and course outcomes: The impact of delivery mode, learning goal orientation, and perceived barriers and enablers. *Personnel Psychology, 59*(3), 665–702.

Kraiger, K. (2003). Perspectives on training and development. *Handbook of Psychology.* Wiley Online Library.

Kraiger, K., & Culbertson, S. S. (2013). Understanding and facilitating learning: Advancements in training and development. *Handbook of Psychology*, vol. 12. (pp. 244–261). Wiley Online Library.

Kraiger, K., Ford, J. K., & Salas, E. (1993). Applications of cognitive, skill-based, and affective theories of learning outcomes to new methods of training evaluation. *Journal of Applied Psychology, 78*(2), 311–328.

Lim, D. H., & Morris, M. L. (2006). Influence of trainee characteristics, instructional satisfaction, and organizational climate on perceived learning and training transfer. *Human Resource Development Quarterly, 17*(1), 85–115.

Mayer, R. E. (1989). Models for understanding. *Review of Educational Research, 59*(1), 43–64.

Miller, L., Ho, M., Frankel, D., Jones, M., & Bello, B. (2014). *2014 State of the Industry.* Alexandria, VA: American Society for Training and Development.

Noe, R. A., & Colquitt, J. A. (2002). Planning for training impact: Principles of training effectiveness. In K. Kraiger (Ed.), *Creating, implementing, and managing effective training and development* (pp. 53–79). San Francisco: Jossey-Bass.

Oser, R. L., Cannon-Bowers, J. A., Salas, E., & Dwyer, D. J. (1999). Enhancing human performance in technology-rich environments: Guidelines for scenario-based training. *Human Technology Interaction in Complex Systems, 9,* 175–202.

Salas, E., & Cannon-Bowers, J. A. (2000). The anatomy of team training. In L. Tobias & D. Fletcher (Eds.), *Training and retraining: A handbook for business, industry, government, and the military* (pp. 312–335). New York: Macmillan.

Salas, E., & Cannon-Bowers, J. A. (2001). The science of training: A decade of progress. *Annual Review of Psychology, 52*(1), 471–499.

Salas, E., & Stagl, K. C. (2009). Design training systematically and follow the science of training. In E. A. Locke (Ed.), *Handbook of principles of organizational behavior: indispensable knowledge for evidence-based management,* (2nd ed.) (pp. 59–84). Chichester: John Wiley & Sons, Ltd.

Salas, E., Tannenbaum, S. I., Kraiger, K., & Smith-Jentsch, K. A. (2012). The science of training and development in organizations: What matters in practice. *Psychological Science in The Public Interest, 13*(2), 74–101.

Salas, E., Wilson, K. A., Burke, S., & Priest, H. A. (2006). What is simulation-based training? *Forum, 24*(2), 12.

Sitzmann, T., Bell, B. S., Kraiger, K., & Kanar, A. M. (2009). A multilevel analysis of the effect of prompting self-regulation in technology-delivered instruction. *Personnel Psychology, 62,* 697–734.

Sitzmann, T., Kraiger, K., Stewart, D., & Wisher, R. (2006). The comparative effectiveness of web-based and classroom instruction: A meta-analysis. *Personnel Psychology, 59*(3), 623–664.

Smith-Jentsch, K. A., Salas, E., & Baker, D. P. (1996). Training team performance-related assertiveness. *Personnel Psychology, 49,* 909–936.

Stevens, C. K., & Gist, M. E. (1997). Effects of self-efficacy and goal-orientation training on negotiation skill maintenance: What are the mechanisms?. *Personnel Psychology, 50*(4), 955–978.

Tannenbaum, S. I., & Cerasoli, C. P. (2013). Do team and individual debriefs enhance performance? A meta-analysis. *Human Factors: The Journal of the Human Factors and Ergonomics Society, 55*(1), 231–245.

Taylor, P. J., Russ-Eft, D. F., & Chan, D. W. (2005). A meta-analytic review of behavior modeling training. *Journal of Applied Psychology, 90*(4), 692.

Villado, A. J., & Arthur Jr, W. (2013). The comparative effect of subjective and objective after-action reviews on team performance on a complex task. *Journal of Applied Psychology, 98*(3), 514.

Warr, P., & Bunce, D. (1995). Trainee characteristics and the outcomes of open learning. *Personnel Psychology, 48*(2), 347–375.

Wexley, K. N., & Baldwin, T. T. (1986). Post-training strategies for facilitating positive transfer: An empirical exploration. *Academy of Management Journal, 29*(3), 503–520.

19 How Much Effort Will I Put into My Work? It Depends on Your Type of Motivation

Anja Van den Broeck, Joseph Carpini, Hannes Leroy and James M. Diefendorff

Overview

Why do some employees put a lot of effort into their job, while others don't? Several motivational theories have shed light on this issue, resulting in a vast literature of diverging theories, all of which propose various determinants of employee motivation. Classical theories include reinforcement theory, Maslow's need hierarchy, expectancy–value theory, and goal setting theory. Recently, self-determination theory (SDT) has been introduced in the field of work motivation, and provides an encompassing framework to understand the (proximal and distal) personal and situational influences of motivation. SDT starts from a positive perspective on people and proposes that employees put the most effort in their job when they are satisfied in their needs for autonomy, competence and relatedness. The level of need satisfaction experienced on the job relates to the way that individuals feel motivated to perform their work, ranging from intrinsic motivation, on the one hand, (which is the most autonomous form of motivation) to extrinsic motivation, on the other, (which is the most controlled form of motivation). It also relates to one's intrinsic and extrinsic values. After describing the classical views on motivation, this chapter presents each of the personal influences of motivation, and describes their relation with work effort and other outcomes, as well as their situational antecedents. Building on SDT, this chapter provides an overview of various motivational factors that stimulate employees to put effort into the job.

19.1 Introduction

Sara drags herself to work. She hardly takes any initiative and really only works for the money. She picks up her 'real life' every evening and weekend. At work, she has to be directed from one task to another and must be closely supervised. Doing the

An Introduction to Work and Organizational Psychology: An International Perspective,
Third Edition. Edited by Nik Chmiel, Franco Fraccaroli and Magnus Sverke.
© 2017 John Wiley & Sons, Ltd. Published 2017 by John Wiley & Sons, Ltd.

bare minimum to make sure she doesn't get fired, she doesn't put a lot of effort into her work and feels drained at the end of the day. David, on the other hand, is highly energized, consistently trying to do his best. He often seeks new challenges and goes the extra mile in new projects. David's performance exceeds not only his supervisor's expectations but also his own goals.

Sara and David clearly differ in how much effort they put into their work, but how can such differences be explained? Motivational psychologists contend that people put effort in their work (or work hard) when they have the motivation to do so, that is, when they have the energy that directs their behaviour and determines its form, direction, intensity and duration (Pinder, 2008, p.11). Throughout the years, work motivation has been studied from various perspectives. Influential frameworks to understand motivation in the context of work include reinforcement theory (Thorndike, 1911; Skinner, 1969), Maslow's need hierarchy (Maslow, 1943), expectancy–value theory (Vroom, 1964), the theory of planned behaviour (Ajzen, 1991), as well as goal setting theory (Locke & Latham, 1990), to name a few. We elaborate on some of these theories next (see Ambrose & Kulik, 1999 for an overview).

19.2 Classical Motivational Theories

19.2.1 Reinforcement theory

Throughout history, motivation has been approached from different perspectives by practitioners and scholars alike. One of the oldest perspectives on motivation is reinforcement theory, which is grounded in the behaviourist tradition (Thorndike, 1911; Skinner, 1969). Rather than focusing on people's internal states, reinforcement theory focuses on the idea that people's behaviour is determined by its consequences, with rewards increasing the likelihood of a behaviour and punishment decreasing the likelihood of a behaviour. In an organizational context, reinforcement theory could be used to modify behaviour by rewarding individuals for engaging in desirable behaviour and punishing them for engaging in undesirable behaviour. Over time, this would produce more desired behaviour and fewer undesired behaviour. For example, David may receive a bonus for his exceptional effort on a project, while Sara could be reprimanded for checking Facebook during office hours. In both instances, the consequences attached to these behaviours will impact the likelihood of the behaviour being repeated in the future. Reinforcement theory is still valuable in understanding the impact of different pay schemes, such as pay for performance, piece rate and profit-sharing (Fall & Roussel, 2014).

19.2.2 Maslow's need theories

Although reinforcement theory remains popular in many organizations, scholars such as Maslow (1943) have criticized reinforcement theory, arguing that not all rewards (or punishments) would have the same effect on all employees. Maslow contended the effect of rewards and punishments would depend on the degree to which the rewards and punishments influenced employees' current needs. Specifically, Maslow theorized five hierarchical needs: (1) physiological needs (e.g., hunger, thirst, air), (2) safety needs (safe and predictable environment, free of illness), (3) belongingness and love (e.g., interaction and affection from others), (4) esteem (stable high self-esteem and esteem from others), and (5) self-actualization, the growth need where one 'becomes everything one is capable of becoming'. Maslow's theory of inherent needs brought the importance of needs – and psychological processes in general – to the attention of organizational researchers and managers as a source of motivation in workers and raised awareness of other need theories, such as the socialized needs for achievement, power and affiliation (McClelland, 1965; Murray, 1938).

Empirical research shows that the satisfaction of all Maslow's theorized needs contributes to people's well-being (Tay & Diener, 2011) and Maslow's argument that the general work environment needs to be tailored to satisfy employees' needs is currently reflected in the literature on idiosyncratic deals, in which employees negotiate for more flexibility, developmental opportunities or better working conditions to satisfy their needs (Rousseau, 2001). Although these further developments of Maslow's theory are fruitful and Maslow's hierarchy of needs itself has received some empirical support, many of the tenets of Maslow's theory remain unsupported by empirical evidence and thus should not be leveraged as part of evidence-based organizational practices.

Maslow's theory also gave rise to the differentiation between Theory X and Y by McGregor (1960), which represent two different points of view on employees that managers may hold. Theory Y argues that employees are motivated by Maslow's growth need of self-actualization and want to work, develop their talents and take responsibility. This contrasts with Theory X stating that employees are only motivated by Maslow's lower order needs, are lazy and will engage in work only when they are closely monitored, controlled and rewarded. Notably, when taking the latter perspective, managers assume that employees likely want to do nothing at all and need to be directed around, as is the case for Sara in our opening example. Although such an approach may cause employees to move, true motivation will still be lacking. For employees to be truly motivated – that is, to be energetic, directed towards a goal and persistent – managers need to adopt a Theory Y perspective, in which employees are assumed to be inherently energetic. From a Theory Y perspective, managers only need to nourish and channel the inherent energy employees have so that the employee can direct themselves and persist, for example, in putting effort into their work. When managers assume all employees are like David, they just have to make sure to provide their employees with enough variation and challenges. The differentiation between Theory X and Y shows that managers' view on motivation causes them to rely on different motivation theories and managerial practices.

19.2.3 Expectancy–value theory

In contrast to Maslow's needs hierarchy, expectancy–value theory (Vroom, 1964) reflects a cognitive decision-making process in which motivation for an activity (and perhaps a job) is a result of the evaluation of extent to which (1) exerting effort will result in a particular level of performance (expectancy), (2) performing the activity will lead to valued outcomes (instrumentality), and (3) the outcomes associated with an activity are desirable (valence). The combination of these three factors produces the overall motivational force for the activity. When deciding what task to pursue (or perhaps the level of performance for which one should strive), individuals are theorized to choose the option with the highest motivational force. For example, David may choose to engage in additional projects because he feels competent in taking charge (expectancy) and is convinced doing well on these projects will help him obtain a promotion (instrumentality), which is something that he greatly values (valence). Expectancy–value theory has received some support, but is generally better in predicting employees' attitudes than their performance (Van Eerde & Thierry, 1996).

Elements of expectancy–value theory have been incorporated into the theory of planned behaviour (Ajzen, 1991), which added the social context as an important determinant of individual motivation. The theory of planned behaviour suggests that perceived behavioural control (similar to expectancy) and attitude (similar to valence) towards a particular behaviour are important in determining motivation, but the social context (social norms or what others will think) will also play a role. Moreover, these factors are expected to predict behavioural intentions, which have the most proximal connection to actual behaviour. For example, David may see himself as capable of taking on additional projects (perceived behavioural control) and see it as valuable to develop his leadership skills (attitude); however, his intention to engage in additional projects may – to some degree – also depend on whether or not he thinks his coworkers or boss are likely to appreciate it (social context). Although incorporating social norms is conceptually useful, research suggests that this factor may be the least important antecedent (Armitage & Conner, 2001).

19.2.4 Goal setting theory

Goal setting theory is among the most well-known theories of employee motivation (see Chapter 4 in this volume). Hundreds of studies have been conducted in support of this theory, showing that difficult, specific goals that are accepted by employees result in better performance than easy or 'do your best' goals (Locke & Latham, 2002). Goal specificity is beneficial because individuals know precisely what is expected of them, making subsequent feedback about one's performance more meaningful. Goal difficulty is a function of goal level and the experience or capabilities of the employees. As such, it is important for managers to understand how to appropriately calibrate individuals' goals so that they are not too difficult (resulting in low commitment or low acceptance) but not too easy (resulting in the employee not reaching his/her potential). Another thing to consider is the ways in which managers can foster employee goal acceptance and commitment. One way to foster commitment is to engage in participative goal setting, which is when the manager and employee jointly determine the goals that an employee will pursue. Having a say in one's goals has been shown to lead employees to feel more ownership for the goals and be more likely to strongly commit to pursuing them (Locke & Latham, 2002).

Goal setting theory has led to management practices such as management by objectives, where employees are involved in setting the goals for the company, and popular motivational concepts such as the formulation of SMART-goals, that is, specific, measurable, attainable, realistic and timely goals.

19.3   The Current State of Motivation Theory

In recent years, several motivational theories have been proposed emphasizing factors such as the difference between learning and performance goals, basic tendencies to approach valued objectives versus avoid unwanted outcomes, the importance of fit between the employee and the organization, the importance of employee feelings of fairness with regard to rewards, organizational processes, and interpersonal treatment, as well as the need to design jobs that enhance worker motivation. In job design research, employees are assumed to be most motivated when they can use their skills, strongly identify with their work, see the benefit of their work in the lives of others, have autonomy, and get informative feedback (Hackman & Oldham, 1976). The plethora of theories, that each only describe some aspects of motivation, has led some scholars to characterize the current state of motivation theory as being dominated by mini-theories – lacking an integrative and overarching theory.

Efforts to integrate the older well-established theories and the current mini-theories have resulted in the classification of work motivation determinants in terms of personal and situational factors. According to this framework, motivation develops from an interplay between personal (e.g., personality, affect) and situational (i.e., HR practices, one's job) factors that can be distal, serving as a background against which employees engage in a particular behaviour (such as personality and HR practices), or proximal, closely attached to the context in which the behaviour occurs (such as affect and one's job). As outlined in Figure 19.1, employees' engagement in particular tasks and hence their work behaviour and well-being are mostly determined by proximal personal factors (Diefendorff & Chandler, 2011). These, in turn, are shaped by more distal personal influences (e.g., stable personality and values) as well as proximal external influences (e.g., job design, equity and fairness), and distal external influences (e.g., national and organizational culture).

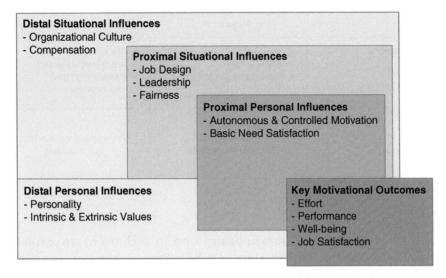

Figure 19.1: Overview of the different determinant of motivation (Adapted from Diefendorff & Chandler, 2011, Figure 3.1, p. 69. Reproduced with the permission of the American Psychological Association.)

One modern motivational theory that attempts to bridge the micro-theories and addresses both personal and situational influences on motivation is self-determination theory (SDT; Deci & Ryan, 2000). As a result, SDT has been called a 'grand theory' of motivation. SDT has been used to understand people's motivation in a variety of life domains, including education, sports, health care, and organizational contexts (Deci & Ryan, 2008). In adopting a broad perspective, SDT incorporates various aspects of different theories, but also adds to the field by arguing that different types of motivation (i.e., different reasons for pursuing activities) may lead to qualitatively different outcomes for individuals and organizations. In other words, what is important is not just the amount of motivation, but also the nature or source of the motivation.

We focus on SDT in this chapter as a means to understand why employees put effort in their job and focus on three important elements: (1) psychological need satisfaction, (2) the distinction between qualities of motivation (autonomous and controlled motivation), and (3) intrinsic and extrinsic values.

19.4 Meta-Theory of Human Motivation

19.4.1 SDT's view of humanity

SDT is based on the assumption that individuals are growth-oriented, (inter-) active organisms (Deci & Ryan, 2000). Rather than seeing employees as passive, reactive entities which need to be forced into particular behaviour, SDT

View	Negative	Positive
Basic assumptions: Employees ...	• Are passive • Are reactive • Need to be controlled	• Are active • Are growth-oriented • Interact with their environment
Motivational Practices: Managers need to ...	Push and pull employees around	Provide a good working environment

Figure 19.2: SDT's view on humanity

argues that people are active human beings who are inclined to strive towards intra- and interpersonal growth (Figure 19.2). People thus aim to actualize their inherent potential: they want to continuously learn, develop their talents and integrate their experiences into a coherent and meaningful sense of self and therefore grow as a person. Moreover, at the social level, people's growth orientation stimulates people to connect with others and to engage in meaningful interactions that are based on mutual care and respect. According to SDT, people aim to build important social relationships and want to be interconnected with others. To realize this growth, people are assumed to actively interact with their environment and to engage in activities that support their development and connectedness with others. Rather than merely responding to their environment or being pushed and pulled around, they actively seek to interact with the environment and potentially even shape their own environment.

19.4.2   Comparing and contrasting SDT against other theories of motivation

SDT's positive view on mankind contrasts with many other motivational theories (Sheldon, Turban, Brown, Barrick, & Judge, 2003). First, not all theories assume that people are active by their very nature. For example, reinforcement theory assumes that people can only be motivated to put effort in their job by rewarding or punishing them, thus assuming people are simply re-active rather than active. Second, not all theories expect people to be directed toward personal growth. For example, goal setting theory argues people set goals (or commit to assigned goals) that create a difference between their current situation and a desired situation. The difference thus causes psychological tension that motivates individuals to pursue the goal with the intension of alleviating the tension and thus returning to a state of homeostasis. This view does not directly acknowledge the importance of higher-level goals related to personal growth and integration that can shape the selection of lower-level work goals.

SDT's positive view of mankind is similar to several existing theories of human motivation, including Maslow's hierarchy of needs (1943) and Theory Y (McGregor, 1960), assuming that people are – in essence – growth-oriented. Despite assuming all people are active growth-oriented individuals who interact with the environment, SDT also acknowledges that this growth orientation does not come about automatically. For people to realize this inherent positive tendency, they need to satisfy their basic needs for autonomy, competence and relatedness, which are considered to nourish human motivation and individual thriving.

19.5 Basic Need Satisfaction

19.5.1 Definition of SDT's basic needs

Consistent with Maslow's argument that needs are fundamental aspects of employee motivation, SDT maintains that needs play an essential and proximal role in understanding and determining people's motivation (see Figure 19.1). According to SDT, employees (and people in general) require that their needs for autonomy, competence and relatedness are satisfied in order to function well psychologically, as much as plants need water, sunshine and minerals to flourish.

The need for *autonomy* is defined as an individual's inherent desire to act with a sense of choice and volition, and to feel psychologically free. This need aligns with the construct of locus of control which describes the feeling of being the author of one's actions rather than a pawn being pushed and pulled around by others. Importantly, this does not mean that people always need to decide for themselves and be independent. Independence and the satisfaction of the need for autonomy are not synonymous nor are they necessarily linked. For example, employees may execute a task assigned by their supervisors and act in a non-independent manner, but if they see value in that task and volitionally engage in it, they will feel satisfied in their need for autonomy. In contrast, if supervisors adopt a *laissez-faire* leadership style, that is, if they leave their employees all by themselves, without giving any guidance or support, employees might be independent but feel little satisfied in their need for autonomy, as they would rather have some instruction and attention from their supervisor.

The need for *competence* is the desire to feel capable of mastering the environment and to bring about desired outcomes. This need shares a resemblance with notions such as expectancy and feeling capable of reaching one's goals as outlined in expectancy–value theory and goal setting theory, respectively. People feel satisfied in their need for competence when they explore and actively seek out challenges in which they can extend their physical and psychological skills. Satisfaction of the need for competence helps people to develop their skills and to adapt to complex and changing environments.

The need for *relatedness* is the inherent propensity to feel connected to others, to be a member of a group, to love and care for others and to be loved and cared for in return. The need for relatedness is satisfied when people experience a sense of communion and maintain close and intimate relationships. Employees who feel part of a team and feel free to express their personal concerns and positive experiences are more likely to have their need for relatedness met than employees who feel lonely and lack social support. The notion of relatedness is acknowledged in the role of social support and the motivating power of helping others (Grant & Parker, 2009).

19.5.2   Distinguishing SDT's needs from other need theories

SDT's construct of basic psychological needs differs somewhat from other need concepts. Maslow, Murray and McGregor (mentioned above) have mostly defined need constructs that people develop during their life span through socialization or particular life experiences. For example, employees who have frequently been praised after accomplishing a task may develop a strong need for achievement. The strength of these needs will subsequently drive employee behaviour until those particular needs are satisfied and homeostasis is reached. In this view, need strength is an individual difference variable and should therefore only be seen as a distal personal influence on motivation (Diefendorff & Chandler, 2011).

In contrast to these ideas, SDT postulates that the needs for autonomy, competence and relatedness are innate and do not necessarily develop as a result of particular experiences. Rather, each of the needs is an inherent part of human nature and all people have these needs, whether or not one is conscious of them. Thus, the focus is not on how strong one's need is, but rather on the extent to which one's need is satisfied, which is then a proximal determinant of motivation (Figure 19.1). This approach is analogous to a focus on physical needs in which it is not the variation in the need for food that is predictive of people's physical well-being, but rather the degree to which people feel their need for food is satisfied (Deci & Ryan, 2000). Although employees from different age groups and different cultures may express and satisfy their basic needs in different ways, everybody is likely to benefit from having the basic psychological needs satisfied (Deci & Ryan, 2000). This focus on need satisfaction thus allows for a focus on needs as proximal personal antecedents of employee motivation.

19.5.3   Evidence supporting the consequences of SDT's needs

Although Maslow's need hierarchy and related theories are often mentioned in the management literature, empirical support for their assumptions is often limited. In contrast, the beneficial effects of need satisfaction from an SDT perspective have frequently been supported. A recent meta-analysis of about 100 empirical studies (Van den Broeck, Ferris, Chang, & Rosen, 2016) provides strong support for the argument that basic need satisfaction at work allows employees to put effort into their job, have positive attitudes towards work, and feel well. Specifically, satisfaction of each of the basic needs is associated with a series of positive behavioural outcomes, including productivity, creativity and proactivity. Employees who feel satisfied in their needs show less deviant behaviour and are absent less than employees who lack the satisfaction of their basic psychological needs. Need satisfaction also promotes positive attitudes such as job satisfaction, organizational commitment, and increases well-being in terms of positive affect and engagement, while preventing burnout and strain.

Need satisfaction therefore represents a prerequisite for employees to put effort in their jobs, become deeply engaged in their work, develop positive attitudes towards their jobs, and feel well at work. This is a particularly important conclusion given very few other theories of motivation have extended the criterion space beyond performance to include factors such as employee well-being and attitudes.

19.5.4   Research on SDT's needs: The antecedents

When looking at the antecedents of need satisfaction, both personal and contextual influences come into play, as also mentioned in the overarching framework of motivation of Diefendorff and Chandler (2011). With regards to distal personal influences, it may be that some employees tend to have an easier time in satisfying their psychological needs. These employees are usually optimistic, mindful, proactive, have secure self-esteem, and score high on the Big Five personality factors. For example, employees who are highly agreeable, like to bond with others, and are emotionally stable generally have an easier time forming close and meaningful relationship at work, thus satisfying their need for relatedness.

With regard to the situational influences on motivation, the work environment can also play an important role in satisfying the basic needs, as employees encountering high job demands, role stressors, work–family conflict or job insecurity find it more difficult to satisfy their basic psychological needs, whereas more need satisfaction is experienced when jobs contain various job resources ranging from opportunities to use various skills, task identity, autonomy, social support, and feedback (see Hackman & Oldham, 1976). Going beyond job characteristics, needs satisfaction is also fostered when supervisors are authentic or transformational (see Chapter 8 in this volume) as well as when organizations support employees and strive for fair exchanges, allow little politics and support feelings of fit with the employees. In short, the literature has linked various personal and contextual influences to basic need satisfaction, providing managers with various pathways through which they can enhance employee motivation (Van den Broeck et al., 2016).

According to SDT, the basic needs are the key to understanding why people put effort in their jobs and are the cornerstone of employee motivation. We can expect that Sara feels little need satisfaction at work, while David is likely experiencing autonomy, competence and relatedness, and as a result, thrives in his job. Need satisfaction is also closely intertwined with other important aspects of motivation, including different types of motivation (as another proximal personal antecedent of motivation) and the pursuit of values (as a distal personal antecedent of motivation). These aspects are highlighted in the following paragraphs.

19.6 Autonomous and Controlled Motivation

19.6.1   Intrinsic and extrinsic motivation in motivation theories

Although several factors may serve as proximal personal influences on work motivation (Diefendorff & Chandler, 2011), in addition to need satisfaction, SDT predominantly points to the importance of different types of motivation as proximal determinant of motivation (Figure 19.1). SDT begins by differentiating between intrinsic and extrinsic motivation, which are thought to reside at the extreme ends of their motivation continuum (Deci & Ryan, 2000). *Intrinsic motivation* is the engagement in an activity because it is fun, inherently interesting, or otherwise enjoyable. David may, for example, genuinely like and enjoy his work and feel satisfied by engaging in it. *Extrinsic motivation,* in contrast, reflects engagement in an activity in order to obtain an outcome that is separable from the activity itself (i.e., obtain a reward or avoid a punishment). Sara may mostly put effort in her work to receive a paycheck. The importance of intrinsic motivation has been acknowledged by several other theories within the work context, for example, when considering the added value of motivational job designs.

19.6.2   Different types of extrinsic motivation

Perhaps it goes without saying, but not all jobs are intrinsically enjoyable. Indeed, many jobs contain boring, stressful, or mind-numbing tasks that can only be done out of extrinsic motivation (Sheldon et al., 2003). This may be problematic, as various laboratory studies have found that extrinsic motivation can be harmful to individual well-being (Deci, Ryan, & Koestner, 1999). Interestingly, SDT argues that not all extrinsic motivation is the same and that it can vary in the extent to which it is experienced as controlling or autonomous. Specifically, SDT identifies four types of extrinsic motivation that are arranged on a continuum from completely external and controlled to more internal and autonomous (Deci & Ryan, 2000, see Figure 19.3).

Starting with the most controlling form of extrinsic motivation, *external regulation* refers to the engagement in an activity to obtain external rewards or to avoid punishments administered by others. Such rewards and punishments can be material, such as when a consultant puts effort in his job to obtain a bonus or job security, but rewards and punishments can also be social in nature, such as when interns work hard to be praised and not ignored by their supervisors. The central role of both rewards and punishments is consistent with earlier behaviouristic reinforcement theories. Moving along the extrinsic continuum, *introjected regulation* refers to being motivated by internalizing the extrinsic pressures to perform, resulting in the motivation to perform an action so as to feel proud or to avoid guilt and shame. For example, a consultant who works overtime on a project to avoid feeling ashamed and embarrassed for not meeting a client's

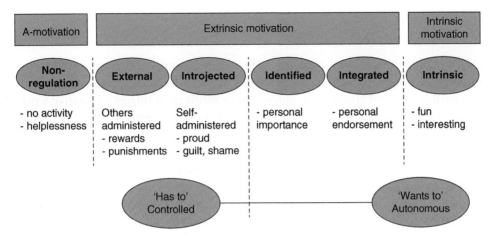

Figure 19.3: Different types of motivation according to SDT

deadline would experience introjected regulation. Moving further along the continuum, *identified regulation* involves employees endorsing the reason for the behaviour and considering the behaviour to be important or valuable. This is an autonomous form of extrinsic motivation. Consultants may spend hours preparing projects for clients, not because they enjoy it, but because they feel the project is important and will have a positive impact on the client's organization and its members. The most autonomous form of extrinsic motivation is *integrated regulation*, employees see the activity as aligned with their broader set of values, beliefs and – ultimately – their identity. Consultants identifying or internalizing their jobs would, for example, put in extra time and effort in working with clients because they see helping clients achieve their outcomes as consistent with who they are as individuals.

19.6.3   Types of motivation: Autonomous and controlled

External and introjected regulations are typified by a lack of internalization and by feelings of pressure, derived from others or one's self. These types of motivation are therefore considered to be *controlled* in nature (Deci & Ryan, 2000). In contrast, in the case of identified and integrated regulation, employees experience a sense of volition. These types of motivation are grouped into *autonomous motivation* together with intrinsic motivation, which reflects individuals' inherent, spontaneous interests in a particular activity (Deci & Ryan, 2000). In sum, SDT replaces the classic distinction between intrinsic and extrinsic motivation with the grouping of the motivational types into autonomous and controlled motivation. Autonomous motivation is fuelled by the satisfaction of the three basic needs and fosters the ability of employees to put effort in their jobs, while still feeling well. Controlled motivation, in contrast, frustrates the basic needs and is suggested to be detrimental for both employee well-being and performance.

19.6.4   Consequences and antecedents of autonomous and controlled motivation

SDT's assumptions on the consequences of autonomous and controlled motivation are supported by an increasing body of research. Because of its close relationship with basic need satisfaction, autonomous motivation relates to positive work behaviour, favourable attitudes, and higher well-being (Gagné et al., 2015), while controlled motivation is generally unrelated to these beneficial outcomes and may even be detrimental to employees. Recent research has revealed profiles in autonomous and controlled motivations, resulting in situations in which individuals can be low in both, high in both or high in only one form of motivation. The results of several studies suggest that in the presence of high autonomous motivation, the degree of controlled motivation (low or high) did not negatively impact employee performance or well-being. However, when autonomous motivation was low, having high controlled motivation was linked to deficiencies in performance (Moran, Diefendorff, Kim, & Liu, 2012) and well-being (Van den Broeck, Lens, de Witte, & Van Coillie, 2013). These findings suggest that controlled motivation might not always be problematic, as long as it is combined with high levels of autonomous motivation.

Antecedents of autonomous and controlled motivation have focused on personal and situational influences. In terms of (distal) personal influences, several traits seem relevant: those who are high in self-esteem, emotional stability, and internal locus of control are more likely to be autonomously motivated than those scoring low on these personality dimensions. Some employees have also learned – through socialization – to search for the meaning and pleasure in their activities, while others are mostly driven by controls in the external environment or inside themselves. These employees are said to have an autonomous and controlled general causality orientation, respectively (Baard, Deci, & Ryan, 2004). In terms of environmental influences, distal factors such as an organization's culture and compensation system can shape employees' motivation (Gagné et al., 2015). More proximal factors including job design, perceptions of equity and fairness, as well as leadership can also shape employees' motivation at work (Diefendorff & Chandler, 2011) and may contribute to the tendency to experience work as autonomously motivated or controlling.

In sum, SDT differentiates between different types of motivation and argues that controlled and autonomous motivations lead employees to expend effort, but autonomous motivation results in enhanced well-being and thriving, whereas controlled motivation results in decreased well-being and the thwarting of one's psychological needs. Indeed, this is a primary contribution of SDT over theories like goal setting theory, which focuses on simply trying to increase effort toward goal attainment. SDT argues that, while goals can lead individuals to action, controlling goals can do so at the cost of personal well-being, whereas autonomous goals can enhance well-being. Returning to Sara and David, we see that Sara is high in control motivation and feels she *has* to work which also means she finds her work draining and exhausting. David, on the other hand, is autonomously motivated and *wants* to work which is why he feels energized at work and is actively engaged in his tasks.

19.7   Intrinsic and Extrinsic Work Values

19.7.1   Values across motivational theories

The distal personal antecedents of work motivation include a variety of individual differences caused by genetic, biological and development influences (Diefendorff & Chandler, 2011). Within SDT, individual differences are mostly studied in terms of *values* (Figure 19.1). Values are defined as enduring beliefs that particular modes of conduct or outcomes are more preferred than others. They therefore serve as guidance for the development of our attitudes, choices and behaviour (Rokeach, 1973).

The pursuit of values is a critical aspect in motivational theories. Most scholars have addressed how strongly employees value work or its aspects. Working from expectancy–value theory, scholars would argue Sara chooses to put little effort into her work because she does not really value what she is doing. If she valued her work more, she would be more likely to actively engage in her work tasks. Similarly, in goal setting theory, scholars state that employees are motivated to achieve the goals they highly value. The more David is committed to his projects, the more effort he will put into completing them. Other scholars have adopted a slightly different approach by also considering the content of values. Schwartz (1999), for example, postulates that employees may hold several different values and therefore strive for different outcomes. For example, Sara might value hedonism (seeking pleasure and enjoyment) more than she values achievement. These values would translate into Sara coasting through work and avoiding demanding tasks instead of putting in a great deal of effort.

19.7.2   Intrinsic and extrinsic values in SDT

SDT suggests the pursuit of different values may lead to qualitative different outcomes, even when both values are closely attached to work. Specifically, SDT differentiates intrinsic from extrinsic work values (which are not to be confused with intrinsic and extrinsic motivation) (Figure 19.4). *Intrinsic values* are prosocial in nature. They include contributing to the community, affiliating to others, and developing oneself. *Extrinsic values*, in contrast, are oriented towards materialism and refer to accumulating wealth, acquiring fame and achieving power (Kasser & Ryan, 1993). According to SDT, striving for intrinsic values aligns with people's growth-oriented nature, supporting the satisfaction of the basic needs and results in more adaptive outcomes, as opposed to the pursuit of extrinsic values, which are less likely to contribute to the

Intrinsic Values	Extrinsic Values
• Community Contribution • Personal growth • Affiliation	• Wealth • Fame • Image

• Positive growth tendency • Basic psychological needs	• Frustration growth tendency • Frustration of the basic psychological needs

Figure 19.4:   Extrinsic and intrinsic values

satisfaction of an individual's basic needs and growth-oriented nature, and may in fact undermine one's needs (Vansteenkiste et al., 2007).

19.7.3   Consequences of intrinsic and extrinsic values

Although a vast amount of research supports SDT's view of intrinsic and extrinsic values in the educational or marketing context, research within the work domain is still scarce (e.g., Vansteenkiste, Lens, & Deci, 2006). Initial research in the work context suggests that holding extrinsic values might result in fleeting feelings of satisfaction, while employees holding intrinsic values are more likely to experience long-term engagement, job satisfaction, as well as reduced emotional exhaustion and turnover intentions (Vansteenkiste et al., 2007). The pursuit of extrinsic values has also been shown to prevent unemployed people from adapting flexibly to the labour market, even though a more flexible approach might increase their chances of finding high-quality employment (Van den Broeck, Vansteenkiste, Lens, & De Witte, 2010).

Apart from these main effects, an intrinsic versus extrinsic orientation may also help employees to interact with the environment to realize an employee's growth potential. Employees who endorse intrinsic values are more likely to benefit from learning opportunities and increased levels of autonomy at work, than those who attach less importance to intrinsic values. This pattern was observed in terms of work engagement and exhaustion such that the endorsement of intrinsic values supported work engagement and decreased exhaustion (Van den Broeck, Van Ruysseveldt, Smulders, & De Witte, 2010). Recently, these results were replicated at the within-person level, meaning that intrinsically oriented employees experience high levels of work engagement on days they have opportunities to develop their skills, while being little engaged on days they cannot use their skills so much (Van den Broeck, Schreurs, Guenter, & van Emmerik, 2015).

19.7.4   Intrinsic and extrinsic values as situational influences

Apart from values as personality traits, studies also provide evidence for the beneficial (vs. detrimental) effects of intrinsic (vs. extrinsic) team and organizational values. They show, for example, that team members are more engaged when they see their team as holding more intrinsic as compared to extrinsic values (Schreurs, Van Emmerik, Van den Broeck, & Guenter, 2014), and see more flexibility in doing different jobs with their employer when they see their organization as promoting intrinsic rather than extrinsic values (Van den Broeck et al., 2014). SDT's differentiation between intrinsic and extrinsic values thus not only provides insights in the distal personal antecedents of employee task engagement, but may also provide a fruitful framework to study team or organizational – or even national – culture, which is one among the most important distal environmental determinants of motivation (Diefendorff & Chandler, 2011).

Interestingly, the beneficial effects of individual intrinsic values and organizational intrinsic supplies align with the person–environment fit perspective (see Chapter 16 in this volume). While a suitable fit between the individual's values and the organization's values may be desirable, a fit in extrinsic values seems to result in less beneficial results. In contrast to the person–environment fit perspective, but in line with SDT, research among students shows that a focus on extrinsic values leads to lower levels of effort, persistence and well-being even when the context is rather extrinsic (Vansteenkiste, Timmermans, Lens, Soenens, & Van den Broeck, 2008).

Summary

In sum, motivation is a critical determinant of whether and in what ways employees will put effort into their jobs. Various motivational theories exist providing a range of distal and proximal, contextual and personal influences on whether or not employees work hard. In this chapter, we focused on self-determination theory (SDT) as one of the most encompassing contemporary theories of motivation, which can provide a multilayered answer as to why employees may put effort into their work. To truly motivate, managers should focus on the satisfaction of the basic psychological needs for autonomy (feeling psychologically free), competence (can complete tasks and be challenged) and relatedness (feel connected to, and cared for by work colleagues) to stimulate work effort. Managers could also increase employees' work effort by explaining the importance of the work, as well as by making work pleasurable and interesting as a way to enhance autonomous motivation (another proximal personal antecedent), and by focusing on how the job may allow one to develop and contribute to society to highlight intrinsic values (a distal personal antecedent). Interestingly, research on motivation in general, and SDT in particular, provides several insights explaining how proximal (e.g., job design) and distal (e.g., organizational culture) contextual factors can impact work motivation. Given the right circumstances, all employees, including Sara and David, can truly flourish at work.

Discussion Points

1 Which needs would you consider essential for humans to realize their potential? Which of the needs do you see reflected in the other chapters of this volume?
2 Think about an organization with which you are familiar. Think of this organization in terms of its compensation systems, management style, and the type of work it assigns employees. Which theory or theories of motivation do you believe drives the organization's decisions? How would you modify these systems and/or practices in light of what we know about employee motivation?

Suggested Further Reading

Deci, E. L., & Ryan, R. M. (2000). The "what" and "why" of goal pursuits: Human needs and the self-determination of behavior. *Psychological Inquiry, 11*(4), 227–268. doi:10.1207/S15327965PLI1104_01. This is the article that introduced self-determination theory.

Diefendorff, J. M., & Chandler, M. M. (2011). Motivating employees. In S. Zedeck (Ed.), *APA handbook of industrial and organizational psychology*, Vol 3, *Maintaining, expanding and contracting the organization*. (pp. 65–135). Washington, DC: American Psychological Association. In this chapter, you will find a broad overview of the many mini-theories that have been used to understand employee motivation, arranged in terms of the distal and proximal situational and personal antecedents of motivation.

Online resources

SDT: www.self-determinationtheory.org This website explains SDT, groups all the articles that have been published on the theory across different domains, provides a list of scholars working on the theory and much more.

SDT: http://www.youtube.com/watch?v=u6XA-PnuFjJc&feature=youtu.be This is a video in which Daniel Pink provides an overview of the most important aspects of SDT.

References

Ajzen, I. (1991). The theory of planned behavior. *Organizational Behavior and Human Decision Processes, 50*(2), 179–211. Available at: http://doi.org/10.1016/0749-5978(91)90020-T

Ambrose, M. L., & Kulik, C. (1999). Old friends, new faces: Motivation research in the 1990s. *Journal of Management, 25*(3), 231–292.

Armitage, C. J., & Conner, M. (2001). Efficacy of the theory of planned behaviour: A meta-analytic review. *The British Journal of Social Psychology, 40*(4), 471–499. Available at: http://doi.org/10.1348/014466601164939

Baard, P. P., Deci, E. L., & Ryan, R. M. (2004). Intrinsic need satisfaction : A motivational basis of performance and well-being in two work settings. *Journal of Applied Social Psychology, 34*(10), 2045–2068. Available at: http://doi.org/10.111/j.1559-1816.2004.tb02690.x

Deci, E. L., & Ryan, R. M. (2000). The "what" and "why" of goal pursuits: Human needs and the self-determination of behavior. *Psychological Inquiry, 11*(4), 227–268. Available at: http://doi.org/10.1207/S15327965PLI1104_01

Deci, E. L., & Ryan, R. M. (2008). Facilitating optimal motivation and psychological well-being across life's domains. *Canadian Psychology, 49*(1), 14–23. Available at: http://doi.org/10.1037/0708-5591.49.1.14

Deci, E. L., Ryan, R. M., & Koestner, R. (1999). A meta-analytic review of experiments examining the effects of extrinsic rewards on intrinsic motivation. *Psychological Bulletin, 125*(6), 627–668.

Diefendorff, J. M., & Chandler, M. M. (2011). Motivating employees. In S. Zedeck (Ed.), *APA handbook of industrial and organizational psychology*, vol. 3, *Maintaining, expanding and contracting the organization.* (pp. 65–135). Washington, DC: American Psychological Association.

Fall, A., & Roussel, P. (2014) Compensation and work motivation: Self-determination theory and the paradigm of motivation through incentives. In M. Gagne (Ed.). *The Oxford handbook of work engagement, motivation, and self-determination theory* (pp. 199–217). New York: Oxford University Press.

Gagné, M., et al. (2015). The multidimensional work motivation scale: Validation evidence in seven languages and nine countries. *European Journal of Work and Organizational Psychology, 24*(2), 178–196. Available at: http://doi.org/10.1080/1359432X.2013.877892

Grant, A. M., & Parker, S. K. (2009). Redesigning work design theories: The rise of relational and proactive perspectives. *Academy of Management Annals, 3*(1), 317–375. Available at: http://doi.org/10.1080/19416520903047327

Hackman, J. R., & Oldham, G. R. (1976). Motivation through the design of work: Test of a theory. *Organizational Behavior and Human Performance, 16*(2), 250–279.

Kasser, T., & Ryan, R. (1993). A dark side of the American dream: Correlates of financial success as a central life aspiration. *Journal of Personality and Social Psychology, 65*(2), 410–422.

Locke, E. & Latham, G. (1990). Work motivation and satisfaction: Light at the end of the tunnel. *Psychological Science, 1*(4), 240–246. Available at: http://doi.org/10.1111/j.1467-9280.1990.tb00207.x

Locke, E. A., & Latham, G. P. (2002). Building a practically useful theory of goal setting and task motivation: A 35-year odyssey. *American Psychologist, 57*(9), 705–717. Available at: http://doi.org/10.1037//003-066x.57.9.705

Maslow, A. H. (1943). A theory of human motivation. *Psychological Review, 50*(4), 370–396. Available at: http://doi.org/10.1037/h0054346

McClelland, D. (1965). Toward a theory of motive acquisition. *American Psychologist, 20*(5), 321–333.

McGregor, D. (1960). *The human side of enterprise.* (pp. 166–171). New York: McGraw-Hill.

Moran, C., Diefendorff, J., Kim, T., & Liu, Z. (2012). A profile approach to self-determination theory motivations at work. *Journal of Vocational Behavior, 81*(3), 354–363. Available at: http://doi.org/10.1016/j.jvb.2012.09.002

Murray, H. (1938). *Explorations in personality.* New York: Oxford University Press.

Pinder, C. (2008). *Work motivation in organizational behavior* (2nd ed.). New York: Psychology Press.

Rokeach, M. (1973). *The nature of human values.* New York: Free Press.

Rousseau, D. M. (2001). Flexibility versus fairness? *Organizational Dynamics, 29*(4), 260–273.

Schreurs, B., Van Emmerik, I. J. H., Van den Broeck, A., & Guenter, H. (2014). Work values and work engagement within teams: The mediating role of need satisfaction. *Group Dynamics: Theory, Research and Practice, 18*(4), 267–282. Available at: http://dx.doi.org/10.1037/gdn0000009

Schwartz, S. H. (1999). A theory of cultural values and some implications for work. *Applied Psychology: An International Review, 48*(1), 23–47. Available at: http://doi.org/10.1080/026999499377655

Sheldon, K. M., Turban, D. B., Brown, K. G., Barrick, M. R., & Judge, T. A. (2003). Applying self-determination theory to organizational research. *Research in Personnel and Human Resource Management, 22,* 357–393. Available at: http://doi.org/10.1016/S0742-7301(03)22008-9

Skinner, B. (1969). *Contingencies of reinforcement: A theoretical analysis.* New York: Meredith Corporation.

Tay, L., & Diener, E. (2011). Needs and subjective well-being around the world. *Journal of Personality and Social Psychology, 101*(2), 354–365. Available at: http://doi.org/10.1037/a0023779

Thorndike, E. (1911). *Animal intelligence.* New York: Macmillan.

Van den Broeck, A., De Cuyper, N., Baillien, E., Vanbelle, E., Vanhercke, D., & De Witte, H. (2014). Perception of organization's value support and perceived employability: insights from self-determination theory. *The International Journal of Human Resource Management, 25*(13), 1904–1918. Available at: http://doi.org/10.1080/09585192.2013.860385

Van den Broeck, A., Ferris, D., Chang, C., & Rosen, C. (2016). A review of self-determination theory's basic psychological needs at work. *Journal of Management.* Available at: http://doi.org/10.1177/0149206316632058

Van den Broeck, A., Lens, W., De Witte, H., & Van Coillie, H. (2013). Unraveling the importance of the quantity and the quality of workers' motivation for well-being: A person-centered perspective. *Journal of Vocational Behavior, 82*(1), 69–78. Available at: http://doi.org/10.106/j.jvb.2012.11.005

Van den Broeck, A., Schreurs, B., Guenter, H., & van Emmerik, I. H. (2015). Skill utilization and well-being: A cross-level story of day-to-day fluctuations and personal intrinsic values. *Work & Stress, 29*(3), 306–323. Available at: http://doi.org/10.1080/02678373.2015.1074955

Van den Broeck, A., Van Ruysseveldt, J., Smulders, P., & De Witte, H. (2010). Does an intrinsic work value orientation strengthen the impact of job resources? A perspective from the Job Demands–Resources Model. *European Journal of Work and Organizational Psychology, 20*(5), 581–609. Available at: http://doi.org/10.1080/13594321003669053

Van den Broeck, A., Vansteenkiste, M., Lens, W., & De Witte, H. (2010). Unemployed individuals' work values and job flexibility: An explanation from expectancy-value theory and self-determination theory. *Applied Psychology, 59*(2), 296–317. Available at: http://doi.org/10.1111/j.1464-0597.2009.00391.x

Van Eerde, W., & Thierry, H. (1996). Vroom's expectancy models and work-related criteria: A meta-analysis. *Journal of Applied Psychology, 81*(5), 575–586.

Vansteenkiste, M., Lens, W., & Deci, E. L. (2006). Intrinsic versus extrinsic goal contents in self-determination theory: Another look at the quality of academic motivation. *Educational Psychologist, 41*(1), 19–31. Available at: http://doi.org/10.1207/s15326985ep4101_4

Vansteenkiste, M., Neyrinck, B., Niemiec, C. P., Soenens, B., Witte, H., & Broeck, A. (2007). On the relations among work value orientations, psychological need satisfaction and job outcomes: A self-determination theory approach. *Journal of Occupational and Organizational Psychology, 80*(2), 251–277. Available at: http://doi.org/10.1348/096317906X111024

Vansteenkiste, M., Timmermans, T., Lens, W., Soenens, B., & Van den Broeck, A. (2008). Does extrinsic goal framing enhance extrinsic goal-oriented individuals' learning and performance? An experimental test of the match perspective versus self-determination theory. *Journal of Educational Psychology, 100*(2), 387–397. Available at: http://doi.org/10.1037/0022-0663.100.2.387

Vroom, V. (1964). *Work and motivation.* New York: Wiley.

How Do We Handle Computer-Based Technology? What Is the Cost/Benefit Ratio of Technology for Workers?

20

Fred R. H. Zijlstra and Anne-Sophie Nyssen

Overview

This chapter focuses on the question of how to deal with technology. Technology has changed our life, it has changed how we communicate with each other, and how we work, and also when and where we work. It is important to understand how and why it has changed our life, and what consequences this has. Technology may affect our (mental) health and well-being. In this chapter we present an overview of factors that need to be taken into account when designing technology. First, a historic perspective is presented in order to understand the development of technology in the work context. Technology at work is generally believed to help us, but this is not always the case. Technology can also make work complex; it can also lead to health problems, in particular when wrong decisions are made while designing technology. A core issue is to what extent people are still in control of technology. The main question is to understand how individuals are affected by technology at work, and know how technology should be handled.

20.1   Introduction

A work situation without computer-based technologies is unthinkable nowadays. The term computer-based technology applies not only to Information and Communication Technology (ICT), such as email and the internet, but includes all kinds of artefacts that people use. The range of applications varies from 'simple' technology such as personal computers, or infusion pumps that are used to administer medicines, to large-scale automated systems in advanced socio-technical systems such as cockpits in commercial jets, control rooms in nuclear power plants, or to perform robotic surgery. In general, people will agree that technology can have great advantages in terms of increased production, accuracy

An Introduction to Work and Organizational Psychology: An International Perspective,
Third Edition. Edited by Nik Chmiel, Franco Fraccaroli and Magnus Sverke.
© 2017 John Wiley & Sons, Ltd. Published 2017 by John Wiley & Sons, Ltd.

of work and safety. For instance, air traffic would not be possible on the present scale without technology. On the other hand, technology has also changed the nature of work for those people who have to use these systems; it has made work much more complex and has created new types of health problems. Whereas originally musculoskeletal problems due to a static working posture received most attention, nowadays the focus is more on psychological health issues, like frustration and anger when the technology does not 'behave' as expected, and also mental fatigue, boredom, or stress are currently important issues. This raises a number of important questions: How do individuals handle these issues? What are the options for dealing with, or avoiding, these problems? What are the advantages and disadvantages of technology for organizations and for the individual? What is the cost/benefit ratio in terms of well-being at work? In order to answer such questions, we need to have an understanding of the origin of the problems. This will be the main focus of this chapter.

People's fascination with new technology has often obscured their insight that technology transforms both work and workers. Understanding how new technology affects people is important when knowing how to design and use future technology, and technology-based work. A historic perspective may help an understanding of how the relationship between human and machine has developed and how this has changed both work and the workers. This chapter will describe the development of technology (for a brief summary of various phases see Box 20.1; see also chapters 6 and 7 of this volume), and outline some of the consequences of using technology at work and the risks they may entail for workers' health. Furthermore, we will explore several ways to humanize the impact that technology may have on work environments of the future.

Box 20.1:   The five phases of technology change

1. *Mechanization*: This reflects the period until approximately the 1960s, in which machines were primarily used to replace human muscle power, where simple and repeating operations were required. In particular, agriculture and industry were mechanized. As a consequence, many jobs disappeared in the agricultural sector.

2. *Automation*: The 1970s and 1980s were characterized by automation; technology had advanced and features such as coordination and timing of various activities could be included which allowed the series of simple operations to be connected to form more complex operations in the production process. In this period the first computers were introduced into offices, and office automation began.

3. *Computerization*: The microchip allowed programming of operations, and thus building and applying algorithms ('if x, then y') in clearly defined situations. The implication was that machines could also make (simple) 'decisions' and become an 'agent' in the work process. The rapid development of microchips allowed more powerful and faster computers to be built that were connected so that they could communicate with each other and exchange data.

4. *'Robotization'*: When in the 1980s the microchip was introduced, more complex operations could be programmed into more autonomous machines, and consequently robots could help to realize very precise operations, such as in robotic surgery, or even handle large parts of the process, for example, in car manufacturing or in aviation.

5. *Information and communication technology*: Around 1990, the development of ICT facilitated the sharing of information between all kinds of parties: colleagues, but also customers and suppliers. It made the transfer of information much faster, which was particularly useful for people working at a distance but, in turn, transformed the way people communicate with each other.

20.2 Mechanization, Automation and Robotization: Technology as a Substitute for Workers

During the Industrial Revolution (around 1880) in Britain, production changed from craftsmanship, based on skills and expertise, to large-scale mass production based on standardization, quantity and mechanization. The English philosopher Adam Smith (1723–1790) published his work *On the Wealth of Nations* (1776), in which he propagated the principles of a 'free market' and the 'division of work' as leading principles for society. A more rational division of work would lead to specialization and hence to the improvement of skills, and consequently more efficient production. A number of years later, the English mathematician Charles Babbage (1791–1871) applied those principles to a cognitive activity: mathematical work. He divided mathematical work between 'mathematicians' who developed algorithms, and 'senior workers' who translated the algorithms into work procedures, and 'calculators' who had to apply those procedures to make simple calculations. In this way a rather complex activity (calculating) was divided into a series of operations that varied considerably in complexity. The 'mathematicians' were responsible for the most complex work, and the 'calculators' had the simplest work. As a consequence, not every employee had to be equally educated and skilled, which meant that not all employees earned the same wages (the 'calculators' were much cheaper to employ). After having applied this principle of 'splitting up complex work' into a sequence of simpler operations, the next step was that Babbage developed a machine that could perform those simple operations (which he called 'the Difference Engine' in 1853 and this is considered to be the forefather of programmable computers), and the machine that took over the work of the 'calculators'.

In the USA, Frederic Taylor (1865–1915) built further upon these ideas. Where Babbage introduced the division of work, which caused a shift in job content, Taylor added the principle of division of 'head labour' and 'hand labour', now known as 'Taylorism'. This further reduced the influence workers had over how they would do their own work. It resulted in simple and monotonous work and reduced the worker to a 'mechanical instrument', which further excavated the role of workers in the work process. In the USA, Henry Ford (1863–1947) applied these principles and added another element resulting in 'the assembly line'. Whereas previously groups of employees moved from one spot to the next work spot to assemble cars, Ford introduced that the cars would move through the hall, and the workers would stay at their own spot. This imposed a certain speed of work on people, and restrained workers even further. Because work was increasingly 'simplified' and 'dismantled', the ultimate consequence was that it could be taken over by automated systems and 'robots'.

From that point, the human operator's main role was to supervise the automatic process. Sheridan (1987) used the term 'supervisory control' to describe the new roles of humans at work in relation to this development. These supervisory roles include: (1) planning what tasks to do, and programming the computer, (2) on-line monitoring of the automatic actions to make sure all is going as planned, (3) detecting failures, and (4) intervening in case of surprises or unanticipated situations (1987, p. 1248). This applies to large-scale processes in the chemical industry, nuclear power plants, healthcare, aviation and many other work settings. Airplanes are nowadays 'flown' by their computers in most phases of flight, during which pilots monitor the situation and make decisions about a suitable course of action, and then program the computers to do it and oversee the adequate functioning of the systems. Only in specific phases of flight (such as 'take-off') or when incidents occur, such as technical failures, do they need to fly the airplane manually. Usually, mode changes (transition from one automatic control logic to another one) are initiated by the human operator. However, in advanced technological systems, mode changes can also be the result of system input. For example, in aviation, the pilot can initiate a transition of mode by entering a command to the computer-system, but it can also be initiated by the system itself, for instance, when the system detects that the airplane has reached a certain prescribed altitude, or if the pilot is putting the plane into an unsafe configuration. This illustrates that the functions (or roles) are not allocated to either the human or to the automated system, as recommended by the famous Fitts' list (1951; see Box 20.2, including Table 20.1), but is a result from the interaction between the two, where both have to operate as a 'team player' (Klein et al., 2004). This increases the complexity for users and necessitates monitoring the joint performance of the operator and the automated system. And this can easily create a mismatch between what the pilot observes and what the pilot expects to see, if the indirect input on the process is not detected or known. Woods and Hollnagel (2006) use the term 'automation surprise' to describe the 'miscommunication and miss-assessment' between the user and the automated system, which leads to a gap between the user's understanding of what the automated systems are set up to do, what they are doing, and what they are going to do' (pp. 120–121).

> ## Box 20.2:   The Fitts' list
>
> The Fitts' list (1951) proposes a list of 11 statements to guide the allocation of functionality based on whether the machine or the human operator performs the task better. The list is reproduced in Table 20.1. Since then, the Fitts' list has received a lot of criticism, including that the list does not take into account aspects like dynamic allocation, contextual variations and the psychological needs of humans at work (job satisfaction, motivation, psychosocial aspects, stress) (Hancock, 2009; Winter & Dodou, 2014).
>
> Table 20.1: Fitts' list (Fitt, 1951, p. 10) as quoted by Winter & Dodou (2014).
>
> | Humans appear to exceed present-day machines with respect to the following: | Present-day machines appear to exceed humans with respect to the following: |
> | --- | --- |
> | 1. Ability to detect a small amount of visual or acoustic energy | 1. Ability to respond quickly to control signals and to apply great force smoothly and precisely |
> | 2. Ability to perceive patterns of light or sound | 2. Ability to perform repetitive, routine tasks |
> | 3. Ability to improvise and use flexible procedures | 3. Ability to store information briefly and then to erase it completely |
> | 4. Ability to store very large amounts of information for long periods and to recall relevant facts at the appropriate time | 4. Ability to reason deductively, including computational ability |
> | 5. Ability to reason inductively | 5. Ability to handle highly complex operations, i.e. to do many different things at once |
> | 6. Ability to exercise judgment | |

20.3   Technology as a Tool

Technology aims to make our job easier, more effective or more efficient. It is used at work either: (1) to replace the human, (2) to circumvent certain limitations that human beings have, or (3) to extend the capabilities of humans beyond what they can achieve alone. Computers are particularly good examples of the latter: they are much better at storing information and making calculations than humans. However, over the years, accumulated research has shown that interaction with technology does not always make the job easier. Weiner (1989) noted that automation can actually increase the workload. Wickens (1999) suggested that extensive use of automation may cause an operator's manual skill to deteriorate, or even disappear, because the worker becomes a mere passive bystander, or observer, instead of an active participant. For that particular reason, various professions have rules that people in their professions must spend a minimum amount of hours per year practising their skills. Several physiological and subjective reports suggest that vigilance tasks reduce task engagement and increase distress (Miller, 2012). For instance, Johansson and Aronsson (1984) demonstrated that workers who had no control over the pace of their work reported more psychological health complaints (i.e., feelings of depression, apathy, feelings of anxiety and unhappiness, low levels of self-confidence, negative self-image, etc.). Another study (Ekkers, Brouwers, Pasmooij, & Vlaming, 1980) found that, in highly automated systems, operators spent only 2.6% of their time on 'operating' the system and reported low levels of achievement and job satisfaction. Generally, their level of well-being appears to be low and sickness absence relatively high. Furthermore it appears that the difficulty of the task, and poor leadership practices (i.e., unfairness, etc.) are positively correlated with mental health complaints and fatigue.

The level of control that operators have in their work is largely determined by the 'level of automation'. Sheridan and Verplank (1978) described ten levels of automation in man–computer decision-making. The lowest level represents manual systems in which the human operator does the whole job up to the point of turning it over to the computer. At the highest end of the spectrum are fully automated systems in which the computer does the whole job, when it decides it should be done. Between these two extreme situations automation varies in terms of 'authority' and 'autonomy'. At the lower levels of automation, computers might offer suggestions for the user to consider, whereas at the higher levels of automation computers might have the authority to select and execute an action, and then inform the human operator.

An important consequence of this technological development is that a distance is created between the production process and the human operator. There is no longer direct contact with the process itself; the process is represented via information that can be read from displays. Thus 'information' becomes the critical object of work (i.e., 'information work'). This physical distance also leads to a psychological distance. The computer interface serves as a window on the complex process, providing operators with a 'mediated representation' of the process in order to allow them to form an adequate mental model of the process. Operators cannot use their own sensory organs (smell, vision, audio, tactile) to follow the process, but depend on information provided by the interface. Thus, there is a strong need to provide workers with appropriate information and representations of the process, which leads to questions such as: Which information is effectively used by human operators during work? How to represent and integrate this information in meaningful ways on displays? Anyone that has ever looked into the cockpit of a modern airplane immediately understands what is meant here. As a result, the demands of work have become largely cognitive (information processing) demands.

Mental workload has become a critical ergonomic criterion for designing and assessing technology. It can be described as 'the relation between the mental capacities that are demanded by a task and the capacities that can be made available by the human operator' (Parasuraman, Sheridan, & Wickens, 2008, pp. 140–160). Researchers have argued that automated systems can leave the operators with too little to do and consequently operators are exposed to boredom, sleepiness, hypo-vigilance and attention slips. On the other hand, operators can also be confronted with unexpected events or failures of the system which require immediate action. In these situations the operator needs to know as soon as possible what the problem is, and what actions are needed. These situations are often very challenging and constitute a high mental workload, because the operator may have lost a detailed awareness of the situation during the automated phases. In aviation, this has been described as 'falling behind the plane', or as 'losing the bubble' (Woods, Johannesen, Cook, & Sarter, 1994), meaning that the operator has lost his/her internal representation (mental model) of the dynamics of the process.

Bainbridge (1987) referred to this phenomenon as 'the irony of automation': human operators increasingly lose their basic skills because they no longer practise their skills, as their activity is taken over by automated systems in daily operations, but yet they are expected to demonstrate superior skills when they occasionally have to take over from computers in unexpected, surprising, or difficult, and very stressful situations.

These issues have prompted 'human-centred' automation concepts, which aim to improve the relationship between users and automated systems, and look for design solutions that allow 'adaptive automation' that would match the level of automation with the level of operator workload (Scerbo, 1996; Parasuraman et al., 2008).

20.4 Computerization, Information & Communication Technology (ICT): Technology Supporting Workers

The process of 'rationalization' of work processes that we described above, started in industrial settings, but later also spread to offices and the service industry. Tayloristic principles were also applied in the office sector (cognitive Taylorism). As a consequence, specialized typing and data-entry departments, and call centres were created (Braverman, 1974; Carayon & Smith, 2000) that operated 24 hours a day and were located in low wage countries. Increasingly also in offices machines would dictate how people would have to do their job (think of writing a letter with paper and pencil, compared to a word processor). Modern ICT devices, like word processors, smartphones, tablets, have spelling checkers, word suggestions, and other features such as standardized sentences that are meant to facilitate writing letters or emails. It can become very confusing for recipients of messages to assess whether the message came from a human being or from a machine. Machines are programmed with rules and the logic of the machine is often imposed on people, constraining creativity and originality (Besnier, 2012). At the same time, people become increasingly dependent on these technologies that are more and more embedded into our environment. Who nowadays can still remember telephone numbers, since they are stored in the memory of one's mobile phone?

The fact that computers are connected to each other and can be used to communicate has resulted in what we now know as the 'world wide web'. That has introduced new ways of communicating with other people, but has also changed the way we communicate with each other. People nowadays send emails more frequently and more easily than they make phone calls. This is partly because a phone call requires the receiving party to be 'available' to talk. Such 'synchronous interaction' is not required with email (i.e., 'asynchronous interaction'), or other communication devices (i.e., 'whatsApp'). As a consequence, communication between people is mostly 'mediated communication' (i.e., communication via a device as opposed to 'face-to-face'). This has advantages, because asynchronous interaction leaves the message until the recipient has time to read, but it also makes it much more difficult to capture the 'richness' of face-to-face communication (facial expressions, emotional tone, etc.). Therefore mediated communication can easily lead to misunderstandings; that is why people increasingly use so-called 'emoticons' in their messages. Sometimes people think that when an email has been sent, it automatically means that the information is received, read and understood. Since email can be fast, people often expect a quick reply, and people may even feel pressed to respond quickly. A delayed response may also be interpreted as a 'signal', maybe expressing 'disinterest' in the message or sender. An email can also be sent to many recipients at the same time, which has introduced a 'strategic dimension' to communicating with email. People use the 'carbon copy' (cc, or blind cc) to send emails to inform several people at the same time (and the bcc is used to inform others in secret). In addition, email can be sent 24 hours a day, and thus transgresses the traditional boundaries between working time and family time. The result is that a lot of information is distributed to a lot of people at all time. Increasingly, people find it difficult or problematic to handle and filter the information they receive; hence the term 'information overload' has been introduced. Some people have problems handling this continuous stream of information and become addicted to checking their email, or webpages, because they are afraid of missing out on important information. It also means that many people are constantly connected to work, and may start becoming anxious about work (Cropley & Zijlstra, 2011). In both cases this may lead to severe mental health problems.

Recently, companies have started developing protocols for better use of ICT technologies like: not checking work mails after 20:00 hours and at weekends, reducing the number of emails using the 'cc option', thinking about which type of message fits best with what kind of medium, and avoiding emailing a colleague two doors down the corridor but rather go and talk to that person, etc. These protocols aim to regulate the interaction with machines, and try to stimulate people to be aware of how to use the technology and also stimulate some self-reflection in this respect. This may place some constraints on human–machine interaction, emphasizing self-management and self-authority by prescribing how to use particular devices outside the domain of work. For instance, professional mobile phones can be switched off, so that employees are no longer contactable 24 hours a day.

The availability of information in the public domain has increased enormously thanks to the internet (or the 'world-wide web'), probably even more than most people are aware of. This adds to the information overload, but also constitutes other issues that the general public is not aware of. For instance, organizations also use social media. It has been estimated that internet recruitment is the second largest source of income for providers (Maynard, 1997). This can have an impact on employees, job applicants, the selection process and organizations (cf. Chapter 2 of this volume). People are not always aware that Facebook profiles and other information (pictures and news items on websites) that are available on the internet are used by organizations to screen job applicants. All kinds of undesirable or negative information (even on websites by others) are available and can be used. There are examples when people have lost their jobs because of their postings on Facebook or Twitter, which were done in the spur of a moment, without much thought. This makes it even more important to control the information that is available, and to filter information and decide what information is relevant or not. Electronic harassment has become a phenomenon in the social domain, but happens also in work settings (Griffiths, 2002). People can be bullied and stalked with (hate)-mail, or 'pictures' or other private content that is distributed using email or social media.

The impact of the technological evolution on workers is different, depending on the content of their work. Aronsson (1989) observed differential effects for higher, middle and lower level skilled employees: the lower-skilled employees reported a substantial increase in intensified work and job dissatisfaction, whereas the higher-skilled employees reported no changes in their tasks (the middle group was somewhere in between). About 95% of lower level skilled workers expected that their work would be made redundant somewhere in the next five years. Aronsson believed that the explanation for the differences in effects between various groups could be found in the fact that higher-skilled employees (often managers) were more involved, and thus had more influence over decisions regarding what technology would be bought or developed. And thus they benefit more from technology, and consequently have less complaints and more satisfaction (Burkhardt & Brass, 1990). Women appear to have more complaints than men (Lindström, 1991), which could also be explained by the fact that women often have lower-level jobs than men.

Taking the development of the relationship between humans and machines into account, Hancock (2009) foresees three different roles for humans in the future of technology: humans as Masters, Servants or Slaves of the machine.

Hockey (2003) developed a model describing the various modes of control, the subjective states of the operator and the consequences for performance, and effort. This model can be adapted and linked to the different levels of automation and the roles of human operators as perceived by Hancock (2009) in order to predict consequences of automation for workers' health. These are presented in Table 20.2. The 'engaged mode' might correspond to a human-machine system in which the human operators control the machine and understand what is going on. In this role, they can maintain optimal performance while exerting effort, resulting in satisfaction and well-being at work. The 'strain mode' corresponds to a human–machine system in which the machine dictates the boundaries and the constraints of the work. In this interaction pattern, the human operators become the servants of automation. They can maintain nominal performance,

Table 20.2: Levels of automation, roles of human and expected effects on workers' health

Role of human in the technology based environment	Environmental context	Human control mode	Performance	Affective State
Human as Master of machine	High demands high control	Engaged	Optimal	Effort without distress Anxiety 0 Effort + Fatigue −
Human as Servant of machine	High demands low control	Strain	Adequate	Effort with distress Anxiety + Effort + Fatigue +
Human as Slave of machine	Low demands low control	Disengaged	Impaired	Distress without effort Anxiety + Effort − Fatigue 0

Source: Adapted from Hockey, 2003 and Hancock, 2009.

but only with increasing effort, anxiety and chronic fatigue. The 'disengaged mode' might correspond to a fully automated system where the human operators are kept into the task loop to maintain or supervise the automated process, but have no control over the machine. Under these conditions, the operators may lower or even abandon the goals of the task. Consequently, performance will decline while causing high levels of stress, depression and feelings of anxiety for the operator.

20.5   Trust in Technologies and Acceptance

An important factor that will determine how people will handle a technology depends on the level of trust people have in technology (Hancock, Billings, & Schaefer, 2011; Parasuraman et al., 2008). Trust in technology is the result of an adequate match between the user's observation of the 'behaviour' of technology and the user's inference about the technology's intent or its performance. With new technology people are sometimes a little sceptical, and wonder: 'Will it function properly? Will it be quicker than how we did it before?' (Are response times consistent, or sometimes long?). But there are also other questions that relate more to their own position: 'How will it affect my job?', 'Will I still have my job in two years' time?', 'Will I be able to work with the technology' People's perceptions concerning the potential answers to these questions will determine how they will accept the new technology.

Lee and Moray (1992) conducted pioneering research showing that an operator's use of automation to control a simulated plant was directly related to his/her momentary trust, which in turn was related to the type and frequency of the technology's failures. Low levels of trust can lead to not using the system, but it can also make people feel either insecure or frustrated. On the contrary, high levels of trust can be associated with being over-reliant on the system and disregarding other relevant information. Think of using your car navigation system, while the signs along the road suggest that you should take another route. Which system do you trust more, and what information will you follow?

More recently, Hancock, Billings, Schaefer, Chen, de Visser, and Parasuraman (2011) conducted a meta-analysis to better understand the antecedents of trust in technology. They quantified the effects of human-related factors (e.g., demographics, propensity to trust, self-confidence), robot-related factors (e.g., reliability, predictability, level of automation, transparency) and environmental-related factors (e.g., culture, communication, task type) on perceived trust in robots. The robot's performance and attributes were the largest contributors to the development of trust. The human and the environmental factors were found to be only weakly associated with trust.

Yet, the human characteristics (e.g., gender, age, level of experience) have an impact on the overall perception of technology and, consequently, determine how humans might engage with technology. For instance, elderly teachers worry about whether they will be able to keep up with the digitalization of teaching materials in schools, and the changing role of the teacher in this process. They see young children coming to school, for whom Ipads and computers have no surprises, whereas some teachers have just learned how to 'swipe'. With the increasingly rapid evolution of technology, there is danger of creating a divide between technology savvy workers who can easily learn and adapt to using new technology and those for whom technology will always remain a 'closed book' (Hancock, 2009, p. 97).

This indeed is becoming a huge issue, since technology is used in many different economic sectors, and systems have become more and more 'intelligent', and 'self-learning'. Artificial Intelligence has developed so far that machines can beat humans at the most complex board games, like Chess and Go. Technology (robots) is now also considered to be used in the care sector, and the first hotels that are completely based on self-service have emerged. These systems rely completely on intelligent technology. The current debate focuses on whether these increasingly 'intelligent' systems will take over other types of work in the service sector as well, as is demonstrated by the development of self-service cashiers in supermarkets, or therapeutic robots for elderly people in the healthcare sector. For that reason some people are referring to the 'Second Machine Age' (Brynjolfsson & Mcafee, 2014), suggesting that new technologies might make more and more people redundant.

As already cited, Hancock (2009) has asked the very relevant question in terms of well-being at work: to what degree are humans still masters of the machine, rather than servants or slaves?

20.6 Conclusion

In this chapter, the effects of technology on workers' health and well-being in different domains have been presented. Technology can support workers and reduce the workload and stress, but it can also do just the opposite when it is badly designed and deployed. The negative consequences are often much greater than would ever be possible in the non-automated state.

The recent literature on stress-related disorders and psychosocial risks in the workplace explains the pervasive impacts of technology. Having autonomy and being in control over work are two important factors relating to well-being at work, and in particular these aspects are at risk when dealing with technology. With these observations in mind, the conclusion should be that in order to deal with technology, people should be given, or made aware of, the autonomy and control options they have when dealing with technology. And system designers should also look at the psychosocial risks that might potentially loom for human beings. This is the only way to guarantee that humans and machines will be able to work together amicably.

Thus far, system designers have largely focused on functionality and system reliability. Several researchers have presented a *user-centred design approach* (Billings, 1997; Nyssen, 2004; Vicente, 1999; Woods & Hollnagel, 2006) that involves prospective users in the design process in order to better identify the needs and constraints of the users in the context in which the system should be used. Hancock (2009) goes one step further and points to the need to construct a philosophy of technology that examines the moral dimensions of the design process and the use of technology by exploring the notion of 'intention' and 'freedom' in the future human-machine system environments. In this line of reasoning we should not make systems that constrain people and reduce humans to servants or slaves by forcing people to follow the pace and the operations dictated by machines, but researchers and designers should promote innovative design solutions that support autonomy, choice and adaptation. Such a design philosophy will be beneficial to the reliability and resilience of the human–machine system, and good for the development and well-being of workers.

Summary

In this chapter we have examined the development of technology and its effects on workers in different work domains (industry, office, services) from automation to ICT. We are often very fascinated with what new technology has to offer, and that is why we often are blind to the fact that technology transforms both work and workers. We have explicitly emphasized the impact technology can have on workers' well-being: their workload, fatigue and psychosocial risks, by relating the level of automation to the concept of workers' autonomy and control over work. Our intention throughout the chapter has been to provide an overview of current research which aims to improve the interaction between users and their automated environment. Our viewpoint is that we should look for ways of designing adaptive automation, which takes the dynamic nature of the users' needs and constraints in work environments into account. It is our hope that this chapter illustrates that system design is a multidisciplinary effort between experts in human behaviour and engineers. Designers and users should have a broad interest regarding the consequences of technology and ensure that design process takes these aspects into account.

Discussion Points

1 Imagine that you are in a position to order high technology equipment for your organization: which of the issues addressed in this chapter would you find most relevant to take into account in your decision-making process?
2 What kind of tasks can be taken over by machines? Try to think of what the consequences would be for the 'operator', but also for the 'recipient'. Make a list of tasks in the healthcare sector, the service industry, and logistics.

Suggested Further Reading

Brynjolfsson, E., & McAfee, A. (2014). *The second machine age: Work, progress, and prosperity in a time of brilliant technologies.* New York: W.W. Norton & Company, Inc. This book will help you think about what the consequences might be when technology adopts an even more important role in our society.

Hancock, P. A. (2009). *Mind, machine and morality: Toward a philosophy of human–technology symbiosis.* Farnham: Ashgate. This book examines the potential dangerous paths of technology and asks questions about the role of the human operator in man-machine relationships.

Hockey, R. (2013). *The psychology of fatigue: Work, effort and control.* Cambridge: Cambridge University Press. This book explains how we can understand fatigue, and the many aspects of fatigue – mental, physical, sleepiness – and their influence on performance and well-being at work.

Norman, D. A. (2011). *Living with complexity.* Cambridge, MA: MIT Press. Norman describes how poor design solutions can make life very complicated.

References

Aronsson, G. (1989). Changed qualification demands in computer-mediated work, *Applied Psychology: An International Review, 38*(1), 57–71.

Bainbridge, L. (1987). Ironies of automation. In J. Rasmussen, K. Duncan, & J. Leplat (Eds.), *New technology and human error.* London: Wiley & Sons.

Besnier, J. M. (2012). *L'homme simplifié: le syndrôme de la touche simplifiée*. Paris: Fayard.

Billings, C. (1997). *Aviation automation: The search for a human centered approach*. Mahwah, NJ: Lawrence Erlbaum Associates.

Braverman, H. (1974). *Labor and monopoly capital: The degradation of work in the twentieth century*. New York: Monthly Review Press.

Brynjolfsson, E., & Mcafee, A. (2014). *The second machine age. Work, progress, and prosperity in a time of brilliant technologies*. New York: W.W. Norton & Company, Inc.

Burkhardt, M. E., & Brass, D. J. (1990). Changing patterns or patterns of change: the effects of a change in technology on social network structure and power. *Administrative Science Quarterly, Special Issue: Technology, Organizations, and Innovation, 35*(1), 104–127.

Carayon, P., & Smith, M. J. (2000). Work organization and ergonomics. *Applied Ergonomics, 31*(6), 649–662.

Cropley, M., & Zijlstra, F. R. H. (2011). Work and rumination. In J. Langan-Fox, & C. L. Cooper (Eds.), *Handbook of stress in the occupations* (pp. 487–503). Cheltenham: Edward Elgar Publishing Ltd.

Ekkers, C. L., Brouwers, A. A. F., Pasmooij, C. K., & Vlaming, P. D. (1980). *Menselijke stuur- en regeltaken* [Human control tasks]. Leiden: nipg/tno.

Fitts, P. M. (1951). *Human engineering for an effective air navigation and traffic control system*. Washington, DC: National Research Council.

Griffiths, M. (2002). Occupational health issues concerning Internet use in the workplace. *Work & Stress, 16*(4), 283–286.

Hancock, P. A. (2009). *Mind, machine and morality: Toward a philosophy of human-technology symbiosis*. Farnham: Ashgate.

Hancock, P. A., Billings, D. R., & Schaefer, K. E. (2011). Can you trust your robot? *Ergonomics in Design: The Quarterly of Human Factors Applications, 19*(3), 24–29.

Hancock, P. A., Billings, D. R., Schaefer, K. E., Chen, J. Y. C., de Visser, E., & Parasurama, R. (2011). A meta-analysis of factors affecting trust in human-robot interaction. *The Journal of the Human Factors and Ergonomics Society, 53*(5), 517–527. doi: 10.1177/ 0018720811417254

Hockey, G. R. J. (2003). Operator functional state as a framework for the assessment of performance. In G. R. J. Hockey, A. W. K. Gaillard, & O. Burov (Eds.), *Operator functional state: The assessment and prediction of human performance degradation in complex tasks* (pp. 8–23). Amsterdam: IOS Press.

Johansson, G. (1989). Job demands and stress reactions in repetitive and uneventful monotony at work. *International Journal of Health Services, 19*(2), 365–377.

Johansson, G., & Aronsson, G. (1984). Stress reactions in computerized administrative work. *Journal of Organizational Behavior, 5*(3), 159–181.

Klein, G., Woods, D. D., Bradshaw, J. M., Hoffman, R., & Feltovich, P. (2004). Ten challenges for making automation a "team player" in joint human-agent activity. *IEEE Computer Society, 6*, 91–95.

Lee, J. D., & Moray, N. (1992). Trust, control strategies, and allocation of function in human-machine systems. *Ergonomics, 22*, 671–691.

Lindström, K. (1991). Well-being and computer mediated work of various occupational groups in banking and insurance. *International Journal of Human-Computer Interaction, 3*, 339–361.

Maynard, R. (1997). Casting the net for job seekers. *Nation's Business, 85*, 28–29.

Miller, J. (2012). An historical view of operator fatigue. In G. Matthews, P. A. Desmond, C. Neubauer, & P. A. Hancock (Eds.), *The handbook of operator fatigue* (pp. 25–45). Farnham: Ashgate.

Nyssen, A.-S. (2004). Integrating cognitive and collective aspects of work in evaluating technology. *IEEE Transactions on Systems Man and Cybernetics Part A-Systems and Humans, 34*(6), 743–748.

Parasuraman, R., Sheridan, T., & Wickens, C. (2008). Situation awareness, mental workload, and trust in automation: viable, empirically supported cognitive engineering constructs. *Journal of Cognitive Engineering and Decision making, 2*(2), 140–160.

Sheridan, T. B. (1987). Supervisory control. In: G. Salvendy (Ed.), *Handbook of human factors*. New York: Wiley & Sons.

Sheridan, T., & Verplank, W. (1978). *Human and computer control of undersea teleoperators.* Cambridge, MA: MIT Man-Machine Systems Laboratory.

Scerbo, M. (1996). Theoretical perspective on adaptive automation. In R. Parasuraman & M. Mouloua (Eds.), *Automation and human performance*. Mahwah, NJ: Lawrence Erlbaum.

Vicente, J. K. (1999). *Cognitive work analysis: Towards safe, productive, and healthy computer-based work.* Mahwah, NJ: Lawrence Erlbaum Ass.

Weiner, E. L. (1989). *Human factors of advanced technology ("glass cockpit") transport aircraft.* Moffett Field, CA: NASA Ames Research Center.

Wickens, C. (1999). *Engineering psychology and human performance* (2nd ed.). New York, NY: HarperCollins.

Winter, J. C. F., & Dodou, D. (2014). Why the Fitts list has persisted throughout the history of function allocation. *Cognition, Technology & Work, 16,* 1–11.

Woods, D., & Hollnagel, E. (2006). *Joint cognitive systems: Pattern in cognitive system engineering.* Boca Raton, FL: Taylor & Francis.

Woods, D., Johannesen, L., Cook, R., & Sarter, N. (1994). Behind human error: cognitive systems, computers, and hindsight. *Crew Systems Ergonomic Information and Analysis Center,* Dayton, OH: Wright Patterson Air Force Base.

21 Why Do I Put Myself and Others in Danger or Help Increase Safety? Person- and Situation-Related Causes of Safety Behaviours

Nik Chmiel and Gudela Grote

Overview

This chapter focuses on employees' safety-related behaviours: why do workers do things that put them at risk of injury and death, on the one hand, and why do they do things that promote a safer workplace, on the other? The first part of the chapter sets out the types of unhelpful and helpful safety behaviours the chapter is interested in, and then discusses the possible person-related factors involved, including accident proneness and personality, before considering these in relation to employee perceptions of safety aspects of their workplaces, and in turn relating these to other, non-safety-specific psychological processes involved in workers' evaluations of their jobs and work relationships. Thereafter we discuss how workplace situations such as job demands, job resources, technology, an employee's work-group, their leaders, and their organization can affect helpful and unhelpful safety behaviours including the question of what behaviours organizations should or should not try to regulate.

21.1 Introduction

This chapter focuses on what could be termed by organizations behavioural safety. Behavioural safety concerns a person's own safety, but is often also related to the safety of other members of the organization or even to consequences outside of the organization, as in the case of major accidents. We take it as read that organizations have legal obligations (which of course vary across country and region around the world) regarding safety in their workplaces, and that organizations act (due to moral and economic imperatives also) to reduce the level of risk that their workforce is exposed

An Introduction to Work and Organizational Psychology: An International Perspective,
Third Edition. Edited by Nik Chmiel, Franco Fraccaroli and Magnus Sverke.
© 2017 John Wiley & Sons, Ltd. Published 2017 by John Wiley & Sons, Ltd.

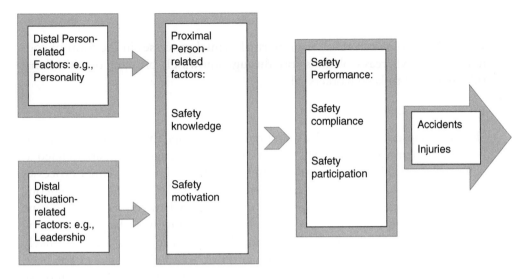

Figure 21.1: Safety Performance Model

Source: Adapted from Christian et al. (2009), Figure 1, p. 1105. Reproduced with permission of American Psychological Association.

to. Normally they will have in place systems of communication to apprise workers of hazards, and training programmes to enable workers to deal with those hazards. We also appreciate that some workplaces and jobs are inherently more dangerous than others: being part of a field team exploring the science of Antarctica is very different to working in an insurance office in a European city. So here we are concerned with why, from a psychological perspective, workers may not behave in as safe a way as their organization thinks they should, and why, on the other hand, they may behave to enhance safety for themselves and work colleagues. We therefore first consider what behaviours we are trying to explain, dividing them into those that are dangerous because they increase the risk of injury, and those that are helpful because they decrease the risk of injury. To help us organize the chapter thereafter we use as a point of departure a model proposed by Christian, Bradley, Wallace and Burke (2009). These authors proposed that safety performance is predicted by both person-related and situation-related factors, such as personality characteristics and job attitudes, on the one hand, and safety climate and leadership, on the other (see Figure 21.1).

21.2 What Behaviours Are We Explaining?

Many behaviours are involved in creating safety at work and just as many can do the reverse. It may sometimes even be difficult to say in advance whether a particular behaviour should be considered harmful or beneficial because only the outcome will tell, as in the case of someone deviating from a rule in good faith. In the following we will concentrate on those behaviours that have received much practical and research attention and are therefore particularly well understood.

21.2.1   Dangerous: cognitive error; violations

Unsafe behaviours can result from normal mental processes in the form of cognitive errors, whereas violations arise through knowingly breaking organizational rules designed to keep workers safe.

21.2.1.1   *Cognitive errors*

Slips and lapses are defined as unintentional errors that result from attentional and memory failures. Mistakes, rule- or knowledge-based, are defined as deficiencies or failures in intentional judgemental and/or inferential processes (Reason, 1990). These types of error have been related to how familiar someone is with their work. Slips and lapses are more likely when connected to routine actions in a highly familiar operating environment involving largely automatic cognitive (perceptual-motor) processing. Rule-based mistakes are more likely when problem-solving but where a situation or set of circumstances has been encountered before, and where the action is governed by the selection and use of stored rules rather than a direct automatic response. Knowledge-based performance is required in novel situations and circumstances, and is dependent on effortful problem-solving and reasoning to work out and decide on a course of action, rather than relying on previously learnt procedures. Almost all people find doing this mentally demanding, so making mistakes in reasoning more likely. All of these types of cognitive error have been implicated in accidents and injuries.

21.2.1.2   *Violations*

Violations are deliberate flouting of safety procedures and rules, and therefore are 'knowing' departures from specified safety rules and procedures. It is possible of course to violate rules unwittingly through ignorance of the rules, and these have been called 'unintentional violations' but 'for all intents and purposes these may be defined as errors rather than violations' (Reason, Parker, & Lawton, 1998, p. 293). Two important categories of deliberate violations have been identified: (1) habitual, or routinized, and (2) exceptional violations.

Reason et al. (1998) suggested there are three major categories of habitual violation: routine, optimizing, and situational. Routine violations typically involve corner-cutting − taking a path of least effort. Optimizing violations involve optimizing non-functional goals ahead of safety, for example, the enjoyment of speeding when driving. These two categories are linked to the attainment of personal goals. Situational violations involve seeing violations as essential 'to get the job done', e.g., because of organizational failings related to the work environment or equipment such as making personal protective equipment hard to access and use. Routine and situational violations have received most attention, with subsequent studies supporting the distinction between routine and situational violations as separable constructs, and finding them to be associated with different psychological processes (Hansez & Chmiel, 2010).

Reason et al. (1998, p. 293) also proposed that 'Recognizing a situation as hazardous and/or a rule as inappropriate is likely to lead to the adoption of self-protective behaviour' and hence would lead to an exceptional violation under certain circumstances, for example, when there are direct threats to life and limb. Exceptional violations need not be 'wrong' behaviours, after all, they are an attempt at self-protection, and may even lead to future rule recommendations in line with that behaviour if the organization thinks it better than what went before. More generally, not following a rule may also be done in good faith, believing the system or others, as well as oneself, may be made safer by doing so. As such, therefore exceptional violations should be kept distinct from 'routinized' violation behaviours, and in fact could in some cases be seen as helpful for future safety.

21.2.1.3   *Helpful: safety compliance, safety participation*

Helpful behaviours can be split into two. On the one hand are behaviours complying with rules and procedures designed to keep you safe, and, on the other, are behaviours which help promote safety, such as volunteering for safety committees, initiating suggestions to improve safety programmes, and helping co-workers to work safely.

21.2.1.4   *Complying with safety rules*

Complying with rules and procedures is generally expected as part of doing one's job and usually is formally prescribed by organizations, whereas not complying would be seen as violating rules and procedures, so compliance and violation can be treated as two sides of the same coin (cf. Beus, Dhanani & McCord, 2015a).

21.2.1.5   *Safety participation: discretionary behaviours*

Interesting are those behaviours that may be more discretionary in natur – employees do not necessarily have to do them as part of their job, but nonetheless they are helpful in reducing risk. Such behaviours have been labelled as 'safety participation' (e.g., Neal, Griffin, & Hart, 2000) and 'safety citizenship' behaviours (Hofmann, Morgeson, & Gerras, 2003).

Neal, Griffin and Hart (2000) measured 'safety participation' by asking employees questions about their: promotion of the safety programme within the organization; any extra effort to improve the safety of the workplace; helping coworkers when they are working under risky or hazardous conditions; and voluntarily carrying out tasks or activities that help to improve workplace safety. Hofman et al. (2003) asked questions in six categories based in part on the organizational citizenship literature. The categories were: safety-related helping (e.g., helping teach safety procedures to new crew members); voice (e.g., speaking up and encouraging others to get involved in safety issues); stewardship (e.g., taking action to protect other crew members from risky situations); whistleblowing (e.g., reporting crew members who violate safety procedures); civic virtue (e.g., maintaining an up-to-date knowledge of safety issues: and initiating safety-related workplace change (e.g., trying to improve safety procedures). Thus safety participation behaviours go above and beyond those usually regarded as part of a job.

Helpful safety participation behaviours are associated with less accidents and injuries and also predict future compliance with safety rules and regulations (Neal & Griffin, 2006).

21.3   Is It Me?

A variety of person-related factors relate to someone's behaviour, ones that come to mind readily include personality and attitudes, and Christian et al. (2009) specifically mention these as person-related factors relevant to safety performance. We begin by briefly reviewing the issues around whether particular people may be deemed 'accident prone', and whether with regard to workplace safety their personalities are responsible. We then discuss other person-related influences on safety at work, including individual employee perceptions of safety-related features of their working environment and other non-safety-specific psychological processes related to jobs and managers.

21.3.1   Am I 'accident prone'?

The idea behind accident proneness is that some people have more accidents than others, more than would be expected by chance, and that the reason is to do with them rather than the situation they are in. That is, they are more liable to be involved in accidents because of who they are. So the first question to ask is whether some people really are involved in more accidents than could be expected by chance.

That a small number of munitions workers had the greatest number of accidents was reported by Greenwood and Woods as far back as 1919. These observations have been taken to imply some people are more liable to have accidents than others. However, there has been controversy surrounding this conclusion. Similar accident distributions to those studied by Greenwood and Woods can be predicted, based on assuming people have equal accident liabilities (McKenna, 1983), suggesting the clustering of accidents in a few people could arise by chance. So is it possible to infer a person's accident liability from their accident record, and support the idea that the people who have more accidents are somehow more prone? In tackling this problem Mintz (1954) observed that two assumptions were necessary. One is that accident liability is not changed by being involved in an accident and does not vary over time. The other is that accident liability varies among people and is distributed in some known manner. Even with these assumptions Mintz showed that there could be people in a group who had more than the mean number of accidents for the group where their probable accident liability was below the mean for the group. However as numbers of accidents increased well above the group mean, so the probability that the accident liability of those people involved would be below the group mean decreased markedly. Recently Visser, Pijl, Stolk, Neeleman and Rosmalen (2007) studied the observed versus expected number of accident repeaters in the general population through a meta-analysis of studies where mean injury rates did not exceed one injury per observation years, concluding that their results indicated that accidents do cluster in the general population and that the clustering was more prevalent than expected by chance. So it appears in answer to our first question we should take the notion that some people are more liable to be involved in accidents than others seriously, but does that mean they are more accident-prone because of who they are?

21.3.1.1   *Personality traits and accidents*

The term 'accident liability' allows for both personal and environmental conditions predisposing people to accidents, but Greenwood and Woods (1919) proposed there was something in a high accident group's personality make-up that accounted for why they had most accidents, giving rise to the notion of 'accident proneness'. Visser et al. (2007, p. 557) define accident proneness as 'the tendency of an individual to experience more accidents than otherwise identical individuals (in terms of basic characteristics like age, gender and place of residence) due to stable personality characteristics'.

A primary question is, does knowing someone's personality characteristics predict their accident involvement? Clarke and Robertson (2005) help answer this question. They used the 'Big Five' or Five Factor Model (FFM) of personality as a framework to meta-analyse relationships between openness, agreeableness, conscientiousness, extraversion, and neuroticism and accidents. They found low agreeableness and low conscientiousness to be valid and generalizable predictors of accident involvement for both work-related and non-occupational accidents. Extraversion was found to predict traffic accidents but not occupational accidents.

21.3.1.2   *Accident exposure and propensity*

Accidents though, as already noted, may not be just a function of a person's characteristics but also of the environment they are working in. 'Exposure' (E) is defined as the number of opportunities for accidents of a certain type in a given time in a given area. For example figures for 2014/15 in the UK show construction workers were twice as likely to sustain an injury compared to those working in education. In short, exposure concerns the hazardous nature of the working environment in general. 'Propensity' (P) is the probability that an accident will occur, given the opportunity for one. In the work environment, propensity could vary as function of a range of organizational and employee-related factors, including, for example, working times, work pressure, the nature and extent of safety regulations, the degree to which workers are inclined to comply with these regulations, and the extent to which employees engage in helpful safety-related behaviours. Thus, propensity concerns the particular circumstances involved in a work environment, separate from the nature of that environment under normal operating conditions. The higher the number of opportunities for accidents (E) and the greater the presence of factors that could increase the likelihood of accidents to occur (P), the more accidents (A) will happen:

$$A = P \times E$$

So how does this consideration of exposure and propensity relate to the idea of accident proneness? A key issue is that people may select themselves into, stay in, or choose to leave different types of job as a function of their personality, interests, and values (Ployhart & Schmitt, 2008). So it is possible that certain personality types prefer to take or accept more risk at work than others. In support of this view, extraversion has been found to predict work domain risk preference – the more extravert, the more preference for risk – whereas people who were more conscientious preferred less risk (Soane & Chmiel, 2005). Thus, personality may play a part in people working in more hazardous sectors of the economy and/or choosing more dangerous jobs. For example, sensation-seekers (an aspect of extraversion) may choose deep sea diving rather than clerical work. This means they will be exposed to more opportunities for accidents. Further, they may also prefer organizations with fewer or minimal safety rules, meaning propensity is higher. Thus, people in those sectors and jobs will be more likely to be involved in more accidents and so we should observe a correlation between personality and accidents because of that. Thus when relating personality and accidents across different industrial sectors and types of organization and job, non-individual difference factors connected to exposure and propensity should be accounted for before we can attribute any remaining effect on accidents to individual causes such as accident proneness.

21.3.1.3   *Personality traits and safety behaviours*

Our discussion of exposure and propensity strongly suggests that if we want to investigate direct effects of personality on accident liability we should be focusing our research attention on what personality may directly affect when doing a job: that is on employees' own safety-related behaviour. This issue has been addressed by Beus, Dhanani and McCord (2015a) using a meta-analysis of 69 studies using the Five Factor Model (FFM) framework. They coded safety behaviours to include both unhelpful and helpful ones, such as using or failing to use safety equipment, following or disregarding safety procedures, and promoting or circumventing workplace safety programmes. In terms of general FFM factors, they found that the strongest relationships were between agreeableness and conscientiousness and safety behaviours: the more agreeable or conscientious, the less people engaged in unsafe behaviours. They also found significant, but weaker, relationships between extraversion and neuroticism with higher scores on both associated with more unsafe behaviours. They found no relationship between openness to experience and unsafe behaviour.

A large number of studies considering liability and accidents have included driving accidents, raising the question that any link can be attributable to driving contexts rather than workplaces. So it is useful that Beus et al. (2015a) compared driving versus non-driving contexts in their analysis and found these contexts made no difference to the strength of the relationships they found between personality characteristics and safety behaviours.

All in all Beus et al. reported that collectively the FFM traits accounted for 13% of the variance in safety-related behaviour with agreeableness explaining the most variance, followed by conscientiousness. They further demonstrated that 2% of the variation in accident outcomes were explained as a result of the FFM traits being mediated by safety behaviours.

21.3.1.4   *Personality facets and safety behaviours*

In addition to broad personality traits researchers have also been interested in particular aspects or facets of those traits. Beus et al. (2015a) looked for relationships between facets of the FFM factors and unsafe behaviours. They found that sensation-seeking had a stronger relationship with unsafe behaviours than did its general factor of extraversion. In contrast, altruism and its agreeableness factor, order and its conscientiousness factor, and anger, impulsiveness and their neuroticism factor did not show meaningful differences. However, one facet of neuroticism, anxiety, showed an effect in the opposite direction to its factor, higher anxiety associated with less unsafe behaviour, which suggests facet level research could lead to further insights into the processes and mechanisms linking personality to accidents. For example, Christian et al. (2009) combined cognitive failure with conscientiousness in their coding scheme on the basis that cognitive failure was reflective of poor dependability, an aspect of conscientiousness. However, Wallace and Vodanovich (2003) found support for the idea that cognitive failure moderated the relationship between conscientiousness and unsafe work behaviours and accidents, and suggested cognitive failure plays an important part in individual safety behaviour, especially when conscientiousness is low.

In an alternative facet-based approach Hogan and Foster (2013) argued for combining different FFM facets into personality-based safety scales to better predict safety-related performance dimensions, derived from a search of the psychological literature on safety and safety incidents reported in the media. The performance dimensions they identified were: following standard operating procedures; handling stress; maintaining emotional control; focusing attention; avoiding unnecessary risks; and pursuing training and development opportunities. They developed personality scales to predict these dimensions labelled respectively: Compliant; Confident; Emotionally Stable; Vigilant; Cautious; and Trainable. As an example, the compliant personality scale correlated with the FFM facets Anger (from the Neuroticism factor) and Compliance (from the Agreeableness factor) among others, leading Hogan and Foster to propose that their compliant personality safety predictor measured characteristics associated with complying with social norms and expectations rather than more compulsive characteristics such as perfectionism, order, achievement orientation, and lack of impulsiveness which are represented by the FFM factor of Conscientiousness. Hogan and Foster report that the composite battery of their developed personality scales correlated positively and significantly with safety performance, and further analyses supported the conclusion that the relationship between their personality scales and safety outcomes, such as accidents and injuries, was mediated by safety performance. Clearly then such an approach implies that if appropriate facets were to be considered, the relationship between personality characteristics and safety behaviours may be stronger than the results from Beus et al. (2015) suggest.

In sum, recent research supports the idea that personality does play a role in behaving safely at work. Since such behaviour affects the likelihood of being involved in an accident, it appears that in part accident liability can indeed be attributed to personality characteristics and so to accident proneness.

21.3.2   Is it how I perceive safety in my workplace?

Although we can argue personality is involved in liability, we have to consider that how workers perceive their working environment with respect to safety also plays a part. Measures of such perceptions have variously been called perceived management commitment to safety, perceived safety climate, and psychological safety climate. Table 21.1 shows the items used by Hansez and Chmiel (2010) to measure such perceptions. Employees were asked how much they agreed or disagreed with each statement.

Table 21.1: Items used to measure perceived management commitment to safety

Management have a positive attitude towards safety.
Due recognition is given by management to employees who practice good safety habits.
Safe procedures at work are given enough publicity.
I am happy with the level of safety training for my job.
The company encourages employees to attend safety meetings and/or safety training.
The company is quick to respond to the safety concerns of their employees.
The company takes the safety ideas of employees seriously
Safety is given a high priority in company meetings and planned activities.
Senior management are actively involved in safety programmes.
Managers take action on employees' non-compliance with safety rules or procedures.
Action is taken by senior management on reports of potential hazards.
The company encourages employees to voice their concerns about safety.
Violations to safety procedures, even when no damage has resulted, are taken seriously by management.

Source: Hansez & Chmiel (2010), Reproduced with permission of American Psychological Association.

Beus et al. (2015a) showed in their meta-analysis that psychological safety climate measures and a combination of agreeableness, conscientiousness and neuroticism explained nearly half (43%) the total variance in safety behaviours, but, in relative terms, safety climate perceptions accounted for nearly two-thirds of the explained variance and the three personality traits combined accounted for a third, with agreeableness contributing more than conscientiousness, and both of those were much more important than neuroticism. Thus, such perceptions potentially appear to play an independent and bigger role than personality in accident liability. Other relevant psychological processes though are also separable from safety climate perceptions and we discuss these next.

21.3.3   Are there other person-related processes?

21.3.3.1   Safety-specific and non-safety specific processes

What other person-related processes, different to those engendered by safety climate perceptions, are there? Hansez and Chmiel (2010) used the Job Demands–Resources (JDR) model to predict safety behaviours (these were two types of violations: one effort-based and the other provoked by the organization) through three different independent processes. One process related to a person's evaluation of their job demands, which entails feelings of job strain and exhaustion (a 'cognitive–energetical' process). A second process related to a person's evaluation of the resources available to them through their job, which entails work engagement and being prepared to put more effort into work (a 'willingness' process), and a third process through safety climate perceptions, which are theorized to influence behaviours through signalling which behaviours will be approved or disapproved of (an 'instrumental' process). Thus, Hansez and Chmiel's findings provide support, from the same sample of workers, that both safety-specific and non-safety-specific processes are involved in predicting safety behaviours.

Chmiel and Hansez (2016), in reviewing the research literature, further identified a fourth process as fundamental to behaving safely. As a result of deciding they have good quality relationships with a supervisor, manager or organization, employees may feel obliged to reciprocate, or give back, the support they feel they receive, and behave more safely as a result if that is what they feel their manager or organization wants (a 'reciprocation' process). As a result of the processes just discussed, four motivational states can be viewed as fundamental to safety behaviours: (1) being mentally exhausted, (2) feeling engaged, (3) feeling rewarded for behaving safely, and (4) feeling obliged to behave safely. A fifth state, valuing safety as important, is also discussed by Chmiel and Hansez as different to the other states, and has been shown to be associated with safety climate perceptions (Neal, Griffin, & Hart, 2000).

21.3.3.2   Attitudes and norms

Constructs such as attitudes, perceived behavioural control and norms are features of the theory of planned behaviour (TPB) that specifies how they should be linked together to predict behavioural intentions and behaviours. The theory has received a huge amount of research attention. In relation to safety, Fugas, Melia and Silva (2011) demonstrated that employees' perceived coworker safety norms, based on perceptions of coworker behaviours towards safety practices, predicted their future helpful proactive safety behaviours. Fugas, Silva and Melia (2013) also showed that groups of transportation workers who engaged in more or less helpful safety behaviours could be differentiated along several dimensions. Perceived behavioural control best differentiated the group with more safe (compliance) behaviours than others, whereas perceived behavioural control, attitudes and coworkers' safety norms differentiated groups with respect to proactive safety behaviours. Fogarty and Shaw (2010) used the TPB to model how attitudes, norms, and intentions to violate, predicted violations in their study. In their case, the TPB had to be modified to achieve an adequate fit to the data, and some argue the theory has served its purpose and is less useful now (Sniehotta, Presseau, & Araujo-Soares, 2014) while acknowledging the variables identified in the theory do help predict behaviour. Consistent with this view, Fogarty and Shaw found that attitudes and norms did predict violations through behavioural intentions as expected from the TPB, but also found these two variables predicted violations directly.

In sum, we can say that although personality and safety climate perceptions play a large role in the prediction of safety behaviours, we should at least also include individual differences in cognitive–energetical processes, work engagement, attitudes, support from work relationships, perceived group norms, and perceived behavioural control as aiding our understanding of person-related factors important to safety behaviours at work. Future research can then be directed at understanding how situational factors give rise to and influence these psychological states and processes, and in return how individual employees may act to change their own work environment to make it safer.

21.4   Is It My Situation at Work?

Any behaviour results from the interaction between personal and situational factors. Regarding safety at work, relevant situational factors are similar to those which influence all other work behaviour, that is, characteristics of the job, of the work team, of leadership and of the larger organizational context (Christian et al., 2009). We will review safety-relevant aspects of each of these in the following. The example of a major accident described in Box 21.1 shows that not only personal and situational factors interact, but also the situational factors among themselves.

Box 21.1:   Crash of Air France flight 447

Just after 2 a.m. on 1 June 2009, an Airbus 330 operated by Air France on its way from Rio de Janeiro to Paris stalled over the Atlantic Ocean and crashed into the water, killing all 228 persons on board. The final report of France's Bureau d'Enquêtes et d'Analyses pour la Sécurité de l'Aviation Civile (BEA) stated that inconsistencies between different speed measurements caused the autopilot to disconnect, requiring the cockpit crew to fly the aircraft manually, which they did not manage to do successfully. When flying at high altitude, manual control of an aircraft is generally very demanding and was particularly so in this case due to zero visibility and a heavy storm. Two first officers – the captain as third crew member was still asleep in the cabin – were in charge at the time. The least experienced of the crew was acting as 'pilot flying' and pulled up the aircraft nose to a very steep angle, eventually causing a stall. After a few minutes, the captain joined the two first officers in the cockpit, but the incorrect flight manoeuvres were continued, resulting in the aircraft descending nose up at very high speed until it hit the water. Despite auditory stall warnings, only the captain realized at the very end that the aircraft was stalled. Root causes of the accident concern technological factors (pitot tubes, inadequate information of speed inconsistencies, lacking mechanical feedback from manual flight operations), person-related factors (inexperience, failure to follow procedures related to speed inconsistencies, inadequate situation awareness), and organizational factors (insufficient training for manual flight at high altitudes and for handling inconsistent speed information).

Source: Grote et al. 2009. Reproduced with permission of Springer.

21.4.1   What safety concerns are inherent in my job?

21.4.1.1   *Process safety and personal safety*

First of all, it is important to understand what particular demands regarding safety exist in a job. A fundamental distinction is that between process safety and personal safety. Process safety is directly linked to the primary work task, such as curing patients or producing chemicals. Potential damages result from failures in the execution of processes linked to this task. Breaches of process safety do not necessarily cause harm to the workers involved, such as in the case of a physician causing a patient's death due to false medication. In personal safety, on the other hand, potential damages always concern the workers, but in turn are not necessarily directly linked to the primary work task. In building construction, for instance, the basic process safety requirement is the stability of the structures erected, while personal safety for construction workers concerns incidents such as falling off a scaffold. Protection against common occupational injuries, such as sprains, fractures, cuts, and bruises, is mostly a secondary task, sometimes even interfering with the primary task, as, for instance, in the case of ear protection preventing detection of task-relevant signals such as unusual machine noises. Personal and process safety may or may not be closely related, depending on the primary work task. Pilots put their own just as much as passengers' lives at risk when operating an aircraft. In building construction, structural safety as the core requirement of the work process and personal safety are quite unrelated, except when structures fail during construction already. Furthermore, causal mechanisms involved in promoting personal versus process safety most likely differ due to differences in the visibility and complexity of risks, required competence for risk handling, available incentives for safe behaviour, and conflicts between safety and production requirements. However, to date, there is little conceptual and empirical knowledge on how measures aimed at process safety or personal safety achieve their effects and how they interact. This constitutes a very significant need for future research.

21.4.1.2   Job demands and resources

Two topics dominate discussions on the relationship between safety and job demands and resources: the production-safety trade-off and the impact of job autonomy on safety. With respect to the production-safety trade-off, the main concern is that workers are often confronted with conflicting demands to do their job efficiently and do it safely. This conflict can originate at the organizational level where expenditure of resources for safety and production need to be balanced, but also at the individual level based on short-term cost-benefit considerations concerning behaviours such as wearing uncomfortable protective equipment. The second issue related to job demands and resources concerns the role of job autonomy for promoting safe behaviour. Job autonomy is considered one of the main resources for dealing with job demands. However, in the safety literature, the effect of job autonomy is less clear: Research indicates that autonomy is beneficial mostly for safety participation, that is, proactive behaviours such as providing suggestions for safety improvements and less so for safety compliance, such as rule-following (Turner, Stride, Carter, & McCaughey, 2012). A recent meta-analysis examining the impact of job demands and resources on employee health and safety more generally has shown that job demands created by risks and hazards at the workplace are related to both burnout and adverse safety outcomes, while social support, leadership and safety climate constitute important resources linked to more safety (Nahrgang, Morgeson & Hofmann, 2011).

21.4.1.3   Automation

Much research in the human factors domain has been devoted to examining the effects of increasing automation on safety. The basic concern has been for a long time that people are put in charge of increasingly complex and non-transparent technical systems with decreasing opportunities to active control these systems. This dilemma continues to be the root cause of many accidents and research remains very active in helping to overcome it (Grote, Weyer, & Stanton, 2014). One example which has attracted much attention in recent years because it deeply affects everyday life is autonomous driving, where the debate reaches from jubilant accounts of car accidents becoming a problem of the past to more cautious views which reflect the intricacies of control and accountability in human-technology interaction.

21.4.2   How does my team impact safety?

21.4.2.1   *Social support, psychological safety and group safety climate*

Research has established social support as an important driver for promoting safety (Nahrgang et al., 2011; Turner et al., 2012). A key aspect of social support is psychological safety, which has been defined as the perception that in a team it is safe to take the interpersonal risks involved in, for instance, questioning others' behaviour or admitting to mistakes (Edmondson, 1999). Psychological safety has been studied especially as a prerequisite for speaking up, which in turn has been shown to be related to safety performance (Kolbe et al., 2012).

A long-standing topic in the safety literature is the study of shared perceptions of safety-related policies, procedures, and practices, termed safety climate (Zohar, 1980). Earlier we discussed safety-related perceptions as a person factor and indeed emotional stability and locus of control have been found to be related to more positive safety perceptions at the individual and group level (Beus, Munoz, & Arthur, 2015). But safety perceptions are also influenced by situational factors and the sharedness of perceptions in itself presumably creates an important situational influence on individuals. While some climate measures focus on shared perceptions of managers' behaviours and attitudes (e.g., Zohar & Luria, 2010), others are based on a more generic set of individual safety-related perceptions aggregated to the team level. Generally, strong relationships between group safety climate and safety outcomes are found, which appear to be stronger than the relationships between person-related characteristics and safety (Christian et al., 2009).

21.4.2.2   *Team behaviour*

Besides research on safety-related perceptions and attitudes in groups there is also a strong research stream that addresses actual behaviour in high-risk teams. In particular coordination, that is the management of task interdependencies, has been studied, and related to changing task and situational requirements. Two coordination mechanisms that have received much attention in this respect are explicit versus implicit coordination. Explicit coordination is the deliberate and resource-intensive establishment of common ground and subsequent decision-making based on the information acquired and evaluated in the team. Implicit coordination, on the other hand, relies on shared assumptions and knowledge about the team, the task and the context, enabling team members to coordinate their action in an effortless manner with few demands on information acquisition and assessment. As implicit coordination is less resource-intensive, it is considered most suited for very demanding tasks. However, if these tasks entail unexpected elements, explicit coordination may become necessary. Of particular importance is therefore to help teams realize the need to switch between coordination mechanisms for which speaking up (Kolbe et al., 2012), but also more effortless behaviours such as talking to the room and monitoring team behaviour (Kolbe et al., 2014) have been found to be effective.

21.4.3 How well am I led? How well do I lead?

21.4.3.1 *Leadership styles*

As in the leadership literature more generally, much of the research on safety has been concerned with identifying effective leadership styles. Especially transformational leadership – that is leadership aimed at motivating employees through inspiration and charisma – has generally been found to be positively related to safety outcomes. However, in a recent meta-analysis (Clarke, 2013), it appears that transactional leadership – the counterpart of transformational leadership aimed at an exchange of rewards for fulfilling expectations – supports both safety participation and compliance, while transformational leadership supports mainly safety participation. Zohar and Luria (2010) have shown that transformational leadership is particularly important for promoting safe behaviour when the priority of safety is not sufficiently embedded in company values. The requirement to adapt leadership styles to situational requirements more generally has been demonstrated by Yun, Faraj and Sims (2005), who found that directive leadership in medical emergency teams was more successful in complex cases and with less experienced team members, while an empowering style was effective in less complex cases and with more experienced teams.

21.4.3.2 *Shared leadership*

Another approach to leadership is to define it in functional terms as exerting influence on others in order to determine and achieve objectives. The tasks and processes involved in leadership are emphasized rather than the formal leadership role. This perspective also provides the foundation for the concept of shared leadership, which argues that leadership functions can be fulfilled not only by the formal leader, but by any team member. In high-risk teams, shared leadership has been shown to promote safety, for instance, in shock trauma teams (Klein et al., 2006). The situation becomes even more complex, when several teams interact as so-called multi-team systems, as is the case for cockpit crews and cabin crews (see Figure 21.2). Bienefeld and Grote (2014) analyzed shared leadership within and across cockpit and cabin crews, operationalized in terms of the ratio of leadership behaviours by formal leaders versus by other team members. Data from behaviour observations of 84 aircrews (with two cockpit crew members and four cabin crew members each) handling a simulated emergency (smoke of unknown origin in the cabin) showed that overall successful aircrews – which achieved a safe landing with all passengers adequately protected – were characterized by more shared leadership in the cabin, but not in the cockpit. More leadership by the captain was related to team goal attainment, that is a safe landing, independent of whether the aircrew overall achieved its goal. Furthermore,

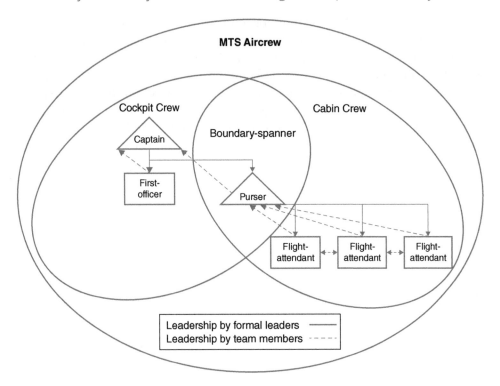

Figure 21.2:   Leadership in a multi-team system

Source: from Bienefeld & Grote, 2014, Figure 1, p. 273. Reproduced with permission of the SAGE Publications.

more leadership of pursers, that is, the formal leaders of the cabin crew, towards the cockpit crew was evident in successful aircrews. The authors discuss their findings in view of the pursers' crucial role as boundary spanners for achieving overall success and the support for this role through shared leadership in the cabin crew. More generally, the study indicates that some caution is needed in judging the benefits of shared leadership. It appears that shared leadership needs to be carefully balanced with leadership by the formal leader. Sharing should concern only delegation of specific leadership tasks, while the overall responsibility should remain with the formal leader, thereby creating some stability and orientation for team members.

21.4.3.3   Substitutes for leadership

Finally, there may be situations where personal leadership is overall less important due to substitutes being in place, such as standards that prescribe work processes in great detail or very experienced employees who know what to do without a leader telling them. In cockpit crews, it was indeed found that better performance in a simulated non-routine situation (landing an aircraft without the flaps and slats on the wings working) was linked to coordination patterns with little leadership and much implicit coordination in highly standardized work phases (take-off and landing) and more leadership during the less standardized work phase of preparing for the unusual landing (Grote et al., 2010). Moreover, substitution may affect different leadership functions differently. For instance, in anaesthesia teams consisting of more experienced nurses and less experienced, but formally responsible residents (i.e., physicians training at a hospital to become a specialist in a particular field of medicine), successful performance was linked to residents being mostly involved with information search and structuring, while nurses took over problem solving (Künzle et al., 2010).

21.4.4   Does my company care about safety?

21.4.4.1   Organizational safety climate and safety culture

Generally, organizational culture concerns shared norms and assumptions guiding behaviour while organizational climate refers to shared perceptions of organizational reality. Applying this distinction to safety culture and safety climate, safety culture can be defined as 'the sum of all safety-related assumptions and norms that are shared by the majority of an organisation's members, and which find their expression in the way safety is actually dealt with in all areas of the organisation' (Müller et al., 1998, p. 25), while safety climate reflects employees' shared perceptions of how safety is managed in the workplace (Zohar, 1980). Given the difficulties inherent in measuring safety culture, much more research has been devoted to studying organizational safety climate, usually measured in terms of the shared perception of aspects such as management commitment to safety, adequate safety management tools and procedures, appropriate risk perception, priority of safety concerns over production pressures, and sufficient knowledge and skills (Flin et al., 2000). Overall, there is ample evidence that organizations which place high importance on safety have better safety performance and outcomes than those that do not (Christian et al., 2009; Nahrgang et al., 2011). Recent research has begun also to consider the reverse relationship: that is, perceptions of a positive safety climate being the consequence of safe behaviour and low accident rates (Stride et al., 2013). Next to safety climate, safety culture remains a hotly debated topic, but mostly with a sense of frustration because culture is often assessed only through climate, it is abused as a catch-all category in accident investigations, and its potential for a deeper systemic understanding of the processes involved in (un)successful safety interventions is not taken advantage of (Silbey, 2009; Strauch, 2015).

21.4.4.2   Safety rules

Inherent in most of the discussions about safety is the assumption that safety requires a firm set of rules which need to be followed by all employees in order to avoid accidents and injuries. This assumption is tied to the basic belief that safety is the result of successfully reducing all uncertainties that could impinge on following the prescribed safe way of doing one's work (Grote, 2015). Accordingly, safety compliance is frequently taken as an indicator of safety. However, in recent years, there has been a shift in the safety literature towards acknowledging the need also to flexibly respond to uncertainties as they are an inevitability in complex systems, expressed, for instance, in safety participation as more proactive behaviour also being considered conducive to safety outcomes (Griffin & Neal, 2000) and in acknowledging possible benefits of rule violations as discussed earlier. This raises the question of what constitutes effective safety rules, given that they should provide sufficient guidance but also leeway for adaptive action. Grote and colleagues (2009) have introduced the construct of flexible rules as a response to this question, which draws on the distinction suggested by Hale and Swuste (1998) between goal, process, and action rules. Goal rules only define the goal to be achieved, leaving open how this is accomplished by the actors concerned. Process rules provide guidance for deciding on the right course of action for achieving certain goals. Finally, action rules prescribe detailed courses of action, possibly without even mentioning the goal to be achieved. Goal and process rules and also those action rules that entail some decision latitude constitute flexible rules. As a rule of thumb on good rule making, action rules should be used when stability of processes can be mostly guaranteed; goal and process rules should be used when high degrees of flexibility are required. Also, there are a number of important prerequisites for using flexible rules well, such as systematic consideration of the uncertainties in a given work process and adequate training of employees (see also Box 21.2).

Box 21.2:   Analysis of rules in the Rule Book of a European railway company (from Grote et al., 2009)

As part of a project conducted to support a railway company and the regulatory agency in evaluating the existing Rule Book and possibly implementing improvements, a rule analysis was carried out. Using coupling and braking of cars during shunting operations and train departure as exemplary work processes, the written rules associated with these two work processes were analyzed using the rule taxonomy developed by Hale and Swuste (1998). Overall, 215 rules were analyzed. The majority of rules were action rules, but many rules contained some decision latitude also. Very few rules were goal rules and up to a third – depending on the work process – were process rules. One important finding was the prevalence of process rules for shunting operations, which in combination with the shunters' comparatively low level of qualification and reluctance to take responsibility for using the decision latitude offered created tensions. For the signallers, somewhat the opposite pattern was found. This highly qualified group had to act on much more defined and prescriptive action rules, but 'stretched' these in order to accommodate non-routine situations. The findings of the study served as input into guidelines for rulemakers to help them make more systematic choices on rule types, taking into consideration the uncertainties inherent in the work situation and the competence profiles of the different actors.

Summary

In this chapter we have provided a review of the literature regarding personal and situational factors involved in (un)safe behaviours. Cognitive errors and violations are crucial unsafe behaviours and safety compliance and safety participation are considered to be important safe behaviours. We have shown that personal dispositions as well as individual attitudes and self-regulatory processes are predictors of safety performance. Subsequently we have discussed relevant situational factors, in particular, characteristics of job design, the work team, leadership and the organization at large. The empirical evidence indicates that situational factors overall are stronger predictors of safety outcomes than personal factors, but the mediating processes still need to be determined. These processes may in themselves contain complex interactions of person and situation, as, for instance, regarding the development of shared perceptions of safety-related policies, procedures, and practices, constituting what has been termed the safety climate and which has been found to be a powerful predictor of safety performance. Thus, any answer to why employees may put themselves in danger or help make a workplace safer has to include an appreciation of the situation they are in and an understanding of their reaction to their situation as a function of their personality, perceptions and attitudes. The difficulties in establishing what is safe behaviour to begin with was discussed in relation to safety compliance, understood as rule following. The more complex and uncertain work processes are, the more likely it is that prescribed behaviours may in fact be inadequate to ensure safety in all cases. Helping employees to make the right choices in these situations is an important leadership task.

Discussion Points

1 Do you think personality is an important influence on safety behaviour in organizations?
2 What are important factors to be considered when designing jobs in view of demands for safe behaviour?

Suggested Further Reading

Chmiel, N., & Hansez, I. (2016). Jobs and safety behavior. In S. Clarke, T. M. Probst, F. Guldenmund, & J. Passmore (Eds.), *The Wiley Blackwell handbook of the psychology of occupational safety and workplace health.* Chichester: John Wiley & Sons, Ltd. This review chapter goes into further detail about the relationships between jobs and safety behaviours, and the variety of possible motivational processes that may help explain them.

Chmiel, N., & Taris, T. W. (2014). Safety at work. In M. C. W. Peeters, J. de Jonge, & T. W. Taris (Eds.), *An introduction to contemporary work psychology.* Chichester: Wiley-Blackwell. This chapter provides a fuller exposition of accident exposure and propensity and uses case studies to illustrate a general approach to relating organizational practices to safety.

Grote, G. (2012). Safety management in different high-risk domains – all the same? *Safety*

Science, 50, 1983–1992. This article provides an overview of contextual factors that should be considered when designing organizations for an optimal support of safety at work.

Grote, G. (2016). Managing uncertainty in high risk environments. In S. Clarke, T. M. Probst, F. Guldenmund, & J. Passmore (Eds.), *The Wiley Blackwell. Chich handbook of the psychology of occupational safety and workplace health* ester: John Wiley & Sons, Ltd. This chapter presents an in-depth discussion of the relationship between safety and uncertainty at the individual, team, and organizational level based on a broad literature review and offers guidance for effectively managing uncertainty at these three levels.

References

Beus, J.M., Dhanani, L.Y., & McCord, A. (2015a). A meta-analysis of personality and workplace safety: addressing unanswered questions. *Journal of Applied Psychology, 100*, 481–498.

Beus, J. M., Munoz, G. J., & Arthur, W. (2015b). Personality as a multilevel predictor of climate: An examination in the domain of workplace safety. *Group & Organization Management, 40*, 625–656.

Bienefeld, N., & Grote, G. (2014). Shared leadership in multi-team systems: How cockpit and cabin crews lead each other to safety. *Human Factors, 56*, 270–286.

Chmiel, N., & Hansez, I. (2016). Jobs and safety behavior. In S. Clarke, T. M. Probst, F. Guldenmund, & J. Passmore (Eds.), *The Wiley Blackwell handbook of the psychology of occupational safety and workplace health*. Chichester: John Wiley & Sons Ltd.

Christian, M. S., Bradley, J. C., Wallace, J. C., & Burke, M. J. (2009). workplace safety: A meta-analysis of the roles of person and situation factors. *Journal of Applied Psychology, 94*, 1103–1127.

Clarke, S. (2013). Safety leadership: A meta-analytic review of transformational and transactional leadership styles as antecedents of safety behaviours. *Journal of Occupational and Organizational Psychology, 86*, 22–49.

Clarke, S., & Robertson, I.T. (2005). A meta-analytic review of the Big Five personality factors and accident involvement in occupational and non-occupational settings. *Journal of Occupational and Organizational Psychology, 78*, 355–376.

Edmondson, A. (1999). Psychological safety and learning behavior in work teams. *Administrative Science Quarterly, 44*, 350–383.

Flin, R., Mearns, K., O'Connor, P., Bryden, R. (2000). Measuring safety climate: Identifying the common features. *Safety Science, 34*, 177–192.

Fogarty, G. J., & Shaw, A. (2010). Safety climate and the theory of planned behavior: Towards the prediction of unsafe behavior. *Accident Analysis, 42*, 1455–1459.

Fugas, C. S., Melia, J. L., Silva, S. A. (2011). The "is" and the "ought": How do perceived social norms influence safety behaviors at work? *Journal of Occupational Health Psychology, 16*, 67–79.

Fugas, C. S., Silva, S. A., & Melia, J. L. (2013). Profiling safety behaviors: exploration of the sociocognitive variables that best discriminate between different behavioral patterns. *Risk Analysis, 33*, 838–850.

Greenwood, M. & Woods, H. M. (1919). *The incidence of industrial accidents upon individuals with special reference to multiple accidents*. Industrial Fatigue Research Board, Medical Research Committee, Report No. 4. London: Her Majesty's Stationery Office.

Griffin, M. A., & Neal, N. (2000). Perceptions of safety at work: A framework for linking safety climate to safety performance, knowledge, and motivation. *Journal of Occupational Health Psychology, 5*, 347–358.

Grote, G. (2015). Promoting safety by increasing uncertainty: Implications for risk management. *Safety Science, 71*, 71–79.

Grote, G., Kolbe, M., Zala-Mezö, E., Bienefeld-Seall, N., & Künzle, B. (2010). Adaptive coordination and heedfulness make better cockpit crews. *Ergonomics, 52,* 211–228.

Grote, G., Weichbrodt, J. C., Günter, H., Zala-Mezö, E., & Künzle, B. (2009). Coordination in high-risk organizations: The need for flexible routines. *Cognition, Technology & Work, 11,* 17–27.

Grote, G., Weyer, J., & Stanton, N. (2014). Beyond human-centred automation: Concepts for human-machine interaction in multilayered networks. *Ergonomics, 57,* 289–294.

Hale, A. R., & Swuste, P. (1998). Safety rules: Procedural freedom or action constraint? *Safety Science, 29,* 163–177.

Hansez, I., & Chmiel, N. (2010). Safety behavior: job demands, job resources and perceived management commitment to safety. *Journal of Occupational Health Psychology, 15,* 267–278.

Hofmann, D. A., Morgeson, F. P., & Gerras, S. J. (2003). Climate as a moderator of the relationship between leader-member exchange and content specific citizenship: Safety climate as an exemplar. *Journal of Applied Psychology, 88,* 170–178.

Hogan, J., & Foster, J. (2013). Multifaceted personality predictors of workplace safety performance: more than conscientiousness. *Human Performance, 26,* 20–43.

Klein, K. J., Ziegert, J. C., Knight, A. P., & Xiao, Y. (2006). Dynamic delegation: Shared, hierarchical, and deindividualized leadership in extreme action teams. *Administrative Science Quarterly, 51,* 590–621.

Kolbe, M., et al. (2012). Speaking up is related to better team performance in simulated anesthesia inductions: An observational study. *Anesthesia and Analgesia, 115,* 1099–1108.

Kolbe, M., Grote, G., Waller, M., Wacker, J., Grande, B., Burtscher, M. J., & Spahn, D. R. (2014). Monitoring and talking to the room: Autochthonous coordination patterns in team interaction and performance. *Journal of Applied Psychology, 99,* 1254–1267.

Künzle, B., Zala-Mezö, E., Wacker, J., Kolbe, M., & Grote, G. (2010). Leadership in anaesthesia teams: The most effective leadership is shared. *Quality and Safety in Health Care, 19,* 1–6.

Mintz, A. (1954). The inference of accident liability from the accident record. *Journal of Applied Psychology, 38,* 41–46.

McKenna, F. P. (1983). Accident proneness: A conceptual analysis. *Accident Analysis & Prevention, 15,* 65–71.

Müller, S., Brauner, C., Grote, G., & Künzler, C. (1998). *Safety Culture: A Reflection of Risk Awareness.* Zurich, Switzerland: Swiss Re.

Nahrgang, J. D., Morgeson, F. P., & Hofmann, D. A. (2011). Safety at work: A meta-analytic investigation of the link between job demands, job resources, burnout, engagement, and safety outcomes. *Journal of Applied Psychology, 96,* 71–94.

Neal, A., & Griffin, M. A. (2006). A study of the lagged relationships among safety climate, safety motivation, safety behavior, and accidents at the individual and group levels. *Journal of Applied Psychology, 91,* 946–953.

Neal, A., Griffin, M. A., & Hart, P. (2000). The impact of organizational climate on safety climate and individual behaviour. *Safety Science, 34,* 99–109.

Ployhart, R. E., & Schmitt, N. (2008). The attraction-selection-attrition model and staffing. In D. B. Smith (Ed.), *The people make the place: Dynamic linkages between individuals and organizations.* New York: Lawrence Erlbaum Associates.

Reason, J. T. (1990). *Human error.* Cambridge: Cambridge University Press.

Reason, J. T., Parker, D., & Lawton, R. (1998). Organizational controls and safety: The varieties of rule-related behaviour. *Journal of Occupational and Organizational Psychology, 71,* 289–304.

Silbey, S. S. (2009). Taming Prometheus: Talk about safety and culture. *Annual Review of Sociology, 35,* 341–369.

Sniehotta, F. F., Presseau, J., & Araujo-Soares, V. (2014). Time to retire the theory of planned behaviour. *Health Psychology, 34,* 1–7.

Soane, E., & Chmiel, N. (2005). Are risk preferences consistent? The influence of decision domain and personality. *Personality & Individual Differences, 38,* 1781–1791.

Strauch, B. (2015). Can we examine safety culture in accident investigations, or should we? *Safety Science, 77,* 102–111.

Stride, C. B., Turner, N., Hershcovis, M. S., Reich, T. C., Clegg, C. W., & Murphy, P. (2013). Negative safety events as correlates of work-safety tension. *Safety Science, 53,* 45–50.

Turner, N., Stride, C. B., Carter, A. J., & McCaughey, D. (2012). Job Demands-Control-Support model and employee safety performance. *Accident Analysis and Prevention, 45,* 811–817.

Visser, E., Pijl, Y. J., Stolk, R .P., Neeleman, J., & Rosmalen, J. G. M. (2007). Accident proneness, does it exist? A review and meta-analysis. *Accident Analysis & Prevention, 39,* 556–564.

Wallace, J. C., & Vodanovich, S. J. (2003). Workplace safety performance: Conscientiousness, cognitive failure, and their interaction. *Journal of Occupational Health Psychology, 8,* 316–327.

Yun, S., Faraj, S., & Sims, H. P. (2005). Contingent leadership and effectiveness of trauma resuscitation teams. *Journal of Applied Psychology, 90,* 1288–1296.

Zohar, D. (1980). Safety climate in industrial organizations: Theoretical and applied implications. *Journal of Applied Psychology, 65,* 89–102.

Zohar, D., & Luria, G. (2010). Group leaders as gatekeepers: Testing safety climate variations across levels of analysis. *Applied Psychology: An International Review, 59,* 647–673.

22

Does It Matter Whether I Am a Happy and Committed Worker? The Role of Identification, Commitment and Job Satisfaction for Employee Behaviour

Rolf van Dick and Lucas Monzani

Overview

Employees, like all human beings, have a need to belong to groups and they have feelings which, to a large extent, determine their actions. Individuals work in organizations. They could feel more or less positive about their jobs. Does this matter, for instance, to their productivity? Organizations have long been interested in fostering a strong attachment of individuals to their job and organization. Why? Does this matter? Research has also been interested in these questions. In this chapter, we first explore the two important concepts that deal with expressions of the need for belongingness and affiliation, namely, organizational identification and commitment. We provide measures of identification and commitment and we demonstrate that identification and commitment can refer to different foci (e.g. workgroup, organization) and that they strongly impact on employee atttitudes and performance. In the second part of this chapter.we explore the concept of job satisfaction as one of the fundamental job attitudes. We provide measures of job satisfaction and we demonstrate that job satisfaction has important consequences for employee performance and ultimately for organizational productivity.

22.1 Does It Matter If Employees Are Committed to the Organization?

All human beings dislike social rejection and isolation. Everyone – albeit to various degrees – has a need for affiliation and belonging (Baumeister & Leary, 1995). Humans satisfy this need for affiliation through their innate ability to form

An Introduction to Work and Organizational Psychology: An International Perspective,
Third Edition. Edited by Nik Chmiel, Franco Fraccaroli and Magnus Sverke.
© 2017 John Wiley & Sons, Ltd. Published 2017 by John Wiley & Sons, Ltd.

psychological attachments towards others (Bowlby, 1988). Once established, people resist the dissolution of existing bonds and groups, because they benefit from attachments with others (e.g. in terms of better mental and physical health and well-being). Thus, establishing safe bonds in early life not only is a major determinant of mental health, but enables people to create new attachments to other social groups as adults. Organizations are a prime source for forming such bonds, as humans spend most of their adult lives working in organizations. Being part of an organization or of related groupings – such as the occupation or profession, teams and departments within one organization or wider networks of multiple organizations – provides people with an answer about where they belong and it satisfies their needs. The strength of the bonds that they form with these entities varies between individuals and can be operationalized as a continuum according to the psychological intensity of the bond towards a given target (e.g., the organization; Klein, Molloy, & Brinsfield, 2012). For example, organizational *identification* and organizational *commitment* are bonds that have similarities but also unique aspects that we will discuss in this chapter. Because both identification and commitment help people understand who they are and where they belong, the degree of identification or commitment has profound implications for a range of work-related attitudes and behaviours that they can influence. Identification typically makes people adhere to the respective group's norms and standards, such as norms for performance. Identification is a bond that demands a strong degree of psychological investment because it implies a sense of *merging* between the person and the target of the bond, after which belonging to a given group is seen as a valued aspect of oneself. Protecting and advancing the interests of such a target (e.g. one's team or the organization as a whole) are a way to protect oneself. Commitment, however, is a type of bond in which this merging does not occur, but it still requires a high degree of psychological investment. Commitment elicits in turn a conscious volition to act in such a way that not only conforms but may even positively exceed the established norms and expectations of its target.

22.1.1   Organizational identification

Tajfel and Turner (1979) formulated social identity theory from their observations that the mere categorization of research participants into arbitrary groups has an impact on their behaviour, such as positive discrimination of fellow ingroup members against members of other groups. This impact is evident even without any scarcity of resources or personal knowledge of an interaction with the other individuals. Social identity theory states that all humans want to have a positive self-concept, i.e., they want to feel good about themselves. Part of this self-concept is determined by one's personal identity which includes the individual characteristics and strengths and weaknesses. Another large part of the self-concept is determined by one's membership in social groups such as the workgroup. When this membership becomes salient, i.e., important in the given context, it has a profound impact on the group members' thoughts, feelings and actions. As soon as a certain social identity becomes salient – for instance, the social identity of being a member of the marketing department because of a resource conflict with the finance department – the members of the marketing department will start seeing other members of the marketing department as more similar to each others and they will exaggerate the difference between members of their own and the other department. They will also more strongly see the common interest of the group as important and start coordinating their activities to accomplish the common goals. According to Ashforth and Mael (1989), an employee's organizational identification helps to answer the question of 'Who am I' and provides guidance about appropriate norms of conduct. Before we review the impact that the degree of organizational identification has on employee attitudes and behaviour, we will provide some examples of how this degree has been measured in survey studies.

22.1.1.1 How can organizational identification be measured?

The most commonly used scale to measure organizational identification has been proposed by Mael and Ashforth (1992). It presents six statements to employees that they are asked to agree or disagree to (e.g. on a five- or six-point answering scale with endpoints 'do not agree at all' and 'fully agree'). Examples are 'When I talk about … [e.g. Deutsche Bank], I usually say "we" rather than "they"', 'When someone criticizes … [e.g. Nokia], it feels like a personal insult', or 'The successes of … [e.g. the school I work for] feel like my personal successes'. The answers to these statements can be averaged and denote the strengths of an employee's perceived overlap between him or herself and the organization. The second most frequently used scale by Doosje, Ellemers and Spears (1995) comprises four items such as 'I feel strong ties with my colleagues at … [e.g. Apple]' or 'I am happy to belong to… [e.g. Microsoft]'. Postmes, Haslam and Jans (2013) suggested a single item measure of social identification ('I identify with … [e.g. General Motors]').

Another operationalization of this overlap has been suggested by Bergami and Bagozzi (2000) who have suggested a Venn diagram to measure the perceived overlap between oneself and the organization as depicted in Figure 22.1.

Finally, another way to measure identification is by analyzing employees oral statements and counting the frequency to which they refer to their organization as 'we' (respectively us, our, etc.) compared to 'I' (respectively me, mine, etc.), Wegge, Schuh and van Dick (2012) used this method in their study on call centre agents.

22.1.1.2 Does organizational identification relate to employee behaviour?

Above, we have shown several ways to measure how much people feel they belong to their organization. But does it matter? Does it influence people's behaviour? Should managers care about maintaining or even increasing their followers' identification because it pays off in terms of more productivity? Yes, it does! Riketta (2005) conducted a meta-analysis of almost one hundred studies that have linked organizational identification to a range of work-related attitudes and behaviours. Some 34 studies, for instance, have looked at the relation between organizational identification and

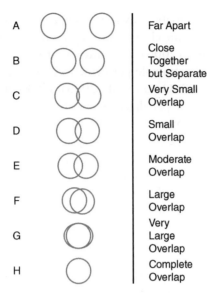

Figure 22.1: Venn diagram to measure organizational identification as the perceived overlap between self and organization

the intention to quit. Riketta found an overall mean effect of –.48,[1] meaning that the more strongly that employees identify with their organization, the less likely they are to quit. We will return to this later when we provide some specific research examples. Riketta also found a moderate but reliable effect of .17 between identification and in-role performance (i.e., the type of performance that concerns an employee's core tasks and duties) and an even stronger relation of .35 between identification and extra-role performance (i.e., the type of behaviour that goes beyond the duties regulated in one's contract, this includes helping colleges, or being proactive) – we will also return to this later with some more specific examples.

Recently, Lee, Park and Koo (2015) conducted an updated meta-analysis and replicated the effect of .35 for the link between identification and extra-role behaviour (based on 53 studies) and calculated an effect of .22 for in-role performance (41 studies). Albeit somewhat weaker, the effects were also reliable when using other people's (coworkers or supervisors) ratings of performance. Morever, Lee and colleagues looked at differences between collectivistic versus individualistic cultures. They predicted a stronger impact of identification in cultures where the group is valued more than the individual and found that the impact of identification on outcomes was positive and significant in individualistic cultures but much stronger in collectivistic societies.

22.1.1.3 Research close-ups: Let's go the extra mile and should I stay or should I go?

Above, we have demonstrated that there are links between organizational identification and important individual variables such as their performance. Now, we would like to look at two of these variables, extra-role behaviour and turnover intentions, in more detail and provide some close-ups of representative studies in these areas.

Van Dick and colleagues (2006) were interested in the link between organizational identification and extra-role performance, also known as organizational citizenship behaviours (OCB; Organ et al., 2005). OCBs are any behaviours that are not directly rewarded (or penalized when absent) nor enforced by the formal work contract but in sum contribute positively to the organization. Typical behaviours in that domain are helping colleagues with a high workload, being always on time and avoiding unnecessary breaks, making innovative suggestions, etc. First, van Dick et al. (2006) conducted a small meta-analysis across 10 different samples from different industries and from different countries within both the public and the private sectors. This meta-analysis closely matched the mean effect found by Riketta (2005) of .36. More importantly, the effect was of the same magnitude but a little stronger in samples of Chinese employees in the manufacturing industry (.41) and a heterogeneous sample of employees in Nepal (.39). These results are in line with the suggested stronger impact of identification in collectivistic cultures (see above). In these ten studies – as in the majority of the research included in the other meta-analyses reported above, the data were collected in the form of employee self-reports and at one point in time. Because of this last point, some may ask if it could be the case that in fact, people identify more because they invested more in the organization by doing more extra-role efforts? Van Dick and colleagues provided evidence against this as they found that the effect of identification on OCB was stronger than the reversed effect from OCB on identification in a longitudinal study of teachers in training across their first six months in school. In a further study of US military personnel, the link between identification and OCB held for data gathered from different sources (identification was reported by soldiers and OCBs were measured by supervisor ratings for each soldier). Finally, in a study of 60 travel agencies, van Dick and colleagues were able to show a mediation process, that is identification of customer service employees led to them showing more OCBs which in turn related to positive outcomes of the travel agencies they were working in – measured by both indicators of financial turnover and the satisfaction of mystery shoppers.

As a second example, we want to look into a study on the link between organizational identification and voluntary employee turnover. Van Dick and colleagues (2004) conducted four different studies with bank employees (two samples), hospital staff and call centre agents. Figure 22.2 illustrates the basic research model which shows that organizational identification was hypothesized to first impact on job satisfaction which in turn related to (lower) turnover intentions. The researchers assumed that highly identified employees would contribute to the organization's well-being which should also increase their own job satisfaction. Ultimately this would be the key mediator responsible for the link between identification and employees' intention to stay rather than quit.

The analyses could confirm the proposed model for all four samples. In the first sample of 350 bank employees, for instance, organizational identification was closely

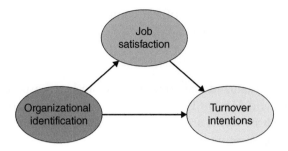

Figure 22.2:   Research model of the link between identification and turnover intentions

related to turnover intentions ($\beta = -.48$, all coefficients from structural equation modeling with latent variables accounting for measurement error) and to job satisfaction ($\beta = .56$). Job satisfaction was also related to turnover intentions as expected ($\beta = -.58$). Most importantly, the direct link between identification and turnover intentions came down to just $-.15$ when job satisfaction was included as a mediator. In the fourth sample of 450 hospital employees, the researchers looked at the impact of the variables on actual turnover. They found that those who had left the hospital in the 12 months after the survey had indeed reported much lower identification and satisfaction and much higher turnover intentions than those who had stayed. These findings provide not only evidence for the proposed model but also show more generally that self-reported attitudes can be predictive of real behaviour.

22.1.2   Organizational commitment

Now, we turn to the second concept that describes the bond between employee and organization: commitment. However, we must first understand what is meant by commitment. Commitment is a force that binds an individual to a course of action (e.g., performing) that is relevant for a given target (e.g. the organization; Meyer & Herscovitch, 2001).

Although research on commitment has a long tradition, the most frequently used modern conceptualization of commitment has been suggested by Allen and Meyer (1990). These authors define commitment as the activation of three states of mind, or mind-sets that summarize the three most recurring themes in the previous commitment literature. These mind-sets are 'desire' (affective commitment; AC), 'obligation' (normative commitment; NC), and 'cost' (continuance commitment; CC). An employee with high affective commitment towards his or her organization stays in the organization because he wants to (desire), employees with high normative commitment stay because they feel that they ought to (moral obligation) and those who stay because of high continuance commitment do so because they perceive that they need to stay because of lack of alternatives and/ or accrued benefits that they would lose if they changed organizations (cost). Continuance commitment is sometimes split into two components 'lack of alternatives' (e.g. lack of job offers) and 'personal sacrifice' (e.g. one would have to give up benefits such as corner office, company car or extra days of vacation accumulated in the current organization).

22.1.2.1 How can organizational commitment be measured?

The three forms of organizational commitment can be measured with the items suggested by Allen and Meyer (1990) which have been shown to be reliable and valid. Each of the three forms are measured by six items and in the following, a few sample items are presented:

- Affective commitment:
  - I would be happy to spend the rest of my career at … [e.g. Chrysler].
  - I really feel that the problems of … [e.g. Volvo] are my own.
  - I do not feel 'part of the family' at … [e.g. Renault] (reversed item).

- Normative commitment
  - I would feel guilty if I left … [e.g. Starbucks] now
  - … [e.g. Walmart] deserves my loyalty
  - I owe a great deal to …[e.g. Waterstones]

- Continuance commitment
  - Too much of my life would be disrupted if I decided to leave … [e.g. Lloyds] now
  - I believe that I have too few options to consider leaving … [e.g. the NHS]
  - If I had not put so much of myself into … [e.g., Electrolux], I might consider working elsewhere

22.1.2.2 Does organizational commitment relate to employee behaviour?

The above scales have been used frequently in employee opinion surveys and research projects. Meyer et al., (2002) conducted a meta-analysis with over 100 samples and more than 50000 employees. Table 22.1 shows the main findings with respect to relevant behaviours or behavioural intentions.

This data shows that affective commitment is the strongest predictor for all criteria. Normative commitment is also significantly and positively related to the

Table 22.1: Average meta-analytic correlations of the three forms of commitment with work-related criteria

Criterion	AC	NC	CC
Turnover	−.17	−.16	−.10
Turnover intentions	−.56	−.33	−.18
Absenteeism	−.15	.05	.06
In-role performance	.16	.06	−.07
OCB	.32	.24	−.01

AC, affective commitment; NC, normative commitment; CC, continuance commitment positive outcomes and negatively related to turnover (intentions) – but the associations are weaker than those for affective commitment. Finally, continuance commitment only relates significantly and negatively to turnover (intentions) but is not related to the other criteria. This means that employees who have high AC or NC are working harder and less likely to leave, wheras those with high CC will also more likely remain in the organization but do not invest more effort.

Meyer and colleagues were also interested in differences between studies conducted in the USA and Canada compared to those in other areas of the world. They found, for instance, that the negative correlation between affective commitment and turnover intentions was greater in studies conducted in North America but that the correlations between normative and continuance commitment and turnover intentions were higher outside North America than in the rest of the world. Similarly, the correlation between normative commitment and performance was larger in studies conducted outside rather than within North America. It therefore seems that there are some cultural influences on the impact of the different forms of commitment.

A more recent meta-anlysis across 54 countries with an overall sample ranging from 133,277 to 433,129 participants show that these differences may be explained because cultures tend to vary in the values they hold as important (Meyer et al., 2012). Some nations give more importance to the individual than the group (individualistic cultures) while others place higher value on group-oriented behaviours (collectivistic cultures). The same occurs for 'power distance', i.e., the importance that different cultures give to hierarchical differences between individuals. The findings show that as it could be expected, normative commitment may be stronger in collectivistic cultures. This may be due to the importance that individuals in collectivistic cultures place on their sense of duty to something larger than oneself.

22.1.2.3   *Profiles of commitment*

From the pattern of correlations between the forms of commitment and criteria it looks as if affective commitment is the most important form. Given that AC and NC correlate quite strongly, some researchers have argued that AC might be the only concept of interest here. However, it has also been proposed that keeping the three forms and looking into them in combination, would help to better understand employee behaviour. Building on Meyer and Allen's work on organizational commitment, Meyer and Herscovitch's (2001) general model of workplace commitment, suggested two main commitment *profiles*. Commitment profiles capture the simultaneous activation of two or more mindsets (e.g., desire and obligation, or obligation and costs).

Recently Meyer and Parfyonova (2010) used the commitment profile approach to explain the mixed findings of normative commitment. They concluded that normative commitment has a dual nature, and that it manifests differently depending on the strengths of other components (affective or continuance). For example, they labelled 'moral imperative' as a commitment profile with a high affective and normative commitment but low continuance commitment. Alternatively, they labelled 'indebted obligation' as a commitment profile with a low affective commitment, but high normative and continuance commitment.

Gellatly, Meyer and Luchak (2006) have provided some evidence for the usefulness of such 'Commitment profile' analysis and have found that the three forms interact in their prediction of turnover intentions and OCB. For turnover intentions, for instance, it was found that the relation to every single form of Commitment was stronger when the other two forms were low than when any of the other forms were also high. Markovits and colleagues (2007) in a large sample of over 1500 Greek employees in the private and public sector also revealed three-way interactions between the forms of commitment in their prediction of intrinsic and extrinsic job satisfaction. While it was the case that when affective commitment alone was high (and the other two forms low), satisfaction was relatively high, the profile with all three forms of commitment being high revealed the highest scores of both intrinsic and extrinsic satisfaction.

22.1.3   Foci of identification and commitment

Both identification and commitment have not only been studied with respect to the organization as a whole but also with respect to other foci. Such studies include identification or commitment to the profession or occupational group, to the leader or most frequently, to smaller units within the organization such as the team or workgroup. Riketta and van Dick (2005) combined all studies that assessed identification or commitment to the team and the organization to a meta-analysis on the differential impact of these two foci of attachment. They predicted and found that attachment to the team was generally stronger than attachment to the organization. This supports the principle of optimal distinctiveness, according to which people prefer smaller to larger groups to identify with because smaller groups satisfy their need for belonging but at the same time allow them to maintain their sense of being unique individuals which is more difficult in large groups. Furthermore, teams are more salient in everyday interactions at work and are the areas where socialization takes place. However, the meta-analysis also revealed that team attachment was more predictive of team-related variables such as workgroup climate or extra-role behaviours on the level of the workgroup. Organizational attachment, on the other hand, was more closely related to extra-role behaviour directed to the organization as a whole or intentions to quit.

22.1.4   Integration of organizational identification and organizational commitment

Although identification and commitment seem to be very similar and empirically highly correlated, there are some marked differences theoretically and also some studies providing evidence for their distinctiveness (Gautam, van Dick, & Wagner, 2004; van Knippenberg & Sleebos, 2006). Meyer, Becker and van Dick (2006) have suggested an integrative model of the concepts that is shown in Figure 22.3 in a simplified version.

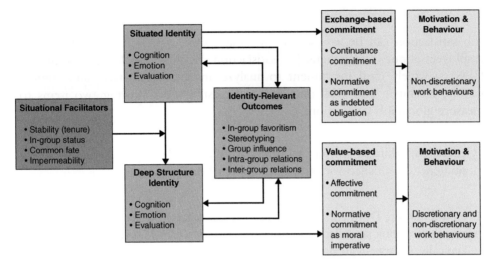

Figure 22.3: Simplified version of the integrative model by Meyer et al. (2006)
Source: Meyer et al. (2006). Reproduced with permission of John Wiley & Sons, Ltd.

As Figure 22.3 shows, Meyer and colleagues suggest that situational factors determine whether an employee's situated (i.e., short-lived, state-like) identity or his or her deep structure (i.e., stable and deeply rooted) identity is activated. The latter impacts on more value-based forms of commitment (AC and some aspects of NC) which in turn drive both in-role and extra-role behaviour. In contrast, the situated identity is more a predictor of exchange-based forms of commitment (CC and other aspects of NC) that in turn are related to non-discretionary work behaviours (mostly turnover) but not necessary to high performance or OCBs.

22.2 Does It Matter Whether Employees are Satisfied in Their Jobs?

It can have a profound impact for both employees and the organizations they work for whether they feel satisfied and happy at work or not. Job satisfaction is the most frequently studied job attitude in psychological research and research on job satisfaction has a long tradition in organizational psychology and management research. It has been defined and conceptualized in numerous ways. Herzberg (1964), for instance, suggested two factors within job satisfaction: motivating and hygiene factors. Hygiene factors, such as workplace safety and security or pay, were supposed to determine whether an employee was dissatisfied or not dissatisfied. Motivators such as recognition or interesting tasks, on the other hand, do influence whether an employee is not satisfied or satisfied. Dissatisfaction and satisfaction are therefore different dimensions of overall job satisfaction. Although Herzberg's original model has been critized and was not well supported by data, it inspired later conceptualizations of extrinsic and intrinsic satisfaction.

22.2.1 How can job satisfaction be measured?

Job satisfaction can be assessed in two ways. One approach would be to ask employees about their general job satisfaction. In their Job Diagnostic Survey (JDS), a widely used instrument to analyze an employee's tasks and context factors, Hackman and Oldham (1975) suggested the following two items to measure global job satisfaction:

> Generally speaking, I am very satisfied with this job.
> I am generally satisfied with the kind of work I do in this job.

As an alternative, Dunham and Herman have suggested a very simple graphical measure presenting so called 'Kunin faces' as depicted in Figure 22.4.

Typically, in large-scale employee opinion surveys or in research projects where job satisfaction is not necessarily the main focus of attention, these global measures are sufficient and valid ways to measure employee satisfaction.

Sometimes, however, a researcher or practitioner wants to be able to go into the details because they want to redesign the job or focus on the areas that are responsible for low levels of overall job satisfaction. When using only the global measure, one would not know, why employees are happy or not. Thefore, the JDS also includes the following items which measure satisfaction with a range of specific aspects:

> How satisfied are you with this aspect of your job …?
> * The amount of job security I have.
> * How secure things look for me in the future in this organization.
> * The amount of pay and fringe benefits I receive.
> * The degree to which I am fairly paid for what I contribute to this organization.
> * The people I talk to and work with on my job.
> * The chance to get to know other people while on the job.
> * The chance to help other people while at work.
> * The degree of respect and fair treatment I receive from my supervisor
> * The amount of support and guidance I receive from my supervisor.
> * The overall quality of the supervision I receive in my work

How satisfied are you with your current job....

very satisfied 🙂 🙂 😐 🙁 ☹️ very dissatisfied

Figure 22.4: Measuring job satisfaction with the Kunin faces scale

Another classic instrument to assess an employee's satisfaction with his or her job is the Minnesota Satisfaction Questionnaire (MSQ, Weiss et al., 1964). It comprises a short form with 20 items measuring general satisfaction and in the long form, it measures the following 20 dimensions with five items each.

Ability Utilization	Moral Values
Achievement	Recognition
Activity	Responsibility
Advancement	Security
Authority	Social Service
Company Policies	Social Status
Compensation	Supervision (HumanRelations)
Coworkers	Supervision (Technical)
Creativity	Variety
Independence	Working Conditions

22.2.2 Are happy employees productive employees?

For a long time researchers thought that the expression 'happy workers are productive workers' was a myth which was not supported by empirical data. Many textbooks still ignore that there actually is a link between job satisfaction and employee performance. This link has been firmly established by Judge and colleagues (2001) who provided an extensive qualitative and quantitative review of the literature. Their meta-analysis of more than 300 studies with more than 50,000 employees shows a clear and positive average association of .3 and an even stronger effect size of .52 for jobs with higher complexity. Also, the correlation was stronger for studies published in top tier journals, for those that have used global measures of job satisfaction and for those that have used peer ratings of performance.

The bottom line is that job satisfaction indeed can predict employee performance. This is corroborated by a more recent meta-analysis by Riketta (2008) on longitudinal studies which showed that the satisfaction-performance link over time was (albeit small) positive and significant whereas the reversed performance-satisfaction link was close to zero. Thus, happiness can indeed make workers productive.

22.2.3 Research close-up

Patterson, Warr and West (2004) studied employees of 39 manufacturing companies in a systematic and longitudinal project. When companies were small, all employees were surveyed, when they were larger, random samples of 500 employees were asked to complete questionnaires. The surveys included a 16-item scale of overall job satisfaction, including the main job features such as physical working conditions and opportunity to use your ability. The surveys were completed by over 4500 employees. The researchers first checked, whether employees within organizations 'agreed' on their levels of job satisfaction which was actually the case – this means that employees within organizations were more similar to each other in their satisfaction than between companies, mainly because of similar working conditions and human resource management procedures that either foster happiness or not. The job satisfaction scores were then aggregated to the company level. Next, the researchers measured company productivity using an index of net sales per employee. Control variables were included in subsequent analyses, namely, company size and sector. First, the researchers controlled for productivity in the year of the surveys and then predicted productivity one year later by job satisfaction. This resulted in a substantial correlation of .44 which further illustrates that happy employees are productive employees.

22.2.4   Can money buy happiness?

Is a salary raise a good way to increase employee happiness? It depends! Robbins and Judge's (2013) data from the USA show that there is a positive correlation between salary level and job satisfaction but only up to a level of about $40,000 annual salary. Beyond this point more money does not necessarily mean more satisfaction. Interestingly, however, Lucas and Schimmack (2009) show linear trends between earnings and life (not job!) satisfaction. They conclude that the effects are small but can create relatively large differences in satisfaction between the richest and poorest groups.

22.3   How Can Identification, Commitment and Satisfaction Be Influenced?

22.3.1   Identity management

We have shown that the need to belong is powerful for employee performance and satisfaction. Therefore, leaders should actively try to positively shape team and organization identities. They can do this by introducing stories (of past and current success), rituals (such as group pictures), or regular team building activities such as retreats which have been shown to increase identification (Hämmelmann & van Dick, 2013). Leaders have been found to be more influential if they are prototypical for the group they lead, i.e., when they represent what the group is about. According to Steffens et al. (2014), leaders can be active managers of the group's identity and therefore also influence their own standing (and prototypicality – 'being one of us') in the group. Steffens et al. suggest that leaders act as identity impressarios ('making us matter'), identity entrepreneurs ('crafting a sense of us') and identity advancers ('doing it for us'). A detailed account of these identity management strategies and their impact can be found in Haslam, Reicher and Platow (2011).

22.3.2   Leadership and organizational commitment

A recent meta-analysis shows that certain leadership styles can shape organizational commitment (Jackson, Meyer, & Wang, 2012). For example, transformational leadership (Bass & Avolio, 1994) relates to both affective ($r = .45$) and normative commitment ($r = .33$). Similarly, transactional leadership, as contingent rewards and active management-by-exception that were related to affective ($r = .37$ and $r = .08$) commitment as well. Also as expected, laissez-faire leadership was negatively related to affective commitment ($r = -.30$).

Again, the degree of individualism/collectivism of the cultures included in this study, moderated these meta-analytic relations for normative and continuance commitment, but not for affective commitment. This means that in highly collectivistic cultures, the relation between these leadership styles and normative commitment was higher. These findings highlight the importance of culture in regards to organizational commitment, but more importantly the role that transformational leaders play in eliciting affective commitment in their followers seems to generalize across cultures.

22.3.3   Job design for high job satisfaction

Above, we presented items to measure specific aspects of job satisfaction. These items already provide an indication for how managers can contribute to higher job satisfaction among their employees, by, for example, providing high security and safety at work; a decent salary; or taking care in harmonious work relationships in groups and teams. The job and tasks themselves are also an important source of satisfaction or dissatisfaction. The Job Characteristics Model (Hackman & Oldham, 1975) suggests (and has been supported by data in many occupations and countries) that job satisfaction increases with tasks that have variety (i.e., using a range of the employees skills), identity (so that employees see the endproduct of what they do), significance (so that employees perceive that what they are doing is meaningful), allow autonomy (because only when employees have leeway over what and how they do, they can feel responsibility) and provide feedback (because only when I have knowledge of the results, I can be either proud of my good work or try to improve). These factors can be used in job design (or redesign activities) by increasing the autonomy or adding tasks to increase variety, etc.

22.3.4   Influence of crises

The job itself does have an impact on whether people are happy or not at work. But what role does the wider environment play? Do, for instance, economic crises impact on employee commitment and satisfaction? Markovits, Boer and van Dick (2014) studied this in samples of Greek employees before (2004) and during (2010) the most recent and on-going financial crisis. Figure 22.5 shows the research model.

Figure 22.5: How a crisis affects employees' morale

About 1000 employees both before and during the crisis completed question-naires on affective commitment, job satisfaction and also on self-regulation. The latter concept refers to Higgins' regulatory focus theory (1998) which suggests that people's actions can have either a promotion or a prevention focus. When people's behaviour has a promotion focus, it is orientated towards achievement and a tolerance for risks. Behaviours with a prevention focus, on the other hand, characterize an individual's aim to avoid risks by all means because they are focused on preventing loss rather than achieving wins.

Markivits and colleagues' analyses confirmed the hypotheses: the crisis negatively affects employee job satisfaction and commitment – which is not trivial because only those people were surveyed who had kept their jobs and did not suffer from being laid off. More importantly, results show that the reductions in satisfaction and commitment were due to the crisis' impact on self-regulation as it increased preven-tion and decreased promotion orientation. The crisis does exactly the opposite of what is required in such a situation, it prevents people from seeking opportiunities, being innovative and trying something new. Furthermore it increases employee's focus on avoiding anything risky with negative effects on their morale.

22.4   Are identification and commitment related to job satisfaction?

As we have discussed above, the concepts of organizational identification and commitment, especially affective commitment, are closely related. But how are these constructs linked to job satisfaction? As van Dick and colleagues (2004, see above) have shown, job satisfaction is indeed related to organizational identi-fication and satisfaction can serve as a mediator which translates organizational identification into outcomes (such as turnover intentions). The links have also been confirmed by meta-analyses. Riketta (2005) found an average correlation between organizational identification and job satisfaction of .54 and Meyer et al.

(2002) showed a strong relation between affective commitment and job satisfaction of .65 and a substantial relation between normative commitment and job satisfaction of .31. Although van Dick and colleagues argue that identification predicts commitment, we can assume that the direction can go both ways: Employees who are more strongly attached to their organization, will probably like their jobs better and vice versa. Finally, both variables can also be influenced by third variables such as good leadership. Therefore, Meyer et al. (2002) consider commitment and satisfaction merely as 'correlates' and do not specify cause and effect.

22.5   Conclusion

For employees, it matters a lot whether they do or do not know where they belong at work and whether they feel happy in their jobs or not. The frequently heard saying that 'people are our greatest assets' all too often is more lip service than guiding managerial action. The annual Gallup surveys of representative employee samples show that the majority of employees have difficulty forming a strong emotional bond with their organization (Gallup, 2014). In 2014, only 4% of the Japanese workforce has a strong emotional attachment to their employer. Although the numbers are a little higher in other countries such as Germany (15%), the UK (13%) or Canada (18%), even the USA only reaches 27% which means that two thirds of employees are not or only weakly attached to their organizations. We have demonstrated in this chapter that high identification, strong organizational commitment and positive job satisfaction all correlate with work-related variables that are good for individual well-being and performance but ultimately also good for organizational productivity and competitiveness. Leaders are therefore well advised to take care of their employee's attachment and satisfaction at work.

Summary

In this chapter, we have reviewed the literature on employee attachment to their organizations and on job satisfaction. We have shown that these aspects of what is sometimes summarized as 'employee morale' can have a large effect on employee well-being and their individual performance which, eventually, is good for organizations. We have shown that attachment can be broken down into organizational identification and organizational commitment – two related, but distinct concepts, and how they can be measured with both longer and shorter scales and also graphical or other methods of assessment. Organizational commitment can be further differentiated into affective, normative, and continuance commitment which together explain employee thoughts and behaviours well.

Continued

Furthermore, we have shown that job satisfaction can be conceptualized as both a general attitude but also as evaluations regarding specific aspects of one's job such as satisfaction with the tasks, pay, or colleagues – and we have provided examples to measure general and specific aspects of job satisfaction. Ways to improve identification and commitment were discuseed, and it was suggested that leadership is the key to establishing a sense of identity and strong commitment. We also briefly discussed how job design can be used to increase employee satisfaction. Finally, we have shown how external influences such as an economic crisis can impact on commitment and satisfaction.

So, in summary, we can conclude that identification, commitment and satisfaction are indeed concepts that do matter at work. They are important for the employees' well-being and performance and eventually also for the organization's functioning. Employees who are strongly identified or committed follow the organization's rules more closely and they are more likely to put effort into their jobs which ultimately is good for the organization but also contributes to their own well-being. Likewise, research has shown a link between employee job satisfaction and both individual performance and organizational productivity.

Discussion Points

1　As a practising manager, which of the concepts described in this chapter would you focus on when you want to improve your employees' morale?
2　Do you believe managers should increase employees attachment to their jobs or to the organization? What are the benefits and limitations of each approaches? How do they interplay?

Note

1　Jacob Cohen (1992) in his book *Statistical Power Analysis for the Behavioral Sciences* developed a method to evaluate how much a variable influences another, independently of the scale used to measure them, which is known as *effect size*. For example, the statistic to compare the strength of pearson's correlations (or in this case, its average) is called Cohen's q. Effect sizes are now conventionally considered small when q is around .10, medium when around .30 and large when larger than .50.

Suggested Further Reading

Haslam, S. A. (2004). *Psychology in organizations: The social identity approach* (2nd ed.). London: Sage.

Klein, H. J., Becker, T. E. & Meyer, J. P. (2009) (Eds.), *Commitment in organizations: Accumulated wisdom and new directions.* (SIOP Organizational Frontiers Series). New York: Routledge.

References

Allen, N. J., & Meyer, J. P. (1990). The measurement and antecedents of affective, continuance and normative commitment to the organization. *Journal of Occupational Psychology, 63,* 1–18.

Ashforth, B. E., & Mael, F. (1989). Social identity theory and the organization. *Academy of Management Review, 14,* 20–39.

Bass, B. M., & Avolio, B. J. (1994). *Improving organizational effectiveness through transformational leadership.* Thousand Oaks, CA: Sage.

Baumeister, R. F., & Leary, M. R. (1995). The need to belong: desire for interpersonal attachments as a fundamental human motivation. *Psychological Bulletin, 117,* 497–529.

Bergami, M., & Bagozzi, R. P. (2000). Self-categorization, affective commitment and group self-esteem as distinct aspects of social identity in the organization. *British Journal of Social Psychology, 39,* 555–577.

Bowlby, J. (1988). *A secure base: Parent-child attachment and healthy human development.* New York: Basic Books.

Cohen, J. (1992). A power primer. *Psychological Bulletin, 112,* 155–159.

Doosje, B., Ellemers, N., & Spears, R. (1995). Perceived intragroup variability as a function of group status and identification. *Journal of Experimental Social Psychology, 31,* 410–436.

Dunham, R. B., & Herman, J. B. (1975). Development of a female Faces Scale for measuring job satisfaction. *Journal of Applied Psychology, 60,* 629–631.

Gallup (2014). The state of the global workforce.Available at: http://www.gallup.com/de-de/181871/engagement-index-deutschland.aspx

Gautam, T., Van Dick, R., & Wagner, U. (2004). Organizational identification and organizational commitment: Distinct aspects of two related concepts. *Asian Journal of Social Psychology, 7,* 301–315.

Gellatly, I. R., Meyer, J. P., & Luchak, A. A. (2006). Combined effects of the three commitment components on focal and discretionary behaviors: A test of Meyer and Herscovitch's propositions. *Journal of Vocational Behavior, 69,* 331–345.

Hackman, J. R., & Oldham, G. R. (1975). Development of the job diagnostic survey. *Journal of Applied Psychology, 60,* 159–170.

Hämmelmann, A., & Van Dick, R. (2013). Entwickeln im Team – Effekte für den Einzelnen: Eine Evaluation von Teamentwicklungsmaßnahmen [Team building – individual effects: An evaluation of a team building intervention]. *Gruppendynamik und Organisationsberatung, 44,* 221–238.

Haslam, S. A., Reicher, S. D., & Platow, M. J. (2011). *The new psychology of leadership: Identity, influence and power.* Hove: Psychology Press.

Herzberg, F. (1964). The motivation-hygiene concept and problems of manpower. *Personnel Administration, 27,* 3–7.

Higgins, E. T. (1998). Promotion and prevention: Regulatory focus as a motivational principle. In M. P. Zanna (Ed.), *Advances in experimental social psychology* (pp. 1–46). New York: Academic Press.

Jackson, T. A., Meyer, J. P., & Wang, X. H. (2012). Leadership, commitment, and culture: A meta-analysis. *Journal of Leadership & Organizational Studies, 20,* 84–106.

Judge, T. A., Thoresen, C. J., Bono, J. E., & Patton, G. K. (2001). The job satisfaction–job performance relationship: A qualitative and quantitative review. *Psychological Bulletin, 127,* 376–407.

Klein, H. J., Molloy, J. C., & Brinsfield, C. T. (2012). Reconceptualizing workplace commitment to redress a stretched construct: Revisiting assumptions and removing confounds. *Academy of Management Review, 37*(1), 130–151. http://doi.org/10.5465/amr.2010.0018

Lee, E.-S., Park, T.-Y., & Koo, B. (2015). Identifying organizational identification as a basis for attitudes and behaviors: a meta-analytic review. *Psychological Bulletin, 141,* 1049–1080.

Lucas, R. E., & Schimmack, U. (2009). Income and well-being: How big is the gap between the rich and the poor? *Journal of Research in Personality*, *43*(1), 75–78.

Mael, F., & Ashforth, B. E. (1992). Alumni and their alma mater: A partial test of the reformulated model of organizational identification. *Journal of Organizational Behavior*, *13*(2), 103–123.

Markovits, Y., Boer, D., & Van Dick, R. (2014). Economic crisis and the employee: The effects of economic crisis on employee job satisfaction, commitment, and self-regulation. *European Management Journal*, *32*, 413–422.

Markovits, Y., Davis, A., & Van Dick, R. (2007). Organizational commitment profiles and job satisfaction among Greek public and private sector employees. *International Journal of Cross-Cultural Management*, *7*, 77–99.

Meyer, J. P., Becker, T. E., & Van Dick, R. (2006). Social identities and commitments at work: Toward an integrative model. *Journal of Organizational Behavior*, *27*, 665–683.

Meyer, J. P., & Herscovitch, L. (2001). Commitment in the workplace: toward a general model. *Human Resource Management Review*, *11*(3), 299–326.

Meyer, J. P., & Parfyonova, N. M. (2010). Normative commitment in the workplace: A theoretical analysis and re-conceptualization. *Human Resource Management Review*, *20*(4), 283–294.

Meyer, J. P., Stanley, D. J., Herscovitch, L., & Topolnytsky, L. (2002). Affective, continuance, and normative commitment to the organization: A meta-analysis of antecedents, correlates, and consequences. *Journal of Vocational Behavior*, *61*, 20–52.

Meyer, J. P., Stanley, D. J., Jackson, T. A., McInnis, K. J., Maltin, E. R., & Sheppard, L. (2012). Affective, normative, and continuance commitment levels across cultures: A meta-analysis. *Journal of Vocational Behavior*, *80*(2), 225–245.

Organ, D. W., Podsakoff, P. M., & MacKenzie, S. B. (2005). *Organizational citizenship behavior: Its nature, antecedents, and consequences*. London: Sage Publications.

Patterson, M., Warr, P., & West, M. (2004). Organizational climate and company productivity: The role of employee affect and employee level. *Journal of Occupational and Organizational Psychology*, *77*, 193–216.

Postmes, T., Haslam, S. A., & Jans, L. (2013). A single-item measure of social identification: Reliability, validity, and utility. *British Journal of Social Psychology*, *52*(4), 597–617.

Riketta, M. (2005). Organizational identification: A meta-analysis. *Journal of Vocational Behavior*, *66*, 358–384.

Riketta, M. (2008). The causal relation between job attitudes and performance: a meta-analysis of panel studies. *Journal of Applied Psychology*, *93*, 472–481.

Riketta, M., & Van Dick, R. (2005). Foci of attachment in organizations: A meta-analysis comparison of the strength and correlates of work-group versus organizational commitment and identification. *Journal of Vocational Behavior*, *67*, 490–510.

Robbins, S. P., & Judge, T. A. (2013). *Organizational behavior*. Boston: Pearson.

Steffens, N. K., et al. (2014). Leadership as social identity management: introducing the Identity Leadership Inventory (ILI) to assess and validate a four-dimensional model. *The Leadership Quarterly*, *25*, 1001–1024.

Tajfel, H., & Turner, J. C. (1979). An integrative theory of intergroup conflict. *The social psychology of intergroup relations*, *33*(47), 74.

Van Dick, R., et al. (2004). Should I stay or should I go? Explaining turnover intentions with organizational identification and job satisfaction. *British Journal of Management*, *15*, 351-360.

Van Dick, R., Grojean, M.W., Christ, O., & Wieseke, J. (2006). Identity and the extra-mile: Relationships between organizational identification and organizational citizenship behaviour. *British Journal of Management*, *17*, 283–301.

Van Knippenberg, D., & Sleebos, E. (2006). Organizational identification versus organizational commitment: self-definition, social exchange, and job attitudes. *Journal of Organizational Behavior, 27,* 571–584.

Weiss, D.J., Dawis, R.V., England, G.W. & Lofquist, L.H. (1964). *Manual for the Minnesota Satisfaction Questionnaire* (Minnesota Studies in Vocational Rehabilitation 22). Minneapolis: University of Minnesota.

Wegge, J., Schuh, S.C., & Van Dick, R. (2012). I feel bad – We feel good!? Emotions as a driver for personal and organizational identity and organizational identification as a resource for serving unfriendly customers. *Stress and Health, 28,* 123–136.

How Does Work Fit with My Life? The Relation Between Flexible Work Arrangements, Work–Life Balance and Recovery from Work

23

Göran Kecklund, Debby G. J. Beckers, Constanze Leineweber and Philip Tucker

Overview

The right balance between work, personal life and daily recovery is an important determinant of employees' well-being, health and experience of stress. One of the most important things in many people's lives is their relationship with their family. Much research has found that various aspects of work, for example, long work hours or high job demands, interfere with family life and time for recovery. This interference can be a source of stress and diminished life satisfaction. Work and home life are the central aspects of most employees' lives, although there are also many other significant aspects of work–life balance, such as leisure, political and spiritual activity, and social engagements. Work–life balance is affected by two forms of interference: work–home conflict and home–work conflict. The interaction between work and home can be negative, for example, when the time spent working leaves too little time for private life; and positive, for example, when a stimulating job enhances one's general mood and life satisfaction. There are many ways to enhance work–life balance and recovery, with one aspect – work flexibility – having received a lot of attention in recent years. In this chapter we review the concepts of work–life balance, recovery from work, and two key components of flexible work–time flexibility and place flexibility. The review focuses on the antecedents of these concepts and their consequences in terms of health, well-being and job-related outcomes.

23.1 Introduction

Stress-related health problems are common around the world, although the causes of stress may differ across cultures and countries. In many societies, one factor contributing to the growing number of stress-related health problems might be

An Introduction to Work and Organizational Psychology: An International Perspective,
Third Edition. Edited by Nik Chmiel, Franco Fraccaroli and Magnus Sverke.

the increase in dual earner families and non-traditional households. Managing the domains of work, private life and family has become a part of everyday life for many, and the work–life imbalance is increasingly prevalent. According to the European Working Condition Survey of 2010, almost one fifth of employees within the EU report that their working hours do not fit well with their family and social commitments outside work. However, work–life balance and recovery is not only a matter of one's work hours. Conflicts between job and family demands can easily interfere with the time devoted to leisure and personal care, and to recovery needs. One way in which work organizations can support work–life balance and recovery is by introducing flexible work arrangements. These help employees balance work, family and home responsibilities, and increase the employees' opportunities for rest and relaxation (Allen et al., 2013). Flexible work arrangements that result in increased job autonomy allow employees to adjust their work hours and place of work, so as to improve the fit with their personal life needs. The current chapter begins with an overview of the concepts of work–life balance and recovery, followed by a summary of the pros and cons of workplace and worktime flexibility.

23.2   The Work–Life Balance: How Do We Manage Work and Non-Work Roles?

In the past few decades scholars have focused much of their attention on the phenomenon of the work–life balance and consequently a plethora of theories has emerged to explain it. Within the field of occupational health psychology one of the most commonly used theories to frame studies on work–life balance is the role strain theory.

23.2.1   The role strain theory

The role strain theory basically assumes that managing several roles is difficult and creates strain. Research on the work–life balance often emphasizes the negative effects of having multiple roles and often refers to work–family conflict. This is defined as 'a form of inter-role conflict in which the role pressures from work and family domains are mutually incompatible in some respect. That is, participation in the work (family) role is made more difficult by virtue of participation in the family (work) role' (Greenhaus & Beutell, 1985, p. 77). Three types of conflict can occur when combining work and family life. *Time-based conflict* refers to the conflict which might occur when time pressure from one domain makes it physically impossible to meet the demands from the other domain, or when one is preoccupied with one domain while attempting to meet the demands of another role. An example of time-based conflict is when working in the evening hampers participation in family-related activities. *Strain-based conflict* refers to strain (e.g., tension, anxiety, irritability, exhaustion or depression), which occurs due to participation in one role making it difficult to fulfil the demands of another role. For example a parent who is tired and exhausted after the working day might have difficulties meeting their children's needs. *Behaviour-based conflict* refers to a situation where the role behaviour in one domain is incompatible with role behaviour in the other domain. An example of behaviour-based conflict is the retired naval officer, Captain Georg von Trapp in *The Sound of Music*, who tries to raise his children using the strict military discipline he knows from his work.

It is important to note that a variety of terms are used to describe the relationship between work and non-work demands, such as 'work–family interference', 'work–home interference', or 'work–home conflict' (Byron, 2005). The latter two highlight the fact that conflict does not necessarily refer to the impact on one's role as a spouse, parent or caregiver but may relate to other aspects of one's non-work life, such as pastimes or hobbies. Another important point is the bidirectional nature of the associations between the 'work' and the 'non-work' domains, highlighting the distinction between work demands that interfere with private life (i.e., work-to-home conflict) and home demands that interfere with work (i.e., home-to-work conflict). These two forms of conflict are moderately correlated, but their antecedents and consequences are somewhat different.

To have several roles, e.g., as a parent and as an employee, not only generates conflicts, but is unarguably associated with many advantages. These include the emancipation of women and a better family income, and it has been argued that work and family roles might facilitate one another. According to this view, experiences in one domain generate resources that can be transferred to the other domain (i.e., enhancement). Thus, work–family enhancement describes how experiences in one role can improve the quality of life in the other role. Nevertheless, it has been consistently shown that negative impacts from work to non-work life are more common than the opposite. Here, we concentrate on the possible negative effects and mainly use the term work–home conflict, although other terms may be used interchangeably. This does not mean, however, that positive effects are less important.

23.3 Recent Perspectives on the Work–Life Balance

Many theories have been presented to explain the interactions between the work and the home domains. The *conservation of resources* (COR; Hobfoll, 1989) theory is a general stress model that offers an appropriate framework in the field of work–life balance. According to this theory, people seek to acquire and maintain resources. If a loss of resources is experienced or anticipated, or if an expected gain in resources is not met, stress reactions will develop. There are two central principles of the COR theory. The first is that resource loss has a more salient impact than resource gain. The second central principle states that resources must be invested in order to recover from resource loss, protect against resource loss or achieve a resource gain. Thus, employees who perceive a loss of resources in one domain are more likely to experience other subsequent resource losses in other domains, leading to work–home conflict. This approach is very close to the Job Demands–Resources model (Demerouti et al., 2001). The model makes the assumption that energy resources are depleted when job demands are too high, i.e., require too much effort and time, such that job resources are insufficient to fulfil the job requirements. On the other hand, when resources are sufficient to meet the job requirements, individuals will be stimulated and energy will be mobilized rather than depleted. In turn, this will facilitate one's functioning in the private domain as well.

A quite different approach is taken by *border theory*. It tries to explain 'how individuals manage and negotiate the work and family spheres and the borders between them in order to attain balance' (Clark, 2000, p. 750). According to this theory, people are border crossers who make transitions between the world of work and the world of family. Both the world of work and the world of the family may satisfy essential but different needs. The borders between work and the family can be physical, temporal, or psychological and are more or less per-meable and flexible. One important aspect of the theory is that weak borders are considered permeable and flexible, and will facilitate the work–life balance if the domains are similar, while strong borders are more functional in the case of very different domains. This theory also has some common features with the boundary management theory (see section of telework in the present chapter).

23.3.1   Antecedents of work–home conflict

A large body of literature has examined antecedents of work–home conflict. Below we present some job characteristics, which are commonly considered as antecedents of work–home conflict and also discuss how gender, family character-istics and age may affect work–home conflict. Figure 23.1 presents some factors related to job demands, job resources and family demands that can influence the work–life balance.

Several *job characteristics* have been suggested as possible antecedents of work–home conflict. Job stressors, such as role conflict, role overload and time demands as well as job involvement have been identified as antecedents of work–home conflict (Michel et al., 2011). In a study that evaluated behaviourally based ante-cedents of work–home conflict, interdependence and responsibility for others at

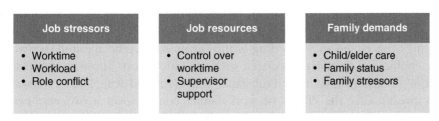

Figure 23.1:   Factors that can affect work–life balance

work predicted work–home conflict (Dierdorff et al., 2008). Job control, a supportive organizational culture, as well as supervisor and coworker support, have all been identified as means of reducing work–home conflict (Michel et al., 2011).

In the past few decades working life has changed dramatically. The introduction of communication technology has led to increased flexibility in working life and today many employees can decide not only on when to work (time flexibility), but also on where to work (place flexibility). These new ways of working may have a number of positive effects, such as enhanced opportunities for balancing work and home demands. However, they might also have their drawbacks, such as an increased risk that individuals are constantly involved in work – even during their free time – which may impair both family life and recovery (Demerouti et al, 2014). It is also unclear if all employees benefit equally from having increased control over their working hours. On the one hand it seems likely that employees with greater family responsibilities (e.g., women) will gain the most. On the other hand, increased flexibility may have adverse consequences for women's work–home balance, as they may end up engaging in more non-work responsibilities.

While there is often an assumption that interference between paid work and family life will burden women more than men, research results are inconclusive and it remains unclear whether men and women report different or equal levels of work–home conflict. A meta-analysis suggests that sex is a poor predictor of work–home conflict (Byron, 2005). However, there are some indications that the lack of difference in work–home conflict between women and men could be at least partly explained by aspects of gender inequality (e.g., work in different occupations, differences in working hours, etc.).

The effect of age has rarely been studied and is hard to separate from the effect of being in different stages of life (e.g., marital status, parenthood, etc.). Evidence regarding the influence of marital status is weak but somewhat clearer findings have been reported with regard to parental status. Work–home conflict has been linked to the presence of children living at home and to the children's age (Geurts & Demerouti, 2003). However those findings were somewhat contradicted by a recent meta-analysis that found that home-to-work conflict was not influenced by the age of the employees' children (Michel et al., 2011).

23.3.2   Consequences of work–home conflict

Many possible consequences of work–home conflict have been suggested, and the list is increasing. They can be divided into health outcomes, work consequences, and family consequences. Regarding *health outcomes*, it has been found that work–home conflict is negatively associated with life satisfaction, burnout, depression, somatic/physical symptoms, and substance abuse (Amstad et al., 2011). A Swedish study investigating the effects of work–family conflict over a two-year period found that while both men and women had an increased odds for emotional exhaustion, only women had an increased odds for poor self-rated health while men had an increased risk of problem drinking (Leineweber, Baltzer, Magnusson Hanson, & Westerlund, 2013). Regarding *work outcomes,* work–home conflict is associated with lower job satisfaction, work performance and organizational commitment, as well as greater turnover intention and absenteeism (Amstad et al., 2011). Work–home conflict may also have negative consequences for private life and has been linked to reduced marital and family satisfaction (Geurts & Demerouti, 2003).

23.3.3 Some concluding remarks

To summarize, research has repeatedly shown that high demands from both work and family contribute to the experience of work–home conflict. This conflict has many important consequences, both for the employee and for the employing organizations. With regard to both the antecedents and consequences of work–home conflict, it is important to remember that the number of longitudinal studies is very small. Most research is based on cross-sectional studies and only a few have assessed whether work–home conflict predicts health outcomes. Thus, little is known about the causality and the direction of the relationships.

23.4 What Is Recovery and Why Is It Important for Our Lives?

Recovery plays a crucial role in the way that work stress affects long-term health. The links between stress, recovery and health have been described by Geurts and Sonnentag (2006), drawing upon the Effort–Recovery model (Meijman & Mulder, 1998) and the Allostatic Load theory (McEwen, 2006). When at work, workers have to expend effort in order to accomplish their tasks. According to the Effort–Recovery model, the impact of this effort expenditure builds up across the working day. When the worker gets home after a demanding day at work, the accumulated fatigue that they feel encourages them to try to relax, mentally 'switch off' and unwind. This process of unwinding after work is when recovery takes place. Recovery is the process by which psychobiological systems that have been activated during the working day return to their 'normal', or 'pre-stressed' state. However, it may not always be possible to unwind and recover during the evening. This may be because the worker continues working after their normal work hours; or because they are unable to stop thinking about work; or because they are exposed to other non-work-related stressors (e.g., domestic problems). Failing to recover in the evening means that the worker returns to work the next morning feeling more fatigued than they otherwise would. Hence they have to expend additional effort to overcome that fatigue. Thus, by the end of that second day their need for recovery is even greater than it was the day before. This can lead to a spiral of accumulating fatigue and need for recovery, which in the long term results in chronic health problems (Meijman & Mulder, 1998).

The allostatic load theory holds that health problems are likely to develop because of failure in the process of *allostasis* (McEwen, 2006). Allostasis is the process by which a person's psychobiological systems control their response to environmental stressors, e.g., increased heart rate and blood pressure, providing the brain and muscles with additional energy. When the stressor is diminished, the psychobiological systems return to pre-activation levels. However, chronic or repeated exposure to job stressors, together with insufficient recovery, may lead to a malfunction of allostasis. The stress-response fails to shut off or fails to respond adequately, leading to malfunctioning of the body's defence mechanisms, as well as excessive wear and tear on those systems.

In addition to the recovery that takes place while a person is awake, sleep is one of the most important means of restoring psycho-physiological resources that have been depleted by activity during the waking day (McEwen, 2006). The failure to unwind and mentally switch off from work (i.e., 'psychologically detach' from work) can cause sleep disturbance, e.g., difficulties falling asleep due to worrying. Hence the negative health effects of failing to recover during the evening may be exacerbated by the detrimental impact that non-recovery has upon subsequent sleep.

23.4.1   How do we recover from work?

Recovery from work effort can occur both within work ('internal recovery') and outside work ('external-recovery'; Geurts & Sonnentag, 2006). Internal recovery (e.g., obtained during rest breaks at work) prevents the accumulation of load effects over the day. Internal recovery is fostered by providing workers with control over the way they perform their job, together with task variety and social support. Having control allows workers to create spontaneous mini-breaks and to adjust their work strategy to their current need for recovery. External recovery occurs during the evenings between workdays, at weekends and during vacations.

There are two mechanisms by which taking a break or stopping work may contribute to recovery; passive recovery and active recovery (Geurts & Sonnentag, 2006). Passive recovery occurs when we cease to be exposed to job demands and stressors i.e., the absence of detrimental activities. Active recovery involves undertaking valued, pleasant and self-chosen non-work activities; the latter reflecting the importance of having control over how one spends one's time.

23.4.2   How does life outside work impact on recovery?

Several studies have examined the way in which activities conducted outside normal work hours may impact upon recovery (Sonnentag & Fritz, 2014). Typically, such studies involve participants completing daily diaries in which they record their free time activities day by day, as well as completing self-report measures of well-being (fatigue, health, vigour, etc.) at bedtime and/or at the start of the next day. Working after normal hours is generally found to impede recovery. This is because demands are made upon the *same* psycho-physiological systems that were already activated while at work. In addition, exposure to stressors outside of normal work hours is a risk because of high sympathetic (cardiovascular) activation, irrespective of whether or not the stressors are work-related. Hence recovery is usually promoted by non-work related, non-stressful activities (Geurts & Sonnentag, 2006). Even if the worker does not actively engage in after-hours work, they may fail to psychologically detach so that physiological activation continues during recovery time e.g., rumination about, and anticipation of, work. Psychological detachment is a core component of recovery from work stress, alongside other recovery experiences such as relaxation, mastery, control, meaning and affiliation (Sonnentag & Fritz, 2014).

There is mixed evidence concerning which non-work activities promote recovery during free time, with much of the research focusing on low-effort activities (e.g., watching TV) and social activities (e.g., meeting with friends or playing sport; e.g., ten Brummelhuis & Bakker, 2012). It seems likely that the nature of the activity *per se* is less important than the way the free time activities are experienced and evaluated (Tucker et al., 2008). For example, social activities in which the person discusses their work may inhibit psychological detachment and recovery. Conversely, reflecting positively on one's work during free time may enrich non-working life (Sonnentag & Binnewies, 2013).

Relaxation activities (e.g., yoga, listening to music, taking a walk in natural environments, progressive muscle relaxation, breathing exercises) have been linked to reductions in health complaints, exhaustion, sleep problems and need for recovery (Sonnentag & Fritz, 2007). Physical exercise is thought to promote recovery through a number of possible routes, including physiological mechanisms (e.g., release of endorphins or monoamines, thermogenic effects on mood), and psychological effects (e.g., distraction from work-related thoughts, experiencing mastery, achievement and self-efficacy).

Household tasks and childcare are potential enhancers of recovery as they draw upon non-work resources and can distract from thoughts of work. However, they are often demanding and are usually compulsory, which could restrict their value for recovery. Early studies, which did not differentiate between household tasks and childcare, typically found no effects on fatigue and wellbeing at bedtime. However, these two forms of activity may differ in several important respects, such as the level of distraction they promote (i.e., attention demanded) and the degree of enjoyment they invoke. A more recent study found that household tasks (along with work-related tasks) lead to decreased feelings of vigour the next morning, through diminished psychological detachment and relaxation, while there were no such negative effects of childcare (ten Brummelhuis & Bakker, 2012).

23.4.3 How do the 'new ways of working' affect recovery?

Mobile technology has increased the opportunities for flexible working for many employees. However, it creates a norm of nomadic working and continual communication, making employees more easily contactable outside

---

Box 23.1: Sleep disturbance

An illustration of the 'double-edged sword' of flexibility is provided by a recent study of work time control and sleep disturbance (Salo et al., 2014). The study was based on a large-scale longitudinal study of public sector employees in Finland who were surveyed on four occasions over 12 years. Among employees who worked up to 40 hours per week, those with better work time control subsequently experienced fewer sleep disturbances. However, the relationship was more complex among those working more than 40 hours per week. Both very low *and very high* levels of work time control were associated with more disturbed sleep. It was suggested that some employees who had a lot of work time control were choosing to work long weekly hours (e.g., in order to earn more overtime pay, or for other reasons), albeit at the expense of being able to unwind and obtain sufficient sleep between work days.

---

normal working hours. Consequently, employees may feel compelled to respond to work-related messages in their free time, thereby inhibiting their psychological detachment from work (Derks et al., 2014). Thus, the increased productivity achieved by staying connected in the evening may be offset by the negative impact that insufficient recovery has upon job performance the next day.

Flexible working allows employees to adjust their work arrangements to fit with non-work aspects of their lives (e.g., family life), which in turn may enhance recovery. However, if flexibility results in more work-related activities being conducted during free time, work–home conflict is likely to increase and well-being may suffer. Also, the blurring of boundaries between work and non-work may make it harder for employees to 'switch off' from work and thus achieve adequate recovery. Moreover, employees with high levels of worktime control may be tempted to work hours that impede recovery (for example, see Box 23.1).

One possible way of resolving the paradoxical effects of new ways of working on recovery is to set clear boundaries between work and non-work aspects of our lives. Within the context of flexible working, this might involve, for example, only working or checking email at home between 19:00h and 21:00h in the evening, thereby allowing for some psychological detachment and unwinding before bedtime.

23.5   Telework, Work–Life Balance and Recovery

Telework is an example of a flexible work arrangement that has become increasingly popular in modern working life. Through the use of information and communication technology (ICT) it is possible to work away from the central office, for example, at home. Such possibilities can provide support for the employee's work–life balance and increase time for recovery, for example by reducing commuting time. However, the pros and cons of telework have been the subject of debate in recent years (see Box 23.2). Telework is common among white-collar workers such as teachers and employees working in the IT sector, whereas it is very rare among blue-collar occupations.

> ## Box 23.2:   Telework
>
> Although telework has increased over time, it is still debated whether this is good or bad for employees and organizations. An example of the controversy is when Yahoo CEO Marissa Mayer in 2013 ended the company's popular 'working from home policy' and claimed that employees are more cooperative and innovative when they are together at the workplace. Mayer's policy statement created a lot of discussion in the media. Many experts in work and organizational psychology claimed that employees working from home can be just as productive as when they are working from the office and that it would be a backwards step to prevent individual's freedom to decide where they want to work.

23.5.1   Definition and prevalence of telework

There is no generally accepted definition of telework. In broad terms, telework refers to working from an alternative location outside the main office (see also Chapter 7 in this volume). Other terms that are often used interchangeably with telework are telecommuting, distance work, distributed work, and flexible work place (Allen et al., 2015). In their recent review, Allen et al. propose a more specific definition: 'Telecommuting is a work practice that involves members of an organization substituting a portion of their typical work hours (ranging from a few hours per week to nearly full-time) to work away from a central workplace – typically principally from home – using technology to interact with others as needed to conduct work tasks'.

A report from 2010 estimated that 7 per cent of the working population in the European Union teleworked from home at least one quarter of their work time, and 1.7 per cent teleworked almost all the time (Eurofound, 2010). It also noted that there had been an increase in telework over time. The opportunities for telework varied between occupations, with the highest use of telework being found in the financial and real estate sectors, and in education. Telework was found to be more common among men. Prevalence statistics for the USA indicate that telework has increased since the early 2000s and that 2.6 per cent of the labour force reported that their home was their main place of work (Allen et al., 2015). However, the average number of hours spent teleworking was still rather modest – around 6 hours per week (Noonan & Glass, 2012).

23.5.2   The benefits and challenges of telework

The main benefits of telework are that it helps employees to manage family demands and household needs, and that less time is spent commuting (Allen et al., 2015). Working from home may also facilitate a better work environment that involves less distractions and interruptions from coworkers. Telework may also involve also some kind of scheduling flexibility since the employee often has more control of their worktime (see next section for an overview of the concept worktime control). It is assumed that, when working from home, work tasks are often partially completed outside the standard office hours and that telework leads to more individualized work hours. For example, it is possible to divide the workday into one morning and one evening period, and to use the free time between the work periods for personal activities such as attending a child's school, household activities, or physical training.

Telework may also be beneficial for work productivity, in particular for employees who have their daily performance peak outside traditional office hours. The increased time and workplace autonomy enables employees to more effectively manage the balance between their work and their private lives, thus suggesting that telework may improve work–life balance and mitigate work–home conflict (Allen et al., 2015). Two meta-analyses support this hypothesis and there is a statistically significant but relatively weak relationship between telework and lower work–home conflict (Gajendran & Harrison, 2007; Allen et al, 2013). The meta-analysis by Allen et al. (2013) distinguished between work–family conflict (WFC) and family–work conflict (FWC), with the association between teleworking and WFC being weakly supported ($r=-0.11$), whereas there was no support for an association between telework and FWC ($r=-0.03$).

One of the key potential negative consequences of telework is the blurred boundary between work and family life, which could increase work-home interference and lead to poorer work–life balance (Kossek et al., 2006). According to the theory of boundary management there are two extreme positions: integration and segmentation. Employees who prefer to integrate work and family in time and space have permeable borders between the two domains, and they mix work and family activities. They may take private calls when they work, and they may work at the kitchen table at home while remaining accessible to their family (Kossek et al., 2006). An employee who prefers a segmentation strategy seeks to have boundaries between work and home and may, for example, turn off the smartphone at the end of the day, not check email outside traditional office hours, and avoid interruptions from the family when at work (Kossek et al., 2006). An integration-oriented strategy can be more attractive for teleworkers and may improve work–life balance. Paradoxically, too much integration may also lead to work–life imbalance and extending working hours, for example, by checking emails in the evening. A blurred boundary between work and home life may cause difficulties switching off thoughts of work, such that work never stops – which may increase stress and impede recovery. The claim that telework is related to blurred boundaries between work and home time is supported by a US study showing that teleworkers worked 5–7 hours more than non-teleworkers, suggesting that home-based telework may have a negative impact on work–life balance (Noonan & Glass, 2012).

The impact of telework and job-related outcomes was examined in a meta-analysis (Martin & MacDonnell, 2012). On the one hand, the results showed that telework is beneficial for self-reported productivity, performance, organizational commitment and retention. On the other hand, it also found that telework may increase social isolation and result in less social support at work.

To sum up, telework can be an effective solution for individuals who have high demands from home, need more control over their work hours and need more family time. However, it is important that employers provide their teleworking employees with advice on how to deal with work and family boundaries, and the need to avoid compromising the work–life balance by working longer hours.

23.6 Worktime Control, Work–Life Balance and Recovery

Worktime flexibility is a key issue in modern work society. Originally, flexibility was predominantly organization-oriented and aimed at promoting efficiency, performance and accessibility of organizations. Organization-oriented worktime flexibility often results in taxing work hours (e.g., long working hours, weekend work, shiftwork) that challenge a proper work–life balance.

Employee-oriented worktime flexibility has become increasingly important during the past decades, as it is often seen as the key to upholding a good work–life balance, increasing labour market participation, and facilitating lifelong workability, even or especially when faced with high work (time) demands. Employee-friendly worktime flexibility provides employees with the freedom to adjust working times to meet their individual needs and preferences. It is also known as 'employee worktime control'. Examples of worktime control include choosing to work part-time, flexitime (employees' control over the starting and ending times of their workdays), leave control (employees' possibilities to self-determine when to take a day off or have a vacation), break control (being able to take a break when needed during the workday), control over which days to work, and control over whether, when and how much to work overtime (Beckers, Kompier, Kecklund, & Härmä, 2012).

The prevalence of worktime control varies considerably between employment sectors, shiftwork vs. non-shiftwork settings, and between countries. A recent survey by Eurofound (2015a) found that on average 20% of European workers report having flexitime, while 6% completely determine their own working times. Other surveys suggest that flexitime is more widespread in other parts of the world. For instance, it has been reported that 41% of US employers allow (at least some) flexitime on a daily basis, 40% provide employees with control over which shifts to work, and 45% allow control over overtime work (O'Caroll, 2015).

Most reports agree that worktime control is on the rise. However, it must be noted that in many countries numerous workers remain dissatisfied with their access to employee-oriented worktime flexibility (Eurofound, 2015b).

23.6.1 How does worktime control influence work–life balance?

Worktime control may promote the work–life balance through two mechanisms: (1) a time-regulation mechanism, and (2) a recovery-regulation mechanism (Nijp et al., 2012).

The first mechanism implies that worktime control allows workers to adapt their work hours to their responsibilities and preferences in their private life (e.g., family commitments, household chores, sport activities, hobbies). For instance, flexible starting and ending times allow employees to bring their children to school in the morning and start work a little later. This time-regulating aspect of worktime control may afford a degree of protection against time-based work–home interference (Nijp et al., 2012).

Worktime control may also help employees maintain a balance between effort and recovery, helping them to avoid high levels of work-related fatigue and strain-based work–home conflict (i.e., the conflict that arises from the employees feeling worn out and stressed from work). This is the second mechanism: 'recovery regulation'. Many occupational health theories advocate job control as a favourable work characteristic that prevents adverse work outcomes such as stress, fatigue and a high need for recovery. Autonomy over the timing of work may have an especially important value for promoting recovery (Nijp et al., 2012). Worktime control can be a resource for internal recovery (i.e., recovery during the workday), as it enables employees to take a break when needed. In addition, worktime control may be a means for external recovery (in-between working days and working periods) as it provides workers with control over the planning of their leave days and the starting and ending times of their workday.

23.6.2 Empirical evidence of the association between worktime control and work–life balance

A meta-analysis by Byron (2005) examining multiple antecedents of work–home conflict found evidence of a favourable association between employee-oriented schedule flexibility and the work–life balance. Similar conclusions were reached by recent systematic review (Nijp et al., 2012) that found proof for this favourable association both in studies that considered the general experience of worktime control and also in studies that focused on sub-dimensions of worktime control, such as flexitime, leave control and compressed workweeks.

An organization may offer its employees the possibility to exert worktime control (e.g., by making it a part of their employment contract), but that does not necessarily mean that the employees will use that facility (e.g., because, in practice, they are discouraged from doing so by their line managers). A meta-analysis which focused on this distinction between 'having access to' and 'use of' worktime control (Allen et al., 2013) found that, contrary to its authors' expectations, flexitime availability was more strongly related to work–home balance than flexitime use. This is in line with a recent study by Nijp, Beckers, Kompier, Van den Bossche and Geurts (2015), who found that use of worktime control was unrelated to the work–life balance. This study among shiftworkers and dayworkers also showed that employees reported higher levels of work–home interference when their 'need for work time control' exceeded the level of worktime control available to them. Thus employees' need for worktime control can be an important factor determining the effects of access to worktime control. It was notable that a large proportion of the employees in the study experienced a negative mismatch between their need for worktime control and the level of worktime control available to them.

Worktime control can be introduced into shiftwork through self-scheduling. Self-scheduling involves the employer using ICT software to set minimum and maximum staffing needs for specific time-units, after which employees submit their preferred schedule for the upcoming month(s). The idea is that individual preferences are met as far as possible while taking staffing needs into consideration. A review by Bambra et al. (2008) identified three prospective studies which showed that health, organizational effectiveness and work–life balance were improved after the introduction of self-scheduling. Similarly, a more recent study by Albertsen et al. (2014) found that the introduction of self-scheduling generally resulted in a decline of work–home conflicts and an increase in work–home facilitation. Interestingly, this study compared several self-scheduling interventions and showed that the exact content of a self-scheduling intervention, along with the implementation process and intervention context, are key factors determining the effectiveness of the intervention. Their findings reflect the fact that self-scheduling can either be a form of organization-oriented flexibility, or employee-oriented flexibility, or a combination of these two. Joyce, Pabayo, Critchley, and Bambra (2010) reached a similar conclusion in their Cochrane Review of flexible worktime arrangements. They found that flexible worktime interventions that increase worker control and choice are likely to have favourable effects, whereas interventions that were motivated or dictated by organizational interests produced equivocal or negative health effects.

23.7 Conclusion

In general, we can conclude that employee-friendly worktime flexibility resulting in more worktime control is a promising tool for promoting a proper work–life balance and daily recovery (Joyce et al., 2010). This is especially so when there is a match between need for worktime control and access to worktime control.

Most of the studies described above focused on moderate levels of worktime control and identified generally positive effects. By contrast, very high levels of worktime control (which are common in several modern initiatives, such as New Ways of Working (NWW)) may actually pose a threat to the maintenance of a proper work–life balance. As noted previously in this chapter, employees who have complete temporal freedom (in NWW combined with spatial flexibility, e.g., telework) run the risk of being 'always on'). That is to say, their work and private lives may become increasingly intertwined and their use of modern ICT (e.g., smartphones) means that they are always contactable by colleagues and clients, and thus risk working longer hours. However, the few high quality studies that have examined the effects of NWW do not appear to bear out such a scenario. A recent quasi-experimental intervention study examined time-independent work (i.e., high access to worktime control) and place-independent work, i.e., (1) working from home at least one or two days a week; and (2) at work, a flexible office without personal work spaces, combined with extensive use of ICT and performance-based management. The findings of this intervention study

---

Box 23.3:   ROWE: Results-Only Work Environment

Kelly and colleagues (2011) describe the characteristics of a Results-Only Work Environment (ROWE) intervention, with attention being paid to both the content of the intervention and the implementation process. ROWE attempts to change the organizational culture so that employee-friendly temporal and spatial flexibility becomes the norm for all employees. Employees are, of course, faced with performance targets, but can largely self-determine their work location and working times. ROWE somewhat overlaps with New Ways of Working (NWW), but often facilitates even higher flexibility than NWW work places do.

ROWE is a team-based intervention and departments that transfer to ROWE usually attend team-level training sessions aimed at developing the ROWE culture. During these sessions, employees get acquainted with the ROWE philosophy, reevaluate their ideas about worktime norms and work location norms, and develop team-level strategies for meeting business goals while simultaneously being given increased control over work hours and work location. Managers are also trained, and employees and managers discuss concerns and decide upon solutions together.

In their quasi-experimental intervention study, Kelly and colleagues (2011) found that the implementation of ROWE resulted in a reduction of work–life conflict and an improvement in work–family fit, through an increase in worktime control. The concern that excessive schedule control would result in an 'always on' culture that could result in more work–life conflict was thus not realized in this study.

---

showed that coworker support, work–home balance, stress levels and fatigue remained favourable and largely unaffected, which implies that it is possible to implement NWW without compromising employee well-being (Nijp, Beckers, Van de Voorde, Geurts & Kompier, 2016). Another form of NWW that features high levels of worktime control is the concept of Results-Only Work Environment (ROWE; e.g., Kelly, Moen & Tranby, 2011), which has also been linked to favourable outcomes for work–home balance (see Box 23.3).

Summary

The present chapter has addressed the question of how work fits within the life of the employee by focusing on two key concepts, namely, work–life balance and recovery from work. Both are beneficial for life satisfaction and positive mood. A positive balance between work and private life reduces work–home conflict and stress, which are important determinants of well-being. One purpose of leisure time is to provide successful recovery after a stressful workday. Recovery outside work hours (i.e., evenings and weekends) refers not only to switching off mentally from work, resting and obtaining adequate sleep, but also to the pursuit of stimulating activities during leisure time such as sports and hobbies. Recovery is also of vital importance for health and is associated with reduced work–home interference. Work organizations can support work–life balance and recovery by offering flexible work arrangements, allowing employees to adjust their work hours and work place to improve the fit with their personal life needs. For example, employee-friendly work hours and increased worktime control promote work–life balance and daily recovery. Telework (working away from the central office using ICT) can be an effective solution for individuals who have high demands from home, need more control over their work hours and more time with their family. However, in extreme cases of new ways of working, excessive levels of worktime control and complete spatial freedom (e.g., telework) can also be a threat to proper work–life balance and recovery. Employees run the risk of being 'always on' as their work and private lives become increasingly intertwined and they work longer hours. A properly designed intervention (that provides actual employee-oriented flexibility) and implementation process are prerequisites for upholding work–life balance when very high levels of worktime and workplace flexibility are introduced into the workplace.

Discussion Points

1 If you were a practising manager, how could you promote your employees' daily recovery and work–life balance, taking both organizational and managerial aspects into account?
2 According to both theory and empirical studies, high worktime control is beneficial for well-being. However, are there situations where, or individuals for whom, high worktime control can have a negative impact on well-being, for example work–life balance and daily recovery? If yes, what are the characteristics of such situations and individuals?

Suggested Further Reading

Demerouti, E., Derks, D., ten Brummelhuis, L. L., & Bakker, A.B. (2014). New ways of working: Impact on working conditions, work–family balance, and well-being. In C. Korunka, & P. Hoonakker (Eds.), *The impact of ICT on quality of working life*. Dordrecht: Springer Science+Business Media. This chapter focuses on advantages and disadvantages of New Ways of Working with respect to the work–life balance.

Grzywacz, J. & Demerouti, E. (2014). *New frontiers in work and family research*. London: Psychology Press. This volume is for students who really want to delve into the field of work–life balance. It seeks to move work and family research forward theoretically and empirically and focus on developing new solutions to problems that remain unsolved.

Nijp, H. H., Beckers, D. G. J., Geurts, S. A. E., Tucker, P., & Kompier, M. A.J. (2012). Systematic review on the association between employee worktime control and work–non-work balance, health and well-being, and job-related outcomes. *Scandinavian Journal of Work, Environment & Health*, 38(4), 299–313. This review is relevant for students who want a deeper understanding of the theory, antecedents and consequences of employee-oriented flexible worktime arrangements.

Sonnentag, S. & Fritz, C. (2014). Recovery from job stress: The stressor-detachment model as an integrative framework. *Journal of Organizational Behavior*, 36, 72–103. This article reviews state-of-the-art evidence on psychological detachment as a core aspect of work-related recovery, also addressing practical implications and need for further research.

References

Albertsen, K., Garde, A. H., Nabe-Nielsen, K., Hansen, A. M., Lund, H. & Hvid, H. (2014). Work-life balance among shiftworkers: results from an intervention study about self-rostering. *International Archives in Occupational and Environmental Health, 87,* 265–274.

Allen, T. D., Golden, T. D., & Shokley, K. M. (2015). How effective is telecommuting? Assessing the status of our scientific findings. *Psychological Science in the Public Interest, 16,* 40–68.

Allen, T. D., Johnson, R. C., Kibruz, K. M., & Shockley, K. M. (2013). Work–family conflict and flexible work arrangements: Deconstructing flexibility. *Personnel Psychology, 66,* 345–376.

Amstad, F. T., Meier, L. L., Fasel, U., et al. (2011). A meta-analysis of work–family conflict and various outcomes with a special emphasis on cross-domain versus matching-domain relations. *Journal of Occupational Health Psychology, 16,* 151–169.

Bambra, C. L., Whitehead, M. M., Sowden, A. J., Akers, J., & Petticrew, M. P. (2008). Shifting schedules. The health effects of reorganizing shift work. *American Journal of Preventive Medicine, 34*(5), 427–434.

Beckers, D. G. J., Kompier, M. A. J., Kecklund, G., & Härmä, M. (2012). Worktime control: Theoretical conceptualization, current empirical knowledge, and research agenda. *Scandinavian Journal of Work Environment & Health, 38*(4), 291–297.

Byron, K. (2005). A meta-analytic review of work–family conflict and its antecedents. *Journal of Vocational Behavior, 67,* 169–198.

Clark, S. C. (2000). Work/family border theory: A new theory of work/family balance. *Human Relations, 53,* 747–770.

Demerouti, E., Bakker, A. B., Nachreiner, F., et al. (2001). The job demands–resources model of burnout. *Journal of Applied Psychology, 86,* 499–512.

Demerouti, E., Derks, D., ten Brummelhuis, L. L., et al. (2014). New ways of working: Impact on working conditions, work–family balance, and well-being. In C. Korunka, & P. Hoonakker (Eds.), *The impact of ICT on quality of life.* Dordrecht: Springer Science & Business Media.

Derks, D., ten Brummelhuis, L. L., Zecic, D., & Bakker, A. B. (2014). Switching on and off … : Does smartphone use obstruct the possibility to engage in recovery activities? *European Journal of Work and Organizational Psychology, 23,* 80–90.

Dierdorff, E. C., & Kemp Ellington, J. (2008). It's the nature of the work: Examining behavior-based sources of work–family conflict across occupations. *Journal of Applied Psychology, 93,* 883–892.

Eurofound (2007). *Combining family and full-time work,* Report from EurWORK.

Eurofound (2010). *Telework in the European Union.* Report from EurWORK.

Eurofound (2015a). *First findings: Sixth European Working Conditions Survey.* Luxembourg: Office of the European Commission.

Eurofound (2015b). *Developments in working life in Europe: EurWORK annual review 2014.* Luxembourg: Office of the European Commission.

Gajendran, R. S., & Harrison, D.A. (2007). The good, the bad, and the unknown about telecommuting: Meta-analysis of psychological mediators and individual consequences. *Journal of Applied Psychology, 92,* 1524–1541.

Geurts, S.A.E., & Demerouti E. (2003). Work/Non-work interface: A review of theories and findings. In M. Schabracq, J. A. M. Winnubst, & C .L. Cooper, (Eds.), *The handbook of work and health psychology* (2nd ed.). (pp. 279–312). Chichester: John Wiley & Sons, Ltd.

Geurts, S. A. E., & Sonnentag, S. (2006). Recovery as an explanatory mechanism in the relation between acute stress reactions and chronic health impairment. *Scandinavian Journal of Work, Environment & Health, 32,* 482–92.

Greenhaus, J. H., & Beutell N. J. (1985). Sources of conflict between work and family roles. *Academy of Management Review, 10,* 76–88.

Greenhaus, J., Collins, K., & Shaw, J. (2003). The relation between work–family balance and quality of life. *Journal of Vocational Behavior, 63,* 510–531.

Hobfoll, S. E. (1989). Conservation of resources: A new attempt at conceptualizing stress. *American Psychologist, 44,* 513–524

Joyce, K., Pabayo, R., Critchley, J. A., & Bambra, C., (2010). *Flexible working conditions and their effects on employee health and wellbeing (Review).* The Cochrane Collaboration. Published by John Wiley & Sons, Ltd.

Kelly, E. L., Moen, P., & Tranby, E. (2011). Changing workplaces to reduce work–family conflict: Schedule control in a white-collar organization. *American Sociological Review, 76*(2), 265–290.

Kossek, E. E., Lautsch, B. A., & Eaton, S. C. (2006). Telecommuting, control, and boundary management: Correlates of policy use and practice, job control, and work–family effectiveness. *Journal of Vocational Behavior, 68,* 347–367.

Leineweber, C., Baltzer, M., Magnusson Hanson, L., & Westerlund, H. (2013). Work–family conflict and health in Swedish working women and men: A 2-year prospective analysis (the SLOSH study). *European Journal of Public Health, 23,* 710–716.

Martin, B. H., & MacDonnell, R. (2012). Is telework effective for organizations? A meta-analysis of empirical research on perceptions of telework and organizational outcomes. *Management Research Review, 35,* 602–616.

McEwen, B. S. (2006). Sleep deprivation as a neurobiologic and physiologic stressor: Allostasis and allostatic load. *Metabolism: Clinical and Experimental, 55,* 20–3.

Meijman, T. F., & Mulder, G. (1998). Psychological aspects of workload. In H. Thierry, & P. J. D Drenth (Eds.), *Handbook of work and organizational psychology* (pp. 5–33). Hove, UK: Psychology Press.

Michel, J. S., Kotrba, L. M., Mitchelson, J. K., et al. (2011). Antecedents of work–family conflict: A meta-analytic review. *Journal of Organizational Behavior, 32,* 689–725.

Nijp, H. H., Beckers, D. G. J., Geurts, S. A. E., Tucker, P., & Kompier, M. A .J. (2012). Systematic review on the association between employee worktime control and work-non-work balance, health and well-being, and job-related outcomes. *Scandinavian Journal of Work, Environment & Health, 38*(4), 299–313.

Nijp, H. H., Beckers, D. G. J., Kompier, M. A. J., Van den Bossche, S. N. J., & Geurts, S. A. E. (2015). Worktime control access, need and use in relation to work-home interference, fatigue and job motivation. *Scandinavian Journal of Work, Environment & Health, 41*(4), 347–355.

Nijp, H. H., Beckers, D. G. J., Van de Voorde, K., Geurts, S. A. E., & Kompier, M. A. J. (2016). Effects of New Ways of Working on work hours and work location, health and job-related outcomes. *Chronobiology International, 33,* 604–618.

Noonan, M. C. & Glass, J. L. (2012). The hard truth about telecommuting. *Monthly Labor Review,* June, 38–45.

O'Caroll, P. (2015). *Working time, knowledge work and post-industrial society.* Basingstoke: Palgrave Macmillan.

Salo, P., et al. (2014). Work time control and sleep disturbances: Prospective cohort study of Finnish Public Sector employees. *Sleep, 37,* 1217–1225.

Sonnentag, S., & Binnewies, C. (2013). Daily affect spillover from work to home: Detachment from work and sleep as moderators. *Journal of Vocational Behavior, 83,* 198–208.

Sonnentag, S., & Fritz, C. (2014). Recovery from job stress: The stressor-detachment model as an integrative framework. *Journal of Organizational Behavior, 36,* S72–S103.

ten Brummelhuis, L. L., & Bakker, A. B. (2012). Staying engaged during the week: The effect of off-job activities on next day work engagement. *Journal of Occupational Health Psychology, 17,* 445–455.

Tucker, P., Dahlgren, A., Akerstedt, T., & Waterhouse, J. (2008). The impact of free-time activities on sleep, recovery and well-being. *Applied Ergonomics, 39,* 653–662.

24

What Happens When I Get Older? Older Workers, Late Careers and Transitions to Retirement

Franco Fraccaroli, Marco Depolo and Mo Wang

Overview

In this chapter, we consider what workers face when they get older. The chapter starts with a concise review regarding the demographic and economic trends in industrialized countries. The aim is to explain why ageing at work is one of the main social issues that needs to be addressed by society at large. We then review age-related stereotypes and discrimination against older workers. In particular, we focus on explicating how stereotypes regarding older workers are associated with reality, discrimination, as well as interpersonal relationships at work. Next, we discuss changes experienced by older workers in terms of their performance, attitudes and motivation. Both Socio-emotional Selectivity theory and the Selection-Optimization-Compensation theory are elaborated in that section. Toward the end of the chapter, we review various organizational practices that may help address issues related to an ageing workforce. We also take the older workers' perspective and discuss how they may smoothly transition from their main careers to full retirement through bridge employment. Specifically, we advocate bridge employment not only as useful post-retirement activity to help older workers adjust to retirement life, but also as a beneficial way for organizations to deal with talent shortage and for governments to improve the sustainability of social security benefits.

24.1 Introduction

Older workers are becoming one of the most crucial concerns for policy-makers. In many so-called industrialized countries, a population that is getting older and older oscillates between the desire to rest after a life spent working and the aspiration (or often the financial need) to continue working. National welfare

An Introduction to Work and Organizational Psychology: An International Perspective,
Third Edition. Edited by Nik Chmiel, Franco Fraccaroli and Magnus Sverke.
© 2017 John Wiley & Sons, Ltd. Published 2017 by John Wiley & Sons, Ltd.

Box 24.1:   Who do we mean by 'older worker'?

Theories which hypothesize the existence of career pattern stages take age as the parameter with which to identify the passage from one stage to the next. But chronological age is too simplistic a benchmark for the complex processes that regulate the final part of a person's work career. Moreover, an age-based categorization entails the assumption that all individuals of the same age have identical work experiences invariant across work situations. The variability among the organizational behaviours of older workers is often greater than the variability between older workers and other age groups (Farr & Ringseis, 2002, p. 41). Given that ageing is a multidimensional process, Sterns and Miklos (1995) identify various approaches to the definition of the 'older worker':

- *the chronological and legal approach*: this defines the older worker on the basis of chronological age and a legal definition of age. For example, the European Community has undertaken initiatives in favour of older workers which define them as being over 45 years old;

- *the functional approach*: this is a performance-based definition of ageing. Individuals are classified as 'older' by an objective measure of performance, health, physical capacity, and cognitive ability. This approach recognizes that people of the same chronological age display marked differences in their functioning;

- *the psychosocial approach*: this definition is based on the social perception of ageing in workplaces and society. An individual is classified as an older worker according to the social perception of what is an 'older worker'. The definition is also based on individuals' self-perceptions of themselves and of their careers as congruent with the social career timetable. Kunze, Raes and Bruch (2015) showed for instance the role of subjective age (how old one feels): employees' subjective age (which is influenced by environmental dynamism and age-inclusive HR practices) drives organizational performance outcomes more than their chronological age;

- *the organizational approach*: this defines the 'older worker' in terms of ageing in organizational roles: it therefore relates to seniority and tenure. Important for this definition are the age norms shared by the members of the organization;

- *the life-span approach*: this approach takes account of the marked variability in the ageing process among individuals and the possibility that behavioural change may occur at any point in the life cycle. These factors give rise to the great specificity of individual careers in adulthood, with the consequent difficulty of constructing age-based typologies.

---

systems, where they exist as in many EU countries, are becoming unable to manage a growing number of older people, and governments are trying to keep older workers longer in the workforce. In most cases, this is regulated by laws regarding the minimum age for retirement.

But what is meant by 'aged' or 'older' worker? It is difficult to establish a precise threshold at which a worker can be classified as an older worker: Box 24.1 presents the main answers that have been given to this question.

Besides the different approaches that one may use to define "older workers", crude demographic figures are calling for our attention. Figure 24.1 shows the projected trend of the old-dependency ratio for the EU-28 and a selection of EU countries.

The old-dependency ratio (population aged 65 and over as a percentage of the 15–64 aged population) is a clear indicator of progressive ageing and changes in the labour market. People aged between 15 and 64 are conventionally considered

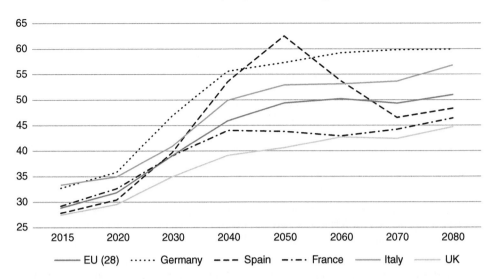

Figure 24.1: Projected old age dependency ratio (i.e. ratio of older than 64 to the aged 15–64)
Source: Eurostat.

to be those who can assume the burden of producing the goods and services necessary for life. It is likewise considered that after age 65 people tend to leave the labour market, becoming consumers and no longer the producers of goods and services. As is apparent the predicted development in the EU-28 countries, Eurostat forecasts that in 2080, people older than 65 will be as much as one half of the 15–64. In other words, every two workers will have to provide resources for one pension receiver, while in 2015 one pensioner is 'fed' by a bit more than three workers. Even without deep economic knowledge, it is easy to conclude that older persons will be required to keep working longer than 65.

That is why a clearer understanding of the factors that might impede or make it more difficult to keep older workers in the labour market is needed. Among the most powerful obstacles we may find are stereotyping and discrimination against older workers, which is the topic of the next section.

24.2 What Is Known About Stereotyping and Discrimination Against Older Workers?

What happens when someone gets older as a worker? One of the main issues that an older worker could encounter in the workplace (and, more generally, in the society) is a (over)generalized system of social beliefs and expectations related to the reduced productivity and efficiency of elderly workers.

Age stereotypes are overgeneralized beliefs, inaccurate perceptions, and distorted knowledge about individuals who are members of a specific age group. Usually the stereotype is active when people infer the characteristics of a person based upon the typical traits of the social group to which this person belongs.

Table 24.1: Negative stereotypes on older workers

Stereotype on older workers	Description of the stereotypes
Poor performer	Older workers are less motivated to work hard and their performance is poorer related to younger or middle age workers. They exert less effort on work activities
Resistent to change	Older workers are more conservative less adaptable and more resistant to organizational and technological changes
Less trainable	Older workers are less motivate to learn, less interested to participate in training and career development activities. In general there are less concerned with achievement
Less healthy	Older workers, due to their advanced age, are more exposed to physical illness and mental diseases
More vulnerable to work-family imbalance	Older workers are more centred on extra-work domain (family; hobbies; community) rather than the work domain
Less trusting	Older workers are less trusting in colleagues and supervisors; Then they are more lonely and they have more difficulties to communicate with others

Source: Adapted from Ng & Feldman, 2012.

For example, someone could consider an older worker less motivated at work because there is a generalized belief that 'older workers' are less motivated at work. The diffusion of age stereotypes in the work context is well demonstrated in scientific research (Ng & Feldman, 2012; see Table 24.1 for a short description of the most diffused stereotypes).

Then, when workers in a work organization become older, it is possible they become a target of prejudice and stereotypes. The attitudes that coworkers and supervisors hold towards them could become less positive; the social context could be less favourable and friendly. The older workers themselves could start wondering whether they are still efficient in carrying out their job. In brief, a psychosocial process named 'ageism' could be activated: prejudices, expectations and beliefs built around an age-based social categorization that could be an antecedent of social discrimination (North & Fiske, 2012). In other words, ageism implies that older workers could be victims of possible discriminatory decisions: less availability of organizational benefits; less training and opportunity to develop competences; more difficulty in being evaluated as a good worker; and higher exposure to inter-generational conflicts.

It becomes clear from these introductory considerations that the scientific study of age stereotypes in the workplace is particularly important for several reasons:

1. *Stereotypes and reality* As for many simplified knowledge systems, stereotypical beliefs are not necessarily true and sometimes they are completely at odds with evidence-based data and reality; then studying stereotypes could be a way to understand specific biases in the perception of workers belonging to different age groups;

2. *Stereotypes and discrimination*: Stereotypes serve as a guide of action and choice of human resource management and supervisors. They are part of the information system that guides organizational behaviours; in other words, age stereotypes could become the basic element for organizational discrimination;

3. *Stereotypes and interpersonal relationships*: The development of a multi-age workforce (a large number of age groups and cohorts working together in organizations) produces greater risks for inter-generational conflict and difficulties in managing age differences. Stereotypes are frequently the basis of conflicting interpersonal relationships, and so could affect cooperation in teams.

24.2.1   Stereotypes and reality

As for the first point, Ng and Feldman (2012) clearly showed that stereotypes described in Table 24.1 often do not reflect objective data. They found that only the lower motivation to learn stereotype has a basis in reality. Moreover, many empirical studies and meta-analyses support the idea that the performance and productivity of older workers is, globally speaking, not strongly different from the performance and productivity of younger workers, reinforcing the hypothesis that behaviour and motivation at work does not necessarily decline with age (see next part of the chapter). Another argument that could be cited for supporting the inconsistency between reality and age stereotypes in the workplace is related to the variation in negative and positive stereotypes about older workers, when compared to younger workers. Some recent research reveals that younger workers are perceived as less conscientious, less motivated, less reliable and less loyal when compared to older workers (Bertolino, Truxillo, & Fraccaroli, 2013; Finkelstein, Ryan, & King, 2013). The presence of such contradictory beliefs about the work capacity and effectiveness of people in different age groups is a strong indicator of the unreliability of this type of shared knowledge. Empirical findings seem to confirm this contradictory set of beliefs in people working as human resource management professionals. Warr and Pennington (1994) interviewed more than 1000 UK personnel managers and found that they considered elderly workers to be more reluctant to accept new technologies, resistant to change, less able to learn, and less interested in training. Contrary to these UK findings, a survey of 774 US human resources managers (Peterson & Spiker, 2005) found that they regarded older workers as having lower turnover, higher levels of commitment, as much ability to acquire new skills, less absenteeism, and greater reliability, when compared to younger workers.

24.2.2   Stereotypes and discrimination

The possibility that human resource managers may not hold realistic views of the capability of older workers is a good introduction for the second point listed above: the relationship between stereotypes and organizational discriminatory behaviours. Stereotyping refers to the process of making generalizations about the characteristics of a particular group (in this case: older workers). This is a cognitive process that concerns the construction of knowledge and schemes characterized by simplification and categorization. In contrast, discrimination involves actual workplace behaviours such as decisions about hiring, career promotion, and giving opportunities for training or developing competences. When people are evaluated for their performance, discrimination could occur if some peripheral attributes (in this case age) are considered but not the central attributes (performance, competences and work capacity). Finally, discrimination could be involved in retention strategies and processes of redundancy when some people have to be dismissed. Thus, stereotyping can be considered a process that may underlie and explain some actual workplace discrimination.

However, the topic of age discrimination in organizations needs to be analysed further. In a recent contribution, Kooij and Van de Vorde (2015) considered three different levels of analysis of age discrimination. The first level refers to general organizational strategies towards older workers: is the organization more oriented to a *depreciation* of older workers or to a *conservation* approach? The 'depreciation' human resource strategy is based on a cultural approach in which the job performance of older workers is seen as declining over time. The 'conservation' approach considers older workers as an asset for the organization because of their competences, experiences and their capacity for preserving organizational culture and values. The second level of analysis focuses on the concrete choices and practices applied in managing age differences in the organization. These actions are usually consequent on the first strategic level, but also depend on other organizational and personal variables (e.g., middle-management culture; leadership style; team characteristics). The third level of analysis concerns how workers of different ages perceive and experience HR practices. This is an individual level of analysis that is important in understanding how workers react to organizational strategies in terms of attitudes, motivation, and behaviours.

24.2.3 Stereotypes and interpersonal relationships

As stated before, stereotypes can have a negative impact also on the quality of the relationships between individuals in the workplace. This is particularly true if we consider the diversity of age groups (people of different age), organizational cohorts (people who joined the organization at different times) and generations (people born in different historical periods) that work in organizations today. In daily working life these different groups are in continuous contact, they tend to share the same work contexts, they have to cooperate in teams and to respond adequately to organizational demands. They are also exposed to the same organizational rules and norms, evaluation systems and rewards. It is evident that reciprocal negative stereotypes between younger and older workers can be an obstacle to the quality of interactions between them, for their satisfaction and well-being, and finally for the effectiveness of the organization.

Beyond the stereotypes that we have already discussed, there is another interesting form of simplified belief that plays an important role in this field: the meta-stereotype (Finkelstein et al., 2013), which means the interpersonal perceptions of 'what other people think of my group'. This type of reciprocal intergroup perception could be affected by erroneous evaluations, biases and oversimplification. For instance, Finkelstein et al. (2013) examined three groups of workers (younger: 18–30; middle-aged: 31–50; and older: over 51) in terms of the relationship between stereotypes and meta-stereotypes. They obtained an interesting result: the younger group had a general positive attitude (stereotype) towards their older colleagues. However, older workers did not expect that younger workers held positive beliefs about them (negative meta-stereotype). In short, there is an incongruent social perception between what younger workers think about older workers, and what older workers believe younger workers think about them. This misalignment could foster misunderstanding, difficult interactions, wrong expectations and, as an extreme consequence, intergenerational conflicts (antagonism between younger and older workers).

Researchers from the perspectives of social identity theory and intergroup relationships have explored some organizational solutions to reduce the negative effects of stereotypes and ageism in workplace relationships. For instance, Iweins et al. (2013) consider the promotion of contacts with an outgroup (i.e., a group that is different from the focal person's own group – the ingroup) and the fostering of a multi-age perspective (group differences should be considered as a resource and should be celebrated in the organization) as possible factors that could reduce intergroup conflict and ageism. These two policies (i.e., facilitate outgroup contacts in an organization and foster a multi-age perspective) could be the basic elements used to build a 'dual identity' among the workers. In essence, this means that people maintain the ingroup-outgroup distinction ('I am an older worker and you are a younger worker'), but also generate a super-ordinate identity ('You and I, we are members of this work team'). This dual identity, in turn, supports more harmonious group relations. Workers with a dual identity are able to accentuate the elements of similarities with people from different age groups because they perceive them as sharing a common identity.

24.3 Performance, Attitudes and Motivation of Older Workers: Decline or Change?

What happens when someone gets older as a worker? Another important issue for answering the basic question of this chapter is related to the ageing-related changes in performance, attitudes and motivation. Does becoming an older worker imply a decline in performance? A change in the attitudes towards job and organizational life? A reduction in the psychological investment in his/her activities? To answer these questions properly, we need to point out a methodological caveat that characterizes the research in this field. Many data available today are obtained using cross-sectional designs, which allows the comparison of workers of different ages at a certain point of time (e.g., younger or middle-aged workers versus older workers). This cross-sectional approach is useful but limited: it is not able to determine the true intra-individual change over time (e.g., how a worker or a group of workers experience changes in performance, attitudes and motivation in different stages of their life). Moreover, the cross-sectional perspective is not adequate to help understand whether the differences between younger and older workers are due to an age effect (differences in chronological ages and in life development stages) or to a cohort effect (differences in historical period that characterize the work and life experiences of the individuals). In fact, the study of intra-individual change is only possible through longitudinal designs, which follow a sample over time with several measurement occasions. These types of studies are rare because of their complexity, length of study period, and the high costs for tracking and measuring participants over a long time period.

24.3.1   Changes in performance

It is not possible to answer the question about age-related change in work performance in a simple way. The variability between individuals in the ageing process is quite large. Moreover, changes in performance and attitudes during the ageing processes are influenced by a large number of factors at the individual, organizational and societal levels.

Some studies have been devoted to understanding the possible decline of cognitive abilities with age. Cognitive abilities are considered as basic elements for successful performance. Memory, attention, reasoning ability, speed of information processing and knowledge are broad examples of these basic elements of performance. But the relationship between cognitive ability and performance is not completely understood in scientific research. Salthouse (2012) provided a good summary of the state of art:

> In summary, it is now well established that cognitive ability has moderate positive relations with a variety of measures of work functioning, including success in training, different measures of performance in the job, and level of occupation achieved. The mechanisms responsible for the relations are still largely speculative, but the research is consistent in documenting that level of cognitive ability is one of the strongest predictors of work success currently available. (p. 204)

Then, exploring the changes in cognitive abilities through age could provide a partial explanation of possible decline in work performance with age. Warr (2001) and Salthouse (2012) summarize the main results regarding cognitive abilities and knowledge in relation to the ageing process. Laboratory studies seem to show, even among persons aged under the age of 65, that certain complex cognitive skills decline with age: the ability to identify relations; draw inferences; understand the connections between facts and objects, and comprehend their implications. A more general finding indicates a modest decline in inductive reasoning and spatial

orientation towards the age of 60, although there are marked inter-individual differences and a more pronounced deterioration of these mental abilities in more
advanced age groups. Older people may encounter difficulties when performing
activities which require rapid reaction times and the processing of complex
information. A concrete example of a job requiring these activities is that of air
traffic controller, where the negative relationship between age, cognitive abilities
and performance seems to be well established (Salthouse, 2012). In this job a
person has to manage a complex system of information in a short period of time,
with inductive and deductive reasoning, and simultaneously has to make decisions
with a high risk level. To avoid the inauspicious negative effects of the decline in
cognitive abilities, in some countries, e.g., the USA, the retirement age of air traffic controllers is set at 56 years old.

In summary, laboratory research shows that monotonic age-related declines in
many cognitive variables have been reported between 20 and 75 years of age. But
the decline is particularly evident for abilities such as reasoning (correlation with
age often ranging from –0.3 to –0.5; Salthouse, 2012). Poorer and slower mental
processing observed in older ages occurs particularly when tasks are complex and
place considerable demands upon the person.

Outside the laboratory, studies conducted in work settings, where the criterion
variable is work performance and not cognitive abilities, provide some different
results. In a meta-analysis reported by McEvoy and Cascio (1989), the average
general correlation between age and work performance was estimated as being
close to zero, with extreme variability in the results obtained. Warr (2001) concludes that work performance is on average constant despite some cognitive limitations and decline in older age. Furthermore, even when cognitive decrements
are found, it has been shown that the magnitude is reduced by a variety of interventions (training, counselling, job design, etc.) (Farr & Ringseis, 2002). Finally,
the conclusion of the review of Salthouse (2012) is that 'there is little evidence of
a negative relation of age (at least within the range of 20 to 75 years of age) and
indices of overall level of functioning in society' (p. 215).

How to explain these contradictory data between laboratory and field studies?
Why, if the cognitive abilities are partially related to work performance and cognitive abilities are shown to partially decline with age, is a relationship between
age and work performance not confirmed by researchers? Using the words of
Salthouse (2012), why is there not a greater consequence of age related cognitive
decline in the real working experience of people?

A partial explanation of this mismatch is attributed to methodological issues.
Following Salthouse (2012), many of the studies examining relations of age and
work performance are exposed to 'selective attrition': the older workers in this
type of research are not representative of their age group because only the most
competent, efficient and healthy workers are still working in their older age. In
other words, others who are less competent and unhealthy have already retired.

But another more salient argument has to be taken into account. Two different types of cognitive abilities could be considered: one is related to the so-called

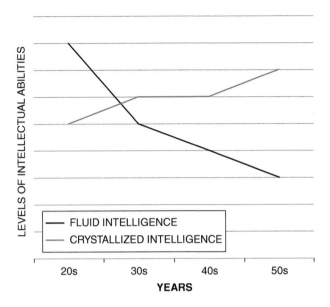

Figure 24.2: Hypothetical trajectories of crystallized abilities and fluid abilities by age group
Source: Adapted from Ackerman 2014. Reproduced with permission of SAGE Publications.

fluid activities like reasoning, managing and transforming information; the other type is related to *crystallized* knowledge accumulated in the mind during the life experiences (Beier & Gilberto, 2015). The two types of cognitive abilities are correlated, but they show a different path during the life-span. Trends of the different abilities with age are well shown in Figure 24.2, that represents the synthesis of research findings in this area (Ackerman, 2014).

What seems to occur in working life is that older people are able to compensate some progressive and partial deficit in fluid cognitive abilities, using a stable or increasing body of knowledge and expertise accumulated during daily activities, training experience, and contacts with colleagues or supervisors.

It is also important to point out that the observable negative association between age and performance is often due to age-related decline in physical well-being. Poor physical well-being can make it difficult for individuals to perform certain job tasks. For example, with ageing, there is a gradual loss of muscle mass and muscle strength (McArdle, Vasilaki, & Jackson, 2002). Because of this age-related loss of muscle strength, maximal exercise capacity declines with age as well (Fielding & Meydani, 1997) and prevents older workers from handling heavy lifting or other job activities requiring great physical strength. Research has also shown a general trend of decreasing energy with ageing, and, as a result, reduced capacity for physically demanding tasks with increasing age. As such, older workers may not be able to work very fast or perform physically demanding activities for long periods of time. Older adults' immune systems also take longer to build up defences against specific diseases. As a result, older adults become more prone to serious consequences from illnesses that are easily defeated by young adults, leading to more absenteeism due to health care needs.

24.3.2   Changes in attitudes

Another psychological aspect that may evolve with age and that could have important implications for personal experiences of older workers and for organizations is their job attitudes. Job attitudes are systems of opinions expressing an evaluation and general tendencies to behave related to specific job aspects. Examples of the most studied job attitudes are job satisfaction (feeling related to the job in general or towards specific aspects of it) and organizational commitment (level of identification and engagement of an individual in relationship to the organization) (see also Chapter 23 in this volume).

Satisfaction and commitment are usually related to task and contextual performance, well-being and quality of organizational relationships (Judge & Kammeyer-Mueller, 2012). On this matter, a systematic meta-analysis has been conducted by Ng and Feldman (2010) of over more than 800 studies. The authors distinguished attitudes under three categories and analysed how each attitude is related to age. The categories included:

1. task-based attitudes (overall job satisfaction, satisfaction with pay, satisfaction with promotions);
2. people-based attitudes (satisfaction towards co-worker and supervisor and their support);
3. organization-based attitudes (organizational commitment, loyalty, justice perceptions, and organizational identification).

In general, they found a range of correlations between age and different job attitudes after controlling for job tenure. The general trend identified in the study was that age is related to more favourable job attitudes: older workers generally have more positive job attitudes than younger workers.

The authors concluded that the overall study findings are in line with the expectations of Socio-emotional Selectivity Theory (SST; Carstensen, 2006). SST focuses on the selection process of goals and motivations across the life-span and considers the perception of time horizons in people as an essential element in this selection process. Becoming older, people see their future as time-limited, thus they adjust their goals and psychological investment accordingly. SST proposes two types of social goals: those related to acquisition of knowledge and those related to emotional regulation. When time is seen with a long perspective (when people are younger), the acquisition of knowledge orientation dominates the motivational perspective of people. When time is perceived as a scarce resource, emotional regulation goals become a priority: i.e., establish good relationship with people; avoid conflicts (Truxillo, et al. 2012). Consistent with SST, Ng and Feldman (2010) found older workers generally show more positive job attitudes because they are more aware of the benefits they receive from their job and organization. More specifically, Ng and Feldman (2008) show that older workers, if compared with younger workers, exhibit more effective *contextual performance*: older workers are more attentive to safety rules and organizational norms, they perform better in terms of organizational citizenship behaviours, and they are less inclined to engage in counterproductive work behaviours (e.g., absenteeism, aggressive behaviour with coworkers or supervisors).

Following the SST, Ng and Feldman (2013) also tried to explain some changes in more specific job attitudes: with ageing and with a reduction of the future time perspective, people are reducing the relative importance of training (i.e., acquisition of knowledge), career and development of their work position (i.e., responsibility and autonomy). In parallel, older workers become more trusting in the organization and in their supervisors, more conscientious and diligent and exhibit higher levels of organizational citizenship behaviour.

The relationship between the ageing process and future time perspectives has been confirmed in a recent longitudinal study over four years. Weikamp and Göritz (2015) analysed the occupational future time perspective in people of different ages. They confirmed that a higher age was associated with perceptions of less remaining time and of fewer remaining opportunities in the work domain. These data are a direct confirmation of the importance of time perspectives for understanding the ageing process at work. The occupational future time perspective may become an interesting variable to study in interplay with the chronological age of workers because it is an indirect measure of some salient psychological elements such as expectations, levels of aspiration, and motivation.

24.3.3 Changes in work motivation

Change in work motivation as a result of ageing seems to follow a trend similar to the one for work performance reviewed earlier, combining loss and decline processes with growth and compensation processes. Following the approach of Kanfer and Ackerman (2004), work motivation continuously adapts during the lifespan with loss of some motivational features and growth of others. Workers try to manage their work experience and organizational roles choosing goals and selecting challenges that allow them to best apply their abilities, skills and knowledge. In a meta-analysis, Kooij et al. (2011) explored the relationship between age and work motivation. They found some trends confirming the complex evolution of work motivation during the ageing process: *growth* motivation (acquiring new responsibilities and autonomy; accepting challenging roles; acquiring new knowledge) decline with age. *Intrinsic* work motivation (doing interesting activities; using the acquired capacities and competences) tend to be improved with age.

The theoretical model of Selection–Optimization–Compensation (SOC Theory), derived from lifespan developmental psychology, explains stability and changes in work motivation in the ageing process (see Box 24.2).

Box 24.2:   Selection, optimization and compensation model

Selection, optimization and compensation are three adaptive strategies people use to fit their changing resources and characteristics with the changing demands of the environment in different life stages. A comprehensive definition of the three components of the SOC model is provided by Müller and Weigl (2015).

The model of selection, optimization, and compensation (SOC) encompasses three processes of action regulation in respect to successful ageing and life-management: Selection refers to the setting and prioritization of goals, based on personal motives and preferences (elective selection) or due to perceived loss of internal or contextual resources (loss-based selection). Optimization involves the obtainment, improvement, and coordinated use of individual means to pursue important selected goals. Compensation involves the acquisition and application of alternative individual means or the utilization of external or technological aids to substitute lost means.

During the transitions in the life stages and developmental phases, people adapt and change their goals and motives, define new priorities, focusing on some objectives but losing some others. They optimize the use and allocation of their physical, psychological and social resources. They try to maintain an acceptable level of cognitive and social functioning through external aids and tools. These SOC adaptive strategies are very useful for preserving good performance at work, maintaining high job satisfaction and commitment, and achieving psychological well-being in the workplace. Many studies confirm these general hypotheses (e.g., Müller & Weigl, 2015). In particular, a recent multi-source data set reported in Weigl et al. (2013) assessed the relationship between individual self-report SOC strategies and supervisors' work ability ratings of health-care workers. The study showed that SOC adaptation interacted with other job characteristics in preserving work ability among older workers.

Both models introduced in this section (the Socio Emotional Selectivity Theory and the Selection, Optimization and Compensation model) encourage the understanding about changes in goals and motives in the ageing process, instead of accepting a generalized decline in motivation with age. In line with these models, one type of motivation seems to be particularly related to late career stage: *generative* motives. These motives stimulate actions in the direction of helping others in the workplace, transferring the knowledge to younger persons and assuming a role of mentor or coach, as well as leaving a legacy at work. Generative motives and needs could be considered as new meanings and contentment during late adulthood facilitating the final part of a work career and a satisfactory life experience during retirement (Miranda-Chan & Nakamura, 2016; Zhan, Wang, & Shi, 2015).

24.4   What Can Organizations Do for an Older Workforce?

Organizations nowadays try to deal with the problems related to an ageing workforce in quite different ways. As mentioned earlier in this chapter, one could expect that a shorter future time perspective (as for the time remaining to be spent on working) is more likely to produce a decreasing engagement and involvement. However, if organizations really invest in keeping older workers involved, they tend to show effort and involvement (cf. James, McKechnie, & Swanberg, 2011).

In principle, many technological (e.g., job design or re-design interventions) or HR-related (e.g., specific training programmes) options are available. In practice, many factors are involved in managerial decisions about implementing them. The Society for Human Resource Management (SHRM, 2014) published the results from a recent survey among US businesses, which offers a useful example to illustrate the problem. About 2000 HR professionals coming from private and governmental agencies responded to an email survey on their opinions and actions about a growing older workforce: more than one-third of respondents said they were preparing by 'beginning to examine internal policies and management practices to address this change', while 20% estimated that their current policies and practices were already sufficient for dealing with an increase in older workforce. Practices seen as sufficient were general management policy/practices (28%), retention practices (33%), and recruiting practices (35%).

However, the awareness of the potential impact of an ageing workforce on organizational success seems less prevalent than expected. Despite the big debate across scientific fields and HR professional forums, according to this survey, US HR professionals seem not to see the ageing workforce as a real problem: in fact, less than one out of three of them considered their organizations as facing a threat as a result of the potential loss of talent due to retirement of workers.

Nevertheless, the same survey reports a number of interventions adopted. More than one-half of HR professionals said their organization had implemented training and/or cross-training programs to transfer knowledge from older workers to younger workers, while mentoring programmes have been implemented in one-third of the firms (33%). However, about one-fifth of respondents said their organizations did not use any strategies to transfer knowledge from older workers to younger workers.

These results pointed to some potential interventions, mainly in two categories (technological interventions and HR interventions):

- *Technological interventions.* As previously discussed in this chapter, changes in performance may be observed in older workers, when specific skills or competences are required by the task. This is the case for decline in some cognitive abilities, such as speed of information processing. In principle, technological changes may be conceived to reduce the impact on performance of such decline. However, financial and organizational reasons often make it very difficult to redesign tasks or jobs in order to make them more suitable for older workers. Indeed, as Charness, Boot, and Czaja (2015) noted, if we want to obtain a real engagement with technology for older workers, technological changes need to be designed well, taking into account the needs, abilities, and preferences of older workers.

- *HR interventions.* SHRM (2015) suggests that, after having completed an *assessment of the state of the ageing workforce in the organization*, interventions should be planned in three main domains.
  - *Recruit mature workers* by hiring (or re-hiring) retirees through targeting recruitment and selection procedures to attract older workers, especially when the turnover rate in the organization is high, and/or affects key organizational positions.
  - *Retain mature workers* mainly by applying flexitime policies, by actions aiming to recognize seniors' contribution to the organization, or by phased retirement plans. As mentioned earlier (e.g.. Kooij et al., 2011), such retention tools rely on research showing that motivational drives tend to switch by age from growth motivation towards intrinsic ones. As an example, enabling older workers to have more choice of when they work can be improved by flexitime policies, part-time or seasonal jobs: such practices seem to fit well with the desire for reconciliation between work and family life. Other factors being equal, older workers more satisfied with time schedules are more likely to show engagement (Armstrong-Stassen & Schlosser, 2008).
  - *Improve skills, training and development* devoted to older workers appears to be another powerful tool of intervention. Helping mature workers to adapt their skills through effective training programmes requires a tailored training design that is able to capture the specific motivational drives for training. Younger workers may perceive training as a tool to develop better career chances, so that the effort and engagement in skill acquisition is seen as profitable for the worker him/herself. The same motivational drive may not be at the same strength among older workers. As such, training programmes should be able to offer learning outcomes closer in time and independent from career progress. However, even if motivational drives may change in the late phase of career, James, McKechnie, and Swanberg (2011) showed that older workers were more engaged when they had the opportunity to access training programmes, compared with those not offered with the same opportunity.

Besides these two main kinds of interventions, more research is needed about HR practices and their impact on senior workers in organization. A recent debate among US experts – researchers, managers, and executives – has proposed (SHRM, 2015) some areas for possible additional research.

First of all, more data are needed to assess the real impact and outcomes of practices for hiring, training, and retaining older workers. As for the potential contribution the older workers may give through their knowledge and vision about work, it is important to know exactly *what knowledge* needs to be transferred from senior workers. Often HR managers do not know exactly what their organizations are losing when senior workers retire. In a similar way, it is important to know more about the *most efficient ways to transfer knowledge* from workers who are approaching their retirement time. Not enough research exists to detect the best practices to do so. Finally, more research needs to focus on examining how small businesses can efficiently hire and retain older workers. The few existing findings are focused on HR problems and practices for medium- or large- sized companies, which are hardly transferable to the small businesses.

24.5   Bridge Employment in the Final Stage of Working Life

Retirement has changed in nature in the twenty-first century. In most industrialized (or so-called developed) countries work and retirement are no longer two opposite and mutually exclusive conditions (Cahill, Giandrea, & Quinn, 2005). Therefore, alternative work practices, going beyond the traditional work and non-work dichotomy, have appeared and questioned the notion of retirement as a single event, proposing to consider it in a proper way as a process that workers go through in different ways and on different time schedules (Shultz & Wang, 2011).

Socio-economic changes in most countries have presented many different ways to manage the withdrawal from the working life. As described by Alcover et al. (2014) in their volume dedicated to 'bridge employment', current times are no longer facing a transition from work to non-work, the notion of trajectory should rather be adopted, leading individuals in different ways and times to a retirement condition.

For example, while growing older, a worker could gradually shorten the hours worked for the same employer: it is called 'phased retirement'. Or a 'partial retirement' could be used: in this case a worker's career job is changed for a new part-time position. In other cases, we may see that workers take a 'bridge job' solution: retirement is approached by changing employer, or even switching to a self-employed job. Others may adopt 're-entry' strategies: the worker, after having taken a break retiring from his/her job, decides to rejoin the labour market in another job (or in the same kind of occupation). Re-entry can be a planned decision, or the result of becoming aware that retirement conditions (in the broadest meaning: financial incomes, life styles, and so on) are different from expected or desired, pushing the individual to look for a further entry into the labour market.

All these behavioural strategies may be labelled as 'bridge employment' strategies. As Gobeski and Beehr (2009) argued, bridge employment covers different ways of prolonging working life approaching the retirement condition, leaving the term 'full retirement' to describe (more or less) final withdrawal from the labour market.

Of course, bridge employment options become more or less easily available (or subjectively attractive) due to the influences of various factors. Based on 12 dedicated national studies from three continents, Alcover et al. (2014) concluded that inter-country differences, arising from local characteristics of national laws, labour market, and economic situation remain very relevant. Following Shultz (2003), bridge employment experiences differ depending on individual attributes (e.g., work history and career, perception of well-being, work attitudes, wealth conditions), and on contextual factors (for instance, organizational HR practices specially aimed to fit older workers' needs, socio-economic or legal country-specific conditions).

Therefore, 'bridge employment' is not a catch-all term for late career jobs, but a useful notion that is able to encompass different behavioural choices or strategies in coping with retirement. Although such strategies may differ considerably, they share one important feature: older workers may use bridge employments to adjust in a proper way to the withdrawal from the labour market (Wang & Shultz, 2010; Wang, Zhan, Liu, & Shultz, 2008). Despite differences in pace and modes, bridge employment seems to offer relevant benefits for people. Across different countries some outcomes have been observed that are beneficial for both individuals and organizations: life satisfaction before and after the retirement; increased satisfaction and well-being at work; more financial security after retirement; less age discrimination; and job positions better fitting the needs and desires of skilled workers who have reached retirement age (mainly due to more flexible working arrangements agreed with the organization. Thus many empirical results (quantitative and qualitative, cross-sectional and longitudinal) have converged sufficiently to allow a list of the main objectives that are achieved by bridge employment (Alcover et al., 2014), including:

1. to extend active life, following the increase in actual life expectancy;
2. to increase financial sustainability of pension and social benefits systems;
3. to help older people to maintain a quite good quality of life, health and welfare;
4. to help organizations to retain the contribution of highly skilled workers;
5. to facilitate the transmission of knowledge between generations.

As one may see, there are enough interesting aspects that can turn into benefits for individuals and for societies, to make bridge employment a crucial topic, able to influence the way each of us is becoming (or will become) older, in relationship with our working lives.

Summary

In this chapter, we argue that the ageing workforce has given a great challenge to society in terms of both sustaining the social security benefits and maintaining older worker well-being and productivity. In particular, our review has shown that older workers often encounter negative stereotypes and age-related discrimination in the workplace. These stereotypes are typically not true and, in addition, at odds with reality.

However, they form the basis for age-related discriminations at work and often produce interpersonal conflicts among workers with different ages. Our review in this chapter also demonstrates that there is little evidence of a negative relation between age and work performance. Rather, older workers seem to exhibit more contextual performance as compared to younger workers. Older workers also show more positive job attitudes than younger workers, and have stronger motivation to engage in emotional regulation. In contrast, younger workers are more motivated to seek development in skill and knowledge acquisitions. Our review summarizes various types of organizational practices that may help address issues related to the ageing workforce. Specifically, we point out that organizations can focus on both technological interventions and human resources-based interventions to maintain older workers' productivity, recruit and retain older workers, and efficiently transfer knowledge from older workers to younger workers. Our chapter also suggests that older workers can use bridge employment as an effective way to smooth their transition from full-time work to full-time retirement. Doing so can both improve their adjustment to retirement and benefit organizations that face talent shortage.

Discussion Points

1 Which kind of solutions could be designed to reduce age stereotypes in society and in the workplace?
2 Human Resource Managers can develop strategies and practices for managing the late career of workers. Consider which types of strategies and intervention are for you the most fruitful and effective.

Suggested Further Reading

Finkelstein, L., Truxillo, D. M., Fraccaroli, F., & Kanfer, R. (Eds.). (2015). *Facing the challenges of a multi-age workforce. A use-inspired approach.* New York: Routledge.

Wang, M. (Ed.), (2013). *The Oxford handbook of retirement.* New York: Oxford University Press.

Wang, M., Olson, D., & Shultz, K. (2013). *Mid and late career issues: An integrative perspective.* New York: Psychology Press.

Work, Aging and Retirement. A journal published by Oxford University Press. http://workar.oxfordjournals.org/

References

Ackerman, P. L. (2014). Adolescent and adult intellectual development. *Current Directions in Psychological Science, 23,* 246–251.

Alcover, C. M., Topa, G., Parry, E., Fraccaroli, F., & Depolo, M. (2014). *Bridge employment: A research handbook.* London: Routledge.

Armstrong-Stassen, M., & Schlosser, F. (2008). Benefits of a supportive development climate for older workers. *Journal of Managerial Psychology, 23*(4), 419–437.

Beier, M. E., & Gilberto, J. M. (2015). Age-related changes in abilities. *Encyclopedia of Geropsychology.* Singapore: Springer Science+Business Media.

Bertolino, M., Truxillo, D. M., & Fraccaroli, F. (2013). Age effects on perceived personality and job performance. *Journal of Managerial Psychology, 7/8,* 867–885.

Cahill, K. E., Giandrea, M. D. & Quinn, J. F. (2005) Are traditional retirements a thing of the past? New evidence on retirement patterns and bridge jobs. *Bureau of Labor Statistics Working Papers,* no. 384, Washington, DC: U.S. Department of Labor.

Carstensen, L. L. (2006). The influence of a sense of time on human development, *Science, 312,* 1913–1915.

Charness, N., Boot, W. R., & Czaja, S. J. (2015) Technology and older workers. *Encyclopedia of Geropsychology.* Singapore: Springer Science+Business Media.

Farr, J. L., & Ringseis, E. L. (2002). The older worker in organizational context: beyond the individual. In C. L. Cooper, & I. T. Robertson (Eds.), *International Review of Industrial and Organizational Psychology.* (vol. 17), (pp. 31–76). Chichester, John Wiley & Sons,

Fielding, R. A., & Meydani, M. (1997). Exercise, free radical generation, and aging. *Aging, 9,* 12–18.

Finkelstein, L. M., Ryan, K. M., & King, E. B. (2013). What do the young (old) people think of me? Content and accuracy of age-based metastereotypes. *European Journal of Work and Organizational Psychology, 22,* 633–657.

Gobeski, K.T., & Beehr, T.A. (2009) How retirees work: Predictors of different types of bridge employment, *Journal of Organizational Behavior, 30,* 401–425.

Iweins, C., Desmette, D., Yserbyt, V., & Stinglhamber, F. (2013). Ageism at work: The impact of intergenerational contact and organizational multi-age perspective. *European Journal of Work and Organizational Psychology, 22,* 331–346.

James, J. B., McKechnie, S., & Swanberg, J. (2011). Predicting employee engagement in an age-diverse retail workforce. *Journal of Organizational Behavior, 32*(2), 173–196.

Judge, T. A., & Kammeyer-Mueller, J. D. (2012). Job attitudes. *Annual Review of Psychology, 63,* 341–367.

Kanfer, R., & Ackerman, P. L. (2004). Aging, adult development, and work motivation. *Academy of Management Review, 29,* 440–458.

Kooij, D. T. A. M., & Van De Voorde, K. (2015). Strategic HRM for older workers. In P. M. Bal, D. T. A. M. Kooij, & D. M. Rousseau (Eds.), *Aging workers and the employee-employer relationship* (pp. 57–72). Dordrecht: Springer.

Kooij, D. T. A., de Lange, A. H., Jansen, P. G. W., Kanfer, R., & Dikkers, J. S. E. (2011). Age and work-related motives: Results of a meta-analysis. *Journal of Organizational Behavior, 32,* 197–225. doi: 10.1002/job.665.

Kunze, F., Raes, A. M. L., & Bruch, H. (2015). It matters how old you feel: Antecedents and performance consequences of average relative subjective age in organizations. *Journal of Applied Psychology, 100*(5), 1511–1526.

McArdle, A., Vasilaki, A., & Jackson, M. (2002). Exercise and skeletal muscle aging: Cellular and molecular mechanisms. *Aging Research Reviews, 1,* 79–93.

McEvoy, G. M., & Cascio, W. F. (1989). Cumulative evidence of the relationship between employee age and job performance. *Journal of Applied Psychology, 74,* 11–17.

Miranda-Chan, T., & Nakamura, J. (2016). A generativity track to life meaning in retirement: ego-integrity returns on past academic mentoring investments. *Work, Aging and Retirement, 2,* in press.

Müller, A., & Weigl, M. (2015). Selection, optimization, and compensation at work in relation to age. *Encyclopedia of Geropsychology.* Singapore: Springer Science+Business Media,

Ng, T. W. H., & Feldman, D. C. (2008). The relationship of age to ten dimensions of job performance. *Journal of Applied Psychology, 93,* 392–423.

Ng, T. W. H., & Feldman, D. C. (2010). The relationships of age with job attitudes: A meta-analysis. *Personnel Psychology, 63,* 677–718.

Ng, T. W. H., & Feldman, D. C. (2012). Evaluating six common stereotypes about older workers with meta-analytical data. *Personnel Psychology, 65,* 821–858.

Ng, T. W. H., & Feldman, D. C. (2013) How do within-person changes due to aging affect job performance? *Journal of Vocational Behavior, 83,* 500–513.

North, M. S., & Fiske, S. T. (2012). An inconvenienced youth? Ageism and its potential intergenerational roots. *Psychological Bulletin, 138,* 982–97. doi:10.1037/a0027843

Peterson, S. J., & Spiker, B. K. (2005). Positive contributory value of older workers: A positive psychology perspective. *Organizational Dynamics, 34,* 153–167.

Salthouse, T. (2012). Consequences of age-related cognitive declines. *Annual Review of Psychology, 63,* 201–226.

SHRM (2014). *Preparing for an aging workforce: Executive report.* Alexandria, VA: Society for Human Resource Management Available at: http://www.shrm.org/Research/Survey-Findings/Documents/14-0765 Executive Briefing Aging Workforce v4.pdf

SHRM (2015). *Preparing for an Aging Workforce: Strategies, Templates and Tools for HR Professionals.* Alexandria, VA: Society for Human Resource Management. Available at: http://www.shrm.org/Research/SurveyFindings/Documents/Preparing for an Aging Workforce - Strategies, Templates and Tools for HR Professionals.pdf

Shultz, K. S. (2003). Bridge employment: Work after retirement. In G. A. Adams, & T.A. Beehr (eds), *Retirement: Reasons, processes, and results,* New York: Springer

Shultz, K. S., & Wang, M. (2011) Psychological perspectives on the changing nature of retirement. *American Psychologist, 66,* 170–179.

Sterns, H. L., & Miklos, S. M. (1995). The aging worker in a changing environment: Organizational and individual issues. *Journal of Vocational Behavior, 47,* 248–268.

Truxillo, D. M., Cadiz, D. M., Rineer, J. R., Zaniboni, S., & Fraccaroli, F. (2012). A lifespan perspective on job design: Fitting the worker to the job to promote job satisfaction, engagement, and performance. *Organizational Psychology Review, 2,* 340–360.

Wang, M., & Shultz, K. (2010). Employee retirement: A review and recommendations for future investigation. *Journal of Management, 36,* 172–206.

Wang, M., Zhan, Y., Liu, S., & Shultz, K. (2008). Antecedents of bridge employment: A longitudinal investigation. *Journal of Applied Psychology, 93,* 818–830.

Warr, P. (2001). Age and work behaviour: physical attributes, cognitive abilities, knowledge, personality traits and motives. In C. L. Cooper, & I. T. Robertson (Eds.), *International Review of Industrial and Organizational Psychology* (vol. 16), (pp. 1–36). Chichester, Wiley.

Warr, P., & Pennington, J. (1994) Occupational age-grading: job for older and younger non-managerial employees. *Journal of Vocational Behavior, 45,* 328–346.

Weigl, M., Müller, A., Hornung, S., Zacher, H., & Angerer, P. (2013). The moderating effects of job control and selection, optimization, and compensation strategies on the age–work ability relationship. *Journal of Organizational Behavior, 34,* 607–628.

Weikamp, J. G., & Göritz, A. S. (2015). How stable is occupational future time perspective over time? A six-wave study across 4 years. *Work, Aging and Retirement, 1,* 369–381.

Zhan, Y., Wang, M., & Shi, J. (2015). Retirees' motivational orientations and bridge employment: Testing the moderating role of gender. *Journal of Applied Psychology, 100,* 1319–1331.

PART IV

ADVISING THE ORGANIZATION

How Do We Work with Organizations?

25

Henry Honkanen and Diana Rus

Overview

In this chapter we provide an overview of how work and organizational (w/o) psychologists engage with organizations. The chapter develops by answering a series of questions such as: What is the context of our work? What are our working models and roles? How do we work? What are our professional ethics?

The chapter starts by considering the context of our work, specifically focusing on the organization as a system, the multidisciplinary nature of developing organizations, and the interplay between client needs and consultancy services. Subsequently, we discuss our profession's working models and roles, with a specific emphasis on change strategies and types of influence as viewed through the lens of various theoretical perspectives. Next, we provide a model of the consulting process and highlight the typical tools and methods applied in the different stages of the consulting cycle as well as the key skills and competencies required for each stage. We conclude the chapter with a short discussion of ethical conduct within our profession.

25.1 What Is the Context of Our Work?

External or internal? As w/o psychology practitioners we can work with organizations from two different vantage points or bases. First, we can work inside the organization as in-house consultants or as HR experts (*Human Resources Managers or Developers*). Second, we can support organizations by providing outside consultancy services in roles such as OD experts (*Organizational Development Consultants*), trainers, coaches, facilitators, assessment psychologists, researchers or data analysts. In practical terms, these two orientations (internal and external) do not differ from each other significantly (O'Mahoney & Markham, 2013). They both approach 'organizations' and the people in them as clients. In addition, a shift seems to be underway with the lines between these roles becoming more blurred: insiders are acting more like external consultants and outsiders are often taking

An Introduction to Work and Organizational Psychology: An International Perspective,
Third Edition. Edited by Nik Chmiel, Franco Fraccaroli and Magnus Sverke.
© 2017 John Wiley & Sons, Ltd. Published 2017 by John Wiley & Sons, Ltd.

on the role of in-house consultants. Finally, both internal and external HR and OD experts need to increasingly 'support the organization to navigate through complexity and chaos' (Cheung-Judge & Holbeche, 2015, p. 1). One advantage of being an outsider to the organization, or at least, being able to distance oneself from the organization, is the ability to get a clearer picture of its structure and internal dynamics. On the other hand, an advantage of being an organizational insider would be a deeper understanding of group and departmental processes and functions. Whereas in this chapter we discuss working with organizations from the external point of view, many of the presented models and methods are also relevant for internal w/o psychologists.

Systemic areas and levels. Any organization can be seen as a complex system, which consists of different functional areas and levels (Figure 25.1). Many of our working models, roles and professional identities are determined by these different areas and levels. That is, phenomena and problems within certain areas or levels of an organization lend themselves to being adequately solved by w/o psychological knowledge and skills, whereas others do not. Hence, not all areas and levels are equally accessible to the w/o psychologist.

As psychologists, our knowledge base is often heavily skewed towards the individual and the group level, as well as towards the interpersonal and intergroup levels. In this respect, we deal with issues such as competencies, motivation, performance, occupational health, coping with job stress, interaction and communication styles, group dynamics, interpersonal conflict management, leadership behaviour, attitude change, job satisfaction, etc. However, as w/o psychologists we also have to deal with the 'socio-technical work system' as a whole (Davis et al., 2014), that is, with issues that are related to organizational processes, structures, technologies and strategies. 'Systemic' in the organizational context means that a change at one level of the system always affects other levels within the system

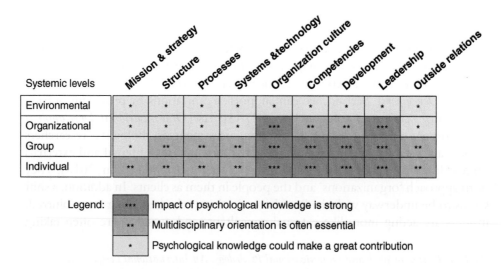

Systemic levels	Mission & strategy	Structure	Processes	Systems & technology	Organization culture	Competencies	Development	Leadership	Outside relations
Environmental	*	*	*	*	*	*	*	*	*
Organizational	*	*	*	*	***	**	**	***	*
Group	*	**	**	**	***	***	***	***	**
Individual	**	**	**	**	***	***	***	***	**

Legend:
- *** Impact of psychological knowledge is strong
- ** Multidisciplinary orientation is often essential
- * Psychological knowledge could make a great contribution

Figure 25.1: Systemic areas and levels of the organization

(Burke, 2011, p. 61). Therefore, in order to be successful in working with organizations, we need to adopt a systemic view of the organization, both in our thinking as well as in our interventions.

Professional expertise and identity. The work of a w/o-psychologist is rooted in two pillars: (1) the science of psychology, and (2) proven professional practice. First, our scientific training enables us to think critically and to differentiate between evidence-based practices and tools and those which find no support in science. This is an essential competence, given that the world of work and organizations is plagued by management fads, consulting products and practices that are not supported by any evidence. Second, we gain expertise from proven professional practice. Given that our professional identity as w/o psychologists is still young and has gradually developed since the late 1980s, our identity and expertise are heavily shaped by 'communities of practice'. Many competencies needed in our work are acquired on the job where we gain work experience and learn from senior colleagues and mentors. In addition, when defining our identity as w/o psychologists, we not only need to consider the difference regarding other areas of psychology but also must act with respect to other professions in the field of work, organizations and management. Given that our work often occurs in a multidisciplinary context, it is important to be aware of these differences. This awareness would allow us to identify potential opportunities to contribute as well as the limitations of our knowledge.

Multidisciplinary context. As w/o psychologists we are not the only profession that provides consulting services supporting organizational effectiveness and efficiency. In fact, a variety of professionals with different disciplinary backgrounds are working in the field of organizational development. For example, management consultants tend to have a background in business administration, economics or engineering. Their work typically focuses at the organizational and strategic levels (see Figure 25.1). Other professionals, such as HR experts, work in domains closer to a w/o psychologist's core areas of expertise, even though their educational background tends to vary widely (e.g., economics, educational science, pedagogy, other behavioural sciences, healthcare). Interestingly, when looking at the types of consulting services and their associated market share, the consulting fields with the highest market share tend to include areas such as IT, strategy, operations, business process improvement, project management and financial consulting. The share of HR (human resources) and CM (change management) consulting varies between 6% and 14% depending on the data source (O'Mahoney & Markham, 2013). As w/o psychologists, we sometimes view HR experts and other professionals as our competitors in the consultancy market, especially since they have a more influential, strategic, opportunity to define developmental agendas compared to us. However, if we consider them to be our colleagues and collaborators, who pursue the same objectives, namely, to enhance organizational performance and well-being, their knowledge and skills can be perfect complements to those of a w/o psychologist.

Client needs. Finally, our clients' needs shape the contents, working models, roles, identity and even the status of our profession. The crucial question here is: Why would the client (i.e. organizations, managers and employees) need outside consultants at all? The most common answer is: to perform some work that the client does not have the time, the skills, and/or knowledge to perform. Other reasons often mentioned for employing consultancy services are: to benefit from original thinking; to be presented with an objective perspective or advice; to temporarily fill in for management; to gain access to a specific methodology; to get tailored solutions; to validate an internal decision or to improve working relationships (O'Mahoney & Markham, 2013). Often, clients use consultants to help them cope with uncertainty or deal with ambiguity. This suggests that their 'problem' might have more to do with emotions than with a lack of knowledge or skills. Consequently, the mere presence of an outsider could be enough to facilitate positive change. However, sometimes consultants are employed solely for legitimization or 'political' purposes. For instance, in an organizational change effort, consultants can be used to validate or provide an excuse for difficult decisions, such as reorganizations that involve lay-offs or other cost-cutting measures.

Client needs vs. consultancy services. Very often, the relationship between clients and consultants tends to be complicated. Consultants and their clients (i.e. managers) are independent, autonomous systems with their own realities. In order to arrive at a mutually beneficial consulting relationship, these systems must become interconnected. Now let us take a look at what management and consultant work entails. We can describe management work as a series of tasks and functions that have to be performed in an organization or a team. Consulting is a service function, the aim of which is to support the fluent performance of different management functions in the organization. Hence, the link between consultancy and management work should be self-evident: consultants can help managers improve their own and their organization's performance. However, in practice, aligning the perspectives and interests of managers and consultants can prove to be tricky. Managers might ask for services and methods that do not fit the problem at hand. Alternatively, consultants might offer solutions and models that reveal their poor understanding of the client's needs or of the organization's culture and climate. Hence the important question would be: What can be done to achieve a better match? One crucial step in this respect is to ensure that information about goals, expectations, needs and values is thoroughly exchanged. This process of sharing information and establishing common ground in terms of what each party expects from the working relationship is often called psychological contracting (Honkanen & Schmidt-Brasse, 2008). If managers and external experts (e.g., organizational development consultants or w/o psychologists) succeed in aligning their perspectives, the ensuing collaboration can create value and help the organization 'anticipate, adapt, and respond to transformation and change' (Rothwell, Stavros, & Sullivan, 2016, p. 16).

25.2 What Are Our Working Models and Roles?

The continuum of roles. In organizations, the w/o psychologist often needs to employ a variety of approaches and to assume different roles. One crucial variable that defines our role as consultants is how directive vs. non-directive our working model is. In the directive mode, the consultant takes responsibility for solving the client's problems. That is, he/she does things on behalf of the client. In the non-directive mode, the client is the one that takes responsibility and engages in action. In this case, the consultant's role is reduced to helping and facilitating. A spectrum of different roles can be described along this continuum (Figure 25.2).

Following a similar logic, Schein (1999) describes three consulting approaches, each one embodying different goals, roles and working models:

- *The expertise model.* In this 'selling and telling' mode a consultant provides information and professional expertise. For instance, the expert mode for a w/o psychologist could mean using psychological testing to assess a job candidate's suitability for a job during the recruitment process.
- *The doctor-patient model.* In this model, a consultant diagnoses and provides advice or prescribes 'medicine' to cure problems. This analyst role could, for instance, entail carrying out surveys and interviews in order to identify problems and developmental areas in an organization.
- *The process consultation model.* In this model, the consultant acts as a helper, a facilitator or a catalyst. He/she tries to help the client solve problems by supporting the client to create the necessary internal conditions for change. Concretely, this could mean asking the 'right' questions, actively participating, and providing coaching and counselling.

For a w/o psychologist the helper/facilitator role is often the most natural choice whereas management consultants usually tend to assume the expert role. Whereas it is possible to be successful in more than one role, we normally tend to favour one of them where we feel the most authentic and effective. In addition, displaying more than one of these approaches in the same project could be seen as

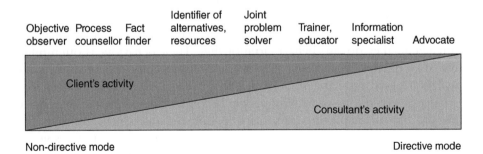

Figure 25.2: The range of consultative roles

Source: Lippitt & Lippitt, 1986, figure 4, p. 61. Reproduced with permission of John Wiley & Sons.

inconsistent by the client and cause problems. For instance, if the consultant initially adopts the role of the expert and provides the client with facts, instructions, and directions, the client will expect the same type of behaviour in the future. It can be very confusing for the client if the consultant suddenly switches to the facilitator role and instead of providing answers starts asking questions and tries to get the client to find his/her own solutions to problems.

Working with change. Typically, when working with organizations, there is a need to develop or change something. This could mean creating a new strategy, implementing a new technology, redesigning the organization, redefining tasks, enhancing performance, learning new things, preventing accidents or managing work conflicts. Changes usually include both structural and behavioural changes. In this respect, there are two partially overlapping doctrines or approaches to organizational change: change management (CM) and organization development (OD) (Creasey, Jamieson, Rothwell, & Severini, 2016). Whereas the underlying models of CM and OD tend to be multidisciplinary, both rely on knowledge gained from w/o psychology research and practice. As w/o psychologists, our added value in working with change derives heavily from our knowledge of behavioural change phenomena. Ultimately, the aim of inducing behavioural change in organizations is to change people's cognitions (Gardner, 2006). That is, we try to change or influence people's thoughts, beliefs, attitudes, values, preferences and decisions.

In their classic work, Chin and Benne (1985) introduced three general strategies for changing human systems: (1) empirical-rational, (2) normative-reeducative, and (3) power-coercive. Below we present an adapted model of Chin and Benne's (1985) model, which entails four general strategies for inducing change in human behaviour (Honkanen, 2006; 2016). Importantly, each general strategy is driven by a different set of underlying assumptions:

- *Rational strategies.* Here, the underlying assumptions are: (1) people are rational and driven by self-interest, and (2) people will take proper action, provided they have sufficient information and the right conditions are in place. From this perspective, typical strategies for change are education, perceptual and conceptual clarification, providing information, and using persuasive reasoning.
- *Psychological strategies.* Although we accept that people can be rational and intelligent, they do also behave 'irrationally'. Their behaviour is often influenced by unconscious forces, such as social norms, emotions, or subtle cues, which trigger automatic responses. From this perspective, typical change strategies would involve helping people become aware of their mental models and habits, supporting personal development, introducing re-educative programmes, appealing to their emotions, or framing choices in ways which exploit heuristics (i.e. mental shortcuts) in decision-making.
- *Situational strategies.* Here the underlying assumption is that people's behaviour is strongly influenced by contextual characteristics and forces within their

immediate environment. Therefore, if we want people to behave differently, we should change the environment they are working in. From this perspective, typical strategies for behavioural change would include redesigning the organization and work processes, changing the physical space or employing various framing techniques (i.e. changing the way choices are framed in order to subtly change people's behaviour).

- *Power strategies.* Here the underlying assumption is that behavioural change is evoked by using power. Power is typically defined as 'asymmetric control over valued resources in social relations' (Galinsky, Rus, & Lammers, 2010). This implies that in any given social interaction, one party has more control over some valued resource, which can range from material goods to more intangible resources such as information or affection. One way to use power would be to employ coercive power strategies such as withholding important information or threatening with negative consequences. Whereas these strategies might lead to short-term changes in behaviour, they are highly ineffective in engendering long-term behavioural change. Therefore, a more suitable way to influence others would be to use 'soft' power strategies that rely on expert, referent, or informational power (Yukl & Falbe, 1991). (See also Chapter 10 in this volume.)

Recent developments in the field of cognitive psychology, especially the dual-process theory of reasoning (Kahneman, 2011), have some important implications regarding the relevance and potential effectiveness of these different change strategies. Rational strategies rely on influencing conscious cognitive processes. Whereas providing information (a typical rational strategy) is a critical intervention for inducing behavioural change, it is not enough to enable the individual to engage in meaningful change. Hence, on their own, rational strategies, although popular, tend to be relatively limited in terms of potential effectiveness (Cheung-Judge & Holbeche, 2015). Psychological or situational strategies focus on automatic processes and rely on changing behaviour by altering the framing of a situation or the context within which people act. In this respect, language, for instance, provides a powerful way to 'frame' the context and direct behaviours by triggering associations regarding appropriate or inappropriate behaviour (Thaler & Sunstein, 2009). For example, in an attempt to change a culture of silence and blame, the head of a children's hospital successfully introduced a policy of 'blameless reporting', whereby words such as 'errors' and 'investigations' were replaced by words such as 'accidents' and 'analysis' (Garvin, Edmondson, & Gino, 2008). In practice, given the systemic nature of organizations, employing a mix of these different types of strategies is more likely to be effective, than any individual strategy alone. Hence, real change within the organization can only occur by employing both behavioural and structural change approaches and by ensuring that they are aligned with each other. Indeed, "individual performance improvement can only occur when the surrounding work environment supports it" (Rothwell, Stavros, & Sullivan, 2016, p. 2).

Two different paths to influence. As a w/o psychologist you are the instrument of change (Rothwell et al., 2016, p. 47). However, you can use your knowledge and skills to effect change by following two very different paths. The first path relies on personal influence and involves direct interaction with the client system. In this case, your success depends not only on your professional consultation skills, but also on the quality of your interaction with the client, your communication skills and personal attributes. The second path relies on influence via design and involves designing the psychological, social or physical environment for your client. Here, your success depends on your design skills (Honkanen, 2016).

In this respect, one useful perspective could be offered by design thinking, an approach that has recently received increased attention in the area of management and organizational development. The roots of this approach can be found in fields such as service design, user experience design (UX-design) and graphic design (Polaine, Lovlie, & Reason, 2013). Central to the design thinking process is a focus on the needs of the user when defining a problem and implementing solutions. At the core of the approach lies a bias towards action and experimentation, with the assumption being that only by creating and testing something, can you learn and improve upon your initial ideas. Key principles of design thinking revolve around (1) empathizing with the users by immersing yourself with their experiences in order to fully understand their perspectives, (2) defining the problem from the perspective of the user, (3) generating a large array of possible solutions, (4) creating prototypes that would allow learning and refinement of the original idea, and (5) testing the prototypes with the user and refining them based on user feedback. According to Kolko (2015), design thinking in the organizational context implies applying the principles of design to the way people work. In that sense, design thinking fits well with the OD tradition given the emphasis on participation, a focus on the client and identifying the client's real need, dealing with emotions, learning by trial and error, and adapting an iterative working model.

25.3 How Do We Work? The Consulting Process

Whenever we work with a client to solve a problem, we begin a process that starts and ends somewhere. In the CM field, there are a number of different models depicting change processes and their associated phases. For instance, the famous Lewinian model of planned change consists of only three phases: unfreeze, move, refreeze. In the OD or action research field, the process is usually described as follows: (1) entry and contracting, (2) data collection and diagnosis, (3) interventions, (4) evaluation, and (5) termination (Cheung-Judge & Holbeche, 2015). A similar process model is used by Lunt, Peiro, Poortinga, and Roe (2015) to describe psychologists' competences in the *EuroPsy* programme (European Certificate in Psychology). In Figure 25.3, this change process model is presented in a slightly modified and simplified form. The essence of the model is an

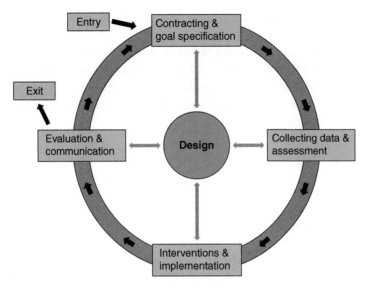

Figure 25.3: The phases of the consulting process

understanding of how the competences needed in w/o psychologists' work are determined by our typical work process.

25.3.1 Phase 1: Contracting and goal specification

Before a w/o psychologist starts to work with a client (be it an individual, a team, or an organization), he or she needs to make initial contact, establish a working relationship and negotiate a contract with the client. These initial steps determine who our clients are, what they need and whether we might be able to help them. In this respect, we typically carry out different kinds of needs analyses to gain an understanding of the situation. For instance, extensive upfront discussions with the client typically help uncover essential information and generate a comprehensive overview of the problem space. Additionally, consultants can use systematic interviews, surveys, field observations or archival data from the client organization to generate a thorough understanding of the situation.

The ultimate purpose, at this stage, is to negotiate and reach an agreement with the client regarding the project goals and the measurement of success. It is critical to ensure that the goals are realistic, feasible and that the criteria for measuring success are specific and clear. In the contracting phase, the most contentious issues usually arise around the psychological contract (i.e. the tacit set of expectations of the w/o psychologist and the client about what each will give and receive in the relationship). Attempts to make these expectations fully explicit often prove difficult. According to Schein (1999), these attempts are neither feasible nor fruitful, given that there will always be 'black holes' in creating a shared understanding. Moreover, 'reality' will inevitably change during the course of the project, as new information will likely be uncovered and some initial assumptions may no longer hold.

According to the EuroPsy model (Lunt et al., 2015), key competencies at this stage are mastery of needs analysis and goal setting. In addition, interpersonal skills, analytical capabilities and perspective-taking (i.e. the ability to understand another person's point of view) are critical for accurately assessing the situation and reaching an agreement with the client.

25.3.2   Phase 2: Collecting data and assessment

In the diagnostic phase, we can select from a number of different methods, tools, and approaches to collect data. Assessment can be performed at different systemic levels: individual, group, organizational, and strategic/environmental. For instance, we can employ psychological tests to assess employee competences, use climate surveys to identify strengths and weaknesses at the group or organizational level, or map potential opportunities and threats in the organizational environment. However, it is often necessary to take a systemic view in our analytic approach and address all these different levels. That is, we can increase our chances of creating a comprehensive view of the organization and its needs by focusing on the different levels within the system as well as their interrelationships. This approach would allow us to identify a context where individuals, teams and organizations can thrive. In the EuroPsy model this type of assessment is called a situational assessment.

Additionally, we can improve the quality of our engagement with the clients, by encouraging them to use the diagnostic tools by themselves or by collaboratively analysing and interpreting the results. If we encourage the clients to use diagnostic tools on their own, it is important that they receive the necessary training and/or certifications. Moreover, it is crucial that we choose tools and methods that are valid, reliable and appropriate for the questions we are trying to answer. Given that the resulting data will provide the basis for our interpretations, recommendations, and decisions regarding future courses of action, it is essential that the initial diagnosis is as accurate as possible. It goes almost without saying, that starting a change process with a faulty diagnosis will most likely not bode well for its success. In addition, sometimes we have to be careful about how much detail we provide to the client regarding the results of our assessment. For instance, if we conduct a survey on well-being in the whole organization, we might want to think about how to aggregate the data in such a way, that no single individual is identifiable. For ethical reasons, we have to honour the anonymity of individual respondents, hence, we should be careful to safeguard that. In short, we have to help the client use the insights from the data to make informed decisions, while at the same time safeguarding individual anonymity, and following other ethical guidelines.

To help us inform our data collection, analysis and interpretation, as well as guide our planning of the necessary interventions, we may need to choose a theoretical model. This can be regarded as our *theory input* (Cockman, Evans, & Reynolds, 1999) and is rooted in the knowledge base produced by w/o psychology – theories, models, and research results. In practice, our theory input can also materialise in processes such as giving feedback, providing coaching, training, or developmental programmes. Here, we are, however, already taking a step towards the next phase in the consulting cycle.

In this phase, critical competencies revolve around a broad range of diagnostic skills. Importantly, within organizations, there is an increasing trend towards the use of more sophisticated measurement methods and a reliance on Big Data. This would require w/o psychologists to be skilled in advanced data analytics methods, such as predictive behavioural analytics (combining an understanding of statistics, computer science, and data modelling), which unfortunately does not seem to be the case (Sesil, 2013). Hence, w/o psychologists would need to constantly update their skillset, if they want to remain relevant and be able to create value for organizations.

25.3.3   Phase 3: Intervention and implementation

In phase 3 we plan and carry out interventions that satisfy a number of criteria: they are appropriate for achieving the goals (defined in phase 1), are based on the insights gained from the diagnostic phase (phase 2) and are rooted in our work during the design phase.

In practice, the consulting contract can finish at the end of phase 2. This is the case, for instance, if the client only needs the w/o psychologist to help with data collection, diagnostics, and planning future developments. In this type of situation, the assessment and its impact on the client system can be seen as the actual 'intervention'. However, if we proceed to phase 3 of the consulting process, which involves intervening, implementing change, and being an active change agent, we move into an area of consulting which requires a different skill-set and methods than the earlier phases.

In terms of change implementation, a successful w/o psychologist might need interpersonal skills and tools to successfully deal with issues such as group dynamics, behavioural change, resistance to change, and adult learning. Here, our job consists of monitoring, mentoring, encouraging, supporting, confronting, opening doors, counselling or training (Cockman et al., 1999). However, interventions can also be more 'structural' or indirect in their nature. That is, they might focus on situational factors or the context people are working in, and, thereby, involve the re-design of the psychological, social or physical environment. In this type of scenario, it is crucial that we intervene at the 'appropriate' systemic areas and levels within the organization. Surely, our ability to do so is highly dependent on the quality of the diagnostic work we have done in phase 2. Nonetheless, as w/o psychologists we have to be acutely aware of the fact that focusing on change at the individual level does not necessarily translate into changes at the organizational level. Instead we need to take a systemic approach and ensure that our interventions are aligned across different areas and levels. For instance, our goal might be to enhance organizational innovation. To this end we cannot only focus on increasing individual innovativeness, but also need to ensure that the reward systems, performance management systems, work processes, and even the physical space are redesigned to be conducive to innovation.

Lunt and colleagues (2015) define three distinct key intervention types and their associated competences. The first type implies applying intervention methods that directly affect one or more individuals. This can be, for instance, selection, training, career development, or behavioural change interventions. The second type involves applying intervention methods that directly affect selected aspects of the situation. This could mean, for instance, the implementation of new tools, methods, procedures, schemes or introducing changes in the work environment. The third type implies applying intervention methods that indirectly enable individuals, groups and organizations to learn and make decisions. In practice this could mean guiding or training managers and employees. In addition, important competencies are the ability to plan interventions and the ability to implement services, methods, procedures that create value for the clients.

Whereas the mastery of different intervention tools is essential, it is not enough. As professionals, we should be able to adapt to the environment and flexibly adapt and apply the tools in different contexts and situations (see the Role of design for more explanation).

25.3.4   Phase 4: Evaluation and communication

Evaluation is the process of assessing whether the goals of the developmental/ change intervention have been achieved and whether expectations have been met. Importantly, it entails assessing the intended and unintended consequences of the intervention. Continuous learning and development are the result of feedback, reflection and taking corrective action. That is, from an open system theory perspective, feedback is a means to evaluate the consequences of one's intervention and take necessary corrective actions, in other words, to learn. When it comes to evaluating change processes, the main challenge stems from the fact that they do not follow a linear path. Whereas we plan the change process in a linear fashion, in reality, it is anything but linear. Implementation is often messy, chaotic and unintended consequences do occur. Figure 25.4 presents a model of the nonlinear nature of the planned change process. The essence of the model is that realized change is rarely the same as the intended or planned change. Typically, there will be emergent forces and social processes that will critically impact the output.

The most important factor determining what we can learn about the outcomes of the change process is the quality of the evaluations. That is, the quality of the data collected will determine the extent to which we can learn anything about the effects of the intervention. Second, learning depends on the manner in which results are communicated and the way they are understood by various partners and stakeholders. Third, very often, evaluations focus solely on whether

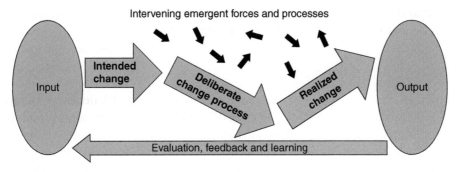

Figure 25.4: The nonlinear nature of the change process

Source: Adapted from the related strategy process model presented by Mintzberg 2007, p. 6.

the intended goals have been achieved. However, due to the nonlinear nature of the change process, a focus on outcomes alone can provide a biased view of the change process and its results. That is why it is crucial that the process itself is evaluated. Fourth, evaluation should be planned, structured and deliberate. However, in reality, unplanned, unofficial evaluations occur throughout the change process as people share their experiences and beliefs. To maximize learning about the process, it is therefore important to also capture this serendipitous feedback.

According to the EuroPsy model (Lunt et al., 2015), the key competences for this phase of the consulting cycle, are mastery of evaluation planning, measurement, and analysis. In addition, strong communication and interpersonal skills as well as flexibility and proactivity are the cornerstone of being a successful change agent.

Re-entry or exit? The consulting cycle depicted in Figure 25.3 is based on the underlying assumption that after evaluation and feedback, we can either exit the process or restart the cycle by renegotiating and resetting goals. In the latter case, we would launch a second loop of the developmental process. This notion that development and change are an iterative process is one of the core principles of the traditional action research model. Importantly, this second developmental loop need not occur at the same systemic level as before. For instance, if our original consulting cycle was focused on the individual level, the second loop could be focused on the group or the organizational level. The decision as to which level to focus on in this second loop would be contingent on the insights gained from the evaluation phase.

Any consulting cycle has to eventually reach an end and there comes a time to exit the process. Exiting or disengaging is an important step for both the client and the consultant, a step which, too often, is poorly executed. Both the client and the consultant need to be able to "say goodbye" and achieve closure, ideally on amicable terms. In this respect, farewell rites or heart-to-heart conversations can be useful in reaching closure. That being said, within the client organization, the change momentum would need to be maintained, which also implies that the results of the change process would need to be evaluated over time. This could mean that the consultant might return for follow-up evaluation meetings, which would be useful for both client and consultant learning.

25.3.5   The role of design

The design element is an essential component of the model depicted in Figure 25.3. In the Lunt et al. (2015) EuroPsy model, design is conceptualized in terms of planning and product development and essentially happens 'backstage'. They focus on how a w/o psychologist plans and develops the tools and services employed in the consulting cycle. In this respect, the design process starts by defining the purpose of the tools/services, and identifying the relevant stakeholders and any potential requirements and constrains. The next step in the design process involves designing and adapting the tools/services to fit the context within which they are to be employed. This involves carefully considering the requirements and drawing up specifications, all the while keeping the contextual constraints in mind. The third step entails testing the tools/services and assessing them in terms of feasibility, reliability and validity. Finally, the tools/services would need to be evaluated with respect to a number of aspects such as their utility, user friendliness, costs, and client satisfaction. (See also Chapter 26 in this volume.)

At a more abstract level, we can conceptualize design (or *design thinking*) as a constant process of improving, diversifying and adapting a w/o psychologist's skills and methods in order to better meet the clients' needs. This implies that our design work not only happens 'backstage' but also 'onstage' whereby we adopt a client-centred, experimental, iterative approach, ask for frequent feedback, learn 'online'and integrate our learning into the design process. Importantly, from this perspective, the w/o psychologist needs to be comfortable with ambiguity, be open to having his/her assumptions challenged, view failure as an opportunity to learn, and place a premium on quick prototyping and learning via trial and error.

25.4   What Are Our Professional Ethics?

The work of w/o practitioners has the potential to have a profound impact on individuals, groups and organizations. Therefore, it is critical that consultants act responsibly and carefully weigh the possible consequences of their involvement in the client system. Hence, practitioners should follow professional standards and norms as officially stipulated by professional associations as well as use self-reflection and consultation with peer colleagues to determine appropriate courses of action, especially when facing ethical dilemmas.

In terms of professional associations, the European Federation of Psychologists' Associations (EFPA 1995/2005) has published an ethical meta-code for psychologists which highlights four specific principles: (1) respect for a person's rights and dignity; (2) competence; (3) responsibility; and (4) integrity.

The first principle entails that we are bound to respect individuals' free will and ensure that their participation in any type of intervention is voluntary. In addition, we need to guarantee the confidentiality of the information we collect. One potential dilemma we could face is that the client (employer) tries to gain access to individual information that was collected under the promise of confidentiality. In this type of situation, we need to be aware of the limits of what we are allowed to share and do not release any information without the explicit consent of the individual.

The second principle implies that it is our obligation to continuously develop and update our skillset and competencies, including our ethical awareness. To ensure the quality of our work, we need to follow recent developments in the science and practice of w/o psychology as well as in related fields. This implies not only staying up to date by reading and attending conferences, but also actively interacting with and collaborating with others in our field and asking for critical feedback.

The third principle entails that it is our responsibility to ensure that our knowledge and work is not misused and does not lead to any harm. This is especially important given that we might come across highly sensitive information about individuals. In addition, we need to be able to recognize ethical dilemmas and, if unable to resolve them on our own, we should consult with colleagues and/or professional associations.

Finally, integrity implies that we are aware of our own limitations, are honest and open in our interactions with clients, and steer away from any potential conflicts of interest in our work engagements. Integrity is critical in the consulting process, given that the client-consultant relationship is based on trust.

Summary

As w/o psychology practitioners we are increasingly faced with the task of helping organizations successfully navigate through fast-paced changes, daunting complexity and uncertainty. First, the context of our work clearly requires us to adopt an interdisciplinary approach, treat organizations as systems of interrelated parts and be mindful of matching client needs to proposed interventions and solutions. We can only add value to organizations if we constantly update our competencies and skillsets by keeping abreast of developments in w/o research and practice. Second, there is a wide range of working models and potential roles we can assume when working with organizations. To this end, we can only be successful if we are flexible and able to adapt our working models to the requirements of the situation at hand. In addition, adopting a design thinking approach, with a clear focus on client needs, experimentation, and iterative development based on learning from trial and error is critical. Third, the different phases of the consulting process require mastery of a variety of tools and methods. Whereas proficiency in different tools and methods is a prerequisite for success, it is not enough. We need to be and stay curious and also develop "soft skills" such as interpersonal sensitivity, communication skills, the ability to deal with ambiguity, and open-mindedness. Finally, we need to be aware of the potential impact of our work on the client system and ensure that we uphold ethical principles in our work.

Discussion Points

1 If you were a w/o psychologist, which of the different types of roles discussed in the chapter would fit you best and why?
2 If you were a w/o psychologist, how would you incorporate design thinking into your daily practice?

Suggested Further Reading

Brown, T. (2009). *Change by design: How design thinking transforms organizations and inspires innovation.* New York: HarperCollins.

Cheung-Judge, M. Y., & Holbeche, L. (2015). *Organization development: A practitioner's guide for OD and HR.* (2nd ed.). London: Kogan Page.

Rothwell, W. J., Stavros, J. M., & Sullivan, R. L. (2016). *Practicing organization development: Leading transformation and change* (4th ed.). Hoboken, NJ: Wiley.

Schein, E.H. (1999). *Process consultation revised: Building the helping relationship.* Reading, MA: Addison-Wesley.

References

Burke, W. W. (2011). *Organization change: theory and practice* (3rd ed.). Los Angeles: Sage.

Cheung-Judge, M. Y., & Holbeche, L. (2015). *Organization development: A practitioner's guide for OD and HR.* (2nd ed.). London: Kogan Page.

Chin, R., & Benne, K. D. (1985). General strategies for effecting changes in human systems. In W. G. Bennis, K. D. Benne, & R. Chin (Eds.), *The planning of change* (4rd ed.), (pp. 22–43). New York: Holt, Rinehart & Winston.

Cockman, P., Evans, B., & Reynolds, P. (1999). *Consulting for real people: A client-centred approach for change agents and leaders.* London: McGraw-Hill.

Creasey, T., Jamieson, D. W., Rothwell, W. J., & Severini, G. (2016). Exploring the relationship between organization development and change management. In W. J. Rothwell, J. M. Stavros, & R. L. Sullivan (Eds.), *Practicing organization development: Leading transformation and change* (4th ed.), (pp. 330–338). Hoboken, NJ: Wiley.

Davis, M. C., Challenger, R., Jayewardene, D., & Clegg, C. (2014). Advancing socio-technical systems thinking: a call for bravery. *Applied Ergonomics, 45*(2), 171–180.

EFPA (1995/2005) Guidance for the content of the Ethical Codes. Adopted by the General Assembly 1995, July in Athens. Revised by the General Assembly 2005, July in Granada. European Federation of Psychologists' Associations. http://ethics.efpa.eu/meta-code/)

EuroPsy (July, 2015). *The European Certificate in Psychology.* EFPA, European Federation of Psychologists Associations.

Galinsky, A. D., Rus, D., & Lammers, J. (2010). Power: A central force governing psychological, social, and organizational life. In D. De Cremer, R. van Dick, & J. K. Murnighan (Eds.), *Social psychology and organizations* (pp. 17-38). London: Psychology Press.

Gardner, H. (2006). *Changing minds: The art and science of changing our own and other people's minds.* Boston: Harvard Business School Press.

Garvin, D. A., Edmondson, A. C., & Gino, F. (2008). Is yours a learning organization? *Harvard Business Review, 86*(3), 109–116.

Honkanen, H. (2006). *Muutoksen agentit, muutoksen ohjaaminen ja johtaminen* [The

Agents of Change: Consulting and Managing Change]. Helsinki: Edita Publishing.

Honkanen, H. (2016). *Vaikuttamisen psykologia, mielen muuttamisen tiede ja taito* [The Psychology of Influence: the Science and Art of Mind-changing]. Helsinki: Arena-Innovation.

Honkanen, H., & Schmidt-Brasse, U. (2008). Roles and methods of work and organizational psychology practitioners. In N. Chmiel (Ed.), *An introduction to work and organizational psychology, A European perspective* (2nd ed.), (pp. 441–464). Oxford: Blackwell.

Kahneman, D. (2011). *Thinking fast and slow.* London: Penguin Books.

Kolko, J. (2015). Design thinking comes of age. *Harvard Business Review,* 93(9), 66–71.

Lippitt, G. & Lippitt, R. (1986) *The consulting process in action* (2nd ed.). San Francisco: Jossey-Bass/Pfeiffer.

Lunt, I., Peiro, J. M., Poortinga, Y., & Roe, R. A. (2015). *EuroPsy: Standards and quality in education for psychologists.* Göttingen: Hogrefe Publishing.

Mintzberg, H. (2007). *Tracking strategies: Toward a general theory.* Oxford: Oxford University Press.

O'Mahoney, J., & Markham, C. (2013). *Management consultancy.* Oxford: Oxford University Press.

Polaine, A., Lovlie, L., & Reason, B. (2013). *Service design: From insight to implementation.* New York: Rosenfeld Media.

Rothwell, W. J., Stavros, J. M., & Sullivan, R. L. (2016). *Practicing organization development: Leading transformation and change* (4th ed.). Hoboken, NJ: Wiley.

Rothwell, W. J., Sullivan, R. L., Kim, T., Park, J. G., & Donahue, W. E. (2016) Change process and models. In W. J. Rothwell, J. M. Stavros, & R. L. Sullivan (Eds.), *Practicing organization development: Leading transformation and change* (4th ed. pp. 42–60). Hoboken, NJ: Wiley.

Schein, E. H. (1999). *Process consultation revised: Building the helping relationship.* Reading, MA: Addison-Wesley.

Sesil, J. C. (2013). *Applying advanced analytics to HR management decisions: Methods for selection, developing incentives, and improving collaboration.* Upper Saddle River, NJ: Pearson.

Thaler, R. H., & Sunstein, C. R. (2009). *Nudge: improving decisions about health, wealth and happiness.* London: Penguin Books.

Yukl, G. A., & Falbe, C. M. (1991). Importance of different power sources in downward and lateral relations. *The Journal of Applied Psychology, 76,* 416–423.

CASE STUDIES

A Strategic Approach to Improving Well-Being in a Large Railway Company

Ivan Robertson, Matthew Smeed and Victoria Ward

26.1 Background

Network Rail is the largest owner and operator of railway infrastructures in the UK, with a diverse workforce. Like many similar, large-scale, engineering-based organizations, Network Rail has a long history of focusing on the health and safety of their employees. People working in hazardous environments represent an obvious focus for health and safety but Network Rail wanted to innovate and extend the scope of their work in this area. In particular, they wanted to move away from the approach that most corporate health strategies take, i.e. a focus on the outcomes of poor physical health, such as obesity or heart disease, and they wanted to target both physical and psychological health in a positive way.

With these goals in mind, the Head of Occupational Health and Well-being Strategy at Network Rail approached Robertson Cooper Ltd to design and implement a data-driven approach that connected employee well-being with positive outcomes (including productivity gains) for employees and the organization as a whole.

The scale of the task was considerable. Network Rail has over 35,000 employees, operating 24/7 across the UK ,and the health and well-being initiative needed to be conducted in a way that engaged all of the staff, from corporate staff working in office locations to shift workers on the tracks.

26.2 Theoretical and Practical Issues

Theoretical and empirical research into well-being in the workplace has a long history and has produced some significant findings that provide a platform for practical interventions.

The first key area of research concerns the relationships between psychological health and physical health. Research has revealed that psychological health is linked to serious physical health consequences, including cardiovascular disease, obesity, diabetes and immune system functioning. The strongest and most extensive evidence concerns the consequences of psychological well-being factors for cardiovascular disease. For example, in a review of prospective cohort studies of coronary heart disease patients, Hemingway and Marmot (1999) found strong evidence of links between psychological ill health (6/6 studies), social support (9/10 studies) and coronary heart disease. For healthy populations, Hemingway and Marmot (1999) also found that psychological ill health (11/11 studies), social support (5/8 studies) and psychosocial work characteristics (6/10 studies) were possible causal factors in coronary heart disease. Research has also established a relationship between work-related psychosocial stress and heart disease and some understanding of the mechanisms that cause this relationship (Chandola et al., 2008). The second key area of research concerns the links between employee well-being and important business outcomes. For example, Ford et al. (2011) examined data from 31 different samples, covering a total of over 10,000 employees and revealed a positive relationship between psychological well-being and overall performance.

The research noted above provides evidence that better psychological well-being at work confers benefits on both employers and employees and that it is a significant causal factor in overall health and well-being. A third important stream of research has focused on the workplace factors that influence people's psychological well-being at work. Psychological factors such as work demands and the degree of control experienced by the worker have been identified as critical factors that influence employees' psychological health and well-being. Original work by Karasek (1979) focused on the key role of demands and control. More recent models (e.g. Bakker & Demerouti, 2007) also include the role of resources in determining the psychological well-being of employees. The essential theory behind these models is that the psychological experience of employees is dependent on the work that they do and the extent to which factors such as levels of demand, resources and the degree of control that they experience are in balance and do not create a level of demand that employees cannot cope with. Importantly the best jobs are not those that are low on demands – rather the most psychologically healthy jobs involve high levels of demand matched by high degrees of support, resources and control.

Robertson Cooper drew on this research base to develop a detailed model of the key workplace factors ('six essentials' http://www.robertsoncooper.com/6-essentials-of-workplace-well-being) that influence employees' well-being at work. Interventions to improve well-being are more effective if they are based on accurate knowledge of current challenges to well-being, and alongside the model of the key workplace factors Robertson Cooper also developed a survey tool (the ASSET model, Johnson, 2009) to measure employees' experiences of the key factors (Figure 26.1).

RESOURCES & COMMUNICATION

Resources includes everything from specialised training to IT systems-basically having all the knowledge and equipment you need to be able to do your job properly. Communication means knowing enough about what's going on in your organisation, and getting feedback on how you're playing your part.

CONTROL

A strong sense of control (aka autonomy) is linked to positive well-being. You need to feel that you have some say over how you do things and what happens around you (think living in a democracy, rather than a dictatorship). Feeling in control will also help you handle other pressures, like difficult working relationships or a heavy workload.

BALANCED WORKLOAD

There are two aspects to a balanced workload: Having a good work life balance, e.g. being able to get away from work to enjoy other activities, and not being asked to complete too much work, or work that is too hard.

JOB SECURITY & CHANGE

It's understandable that we might find it more difficult to cope when we feel insecure about our job. Change can also feel a little daunting sometimes, even if it ends up being for the better. Being able to greet change with enthusiasm rather than apprehension, and to persevere in the face of uncertainty, will help keep your well-being and performance on track.

WORK RELATIONSHIPS

Good working relationships are one of the most important sources of well-being, while a relationship gone bad can be hugely draining. Work relationships are at their best when they are a healthy mix of challenge and support.

JOB CONDITIONS

Job conditions are the elements that add up to a sense of job satisfaction. This can be everything from having the right work environment, to feeling as though you are paid fairly.

Figure 26.1:   The six essentials

26.3 Action and Outcome

As noted above, the initiative involved Network Rail in a new and innovative approach to well-being. Previous work had focused much more on health and an important goal for the intervention involved ensuring the engagement of staff at all levels in the organization. The Head of Occupational Health and Well-being Strategy described it in the following way:

> Managers were either sceptical and viewed it as unimportant or wanted to do something about it, but didn't know what to do. Employees, on the other hand, often distrusted why the business was interested in their health, because many of our roles require a certain level of medical fitness to be able to perform them safely.

One key aspect of the approach for Network Rail was that the use of the six essentials framework and associated model provided a clear and objective framework that describes the main barriers and enablers of well-being in the workplace. The six essentials framework and core concepts provided a conceptual model of the workplace factors that affect well-being and hence enabled discussion of these key factors and how they impact on people's day-to-day experience of work. Managers' and others, throughout the organization had a vocabulary and set of ideas that framed their thinking and conversations about well-being. Research (Gilbreath & Benson, 2004) has identified the key role that line managers play in employees' everyday experience of work. Network Rail recognized this and, at an early stage in the intervention, worked with Robertson Cooper, to develop and deliver a series of training courses for managers across the organization. The aims and objectives of the training courses were as follows:

- Understand the relationship between work pressure, performance, morale (well-being) and resilience.
- Learn how to build and maintain high levels of personal resilience in yourself and your team.
- Understand and develop your leadership strengths and learn how to manage your risks.
- Identify specific actions to take forward for your development and to support people in your team through change.

The full-day course was broken down into three core modules. The first focused on knowledge transfer, building the understanding of managers when it came to the key areas of pressure, well-being, resilience and the impact on performance. They were also introduced to the key models such as the six essentials, the idea being that this helped to build a common vocabulary for them to use with their teams.

The second module looked at the leadership style of the managers themselves. Using Robertson Cooper's proprietary psychometric tool, Leadership Impact, managers were asked to consider their natural strengths and risks when leading their team and how this might impact on the well-being of others.

Finally, the third module was used to provide the managers with a number of practical tips, techniques and exercises that they could use to build resilience in themselves and their teams. This included group activities to share strengths and using cognitive behavioural therapy techniques to have a constructive conversation about well-being with a team member. Managers consolidated their learning at the end of the session and committed to a number of actions that they would carry out when back in the workplace.

These sessions measurably improved managers' confidence in their ability to hold conversations about well-being or stress (14% improvement) and their ability to spot early signs of stress (18% improvement).

The measurement work began with an organization-wide survey using the ASSET tool to assess the six essentials and the related outcomes that are associated with employee well-being. The (anonymized) data obtained from the ASSET survey provided a starting point in understanding well-being levels across the organization and how things differed in various divisions, locations and job roles. These results provided useful management information but Network Rail wanted to go beyond the standard annual survey approach and, again with the help of Robertson Cooper, designed a short 'Snapshot' questionnaire containing items covering social, psychological and physical well-being. This questionnaire was made available to employees on an on-going basis, so that they could complete it and receive a report on their well-being levels (Figure 26.2). The report also provided employees with a well-being age score. On-going access to the questionnaire and reports enables employees to track their well-being levels. The report also contains tailored advice and support options, available within Network Rail and elsewhere, to encourage employees to make beneficial changes in their lifestyles.

The management information provided by the survey data enables the organization to focus on key risk areas where further intervention is needed. These key areas may be certain employee roles, geographical locations, or categories of employee (e.g. male workers aged 40–50 years). On-going monitoring enables the organization to retain an up-to-date snapshot of well-being issues

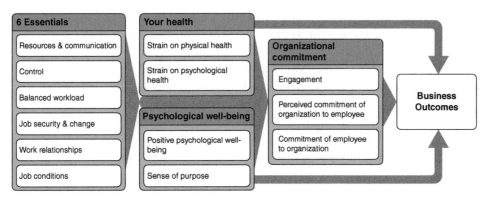

Figure 26.2: The well-being dashboard

throughout the organization. And to tackle them in a systematic, evidence-based way. For example, the data showed that the significant change occurring within the business was creating a level of job insecurity for certain parts of the business. To support people, managerial training, as outlined above, was implemented in these parts of the business first. This allowed line managers to build the resilience of their team members during these challenging times and to have a constructive conversation about job insecurity and the effect of change on individual well-being.

Network Rail calculated that by properly supporting employees in the lowest 10% for well-being, they could save an estimated £1 million per annum in productivity, as well as improving the lives of people across the organization.

26.4   What Would We Do Differently Next Time? Learning Points

The main learning points relate to increasing the use of the online assessment by staff. For example, in the first year after the tool was launched, over 10% of the population used the assessment – 4,142 unique users in total. In the second year this was increased to 22%, with over 8,000 unique users downloading their personal report.

However, the challenge still remains to increase this response across the business and in particular in certain parts of the business. While the response rate in some office-based parts of the business was pushing 50%, it was harder to reach some areas, such as the function responsible for the safe operation and maintenance of the railways, which includes track workers in each of the different routes across the country. The function is very large with c. 25,000 full-time equivalent workers, but is hard to target because they are so geographically spread and also work away from computers. To increase the response in this area, a number of potential activities have been planned, including:

- the creation of a network of Occupational Health managers based specifically in each of the routes;
- developing the assessment so that it is accessible on a mobile device;
- incentivizing employees to complete the assessment where possible, for example, by offering free gym sessions from an external provider;
- simplifying the assessment to reduce the time it takes to complete;
- potentially creating different versions of the report based on employee reading style and the length of assessment that they have filled in.

The other main learning point is about developing a way to get the aggregated group data into the hands of line managers across the business more quickly. This will be done by advancing the online system and also by training managers to use the results with their teams.

References

Bakker, A. B., & Demerouti, E. (2007). The Job Demands–Resources model: State of the art. *Journal of Managerial Psychology, 22,* 309–328.

Chandola, T., et al. (2008) Work stress and coronary heart disease: What are the mechanisms? *European Heart Journal, 29,* 640–648.

Ford, M. T., Cerasoli, C. P., Higgins, J. A., & Decesare, A. L. (2011) Relationships between psychological, physical, and behavioural health and work performance: A review and meta-analysis. *Work & Stress, 25,* 185–204.

Gilbreath, B. & Benson, P. G. (2004) The contribution of employee supervisor behaviour to employee well-being. *Work & Stress, 18,* 255–266.

Hemingway, H., & Marmot, M. (1999) Psychosocial factors in the aetiology and prognosis of coronary heart disease: Systematic review of prospective cohort studies. *British Medical Journal, 318,* 1460–1467.

Johnson, S. J. (2009) Organizational screening: The ASSET Model. In S. Cartwright, & C. L. Cooper (Eds.), *The Oxford handbook of organizational well being.* Oxford: Oxford University Press.

Karasek, R. (1979). Job demands, job decision latitude, and mental strain: Implications for job redesign. *Administrative Science Quarterly, 24,* 285–308.

27 Humiliation: Why We Deserve Respect at Work

Barbara Kożusznik

27.1 Background

The aim of this case study is to provide an example of a situation in which an employee felt humiliated by his supervisor. Humiliation is a formative experience and theoretical discussions describe humiliation acts as being connected with additional control, and the re-establishment of hierarchy and obedience. In a service company employing over 200 workers, there was a team X in the marketing department composed of young and enthusiastic people willing to win new customers, both via the internet and through organizing varied campaigns and events. The service company was fighting in the market and in this context it is not easy to survive. The strategy of the top management was based on allowing very competitive relations in the departments. In the centre of the organization was a group of the most dynamic, aggressive, and demanding managers who were very efficient at winning clients. All this created a 'rat race' climate in the company.

One day a boss came into the room occupied by team X, and in the presence of all the people gathered there – actually there were seven team members present, so almost the whole team – said to one of the youngest employees, the very talented and resourceful Eric: 'I have read your email sent to Director Smith and I hadn't known that you could be so ignorant! You've overlooked an essential matter which was the main topic of the email, and what's more, you worded a sentence so incorrectly as if you were a first-form pupil. I didn't think you were as stupid as a donkey. Can you please stop smiling foolishly when I am talking to you? It is not funny at all. If you took your work seriously, everything would be fine.'

Obviously, Eric felt a fool, but he also felt how unfair his boss's attack on him was. He had not made such a big mistake after all, it was only an oversight! Everybody understood that! He forced a smile and apologized, but he could hear muffled chuckles from his colleagues.

An Introduction to Work and Organizational Psychology: An International Perspective, Third Edition. Edited by Nik Chmiel, Franco Fraccaroli and Magnus Sverke.
© 2017 John Wiley & Sons, Ltd. Published 2017 by John Wiley & Sons, Ltd.

From that moment on, this situation was engraved on his memory. Eric consulted the Human Resources (HR) section of the company and asked for help because he was upset and he was not able to sleep well. HR suggested he see a psychologist and provided access to one. During the meetings with the psychologist, Eric told her about his emotions and how he felt. The psychologist met him several times, and first carried out a diagnosis in order to assess his personality traits that could possibly underlie his problems (such as narcissism or neuroticism) and to discover the reason he was vulnerable. Then the psychologist focused on Eric and his response to the humiliation and how he could cope with it. She explained to Eric that he was a very intelligent person and that his system of values should not change as a result of such an insignificant event at work. She suggested ways to take care of psychological and health problems in the future so he could be more resilient.

Imagine you were Eric, do you think that his work situation and well-being improved as a result of the interventions by the psychologist? An understanding of the theoretical background will help to answer this question.

27.2 Theoretical and Practical Issues

The humiliation of an employee can be perceived from various perspectives. The broader picture of this phenomenon is based on defining humiliation as 'a nuclear bomb of emotions' (Hartling, Lindner, Spalthoff, & Britton, 2013). A person/group (or even society) is reduced to a lower position in their own eyes or in the eyes of others. These authors believe that humiliation is the most toxic social dynamic of our age (Hartling et al., 2013) and state that humiliation can be viewed from the perspective of being: (1) an internal experience (feeling, emotion), (2) an external event (degradation, abuse, bullying), and (3) systemic social conditions (poverty, discrimination, forced dislocation). Studies of humiliation in today's world also link the dynamics of humiliation to violence (Lindner, Hartling, & Spalthoff, 2012; Hartling, & Luchetta, 1999), although the particularities of this experience should be understood within the social, cultural and historical context in which humiliation occurs (Whack, 2013).

Research studies show that the children whose parents subjected them to humiliation for disciplinary reasons have grown up to be less confident and more susceptible to mental disorders, such as depression or anxiety (Loader, 1998; Solomon & Serres, 1999). While the most potent form is the recurrent and gross humiliation of a young person, experts explain that even occasionally putting children to shame in the presence of a bigger group of people may do them harm. Parents ridiculing their children create in them a sensation of despair and develop their conviction that their life is irrevocably destroyed (Graham-Bermann, Miller, Howell, & Grogan-Kaylor, 2015; Kersey, 2012).

Humiliation carries a strongly negative meaning in life, and in the working environment, 'it is not an ordinary experience' for the individuals involved. Czarniawska (2008) considers humiliation to be a type of bullying, while, according to Ellis (1997), it is the second most frequent type of bullying after aggressive shouting. He quoted the result of a survey indicating that one in two UK employees have been bullied, mostly by their supervisors, at work during their working careers. Humiliation is an important experience in forming, building and shaping a person (Czarniawska, 2008). Humiliated people often view themselves through the prism of a failure and defeat. Frequent humiliation at work results in the perpetuation of low self-esteem – we perceive ourselves as worse, weaker and dependent, which often evokes a desire to exact vengeance. Unfortunately, we rarely respond since we dread being dismissed, and we get used to being humiliated, and so treat it as painful but 'normal' at work.

There are many ways to humiliate a worker: the most direct way is through name-calling ('you are the stupidest person who has ever worked here'); insults (certain words can cut through a person like a knife when using unfavourable comparisons such as 'an idiot'); getting someone to admit they were wrong and confessing to it in public; and asking someone to apologize in front of coworkers ('I want you to tell everyone how badly you have messed up'); treating someone like a child or like a servant (asking someone to fetch something, or perform menial tasks); making a person run errands that are not a part of their work (buying a gift for the boss's wife); ordering them to do something which contradicts their morals (lying to the boss); and bringing up for public discussion something personal that was said in confidence to an employer.

Many contemporary organizations (depending on their cultural and economic position, and phase of development) may focus mostly on a sense of maintaining their position and securing it against competitors, resulting in an increase in internal control (Barnes, 1981; Kożusznik & Polak, 2016). It can easily be observed that two essential ways of building up a sense of security in social relations at work, i.e., control and trust, remain in conflict with each other. In practical terms, increasing control usually means decreasing trust. Such a situation is described as the paradox of trust (Barnes, 1981) and the more control we experience and demonstrate, the less trust we express and feel. Consequently, the less trust we feel, the more willing we are to control others without it. A sense of security decreases in situations of increased risk and considerable uncertainty. It is natural that in such situations people show a tendency to increase their influence and power (see Chapter 10 in this volume).

Humiliation can be seen therefore as a means of social control (Silver et al., 1986), as the result of an organizational system rather than just the result of the behaviour of an individual person. In this case, those who witness and/or participate in the humiliation of another are themselves subject to a system that affects their actions, maintaining the perception that they are, indeed, inferior also (Smith, 2001). In such circumstances humiliation is not only destructive for an humiliated individual but it also has a demoralizing effect on the organization because it maintains the conviction that it is impossible to express a socially accepted reaction to the situation where a person is being deprived of their own dignity (Czarniawska, 2008).

In interpreting the situation affecting Eric, we can refer to a phenomenon of rankism (Kostera, 2012), the violence encoded in hierarchical organizations in a covert manner observed by Robert W. Fuller (2003). Fuller presented this type of injustice that typically manifests itself in aggressive behaviour towards people who occupy lower positions in the hierarchy. Rankism consists in using the power ascribed to one's post for goals other than fulfilling one's duties in the organization. As a result of rankism, people are humiliated, offended and intimidated. It is an assault on their dignity, potentially very serious, as dignity belongs to the basic rights of every person. Czarniawska (2008) presents humiliation as a typical side effect of organizations, and suggests humiliation refers not only to personal matters (e.g., supervisor's remarks about Eric's facial expression and 'foolish' smile) but also affects many other spheres of the organization's activities. Humiliation is a negative result of organizational authority, a phenomenon that is very common but not well documented. Humiliation denies employees their basic rights as an organizational citizen. On one hand, depriving employees of their participation rights is a result of abuse of power and, on the other hand, it is in itself a source of further power abuse. People who have been humiliated in public (like Eric) are more easily controlled and subjected to negative practices. The spread of such practices makes it easier for the perpetrators to use them. The observers (i.e., Eric's colleagues) become accustomed to them and do not protest when they see their colleague being humiliated. Some adopt these practices themselves and use them on those who are weaker than they are.

There are many possible explanations for why some supervisors choose to humiliate others rather than behave respectfully. For the people who consider that their individual interests are more significant, there is only one way to support their power: by controlling subordinates' behaviour. Humiliation is probably treated as an instrument of social control not only of these humiliated ones but also of those who watched and/or participated in the humiliation (Silver et al., 1986). The aim of humiliation is to instil powerlessness and helplessness in subordinates. Individuals and groups may develop their ability to overpower others (probably aimed at achieving their own interests) in an effort to avoid being overpowered (Silver et al., 1986).

We might therefore suppose that supervisors who behave in a respectful way will concentrate on organizational effectiveness as well as on task performance. Respect for subordinates is a natural and professional approach to coordinating common effort among workers in order to achieve high performance.

27.3 Action and Outcome

What happened in the situation described above? The events that occurred correspond to the above-mentioned definition of humiliation: Eric lost face and was humiliated by his superior in front of other people. In our society and at work, an adult person, and so Eric, should be treated with respect, should be met with rational arguments, be able to discuss his duties and carry them out without being made a fool of. In the case of a disagreement, a worker should be offered an explanation of the motives behind a supervisor's decision (Czarniawska, 2008). We did not observe this kind of rational behaviour in Eric's case, described above, and this account provides an example of bullying and lack of respect for others. We should remember that, although humiliation can be viewed as a form of bullying, bullying is usually defined as a recursive and systematic behaviour, taking place over time, whereas when we talk about humiliation, we are considering an event at a particular moment in time. Nonetheless it's likely that humiliation was used as a means of social control not only of the person being humiliated (Eric) but also of those who were onlookers (Eric's colleagues) with the aim of reinforcing their subordinate status and their self-perception that they are inferior.

In the situation described above, Eric felt helpless and powerless and, even after attending a professional psychologist, he was not able to function in the environment that had generated humiliation. Yes, he slept better, he stopped making any mistakes in letters and emails, he read them over and over again before sending them, however, he did not forget the words he had heard and the humiliation he had experienced in front of his colleagues. He could not forget being ashamed and he still felt hatred towards the manager and his scoffing smiles; he could even hear his chuckles in his dreams.

Every time he talked with his colleagues from the team, he wondering whether they remembered that situation when he had been so degraded and whether it had affected his relations with other team members. Since the incident, he had lost trust in his coworkers, and his enthusiasm for his work, and as soon as the first opportunity arose, he changed his job.

Why was there no response from Eric's colleagues? First of all, they felt embarrassed for the victim, being, on one hand, witnesses to 'bad performance of a character', and to 'the performance of bad character' on the other. Second, they were simply afraid that they would be further humiliated as well, and, third, it must be emphasized that humiliation was perceived in the organizational context as 'natural' and occurring very often, so employees viewed it as 'normal'. Finally, although a psychological intervention was provided, it helped only in the short run to make Eric think about the situation more clearly and helped him in decision-making. It is very probable that his psychological help contributed to him leaving his workplace because Eric started to become more aware of his values and of their violation by company rules which were not being changed.

Eric's company had a culture based on rivalry and competition, A further factor contributing to the development of a 'humiliation culture' is the presence of a distinct hierarchy in which some groups are more powerful than others. Thus, only basic changes in the nature of work relations could possibly eliminate the emergence of the systemic factors promoting humiliation. There are organizations, for example, in Sweden, where, according to Ellis, 'you are more likely to be bullied by your peers than by your manager'

(Ellis, 1997, p. 18). The author explained that one reason for this comment is that laws relating to workplace bullying are much tougher in Sweden and employers may spend a lot of money to provide training courses for managers in effective management techniques (Ellis, 1997). Barbara Czarniawska (2008) also reports that she could not find any reports or stories of humiliation from organizations in Sweden or Norway.

27.4   What Would We Do Differently Next Time? Learning Points

Empirical support for a relational shift in psychology is growing (Baumeister, Leary, Higgins, & Kruglanski, 2000; Fiske, Fiske, Kitayama, & Cohen, 2007). Robert Putnam (2001) concluded, even within the highly individualistic culture of the United States, studies have established beyond reasonable doubt that social connectedness is one of the most powerful determinants of our well-being (Putnam, 2001, p. 326).

Respect is a basic right of each human being as a member of their society, and similarly each worker may be called 'an organizational citizen'. Humiliation violates this basic right. 'The workplace is not only unhealthy for those being bullied but also for organizations which are allowing this to continue' (Ellis, 1997, p. 1). Bullying and humiliation might lead to higher costs for organizations, due to increased absenteeism, high turnover and decreased commitment and productivity (Ashford, 1997; Salin, 2003). All these authors claim that it should be prevented and condemned because it is morally wrong.

People value their dignity most in the workplace, not money, power or prestige (Dalton, 1959; Crozier, 1964; Kanter, 1977). Margalit says that 'wounds of insult and humiliation keep bleeding long after the painful physical injuries have crusted over' (2002, p. 120). Humiliation in the workplace is possible due to social tolerance of certain ways of exerting power, and that is why the law and trade unions must support people to resist humiliation, because only collective resistance will stop the use of humiliation as a control tool, and Czarniawska (2008) suggests solidarity between relevant stakeholders is one of the antidotes to abuse of power.

An antidote to humiliation at work is respect for the other person. Therefore, when an employee makes a mistake, a manager should act according to the following rules:

- Inform an employee of his mistake face to face, without others present.
- Discuss the consequences which are predictable and proportionate to an act.
- Explain why a given behaviour is inappropriate.
- Try to build a work relationship with a subordinate based on reciprocal understanding and respect.

If we are aware of a global and mutual connection and reciprocal dependencies, we should come to the conclusion that development of sound relations at all levels of human experience is not a whim but a necessity. Rather than separation and domination, a mutually beneficial connection is the currency of sustainable security.

References

Ashford, B. (1997). Petty tyranny in organizations: A preliminary examination of antecedents and consequences. *Canadian Journal of Administrative Sciences, 14,* 126–140.

Barnes, L. B. (1981). Managing the paradox of organizational trust. *Harvard Business Review, 59,* 107–116.

Baumeister, R. F., Leary, M. R., Higgins, T. E., & Kruglanski, A. W. (2000). The need to belong: Desire for personal attachments as a fundamental human motivation. In E. T. Higgins, & A. Kruglanski (Eds.), *Motivational science: Social and personality perspectives* (pp. 24–49). Philadelphia, PA: Psychology Press.

Crozier, M. (1964). *The bureaucratic phenomenon.* Chicago: University of Chicago Press.

Czarniawska, B. (2008). Humiliation: A standard organizational product? *Critical Perspective on Accounting, 19,* 1034–1053.

Czarniawska, B. (2010). *Trochę inna teoria organizacji* [A little different theory of organizing]. Warsaw: Poltext.

Dalton, M. (1959). *Men who manage.* New York: Wiley.

Ellis, A. (1997). *Workplace bullying.* Available at: www.stressatwork.ac.uk. (accessed 2 May 2015).

Fiske, A. P., Fiske, S. T., Kitayama, S., & Cohen, D. K. (2007). Social relationships in our species and cultures. In S. Fiske, D. T. Gilbert, & G. Lindzey (Eds.), *Handbook of cultural psychology* (pp. 283–306). New York: Guilford Press.

Fuller, R. W. (2003). *Somebodies and nobodies: Overcoming the abuse of rank.* Toronto: New Society Publishers.

Graham-Bermann, S. A., Miller, L. E., Howell, K. H., & Grogan-Kaylor, A. L. (2015). An efficacy trial of an intervention program for children exposed to intimate partner violence. *Child Psychiatry and Human Development, 46,* 928–939.

Hartling, L. M., Lindner, E., Spalthoff, U., & Britton, M. (2013). Humiliation: A nuclear bomb of emotions? *Psicologia Politica, 46,* 55–76.

Hartling, L., & Luchetta, T. (1999). Humiliation: Assessing the impact of derision, degradation, and debasement. *The Journal of Primary Prevention, 19,* 259–270.

Kanter, R. M. (1977). *Men and women of the corporation.* New York: Basic Books.

Kersey, K. (2012). *101 principles of positive guidance with young children.* New York: Allyn & Bacon.

Kostera, M. (2012). *Organizations and archetypes.* Warsaw: Wolters and Kluwer Polska, Edward Elgar Publishers.

Kożusznik, B., & Polak, J. 2016. Regulation of influence: An ethical perspective on how to stimulate cooperation and trust in innovative social dialogue. In P. Elgoibar, M. Euwema, & L. Munduate (Eds.), *Building trust and constructive conflict management in organizations* (pp. 169–184). New York: Springer.

Lindner, E., Hartling, L. M., & Spalthoff, U. (2012). Human dignity and humiliation studies: A global network advancing dignity through dialogue. In T. Besley, & M. A. Peters (Eds.), *Interculturalism, education, and dialogue* (pp. 386–396). New York: Peter Lang.

Loader, P. (1998). Such a shame. A consideration of shame and shaming mechanisms in families. *Child Abuse Review, 7,* 44–57.

Margalit, A. (2002). *The ethics of memory.* Cambridge, MA: Harvard University Press.

Putnam, R. D. (2001). *Bowling alone: The collapse and revival of American community.* New York: Simon & Schuster.

Salin, D. (2003). The significance of gender in the prevalence, forms and perceptions of work-place bullying. *Nordiske Organisasjonsstudier, 3,* 30–50.

Silver, M., Conte, R., Miceli, M., & Poggi, I. (1986). Humiliation: Feeling, social control and the construction of identity. *Journal for the Theory of Social Behavior, 16,* 269–283.

Smith, D. (2001). Organizations and humiliation. *Organization, 8,* 537–560.

Solomon, C. R., & Serres, F. (1999). Effect of parental verbal aggression on children's self-esteem and school marks. *Child Abuse & Neglect, 23*(4), 339–351.

Whack, R. C. (Executive Producer). (2013). Guest biography: Kofi Annan (Webpage and audio download). *Maya Angelou's Black History Month Special 2013.* 'Telling our stories'. Available at: http://mayaangelouonpublicradio.com/guest-bios/kofi-annan/

28 Resilience Development Through an Organization-Led Well-Being Initiative

Katharina Näswall, Sanna Malinen and Joana Kuntz

28.1 Background

This case study describes a set of innovative initiatives implemented by a New Zealand organization in order to address low staff morale and well-being following a natural disaster. The challenges and initiatives were documented by the research team through a collaborative process over a two-year period. The initiatives resulted in increased well-being among staff, as well as other positive outcomes that had not been the main target for the initiatives. The staff became more resilient and better able to proactively engage in their work and contribute to improved organizational outcomes. In addition, the initiatives resulted in long-term changes to the organization's culture, which paid more attention to employees and became more well-being focused.

28.1.1 The local context

The organization under study is a regional subsidiary of a large financial institution with its headquarters located outside of New Zealand. The particular subsidiary in focus is located in Christchurch, the largest city on the South Island of New Zealand, where a series of large-scale earthquakes occurred between 2010 and 2011. The largest earthquake, on 22 February 2011, reached a magnitude of 6.3 and caused serious damage to the land and the city's infrastructure, and resulted in 185 deaths and thousands injured. The February earthquake and the thousands of aftershocks that followed caused major disruption to businesses and individuals in the area, including displacement from homes and schools, drawn-out insurance claim processes, and stress-induced health issues. Many businesses had to close or relocate to other parts of the city due to building damage.

An Introduction to Work and Organizational Psychology: An International Perspective,
Third Edition. Edited by Nik Chmiel, Franco Fraccaroli and Magnus Sverke.
© 2017 John Wiley & Sons, Ltd. Published 2017 by John Wiley & Sons, Ltd.

28.1.2   The organization

The case organization was not only negatively impacted by the damage to infra-structure and the disruptions in the city, but also by organization-wide changes that resulted in restructuring and downsizing one year after the main earthquake. At the outset of the study described here, the organization did not offer any health pro-motion programmes or provisions for employee well-being, beyond the health and safety plan, which focused on physical safety and injury prevention. The health aspects mainly addressed lifestyle choices, such as weight loss and smoking cessation. How-ever, a number of issues had started to surface among employees which could not be satisfactorily explained without considering the impact of stress and low well-being. The problems included longer absences from work for minor complaints (e.g., colds), performance issues, and regional productivity levels well below national standards – along with a general sense of pessimism and lack of a positive climate.

These issues inspired the HR team to explore solutions which had not been tested before in the organization (which had quite a traditional culture). Among other initiatives, the HR team contacted the researchers for advice. Workshops with middle managers were facilitated by the research team in order to provide some research-based information and explore existing challenges. The middle managers were the ones most affected by the changes.

The themes that came out in the workshops presented a picture of a group of middle managers under significant stress, and with a strong commitment to pro-tect their staff from experiencing stress. The managers described how their roles had changed and expanded dramatically after the earthquakes, from being pri-marily focused on task-related issues to dealing with new earthquake-related issues among both employees and clients. Resource shortages had led to middle managers having to step out of their management role to help the frontline staff, resulting in increased workload. Staff members needed more support, both emotionally and technically, and new skills were needed to address a range of earthquake-related client concerns, from financial issues to personal hardship. These were exactly the same issues a number of staff members and managers were facing outside of work. Many reported a high degree of emotional labour and difficulties detaching from work, and that their own earthquake-related problems were making it difficult for them to carry out their work. Most reported overwork, deteriorated health, and that they could not take time off work if they were sick.

In addition to earthquake-related factors, it was clear that the perception of support from the wider organization was very low; the managers felt as if their senior leaders were largely unaware of their struggles and, even worse, that the senior levels of management, who were located outside of the region, were not that interested in learning more about the severe challenges faced by the middle managers and the staff in the region. Also, the managers felt that their resources for handling both new and recurring challenges at work had been restricted by invasive restructuring and staff reductions. In spite of these largely negative com-ments, the managers expressed a strong commitment to their team, and presented ideas for how things could be turned around if they were given the chance.

The results of the workshops were communicated to the HR team and the leaders of the middle managers. While most of the results were not surprising to the HR team and the leaders (but still not known by the senior management team), there was a clear sense of urgency to take action to support their staff. This led the HR manager and the leaders to investigate existing well-being programmes, focusing on programmes that were based on research and available at a low cost, as no funding was available from the organization. Despite the need to act quickly, the HR manager made sure that this preliminary work was done carefully to avoid rushing into something that was not appropriate for the organization and its culture. The HR manager and her team consulted with various organizations and mental health agencies. The result of this consultation process, which lasted for several months, was the development of an organization-specific, non-intrusive, very low cost, well-being initiative, based on the *Five Ways to Well-being,* which originated from a study by the UK Government Office for Science in 2008 (Aked et al., 2009). It had first been implemented in New Zealand as part of the 'All Right?' campaign (see http://www.allright.co.nz/) in late 2012 following the Canterbury earthquakes, to address the emerging need for mental health initiatives in the region (http://www.mentalhealth.org.nz/).

28.2   Theoretical and Practical Issues

The *Five Ways to Well-being* is a framework based on the notion that it is possible to increase well-being by engaging in everyday actions that direct attention towards things that bring pleasure and meaning (Aked et al., 2009). The framework emphasizes that people can experience well-being in many different ways, the main ones in this particular framework being *Connect, Give, Take Notice, Keep Learning,* and *Be Active* (see Figure 28.1; Mental Health Foundation, 2015).

Figure 28.1:   The Five Ways to Well-being
Source: The Mental Health Foundation of New Zealand.

Connect involves social relationships, interacting with others and social support. *Give* encourages giving, in any form, such as time, information, or support, to others. Based on mindfulness principles, *Take Notice* encourages focusing on everyday things that bring enjoyment. *Keep Learning* emphasizes the positive outcomes of gaining new knowledge and skills. Finally, *Be Active* encourages some sort of enjoyable, physical activity. All Five 'Ways' are supported by research to relate to improved well-being. By focusing on any of these five ways in everyday life, people's attention is turned to aspects of life that make them feel better. This approach is similar to aspects of the Broaden-and-Build model (Fredrickson, 2001), which highlights the importance of positive experiences and emotions for well-being.

A prominent feature of the Five Ways to Well-being is that participants are able to choose which of the Five Ways they prefer to focus on, and whether to focus on one or several, introducing flexibility and autonomy. The availability of free information on the framework and related materials made it accessible to everyone and affordable to the organization (http://www.mentalhealth.org.nz/home/ways-to-wellbeing/).

The initiative did not explicitly focus on changing any organizational factors. The main goals were to help staff find simple ways to deal with their accumulated stress, and show organizational support. The overall aim was to increase well-being and help staff devise strategies to cope with challenges at work.

The choice to focus on staff well-being and not on changing working conditions may seem short-sighted, especially since a number of the problems identified related to organizational factors (e.g., low support, resource constraints, and low decision-making autonomy). However, many of the challenges facing the staff were not within the control of the regional offices, such as resource allocation and staffing decisions, and could not be addressed by the local leadership team. Furthermore, there is research to support addressing well-being issues in the first instance, and then tackling organizational issues. As greater psychological well-being has been associated with having fewer health complaints (Cohen, Alper, Doyle, Treanor, & Turner, 2006), well-being-focused interventions may lead to a decrease in health-related absenteeism and associated costs, and positively impact productivity. Employees who are low in well-being are less likely to engage in proactive behaviours and will be less able to cope with challenges at work (Bakker & Costa, 2014). Higher well-being enables employees to cope with on-going changes by engaging in the development of their work roles (Ilies et al., 2015), and job crafting activities (Tims et al., 2013), which have been related to positive outcomes for employees and organizations (Bakker, 2015). Thus, addressing the well-being of employees became an important building block for increasing resilience in this organization, which in turn led to positive organizational outcomes.

28.3 Action and Outcome

Rather than launching a large-scale intervention programme in the organization, the HR team initiated what they called the "Well-being Movement." It introduced small changes to policies and procedures, such as revamping the existing Employee Assistance Programmes to focus more on well-being, making self-care coaching available (but not mandatory) for the middle managers, introducing a Well-being Hub to the organization, and, most noticeably, introducing the terms from the Five Ways to Well-being campaign into everyday corporate conversations. In order to promote these small changes to managers and staff, the HR manager recruited a leader to assist as a well-being champion, and to act as a well-being role model.

The subsequent more formalized implementation included the running of a well-being focused workshop (participation was completely voluntary), developed in consultation with outside mental health agencies. This workshop was led and designed by the local leaders (the level of management above the middle managers), allowing the complete tailoring of the workshop to the organization and its specific needs. The workshop was only advertised among the small group of middle managers, and no additional workshops were planned after the first one. Rather, the HR team waited until word spread and other managers showed interest in participating. This created a 'buzz' in the organization, and when the next round of workshops were held, they were fully booked and staff were attending on their own initiative.

The initial initiatives directly targeted the middle managers, who were encouraged to then implement well-being initiatives among their own teams of frontline staff, inspired by the Five Ways to Well-being framework. Leaders and senior management were gradually included in these initiatives, but the main focus was to support middle management, as they had the most direct contact with the staff and were also under the greatest pressure at the start of the programme.

28.3.1 Evaluation

To date, the information gathered through follow-up focus groups with middle managers, interviews with the HR manager and the middle managers, and brief surveys of middle managers and their staff suggests that the overall initiative has had a number of positive outcomes. For example, a number of the challenges identified by the managers at the start of the collaboration have to some extent been addressed, and there is now an explicit well-being focus in the organization. Middle managers have been given more autonomy and have formed a Managers' Board, providing a forum for the managers and their staff to propose suggestions for improving organizational processes. This change in agency can be partly attributed to the increased well-being among managers and to the fact that the organization, through the well-being initiative, also has, to some degree, become more open to new ideas.

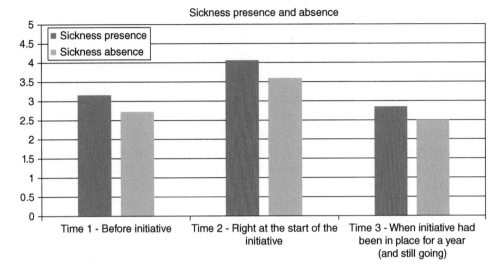

Figure 28.2:   Self-reported absence due to illness (sickness absence) and days at work while feeling ill enough to stay home (sickness presence)

The Five Ways to Well-being have been incorporated into everyday business, which has resulted in creative ways of working. One team even dedicates each day of the week to one of the Five Ways, using the particular Way of the Day as a theme at their morning meetings. Sick-leave numbers have not increased over the past year, and self-reported sickness presence and absence have decreased during the initiative (see Figure 28.2). Voluntary turnover has decreased over the past year, turning around a negative trend. The organization's hiring strategy has changed from being focused on numbers to emphasizing the well-being focus in the organization when interviewing candidates.

The initiative addressed well-being but it is not a traditional resilience training or wellness programme. The initiative is unique, given its focus on everyday practices at work that make people feel better (i.e., the Five Ways), and the possibility of carrying out work tasks with these practices in mind. The initiative has enabled employees by making it acceptable to focus on 'softer' aspects of work such as well-being. As a result of employees feeling better, they are more willing and able to participate in decision-making and contribute to improved work practices. The formation of the Board by the middle managers is one step in this bottom–up movement, as the Board focuses not only on individual well-being, but also on ways of improving procedures and structures. In general, the important shift in mindsets that the initiative has led to among staff and leaders has contributed to the development of a well-being culture. The activities associated with this initiative have become part of everyday work in this organization (Landsbergis & Vivona-Vaughan, 1995), resulting in increased middle management capacity to support the well-being of their staff (Skakon et al., 2010), and, at these particular regional offices, the workplace is a source of well-being for the employees.

28.4 What Would We Do Differently Next Time? Learning Points

28.4.1 What did we learn from this initiative?

- Having a good grasp of the organization's context (e.g., culture and business environment) allows for a better understanding of specific staff needs and resources available to facilitate a well-being initiative.
- Focusing on well-being can be a great springboard for changing other aspects of day-to-day work and relationships within the team and the organization.
- Starting a movement takes time, but once it gains momentum, it can be powerful.
- The flexibility of the Five Ways to Well-being was key, enabling it to be tailored to the team climate and the organizational culture, as well as allowing the use of personal preferences for activities that increase well-being.
- The movement did not imply 'doing well-being' to people – it was about empowering them to take initiatives that improve their own well-being.
- As a staff-led initiative, there was a positive sense of ownership and empowerment in addressing their needs and goals.
- Listening to people and acknowledging their goals and circumstances is important.
- Low organizational support has a detrimental effect on staff morale and well-being and generates an 'us–them' mindset that undermines a positive climate.
- Spending time and thought on finding the right champions who can model the behaviours and inspire others to get on board (those who may not appear initially to be the best ones) is vital for success.

28.4.2 How could we have evaluated the initiative better?

- Including measures of different aspects of well-being as well as indicators of performance, both before and during the initiative to study trajectories of change.
- Tracking people over time, to allow for the study of within-person processes.
- Taking into account parallel organization-wide processes to include as explanatory variables.
- Including measures of client satisfaction to provide information on how changes are reflected in the business.

28.4.3 What suggestions would we make to others wanting to try this initiative?

- Spend more time and resources on getting the senior management team on board early on in the process, the earlier the better.
- Focus on senior leadership development to support and inform the organization about well-being initiatives.

- Act sooner rather than later, before things reach a critical state. Be proactive.
- Tailor the initiatives to the organizational culture, both on the team and individual level, and allow for different ways of engaging with the initiatives (cf. The Five Ways to Well-being).

References

Aked, J., Marks, N., Cordon, C., & Thompson, S. (2009). *Five Ways to Wellbeing: A report presented to the Foresight Project on communicating the evidence base for improving people's well-being.* London: Nef.

Bakker, A. B. (2015). Towards a multilevel approach of employee well-being. *European Journal of Work and Organizational Psychology*, 1–5. doi: 10.1080/1359432X.2015.1071423

Bakker, A. B., & Costa, P. L. (2014). Chronic job burnout and daily functioning: A theoretical analysis. *Burnout Research, 1*(3), 112–119. doi: http://dx.doi.org/10.1016/j.burn.2014.04.003

Cohen, S., Alper, C. M., Doyle, W. J., Treanor, J. J., & Turner, R. B. (2006). Positive emotional style predicts resistance to illness after experimental exposure to rhinovirus or influenza A virus. *Psychosomatic Medicine, 68*(6), 809–815. doi: 10.1097/01.psy.0000245867.92364.3c

Day, A., & Randell, K. D. (2014). Building a foundation for psychologically healthy workplaces and well-being. In A. Day, E. K. Kelloway, & J. J. Hurrell (Eds.), *Workplace well-being: How to build psychologically healthy workplaces* (pp. 3–26). Chicester: Wiley-Blackwell.

Fredrickson, B. L. (2001). The role of positive emotions in positive psychology: The broaden-and-build theory of positive emotions. *American Psychologist, 56*(3), 218–226. doi: 10.1037/0003-066X.56.3.218

Ilies, R., Aw, S. S. Y., & Pluut, H. (2015). Intraindividual models of employee well-being: What have we learned and where do we go from here? *European Journal of Work and Organizational Psychology, 24*(6), 827–838. doi: 10.1080/1359432X.2015.1071422

Landsbergis, P. A., & Vivona-Vaughan, E. (1995). Evaluation of an occupational stress intervention in a public agency. *Journal of Organizational Behavior, 16*(1), 29–48. doi: 10.2307/2488611

Mental Health Foundation. (2015) *Best practice guide.* Available at: http://www.mentalhealth.org.nz/assets/Five-Ways-downloads/mentalhealth-5waysBP-web-single-2015.pdf

Näswall, K., Kuntz, J., Hodliffe, M., & Malinen, S. (2015). *Employee Resilience Scale (EmpRes) measurement properties.* Resilient Organisations Research Report 2015/04. Available at: www.psyc.canterbury.ac.nz/research/empres/pubs.shtml

Nilakant, V., Walker, B., Kuntz, J., de Vries, H., Malinen, S., Näswall, K., & van Heugten, K. (2016). Dynamics of Organizational Response to a Disaster: a Study of Organizations Impacted by Earthquakes. In C. M. Hall, S. Malinen, R. Wordsworth & R. Vosslamber (Eds.), *Business and Disaster Management: Business, organisational and consumer resilience and the Christchurch Earthquakes* (pp. 35–47). New York: Routledge.

Skakon, J., Nielsen, K., Borg, V., & Guzman, J. (2010). Are leaders' well-being, behaviours and style associated with the affective well-being of their employees? A systematic review of three decades of research. *Work & Stress, 24*(2), 107–139. doi: 10.1080/02678373.2010.495262

Tims, M., Bakker, A. B., & Derks, D. (2013). The impact of job crafting on job demands, job resources, and well-being. *Journal of Occupational Health Psychology, 18*(2), 230–240. doi: 10.1037/a0032141

29 Positive Action: Effectively Increasing Diversity at the Top

Nic Hammarling

29.1 Background

The lack of diversity at senior levels continues to be a source of frustration for many in today's organizations. Societal norms, conscious and unconscious bias all play a role in maintaining this status quo, and increasingly there is recognition of the need to maximize the potential of all employee populations, rather than simply the 45% or so who are white men.

Organizations are increasingly turning to positive action schemes to address this stubborn lack of diversity. In essence, the term positive action refers to initiatives that are designed to attract under-represented people to apply to organizations, such as Transport for London's recruitment campaign to attract more female tube drivers, or to give additional support to existing employees who are under-represented at more senior levels, such as the programme to support the development of black and minority ethnic (BAME) and disabled employees in the Senior Civil Service in the UK. It is important to note that positive action is *not* positive discrimination, which, in contrast, is giving someone preferential treatment based on their demographic status irrespective of merit. Positive discrimination is illegal within the UK, barring a couple of very specific circumstances.

All too often, positive action programmes are viewed with suspicion by majority employees, who suspect that others are receiving preferential treatment over them. Ironically, they are also frequently viewed with suspicion by the intended beneficiaries as well, who frequently do not want to be classified as needing 'additional help'. The failure to consider the psychological impact of these positive action initiatives on both majority and minority employees ultimately leads to the failure of the initiative itself.

In this case study, therefore, we explore the importance of understanding the psychological impact of positive action schemes on both beneficiaries and

An Introduction to Work and Organizational Psychology: An International Perspective, Third Edition. Edited by Nik Chmiel, Franco Fraccaroli and Magnus Sverke.
© 2017 John Wiley & Sons, Ltd. Published 2017 by John Wiley & Sons, Ltd.

non-beneficiaries, and how, effectively applied, psychological research can result in very effective positive action schemes.

29.2   Theoretical and Practical Issues

In essence, the psychological impact of positive action programmes can be understood by answering four key questions:

- Do we really need positive action?
- Is positive action fair?
- How can we ensure employees support the positive action?
- How can we avoid any negative consequences of running a positive action programme?

29.2.1   Do we really need positive action?

A key influencing factor in whether employees are likely to support positive action programmes is the extent to which they believe that the beneficiary group is subject to unfair discrimination. Greater denial or minimizing the existence of racism is significantly linked to increased opposition to positive action programmes, and indeed explains more variance than overt measures of racial attitudes (Awad, Cokley, & Ravitch, 2005; Harrison, Kravitz, Mayer, Leslie, & Lev-Arey, 2006; Oh, Choi, Neville, Anderson, & Landrumbrown, 2010). Increasing understanding of the biases that exist in today's organizations is a good method of paving the way to employees understanding and acceptance of the need for positive action.

29.2.2   Is positive action fair?

Organizational justice is, in essence, the extent to which employees feel their treatment, as well as that of other employees, is fair. There are three key forms of organizational justice: (1) procedural justice, (2) distributive justice and (3) interactional justice – all of which have been found to be affected by the introduction of positive action measures.

The strength of the positive action has a significant influence on whether employees think it is fair or not. Employees are significantly more likely to support weaker forms of positive action, such as recruitment programmes and policies on eliminating discrimination, while stronger forms of positive action, including the provision of additional training, tiebreak scenarios and preferential treatment, result in lower ratings of all three forms of organizational justice (Cropanzano, Slaughter, & Bachiochi, 2005; Levi & Fried, 2008).

The perceived fairness of a programme has also been found to explain 28% in variance of whether ethnic minority employees are willing to participate in a positive action programme (Slaughter, Sinar, & Bachiochi, 2002). Developing a positive action programme that is clearly and overtly based on merit is key in overcoming this concern over fairness.

29.2.3   How can we ensure employees support the positive action?

One of the most common mistakes that we see with regard to positive action programmes is the assumption that the intended beneficiaries, often BAME, female, or disabled employees, will automatically welcome the scheme, while non-beneficiaries (often white men), will not take much notice of the scheme because it does not directly affect them. These assumptions are both wrong and dangerous for the subsequent success of the positive action programme. Indeed, research has consistently found that positive action programmes need the support of both beneficiaries and non-beneficiaries if they are going to be successful, achieve their objectives (e.g., Hitt & Keats, 1984) and avoid backlash effects (Kidder, Lankau, Chorbot-Mason, Mollica, & Friedman, 2004).

Intended beneficiaries are significantly more likely to engage in the positive action programme if their participation is based on their ability rather than their group status. A key factor in securing the support of majority employees is developing their sense of psychological ownership. In essence, psychological ownership is a phenomenon whereby an individual becomes personally invested in ensuring a positive outcome of something; the sense of ownership they feel for something can result in feelings of responsibility for its success. In their 2011 paper, Hideg, Michela and Ferris found that both white participants and male participants were indeed more supportive of the positive action programme if they were given the opportunity to provide comment on the policy that was being developed.

29.2.4   How can we avoid any negative consequences of running a positive action programme?

If the positive action programme is badly managed, or if there is poor communication about it, then two key negative consequences can result: stereotype threat, and attribution error.

29.2.4.1   Stereotype threat

There is significant evidence that those who believe they have benefitted from positive action programmes may experience negative emotions and subsequent self-doubt about their ability. For example, when women thought they were beneficiaries of a positive action programme, they subsequently made lower performance evaluations and competency ratings of other women, but not men (Heilman, Kaplow, Amato, & Stathatos, 1993; see also Crosby, Iyer, Clayton, & Downing, 2003).

29.2.4.2   Attribution error

One of the most dangerous unintended consequences associated with positive action programmes is a form of attribution error, whereby majority employees misattribute the success of their minority colleagues to their participation in these positive action programmes, rather than to the abilities of the individual themselves.

This is especially evident in organizations that have taken a poor, numbers-driven approach to communicating about the need for the programme, and in organizations where the success of the programme is communicated in terms of numbers rather than focus on enhanced skills for the organization. For example, Heilman, Block and Lucas (1992) found that participants made lower competency ratings of mock job applicants who were described as being part of a positive action hiring programme than they did for those who were not. In another study, university applicant details were left completely unchanged, but instead researchers varied whether the graduate school admissions policy was described as giving 'particular consideration' to women and minority applicants. Even under this association condition, where participants thought that the university had a positive action policy, minority applicants were rated as having less likelihood of success and – interestingly – were also rated as having lower qualifications (Heilman & Blader, 2001).

29.3 Action and Outcome

These key research findings played a significant role in shaping a positive action programme that was recently completed in a large media organization, which for the purposes of this case study we'll call *Invenire*. As is often the way, the lack of diversity at senior levels in *Invenire* was starting to raise questions; there were good levels of diversity across the organization at junior and mid-management levels, but as soon as senior grades were entered, the numbers of ethnic minority and disabled employees fell dramatically. The need for a positive action programme became apparent, and design got underway.

The design of the programme was driven by the research findings outlined above, with two key principles at the core: first, participation in the programme was entirely based on merit, and, second, that participation in the programme was not exclusive to under-represented employees.

The programme itself was designed to cover a 12-month period for each participant. A critical first step was to develop a clear communications plan which spanned the entire life of the programme. The communication focus was on the ways in which *Invenire* could benefit from maximizing the potential of highly talented employees: although a lack of diversity at senior levels was referenced, numbers of minority employees and the desire to increase these numbers were not. Later communications focussed on the skill development aspects of the programme, and the importance of merit, sending a clear message that generated kudos for those who made it onto the programme itself. Interviews with participants about how they had practically applied their new skills in *Invenire* were also included. This communication was absolutely key to avoiding attribution errors and encouraging more applications for later cohorts.

Employees who applied to be included in the programme went through a rigorous assessment process, including an interview exploring their motivation, together with a one-day assessment centre to assess potential against *Invenire*'s leadership competencies. At the end of the selection process, participants described feeling proud to have made it through to the programme itself, a key factor in avoiding stereotype threat.

Critically, the programme was made available to all employees at the required grades – regardless of whether they were from a majority or minority background. All participants had to pass a cut-off in order to make it through to the programme, and the number of places available for minority employees was ring-fenced in order to ensure that ultimately the programme benefited those from under-represented groups.

The development component of the positive action programme comprised three key parts: (1) a two-day development centre, (2) on-going mentoring support, and (3) a range of follow-up activities.

The two-day development centre was designed as a stretch event. The exercises, which were designed by a panel of majority and minority employees with external specialist diversity and inclusion support, were designed around the *Invenire* leadership competencies. Throughout the event, participants were observed by a dedicated coach and given regular feedback about their strengths and areas for development against these competencies. Through this process, participants left with a crystal-clear picture of how they could make the most of their strengths and the development areas they needed to address, together with a clear, practical and robust development action plan.

The development activities did not, however, stop at the end of the two-day event. In line with research highlighting the importance of internal mentors in career progression (e.g., Ibarra, Carter, & Silva, 2010; Morrison, et al., 2014), each participant was paired with a mentor from the senior executive team. The mentors themselves received training on how they might best support their mentees, as well as some of the issues experienced by under-represented employees in their organization. The involvement of mentors in the programme was a significant factor in increasing psychological ownership among the leadership team for the success of the programme.

Follow-up activities for participants were held throughout the 12 months following their attendance at the development centre, including establishing action learning sets and delivery of workshops targeting common development areas highlighted by the development centre. These follow-up activities were key in maintaining momentum as well as providing on-going support.

The programme ran for three years, with several cohorts participating each year. Individual success stories came in thick and fast, and mentors also gave evidence of having benefited significantly from their involvement in the programme. By the end of the three-year programme, the talent pool at mid-level and associated succession plans were significantly more diverse. Critical, however, is the evidence found in the subsequent promotion levels. Within 12 months of having completed the programme, 20% of participants had been promoted to a more senior level, a figure which hugely outstripped average promotion rates for *Invenire*. When the data was cut to examine the promotion rate for the target minority groups involved in the programme, a whopping 37% had been promoted to the senior team.

It is clear then, that positive action programmes, when run successfully and when mindful of the key psychological research in the area, can have a huge impact on the successful career development of minority employees. The programme significantly over-achieved its stated objectives but there is always something that can be improved.

29.4   What Would We Do Differently Next Time? Learning Points

A key lesson from the first year of running the programme was that a tap-on-the-shoulder is not all bad. Initially, the application rate from minority employees was low, prompting us to have to go through line managers and department heads to take a tap-on-the shoulder approach to encourage people to apply. Many indicated that they did not yet feel they had the skills required to apply for the programme. In subsequent years, we also made better use of informal internal employee networks, with those who had participated in an earlier cohort actively encouraging their colleagues to attend.

Second, the programme highlighted the importance of getting the mentor-matching process right to start with. Due to time restrictions, mentor-matching was largely based on the expertise areas that mentees had stated in their application form that they wanted to develop. There was no opportunity for mentors and mentees to get to know each other first, and this was a missed opportunity for raising awareness among mentees of other departments or connecting with senior people with whom they had previously had very little contact. Encouraging this cross-fertilization within an organization is good not only for levels of creativity, but also great for generating the crucial sponsorship of under-represented employees.

In summary, the programme was noted as a significant success for all concerned: support for the programme existed among majority employees, under-represented employees improved their promotion rates and the organization was in a stronger position to make the most of its employee talent. The application of psychological research was central in bringing about this success.

References

Awad, G., Cokley, K., & Ravitch, M. (2005). Attitudes towards affirmative action: A comparison of color-blind versus modern racist attitudes. *Journal of Applied Social Psychology, 35,* 1384–1399.

Cropanzano, R., Slaughter, J. E., & Bachiochi, P. D. (2005). Organizational justice and black applicants' reactions to affirmative action. *Journal of Applied Psychology, 90*(6), 1168–1184.

Crosby, F. J., Iyer, A., Clayton, S., & Downing, R. A. (2003). Affirmative action: Psychological data and the policy debates. *American Psychologist, 58*(2), 93–115.

Harrison, D. A., Kravitz, D. A., Mayer, D. M., Leslie, L. M., & Lev-Arey, D. (2006). Understanding attitudes towards affirmative action programs in employment: Summary and meta-analysis of 35 years of research. *Journal of Applied Psychology, 91*(5), 1013–1036.

Heilman, M. E., & Blader, S. L. (2001). Assuming preferential selection when the admission policy is unknown: The effects of gender rarity. *Journal of Applied Psychology, 86,* 188–193.

Heilman, M. E., Block, C. J., & Lucas, J. A. (1992). Presumed incompetent? Stigmatization and affirmative action efforts. *Journal of Applied Psychology, 77,* 536–544.

Heilman, M. E., Kaplow, S. R., Amato, M. A., & Stathatos, P. (1993). When similarity is a liability: Effects of sex-based preferential selection on reactions to like-sex and different-sex others. *Journal of Allied Psychology, 78,* 917–927.

Hideg, I., Michela, J. L., & Ferris, D. L. (2011). Overcoming negative reactions of nonbeneficiaries to employment equity: The effect of participation in policy formation. *Journal of Applied Psychology, 96*(2), 363–376.

Hitt, M. A., & Keats, B. W. (1984). Empirical identification of the *criteria* for effective affirmative action programs. *Journal of Applied Behavioral Science, 20,* 203–222.

Ibarra, H., Carter, N. M., & Silva, C. (2010). Why men still get more promotions than women. *Harvard Business Review, 88*(9), 80–85.

Kidder, D. L., Lankau, M. J., Chorbot-Mason, D., Mollica, K. A., & Friedman, R. A. (2004). Backlash toward diversity initiatives: Examining the impact of diversity programme justification, personal and group outcomes. *International Journal of Conflict Management, 15,* 77–102.

Levi, A. S., & Fried, Y. (2008). Differences between African Americans and whites in reactions to affirmative action programs in hiring, promotion, training and layoffs. *Journal of Applied Psychology, 93*(5), 1118–1129.

Morrison, L., Lorens, E., Banidera, G., et al. (2014). Impact of a formal mentoring program on academic promotion of Department of Medicine faculty: A comparative study. *Medical Teacher, 36*(7), 608–614.

Oh, E., Choi, C., Neville, H. A., Anderson, C. J., & Landrumbrown, J. (2010) Beliefs about affirmative action: A test of the group self-interest and racism beliefs models. *Journal of Diversity in Higher Education, 3*(3), 163–76.

Slaughter, J. E., Sinar, E. F., & Bachiochi, P. D. (2002). Black applicants' reactions to affirmative action plans: Effects of plan content and previous experience with discrimination. *Journal of Applied Psychology, 87*(2), 333–344.

Age Management

30

Christian Stamov-Roßnagel

30.1 Background

In most industrialized countries, workers over 50 years old have begun to outnumber their younger colleagues. The percentages of younger workers are shrinking (Piktialis & Morgan, 2003; Dychtwald, Erickson, & Morison, 2006), while more people are continuing to work past traditional retirement ages (Alley & Crimmins, 2007; Noone, Alpass, & Stephens, 2010). As a result, workforces are becoming increasingly age-diverse. Numerous organizations are engaging in *age management* to deal with the implications that demographic change might have for organizations and workers alike (Chand & Tung, 2014). Quite often, organizations seek external consulting or attempt to develop evidence-based age management solutions through research collaborations. Given the multidimensional nature of age management, working in that field is clearly an exciting opportunity to put theories to good use.

As a case in point, a project we ran with five German call centre sites of a UK-based international telecommunications provider will be discussed. The company had invited tenders for that project as they sought research-based consulting on what they called a 'demography-proof personnel management strategy'. Their general concern was that the average age of the employees in their call centre was 43 years. As the company had been a state-owned public provider in the past, most employees were tenured. Budget restrictions precluded large numbers of new hires. As a consequence, the company's labour force was ageing linearly, reaching an average age of over 50 years old by 2020. With that background, the aim of the project was to work out the cornerstones of a personnel management strategy that would help the company secure the productivity of their employees throughout their entire work life. Furthermore, the project was to develop the essential instruments required to implement that strategy. Finally, the effectiveness

An Introduction to Work and Organizational Psychology: An International Perspective,
Third Edition. Edited by Nik Chmiel, Franco Fraccaroli and Magnus Sverke.
© 2017 John Wiley & Sons, Ltd. Published 2017 by John Wiley & Sons, Ltd.

of those instruments was to be evaluated. Given these initial specifications, we signed a three-year contract. We worked with the head of personnel development, the managers of the five call centres, and two labour representatives.

30.2   Theoretical and Practical Issues

While it might seem rather obvious that, say, health management manages employees' health, it is less obvious what age management actually manages. Of course, rather than age itself, age management is about the effects of ageing, but how can those effects best be captured, given that ageing is multidimensional? (For a summary, see Zacher, 2015.) On the physical dimension, age-related changes in, for instance, sight, hearing and physical strength might influence productivity. Closely related is the cognitive dimension of age-related changes in attention and memory. If the physical and the cognitive dimensions were the only drivers of age-related changes in productivity, age management practitioners and researchers would have a relatively easy job. Most physical and cognitive indicators of performance capability can be measured objectively and it would be quite straightforward to assess how certain job characteristics (e.g., time pressure, task complexity) are related to physical and cognitive indicators. Knowledge of such relationships would help to design 'age-friendlier' jobs. However, ageing also has a motivational dimension so that employees in different age groups value different aspects of their jobs and strive for different work-related goals (Ng & Feldman, 2010; Stamov-Roßnagel & Biemann, 2012). Finally, age stereotypes play an important role. Those widespread beliefs about older employees' capabilities co-determine a company's *age climate* that influences both managers' and personnel executives' expectations, as well as those of older employees (Boehm & Kunze, 2015). In sum, therefore, ageing in the workplace is multidimensional, which has both methodological and practical implications (see also Chapter 24).

On the methodological side, consultants and researchers need to be aware that, to date, there is no single integrative theory of ageing in psychology (see Zacher, 2015). Instead, various theories specialize in the aforementioned dimensions of ageing. *A priori*, none of those dimensions is inherently more important than any of the others; they are interrelated and thus all contribute to age differences in productivity. Consequently, more likely than not, assessing all four levels of ageing (physical, cognitive, motivational and stereotypical) might be necessary to identify the starting points of a specific organization's age management initiatives. However, a 'multidimensional questionnaire' designed for that assessment might be overly long. Moreover, some of the information of interest (e.g., cognitive job analysis data) might already be available. Therefore, one would screen existing data (e.g., from previous employee surveys) and develop an initial 'working model' prior to collecting primary data. That working model is specific to a given organization and describes the most important determinants of the outcome(s) in question (here: productivity).

On the practical side, the stereotypes dimension can make ageing in the workplace a delicate issue. While managers try to steer clear of any sort of age discrimination, employees feel age management is just that. Transparency to all stakeholder groups about the project phases and goals is thus indispensable, as are trust and relationship building during the project set-up. Therefore, it is a good idea to have the general design worked out, but to leave room for modifications of details when speaking to the company research partners. When presenting that general design, the main stakeholder groups should be involved in finalizing the design. Such collaboration will build trust and increase buy-in through participation and transparency, which will not only boost response rates, but also ensure high data quality. Participants will be much more likely to report their 'real' attitudes and not just half-heartedly 'tick the boxes'. This is not the only benefit of collaborating, however. By adding their perspectives, company research partners might contribute to richer hypotheses. Another key to trust building is a clear statement on how both the organization and employees will benefit from age management and how the specific project will help secure those benefits. Trust building involves, of course, managing stakeholders' expectations. Because of the multidimensionality of ageing, there is no one tool of age management. Rather, successful age management requires the cooperation of all stakeholders. Even with best intentions, age management is not something organizations can do 'for' their employees, but only together with them.

30.3 Action and Outcome

Consistent with the multidimensional view on ageing outlined above, we devoted the first two months to a comprehensive clarification of the project goals. All stakeholder groups listed their expectations of a successful project and we negotiated a detailed project plan before collecting or analysing any empirical data. As the core of a working model, we agreed on the assumption that resources management should be the core of age management and that general models of developmental regulation from lifespan psychology should be an appropriate conceptual framework. In such models (e.g., Baltes & Baltes, 1990; Brandtstädter, 1999; Heckhausen, 1997), employees' cognitive, motivational, social, etc. development is seen to continue over the entire lifespan. Employees do not 'passively undergo' that development. Rather, they actively co-regulate it by trying to match their resources to external demands. The physical, psychological, social or organizational aspects of a job that help workers achieve their work goals, reduce job demands, and that may stimulate personal growth, learning and development (Demerouti, Bakker, Nachreiner, & Schaufeli, 2001) count as *job resources* (e.g., an organization's supportive learning climate). Personal resources are positive self-evaluations that facilitate goal achievement and protect an employee against the physical and emotional costs of work-related demands (Hobfoll, Johnson, Ennis, & Jackson, 2003). Personal resources refer to one's sense of the ability to control and successfully influence one's environment.

In an initial survey (n = 1781) in the first project phase, we assessed employees' levels of crucial job and personal resources. We found that higher levels of personal resources such as learning-related self-efficacy and job resources such as supervisor support were associated with higher self-reported and supervisor-reported productivity. However, even high levels of job resources were negatively related to productivity when personal resource levels were low. On the other hand, high levels of personal resources buffered the impact of job demands such as work pressure and strain. Age moderated these relationships so that the beneficial effect of personal resources was stronger for employees over 50 years old.

In the second project phase, we used these findings to design a resource-oriented intervention. It was based on the fact that resource effects depend on employees' appraisal of those resources (see Karasek & Theorell, 1990). For instance, employees who might initially feel that their job experience left them 'stuck in a mental rut' might learn to see the beneficial side of such experience (e.g., in terms of facilitating decision-making) and thus, through a change in appraisal, turn a perceived obstacle into a resource. The intervention focused on the personal resource of *learning-related self-efficacy*, i.e., employees' beliefs in how well they are able to self-regulate their work-related learning and development; this belief had emerged from the survey as a crucial personal resource for mastering increasing job demands and keeping up productive work.

We tested the intervention (see Table 30.1) with 240 participants (M_{Age} = 51.7 years) from all five call centres who were randomly recruited from the survey participants. The intervention was designed as a small-group training comprising four training sessions (two hours each) in four consecutive weeks and one evaluation session of one hour, all taking place in the company's training centre. We started by having participants establish their individual 'development model' that indicated what they considered to be 'successful development' and what influences they saw as facilitating or impeding that development. Exercises on cognitive restructuring (see Box 30.1) served to help participants rephrase negative development-related beliefs that lowered self-efficacy and invoked negative affective experiences.

Table 30.1: Overview of the resource-building intervention

Intervention				Evaluation
Session 1	Session 2	Session 3	Session 4	Session 5
Setting personal intervention goals	Myths and facts on cognitive ageing	Revisiting negative learning attitudes	Setting future change goals	Studying training materials on mobile phone technologies
Exploring subjective learning beliefs	Essential learning strategies	Reappraising learning-related self-efficacy	Developing personal transfer plan	Knowledge test
Learning attitudes questionnaire	Individual resources portfolio		Dealing with setbacks	Learning attitudes questionnaire

---

Box 30.1: Cognitive restructuring in a nutshell

Using a five-column thought record protocol, participants recalled as vividly as possible a specific learning-related episode at their workplace and recorded the negative thoughts they had had in that situation, together with a rating of the strength of negative emotions in that situation. Participants then rephrased those negative thoughts into positive ones, imagined the same situation in light of those positive thoughts and rated the emotions they now felt. In a moderated group discussion, participants elaborated on the insight that the way they think about learning drives negative attitudes, rather than negative attitudes driving participants' thoughts and emotions. Participants discussed how they might use this insight to revise their attitudes towards learning.

In the evaluation, intervention participants and a comparison group of non-participants studied work-related training materials on specific mobile phone technologies, on which they took a knowledge test. As one main result, learning efficiency was considerably higher in the intervention group. While both groups performed similarly well on the knowledge test, the intervention group took 20% less time to study materials. Moreover, participants in the intervention group reported higher confidence in their learning. Finally, before the intervention, both groups had not differed significantly in their beliefs about learning and development or in learning-related self-efficacy. After the intervention, participants reported more favourable beliefs and higher self-efficacy than the control group. Given that we evaluated the intervention three months after the last session, the benefits of the intervention appear to be more than just short-lived.

30.4 What Would We Do Differently Next Time? Learning Points

All in all, the project was quite successful; the self-efficacy intervention has become a regular part of our company partner's training and development offers. Still, we have learnt a few things that might help make projects like these run even more smoothly.

As for the survey part, company partners are likely not to accept the initial questionnaire right away, but discuss ways to shorten it. This holds especially if the questionnaire takes longer than 20 minutes to complete and for sample sizes of more than, say, 200 participants. Therefore, it is a good idea to include in the first questionnaire version scales that it would be 'nice to have', but that can be dropped without losing the essence of the study. While the questionnaire is in the field, regular updates and feedback are essential. Stakeholder groups should be proactively informed of the number of questionnaires completed and involved in sending out reminders. Participants may get back with questions; answering them will ensure high response rates and low attrition rates.

On the modelling side, sophisticated as our initial models may have been, our research partners considered them relatively simplistic and suggested several other predictors they thought we should take into account. Therefore, in our on-going projects, we work even more closely with our company partners. We cooperate more closely with trainers, involving them from the start in the development of intervention designs to maximize the effectiveness of the interventions. After all, running intervention workshops requires a set of skills many researchers might not have acquired in their academic teaching. Experienced trainers can help to find the most appropriate established workshop techniques beyond mere lecturing and they are very helpful reviewers of workshop designs. They might even run the actual workshops together with researchers. As company 'insiders', they have usually built a working relationship with the target group, which will contribute tremendously to the effectiveness of the intervention.

References

Alley, D., & Crimmins, E. M. (2007). The demography of aging and work. In K. S. Shultz, & G. A. Adams (Eds.), *Aging and work in the 21st century* (pp. 7–23). Mahwah, NJ: Lawrence Erlbaum.

Baltes, P. B., & Baltes, M. M. (1990). Psychological perspectives on successful aging: The model of selective optimization with compensation. In P. B. Baltes, & M. M. Baltes, (Eds.), *Successful aging: Perspectives from the behavioral sciences* (pp. 1–34). New York: Cambridge University Press.

Boehm, S. A., & Kunze, F. (2015). Age diversity and age climate in the workplace. In P. M. Bal, D. T. A. M. Kooij, & D. M. Rousseau (Eds.), *Aging workers and the employee-employer relationship* (pp. 33–55). Cham: Springer.

Brandtstädter, J. (1999). The self in action and development: Cultural, biosocial, and ontogenetic bases of intentional self-development. In J. Brandtstädter, & R. M. Lerner (Eds.), *Action and self-development: Theory and research through the life span* (pp. 37–65). Thousand Oaks, CA: Sage.

Chand, M., & Tung, R. L. (2014). The aging of the world's population and its effects on global business. *Academy of Management Perspectives, 28,* 409–429.

Demerouti, E., Bakker, A. B., Nachreiner, F., & Schaufeli, W. B. (2001). The job demands–resources model of burnout. *Journal of Applied Psychology, 86,* 499–512.

Dychtwald, K., Erickson, T. J., & Morison, R. (2006). *Workforce crisis: How to beat the coming shortage of skills and talent.* Boston, MA: Harvard Business School Press.

Heckhausen, J. (1997). Developmental regulation across adulthood: Primary and secondary control of age-related challenges. *Developmental Psychology, 33,* 176–187.

Hobfoll, S. E., Johnson, R. J., Ennis, N. E., & Jackson, A. P. (2003). Resource loss, resource gain, and emotional outcomes among inner-city women. *Journal of Personality and Social Psychology, 84,* 632–643.

Karasek, R. A., & Theorell, T. (1990). *Healthy work: Stress, productivity and the reconstruction of working life.* New York: Basic Books.

Ng, T. W. H., & Feldman, D. C. (2010). The relationship of age with job attitudes: A meta-analysis. *Personnel Psychology, 63,* 667–718.

Ng, T. W. H., & Feldman, D. C. (2012). Evaluating six common stereotypes about older workers with meta-analytical data. *Personnel Psychology, 65,* 1744–1765.

Noone, J., Alpass, F., & Stephens, C. (2010). Do men and women differ in their retirement planning? Testing a theoretical model of gendered pathways to retirement preparation. *Research on Aging, 32,* 715–738.

Piktialis, D., & Morgan, H. (2003). The aging of the U.S. workforce and its implications for employers. *Compensation Benefits Review, 35,* 57–63.

Stamov-Roßnagel, C., & Biemann, T. (2012). Ageing and work motivation: A task-level perspective. *Journal of Managerial Psychology, 27,* 459–478.

Zacher, H. (2015). Successful aging at work. *Work, Aging, and Retirement, 1,* 4–25.

Index

Printed and bound by CPI Group (UK) Ltd, Croydon, CR0 4YY

27/11/2024

14600248-0001